D0843860

UPDATE...NOVEMBER 1991

Twenty-eight years after the shots that changed history, Americans are talking about the Kennedy assassination all over again. The cause is the movie *J.F.K.*, Hollywood's first real attempt to tackle the subject, and—according to a Gallup poll— seventy percent of people between the ages of eighteen and fifty-four are keen to see it.

Those who have long labored to uncover the truth about Dallas might be expected to be happy about *J.F.K.* In a sense they are, because—after all these years of thankless digging, in the face of appalling negligence by the mainstream media—a powerful medium is bringing a vital issue back to the front pages, and to the forefront of the American mind.

Even before the movie appeared, though, it was causing enraged debate. Three-time Oscar winner Oliver Stone, director of *Platoon*, *Born on the Fourth of July*, *Salvador*, and screenwriter of *Midnight Express*, has made some bizarre decisions. From a vast array of scholarship, he picked a book by Jim Garrison, former District Attorney of New Orleans, as his main source work. Garrison, many will recall, is the strange figure—considered crazy by some, crooked by others—who in 1967 brought a prominent local citizen to trial for conspiracy to murder President Kennedy. It took a jury less than an hour to declare the accused man, Clay Shaw, not guilty.

You will find only a sprinkling of references to Garrison in this book. His probe has long been recognized by virtually everyone—including serious scholars who believe there was a conspiracy—as a grotesque, misdirected shambles. As *Esquire* magazine pointed out this November, there were things director Stone did not at first know about Garrison. About his separation from the U.S. Army, "following diagnosis that he was in need of long-term psychotherapy." About his "close association with organized crime, whose soldiers and capos he rarely prosecuted..." About "the bribery and income-tax evasion trials in which he was exonerated."

Yet, even when he did learn these things, Stone persisted in his association with Garrison and a bunch of other buffs, so-called witnesses and experts whom serious observers dismiss as cranks or worse. As a cheap gimmick, he even let Garrison act in the movie—in the role of Earl Warren, the Chief Justice who gave his name to the original official investigation. A glimpse of an early script for *J.F.K.* disclosed so many howlers and historical distortions that one critic— aware that the Garrison role would be played by Kevin Costner, of *Dances with Wolves* fame—suggested that the movie's title be changed to *Dances with Facts*.

As this book went to press, it was yet to be seen whether *J.F.K.*, perhaps the last chance in our time to bring some of the truth before the public, will end up precisely as so many in authority would prefer— exposed as travesty, enmired in ridicule.

Whatever its fate, this new movie is a prime example of a sad trend. For a long time now, publishers and moviemakers have preferred historical fiction to nonfiction, filmed drama to documentary. Facts are less profitable than sensational fable. In the end, though—even in our Age of Illusion—it is the facts that really matter.

This book was originally written to sort fantasy from fact. Now, as this edition goes to press, I offer fresh information—too new for inclusion in the main text—but essential knowledge for those to whom Dallas, 1963, means more than entertainment.

Ironically, a neat way into the new information is a footnote in a report by Congress's Assassinations Committee. It observes that in 1967—at the height of his ill-fated probe—*J.F.K.'s* hero Jim Garrison met in Las Vegas with top mobster Johnny Roselli. Roselli, who had been a key figure in the CIA-Mafia plots to kill Fidel Castro, was at that same time industriously spreading a story that the Cuban leader had been behind Kennedy's murder.

While virtually everyone agrees that Castro did no such thing, there is reason to suspect that Roselli—with Mafia associates and rogue elements of the U.S. Intelligence—was indeed involved. The latest leads came this year, in developments reported by the author after interviews with one of John Kennedy's lovers, Judith Exner. It has been known since 1975, following a leak by the Senate Intelligence Committee, that Exner carried on an affair with Kennedy from 1960 to 1962, while also meeting frequently with Roselli and Chicago mob chieftain Sam Giancana. Now, with compelling support from White House logs and other documents, Exner has alleged there was more to it than a presidential romance and a social acquaintance with top mafiosi.

According to Exner, Kennedy used her as a courier to carry packages to Giancana and Roselli. At first, while still campaigning for the White House, he sent her to Giancana with bags stuffed with cash to be used by the mobster in rigging key elections. Then, during the presidency, he sent Giancana an envelope which—Kennedy told Exner—contained "intelligence material" connected with the "elimination" of Fidel Castro.

As recently reported in detail by this author in the *New York Daily News*—there are compelling grounds for believing Exner's account. A mass of information suggests the Kennedys did have compromising links with organized crime before the presidency began, and that these continued during Kennedy's first two years in the White House. Then something went badly wrong.

A skein of evidence, some of it drawn from FBI wiretaps, indicates that the mobsters—harried as never before by the Justice Department, on the orders of Attorney General Robert Kennedy—felt the President had broken faith with them. Mafia boss Santos Trafficante, an accomplice of Giancana and Roselli in the CIA/Mafia plots, told an associate in late 1962 that the Kennedys were "not honest. They took graft and they did not keep a bargain...this man Kennedy is in trouble, and he will get what is coming to him...he is going to be hit."

To be hit by whom? Almost certainly not by the mobsters acting alone. The case is littered with the fingerprints of U.S. Intelligence, and especially of the CIA. Elements of the CIA, as explained in these pages, had their own reason for rage against John Kennedy.

A forthcoming book written by Sam Giancana, godson and nephew of his mobster namesake, will assert that President Kennedy indeed used several people—not only Judith Exner—for his covert contacts with the Mafia, and that his uncle—in league with U.S. Intelligence contacts—was indeed involved in the assassination.

New research, reported here for the first time, indicates that the CIA Chief of Operations at its Miami anti-Castro headquarters, David Morales, was in direct contact with "Maurice Bishop," the cover name used by a CIA officer once seen with the President's alleged assassin, Lee Harvey Oswald. According to Bradley Ayers, a former Army Captain seconded to the CIA at the time, Morales personally controlled mobster Roselli—and Roselli was seen with him and another senior CIA officer, William Harvey, as late as summer 1963, after the Agency had supposedly severed its connection with the Mafia.

Here the story comes full circle, back to New Orleans, the city where Oswald lived in the months before the assassination, and where District Attorney Garrison would one day stage his farcical trial. Johnny Roselli reportedly came to New Orleans in 1963 to meet with Guy Banister, a former FBI agent and extreme rightwinger then running anti-Castro operations out of an office at 544 Camp Street. The source of this information, Banister's former secretary, told the author that another visitor to the office was Oswald himself. The alleged assassin, she gathered, was involved in "undercover" activity sanctioned by Banister.

For the first time, here is a direct chain of association. CIA officers controlling a top mafioso, who meets in 1963 with an anti-Castro operative suspected of manipulating—perhaps of setting up—the young man who is supposed to have murdered the President of the United States.

It always has been clear that New Orleans held crucial evidence, evidence that could be the key to unlocking the mysteries of the Kennedy assassination. If the key in that lock is to be turned in the lifetime of this generation, more responsible work is urgently needed.*

And so back to this new movie, *J.F.K.* What angers investigators most about its hero, Jim Garrison, is that his cockeyed caper in 1967 was more than an abuse of the justice system. It was an abuse of history, and—more than any other single factor—it discredited and stalled genuine research for a full decade, a decade in which witnesses died and evidence was further obscured.

It would be tragic if, by making a movie he honestly intended to open the eyes of the American public, but by falling for Garrison's hokum, Oliver Stone destroyed the last lingering chance of solving the crime of the century.

Anthony Summers
December 1991

---

*The Assassination Archive and Research Center is a nonprofit tax-exempt organization devoted to collating information on American political assassinations, and to furthering research. Contributions, however small, are welcomed at: Assassination Archive and Research Center, 918 F Street NW, Room 1510, Washington D.C. 20004. Telephone: 202-393-1917.

Praise for the original edition of CONSPIRACY

". . . a monumentally important new book on the assassination of President John F. Kennedy."

—*Philadelphia Daily News*

"CONSPIRACY proves to any reasoning reader that at all events the Oswald story handed to the public was a pack of lies . . . a book which tops the drama of any fictional thriller."

—*New York Post*

". . . Don't miss this brilliant book."

—*Cosmopolitan*

"This authoritative book opens a box of secrets. It offers disquieting, even terrifying, answers to the questions we have all been asking . . ."

—*Len Deighton*

"One does not have to accept Mr. Summers' conclusions to recognize the significance of the questions raised in this careful and disquieting analysis of the mysteries of Dallas."

—Arthur Schlesinger, Jr.,
former Special Assistant
to President Kennedy

"Summers' argument is so lucidly arranged and so forcefully mounted that I now feel compelled to believe that there was a conspiracy to kill President Kennedy."

—Robert MacNeil,
Executive Editor of
the MacNeil-Lehrer News Hour

"Of all the books written about the Kennedy assassination, this is the first one that has convinced me there is a plausible trail of evidence leading to a conspiracy—a trail that for some reason was not adequately pursued by the Warren Commission."
—Ambassador William Attwood,
former Special Assistant to
the U.S. Delegation at the U.N.
and former Publisher of Newsday

"Mr. Summers has written a thoughtful and responsible book. While I disagree with his argument about the role of U.S. intelligence, his opinion that the assassination inquiry is not over, and that it should not end with the House Assassinations Committee Report, is right on the mark."
—Congressman Judge Richardson Preyer,
former Chairman of Kennedy Subcommittee,
House Select Committee on Assassinations

"I do not subscribe to all of Summers' thesis, but his book deserves to be read and taken seriously by all those who care about truth or justice."
—Professor Robert Blakey,
former Chief Counsel of
the House Select Committee
on Assassinations

"This is a brilliant investigation. Mr. Summers has sought out the evidence with patience and courage, and evaluated it responsibly. The result is both fascinating and disquieting. Some details may remain in doubt, but it is now clear that President Kennedy was the victim of a conspiracy: a conspiracy in which, it seems, uncontrolled U.S. intelligence agents were involved with embittered Cuban exiles and organized crime."
—Professor Hugh Trevor-Roper,
Regius Professor of Modern History,
Oxford

". . . If you've ever been curious about the mysterious 'Maurice Bishop' of the C.I.A., or the role of Loran Hall, or whether New Orleans prosecutor Jim Garrison really had the goods, or which Mafia chieftain said Kennedy was going to get his, the Silvia Odio incident, or Jack Ruby's alleged visit to Santos Trafficante in a Cuban prison, 'CONSPIRACY' is the place to look . . ."

New York Times Book Review

"Until very recently, I, for one, have resisted conspiracy interpretations . . . No more. I now think that it is possible that the Kennedy assassination was the most far reaching state crime ever committed in this country. If so, the culprits are undetected, and some are still alive . . . If not so, we need to know that too . . . The excuses are understandable in hindsight; they don't suffice now."

—Eliot Freemont-Smith,
The Village Voice

"Superb investigative disciplines . . . and so readable."

—Norman Mailer

"Anthony Summers, a British investigative reporter for the BBC, who certainly cannot be dismissed as a crank or a publicity seeker, here offers this meticulously documented account of his examination of the case, and his findings, understated as they may be, are likely to disturb the reader. Summers aduces testimony to substantiate what some Americans have long supposed, namely, that the assassination was not the work of an unstable Lee Harvey Oswald alone but a carefully planned conspiracy . . ."

—*John Barkham Reviews*

"This powerful book by a BBC documentarist and leading British journalist stands out among the vast number of works on the John Kennedy assassination."

—*Publishers Weekly*

"Exceptionally well written, with all the tone and tension of an Eric Ambler thriller . . . An important piece of work, both in literary and public terms . . . A book that must be read."

—*New York Review of Books*

BY ANTHONY SUMMERS

The File on the Tsar (with Tom Mangold)

Goddess: The Secret Lives of Marilyn Monroe

Honeytrap: The Secret Worlds of Stephen Ward
(with Stephen Dorril)

CONSPIRACY

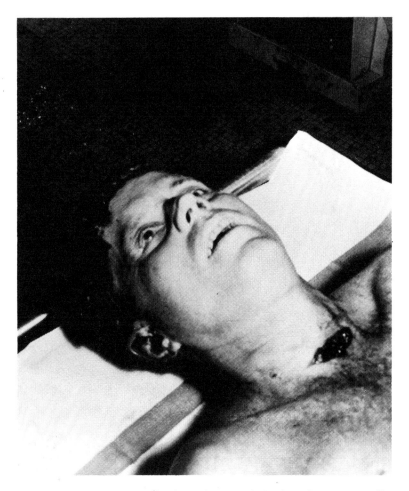

A president in death. The last picture of the face known to millions, taken at autopsy in Washington. Post-mortem photographs were first seen by U.S. television viewers in 1988, on PBS' *Nova* program, presented by Walter Cronkite. Many say such pictures should not be published, but they are relevant as well as shocking. The neck wound, shown in this picture, remains the subject of medical controversy.

CONSPIRACY

by

ANTHONY SUMMERS

Updated and expanded edition

PARAGON HOUSE
New York

for Joanne Bario,
David,
and
Anna

First published in the United States by McGraw-Hill Book Company

First Paragon House paperback edition 1989

Copyright © 1980, 1981, 1989 by Anthony Summers

Paragon House
90 Fifth Avenue
New York, NY 10011

All rights reserved. No part of this book may be reproduced
in any form, without written permission from the publishers,
unless by a reviewer who wishes to quote brief passages.

Library of Congress Cataloging-in-Publication Data

Summers, Anthony.
Conspiracy / by Anthony Summers.—
Updated and expanded ed. p.   cm.
Includes bibliographical references.
ISBN 1-55778-286-5
1. Kennedy, John F. (John Fitzgerald),
1917–1963—Assassination.   I. Title.
E842.9.S9   1989
973.922—dc20   89-16405
                                                CIP

The paper used in this publication meets the minimum requirements
of American National Standard for Information Sciences—Permanence
of Paper for Printed Library Materials, ANSI Z39.48-1984.
10   9   8   7   6

Contents

IV ENDGAME *Deception and Tragedy*

Acknowledgments

Those independent researchers of the Kennedy case who work on, in spite of passing years and press mockery, set themselves a thankless task. They are perennially assailed as sensationmongers or cranks, and in some cases that criticism has been justified. Others, however, with their scholarship and persistence, have filled a gap left by poor official investigation and shoddy journalism. Their best reward has been recent reinvestigation by Congressional committees, a sign that a tiny handful of citizens can still budge a resistant establishment. The best of the private students of the case, those of whom the public hears little, have been vindicated by the formal finding, in 1979, that President Kennedy's death was probably the result of a conspiracy. They are not yet, however, satisfied. Reasonably enough, they now press for the location and prosecution of those who plotted the President's death. Many of these zealous citizens were of great help to me.

Over the years, two people in particular gave me access to a unique fund of knowledge and research material and guided me away from red herrings. They are Mary Ferrell of Texas and Paul Hoch of California. Mrs. Ferrell is rightly known to reporters and researchers around the world for her tireless and meticulous research. She has been personally responsible for important breakthroughs and deserves the bulk of the credit for the detective work that led to an official conclusion that there were two gunmen in Dealey Plaza. Paul Hoch, equally persistent, has also labored quietly over many years to earn a reputation for scholarship and innovative insight. I am indebted to both these researchers for their friendship and guidance, and both read this book before its original publication.

Of the handful of professional reporters who have worked diligently on the case, one has been of enormous help to me as a colleague and friend. This is Earl Golz, formerly of the *Dallas Morning News,* who has continued to work the story—sometimes in the face of editorial reluctance.

Special thanks are due to the late Sylvia Meagher, whose analysis of the Warren Commission's failings, published as *Accessories after the Fact,* did much to convince Congress that the case should be reopened. Ms. Meagher helped me greatly and her passing has saddened all long-term students of the case. I am grateful to Gary Shaw, from Texas, a persistent researcher who is presently organizing a JFK Assassination Information Center for Dallas—a project that deserves support.

Others who have helped unselfishly are: Mark Allen; Professor Peter Dale Scott; Bernard Fensterwald and James Lesar of the Assassination Archives and Research Center in Washington, D.C.—an indispensable source for any serious scholar of the assassination; Jeff Goldberg; Jones Harris; Larry Harris, an expert on the Tippit case; Harry Irwin; Tom Johnson; Penn Jones; Seth Kantor, *Atlanta Constitution* correspondent and specialist on Jack Ruby; David Lifton; Gary Mack; Jim Marrs of the *Fort Worth Star-Telegram;* Dick Russell; Alan Weberman; Harold Weisberg; Jack White; and Les Wilson.

For his advice, I am indebted to Dr. Vincent Guinn, the metals analyst whose work on the ballistics evidence was central to recent Congressional study. Dr. Cyril Wecht, the combative forensic pathologist from Pennsylvania, corresponded with me patiently over many months. His passionate dissent from official certainties has made him a salutary thorn in the side of apathetic authorities. Former British Detective Superintendent Malcolm Thompson helped with his photographic expertise. In the intelligence area, I thank John Marks of the Center for National Security Studies; Ray Cline of the Center for Strategic and International Studies; and Fletcher Prouty, former Focal Point Officer between the Department of Defense and the CIA. Marion Johnson of the National Archives extended me the infinite patience he has long given to Kennedy researchers. Dave Powers, curator of the John F. Kennedy Library, was most helpful. In Congress, I thank Senator Richard Schweiker, Representative Richardson Preyer, and a number of dedicated Congressional Staff who must—in many cases—remain anonymous. In Cuba, I found officials cooperative and generous with facilities.

My work on this case began as producer of a television documentary shown on the BBC and around the United States. My continued interest was helped along by the hard work and enthusiasm of the staff who created that program. The researchers, Katherine Kinsella and Scott Malone, were indefatigable. So too was the skillful part played by *Panorama* reporter Michael Cockerell and the program's editor, Christopher Capron. The late Ian Callaway, the veteran *Panorama* film editor, gave the sterling service for which a generation of television journalists will long remember him. Independent film-makers Dick Fontaine and Ronan O'Rahilly gave me further research opportunities and encouragement. Neither of the film operations could have been achieved without the skill and comradeship of cameraman Raymond Grosjean and sound engineer Georges Méaume. These last two outstanding professionals worked with me loyally over fifteen years, in some of the most difficult and dangerous situations a journalist can encounter. In thanking them for their work on this case, I thank them for their labors during those years.

A number of people extended their friendship to include help and encouragement with this assignment. They include Kathy Anday, Fenella Dubes, Mariko Fukuda, Esme and Larry Gottlieb, Willie and Bríd Henry, Vicky Mason, Jane Rosemond, Ellen Shapley, and James Villiers-Stuart. Susan Rostochil, who typed the manuscript, was an unfailing source of help, as was Charlie Holland, who provided vital liaison and research in the United States. In the final stages, Cynthia Rowan urged me on and applied an eagle eye to the manuscript. Ms. Ziman, of the University of London Library, gave splendid cooperation. My editors, Helen Fraser, Victoria Petrie-Hay, and Barbara Boote in London, and Bruce Lee in New York, were tireless. I owe special thanks to PJ Dempsey, at Paragon House, for her initiative in creating this new edition.

Most of all, I thank those who agreed to talk to me of their own experiences—some of them possibly at considerable personal risk.

Preface

No American, whether he loved or loathed President John F. Kennedy, has been immune to the impact of his assassination. The very date—November 22, 1963—is now perceived as a turning point, a lurch toward decline in the fortunes of the world's most powerful people. Whatever Kennedy's own merits, few would now champion his successors. The United States has been led into military disaster by one President, into shame and scandal by the moral turpitude of another, into the doldrums by a third, and into floundering unease under the nondescript government of a fourth. In 1981, as Americans cast around once again for a new leader, some clamored for the sole surviving brother of the Kennedy who died in Dallas. Their yearning had its roots as much in legend as in earned respect, and the search for true quality was sidetracked by the very name Kennedy. In 1988, until scandal wiped his name off the ballot, some flocked to Gary Hart because he was said to *look* a little like John Kennedy. In a nation now introspective, with more than its share of recent martyrs, there is another element to this obsession. Long after John Kennedy's death, Americans still argue the manner of his passing. They are weary of the issue, but they do not let it drop.

The first official inquiry into the assassination—the Warren Commission—concluded that one man, Lee Harvy Oswald, murdered President Kennedy. He was said to have fired at the President as he drove through the Texan city of Dallas. This lone sniper, said the Commission, had lain in wait in the window of a warehouse, then picked off his victim with two accurate rifle shots. There had been no conspiracy. Yet, while the Commission made no suggestion that Oswald was insane, it failed to explain *why* he would have wanted to kill the President. The fact is that, on the contrary, Oswald had frequently expressed his liking for President Kennedy. Other factors, and many rumors, made the flat official verdict seem implausible. Oswald himself had been killed within days, and his executioner, Jack Ruby, had criminal connections. Oswald had an extraordinary personal history. Before his death, at the age of twenty-four, he had served as a radar operator at a top-secret base for American espionage operations, had spent years in the Soviet Union as a supposed defector, and—back in the United States—had dabbled in Cuban revolutionary politics. His apparent posture, that of the left-wing malcontent, seemed riddled with inconsistency. The Warren Commission account of Oswald's actions failed to satisfy the American public for long.

For a dozen years, in the face of official disdain, a small number of private citizens, convinced that the truth had not been told, worked doggedly to have the case reopened. In 1976, after a number of false starts, and after the cumulative shock of other political murders, they succeeded. By an overwhelming majority, Congress voted to conduct its own probe into President Kennedy's death and that of civil-rights leader Martin Luther King, shot down in 1968. The mandate was to make a "full and complete investigation," and the instrument was the specially formed body that became known as the "House Assassinations Committee." Its first chairman went so far as to tell the House, "In the case of President Kennedy, I am convinced there was a conspiracy involved." By 1978 that statement seemed rash and premature, and the Committee's final report was expected to be a damp squib. The fresh inquiry had placed the emphasis on hard scientific data rather than fickle human testimony, and science had produced nothing to alter the original findings. Then, in mid-summer 1978, the Committee was forced into a major reappraisal.

A distinguished acoustics expert, appointed to analyze a sound-recording made on the day of the assassination, came to a cautious yet sensational conclusion. He reported that the recording indicated not three shots, as had previously been thought, but four. Oswald alone could not possibly have fired four shots in the time available. Moreover, the expert noted, the third shot appeared to have originated in front of the President. It could not have been fired by Oswald, who had allegedly fired from behind his victim. If this latest information was sound, at least two gunmen had fired at the President in Dallas. Two gunmen would indicate a conspiracy, however limited. The Assassinations Committee ordered further expert study, and thus it was that two more scientists came to give last-minute testimony in the final hours of the Committee's mandate. Their report stated, to a scientific certainty, that there had indeed been more than one gunman. The Committee's Chief Counsel said flatly, "That there were two shooters, and thus a conspiracy, is a scientifically based fact."

Months later, in the summer of 1979, the Committee reported accordingly. The American people were told that President Kennedy "was probably assassinated as a result of a conspiracy." The scientific evidence, said the report, compelled acceptance of that fact and demanded "a re-examination of all that was thought to be true in the past." The Committee still believed that Oswald's finger was on the trigger of the gun that actually killed the President. Now, however, it expressed suspicion that elements of the Mafia, or anti-Castro activists, or both, may have taken part in the plot. It said pointedly that two specific living Mafia bosses, Carlos Marcello and Santos Trafficante, "had the motive, means, and opportunity to assassinate President Kennedy." It uncovered, for the first time, "credible associations" relating both Oswald and Jack Ruby—through others—to Marcello's crime organization. The Committee's Chief Counsel has said, "If history is well-served by truth, we have done history a favor." Others are not so sanguine. The Assassinations Committee has prolonged doubt and provoked new debate. As this edition will report, the Committee's experts remain at odds with others, not least with the National Academy of Sciences.

Of the twelve members of the Committee, three felt the conclusion about a second gunman was precipitate and perhaps in error. Another—and the Chief Counsel—believed there might have been as many as three gunmen. Meanwhile, independent researchers have been swift to pounce on the weaknesses in the Committee's report. These center on the role of Oswald. If he was, as he appeared, a zealous left-winger, how does he fit into a conspiracy inspired by the Mafia? If, as some have suggested, it was intended that he alone should take the blame, how to account for the Committee's second gunman? If he had been caught, as was perfectly possible at the time, what place did he have in a "lone left-wing gunman" scenario? The Committee could only admit weakly that "the assassin and the man who murdered him still appear against a backdrop of unexplained, or at least not fully explained, occurrences, associations and motivations." In spite of strong circumstantial evidence against Oswald, some sane, open-minded researchers believe he may have been framed. This possibility is not seriously considered in the Committee's report.

The Committee dismissed suggestions that either of the U.S. intelligence agencies, the Central Intelligence Agency or the Federal Bureau of Investigation, were involved in the assassination. While that seems quite correct, the report sidestepped the possible meaning of some of its own findings. The Committee concluded that FBI officials had destroyed evidence—a note from Oswald. It called this a "serious impeachment" of the credibility of the officers concerned. The Committee considered evidence that, within months of the assassination, Oswald had been separately reported in the company of two extreme right-wingers, one of them the former Agent-in-Charge of the Chicago FBI, a man with enduring Bureau connections. The Committee found some of this evidence "credible and significant" and left it at that. It avoided committing itself fully on whether Oswald ever had links with the CIA or other intelligence agencies. Yet the Committee admitted it was "extremely troubled" by the discovery that the CIA file of an official who had met Oswald in Russia was "segregated" as "a matter of cover." The CIA was "unable to explain" the reference to cover, and the Committee remained unsatisfied by the agency's explanation of the handling of the file. In the course of other research, the Committee found itself "inhibited by the refusal of the CIA to make available its sources . . ." on an important area.

The Committee established that one of Oswald's closest associates had contacts with a CIA agent in Dallas and later with a senior official of military intelligence. It was unable to confirm a claim that Oswald himself had been seen in the company of an American intelligence officer shortly before the assassination. Yet, when it received persuasive information that the officer named had existed, either at the CIA or within "one of the military intelligence agencies," intelligence headquarters pleaded ignorance. Some now firmly believe that the vital information has been withheld or destroyed. The Committee did discover that U.S. Army

Intelligence possessed a file on Oswald before the assassination. The Army failed, however, to make it available to the Warren Commission and has since destroyed it. In the light of this astonishing development the Committee concluded dryly. "The question of Oswald's possible affiliation with military intelligence could not be resolved."

The Committee extracted nothing material from the fact that, of the Mafia criminals suspected of involvement in the assassination, several had long been involved in illicit CIA plotting to murder Fidel Castro. Nevertheless, few would argue with the conclusion of one eminent witness. He testified that he believed the CIA was still concealing and falsifying information about its assassination projects.

The American press, to its discredit, has generally played down the achievements of the Assassinations Committee or brushed its conclusions aside. This lethargy may stem in part from the fact that—sixteen years ago—there was no serious attempt at investigative reporting of the Kennedy assassination. In those days, before Vietnam and Watergate, investigation was left to the government. Ever since, editors have been content to denigrate the efforts of those citizens who threw doubt on the original findings. In some cases they were right; there were gold-diggers and headline-seekers. Today, however, a massive and sober Congressional inquiry has vindicated the serious researchers. The press should now be prepared, at the very least, to treat the case seriously.

For more than two years I immersed myself in the massive documentation of the Kennedy case and traveled widely to question a great number of witnesses. This last was an opportunity denied to many students of the case, who must rely on scholarly research alone. It is, I suppose, a further comment on press performance that I know of no professional colleague who was ever assigned to delve so deeply or so long into the case. With those qualifications, and the patient help of serious students of the case, I have assembled this presentation of the crime—and the controversy—of the century.

There are those who may by now find it tedious to read forensic and ballistic details of the assassination. This is not a technical study, and I leave that work to the specialists. Yet the scientific aspects must be covered, not least because science has recently posed a major challenge to the Warren Commission verdict. Beyond the science lies a mass of troubling information. It all has its place when the evidence comes to be weighed.

From the plethora of past theories as to who killed Kennedy and why, the key targets of suspicion can now be distilled to three—members of the Mafia, American intelligence personnel, and anti-Castro activists. Elements of all these groups, accomplices in crime that they indubitably were in the Sixties, may have been involved. The Chief Counsel of Congress' Assassinations Committee, Professor Robert Blakey, has declared a personal belief that organized crime figures killed the President. He stresses that this is his personal opinion, not the Committee's. It is clear, from conversations with a number of former staff members, that the Committee staff wound up its work without reaching a consensus. One lawyer told me that "the idea of unique organized crime involvement is an unjustified poetic leap—there were too many unanswered questions in other areas." Specifically, he added, "Intelligence involvement in the assassination remains an open question." A staff investigator told me that, in particular "the Military Intelligence angle was not covered adequately . . . the Defense Department held out on us, and that—after all—is the department that destroyed the Oswald file." A number of clues suggest that Oswald was, before the assassination, the tool of some part of American intelligence. Such disturbing leads demand urgent further inquiry. Nobody I spoke to on the Assassinations Committee—whatever his personal opinion on the evidence—felt that the case had yet been exhaustively investigated. All agree that lack of time and funds forced the Committee to leave important research unfinished.

As he left office, the Committee's Chief Counsel said of the original inquiries into the Kennedy and King assassinations, "To see how poorly this was done in 1964 and 1968 has been the single most soul-shattering experience that I've had. And I would be deeply disappointed in the agencies of my government, and in the people who currently run them, if these cases were simply allowed to die." Chief Counsel Blakey said he believed that perhaps—

given further investigation, backed by the clout of the Justice Department—he could come close to bringing "an indictment that would secure a conviction." That statement was, by any standards, a remarkable development. Coming from a public figure of "Professor Blakey's standing, it should surely have prompted a firm, positive response from the law-enforcement authorities. Instead, the Justice Department responded with delays and diversions.

In March 1979 the Assassinations Committee asked the Department of Justice, formally, to arrange specialist examination of some films shot in Dealey Plaza, to study the acoustics evidence, to review the Committee's findings, and to report whether further investigation was justified. It took the Department *nearly a decade*—till March 1988—to send its brusque, five-page conclusion to Congress. This document offered a thin pretext for having failed to examine the films. It shrugged off the acoustics issue on the basis of new negatives, without conducting further studies that could go far towards resolving the matter. The Department concluded blandly that "no persuasive evidence can be identified to support the theory of a conspiracy" in the assassinations of either President Kennedy or Martin Luther King. "No further investigation appears to be warranted," said the Department, "unless new information . . . sufficient to support additional investigative activity, becomes available."

So much for Congress and its six-million dollar inquiry. Former Assassinations Committee Chief Counsel, Professor Blakey, is now a disillusioned man. "The fiasco with the acoustics," he says, "is incredibly disappointing. Instead of setting out to find out whether what we did is correct, they simply set out to refute it. I think I was naive to believe this was a question of evidence, and science. I see now that it is a question of a public controversy, in which evidence plays a minimal role."

"You get the feeling," says Blakey of the Justice Department study, "that—instead of science—it was an effort to lay to rest inconvenient information. I think that from beginning to end, the staff people—and I include the FBI—thought the whole thing a waste of time and money. It was politics for them. . . . One thing I've learned from this is the wonderful capacity of the human mind to be incapable of sustained analysis and balanced judgement . . .

The whole assassination just has not received serious, sustained study."

The Professor believes the Justice Department ignored the totality of the evidence, evidence that still leads him to believe President Kennedy was killed as a result of a conspiracy.

Given the Justice Department's failure to pursue that evidence, there is now virtually no hope of a judicial solution to the greatest murder mystery of our time. In the face of the government's negligence—at best—it remains for ordinary people to weigh the available information as best they may. I have added a new Aftermath to this edition of *Conspiracy*, to include significant developments since 1980—all of them troubling, all of them ignored by officialdom. The full truth may never out, but the facts in this book offer a glimpse of it.

A.S.
May 1989.

Cast of Main Characters

JOHN F. KENNEDY: President of the United States
ROBERT F. KENNEDY: Attorney General of the United States

The Oswald Family

OSWALD, LEE HARVEY: at first officially credited with sole responsibility for murdering the President. Latest formal findings indicate he had at least one accomplice; doubt remains whether he actually fired shots on November 22.
OSWALD, MARINA: (née Nikolaevna Prusakova): abruptly married Oswald in the Soviet Union and returned with him to the United States.
OSWALD, MARGUERITE: Lee's mother.
OSWALD, ROBERT: Lee's eldest brother.
MURRET, CHARLES "Dutz": Oswald's uncle in New Orleans; had connections with organized crime.
MURRET, LILLIAN: wife of Charles.

Individuals who either appear more than once or play a role of significance

ALBA, ADRIAN: garage proprietor who knew and observed Oswald in New Orleans.
ALEXANDER, WILLIAM: Assistant District Attorney of Dallas.
BANISTER, GUY: former senior FBI agent and reportedly Naval Intelligence operative—allegedly became involved with Oswald in New Orleans.
BOOTHE LUCE, CLARE: writer and diplomat, financial supporter of anti-Castro exiles.

BRADLEE, BEN: then Washington Bureau Chief of *Newsweek* and friend of Kennedy family; learned of Hoffa threat against Robert Kennedy and urged President to see French correspondent Jean Daniel before he traveled to Cuba.

BROWDER, EDDIE: Florida arms dealer involved in Cuban activities.

BUCHANAN, JAMES: wrote article suggesting Oswald had engaged in pro-Castro activities in Miami.

BUCHANAN, JERRY: brother of James, anti-Castro activist and solider of fortune.

BUTLER, GEORGE: Dallas police lieutenant involved in unmasking early mob attempt to move into Dallas; was part of basement security operation when Ruby killed Oswald.

CAMPBELL, ALLEN: worked for Guy Banister Associates in New Orleans—date uncertain.

CAMPBELL, DANIEL: brother of Allen, worked for Guy Banister in 1963.

CLARK, COMER: British reporter who claimed to have interviewed Fidel Castro about Oswald visits to Cuban Embassy in Mexico City.

CONNALLY, JOHN: Governor of Texas, seriously wounded in shooting which killed the President.

CONTRERAS, OSCAR: Mexican newspaper editor, formerly member of Mexican left-wing student group; reports meeting a man who identified himself as Oswald.

CURRY, JESSE: Dallas police chief at time of assassination.

DELGADO, NELSON: Marine who served with Oswald in California.

DE MOHRENSCHILDT, GEORGE: Russian emigré, with links to U.S. intelligence, who befriended Oswald on his return from the Soviet Union.

DE MOHRENSCHILDT, JEANNE: wife of George—also spent time with the Oswalds.

DESLATTE, OSCAR: New Orleans truck dealer who reported the use of the name "Oswald" by anti-Castro movement as early as 1961.

FERRIE, DAVID: former airline pilot with alleged links to the CIA and definite links to the Mafia; he reportedly associated with Oswald.

FRITZ, Captain WILL: Chief of Homicide for Dallas police department.

GARRISON, JIM: New Orleans district attorney who reopened Kennedy investigation in 1967.

GARRO, ELENA: Mexican right-wing writer with reported connections to American Embassy; made inflammatory allegations about an Oswald relationship with Cuban Embassy staff.

GLENN, JOHN: former U.S. Air Force intelligence operative who subsequently joined Fair Play for Cuba; his career had intriguing parallels to that of Oswald.

HEMMING, GERRY: former Marine, later anti-Castro fighter; he claims to have encountered Oswald as early as 1959 and to have recognized him as a military intelligence agent.

"HIDELL, ALEK": pseudonym used by Oswald to refer to a supposed colleague in his "pro-Castro" activities; the name was also used to purchase the rifle found at the Texas School Book Depository; "Hidell" was a nickname applied to John Rene Heindel, a Marine who served with Oswald in Japan.

HUNT, H. L.: Texas oil magnate.

HYDE, MARIE: encountered Oswald in Minsk after joining American tourist party in unusual circumstances; was involved in taking photographs that featured Oswald.

JOHNSON, LYNDON B.: Vice President in 1963; he acceded to Presidency on death of President Kennedy.

KANTOR, SETH: Washington correspondent who encountered Jack Ruby at hospital where the President died; has since become specialist on Ruby aspects of the case.

KRAMER, MONICA: encountered Oswald in Minsk and—according to her friend Rita Naman—also in Moscow; her camera was used to take a photograph featuring Oswald.

MANN, THOMAS: American ambassador in Mexico City.

MARTIN, JACK: employee of Guy Banister in New Orleans; later reported that he suspected a connection between Oswald and David Ferrie.

MARTIN, JOHN: president of Chicago Scrap Iron and Junk Handlers' Union in 1939, when Jack Ruby was "bagman"; his accession marked the intervention of organized crime in union affairs.

MCKEOWN, ROBERT: gun runner who reported visit by Jack Ruby in connection with Cuban intrigue; he later claimed he had also met Lee Oswald.

MCVICKAR, JOHN: assistant consul at U.S. Embassy in Moscow, met Oswald.

"YURI MEREGINSKY": intermittently identified by Marina Oswald as the man who introduced her to Oswald.

NAMAN, RITA: American tourist who reports encountering Oswald in both Moscow and Minsk; was involved in taking pictures of him in Minsk Square.

NOSENKO, YURI: KGB officer who defected to the United States shortly after assassination; in spite of grave doubts about his motives, is now working for the CIA.

PAINE, RUTH: befriended Marina Oswald in Texas; Oswald stayed at her house on the eve of the assassination.

PRUSAKOV, ILYA: Marina Oswald's uncle, a lieutenant colonel in Soviet Ministry of the Interior.

ROBERTS, DELPHINE: New Orleans right-wing activist and secretary to Guy Banister (her daughter is also called Delphine).

RODRIGUEZ, ERNESTO: New Orleans language-school proprietor who met Oswald.

RODRIGUEZ, ERNESTO: former CIA contract agent in Mexico City; says Oswald told Cuban authorities about CIA plans to kill Fidel Castro.

RUBY, JACK (né Rubenstein): Dallas nightclub owner with lifelong links to organized crime; he killed Lee Oswald.

SAPP, Capt. CHARLES: member of Miami police intelligence section; he warned of potential threat to U.S. officials by anti-Castro exiles; learned of menacing remarks by Joseph Milteer, and says there was a security alert during President's visit to Miami on November 18.

SNYDER, RICHARD: consul at U.S. Embassy in Moscow, with intelligence background, who met Oswald.

THORNLEY, KERRY: served in Marines with Oswald.

TIPPIT, J.D.: Dallas police patrolman shot shortly after the President's murder; Oswald was officially identified as his lone killer.

VOEBEL, EDWARD: New Orleans school friend who was in Civil Air Patrol with Oswald.

WALKER, Major General EDWIN: right-wing agitator and victim of an assassination attempt in April 1963; Oswald has been officially named as being involved, but evidence suggests more than one person took part.

WEBSTER, ROBERT: technician with Rand Development Corporation; his defection to Russia had intriguing similarities to Oswald's.

ZAPRUDER, ABRAHAM: took film of assassination which became key evidence.

Individuals associated with U.S. intelligence activities

ANGLETON, JAMES: CIA Chief of Counterintelligence; handled many matters connected with Kennedy assassination investigation.

"FRANK BENDER": cover name of CIA director of preparations for Bay of Pigs invasion.

"MAURICE BISHOP": cover name reportedly used by CIA officer alleged to have met Oswald before the assassination and to have tried to fabricate evidence linking him to Cuban diplomats; "Bishop" was the subject of a national appeal for information which might help identify him.

"B. H.": pseudonym given by Congress' Assassinations Committee to former CIA covert operative who says he knew "Bishop."

"RON CROSS": pseudonym given by Assassinations Committee to former CIA case officer who believes "Bishop" was a cover name used by CIA officer David Phillips.

DAVIS, THOMAS: criminal, with apparent CIA connections, believed to have known Jack Ruby.

DAVISON, Capt. ALEXIS: Assistant Air Attaché at U.S. Embassy, Moscow; met Oswald.

"D.C.": pseudonym given by Assassinations Committee to former Deputy Chief, CIA Soviet Bloc Division.

DULLES, ALLEN: Director of CIA till late 1961, later member of Warren Commission.

FITZGERALD, DESMOND: CIA official who claimed to represent Robert Kennedy when discussing anti-Castro coup with Rolando Cubela, disaffected aide to the Cuban leader.

FOX, Col. THOMAS: Chief of Clandestine Services for Defense Intelligence Agency.

GALLEGO, RODRIGUEZ ALBERTO: alleged CIA operative said to have operated observation post opposite Cuban Embassy in Mexico City.

GAUDET, WILLIAM: CIA operative whose name appeared next to Oswald's on Mexico City visa list.

"DOUG CUPTON": cover name of CIA special operations official; does not recall David Phillips using the name "Maurice Bishop".

HARVEY, WILLIAM: senior CIA official who coordinated CIA-Mafia plots to kill Castro and handled "Executive Action"—the CIA blue-print for foreign assassinations.

HELMS, RICHARD: CIA Deputy Director for Plans (in charge of covert operations) at the time of assassination, later senior liaison officer with Warren Commission.

HUNT, E. HOWARD: chief CIA political officer for anti-Castro exiles; one of the earliest to recommend assassination of Fidel Castro.

JONES, Lt. Col. ROBERT E.: operations officer, U.S. Army 112th Military Intelligence Group, at time of assassination; says Army had file on Oswald.

KAIL, Col. SAM: U.S. Army attaché in Havana after revolution, reportedly mentioned by "Maurice Bishop"; in 1963 was involved in Army Intelligence talks with Haitian representative Clemard Charles.

MAHEU, ROBERT: former Chicago FBI agent, chosen as liaison man between CIA and Mafia.

MARCHETTI, VICTOR: former executive assistant to Deputy Director of CIA, with previous specialist experience of CIA's Soviet operations.

MCCONE, JOHN: CIA Director from 1961 until after President Kennedy's death.

"MR. MELTON": pseudonym for American intelligence officer who allegedly trained Antonio Veciana in Havana.

MILLER, NEWTON: former Chief of Operations, CIA Counterintelligence.

MOORE, J. WALTON: CIA Domestic Contacts Division representative in Dallas.

OTEPKA, OTTO: Chief Security Officer at State Department.

PAWLEY, WILLIAM: former American diplomat involved in antiCastro campaign.

PHILLIPS, DAVID: former senior CIA officer concerned with antiCastro operations; posts included Chief, Western Hemisphere Division, CIA Directorate of Operations, covert operative, Havana, 1960; a Chief of Covert Operations, 1961–3; in Mexico City at time of Oswald visit in autumn, 1963.

POWERS, GARY: pilot of U-2 spy plane that crashed in Soviet Union in 1960.

PROUTY, Col. FLETCHER: Department of Defense Focal Point for liaison with CIA.

QJ/WIN: code name for foreign citizen with criminal background recruited by CIA to spot potential assassins.

FBI officers

DE BRUEYS, WARREN: New Orleans special agent, has refuted an allegation that he knew Oswald.

DOYLE, DANIEL: Atlanta agent reported to have resigned because Cuban aspects of the post-assassination inquiry were suppressed.

FLYNN, CHARLES: Dallas agent who used Jack Ruby as an informant in 1959.

HOOVER, J. EDGAR: Director of the FBI.

HOSTY, JAMES: Dallas agent who handled Oswald case before assassination; he admits destroying a note sent to the FBI by Oswald.

KAACK, MILTON: New Orleans agent involved in security investigation of Oswald before assassination.

KENNEDY, REGIS: New Orleans agent involved in assassination investigation; he defended Mafia boss Carlos Marcello.

MURTAUGH, ARTHUR: Atlanta agent who has criticized FBI handling of both Kennedy and King inquiries.

QUIGLEY, JOHN: New Orleans agent who responded to Oswald's request to see an FBI representative in summer 1963.

SHANKLIN, GORDON: special agent-in-charge in Dallas at the time of the assassination; alleged to have ordered Hosty to destroy Oswald's note.

SULLIVAN, WILLIAM: Assistant Director of FBI.

WOOD, JAMES: agent who questioned George de Mohrenschildt in Haiti.

Individuals involved in the conflict over Cuba

ALVARADO, GILBERTO: sell-avowed Nicaraguan agent whose allegations linked Oswald to Cuban diplomats in Mexico City.

"ANGEL" (or "ANGELO"): one of the Latins who visited Silvia Odio in the company of a man introduced as "Leon Oswald"; claimed to be a member of JURE, or Junta Revolucionaria Cubana.

ARCACHA SMITH, SERGIO: former official under Cuban dictator Batista; in 1961 set up Cuban Revolutionary Council office at 544 Camp Street, New Orleans.

ARTIME, MANUEL: key figure in CIA's Bay of Pigs invasion and close friend of Howard Hunt.

ATTWOOD, WILLIAM: special adviser to United States delegation at United Nations; carried rank of ambassador.

AZCUE, EUSEBIO: Cuban consul in Mexico City; met visitor called "Oswald" but believes he was bogus.

BRINGUIER, CARLOS: New Orleans representative of DRE, or Directorio Revolucionario Estudiantil; clashed with Oswald over Cuba.

CAIRE, RONNIE: New Orleans advertising man and supporter of Crusade to Free Cuba; he "seemed to recall" a visit from Oswald.

CARDONA, JOSE MIRO: president of the CRC—Cuban Revolutionary Council—until April 1963, when he resigned in protest
against President Kennedy's Cuba policy.

CASTRO, FIDEL: leader of the Cuban revolution and subsequently
Prime Minister.

CUBELA ROLANDO: disillusioned hero of the Cuban revolution
recruited by the CIA and code-named AM/LASH; he took part in
one of the many plots to kill Castro.

DANIEL, JEAN: prominent French journalist (for L'Express); on
the day of President Kennedy's assassination he was with Fidel
Castro, providing a degree of informal contact between the two
leaders.

DURAN, SYLVIA: secretary to Cuban consul in Mexico City; processed a visa request in the name of Oswald, although controversy still surrounds the true identity of the applicant.

GONZALEZ, PEDRO: president of Cuban Liberation Committee in
Abilene, Texas; reportedly received message signed "Lee Oswald" five days before the assassination.

GONZALEZ, REINALDO: national coordinator in Cuba of the left-
tending anti-Castro movement MRP—Revolutionary Movement of the People, arrested on Odio estate after involvement
in assassination attempt on Castro organized by Antonio Veciana.

HALL, LORAN: worked with one of CIA-backed Free Cuba groups
and was arrested for defiance of ban on military activity; after
assassination his "fabrication" defused the Odio evidence.

HARKER, DANIEL: Associated Press correspondent in Havana;
interviewed Castro in September 1963.

HOWARD, LISA: correspondent for American Broadcasting Company; following interview with Castro, she helped Ambassador
Attwood in his diplomatic dialogue with Havana.

KOHLY, MARIO: son of anti-Castro exile politician of the same
name; believes his father, who called himself President-in-exile,
had inside knowledge about the assassination.

LECHUGA, CARLOS: Cuban ambassador to the United Nations,
involved in Castro-Kennedy peace feelers just before assassination.

"LEOPOLDO": the Latin who led the group of three men who

visited Silvia Odio; introduced one of the party as "Leon Oswald"; claimed to be a member of JURE, or Junta Revolucionaria Cubana.

MARTINEZ, JORGE: anti-Castro exile who reportedly talked in sinister terms about a Marine marksman called "Lee" before the assassination.

MASFERRER, ROLANDO: crony of former Cuban dictator Batista; became prominent in exile movement.

MIRABAL, ALFREDO: incoming Cuban consul to Mexico City; observed visit to Cuban Embassy by individual who said he was Oswald.

MOORE, JOSEPH (possibly pseudonym): representative of Friends of Democratic Cuba who in 1961 asked that name "Oswald" be placed on truck order.

ODIO, SYLVIA and ANNIE: daughters of wealthy Cuban political activist Amador; recalled visit before assassination by two Latins accompanied by man introduced as "Leon Oswald." Silvia, a supporter of JURE, was told that "Leon" recommended the President's assassination.

PENA, OREST: anti-Castro activist in New Orleans; claimed that he saw Oswald in his bar with a U.S. agent and that he was intimidated after assassination by FBI agent; he assisted Bringuier when in police custody.

PRIO, CARLOS: former President of Cuba with links to organized crime.

QUIROGA, CARLOS: anti-Castro militant, friend of Carlos Bringuier; went to visit Oswald following the New Orleans street fracas.

SAN ROMAN, PEPE: commander of invasion brigade at Bay of Pigs.

STURGIS, FRANK (né Fiorini): early pro-Castro fighter, then "Inspector" of Havana casinos, then anti-Castro militant; spread story linking Oswald to pro-Castro intelligence. Later was one of Watergate burglars.

DEL VALLE, ELADIO: headed Free Cuba Committee in Florida, reportedly linked to Santos Trafficante, and close friend of David Ferrie.

VALLEJO, Dr. RENE: senior Castro aide who acted as liaison in Washington-Havana contacts shortly before assassination.

DE VARONA, ANTONIO: vice president, then leader, of Cuban Revolutionary Council; reported to have taken part in CIA-Mafia plot against Castro through liaison of Santos Trafficante.

VECIANA, ANTONIO: anti-Castro militant, key figure in Alpha 66; claims that his CIA mentor, "Maurice Bishop," was involved with Lee Oswald before assassination.

Individuals mentioned in chapters related to organized crime or to Jack Ruby

ALEMAN, JOSE: Cuban exile, son of former government minister; reported Santos Trafficante as saying that President Kennedy was "going to be hit."

ANDREWS, DEAN: New Orleans attorney; says that Oswald visited his office in summer 1963 and that following the assassination he was asked to act as Oswald's legal representative.

BAKER, ROBERT "BARNEY": aide to Jimmy Hoffa; he spoke to Jack Ruby on the telephone twice, two weeks before the assassination.

BECKER, EDWARD: sometime casino employee, later investigator; reports that Carlos Marcello discussed murder of President Kennedy.

BRADING, EUGENE (changed his name to Jim Braden in 1963): was briefly detained after assassination for reportedly "acting suspiciously."

BRUNEAU, EMILE: associate of Marcello aide Nofio Pecora; intervened to bail out Oswald after street dispute in New Orleans.

CAMPISI, JOSEPH: owner of Egyptian Restaurant in Dallas; visited Jack Ruby in jail.

CIVELLO, JOSPEH: reportedly ran Dallas operations for Carlos Marcello.

CRIMALDI, CHARLES: former Chicago contract killer turned Government informant.

DANIELS, "HAWK": federal investigator, later judge; listened in on phone conversation between Jimmy Hoffa and an aide with reference to a plan to kill Robert Kennedy.

DEAN, Sergeant PATRICK: played central role in police security operation before Ruby killed Oswald.

DOLAN, JAMES: contact of Jack Ruby, linked to Santos Trafficante and to Marcello network.

EXNER, JUDITH: had relationship with President Kennedy and with Mafia boss Sam Giancana.

GIANCANA, SAM: Chicago Mafia boss and coordinator of CIA-Mafia plans to murder Fidel Castro.

GILL, WRAY: lawyer for Carlos Marcello; David Ferrie worked for him.

HARRISON, WILLIAM "BLACKIE": Dallas policeman involved in basement security operation before Ruby shot Oswald.

HOFFA, JIMMY: head of Teamsters Union; reported to have planned murder of Robert Kennedy.

HOWARD, TOM: Jack Ruby's first lawyer.

JONES, PAUL ROLAND: took leading part in early mob attempt to move into Dallas; friend of Jack Ruby.

KOHN, AARON: director of New Orleans Crime Commission.

LIVERDE: name of man identified by Edward Becker as being at meeting when Marcello discussed murder of President Kennedy.

MARCELLO, CARLOS (né Calogero Minacore): today still a powerful organized-crime leader in the United States; based in New Orleans. Is reported to have discussed plan to murder President Kennedy about a year before the assassination.

MARTIN, JACK: investigator for Guy Banister; he suspected link between David Ferrie and Oswald.

MARTINO, JOHN: involved with organized crime, U.S. intelligence, and anti-Castro movement; reported as saying that Oswald was "put together" by the "anti-Castro people."

MATTHEWS, RUSSELL D: worked in Havana casino operated by Santos Trafficante, was reportedly involved in plot to murder Fidel Castro, and knew Jack Ruby; call was made by Ruby to Matthews' wife's phone in October 1963.

MCLANEY, MIKE: sometime owner of the National Casino in Havana.

MCLANEY, WILLIAM: brother of Mike, once operated from Tropicana Hotel in Havana; controlled property near New Orleans raided in July 1963 because of anti-Castro activities.

MCWILLIE, LEWIS: friend of Jack Ruby, formerly manager of Tropicana nightclub in Havana, then owned by associate of Santos Trafficante.

MILLER, MURRAY "DUSTY": senior aide to Jimmy Hoffa; Ruby called him two weeks before the assassination.

OLSEN, HARRY: Dallas policeman who talked at length with Jack Ruby during the night following the assassination.

PARTIN, EDWARD: aide to Jimmy Hoffa who reported that Hoffa planned the murder of Robert Kennedy; he believes Hoffa was also a threat to President Kennedy himself.

PAUL, RALPH: Dallas restaurant owner and friend of Jack Ruby, who called him repeatedly following the assassination.

PECORA, NOFIO: associate of Carlos Marcello; knew Oswald's uncle Charles Murret. Jack Ruby called his office number in New Orleans less than a month before the assassination.

REID, ED: Pulitzer Prize-winning author on Mafia who first reported alleged discussion by Carlos Marcello of plan to murder President Kennedy.

ROPPOLO, CARL: oil geologist; according to his associate, Edward Becker, he attended meeting at which Marcello discussed plan to murder President Kennedy.

ROSELLI, JOHN: gangster; go-between in CIA-Mafia plots to assassinate Fidel Castro.

SAIA, SAM: associate of Carlos Marcello and of Oswald's uncle, Charles Murret.

SEHRT, CLEM: lawyer with suspected underworld connections in New Orleans; Oswald's mother consulted him when her son tried to join the Marines while underage.

SENATOR, GEORGE: Jack Ruby's roommate; was with him in the hours before he killed Lee Oswald.

SERE, RAOUL: New Orleans lawyer, reportedly under influence of Marcello organization; advised Oswald's mother when her son defected to the Soviet Union.

TANNENBAUM, HAROLD: New Orleans club manager; called Jack Ruby shortly before assassination.

TERMINE, SAM: Marcello henchman; knew Oswald's mother.

TODD, JACK: associate of Santos Trafficante who knew Jack Ruby; his phone number was found in Ruby's car after the murder of Oswald.

TRAFFICANTE, SANTOS: today a powerful organized-crime figure in the United States; was key figure in CIA-Mafia plots to kill Fidel Castro, may have been visited by Jack Ruby in Cuba in 1959, and allegedly said in advance of the assassination that President Kennedy was "going to be hit".

WEINER, IRWIN: financial adviser to Jimmy Hoffa; has produced conflicting explanations of a phone conversation with Ruby less than a month before the assassination.

WEST, JEAN: was staying at Cabana Motel in Dallas on the eve of the President's assassination; David Ferrie called her apartment house in Chicago eight weeks earlier.

WILSON (HUDSON), JOHN: was in detention camp in Cuba along with Santos Trafficante in 1959; after the assassination he reported that a "gangster type named Ruby" visited "Santos" in the prison.

Read not to contradict and confute, nor to believe and take for granted . . . but to weigh and consider.

—Francis Bacon

CONSPIRACY

CHAPTER 1

Ambush

*It may be that he shall take my hand
And lead me into his dark land
And close my eyes and quench my breath. . . .
But I've a rendezvous with Death*

—Lines from battle poem quoted by President Kennedy

In his office at the White House, the President looked gloomily across the desk at his press secretary. "I wish I weren't going to Dallas," he said. The secretary replied. "Don't worry about it. It's going to be a great trip."

It was November 20, 1963. The President had received warnings about Dallas from all sides. Senator William Fulbright had told him, "Dallas is a very dangerous place. I wouldn't go there. Don't you go." That morning Senator Hubert Humphrey and Congressman Hale Boggs had advised him not to go, the Congressman saying, "Mr. President, you're going into a hornet's nest."

The President knew he had to go. Dallas, a thousand miles away, had voted overwhelmingly for Richard Nixon in the last presidential election. This time around, the state of Texas as a whole was sure to be tough territory for the Democrats, and Kennedy was determined to take the initiative.

Yet Texas was a menace. Dallas, sweltering in its interminable summer, was dangerously overheated in a different way. It was a mecca for the radical right. Leading lights of the community included a racist former Army general, a Mayor who reportedly sympathized with the city's flourishing and furiously right-wing John Birch Society, and a vociferous millionaire obsessed with the Communist menace. Men of their ilk cried "treason" at Kennedy's talk of racial integration, his nuclear test ban treaty, and accommodation with the Communist world. It was only a year since the Cuban missile crisis, and the President was now showered with accusations that he had gone soft on Fidel Castro. Right-wing extremism was the boil on the face of American politics, and Dallas the point where it might burst. But John Kennedy had set his mind on going.

On November 21 the President flew south from Washington to San Antonio, his first stop on the Texas tour. All went well there, and Kennedy made a speech about the space age. "We stand on the edge of a great new era . . ." He went on to Houston and talked about the space program again. "Where there is no vision, the people perish . . ." Before the President arrived in Fort Worth, at midnight, he had traveled safely in four motorcades.

November 22 began with a speech in the rain and a political breakfast. Then, back in his hotel room, Kennedy read the newspapers. In the *Dallas Morning News* he saw an advertisement placed by "The American Fact-Finding Committee." Headlined WELCOME MR. KENNEDY TO DALLAS, it inquired, "Why do you say we have built a 'wall of freedom' around Cuba when there is no freedom in Cuba today? Because of your policy, thousands of Cubans have been imprisoned . . . the entire population of 7,000,000 Cubans are living in slavery. . . ." The advertisement, whose leading sponsors included a local organizer of the John Birch Society and the son of H. L. Hunt, the Dallas oil millionaire, prompted the President to turn to his wife and murmur, "You know, we're heading into nut country today."

Four days earlier, when the President visited Miami, there had apparently been a security flap. A motorcade was reportedly canceled following concern about disaffected Cuban exiles. The Secret Service had information that a right-wing extremist had talked about a plan to shoot the President "from an office building with a high-powered rifle." Perhaps his personal escort had mentioned it to Kennedy, for now—in Fort Worth—he murmured to an aide, "Last night would have been a hell of a night to assassinate a President . . . Anyone perched above the crowd with a rifle could do it." John Kennedy even crouched down and mimed how an assassin might strike.

Just before noon the President arrived in Dallas. There were welcoming crowds at the airport, and then he was traveling to the city center in an open limousine. As Kennedy passed, one spectator said to her husband, "The President ought to be awarded the Purple Heart just for coming to Dallas."

At 12:29 P.M. the motorcade was amidst cheering crowds, moving slowly through the metal and glass canyons of central Dallas.

For a while there had been no talking in the President's car. Then, with the passing crowd a kaleidoscope of welcome, the wife of the Governor of Texas, Nellie Connally, turned to smile at the President. It was now that she said, "Mr. Kennedy, you can't say Dallas doesn't love you."

The President, sitting behind her and to her right, replied, "That is very obvious." With his wife Jacqueline beside him, he continued waving to the people.

Ponderously, at eleven miles an hour, the procession moved on to Elm Street and into an open space. This was Dealey Plaza, a wide expanse of grass stretching away to the left of the cars. To the right of the President towered the Texas School Book Depository, a warehouse, the last high building in this part of the city. Its far end marked the end of the urban ugliness and the end of likely danger to the President during the motorcade. Here there was a grassy slope, topped by an ornamental colonnade. In the lead car an officer looked ahead at a railway tunnel and said to a colleague, "We've almost got it made." It was now twelve seconds past 12:30 P.M.

The several shots rang out in rapid succession. According to a Secret Serviceman in the car, the President said, "My God, I'm hit."[1] He lurched in his seat, both hands clawing toward his throat. Directly in front of the President, Governor Connally heard one shot and was then hit himself. He screamed. For five seconds the car actually slowed down. Then came more gunfire. The President fell violently backwards and to his left, his head exploding in a halo of brain tissue, blood and bone. To Mrs. Connally it "was like buckshot falling all over us." As the car finally gathered speed, Mrs. Kennedy believed she cried, "I love you, Jack." From the front seat the Governor's wife heard her exclaim, "Jack . . . they've killed my husband." then "I have his brains in my hand." This last Mrs. Kennedy repeated time and time again. It was over.

Half an hour later, in an emergency room at nearby Parkland Hospital, a doctor told the President's wife what she already knew, "The President is gone." Governor Connally, though seriously wounded, survived.

The dying of President Kennedy was brutally brief. Yet it has taken some time, and care, to write this summary of the shooting with integrity. Twenty-six years on, little is clear about what happened in Dealey Plaza except its stark tragedy. Few murders in history had such a massive audience or were caught in the act by the camera, yet for millions the case remains unsolved. No assassination has been analyzed and documented so laboriously by public officials and private citizens. Yet thinking people remain uncertain who killed the President. Why the murder was committed, only the arrogant or the opinionated can pretend to know for sure. Weary though we may be after years of controversy and nitpicking, any serious inquiry has to begin where life ended for John Kennedy—the moment the shots were fired in Dealey Plaza.

I

DALLAS

The Open and Shut Case

CHAPTER 2

The Evidence Before You

Detection is, or ought to be, an exact science, and should be treated in the same cold and unemotional manner.

—Sherlock Holmes, in *The Sign of the Four*

In any fatal shooting inquiry, the primary factors are ballistics and wounds. Human testimony, though often crucial, must be weighed against the picture presented by hard evidence. In the Kennedy assassination they are the raw material for the answers to vital questions. How many gunmen fired how many bullets, and from what position? Obviously, if gunfire came from more than one vantage point, there must have been more than one assassin. Similarly, if more shots came from one position than could be fired by one gunman in the available time, it follows that accomplices were at work.

Evidence there was in profusion, and it was all poorly handled in the first investigation. This is what we are left with in 1989— leaving aside for the moment the question of assigning guilt for the shooting.

Dealey Plaza provided a field day for the ballistics experts. Soon after the assassination a policeman found three spent cartridge cases lying near an open window on the sixth floor of the Texas School Book Depository, the large warehouse to the right rear of President Kennedy's car at the time of the attack. Within an hour, another policeman spotted a bolt-action rifle,[2] the now infamous 6.5 Mannlicher-Carcano, stashed behind a pile of boxes and also on the sixth floor. A number of bullet fragments were recovered—from the wounds suffered by the President and Governor Connally, and in the Presidential limousine. One intact bullet,[3] virtually undamaged to the layman's eye, turned up on a stretcher

at the hospital where the victims had been treated. Suffice it to say
at this point that firearms experts have firmly linked the cartridge
cases to the rifle; they are sure the whole bullet and the bullet
fragments came from the same gun. Bullet damage was also noticed on the inside of the windshield of the Presidential car and on
a section of the curb in Dealey Plaza. No other gun or missiles
were recovered immediately after the assassination.[4] The catalogue of ballistics evidence is at least clear-cut, but the accounting
of the wounds is a different matter. The autopsy on President
Kennedy, perhaps the most important autopsy of our time, was
seriously flawed. Had it not been, much of today's wearisome
doubt could have been avoided.

An hour and a half after the shooting of the President there
came a struggle over his corpse. At the hospital, as the Secret
Service team prepared to take the body to Washington, Dr. Earl
Rose, the Dallas County Medical Examiner, backed by a Justice of
the Peace, barred their way. The doctor said that, under Texas
law, the body of a murder victim may not be removed until an
autopsy has been performed. And the J.P., Judge Ward, declared,
"It's just another homicide as far as I'm concerned."

"Go screw yourself," replied Kenneth O'Donnell, Special
Assistant to the dead President.

The Secret Service agents put the doctor and the judge up
against the wall at gunpoint and swept out of the hospital with the
President's body. They were wrong in laws, and with hindsight
they denied their President an efficient autopsy. That evening, at
eight o'clock, three doctors at Bethesda Naval Hospital began the
examination to determine precisely how the President had died.
Incredibly, according to the expert study commissioned by Congress' Assassinations Committee, the doctors "had insufficient
training and experience to evaluate a death from gunshot
wounds." None of them were forensic pathologists, full-time experts in determining the cause of death in criminal cases.

The late Medical Examiner for New York City, Dr. Milton
Helpern, said of the President's autopsy, "It's like sending a
seven-year-old boy who has taken three lessons on the violin over
to the New York Philharmonic and expecting him to perform a
Tchaikovsky symphony. He knows how to hold the violin and

bow, but he has a long way to go before he can make music." In 1978 the chairman of the medical panel for Congress' Assassinations Committee, Dr. Michael Baden, said formally that the autopsy was deficient in "the qualification of the pathologists . . . the failure to inspect the clothing . . . the inadequate documentation of injuries, lack of proper preservation of evidence, and incompleteness of the autopsy."

Four wounds were reportedly found in the President's body during this breathtakingly inefficient procedure. The autopsy doctors reported finding a massive defect in the skull, a much smaller wound at the back of the skull, a wound in the right back area, and a hole in the throat.

The skull damage—the fatal wound—was seen as a hole thirteen centimeters wide on the right side, extending both forward and back. This the doctors deemed a wound of exit. The small head wound, judged to be a wound of entry, was 2.5 centimeters to the right and slightly above the protuberance at the back of the skull. The bullet hole in the back was considered an entry wound, and the doctors placed it 14 centimeters below the right mastoid process—a bump at the rear of the skull. An autopsy sketch of the same wound, however, placed it much lower. The doctors were at first misled by what appeared to be merely a surgical tracheotomy incision in the throat, and learned only next day—in a call to the hospital in Dallas—that the hole cut to give the President air had been adapted from an existing bullet wound. They now concluded that the original throat wound was in fact the point of *exit* for the bullet which had entered the President's back. The positioning of the wounds was, of course, central to the key questions about the number of wounds and the source of the shots. It should have been definitive. Sadly, though, the doctors omitted an elementary autopsy procedure—that of establishing the path of the bullets in the body. The wound in the back was merely probed, instead of being fully opened up and tracked to its destination. The conclusion that it linked up with the throat wound was mere guesswork. Why was the wound not tracked? With the President's relatives huddled in a nearby room, and with the autopsy room itself crowded with military brass hats and FBI men, the atmosphere was far from the calm and quiet in which the doctors should have worked. In 1979,

Congress' Assassinations Committee concluded that, under pressure to work quickly, the presiding pathologist, Dr. James Humes, decided not to dissect the wound. His colleague, Dr. Pierre Finck, remembers it rather differently. He believes the order came from somebody else, perhaps an army general. Another official, he recalls, prevented him from examining the President's clothing—an essential procedure in a firearms case.

For the same reasons as the back wound, the fatal head wound should have been traced in minute detail. To this end, in line with normal procedure, the President's damaged brain was removed from the body and preserved "for future study." Normally, after a waiting period while the brain was fixed in formaldehyde, it would have been sectioned. Instead it was only superficially examined. Dr. Cyril Wecht, a former president of the American Academy of Forensic Sciences, was in 1972 the first non-government pathologist to examine the surviving Kennedy medical evidence. More recently he served on the medical panel of the Assassinations Committee. Wecht regards with high scorn the explanation recorded by the autopsy doctors—that they omitted to section the brain "in order to preserve it." He has observed, "To voluntarily omit such an examination is to be incompetent or a fool, and I do not believe the autopsy pathologists were either. I believe they were *instructed* not to do a complete examination of the brain. . . ."

The brain, along with other autopsy materials, including X rays and photographs, was apparently first delivered to President Kennedy's former secretary for safekeeping. Safe it was not—at least from the point of future investigators. In 1966, after the materials had passed into the care of the National Archives, it was discovered that the President's brain was missing. Also absent were tissue sections, blood smears, and a number of slides. Nor have any photographs of the interior of the President's chest survived, even though the chief autopsy doctor and an official photographer remember them being taken. In 1979 the Assassinations Committee failed to discover any trace of the missing brain, or of the other material. It favored the theory that the President's brother, Robert Kennedy, disposed of it to avoid tasteless display in the future. Whatever the reason, the certain result has been to hamper the work of later forensic pathologists. Dr. Wecht notes that the brain and the chest pictures would have been an immense help in determining the crucial matter of bullet paths through the President's body.

In the wake of autopsy chaos, and as controversy grew over the facts of the Kennedy assassination, various forensic scientists had the opportunity to review the forensic evidence. With the body long buried, they have had to make do with the extensive surviving X rays and photographs. In 1966 these were examined by the original autopsy doctors, who unbelievably had never before seen the photographs taken of the post-mortem they had themselves supervised. The material—and the President's clothing—has since been scrutinized five times—by an Attorney General's medical panel in 1968, by the Rockefeller Commission panel in 1975, and finally by the pathologists for Congress' Assassinations Committee.* This last study has attempted to end argument over the precise location of the wounds. It dismissed the autopsy sketch showing a back wound well down from the shoulder, concluding that this had been merely a "crude representation . . . not necessarily an exact representation of the wound." Lifelike illustrations, expertly copied from the original photographs in the interests of good taste, were made public in 1979. One of these shows the back wound in a position which Assassinations Committee doctors found compatible with a shot passing through the President to exit through the throat. A second illustration (*see illustration 5*) demonstrates what they regard as a glaring mistake by the original doctors. This, along with supporting X ray evidence, places the small wound of entrance about *four inches* higher than recorded in the autopsy report. Dr. Michael Baden, head of the latest medical panel, pointed out that this wound in the back of the head can be seen in the photographs, high above the hairline. A smaller spot on the photograph, in the area of the hairline, is dismissed by a majority of the Assassinations Committee experts as dried debris, probably brain tissue. Quite how the doctors on the spot could

* The photos and X-rays were also seen by consultants for the Boston Globe, in 1981, and—for the TV program *Nova*—by three of the Dallas doctors, in 1988. See Aftermath, p. 473.

have made such a seemingly huge error, when they had their subject in front of them to probe and explore, remains bewildering.

The Assassinations Committee's study of the autopsy photographs led to a scandal over disquieting snooping involving the CIA. Throughout the inquiry, the Committee's Chief Counsel maintained strict security—not least in the case of the gruesome photographs, which he feared might find their way into the hands of sensation seekers. The pictures, along with X rays and ballistics evidence, were housed in a separate safe in a special room. They could not be examined, even by the staff concerned, without the chief counsel's personal permission. This was granted separately on each date of access, and items studied were meticulously logged in and out. One day in June 1978, however, an interloper found a loophole in the precautions. A staff member, on legitimately taking photographs to a nearby office, left the safe closed but not locked. By the time the researcher returned, the safe had been opened and the sensitive material seriously disturbed. A folder had been taken out of the safe and one photograph of the dead President ripped out of its cover. There was an immediate investigation, with disturbing results. A fingerprint check showed that the only unauthorized person who had handled the files was a CIA employee. He was Regis Blahut, a liaison officer who had been assigned to supervise and assist with secret CIA material stored in the Committee premises. He worked in a secure area quite separate from the room where the photographs were held and had no business being in that room at all. Bluhut was interrogated both by Committee staff and by superiors at the CIA. At first he denied the whole thing, and then—faced with the incontrovertible evidence—Blahut simply maintained there was an innocent explanation. In one brief conversation with a reporter, he said darkly, "There's other things involved that are detrimental to other things." He declined to elaborate, and the CIA told the Committee Blahut had acted out of "mere curiosity." Blahut was fired. Some Committee staff, however, were not satisfied with the CIA explanation. They said that curiosity was inconsistent with the fingerprint evidence, and with the way the autopsy material had been handled. It seems that Blahut was disturbed—in the midst of his tampering—by the returning Committee employee. One of the pictures which had attracted his specific interest was a photograph of the late President's head. The pictures of the head are, of course, at the center of controversy over the source of the shot or shots that caused the President's fatal head injury.[5] Whatever the CIA officer's true purpose, his mischief is one more example of the kind of conduct that has led to public distrust of the agency—and specifically where the Kennedy case is concerned. The matter was to have been further investigated in Congress, but has since been quietly forgotten.

Apart from the evidence of body and bullets, there is one further invaluable aid to any analysis of the assassination. This is the short but infinitely shocking film made by an amateur cameraman in the crowd, Abraham Zapruder. After initially leaving his camera at home, Zapruder had hurried home to fetch it at the last moment. Thus it was that he came to make eighteen seconds of truly apocalyptic film, the subject of diverse interpretation by students of the President's murder. The most famous amateur movie in the world was shot from a vantage point on a low concrete wall to the right front of the approaching President. For all its fame, and although no description can replace actual viewing of the Zapruder film, its contents must be summarized here.

As the motorcade turns to come straight toward his lens, Zapruder catches the last uneventful seconds of the motorcade, with the President and his wife smiling and waving in the sun. Then the limousine vanishes for a moment behind a street sign. When it emerges, the President is clearly reacting to a shot—his hands clenched and coming up to his throat. Governor Connally turns around to his right, peering into the back seat. He begins to turn back, then goes rigid and shows signs that he, too, has been hit. Jacqueline Kennedy looks toward her husband, who is leaning forward and to his left. There is an almost imperceptible forward movement of the President's head, and then, abruptly, his skull visibly explodes in a spray of blood and brain matter. He is propelled violently back into the rear seat of the car, then bounces forward and slides to the left, into Mrs. Kennedy's arms. The savage backward lurch by the President occurs, to the eye, at the instant of the fatal shot to the head. Then, as Mrs. Kennedy reaches desperately for a fragment of her husband's skull on the back of the car, a Secret Service agent jumps aboard from behind, and the limousine finally accelerates away.

Abraham Zapruder sold his film to *Life* magazine for a quarter of a million dollars. The magazine later published still frames from the material, but the moving footage was not shown on television until March 1975. The film has been a key tool for both official investigations, not least because it provides a near precise time frame for the assassination. In 1978 it took on new importance, for its use in conjunction with a hitherto neglected item of evidence. This, the subject of continuing controversy, was greeted as the most momentous single breakthrough in the case since 1964. It followed news that the sounds in Dealey Plaza had apparently been recorded and included identifiable gunshots.

This evidence, if evidence it is, had been ignored for sixteen years. This was a battered blue "dictabelt," a routine recording of police radio traffic which had been made on the day of the President's murder just as on any ordinary day. To the layman it is a mishmash of barely comprehensible conversation between policemen in the field and their dispatch office at headquarters. The gaps between speech seem a meaningless blur of distorted sound and static. That certainly is what was assumed by the Dallas police and the Warren Commission, who used the recording only to establish police movement and messages. For years the dictabelt lay abandoned in a filing cabinet at Dallas police headquarters, until in 1969 a director of the Intelligence Division took it into his personal care. He later took the dictabelt home, and there it languished. The belt might well have stayed there were it not for the keen archival mind of a Dallas private researcher, Mary Ferrell. Mrs. Ferrell is a private citizen who has researched the Kennedy case from the very beginning, with an exemplary combination of zeal and discipline. She had long been aware of the recording and drew the attention of the Assassinations Committee to its possible significance. In 1978, when the original dictabelt was recovered, it was submitted to Dr. James Barger, chief acoustical scientist for the firm of Bolt, Beranek and Newman. That company specializes in acoustical analysis, working more routinely on such projects as underwater detection devices for the Navy. It has also studied matters of national importance and public interest. In 1973, at the Watergate trial, the firm advised on the famous gap in the White House tapes. Earlier, its expertise was used in the Government prosecution of National Guardsmen involved in the shooting of students at Kent State University. Nobody expected very much from the crackly recording submitted to Dr. Barger. Yet it was his work, along with further study performed by two scientists at the City University of New York, which turned out to be pivotal to the deliberations of Congress' Assassinations Committee. Technical processes, including the use of equipment not available in 1963, enabled Barger to produce a visual presentation of the sound wave forms on the vital part of the tape. With his New York associates, Professor Mark Weiss and Ernest Aschkenasy, he designed an acoustical reconstruction in Dealey Plaza. Early one morning in 1978, guns boomed once again at the scene of President Kennedy's murder. The results showed that impulses on the police recording matched sound patterns unique to the scene of the crime. Certain impulses, the scientists firmly decided, were indeed gunshots. They were distinguishable as rifle fire, rather than the noises produced by, say, a pistol or a car's backfire. The scientists were able to say that the sounds had been picked up by a microphone moving along at about eleven miles per hour at the time of the assassination. They surmised that this was mounted on the motor-cycle of a police outrider in the Presidential motorcade, and that the recording had been made because the microphone button was stuck open at the time. From photographs and testimony, Assas-sinations Committee staff identified the motorcycle as one ridden by Officer H. B. McLain. When the Assassinations Committee prepared its report, it appeared that the scientists and the investi-gators had achieved a *tour de force* of detection. They had sound answers to the predictable chorus of objections.

Investigators were at first perplexed, and skeptics encour-aged, by the sound of a bell on the recording. There was no bell in Dealey Plaza. It was puzzling that there seemed to be no crowd noise, and that the sound of police sirens did not start until two minutes after the assassination. These phenomena have now been adequately explained. There is no proof that McLain switched on his own siren, and the nearest siren known to have been switched

on after the shooting was too far away to register on his microphone. General background noise, as from a crowd, would not
have exceeded the roar made by the motorcycle's engine. As for
the mysterious bell, it was determined that the police broadcast
system permitted more than one transmission to operate at the
same time. The logical explanation for the bell, therefore, was that
the dispatch tape recorded more than one transmission at a time—
one of them originating at a police microphone *outside* Dealey
Plaza. Committee experts remained convinced, therefore, that the
sounds identified as gunfire are uniquely those of patterns produced by rifle shots in Dealey Plaza. The mobility of the microphone was established well before anybody realized that Officer
McLain and his radio were on exactly the right route at exactly the
right time.

Acoustics is today a science in its own right, concerned with
analysis of the nature and origin of sound impulses. The firm which
handled the police recording have been pioneers in using recordings to establish the timing and direction of gunfire. After the Kent
State University shootings, its study of a tape was admitted into
evidence to help determine which guardsmen started the firing.
There can be no denying acoustics its place in forensic science,
along with ballistics and all the more familiar aids to detection. It
forced Congress' Assassinations Committee, somewhat to the consternation of three members, into a dramatic reassessment.
Acoustics appeared to provide clinching answers to the crucial
questions about the source and number of the shots fired at President Kennedy.

The 1979 expert conclusion—beyond a reasonable doubt
was—it was claimed that gunfire came from in front of the President as well as from behind him. At least two gunmen were
therefore involved in the assassination. Since 1979, other experts
have cast doubt on the conclusion. First the FBI, then a panel of
scientists for the National Academy of Sciences, said the Committee's analysis did not stand up.*

The Committee's experts, however, have not accepted the

---

* The acoustics controversy will be reported in greater detail in the
Aftermath chapter.

criticism. While shaken by the attacks on what he was advised was scientific certainty, Committee Chief Counsel Blakey insists, "I think our approach was correct, and I think our conclusion was correct. On balance I say there were two shooters in the Plaza—apart from the acoustics. Indeed it's the existence of all the other evidence and testimony that makes me think the acoustics is right."

The fact of the matter is that science has produced no certainties. What the Assassination Committee's technical experts did do—in conjunction with its study of all the other available information—was to rock the old "lone gunman" theory to its foundations. In that sense, the Assassinations Committee has surely changed history.

CHAPTER 3

The Science of Conspiracy

*"The great tragedy of Science—the slaying of a
beautiful hypothesis by an ugly fact."*
—Thomas H. Huxley, evolutionist, 19th Century.

Of 178 people in Dealey Plaza—says an Assassinations Committee
survey—no less than 132 later came to believe that only three shots
had been fired. Three spent cartridges were found near the window of the Texas School Book Depository. Initially, then, a count
of three shots seemed rational, if not conclusive. It was certainly
convenient. The testimony of the "ear witnesses" alone, though,
was always a shaky basis for decision. It must be borne in mind
that almost all witnesses gave statements hours—and, in some
cases, weeks—later, when the generally published version of the
assassination had already put the total of shots at three. A few
people, including Mrs. Kennedy and a Secret Service agent in the
follow-up car, thought they had heard as few as two shots. Others
thought they heard more than three, some speaking of as many as
six or seven. Ballistics and acoustics specialists have examined how
and why people become mixed up in their memory of gunfire. The
sound of a first shot comes upon a witness when he does not expect
it, subsequent shots compound the surprise, and muddle ensues.
Further confusion may be caused by the fact that a rifle shot
actually makes three minutely separated sounds—the muzzle
blast, the sound of a bullet breaking the sound barrier, and finally
the impact on the target. On the other hand, say the experts, those
listening in the immediate target area probably receive the least
distorted impression of gunfire.

Oddly, and unforgivably, the vital first inquiry produced no statement of any kind from the two police outriders traveling to the right rear of the President—in a fine position to listen and observe. Twelve people in the target area did go on record. All but one of the five in the car itself, and two other outriders, spoke of three shots. Their predicament, however, was hardly conducive to rational recall. Mrs. Kennedy, naturally, confessed herself "very confused." Governor Connally was himself severely injured during the shooting, and Mrs. Connally was preoccupied trying to help him. The two outriders to the President's left rear were shocked by being spattered with the President's blood and brain matter. The two Secret Servicemen in the car, one of them the driver, had to make vital decisions. Both, however, did have interesting comments on the shots. Agent Kellerman said later that the last sound he recalled was "like a double bang—bang! bang! . . . like a plane going through the sound barrier." Agent Greer, the driver, also said the last shot cracked out "just right behind" its predecessor. This could conceivably mean the two agents heard a single bullet breaking the sound barrier, but it also suggests they heard two shots very close together indeed—far closer together than one man could achieve with a bolt-operated rifle. Agent Kellerman later expressed the opinion, based on what he heard and the wounds he saw later at the autopsy, that "there have got to be more than three shots."

In spite of being himself shot in the hail of gunfire, Governor Connally—who was an experienced hunter—remembered that because of the "rapidity" of the shots, "the thought immediately passed through my mind that there were two or three people involved, or more, in this: or that someone was shooting with an automatic rifle."

As for the bystanders nearest to the offside of the President's car, one, Mary Moorman, made estimates ranging from two to four shots. Like those in the car, she was first preoccupied and then so panicky that she was distracted. (She was taking a photograph as the limousine approached and then threw herself to the ground, shrieking, "Get down! They're shooting!") Near her, Charles Brehm thought he heard three shots. Mary Moorman's

friend, a schoolteacher called Jean Hill, says she was paying special attention to the motorcade because one of the police outriders
was her boyfriend of the moment. She was sure there were more
than three shots. In 1978 she told me, "I heard four to six shots,
and I'm pretty used to guns. They weren't echoes or anything like
that. They were different guns that were being fired."

Gayle Newman, standing on the curb on the near side of the
President's car, thought there could have been four shots. Then
there was Maurice Orr, who also stood on the nearside pavement
and was one of those closest to the President. Orr, questioned a
few minutes after the tragedy, thought there could have been as
many as five shots. So four witnesses, in the target area and not
otherwise distracted, had the impression that more than three
shots had been fired. The Warren commission chose to ignore
them and favored the silent testimony of the three cartridges lying
near the sixth-floor window. In 1978 came the acoustics evidence,
casting further doubt on the Warren Commission.

On the last day of the Assassinations Committee hearings, the
three acoustics scientists spent hours trying to explain technical
complexities to a rather baffled group of Congressmen and lawyers. When he lost the audience with his talk of sound velocity and
echo-generating surfaces, one of them insisted his work was "not
an arcane science. . . . It is taught in high school and college-level
physics . . . and I think it can be understood by anybody who has
ever heard an echo." He demonstrated that movement of sound
can be measured using equipment as basic as a hand calculator,
pins, and a piece of string. In the end, it was left to the Committee's Chief Counsel, Professor Robert Blakey, to distill the scientists' conclusions into simple language. He summarized, "According to the acoustical analysis conducted by the Committee, four
shots, over a total period of 7.91 seconds, were fired at the Presidential limousine. The first, second and fourth came from the
Depository; the third came from the grassy knoll. . . ." Four
shots, including one from the raised ground to the right front of
the President, meant at least two accomplices.

The acoustics study also provided a time frame for the shooting. Taking zero as the time of the first shot, the second was fired

1.66 seconds later, the third at 7.49 seconds, and the fourth at 8.31 seconds. The brevity of the pause between the first and second shots, both fired from the rear, raised questions as to whether one lone gunman could possibly have fired both. These will be dealt with later, along with the possibility that more than one assassin fired from the rear. Meanwhile, the fractional pause between the third shot, from the knoll, and the fourth, from the rear, may explain a great deal. With less than a second between them, the two shots may well have sounded like one to those who believed only three were fired altogether. It would also make sense of the comments of two of those in the target area and best placed to hear the gunfire. It explains Governor Connally's impression that someone was shooting with an automatic rifle, Agent Greer's observation that the last shot was "just right behind" its predecessor, and Agent Kellerman's recall of a "double bang"—like the sound barrier being broken. Kellerman felt there must have been more than three shots. If the Assassinations Committee's acoustics verdict is valid, the Secret Service agent was right.

On hearing the acoustics verdict, the chairman of the Assassinations Committee, Louis Stokes, asked one of the scientists if he was aware of the enormous impact of his testimony in terms of history. Professor Weiss, whose work had concentrated on the third shot—the one from the grassy knoll—said he was certain "with a confidence level of 95 percent or higher, which I guess if I were a lawyer, I might well express as beyond a reasonable doubt. . . ."

The acoustics work indicated that all but the third shot originated "in the vicinity of the sixth-floor southeast corner window of the Texas School Book Depository." Because that window is so close to the edge of the building, scientists believe further tests might show that some of the shooting came from the Daltex building next door. So far, the most refined study has been reserved for the third shot because the Committee was acutely aware of the need to be positive there really was a sniper on the knoll. They concluded that the third shot was "fired from a point along the east-west line of the wooden stockade fence on the grassy knoll, about eight feet west of the corner of the fence." (*See illustrations 3 and 4.*) Professor Weiss and his colleagues allowed a margin of error of five feet in either direction, but they were positive the shot had come from behind the fence. A mass of evidence seemed, at last, to fall into place.

Onetime Congressman, later President, Gerald Ford served on the Warren Commission. He later wrote, "There is no evidence of a second man, of other shots, or other guns." That was bunkum, even in 1964. Of 178 witnesses whose statements were available to the Warren Commission, 49 believed the shots came from the Texas School Book Depository, 78 had no opinion, and 30 came up with answers that fit in with none of the other evidence; 21, though, believed the shots had come from the grassy knoll. Another sample of the statements suggests 61 witnesses believed that at least some of the gunfire originated in front of the motorcade. A number of others said as much in statements to newspapers or private researchers.[6] Perhaps Gerald Ford didn't know about them because so few of these witnesses were called to testify. Or perhaps because, although he attended more than the other Commissioners, Ford did not appear at all the sessions.

"As a matter of history," says former Assassinations Committee Chief Counsel Blakey, "I surely came to examine all the other things because of the acoustics. And I find on balance that the earwitness and eyewitness testimony is credible." The voice of human memory deserves an attentive hearing, in view of the acoustics evidence, and also in its own right.

These are the opinions of the fifteen people in the immediate target area, where experts say sound impressions are least distorted. Of those in the car, Mrs. Kennedy had no opinion on where the shots came from. Governor Connally—injured before the fatal shot—thought he heard shooting behind him. His wife said on one occasion that she believed all shots came from the rear, on another, "I had no thought of whether they were high or low or where. They just came from the right." Agent Greer, the driver, said the shots "sounded like they were behind me;" Agent Kellerman said only that his main impression was of sound to the right—perhaps to the rear. Two police outriders to the left rear of the car, the two splattered with blood and brain, not surprisingly had no idea where the shooting originated. Those at the eye of the storm were hardly well placed for rational recall, as we have noted. The two policemen to the President's right rear, and very close to him indeed, were excellently placed; one of them, Officer James Chaney, closest to the President, thought some shooting came from "back over my right shoulder." He also said, however, that "when the second shot came, I looked back in time to see the President struck in the face by the second bullet. . . ."

Mary Moorman, to the offside of the limousine, and busy taking pictures, could not tell where the shots came from. Maurice Orr, opposite her, was also too confused. Charles Brehm, not far away, said in a formal statement that shots came from behind him. On the day of the assassination, though, he was reported as saying he thought "the shots came from in front of or beside the President." Jean Hill, the schoolteacher standing with Mary Moorman, said, "I frankly thought they were coming from the grassy knoll. . . . I thought it was just people shooting from the grassy knoll." Although she was questioned four times, her testimony was omitted from the section of the Warren Report called "The Witnesses." On the other side of the street, standing on the grass with their children, were William and Gayle Newman. Mr. Newman's affidavit, sworn just after the assassination, said, "I was looking directly at him when he was hit in the side of the head. . . . I thought the shot had come from the garden directly behind me, that was on an elevation from where I was right on the curb. Then we fell down on the grass as it seemed we were in the direct path of fire." The Commission omitted both Newman statements from its "Witnesses" section. Sixteen people in or outside the Book Depository, behind the President, indicated some shooting came from the knoll. They included the Depository manager, the superintendent, and two company vice presidents. Secret Service Agent Forrest Sorrels, travleing in the lead car and nearing the end of the knoll at the moment of the fatal shot, also stared instinctively at the knoll. He first reported, "I looked toward the top of the terrace to my right as the sound of the shots seemed to come from that direction." Only later, in his Commission testimony, did Sorrels go along with the conventional wisdom that the source of the gunfire was exclusively to the President's rear.

Secret Service Agent Paul Landis, in the car behind the President, made an interesting distinction. He said, "I heard what sounded like the report of a high-powered rifle from behind me." Landis drew his gun, and then, "I heard a second report and saw the President's head split open and pieces of flesh and blood flying through the air. My reaction at this time was that the shot came from somewhere toward the front . . . and looked along the right-hand side of the road." Landis was not called to testify before the Warren Commission.

Several police officers also thought the shots came from the knoll area. The reaction of the Dallas County Sheriff, Bill Decker, riding in front of the President, was to bark into the radio, "Notify station five to move all available men out of my department back into the railroad yards." The railroad yards were just behind the fence where the committee acoustics experts placed a gunman.

Loosely speaking, the "grassy knoll" is the whole area the President's limousine passed after leaving the Book Depository to its rear (*see page 25*). It is easiest to describe it as three sectors. First there is a narrow slope topped by trees and bushes. Then comes a much longer slope up to a semicircular colonnade, with access steps and a retaining wall. Beyond that the slope continues beside the road, topped by more vegetation and a fence. The fence makes a right angle which, in 1963, faced directly toward the oncoming motorcade. By the last stage of the shooting the President's limousine was a mere thirty-five yards from the point on the fence where where Committee acoustics experts placed a gunman.

About a dozen people were actually on the grassy knoll when the President was shot, and almost all of them believed some of the gunfire came from behind them, high up on the knoll itself. For several, there could be no talk of illusions or echoes. The shooting was frighteningly close. Their stories, for the most part never heard by the official inquiry, are jolting, even after sixteen years.

In 1963 Gordon Arnold was a young soldier of twenty-two. On November 22 he was home briefly on leave. Armed with his movie camera, Arnold walked to the top of the grassy knoll just before the President arrived, looking for a good vantage point. He went behind the fence, trying to find a way to the railroad bridge which crossed the road right in front of the motorcade route. From

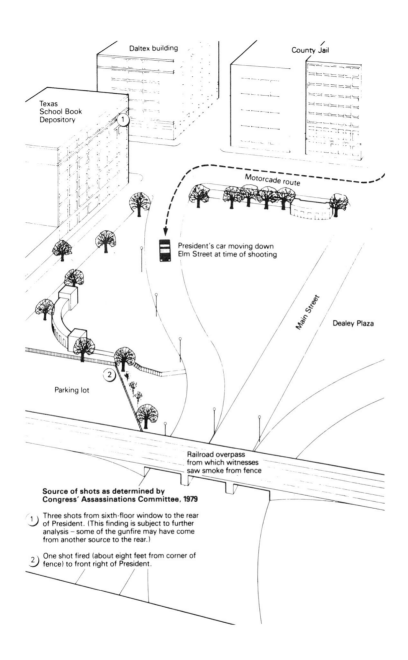

Daltex building

County Jail

Texas
School Book
Depository

①

Motorcade route

President's car moving down
Elm Street at time of shooting

Main Street

Dealey Plaza

②

Parking lot

Railroad overpass
from which witnesses
saw smoke from fence

**Source of shots as determined by
Congress' Assassinations Committee, 1979**

① Three shots from sixth-floor window to the rear
of President. (This finding is subject to further
analysis – some of the gunfire may have come
from another source to the rear.)

② One shot fired (about eight feet from corner of
fence) to front right of President.

Dealey Plaza, November 22, 1963

there his view would be perfect. Arnold was moving along the fence—on the side hidden from the road—when ". . . this guy just walked towards me and said that I shouldn't be up there. He showed me a badge and said he was with the Secret Service and that he didn't want anybody up there." It sounded sensible enough, and Arnold retreated to the next best spot—beside a tree on the road side of the fence, high on the grassy slope beyond the colonnade. Then the motorcade arrived.

Arnold maintains, "The shot came from behind me, only inches over my left shoulder. I had just got out of basic training. In my mind, live ammunition was being fired. It was being fired over my head. And I hit the dirt." All Arnold ever heard was the shooting over his shoulder. It was so close he heard "the whiz over my shoulder. I say a whiz—you don't exactly hear the whiz of a bullet, you hear just like a shock wave. You *feel* it . . . you feel something and then a report comes just behind it."

According to Arnold, he was still on the ground when a policeman rushed up and booted him to his feet. Then came another policeman, this one toting a shotgun. Arnold said he gave the police his film and then left the chaos of Dealey Plaza. Two days later he flew to his new post in Alaska. Nobody took Arnold's name at the time, and no official body has ever taken his testimony. In 1978 the House Assassinations Committee learned about him but failed to interview him.

Arnold's story sounds fantastic. Once published, however, as it was in 1978, his account did find some support. Texas Senator Ralph Yarborough, who in 1963 rode in the motorcade two cars behind the President, happens to recall seeing a man in Arnold's position. Yarborough says, "Immediately on the firing of the first shot I saw the man . . . throw himself on the ground . . . he was down within a second, and I thought to myself, 'There's a combat veteran who knows how to act when weapons start firing.' " Arnold cannot be seen in photographs of the knoll at the relevant time, but the nature of the photographs does not preclude his having been at the position he now specifies. Above all, though, Arnold's statement is credible because it fits into a pattern. Like Arnold, a railway supervisor on the bridge also observed "a plainclothes detective or FBI agent or something like that" before the shooting. He will appear in this story again. Policemen did run up the grassy slope immediately after the murder. Arnold could, of course, have read all this in the newspapers an made up his story. But then, among the people in the grassy-knoll area, Arnold's account of the shooting is not unique. It is typical.

Mary Woodward, Maggie Brown, Aurelia Lorenzo, and Ann Donaldson all worked at the *Dallas Morning News*. They spoke of "a horrible, ear-shattering noise coming from behind us and a little to the right." Although what they said was in the press next day, all four witnesses went unmentioned and unquestioned by the Warren Commission.

John Chism said, "I looked *behind* me, to see if it was a fireworks display." His wife, Mary, said, "It came from what I thought was *behind* us." The Chisms were not called by the Warren Commission.

A. J. Millican, who had been standing in front of the colonnade, said of the final gunfire, "I heard two more shots come from the arcade between the bookstore and the underpass, and then three more shots came from the same direction only farther back. Then everybody started running up the hill." Mr. Millican was not called by the Warren Commission.

Jean Newman* stood halfway along the grassy knoll and said that her first impression was that "The shots came from my right." Ms. Newman was not called by the Warren Commission.

Abraham Zapruder, of film fame, was using the concrete wall on the grassy knoll as a vantage point. A Secret Service report of an interview with him reads: "According to Mr. Zapruder, the position of the assassin was behind Mr. Zapruder." In testimony to the Warren Commission, Zapruder recalled that one shot reverberated all around him, louder than all the others. This would be consistent with a shot fired on the knoll itself, much closer to Zapruder than gunfire from the Book Depository.

The next witness became well known after the assassination

---

*Not to be confused with the married couple of the same name, who also witnessed the shooting.

because of what then seemed a lonely tale—puckishly contrary to the official story. He is Sam Holland, the elderly signal supervisor who stood at the parapet of the railway bridge over the road, directly facing the President's car as it approached (*see page 57*). Holland also had an excellent view of the fence on the knoll near where the young soldier, Gordon Arnold, was to hear bullets "whizzing" right over him.

Immediately after the assassination Holland told the police firmly that there had been four shots and that he had seen "a puff of smoke come from the trees." He stuck to his story in spite of official skepticism, maintaining that at least some of the firing "sounded like it came from behind the wooden fence. . . . I looked over to where the shots came from, and I saw a puff of smoke still lingering underneath the trees in front of the wooden fence." Pressed on where the shots came from, Holland replied confidently, "Behind that picket fence—close to the little plaza—there's no doubt whatsoever in my mind."

Sam Holland did testify to the Warren Commission, though his evidence was ignored. Skeptics have suggested he saw smoke or steam from a locomotive. Clearly that is not what he saw; the railway line itself is much too far from the fence at the top of the knoll. Others, the latest among them a Congressman on the Assassinations Committee, have questioned whether rifles in fact emit smoke. Experts confirm that they do. Holland's account was in fact corroborated and buttressed by others. He was backed up— with variations as to the precise location of the smoke—by eight witnesses who had been standing on the same bridge, most of them fellow railway workers. Other people saw the same phenomenon from other vantage points.

Jean Hill, standing to the left of the President's car, in the central reservation of Dealey Plaza, also saw smoke at the top of the knoll. In 1978 she told me, "The President was killed, and then of course pandemonium reigned . . . and I looked up, and at the time I looked up across the street I saw smoke like from a gun coming from the parapet, that built-up part on the knoll." One witness was in a better position than anyone else to observe suspicious activity by the fence at the top of the grassy knoll. This was railway worker Lee Bowers, perched in a signal box which commanded a unique view of the area *behind* the fence. Bowers said that, just before the shots were fired, he noticed two men standing near the fence. One was "middle-aged" and "fairly heavy-set," wearing a white shirt and dark trousers. The other was "mid-twenties in either a plaid shirt or plaid coat . . . these men were the only two strangers in the area. The others were workers that I knew." Bowers also said that when the shots were fired at the President "in the vicinity of where the two men I have described were, there was a flash of light, something I could not identify, but there was something which occurred which caught my eye in this immediate area on the embankment . . . a flash of light or smoke or something which caused me to feel that something out of the ordinary had occurred there." Lee Bowers was questioned by the Warren Commission but was cut off in mid-sentence when he began describing the "something out of the ordinary" he had seen. The interrogating lawyer changed the subject.

Then there were the witnesses who actually claimed to have smelled gunpowder in the air—surely a farfetched notion. Yet there were six of them, all either distinguished public figures or qualified to know what they were talking about. Three witnesses in the motorcade—the Mayor's wife, Mrs. Cabell, Senator Ralph Yarborough, and Congressman Ray Roberts—all later mentioned the acrid smell in the air. It is highly improbably that any of these people—sweeping past in the motorcade—could have picked up the smell of gunpowder from a sixth-floor window high above them. It is remarkable too that they could have smelled it from the grassy knoll, but it seems it was in that general area they did notice it. Police Officer Earle Brown, on duty at the railway bridge, and Mrs. Donald Baker, at the other end of the knoll, reported the same distinctive smell. Another policeman, Patrolman Joe Smith, was holding up traffic across the road from the Texas School Book Depository when the motorcade passed by. He heard gunfire, and when a woman cried out, "They're shooting the President from the bushes!" Smith ran to the grassy knoll, the only bushy place in the area. In 1978 he still remembered what he reported shortly after the assassination, that in the parking lot, "around the hedges, there was the smell, the lingering smell of gunpowder."

Congress' Assassinations Committee subjected known photographs taken at the time of the assassination to intensive expert analysis. One appeared to show a human figure standing behind the concrete retaining wall on the knoll, about forty feet to the right of where the acoustics experts place a gunman. Special enhancement techniques confirmed that this was indeed an adult person wearing dark clothing. In a photograph taken very shortly afterward, the figure has vanished. Study of the first picture showed that, in the region of the person's hands, there is a "very distinct straight-line feature." The focus was not good enough to determine whether or not it was a weapon.

There is continuing interest in another photograph, which shows the very fence where acoustics evidence places a knoll gunman. The Assassinations Committee photographic panel examined the picture, a Polaroid taken at the moment of the fatal shot by bystander Mary Moorman, long before the acoustics evidence pinpointed the fence area as the source of the shots. A shape that may be a man's head can be seen in the fenced area specified by the acoustics report (*see illustration 3*). The shape is no longer there in subsequent photographs. One Committee photographic consultant, Robert Groden, is confident that a man can be seen behind the fence in prints of the Moorman photograph held by United Press International and Associated Press. The Committee's photographic panel have recommended, in the light of the acoustics evidence, that the photograph be re-examined. This was done recently, by researchers at Polaroid and the Massachusetts Institute of Technology, using image enhancement techniques.* While they felt there might be a man there, the picture is just not clear enough for certainty.

In 1978, amidst the excitement over the formal conclusion that two guns were fired at President Kennedy, rather less attention was given to the Committee's decisions on a secondary but equally vital question. Which of the shots actually hit the President?

If the only comprehensive visual record of the Kennedy assassination had been shown on television on November 22, 1963, most

---

*For PBS TV *Nova* program, Nov. 15, 1988.

people in the United States would have gone to bed that night certain that their President has been shot from the front and only perhaps—by an earlier shot—from behind. Americans were of course not shown the full Zapruder film until more than a decade later. They were, within days, given a verbal description of the footage on CBS television. Dan Rather, a television correspondent who had been permitted to view the film, was the narrator. Rather said that at the fatal head shot the President "fell *forward* with considerable violence." He omitted to say what in fact is mercilessly obvious from any alert viewing of the film. It is manifestly clear that the President jerked *backward* at the moment of the shot that visibly exploded his head. Members and staff of the Warren Commission did see the Zapruder film, yet nowhere in its report is the backward motion mentioned. Indeed, although still frames from the film were published in the Warren Commission volumes, the two frames following the head shot were printed in reverse order. This has since been explained by J. Edgar Hoover as a "printing error" at the FBI. Others have seen the omissions and errors as a sinister attempt to conceal the truth from the public. The truth for such critics is that the President was knocked backward by a bullet originating in front of him, from the direction of the sniper on the grassy knoll. That has been the layman's impression and it has been echoed, from time to time, by the scientist.

One physicist, Dr. R. A. J. Riddle, then with the University of California at Los Angeles and a member of its Brain Institute, ventured, "Newton's second law of motion has remained inviolate for three centuries. No physical phenomenon is known that fails to obey it; basically this law says that an object hit by a projectile will be given a motion that has the same direction as that of the projectile. At a shooting gallery, for instance, the ducks fall away form the marksman, not toward him. Thus if someone is shot, and the shot strikes home, the general direction of recoil will be away from—not toward—the marksman." Dr. Riddle pointed out that the President's backward movement cannot be accounted for by acceleration of the car; this had not yet occurred, and the film shows no similar movements by other occupants of the limousine. Riddle thus found himself forced to disagree with the finding of the

Warren Commission that all the shots, including the fatal one to
the head, originated to the rear of the President, in the book
Depository. Others noted gory details which seemed to reinforce
the thesis of a hit from in front. Both motorcycle officers riding to
the left *rear* of the President were splattered with blood and brain
coming toward them. Officer Hargis, who was only a few feet from
Mrs. Kennedy, said later that he had been struck with such force
by the brain matter that for a moment he thought he himself had
been hit. Riding on Hargis' left was Officer B. J. Martin, who later
testified that he found blood and flesh on his motorcycle windshield, on the left side of his helmet and the left shoulder of his
uniform jacket. A young student, Billy Harper, was later to pick
up a large piece of the President's skull in the street, at a point
more than ten feet to the *rear* of the car's position at the time of
the fatal shot. The evidence is that such human debris, including
other skull fragments, was driven backward. Some researchers,
making light of the fact that people in the front of the car were also
"covered with brain tissue," see this as further evidence of a hit by
the knoll gunman. In 1979 the Assassinations Committee said this
was quite wrong. Only two of the four shots fired, said the Committee, found human targets. Both, including the fatal head shot,
were fired from the rear, and almost certainly from the sixth-floor
corner window of the Book Depository. Drawing together medical, ballistics, film, acoustics, photographic, and trajectory analysis, the Committee ended up with this reconstruction of the assassination.

A first shot, fired from the Book Depository, missed. The
second, again from the Depository, entered the President's back,
came out through his throat, traveled on into Governor Connally's
back, and exited through his chest to cause further injuries to his
right wrist and thigh. According to the Committee the third bullet,
fired from the knoll, missed altogether. The fourth, fired from the
Depository, caused the fatal wound to the President's head.

A wound ballistics expert told the Committee that the President's lurch backward, in the Zapruder film, was "a neuromuscular reaction . . . mechanical stimulation of the motor nerves of the
President." The Congressmen accepted this thesis and cited other

evidence indicating that the head shot came from the rear. The Committee's medical panel, with one doctor dissenting, supported the thesis that the backward movement was either "a neurological response to the massive brain damage" or a "propulsive" phenomenon, sometimes known as "the jet effect." Their studies of the X rays and photographs convinced them that the bullet entered in the upper part of the skull and exited from the right front. All the doctors agreed that the rear wound was "a typical entrance wound.*" In spite of the fact that the brain had not been sectioned, as the panel would have preferred, existing pictures of it tend to confirm their opinion that the head shot was fired from behind. The Committee was further convinced by sophisticated modern tests which had not been made sixteen years ago. Dr. Vincent Guinn, a chemist and forensic scientist, broke new ground with his "neutron activation" tests—a process in which the bullet specimens were bombarded with neutrons in a nuclear reactor. The results were impressive, and appear to resolve fundamental areas of controversy.

Dr. Guinn was supplied with all the surviving bullet specimens, the several pieces from the car, tiny fragments removed from the wounds of both the President and Governor Connally, and the full-sized bullet found on the stretcher at Parkland Hospital.[7] He concluded that these represented only two bullets and that it was "highly probable" that both were of Mannlicher-Carcano manufacture—the ammunition designed for the rifle found in the Book Depository. The phrase "highly probable" is the cautious formal language of the scientist going on the record, but a personal interview with Guinn confirms that he is highly confident of his conclusion. He is equally certain about a third conclusion, one that—in conjunction with the ballistics evidence—supports the thesis that the fatal head shot was fired from behind. Guinn's tests show that fragments from the President's brain match the three

---

*The Dallas medical staff, who treated Kennedy, are at the center of renewed controversy over whether there was in fact a grassy knoll hit, which exited at the rear. *See* Aftermath chapter.

testable fragments found in the car and that they in turn come from the same bullet. Since ballistics experts conclude that the fragments in the car were fired by the gun in the Book Depository, it seems certain that a shot from the Depository did hit the President in the head. The Committee decided this was the fourth shot and that it was fatal.

While Dr. Guinn's work is in itself most impressive, his conclusions must be weighed in the context of the data he had to work with. Assassinations Committee Staff were horrified to discover the slipshod way in which the material evidence—including the bullet fragments—had been handled over the years. Some feel this taints any objective analytical conclusions about the evidence. Others have objected that, because several tiny fragments have disappeared since 1963 and because Guinn was unable to test one copper fragment, his identification of only two bullets is meaningless. The Committee, however, found nothing sinister about the fragments vanishing and accepted Guinn's findings. His work also had a major impact on the Committee's deliberations in another vital area. They had to resolve a festering controversy over the cause of the other wounds, those to the President's back and throat, and the multiple injuries to Governor Connally's torso, wrist, and thigh. The Warren Commission had theorized that one bullet—the near pristine specimen found at the hospital—was responsible for all of these wounds. It had, the Warren Report suggested, coursed right through President Kennedy and gone on to injure the Governor. This thesis was born when official investigators analyzing the Zapruder film realized that a lone gunman would not have had time to fire his rifle again between the time the President was first seen to be hit and the moment Governor Connally appeared to react to his wounds. It seemed, back in 1964, that there was only one alternative—that two gunmen had fired almost simultaneously,[8] and the Warren Commission did not believe there were two gunmen. Thus its staff produced the "magic bullet" theory, which over the years has caused more derision and skepticism than anything else.

The most persistent objection to the "magic bullet" was its

remarkable state of preservation. To the layman's eyes, it had sustained virtually no damage (*see illustration 6*). Yet according to the Warren Commission's theory, this bullet first pierced the President in the back, coursed through his upper chest, came out through the front of his neck, went on to strike the Governor in the back, pierced a lung, severed a vein, artery and nerve, broke the right fifth rib, destroying five inches of the bone, and emerged from the Governor's right chest. It then plunged on into the back of the Governor's right forearm, broke a thick bone, and distal end of the radius, came out of the other side of the wrist, and finally ended up in the left thigh. It supposedly fell out of the thigh and was recovered on the stretcher at the hospital.

Ever since 1964, doctors with long experience of bullet wounds have had great difficulty in accepting that a bullet could cause such damage, especially to bones, and still emerge almost unscathed. Typical of such doubt was the considered opinion of Dr. Milton Helpern, formerly Chief Medical Examiner of New York City, of whom the *New York Times* said, "He knows more about violent death than anyone else in the world." Dr. Helpern, who had conducted two thousand autopsies on victims of gunshot wounds, said of the "magic bullet," "The original, pristine weight of this bullet before it was fired was approximately 160-161 grains. The weight of the bullet recovered on the stretcher in Parkland Hospital was reported by the Commission at 158.6.[9] This bullet wasn't distorted in any way. I cannot accept the premise that this bullet thrashed around in all that bony tissue and lost only 1.4 to 2.4 grains of its original weight. I cannot believe either that this bullet is going to emerge miraculously unscathed, without any deformity, and with its lands and grooves intact. . . . You must remember that next to bone, the skin offers greater resistance to a bullet in its course through the body than any other kind of tissue. . . . This single bullet theory asks us to believe that this bullet went through seven layers of skin, tough, elastic, resistant skin. In addition . . . this bullet passed through other layers of soft tissue; and then shattered bones! I just can't believe that this bullet had the force to do what [the Commission] have demanded of it; and I don't think they have really stopped to think out carefully what they have asked of this bullet, for the simple reason that they still do not understand the resistant nature of human skin to bullets."

Dr. Helpern's comments have been echoed and developed by many critics of the official theory and most of all by Dr. Cyril Wecht, former president of the Academy of Forensic Sciences. He had been supported by other researchers, notably Dr. John Nichols of the University of Kansas Department of Pathology. Dr. Robert Shaw, Professor of Thoracic Surgery at the University of Texas, the doctor who treated Governor Connally's chest wounds, has never been satisfied that the "magic bullet" caused all his patient's injuries.

Three of the seven members of the Warren Commission did not fully believe the theory of the magic bullet, even though it appeared in their own report. The Commissioners wrangled about it up to the moment their findings went to press. Congressman Hale Boggs had "strong doubts." Senator Sherman Cooper was, as he told me in 1978, "unconvinced." Senator Richard Russell did not want to sign a report which said definitely that both men were hit by the same bullet; he wanted a footnote added indicating his dissent, but Warren declined to put one in. Years later, in an interview with a researcher, Russell went so far as to say no one man could have done the known shooting. He believed there had been a conspiracy.

In 1979, in spite of this barrage of illustrious disbelief, Congress' Assassinations Committee decided that the Warren Report had been right all along. The "magic bullet," it said, did cause the havoc with which it was credited. In this the Committee had the support of almost all its specialist consultants. The majority of the forensic pathology panel decided the medical evidence was consistent with the one bullet wounding both victims. In saying so the doctors took account of other evidence. They believed that the photographic exhibits, and the Zapruder film in particular, showed that the President and the Governor were lined up in a way "consistent with the trajectory of one bullet." They listened to the opinion of a ballistics witness who said that a Mannlicher-Carcano bullet could indeed emerge only minimally deformed after striking bone. The ballistics experts were satisfied, too, that the "magic bullet" itself had been fired in the Mannlicher-Carcano rifle. Finally, for the first time, the controversial bullet was linked firmly to the wound in Governor Connally's wrist. Dr. Guinn's neutron activation tests revealed that the make-up of the bullet was indistinguishable from fragments found in the Governor's wrist. Guinn says it is "extremely unlikely" that they come from different bullets. It was in the light of all this that the Assassinations Committee decided to restore the "magic bullet" theory to respectability. It retains its place in today's official conclusion, that the President was hit twice from behind and that the first of the hits, not necessarily lethal, passed through both him and the Governor. The second hit struck him in the head and killed him. For some, however, the controversy continues.

One of the Committee's own distinguished forensic pathologists dissented volubly from his colleagues' conclusions. This was Dr. Cyril Wecht, the combative coroner from Pennsylvania who has studied the Kennedy case longer than any of his fellows on the forensic panel. Wecht still rejects the magic-bullet theory and maintains that his fellow doctors' judgment is "semantical sophistry and intellectual gymnastics." He does not accept the argument that the President and Governor were adequately aligned at the moment of the shot and claims the bullet would have had to swerve sharply in mid-air, "a path of flight that has never been experienced or suggested for any bullet known to mankind." Wecht's interpretation of the Zapruder film is that the Governor did not react as soon as he would have done had he been hit by same shot as the President. He does not accept a contention by his colleagues that the wound in Connally's back is consistent with a bullet that was tumbling because it had previously hit the President. Above all, he still refuses to believe that a bullet could emerge almost intact after causing as much bone damage as was done to the Governor. To demonstrate this, Wecht points to the condition of Mannlicher-Carcano ammunition after firing into cotton wadding, a goat carcass—which sustained a broken rib—and through the wrist of a corpse. All the test bullets are visibly more damaged than the bullet alleged to have caused the wounds of the President and the Governor. Wecht deplores the fact that the Assassinations Committee did not try to reproduce the "magic bullet" by performing similar tests and has challenged his colleagues to produce even *one* bullet that had emerged similarly undamaged.

The forensic panel was unmoved by Dr. Wecht's passionate dissent. Its chairman, Dr. Baden, insisted that tests to reproduce a "magic bullet" were "futile." He also claimed he had seen other makes of bullet survive similar battering and emerge virtually undamaged.[10] Nobody, however, has produced such a bullet. Moreover, while modern tests have now linked the magic bullet to fragments removed from Governor Connally's arm, no fragments have survived from the Governor's chest or the President's throat wound. Recent statements, by a former operating-room supervisor and a policeman who guarded the Governor's room, refer to the retrieval of more fragments than could possibly have come from the magic bullet.[11] For some, this arouses again dark suspicions about fragments lost or, worse, deliberately removed. Meanwhile, the fact remains that, for the President's throat wound and the Governor's chest there are no fragments to test against the magic bullet. For Dr. Wecht, this leaves open the possibility that a separate bullet hit the President in the back and emerged through his throat. It was, indeed, a notion which could not be excluded by a leading wound ballistics consultant to the Assassinations Committee. Wecht has speculated that such a bullet could, after coursing through the President, have simply sped past the car and on into thin air.

Dr. Wecht also objected to his colleagues' confidence that there was a single fatal head shot fired from a single position to the President's rear. While the brain remains missing, says Wecht, it is impossible to be categorical about what really happened. He reserves judgment about the mark to be seen in one autopsy photograph, low down on the back of the President's head. While both he and his colleagues accept that this is smeared brain tissue,

Wecht cannot exclude the possibility that it conceals a very small wound on entrance or exit. He also believes it possible that the massive hole in the skull could be the result of not one head shot but of *two* impacting almost simultaneously.

Even Dr. Baden has acknowledged the remote possibility that the fatal headshot "could have been caused by a shot from the grassy knoll, and that medical evidence of it has been destroyed by a shot from the rear a fraction of a second later." While this remains conceivable from the medical point of view, the Committee found it contrary to trajectory data and the time frame reconstructed from acoustics evidence and the Zapruder film. Dr. Wecht, however, does not suggest the President was hit from the grassy knoll. Instead, he theorizes, the President may have been hit, from the right side, at almost the same instant that he was hit from the rear. He has suggested that a soft-nosed bullet, or "relatively frangible ammunition," could have penetrated without leaving fragments in the left side of the brain. A wound ballistics expert, on the other hand, told the Committee that from the evidence of the X rays the President was definitely not hit by a frangible or exploding bullet. So did one of Wecht's pathologist colleagues, and it is hard to see how such a shot could fit into the acoustic record of the shooting.

The chairman of the Assassinations Committee asked Dr. Wecht how ordinary people should react to the fact that he was in a minority of one on a panel of nine eminent forensic pathologists. He replied hopefully that he might be compared to a Supreme Court Justice whose lone dissent many years later becomes the law of the land. In fairness, it must be remembered that, in advance of the acoustics report, Dr. Wecht was the only member of the medical panel to insist there had been four shots. Dr. Wecht has not subscribed to extreme theories, such as recent suggestions by others that the photographic record of the autopsy has been deliberately faked.[12] He has, however, long proposed an intriguing resolution of his problems with the "magic bullet" theory that there may have been two gunmen firing from the Book Depository. This, added to Gunman No. 1 operating on the Depository

sixth floor and to Gunman No. 2 firing from the knoll, would make
a total of three assassins. Dr. Wecht thinks the third assassin may
have fired from a lower floor of the Depository or may have
worked alongside Gunman No. 1 on the sixth floor. In that, Dr.
Wecht may yet turn out to be right.

CHAPTER 4

Gunmen in the Shadows

The physical evidence and eyewitness accounts
do not clearly indicate what took place on the sixth
floor of the Texas School Book Depository at the time
John F. Kennedy was assassinated.

—Dallas Police Chief Jesse Curry, 1969

One fact is not in question. Before and during the shooting, people in the crowd noticed a man, or a man with a gun, in the right-hand window of the sixth floor of the Texas School Book Depository, the window soon to become known as the sniper's perch. Two bystanders, clerks from the nearby county building, noticed him just before the shooting, because he looked "uncomfortable." One actually remarked that the man "must be hiding or some-thing." To the clerks, the man seemed to be looking toward the grassy knoll rather than in the direction from which the President would be arriving. Then there was Howard Brennan, later to become a star witness for the official inquiry. He was standing right across the road from the Depository and was to report seeing a man at the right hand sixth-floor window both before and during the shooting. After the second shot, said Brennan, "this man I saw previous was aiming for his last shot." The gunman then drew back "and maybe paused for another second as though to assure himself that he had hit his mark" and then disappeared. Near Brennan, a fifteen-year-old schoolboy, Amos Euins, also saw a rifle fired from the famous window. "I could see his hand," he said later, "and I cold see his other hand on the trigger, and one hand on the barrel thing." Another youth in the crowd, James Worrell, said he looked up after the first shot and saw "six inches" on a rifle barrel sticking out of the window. Three people traveling in the motorcade itself, the Mayor's wife and two photographers, saw part of a rifle from the window. Neither of the photographers, however, were off the mark fast enough to take a photograph. These witnesses posed no problem to the Warren Commission, and their statements were written into the record. Others, though, were either judged to be mistaken or wholly ignored. They, most inconveniently, had reported *two* men behind the windows of the Book Depository.

Fifteen minutes before the assassination, a bystander called Arnold Rowland asked his wife if she would like to see a Secret Service agent. He pointed to a window on the sixth floor where he had noticed "a man back from the window—he was standing and holding a rifle . . . we thought momentarily that maybe we should tell someone, but then the thought came to us that it is a security agent." Rowland testified that he had seen the rifle clearly enough to make out the telescopic sight and realize it was a high-powered weapon. The man he saw was not in the famous window, at the right-hand end of the sixth floor, but in the far *left*-hand window. Rowland also said that, at the same time, he spotted a second figure, at the famous *right*-hand window. The second man was dark complexioned, and Rowland thought he was a Negro.

The first official inquiry rejected Rowland's comments about a second man, even though a deputy sheriff confirmed that he mentioned the man immediately after the shooting. Rowland said that when he told FBI agents about the second man, during the weekend, ". . . they told me it didn't have any bearing or such on the case right then. In fact they just the same as told me to forget it now. . . . They didn't seem interested at all. They didn't pursue this point. They didn't take it down in the notation as such." The Warren Report ignored and omitted altogether statements that were taken from the FBI from two other witnesses. These also referred to two men, and the first of them appears to corroborate Rowland's account.

Shortly before the assassination a female bystander, Mrs. Ruby Henderson, saw two men standing back from a window on one of the upper floors of the Book Depository. Like Rowland, she particularly noticed that one of the men "had dark hair . . . a darker complexion than the other." At the time, it occurred to her that he might have been a Mexican. She had the impression that the men were looking out, as if "in anticipation of the motorcade. . . ." Mrs. Henderson's sighting can be timed, because she remembered it as occurring after an ambulance removed a man taken ill on the street. The time of the ambulance was logged, so we know Mrs. Henderson saw the two men less than six minutes before the assassination. Yet another witness observed two men just before the assassination, and her report is even more troubling.

Mrs. Carolyn Walther noticed two men with a gun in an open window at the extreme right-hand end of the Depository. Although she did not think of it as quite as high as the sixth floor, it was a window at the extreme right-hand end of the building, and it was open. Photographs, and the location of innocent employees in the fifth-floor windows, establish that she must have been looking at the famous sniper's perch. As Mrs. Walther described it, "I saw this man in a window, and he had a gun in his hands, pointed downwards. The man evidently was in a kneeling position, because his forearms were resting on the windowsill. There was another man standing beside him, but I only saw a portion of his body because he was standing partly up against the window, you know, only halfway in the window; and the window was dirty and I couldn't see his face, up above, because the window was pushed up. It startled me, then I thought, 'Well, they probably have guards, possibly in all the buildings,' so I didn't say anything." If Mrs. Walther had sounded the alarm, it would probably have been too late. She had barely noticed the second man when the President's motorcade swept into view.

Yet another witness did not tell his story in 1963. Although he was an obvious candidate for interview, nobody bothered to ask him questions. Until very recently he was reluctant to speak out for obvious reasons. On November 22, 1963, John Powell was one of many inmates housed on the sixth floor of the Dallas County Jail. The window in his cell was an ideal vantage point for observation of the famous Depository window. Powell, who was spending three days in custody on minor charges, has long told friends and family members that, in the minutes before the assassination, he and his cellmates watched two men with a gun in the window opposite. He claims he could see them so clearly that he even recalls them "fooling with the scope" on the gun. Powell says, "Quite a few of us saw them. Everybody was trying to watch the parade and all that. We were looking across the street because it was directly straight across. The first thing I thought is, it was security guards. . . . I remember the guys." Powell did not seek publicity for his story; a friend contacted a local newspaper much later. Like Mrs. Henderson and Arnold Rowland, Powell recalls, spontaneously, that one of the men appeared to have darker skin than a white American. During the Warren inquiry, an official failed to respond to a specific reminder that observers in the County Jail had had a perfect view and should be questioned.

Today it is impossible to dismiss those who reported seeing two men, at least one of them armed, lurking behind the sixth-floor windows. Fresh material evidence, which surfaced at the eleventh hour of assassinations Committee deliberations, may yet provide corroboration. In late 1978, in a three-page lead story, the *Dallas Morning News* announced the discovery of a film shot six minutes before the assassination, by an amateur cameraman named Charles Bronson. It had lain abandoned in its owner's keeping since 1963, when a cursory FBI viewing dismissed it as irrelevant. In fact it shows the windows of the sixth floor—albeit in the distance—and was filmed within six minutes of the assassination. Senior staff on the Dallas newspaper, viewing the film in 1978, believed they could see distinct movement in more than one window of the sixth floor. They submitted the footage to Robert Groden—a consultant who performed photographic source research for the Assassinations Committee—and his preliminary comments caused something of a sensation. Groden concluded that there was not only movement of what appears to be two men in the sixth-floor window but also—at one point—movement in an arched window to its left. Groden stated: "The fact that there is movement in two windows that are separated by a good eight feet indicates beyond question that there was more than one person up there."

Groden believes the Bronson footage may vindicate those who long ago saw evidence of two men in yet another film. A bystander called Robert Hughes also caught the sixth floor in his lens on November 22, 1963, at the very moment the motorcade was approaching the Book Depository. Some researchers, including Groden, suggest there is human movement in the same windows as in the Bronson film. A still photograph, taken seconds before the shooting, also shows a shape in the arched window (*see illustration 2*). Groden felt sufficiently confident, after optically enhancing the Bronson film and comparing it to the other material, to write: "The man in window No. 1 is moving rapidly back and forth, and the man in No. 3 seems to be crouched down at the window and rocking on his toes. . . . The shape in window No. 2 is slightly less distinct than the other two. . . . I now feel that is a distinctly different person who is probably handing boxes to man No. 1."

The Assassinations Committee photographic specialists, many of whom disagree with Groden's opinions, were much more cautious. The panel did conclude firmly, from still pictures, that boxes were rearranged in the sixth-floor window just *after* the assassination. On the movie film, though, it went no further than noting "an appearance or impression of motion" in the window just before the assassination. Computer enhancement of the Hughes film failed to convince the panel that the movement was caused by human activity, although they admitted it was possible. One panel member, Robert Selzer, commented that there was clearly movement which could be human, and in more than one window. Bronson's film had surfaced in the last days of the Committee's work, and there was no time for sophisticated tests. To that end, as one of its last acts, the Assassinations Committee recommended further examination by the Department of Justice.* That could yet confirm the presence of more than one gunman on the sixth floor. It may be, however, that acoustic analysis once again holds the key to placing the assassins.

For Assassinations Committee staff in 1978, one factor in the new acoustics evidence proved as alarming as the revelation of a gunman on the grassy knoll. They knew now that the gap between

---

* The Department failed to do it, citing unconvincing reasons. See Department letter to Chairman, House Judiciary Committee, March 28, 1988.

shots 1 and 2, both fired from the Depository, was extraordinarily
short. It was, to be precise, a mere 1.66 seconds. Back in 1964,
tests conducted by the FBI had shown that the rifle found in the
Depository could not be aimed and fired in so short a time.
Indeed, the FBI marksmen's best times were as long as 2.25 and
2.3 seconds. If those tests were accurate, the Committee staff well
realized, it followed that two gunmen fired from the Depository on
November 22, 1963. This specter, on top of the confirmation of a
gunman on the grassy knoll, caused a flurry of activity by the
Assassinations Committee. From firearms consultants the staff
learned that the Mannlicher-Carcano can be fired accurately dispensing with the telescopic sight and using only the iron sights.
Indeed, said the experts, the iron sights would have been preferable in the conditions of Dealey Plaza. Committee staff therefore
conducted new tests, and unpracticed volunteers fired at a silhou-
ette over iron sights. They brought down the firing time, but
hardly enough. The best the rifle could be fired was to achieve one
hit out of three, at 150 feet, in average times of 1.65 and 1.75
seconds. A second marksman failed to get his time below two
seconds. In March 1979, when the Committee had already announced its conclusions, further tests were conducted. This time
the men with the guns included four police marksmen and—
delightful image—the learned Chief Counsel of the Committee
and his deputy. None of the police marksmen were able to aim and
fire two consecutive shots within the required time of 1.66 seconds.
The two amateurs from the Committee were able to fire in the
required time, but only by "point-aiming"—not using either the
telescopic or the iron sights. Both men missed with their second
shots. The experiment itself may have been unrealistic. The gun
used was a Mannlicher-Carcano rifle of the type found in the Book
Depository but not the actual weapon found on the day of the
assassination. The original Mannlicher-Carcano was an uncooper-
ative piece of evidence, as army experts discovered after the
assassination. As a spokesman put it, one of them "had difficulty
in opening the bolt in his first firing exercise. . . ." He added that,
as newcomers to the weapon, "The pressure to open the bolt was
so great that we tended to move the rifle off the target. . . ." An
assassin using the Mannlicher-Carcano in Dealey Plaza may, of

course, have known the quirks of his weapon, but this account suggests the gun was hardly ideal for feats of marksmanship. Christopher Dodd, one of the most assiduous Congressmen on the Assassinations Committee, could not agree with a flat conclusion that all the shots fired from the Depository were fired by one man.

Representative Dodd remains unconvinced by the latest tests showing that the rifle could, without proper aiming, be fired in less than 1.66 seconds. Sensibly, he raises a further consideration. If a gunman missed with his first shot, as all the evidence indicates, surely he would take time to aim properly the second time. The second shot, after all, struck home at a target moving along at eleven miles an hour. Dodd is aware of the circumstantial evidence in favor of a lone gunman—three cartridge cases, all found near the sixth-floor window and all linked to the Mannlicher-Carcano. These do seem to indicate three shots from the same gun. However, as Dodd points out, one of the three might have been fired *before* the day of the murder, left in the breach, and simply been ejected before the rifle was used against the President. If the first two shots were not fired by a lone gunman, the Congressman reasons, the investigator is left with only two options. Either the acoustics evidence is in error, or there were two gunmen operating from the rear. Dodd, like the majority of the Assassinations Committee, is convinced by the acoustics evidence. It has led to the momentous finding which places a gunman on the knoll, and it may yet force a finding that there were two assassins firing from behind the President.

There is clearly scope for further scientific study. The Committee's Chief Counsel, Professor Blakey, is open to the possibility that gunfire may have come from more than one source to the rear—perhaps from the Daltex building. The later work of the Committee's acoustics scientists concentrated intensively on the precise location of the gunman on the grassy knoll. Shortage of time prevented final exhaustive research into the shots from the President's rear. For the same reason, the Bronson film has yet to be examined properly for the presence of more than one assassin. As its final act, the Assassinations Committee recommended that the Department of Justice continue to work on the film and on the recording of the shots.

In his comments on the report, Congressman Dodd emphasized, "If further study would resolve any lingering doubts as to the conclusion, failure to pursue the answers would be inexcusable.* On the issue of a President's death we should not deal in shadows of suspected truths when we might have light." It remains to be seen whether the Congressman's hopes will ever be answered.

Conspiracy, as a Supreme Court justice once defined it, is "a partnership in criminal purposes." As the scientific case stands, and as a massive official inquiry has indicated, the Kennedy assassination was the result of such conspiracy. The immediate purpose was tragically obvious. Yet the identity of the partners in crime remains uncertain, their trail perplexing. There is, nevertheless, a trail.

---

* The work recommended was not done. See Preface.

CHAPTER 5

Finding a Fugitive

He didn't think there would be any more work done that day. . . . Oswald's ostensible reason for leaving the scene of the crime,

quoted by the Dallas Chief of Homicide

The last the people of Dallas saw of President Kennedy was his slumped figure, then a Secret Service agent leaping into the back seat of the limousine and another—in the follow-up car—impotently brandishing an automatic rifle. Then confusion reigned in Dealey Plaza, and it was at first the grassy knoll which attracted most attention. Spectators and police seemed to think that was a key place to look for assassins, and—quite apart from the story now told by acoustics—they were probably right.

Rose, the daughter of amateur photographer Philip Willis, had been running alongside the President's car as it passed the knoll. As she ran she caught a glimpse of somebody standing behind the corner of a concrete retaining wall. For some reason he appeared "conspicuous" and seemed to "disappear the next instant." As we have seen, photographs bear out her story. Meanwhile, from his perch on top of a high building nearby, Jesse Price found his attention drawn to something behind the fence on the knoll. A man, about twenty-five and wearing a white shirt with khaki trousers, ran off "towards the passenger cars on the railroad siding. . . ." The man appeared to be carrying something. Lee Bowers, the railway towerman who had seen two strangers behind the fence just before the assassination, had partially lost sight of them in foliage. At the time of the shooting, though, he had observed some sort of commotion behind the fence. Then policemen started pouring into the area. One of the first was patrolman Joe Smith, who rushed into the parking lot behind the fence because a woman said the shots had come "from the bushes." It was there, as we noted, that he smelled gunpowder. It was there that Congress' acoustics evidence places a gunman and there that Smith had a very odd experience.

The patrolman had drawn his pistol as he ran. He was just beginning to feel, as he put it, "damn silly" when he came across a man standing by a car. The man reacted quickly at sight of Smith and an accompanying deputy. As Smith remembered it, "The man, this character, produces credentials from his hip pocket which showed him to be Secret Service. I have seen those credentials before, and they satisfied me and the deputy sheriff. So I immediately accepted that and let him go and continued our search around the cars." It was a decision Officer Smith later bitterly regretted, for there were no authentic Secret Service agents on the grassy knoll.[13]

All Secret Servicemen in Dallas that day are accounted for in official reports. None were on foot either before or immediately after the assassination, and those on motorcade duty stayed with their cars. There were no genuine agents anywhere near the grassy knoll parking lot.

Secret Service agents, in 1963, were the essence of the crew-cut, besuited American young man. The man encountered in the parking lot was different. As Officer Smith put it, "He looked like an auto mechanic. He had on a sports shirt and sports pants. But he had dirty fingernails, it looked like, and hands that looked like an auto mechanic's hands. And afterwards it didn't ring true for the Secret Service." The policeman now says wryly, "At the time we were so pressed for time, and we were searching. And he had produced correct identification, and we just overlooked the thing. I should have checked that man closer, but at the time I didn't snap on it. . . ."

Smith and the deputy sheriff were not alone in their sighting of the "Secret Serviceman." Gordon Arnold, the soldier who found himself virtually in the line of fire during the shooting, recalls encountering a "Secret Service agent" just before the assassination. Jean Hill, who had seen smoke on the knoll, says she met an agent immediately afterward—just before Officer Smith. Hill had run impetuously across the road, dodging between the cars while the motorcade was still going by. She was ahead of the field in the parking lot, and there, she says, she met a "tall and slender man." Today she tells of an experience much like that of Officer Smith—of a man who whipped out Secret Service identification and how she then gave up her chase. Officer Smith did give his information to the Warren Commission. Jean Hill insists she gave her account to the Warren staff. In 1977 former Dallas Police Chief Jesse Curry said of the "Secret Service agent" on the knoll, "I think he must have been bogus—certainly the suspicion would point to the man as being involved, some way or other, in the shooting, since he was in an area immediately adjacent to where the shots were—and the fact that he had a badge that purported him to be Secret Service would make it seem all the more suspicious."*

Jean Hill, in her account of meeting the "agent," says that beyond and behind him she caught sight of a man running. Like the man Price saw, she lost sight of him by the railway lines some twenty yards away. It might all seem fanciful if it were not for the evidence of another policeman. Officer John Tilson was off duty on the day of the assassination but, within minutes of the shooting, happened to be driving with his daughter on the road beyond the railway tracks. Tilson had just heard the first word of the shooting, on the car radio, when he saw a man "slipping and sliding" down the railway embankment.* In 1978 the policeman recalled, "'He came down that grassy slope on the west side of the triple underpass. He had a car parked there, a black car. He threw something in the back seat and went around the front hurriedly and got in the car and took off. I saw all of this and I said, 'That doesn't make sense, everybody running to the scene and one person running from it.' " Officer Tilson, now retired, says his seventeen years of police experience, coupled with the news now pouring over the radio, prompted him to give chase. After a while he lost his quarry, but—as his daughter confirms—he managed to take the

*In 1988 a Dallas witness, Malcolm Summers, told the PBS program *Nova* he encountered a man with a gun on the knoll.

license number of the car. Tilson reported the incident, and the number, to Dallas Police Homicide that afternoon, but heard no more about the matter. Predictably, there were other reports of speeding cars in central Dallas that afternoon. One, it turned out, was carrying stolen Georgia plates. Officer Tilson's account appears to have been passed over in the chaos of the hours that followed, and there is no record of the car number he noted.

Meanwhile, less than five minutes after the shooting, the focus of interest changed sharply. First an officer called in over the radio to say ". . . a passerby states the shots came from the Texas School Book Depository building." At about the same time, three employees at the Depository came forward to say they had been watching the motorcade from a fifth-floor window and had heard suspicious sounds above them. They had heard a clatter like a rifle bolt being operated and, above their heads, what sounded like shells being ejected on to the floor. Slowly, as the police operation became more organized, the Depository was sealed off and a floor-by-floor search began.

Before this bore any fruit, as early as 12:44 P.M., the police radio put out its first description of a suspect in the assassination: "Attention all squads. The suspect in the shooting at Elm and Houston is supposed to be an unknown white male approximately 30, 165 pounds, slender build, armed with what is thought to be a 30-30 rifle . . . no further description at this time."

In what today seems an astonishing failure, the Warren inquiry never did establish the source of this description. Its best guess was that it arose from a police officer's conversation with Brennan, one of the witnesses who claimed to have seen a man with a gun in the sixth-floor window. Whatever the source, policemen in Dallas now had a lead, however vague, a rough description of somebody to be on the lookout for.

Later there would be reports of men apparently running away from the Book Depository. One witness said he noticed a man in his thirties, in a dark jacket, emerge from the "back entrance" of the building and run off down the street. There were other reports and varying descriptions, but these were soon overtaken by events. At 1:16 p.m., forty-five minutes after the assassination, operators at Dallas police headquarters were startled to hear an unknown voice break into official radio traffic. A citizen was relaying news of fresh drama and a second murder:

CITIZEN: Hello, police operator.
OPERATOR: Go ahead, go ahead, citizen using police radio.
CITIZEN: We've had a shooting out here.
OPERATOR: Where is it at?
CITIZEN: On Tenth Street.
OPERATOR: What location on Tenth Street?
CITIZEN: Between Marsalis and Beckley. It's a police officer. Somebody shot him.

A police officer had indeed been shot, a couple of miles from Dealey Plaza, on a leafy street in the district of Oak Cliff. He was patrol-car driver J. D. Tippit, and he was dead. Several people had seen the shooting or its aftermath, and within four minutes police were broadcasting the description of a suspect in this second murder: "A white male approximately 30, 5′ 8″, slender build, has black hair, a white jacket, a white shirt and dark trousers." From all over Dallas, police cars hurried to join the hunt for the murderer of a fellow officer. As they searched surrounding streets, two more ordinary citizens decided they, too, had something to report. A shoe-shop manager, Johnny Brewer, heard police-car sirens wailing and looked up to see a young man walking into the shop entranceway. When the police cars went away, so did the young man, and Brewer later said, "His hair was sort of messed up and looked like he'd been running." Brewer left the shop and spoke to the ticket seller at a movie house a few doors away—the Texas Theater. They decided the mysterious young man had entered the movie house without buying a ticket, and, putting two and two together, they telephoned the police. Within minutes at least fifteen officers descended on the theater, and one of them, Patrolman Nick McDonald, went around to the back entrance. When I talked to him in 1978, he gave me his version of what happened next. By now, the lights were up in the auditorium, and from behind a curtained doorway Brewer, the shoe-shop manager, pointed to a man sitting near the back. It was McDonald's big moment. He walked cautiously up through the almost empty theater, checking a couple of other customers on the way, but always keeping an eye to the man at the back. When he reached the suspect—a nervous-looking young man—McDonald ordered him to his feet. The man started to rise, brought his hands half up, and then punched McDonald between the eyes. Next, according to McDonald, the suspect went for a pistol in his waistband. There was a brief scuffle in which the gun misfired, then more officers arrived, and the Dallas police had their prisoner. The suspect, a slim young man of twenty-four, was hustled out of the theater, through a hostile crowd, and into a police car destined for headquarters. During the scuffle with the policeman he had cried, "Well, it's all over now."

In so many ways, as America knows to its cost, it was by no means all over. The prisoner was Lee Harvey Oswald.

Oswald was to be questioned by the Dallas police, the FBI, and the Secret Service for nearly two days—two days in which he steadfastly denied any part in the murder of either the President or of Officer Tippit. According to the police no record of any kind was kept of the twelve hours of interrogation—although there is reason to doubt this. Captain Will Fritz, the chief of the Homicide Bureau, who led the questioning, has himself referred to keeping "rough notes," yet these were never produced for the official inquiry. We have to rely on retrospective reports written by Fritz and the other officers who talked to Oswald.

Oswald was quite open about his basic background, the outline of a life now well known around the world. He had been born in 1939 in New Orleans, joined the U.S. Marines at the age of seventeen, and then, in 1959, traveled to the Soviet Union. Behaving like a defector who wanted to become a Soviet citizen, Oswald had stayed in Russia for two and a half years. After marriage to a Soviet wife and the birth of a baby daughter, Oswald returned to the United States and to Texas, where his mother lived. During 1963, Oswald told the police, he spent several months in New Orleans, where he began to take an active interest in Cuban politics. He admitted having demonstrated in favor of Fidel Castro, and—for his part in an ensuing street incident—having been arrested by New Orleans police. This, said Oswald, was the only time he had been in trouble with the police, and a check proved him right. The interrogators asked Oswald if he was a Communist, and he replied that he was a Marxist but not a Marxist-Leninist. That was a little too sophisticated for Dallas law-enforcement officers, and Oswald said wearily that it would take too long to explain. Of his recent activity, Oswald described how he had looked for work in Dallas and eventually taken a laboring job at the Texas School Book Depository.

On several occasions, as he was escorted around the police station, Oswald faced a barrage of questions from the world's press. Radio and television microphones recorded his strenuous denial of any involvement in the Kennedy assassination. Asked point-blank "Did you kill the President?" Oswald replied, I didn't shoot anybody, no sir." He told the press this more than once. On the last occasion, as he was being dragged away through the seething crowd of reporters. Oswald said, "No, they're taking me in because of the fact that I lived in the Soviet Union." As he was hustled away. Oswald almost shrieked, "I'm a patsy!"

If Oswald really was just a fall guy, he had been bewilderingly well framed. Even before his arrest, police were finding evidence that was to prove damning, evidence black enough and copious enough to give any prosecutor a good case. Consider now the facts that would have been used against Oswald if he had come to trial.

Half an hour after the assassination, near the famous sixth-floor Depository window, a sheriff's deputy noticed a stack of book cartons. They were stacked high enough to hide a crouching man from a casual observer behind him in the building. There, on the floor, in the narrow space between the boxes and the window, were three empty cartridge cases. A rifle was found soon afterward, by two other officers searching the other end of the sixth floor. From the prosecutor's point of view, it was to provide the clinching evidence against Oswald.

The gun was a bolt-action rifle with a sling and telescopic sight and was stamped with the serial number C-2766. It was the 6.5-millimeter Mannlicher-Carcano, a hitherto undistinguished Italian rifle of World War II vintage. There was a live round in the breach ready for firing. The weapon was examined for fingerprints at

Dallas police headquarters, then flown to FBI headquarters in Washington. Experts there found some traces of fingerprints on the metal near the trigger, but these were too incomplete to be identified. Then, four days later, Lieutenant Day of the Dallas police sent the FBI a palm print which, he said, he had "lifted" from the barrel of the rifle before sending it to Washington. The palm print was firmly identified as that of the right hand of Lee Harvey Oswald.

At dawn on November 23, as Oswald ended his first night in custody, came a discovery that incriminated him even further. In Chicago, the staff of Klein's Sporting Goods Company, searching through their files at the request of the FBI, came upon the records for the rifle with serial number C-2766. Klein's, who did a large mail-order business, had sent such a gun on March 20—eight months before the assassination—to a customer called A. Hidell, at Post Office Box 2915, Dallas, Texas. The order form, which Klein's had received a week earlier, was signed "A. Hidell," in handwriting.

For the early investigators, the case now seemed effectively broken. The serial number at Klein's matched the number on the gun found at the Depository, and that gun had borne Oswald's palm print. The signature "A. Hidell" and the hand-printed part of the order form, were firmly identified by government document examiners as Oswald's handwriting. Dallas police said that Oswald, when arrested, had been carrying a forged identity card, as well as documents in his own name. The forged card bore the name "Alek J. Hidell," yet the photograph attached was Oswald's. Dallas Post Office Box 2915 turned out to belong to Lee Oswald. Nor was that all.

In a crevice on the butt of the rifle was a tuft of cotton fibers. These were examined microscopically at the FBI laboratory, which judged them compatible with fibers in the shirt Oswald was wearing when arrested.

Oswald's wife, Marina, was to tesify—months later—that her husband had owned a rifle. She had seen it, she was to say, in late September, at the house near Dallas where she was then staying. Oswald and his wife were living apart, seeing each other only occasionally, in the months before the assassination. Marina, with her two children, was staying at the house of a friend called Ruth

Paine. Many of Oswald's possessions had been stored in the Paine garage, and it was there that Marina said she had last seen the rifle, wrapped in a blanket. Police saw the blanket during a search of the garage after the assassination. By then there was no rifle, but an FBI examination suggested the blanket had been stretched by hard, protruding objects.

On the eve of the assassination Oswald had asked a fellow employee, Buell Frazier, to drive him to Mrs. Paine's house. Frazier quoted him as saying, "I'm going home to get some curtain rods . . . to put in an apartment." Oswald had then stayed the night with his wife and left the next morning before she was up, at 7:15 A.M. He then walked over to Frazier's house, just a few doors away, to get a lift into work. Frazier's sister noticed that Oswald was now carrying a heavy brown bag, and Frazier asked about it as the two men drove into the city. Oswald said something about "curtain rods," and Frazier remembered he had mentioned rods the night before. At the Texas School Book Depository, Oswald walked ahead into the building, holding the package tucked under his right armpit.

After the assassination, during their search of the sixth floor, police found a brown paper bag large enough to have contained the Mannlicher-Carcano rifle. It appeared to be home-made. The FBI later found a palm print and a fingerprint on the bag, and these matched Oswald's right palm and his left index finger. Fibers found on the paper were very similar to fibers on the blanket in the Paine garage.

The day after the assassination, again in the garage, police made further dramatic finds. They came up with two photographs, both of a man holding a rifle in one hand, two left-wing newspapers in the other, and with a pistol on his hip. The Warren Commission was to decide that the man was Oswald and that the rifle was the assassination weapon. Oswald's wife, indeed, was to say that she had photographed her husband in this odd pose the previous spring. The background in the pictures was the back yard of a house where the couple had lived at that time. An FBI photographic expert determined that the photographs had been taken with an Imperial Reflex camera believed to have belonged to Oswald. On top of all that, there was the ballistics evidence.

As we have already seen, expert opinion is that the "magic

bullet," found on the afternoon of the assassination at Parkland Hospital, was fired in the Mannlicher-Carcano to the exclusion of all other weapons. The three cartridge cases found at the Depository have also been firmly linked with the rifle. The ballistics evidence involved in the policeman's shooting seemed damning too: cases found near the scene of the killing had been fired in the pistol that Oswald was carrying when arrested.

Long before this catalogue of evidence had been prepared, the Dallas authorities expressed great confidence in the case against Oswald. At ten past seven on the evening of the assassination, Oswald was charged with the killing of police officer Tippit. Later that night Assistant District Attorney William Alexander, along with Captain Fritz of Homicide, decided there were also grounds for charging Oswald with the President's murder. Alexander told me in 1978 that the fact of Oswald's departure from the Depository after the assassination, coupled with the "curtain rods" story and the "Communist" literature found among Oswald's effects, was enough to justify the second charge. According to Police Chief Curry, Oswald was brought from his cell sometime after 1:30 A.M. and charged by Judge David Johnston that he "did voluntarily and with malice aforethought kill John F. Kennedy by shooting him with a gun."[14]

The former Police Chief, the late Jesse Curry, commented that Oswald's reaction was "typical." He said, "I don't know what you're talking about. What's the idea of this? What are you doing this for?" Judge Johnston said "Oswald was very conceited. He said sarcastically, 'I guess this is the trial' and denied everything."

All Oswald's denials were later to be dismissed as outright lies, and some of them certainly were. Yet wholesale rejection of Oswald's statements may be ill-judged. A re-examination of what he said may provide clues to his real role in the assassination story.

Oswald and the Mannlicher-Carcano Rifle

Oswald told his interrogators, from the start that he had never possessed a rifle of his own. In later interviews, after the FBI had traced the order for the rifle at the mail-order firm in Chicago, Oswald was asked directly whether he had bought the weapon. He denied it outright but actually volunteered the fact that he had rented Dallas Post Office Box 2915 and indeed that he had been using it at the time the rifle was allegedly sent to that box number. It was never established that it was he who picked up the package containing the rifle at the post office.[15]

Oswald did admit to having used the name "Hidell"—the name in which the rifle had been ordered—saying he "had picked up that name in New Orleans while working in the Fair Play for Cuba organization." At one stage, though, Oswald seemed to contradict himself, saying that he "had never used the name, didn't know anybody by his name, and had never heard of the name before." This, though, was probably just truculent weariness for he went on to snap, "I've told you all I'm going to about that card. You took notes, just read them for yourself if you want to refresh your memory." Why exactly was Oswald reluctant to discuss the card? As it turns out, his use of the name "Hidell" is intriguing.

The Warren Report contained a statement on the subject that was simply untrue. It declared, "Investigations were conducted with regard to persons using the name 'Hidell' or names similar to it. . . . Diligent search has failed to reveal any person in Dallas or New Orleans by that name." In fact, the Warren Commission's own files contain a statement by a John Rene Heindel. He said that "While in the Marine Corps, I was often referred to as 'Hidell'—pronounced so as to rhyme with 'Rydell.' . . ." This was a nickname and not merely a mispronunciation. . . ." Heindel revealed, moreover, that he had served in the Marines with the alleged assassin. They had both been stationed at Atsugi Base in Japan. Finally, Heindel lived in New Orleans, where Oswald was born, spent part of his youth, and lived during the summer of 1963. All this, for the investigator, is of great potential significance.

Any serious study of the Kennedy case must confront the possibility—many would say the probability—that Oswald had some connection with either the CIA or some other branch of American intelligence. If there was such a connection, it may well have begun at Atsugi, where Oswald and Heindel both served and which was an operational base for the CIA. This period will be covered at length later in this book. We shall also see that, if Oswald was drawn into an assassination conspiracy by others, or framed, the process probably began during his New Orleans stay in 1963. These factors make it all the more disturbing that the Warren Report omitted altogether to mention that there was a real "Hidell"—and even untruthfully stated the contrary. None of the thousands of Warren commission documents reflect serious inquiry into whether or not there was any Heindel-Oswald association after the Japan period. Heindel himself was never called to testify before the Warren Commission. The evidence gathered by Congress' Assassinations Committee, as published in 1979, shows no investigation of Heindel. This is all the more remarkable, given the role played by U.S. military intelligence on the day of the assassination and specifically concerning the "Hidell" alias.

There were, from the start, curiosities about the way the same "Hidell" emerged after the assassination. According to later police testimony, an Army draft card in "Hidell's" name was found in Oswald's wallet immediately after his arrest. One of the first two detectives to question Oswald reported that at first Oswald actually pretended his name was "Hidell." Yet, although the immediate rash of police press statements on the case included a mass of incriminating detail, the name "Hidell" did not come up publicly until the next afternoon, *after* the discovery of a mail order in that name for the rifle.[16] The name "O. H. Lee," the inversion of Oswald's real name in which he was registered at his Dallas roominghouse, was provided to reporters within hours of the assassination. "Hidell" was not. Behind the scenes, however, official communication lines hummed with references to the name within a very few hours of the assassination. It now appears that the police and the FBI were only fully alerted to the "Hidell" alias after contact with a third force—part of the U.S. intelligence apparatus. This is what occurred, according to FBI records now available and the recent testimony of a former senior officer in U.S. Army intelligence.

Military intelligence agents were in Dallas on the day of the assassination, backing up the Secret Service in security operations for President Kennedy's visit. At San Antonio, to the north of the Texas border with Mexico, Lieutenant Colonel Robert Jones was operations officer for the 112th Military Intelligence Group. As soon as he heard about the assassination, says Jones, he urgently requested information from his men at the scene of the crime. By early afternoon he had received a phone call "advising that an A. J. Hidell had been arrested. . . ."(Oddly, published information suggests that the call did not mention the name "Oswald," although both names were on documents in Oswald's wallet.) Jones says he quickly located the name "Hidell" in military intelligence files. It cross-referenced, Jones claims, with "a file on Lee Harvey Oswald, also known by the name A.J. Hidell." This in turn contained information about Oswald's past, including his time spent in the Soviet Union and the fact that he had recently been involved in pro-Castro activities in New Orleans. Indeed, according to the Assassinations Committee summary of Jones' testimony, the file had been opened in mid-1963, "under the names Lee Harvey Oswald and A. J. Hidell," following a New Orleans police report of Oswald's activities in support of Castro. With the file in front of him, says Lt. Col. Jones, he promptly got on the telephone to tell the FBI in Dallas about the contents of the Oswald file. One person he spoke to was Agent-in-Charge Gordon Shanklin. That, Jones has testified, was the end of his role in the matter, apart from writing a report summarizing the day's developments.

It is, of course, essential to learn everything possible about Oswald's use of the name "Hidell"—not least because it was mail order in that name which linked him in such a damning fashion to the Mannlicher-Carcano rifle. The Warren Commission specifically asked to see any Army files there might be relevant to Oswald but was never shown the file Jones has discussed on oath. For years independent researchers have asked for them, only to be told they could not be found. In 1978, Congress' Assassinations Committee was informed that the Army's Oswald file had been destroyed in 1973 as a matter of "routine." In a masterpiece of understatement, the Assassinations Committee report said it found the destruction of the military intelligence file "extremely troublesome, especially when viewed in the light of the Department of Defense's failure to make this file available to the Warren Commission."

The Assassinations Committee said it found Lt. Col. Jones' testimony "credible." It contains, however, an apparent flaw—in terms of all the known facts about Oswald's use of the name

"Hidell." Jones has stated that "Hidell" was an alias used by
Oswald and makes it clear that this is why the intelligence index
contained both names. However—and this is important—Oswald
did not actually use the name "Hidell" as an alias in New Orleans.[17] Nor, in all the massive documentation of Oswald's life, is
there any reference to use of that name as an alias—*except* in
ordering the rifle alleged to have been used in the President's
murder and the pistol allegedly used to shoot police officer Tippit.
If Jones' testimony is correct, either Army intelligence had separate knowledge of some use of the name "Hidell" by Oswald or it
was privy to the purchase of the weapons months before the
assassination.* If the former is true, it would have been vital
information for any inquiry. As for the second option, it gives rise
to two other possibilities. Either U.S. military intelligence had
been monitoring Oswald's post-office box since early 1963, when
the guns were mailed to him, or some human source, conceivably
Oswald himself, informed the military of his weapons purchases.

Congress' Assassinations Committee report was written as
though the troubling options raised by Lt. Col Jones' testimony
did not exist. However, when it complained of the Army's destruction of the Oswald file, the Committee noted that "without access
to this file, the question of Oswald's possible affiliation with military intelligence could not be fully resolved." The suspicion that
the alleged assassin had been affiliated to some agency of intelligence is today stronger than ever and will be treated in depth in
this book. Meanwhile, the role of Army intelligence in the early
hours of the investigation, and in connection with the damning
"Hidell" connection, remains obscure and undocumented. For
that, the Army alone is answerable.

One other source mentioned by Lt. Col. Jones might be able
to throw more light on official knowledge of Oswald before the
assassination. This is Dallas FBI Agent-in-Charge Shanklin, with
whom Jones says he spoke on the afternoon of the murder. As will
be discussed later, Shanklin is widely held responsible for ordering
the destruction of correspondence written by Oswald: a letter,

---

*FBI records show Jones telling the FBI that Hidell was an *associate* of
Oswald, not a name used as an alias.

from Oswald to the FBI, was deliberately destroyed after the assassination, when it should have been preserved as evidence. The Assassinations Committee has called this "a serious impeachment" of Shanklin's credibility. Shanklin was interviewed by the Committee in 1978.

As for Oswald's use of an alias—any alias—to buy a gun, it remains perplexing. If this was an attempt to conceal his real identity, as protection against taking blame for future crimes involving the rifle, Oswald was indeed a foolish fellow. Hard though it may be for a European to comprehend, in Texas it is still as normal to own a gun as not—and often with a little thought of hunting four-legged game. In 1963 a man could buy a rifle across the counter in dozens of stores with few or no questions asked. Oswald could have done so and risked nothing more than a future shaky visual identification by some shop assistant. As it is, Oswald not only gave his own post office number of the order for the gun, committed his handwriting to paper, but also invited exposure—so we are told—by going out to murder the President with a "Hidell" identity card in his pocket and a "Hidell" -purchased rifle under his arm. He then identified himself as "Hidell" to one of the first policemen to question him. It is frequently said that criminal cunning is invariably flawed by stupidity, but other evidence suggests Oswald was far from stupid. School records show that in several subjects he was three years ahead of his class, and his intelligence was noted by his officers in the Marines. How, then, to explain this next anomaly? For, while "frantically" denying any part in the assassination, it was Oswald who sent the police straight to some of the most incriminating evidence of all.

On the morning of the day following the assassination, Oswald provided details of where he had stayed in Dallas and where his belongings were kept. Although some of his possessions were kept at his lodgings, Oswald volunteered the fact that he stored many items in the garage of the Paine house, where his wife was staying. Officers armed with a search warrant were soon on their way back to the Paine address, which had already been searched once the previous day. According to the police account, the officers returned to headquarters triumphantly with the two enormously incriminating photographs[18] of Oswald holding a rifle and

with a pistol at his hip (*see illustration 8*). At 6:00 P.M. that
evening, when Oswald was confronted with an enlargement of one
of the pictures, his reaction was confident. According to Captain
Fritz, head of Homicide, "He said the picture was not his; that the
face was his face but that this picture was not him at all and he had
never seen the picture before. When I told him that the picture
was recovered form Mrs. Paine's garage, he said that picture had
never been in his possession. . . . He denied ever seeing that
picture and said that he knew all about photography, that he had
done a lot of work in photography himself, that the picture had
been made by some person unknown to him. He further stated
that since he had been photographed here at the City Hall and that
people had been taking his picture while being transferred from
my office to the jail door that someone had been able to get a
picture of his face and that, with that, they had made the picture.
He told me that he understood photography real well, and that in
time, he would be able to show that it was not his picture, and that
it had been made by someone else."

Oswald's claim that the photographs were faked could reasonably be written off as desperate prevarication by a man refusing
to admit that the game was up. Expert testimony that the pictures
were taken with a camera believed to have been Oswald's, and his
widow's statement that she took them for her husband, have
seemed persuasive evidence that this was so. For all that, Oswald's
claim that the photographs were false continues to find supporters.

In 1977 the commander of the photographic department at
the Canadian Defense Department, Major John Pickard, studied
the Oswald rifle pictures at the request of the Canadian Broadcasting Corporation. He reported, "The pictures have the earmarks of
being faked. The shadows fall in conflicting directions. The shadow of Oswald's nose falls in one direction and that of his body in
another. The photos were shot from a slightly different angle, a
different distance, with the gun in a different hand. So, if one
photo is laid on top of another, nothing could match exactly. Yet,
impossibly, while one body is bigger, in the other the heads match
perfectly, bearing out Oswald's charge that his head was pasted on
an incriminating photograph."

With the backing of the British Broadcasting Corporation,

which was also preparing a documentary on the Kennedy assassination, I retained a consultant for a second opinion. Retired Detective Superintendent Malcolm Thompson is a past president of the Institute of Incorporated Photographers, of the Evidence Photographers' International Council, holder of many other distinctions in photography, and has had a lifetime in police identification work. He was recommended by Scotland Yard and Kodak. After examining the rifle pictures for a week, the Detective Superintendent gave the photographs a dubious report. He said he detected retouching, between Oswald's head and a pillar, and in one of the photographs on the rifle butt. Like the Canadian expert, he noted contradictions in the shadow formations, saying that the body shadows do not relate to other shadows in the picture. Most telling of all, though, in Thompson's opinion, was Oswald's head. "I have seen photographs of Oswald, and his chin is not square. He has a rounded chin. Having said that, the subject in the picture has a *square* chin, while from the upper lip to the top of the head he does appear to be like Oswald. One can only conclude that Oswald's head has been stuck on to a chin which is not Oswald's chin." Thompson also pointed out that one of Oswald's arms "looks as if it had been stuck on to the body." Detective Superintendent Thompson's conclusion was succint. "My opinion is that those photographs are faked. . . . I consider the pictures to be the result of a montage."[19]

All this seemed impressive, but in 1978 the Assassinations Committee took a precisely opposite view. Its photographic panel—all distinguished experts—assembled an impressive mass of data to show that the pictures of Oswald with the rifle were genuine after all. They decided, after exhaustive tests, that all the apparent flaws in the photographs had innocent technical explanations. A suspect line was diagnosed as a water spot, apparent retouching as the shadow of a leaf. Oddities concerning the size of the head in relation to the body were dismissed as the result of camera movement between shots. Detective Superintendent Thompson was consulted, and he deferred to his colleagues' opinion on many points. Both he and Major Pickard have pointed out that they had been obliged to study prints of a later generation and poorer quality than those available to the Committee. Thompson, however, still has trouble with the fact that the chin in the rifle pictures seems so different from the chin he has seen in pictures of the real Oswald. While the Committee's photographic spokesman believes the pictures are genuine, even he has publicly conceded that "it is possible to make a fake photograph that we would not be able to detect." Once again in this frustrating case, the layman looks in vain to the experts for certainties. Nevertheless, I personally accept the weighty opinion of the Assassinations Committee experts. Their technical arguments aside, it may be no coincidence that one of the left-wing newspapers held by Oswald contained, in its correspondence column, a letter from Dallas signed "L.H.". The pictures of Oswald with the suspect rifle are probably what they appear to be. That probability, however, does little to end the mystery surrounding the photographs—why and when were they taken, and with what purpose in mind?

As this book went to print, the Dallas picture show was still running. The puzzles proliferate. Marina Oswald, the reader will recall, first claimed she remembered taking only one photograph of Oswald with the rifle, in their back yard. Then, when there turned out to be two different poses, she said she might have taken two. Most recently, in 1978, she said she could not remember how many had been taken, and that does seem to be her safest tack. Oswald's mother Marguerite referred in her testimony to seeing another photograph, in which Oswald was holding the rifle over his head with both hands. That picture, said Marguerite, was destroyed by her and Marina—just after the assassination—to protect Oswald. Marina was never asked by the Warren Commission about this third photograph, even though it made her claim to have "forgotten" taking more than one photograph less plausible. In fact, there was yet another photograph.

In 1976, when the Senate Intelligence Committee was probing the role of the intelligence agencies in investigating the assassination, it found another pose in the same series of pictures. This was in the possession of a Dallas policeman's widow, the former Mrs. Roscoe White. She said her husband had told her it would be very valuable one day. As the polite prose of the Congressional Assassinations Committee was to put it later, policeman White had "acquired" the picture in the course of his duties after the assassination. A fellow officer has mentioned making "numerous" copies of the Oswald pictures for his colleagues. However, even if this particular print was intended merely as a keepsake, why was there no copy of it in the evidence assembled for the official inquiry? It reflects, at best, astonishingly sloppy handling of evidence. Several officers must have known about this version of the photograph in 1963, for it shows Oswald in a stance with the rifle which was copied in police re-enactment experiments. Perhaps, indeed, they once knew of more copies. The last act of this comedy of police work does nothing to still the suspicions of those who suspect hanky-panky with the rifle poses.

In 1978 a commercial photographer who assisted the police and the FBI with photographic work after the assassination, Robert Hester, declared he had seen a version of the rifle picture on November 22—the day *before* the police said they found the pictures. In addition, he recalled it as a color transparency. The official record makes no mention of any color version of the Oswald photograph.

All this recalls Oswald's outburst suggesting that the Dallas police were trying to frame him with the photograph. His accusation remains just that—Oswald's accusation in a tight spot. Yet there remains the nagging hint of some sort of cover-up—not necessarily involving the police, but other, possibly unknown, Oswald associates.

For the first time in this narrative, the back-yard photographs have raised the ambivalent role of Marina, Oswald's Russian-born wife. In 1977 her authorized biography suggested that the deliberate destruction of copies of the pictures was the act of a loyal wife misguidedly trying to protect her husband—not knowing whether he had really killed the President or not. However, before burning the pictures, Marina did tell the police that Oswald owned a rifle. As the weeks went by, she was to be responsible for a mass of testimony incriminating her husband.[20] As Oswald's wife, of course, she was potentially in an excellent position to supply information about him. As a frightened foreigner, caught in the eye of an American tragic cyclone, it may be that she simply felt bound to cooperate in every way possible. The fact remains that while the Warren Commission used her testimony to help convict her husband in the public mind, its staff did not trust her. They felt, indeed sometimes knew, that Marina had on occasion deceived them. One Commission lawyer wrote in a memorandum, "Marina Oswald has lied to the Secret Service, the FBI, and this Commission repeatedly on matters which are of vital concern to the people of this country and the world." As late as 1979 Congress' Assassinations Committee wrote caustically of her professed ignorance of Oswald's activities. It referred to her past testimony as "incomplete and inconsistent" and noted with relief that it had not relied on her during its investigation. Marina tends to have lapses of memory on the most improbable subjects. Asked if her husband liked photography, Marina said she did not think so. Asked whether he owned a camera, she said she could not remember. Asked if Oswald once did a job involving photography, she pleaded ignorance. That was all very odd given that Oswald did possess cameras and did work in Dallas that specifically involved photographic equipment. On account of that job, Oswald provides yet another tantalizing thought about those strange rifle pictures.

In March 1963, when the rifle photographs were allegedly taken, Oswald was working in the photographic department of Jaggers-Chiles-Stovall, a Dallas graphic-arts company that did work for the U.S. Army. According to a former colleague, ". . . about one month after he started . . . he seemed interested in whether the company would allow him to reproduce his own pictures, and I told him that while they didn't sanction that sort of thing, people do it now and then." With that in mind, it has even been suggested that Oswald *himself*—perhaps with assistance— doctored his own incriminating pictures. Then, if caught committing mayhem with his newly acquired gun, he would be able to show that the photographs were fakes. It would thus appear that he had been framed—just as Oswald claimed at the police station—and he would be on the way to escaping a murder charge. It is a scenario worthy of Agatha Christie—or would she have thought it too farfetched? The journalistic mind quails.

The Assassinations Committee, of course, would have none of this. Its photographic panel, which decided the pictures were genuine, also appealed to common sense. Why, it asked, would a forger treble the risk by making several different versions of his forgery? There is, in fact, another way of interpreting the pictures. This permits them to be authentic images of Oswald but makes them false in a quite different way. It may provide a clue to their purpose.

All the copies of the photograph purport to show Oswald proudly displaying two recognizable left-wing newspapers, *The Worker* and *The Militant*. In that fact lies an apparent contradiction. *The Worker* was the newspaper of the Communist Party of the United States, which was generally aligned towards Moscow. *The Militant* was the organ of the Trotskyite Socialist Workers' Party, which regularly expressed views diametrically opposed to those of *The Worker* and Moscow. The two publications differed violently in terms of ideology, and no genuine self-respecting Socialist would have advertised himself holding both at once. By 1963 Oswald, whatever his failings, was more than familiar with these very basic contradictions. Yet, quite apart from the photographs, Oswald had been corresponding with both Communist factions. It may suggest, as some believe, that Oswald was now merely masquerading as a Marxist while working to some other secret purpose. In that case, if the pictures are genuine, they may have been a private joke—to be shared with some unknown second party.[21] Alternatively, the pictures may be evidence of an operation designed to discredit the vocal left as a whole. Those possibilities, as this unfolding story will show, lie at the very heart of the assassination mystery. Meanwhile, photographic specialists disagree, police inefficiency becomes apparent, and Marina's real knowledge of the back-yard pictures remains obscure. The controversy over the photographs will no doubt sputter on.

Of the material evidence concerning Oswald and the rifle, some points to Oswald having handled the rifle, such as the fibers caught in the rifle butt and the blanket in which the weapon had allegedly been wrapped at the Paine house. These items were circumstantially persuasive, but the FBI did not claim they were forensically conclusive. There is a special point to make about the fibers found on the rifle butt, which the FBI felt "could have come" from the shirt Oswald was wearing when arrested. Oswald himself remarked while in custody, and long before the forensic import of the shirt was known, that he had changed his shirt at his roominghouse after the assassination. If that was true, then the fibers tend to link Oswald to the rifle through a shirt he was not wearing at the time of the murder. They may indicate that he had *previously* handled the rifle, while actually exonerating him from using it in the Book Depository. The same applies to the palm print allegedly found on the underside of the gun.

That print was positively identified as Oswald's. Yet it could not be detected on the rifle when it reached FBI headquarters and was produced days later—by the officer who first processed the rifle in Dallas—as a "lift" he said he had made on the night of the assassination. Some have implied that the print was planted by the Dallas police. The officer concerned may have been derelict in not alerting the FBI to the print earlier,[22] but there is no hard basis for a more sinister interpretation. Today, the most important feature of the palm print is its location. According to the officer who claimed to have found it, it was on the bottom side of the metal barrel—at a place accessible only when the wooden stock was removed. In other words, the print had been impressed on the rifle when the weapon was *disassembled*. Therefore, while the print may be hard evidence that Oswald handled the gun at some point, it is no kind of proof that he was holding the gun at the moment it was supposedly fired at the President.

What, then, of the allegation that Oswald carried the Mannlicher-Carcano to the Depository on November 22?

The Curtain Rods Story

Oswald did admit bringing a package of some sort to work with him on the morning of the assassination but strenuously denied it contained a rifle. He claimed it was merely a bag containing his lunch, made up of a cheese sandwich and an apple. When asked the size of the package, Oswald replied, "Oh, I don't recall. It may have been a small sack or a large sack. You don't always find one that just fits your sandwiches." When he gave this evasive answer, the prisoner was well aware the police had already heard the ominous story about curtain rods from Buell Frazier, the work-mate who drove Oswald to his wife's place the night before the assassination and then back to work the next morning. Oswald denied telling Frazier that he was going there to fetch curtain rods for his rented room and insisted he did not carry a long package the next morning or place it on the back seat of Frazier's car. Both denials are implausible because there is no reason to doubt the word of either Frazier or that of his sister, who also saw Oswald with the long package. Ironically, it was Frazier and his sister who created a slight doubt that Oswald had, in fact, been carrying the murder weapon rather than his "curtain rods." Both insisted Oswald's parcel was a good eight inches shorter than the disassembled Mannlicher-Carcano. Frazier demonstrated this by showing that Oswald could not physically have carried a 35-inch rifle tucked into his armpit with the base cupped in his hand, as Frazier remembered. He could have done so only if the package was shorter. Yet the Commission felt Frazier and his sister were mistaken, and to bolster their theory that Oswald did carry the rifle to the Depository, they had the 38-inch paper bag which had been found by the window on the sixth floor. The bag was firmly linked to Oswald by a fingerprint and a palm print, although it was free from any scratches or oil from the metal parts of a rifle. This is rather strange, because the Mannlicher-Carcano was oily when found. The Warren Commission—and the Assassinations Committee in 1979—concluded that Oswald did carry the rifle to work, and it was not an unreasonable finding. Certainly, Oswald carried something to work and was evasive about it when questioned.

The saga of the paper bag cannot be left without a reference to a real paper-bag enigma which presented itself twelve days after the assassination. On December 4, 1963, an undeliverable package addressed to "Lee Oswald" was retrieved from the dead-letter section to a post office in a Dallas suburb. It was wrongly addressed to 601 W. Nassaus Street, which could approximate to Neches Street, which was near where Oswald had lived. When opened, it turned out to contain a "brown paper bag made of fairly heavy brown paper which bag was open at both ends." Since no postal worker is likely to have tossed aside a package addressed to "Lee Oswald" *after* the name became world famous on November 22, it is reasonable to assume the parcel arrived before the assassination. Who sent it to Oswald, and why, are questions which appear especially pertinent with the knowledge that another paper bag became key evidence. But the Warren Report did not even mention the mystery parcel, and there is no sign that it was forensically tested or further investigated.

This little mystery apart, the evidence against Oswald does strongly suggest that he owned the Mannlicher-Carcano and that he brought it to work on the day of the assassination. But did Oswald, using that rifle, fire three shots at the President on November 22, 1963?

The Cartridge Cases on the Sixth Floor

Nobody disputes the fact that three used cartridge cases were found near the famous sixth-floor window and one live round in the breech. Barely, however, does anybody raise the troublesome fact that *only* these were found—anywhere. Not a single spare bullet for the Mannlicher—Carcano rifle was found on Oswald's person, at his roominghouse, or among his effects stored at the house where his wife was living. Intensive inquiry in Dallas revealed only two stores in the area where a man could buy ammunition suitable for the rifle.[23] One of these was in fact well outside Dallas itself, and both gun shops were sure they had never had Oswald as a customer. In any case, ammunition is normally sold in hundreds or dozens of bullets, not by the handful. The traditional version of the assassination thus assumes, improbably, that Oswald had previously exhausted his supply of ammunition—all save the four bullets accounted for at the Book Depository. It suggests, too, that he set off to shoot the President of the United States confident that he would use only those bullets that day. The four lonely exhibits on the sixth floor justify more thought than they have ever been given. For some, they nourish the suspicion that they were planted to incriminate Oswald.

All the technical evidence shows that the three used cartridge cases had been fired from the Mannlicher-Carcano. All were scored distinctively by marks firmly identified as being caused in the chamber of the Carcano. As we saw earlier, sophisticated modern tests on the magic bullet—and, more importantly, on bullet fragments found in wounds and in the Presidential car—

define them as coming from only two bullets. The same tests narrow down the type of the bullets to either standard Carcano ammunition or one of a very few other bullet types. It is reasonable to suppose, then, that the rifle on the sixth floor was used to fire two shots at the President. The presence of a third cartridge does not, however, necessarily mean that the rifle was used for a third shot at the motorcade.

The reason for doubt was spotted by Assassinations Committee Congressman Christopher Dodd when he struggled to interpret the acoustics evidence indicating how quickly the Depository shots had been fired. Dodd realized that there was an apparent contradiction. In his view, the brevity of the pause between the first and second shot means a likelihood that *two* rifles were at work to the rear of the President that day. Since scientific evidence suggests firmly that the second shot hit both the President and the Governor and was fired from the Mannlicher-Carcano, Dodd reasoned that the first shot must have been fired by his hypothetical second gun. On that basis, Dodd could attribute only two of the recovered cartridge cases to shots fired in the assassination—the one credited with hitting the President and the Governor and the one presumed to have caused the fatal wound to the President's head. What, then, to make of the third used cartridge case on the sixth floor? Congressman Dodd pointed out that the ballistics evidence shows merely that the cartridge cases were fired in the rifle at some point in time. Any or all of them could have been fired at some previous date. In this case, Dodd suggested, the third cartridge case could have been left in the breech after a firing previous to the assassination and ejected on the sixth floor only to make way for the bullets actually used in the murder. This is a tortuous thought, but, as Dodd explains it, it is logical enough.

If Dodd's theory is right, the ballistics evidence in the case against Oswald is reduced—but only by one bullet. The fact remains that an apparently damning chain of evidence still appears to link him to the crime. It is time to recap. The remnants of two bullets come from a rifle ordered in the name of Hideli but in handwriting attributed to Oswald. Fingerprint evidence shows that Oswald had handled that rifle, at least when disassembled. It appears that he brought a package to work on the day of the assassination, and a paper bag bearing his prints was found near the sixth-floor window. It is easy to conclude flatly that it was Oswald—whoever and however many his accomplices—who fired the two shots that killed the President and wounded Governor Connally. Pause, however, once more.

There has been controversy down the years about Oswald's proficiency as a marksman. The official inquiry noted that Oswald's Marine shooting record revealed him—at different times—as a "fairly good shot" and a "rather poor shot." The Warren Report omitted entirely, however, the recollection of Oswald's marksmanship by one of his former Marine comrades that ". . . we were on line together, the same time, not firing at the same position, but at the same time, and I remember seeing his shooting. It was a pretty big joke because he got a lot of 'Maggie's drawers'—you know, a lot of misses, but he didn't give a darn." There is no evidence that Oswald's marksmanship improved dramatically between his Marine career and the time of the assassination. There is therefore a short, unsatisfying answer to the perennial question "Could Oswald have done it with the Mannlicher-Carcano?" It is "Maybe or maybe not."

There is a more important question, of vital relevance to a final judgment about Oswald's guilt. Was Oswald actually on the sixth floor and in a position to shoot at the President at 12:30 P.M. on November 22? In 1979, new evidence increased the uncertainty.

Oswald—Sniping at the President or Eating his Lunch Downstairs?

Predictably enough, Oswald told his interrogators he was nowhere near the sixth floor* when the President was shot. As the head of the Dallas Homicide Bureau reported: "I asked him what part of the building he was in at the time the President was shot, and he said that he was having lunch about that time on the first floor."

---

*References to specific floors of the Texas School Book Depository are rendered in the American style. The American first floor is equivalent to the British ground floor. British readers should therefore subtract one floor to understand the locations mentioned.

His snack, said Oswald, also took him to the second-floor lunch-room, but he claimed he had been on the first floor at the moment the President passed by. Unlike some of Oswald's denials, this cannot be dismissed out of hand.

The official inquiry found it impossible to prove anything about Oswald's whereabouts at the time of the shooting. Three of Oswald's prints were found on two of the book cartons found near the suspect window, but that was proof of nothing. Oswald had worked legitimately on the sixth floor, and his were not the only prints found on the cartons. One identifiable palm print was found and never identified. It did not belong to any of the employees known to have worked with the boxes, nor to official investigators who handled them after the assassination.[24] It remains possible that the prints belonged to an unknown assassin who did fire from the sixth floor.

A chemical test on Oswald's right cheek, to identify possible deposits resulting from firing a rifle, proved negative.[25] In the end, the Warren Report gave great weight to a flimsy claim that Oswald was still on the sixth floor at 11:55 A.M., a full thirty-five minutes before the assassination. This assertion was based on the 1964 testimony of Charles Givens, a Depository worker who said he returned from lunch to fetch cigarettes from the sixth floor and saw Oswald then and spoke with him. It has since emerged, however— from Warren Commission documents—that Givens was himself sought by the police after the assassination because he had a police record—involving narcotics—and was missing from the Deposi-tory. When picked up and questioned, he mentioned nothing about seeing Oswald upstairs after everyone else had left. On the contrary, he said he "observed Lee reading a newspaper in the domino room where the employees eat lunch about 11:50 A.M." "The domino room" is on the *first* floor of the Depository. Even if what he said later is true—about seeing Oswald just five minutes later on the sixth floor—it would mean very little that Oswald was upstairs more than half an hour before the assassination. All other evidence suggests that Oswald not only declared his intention of coming downstairs to lunch but actually did so. It is evidence which, with scandalous disregard for the facts, official inquiries have either investigated lazily or ignored.

The fact is that when Oswald's co-workers left the sixth floor for their lunch break at about 11:45; they left behind them an Oswald vocally impatient to come down and join them. Two, Bonnie Ray Williams and Billie Lovelady, remembered Oswald shouting to them as they went down in the elevator: "Guys! How about an elevator?" and adding words to the effect: "Close the gate on the elevator" or "Send one of the elevators back up." Some time after this, around noon, Bonnie Ray Williams went back to the sixth floor to eat his own lunch in peace and quiet. Later, his lunch bag, chicken bones, and empty pop bottle were found there to prove it. Williams stayed on the sixth floor, at least until 12:15 P.M., perhaps til 12:20. He saw nobody, certainly not Oswald.

Under interrogation, Oswald insisted he had followed his workmates down to eat. He said he ate a snack in the first-floor lunchroom alone but thought he remembered two black employees walking through the room while he was there. Oswald believed one of them was a colleague known as "Junior" and said he would recognize the other man although he could not recall his name. He did say the second man was "short." There were two rooms in the Book Depository where workers had lunch, the "domino room" on the first floor and the lunchroom proper on the second floor. There was indeed a worker called "Junior" Jarman, and he spent his lunch break largely in the company of another black man called Harold Norman. Norman, who was indeed "short," said later he ate in the domino room between 12:00 and 12:15 P.M., and indeed he thought "there was someone else in there," though he couldn't remember who. At about 12:15, Jarman walked over to the domino room, and together the two black men left the building for a few minutes. Between 12:20 and 12:25—just before the assassination—they strolled through the first floor once more, on the way upstairs to watch the motorcade from a window. If Oswald was not indeed on the first floor at some stage, he demonstrated almost psychic powers by describing two men—out of a staff of seventy five—who were actually there. This information is nowhere noted in the Warren Report.[26]

The Warren Report said no employee saw Oswald after 11:55 A.M., when he was still on the sixth floor. This ignored two items of evidence. Bill Shelley, a foreman, said he saw Oswald near the telephone on the first floor as early as ten or fifteen minutes before noon. (It would certainly be interesting to know whether Oswald actually used one of those telephones.) An employee called Eddie Piper said he actually spoke to Oswald" just at twelve o'clock, down on the first floor." The Warren Commission had both these statements but omitted them.

Within hours of the assassination, Oswald told interrogators that he left the first floor for the second-floor lunchroom to get a Coca-Cola to drink with lunch. The staff lunchroom was on the first floor, and the Coca-Cola machine was there. Oswald's statement is supported again by Eddie Piper, who said Oswald told him: "I'm going *up* to eat." Today it is also corroborated by a witness who was never questioned by the Commission and whose story remained buried until I traced her in 1978.

In 1963 Carolyn Arnold was secretary to the vice-president of the Book Depository.[27] An FBI report, omitted altogether from the report, said Mrs. Arnold was standing in front of the Depository waiting for the motorcade when she "thought she caught a fleeting glimpse of Lee Harvey Oswald standing in the hallway." When I found Mrs. Arnold in 1978 to get a firsthand account, she was surprised to hear how she had been reported by the FBI. Her spontaneous reaction, that she had been misquoted, came *before* I explained to her the importance of Oswald's whereabouts at given moments. Mrs. Arnold's recollection of what she really observed was clear—spotting Oswald was after all her one personal contribution to the record of that memorable day. As secretary to the company vice-president she knew Oswald; he had been in the habit of coming to her for change. What Mrs. Arnold says she actually told the FBI is very different from the report of her comments and not vague at all. She said: "About a quarter of an hour before the assassination, I went into the lunchroom on the second floor for a moment. . . . Oswald was sitting in one of the booth seats on the right-hand side of the room as you go in. He was alone as usual and appeared to be having lunch. I did not speak to him but I recognized him clearly." Mrs. Arnold has reason to remember going into the lunchroom. She was pregnant at the time and had a craving for a glass of water. She also recalls the time. It was "about 12:15. It may have been slightly later."

It is of course possible that Oswald scurried upstairs to shoot

the President after Mrs. Arnold saw him in the second-floor lunchroom. Yet one witness, Arnold Rowland, said he saw two men in
sixth-floor windows, one of them holding a rifle across his chest, at
12:15. Rowland's wife confirmed that her husband drew her attention to the man, whom he assumed to be a Secret Service guard.
There was, of course, no such guard, and no other employees were
on the sixth floor at that time. The time detail—12:15—is the vital
point here. It can be fixed so exactly because Rowland recalled seeing the man with the rifle just as a police radio nearby
squawked out the news that the approaching motorcade had
reached Cedar Springs Road. The police log shows that the President passed that point between 12:15 and 12:16. Mrs. Arnold's
given time for leaving her office—12:15 or later—is corroborated
by contemporary statements made by her and office colleagues.
She told the FBI she finally left the building, after visiting the
lunchroom, as late as 12:25 P.M. If Mrs. Arnold saw Oswald in the
lunchroom at 12:15 or after, who were the two men, one of them a
gunman, whom Rowland reported in the sixth-floor windows?

There never was any reliable eyewitness identification of Oswald in the sixth-floor window after he was seen downstairs. The
Commission, however, set great store by the evidence of Howard
Brennan, a spectator in the street who stood directly opposite the
Depository. He said that he saw a man moving around at the
famous "sniper's perch" window between 12:22 and 12:24 and
that, at the moment of the assassination, he looked up to see the
man fire his final shot. Later that day, Brennan was taken to a
police identity line-up, which included Oswald. He failed to make
a positive identification of Oswald as the man he had seen in the
window—even though he had seen Oswald's picture on television
before he attended the line-up. A month after that, Brennan told
the FBI he was sure the man he had seen was Oswald. Three
weeks on, he was saying he couldn't be sure. And many months
later, Brennan told the official inquiry that he could have identified Oswald at the line-up but had been afraid to because he feared
reprisals from the Communists. Brennan's testimony was flawed
with contradiction and confusion. Warren Commission questioning raised serious doubt as to the quality of his eyesight. Brennan
claimed to have been watching as the last shot was fired, yet he saw

neither flash, smoke, nor recoil. Testimony showed that, in the immediate aftermath of the tragedy, he did not at once draw attention to what he claimed to have seen in the Book Depository, but joined others hurrying toward the grassy knoll. Questioning suggested that Brennan at first stated he had seen smoke in the area of the knoll. The Commission was able to conclude only that "Brennan believes the man he saw (*in the Depository*) was in fact Lee Harvey Oswald." In 1979, and wisely so, Congress' Assassinations Committee Report did not use Brennan's testimony at all. Brennan was less consistent than many a witnesses discredited or totally ignored by the official inquiry. He may have seen a gun, or a man with a gun, but in no way does his evidence put *Oswald* in the sixth-floor window. Nor does the physical evidence support that notion.

Lee Oswald was, when caught, wearing a long-sleeved rust-brown shirt with a white T-shirt beneath it. He said that he had changed his clothing since the assassination and that he had been wearing a long-sleeved "reddish colored shirt" at work that day. This may have been the truth. A policeman who saw Oswald after the assassination, but before he left the Depository, said on seeing him under arrest that "he looked like he did not have the same clothes on." The policeman explained that the shirt Oswald had on at work had been "a little darker." Whether Oswald changed or not, neither shirt fits with the clothing described by those who noticed a gunman on the sixth floor between 12:15 and 12:30 P.M.[28] Rowland, who made the earliest sighting, remembered a "very light-colored shirt, white or a light blue . . . open at the collar . . . unbuttoned about halfway" with a "regular T-shirt, a polo shirt" beneath it. Even Brennan, the man the Warren Report credited with recognizing Oswald, described the gunman in the window as wearing "light-colored clothes, more a khaki color." The two clerks from the County Building, who also noticed a man in the sixth-floor window, spoke of an "open neck . . . sport shirt or a T-shirt . . . light in color, probably white" and of a "sport shirt . . . yellow." Mrs. Walther, who saw two men in the window only moments before the assassination, has said, "The man behind the partly opened window had a dark brown suit, and the other man had a whitish-looking shirt or jacket, dressed more like a workman that did manual labor. *It was the man with the gun that wore white*." None of these statements about light-colored clothing fit either the rust-brown shirt Oswald was wearing when arrested or the red shirt he said he had been wearing at the time of the assassination.

The bald fact is that Oswald cannot be placed on the sixth floor either at the time of the shooting or during the half hour before it. The last time he was reliably seen before the assassination was by Mrs. Arnold—in the second-floor lunchroom. The next time Oswald was firmly identified was immediately after the assassination—again in the second-floor lunchroom.

When the shots rang out in Dealey Plaza, one motorcycle policeman, Marrion Baker, thought they came from high in the Book Depository. He drove straight to the building, dismounted, and pushed his way to the entrance. Joined by the building superintendent, whom he met in the doorway, he hurried by the stairs up to the second floor. Just as he reached it, Baker caught a glimpse of someone through a glass window in a door. Pistol in hand, the policeman pushed through the door, across a small vestibule, and saw a man walking away from him. At the policeman's order "Come here," the man turned and walked back. Baker noticed the man did not seem to be out of breath or even startled. He seemed calm and said nothing. Although reports conflict, it seems he may have been carrying a bottle of Coca-Cola.[29] At that moment, as Baker was about to start asking questions, the Depository superintendent arrived and identified the man as an employee. He was, of course, Lee Harvey Oswald, and the room was the second-floor lunchroom, exactly where Oswald had been last seen—at most fifteen minutes before the assassination. Baker let Oswald go, and hurried on upstairs.

The Warren Report reckoned the policeman confronted Oswald one and a half minutes after hearing the shots. It calculated that Oswald, as the gunman on the sixth floor, took slightly less than that to reach the lunchroom door. Other equally impressive reconstructions have suggested that Baker took less time and that Oswald, if he was a sixth-floor gunman, would have taken longer to clear up and get downstairs. The Warren Report just succeeds in getting Oswald downstairs in time to be confronted by Patrolman Baker. After making its own tests at the scene, the Assassinations Committee in 1979 said merely that the available testimony "does not preclude a finding that Oswald was on the sixth floor at the time the shots were fired." Alternative, independent calculations say that, if Oswald had really been a gunman, he could not have reached the lunchroom in time for the meeting with the policeman. The question will never now be resolved, but the evidence that Oswald was down in the lunchroom fifteen minutes before the assassination, and two minutes afterwards, cannot be ignored.

The fresh look at Oswald's whereabouts becomes even more significant in the knowledge that the President was late for his appointment with death. He was due to arrive at his first Dallas appointment at 12:30, and that was about five minutes' drive beyond the Book Depository. Had the motorcade been on time, therefore, it would have passed beneath the windows of the Depository at 12:25 P.M. This fact was evident from the published program, and would clearly have come into the calculations of any would-be assassin. A killer who had planned the assassination would hardly have been sitting around downstairs after 12:15 P.M., as the evidence about Oswald suggests, if he expected to open fire as early as 12:25.

It will be argued that the alleged assassin was merely trying to assure himself of an alibi. If so, it was a curious and unreliable way to go about it, and the lunchroom was an odd spot to choose. That room was deserted at all relevant times, and Oswald was seen there only by chance observers. On the other hand, it is hard to understand why Oswald, known to be interested in politics and politicians, would stay in the lunchroom when he knew the President was about to pass by. We know he did know, because earlier that morning he asked a workmate why the crowd was gathering outside. When told the President was coming and which way he was coming, Oswald said merely, "Oh, I see." Supporters of the official story say, of course, that this was another attempt to establish an alibi, by professing ignorance of the very fact that the President was in town. They are right: Oswald's wide-eyed question does not ring true.

The evidence does certainly cast enormous suspicion on Oswald. Quite apart from the evidence linking him to the rifle, his own statements—above all the implausible "curtain rod" tale—leave him looking guilty of *something*. The evidence does not, on the other hand, put him behind a gun in the sixth-floor window. A mass of information, indeed, suggests that others were manning the sniper's perch. Oswald may have been, as he claimed so urgently before he died, "just a patsy." If he was, it looks as though he realized his predicament the moment the hue and cry started in Dealey Plaza. It was from then on that this same Oswald, who had behaved so coolly in his encounter with the policeman, gradually began to behave like a man in a panic.

Oswald's account of leaving the scene of the crime goes like this. He told his interrogators about getting his Coca-Cola in the second-floor lunchroom, of meeting the policeman, and then going downstairs. In the uproar, said Oswald, he heard a foreman say there would be no more work that day and decided to leave—by the front door. Outside the Depository he encountered a crew-cut young man whom he believed to be a Secret Service agent because he had flashed an identity card. Oswald had directed the "agent" to a telephone, and then traveled home to his lodgings by bus and taxi. All this is supported well enough by other witnesses. A clerical supervisor returning to her second-floor office said she saw Oswald with his Coca-Cola bottle in hand within a couple of minutes of the assassination: "I had no thoughts or anything of him having any connection with it all because he was very calm." The foreman in question was indeed on the ground floor. The "Secret Service agent" was probably Robert MacNeil, a reporter for the National Broadcasting Company, who had abandoned the motorcade after hearing the shots.

Oswald's story of how he got home is corroborated by the bus ticket found in his pocket when he was arrested, and by a Dallas taxi driver. This is all very well, but it is highly improbable that a wholly innocent man would go home within minutes of the assassination of the President of the United States just because he "didn't think there would be any more work done that day." The natural thing for anybody, especially for a politically aware person like Oswald, would have been to linger awhile in the excited atmosphere outside the Depository. Oswald's decision to take a taxi home, which he himself admitted he had never done before, also suggests flight.

Once he did reach his lodgings, many things became mysterious, suggesting neither the innocence he claimed nor the lone guilt official versions have asked the public to accept. As with the evidence in Dealey Plaza, the record suggests that—whatever Oswald's part in the tragic events that day—others were involved.

CHAPTER 6

An Assassin in Seven-League Boots

There is still a real possibility that Oswald was on his way to meet an accomplice at the time of the Tippit murder. I led the Dallas investigation of that aspect of the case and was never satisfied on that point.

—Assistant District Attorney William Alexander, 1977

It was just before one o'clock, half an hour after the assassination, when Oswald's landlady, Earlene Roberts, answered the telephone at her house in the Oak Cliff district. It was a friend calling to tell her what had happened, and Mrs. Roberts turned on the television to catch the news. It was then—at 1:00 P.M.—that her lodger, Lee Oswald, came bustling in. Mrs. Roberts said, "Oh, you're in a hurry" and went on watching television. Oswald went to his room and, as he himself later admitted, changed his clothes and armed himself with a .38 revolver. Within five minutes he was out of the house again, and Mrs. Roberts, looking out of the window, last saw him standing at a bus stop. In that five minutes, Mrs. Roberts had noticed something else, something that has never been explained. While Oswald was in his bedroom, she saw a Dallas police car come slowly by the house and pull up. As it did so, its horn was sounded several times. Mrs. Roberts later described the incident under oath.

LAWYER: Where was it parked?
MRS. ROBERTS: It was parked in front of the house . . . directly in front of my house.
LAWYER: Where was Oswald when this happened?
MRS. ROBERTS: In his room. . . .
LAWYER: Were there two uniformed policeman in the car?

MRS. ROBERTS: Oh yes.
LAWYER: And one of the officers sounded the horn?
MRS. ROBERTS: Just kind of "tit-tit"—twice.

When the car had signaled twice, it moved slowly away, said the landlady. She did not remember clearly the police number on the side of the vehicle and had no reason to note it at the time. But, in repeated statements in the days to come, she was consistent about seeing the car stop and about hearing the signal on the horn. It was a problem for the official inquiry, because a check with the police suggested there was no patrol car at that point at one o'clock. There was, moreover, absolutely no known cause for any police car to visit Oswald's address so early in the case. He had not yet been missed from the Book Depository. The official breakdown of the day's events shows that Oswald's name did not crop up at all until just before 2:00 P.M. According to the record, nobody in authority knew about this rented room till *after* two o'clock, when he volunteered it at the police station. The Warren Report dealt with the mystery in a way it often used when the evidence failed to fit—it buried the incident in an obscure section of the report and implied Mrs. Roberts was mistaken. It remains possible that a police car was innocently in the area and happened, by pure coincidence, to salute an acquaintance by sounding the horn. But, because of skimped investigation at the time, the signaling police car remains a relevant mystery. Its solution may be pertinent to Oswald's movements in the ten minutes after 1:00 P.M., ten minutes which ended in the murder, about a mile away, of a policeman.

The police radio log reveals that at 12:45 P.M. Officer J. D. Tippit, a patrol-car driver, was ordered into the Oak Cliff area. At 12:54 P.M. he reported that he was in the area and was instructed to "be at large for any emergency." At 1:00 P.M., as Oswald reached Mrs. Roberts' house, police headquarters called Tippit on the radio, and he did not reply. Although there is no evidence of any connection between Tippit's silence and the police car outside Mrs. Roberts' house, the time coincidence should be borne in mind.

Tippit did call headquarters again at 1:08 P.M., and this time the police dispatcher failed to reply. We shall never know what

Tippit wanted to tell headquarters, because that was his last call. At 1:16 came the call from a member of the public using Tippit's car radio: "We've had a shooting here . . . it's a police officer, somebody shot him." J. D. Tippit—his friends knew him as just "J. D."—was lying dead in a puddle of blood, beside his patrol car. He had been gunned down in a quiet tree-lined street about a mile from Oswald's lodgings, and the circumstances of his death have never been satisfactorily resolved.

The official Report decided on the following scenario. Tippit, cruising slowly along Tenth Street, came upon Oswald, walking on his own. The policeman pulled up and spoke to Oswald, probably because he looked something like the broadcast description of the suspect in the President's assassination. The two men exchanged a few words through the window of the car, then Tippit got out and began walking around to approach Oswald. Suddenly Oswald pulled a revolver and fired four times, killing the policeman instantly. He ran off, scattering shell cases as he went, and was noticed by a dozen witnesses. Later, after the hue and cry led to Oswald's arrest in a nearby movie theater, five of the witnesses identified Oswald at police line-ups. Crisply summarized in the Warren Report, it all sounded very simple.

The fact is that the Warren Commission showed little interest in a full investigation of the Tippit shooting. When it laid its plans for the Kennedy inquiry, the Tippit angle was oddly neglected. Only a handful of relevant witnesses ever testified to the Commission, and contradictions in the evidence were papered over. Some evidence, which could have changed the picture entirely, was completely ignored.

The star witness to the shooting was Mrs. Helen Markham, a Dallas waitress. She was supposedly the only person to see the shooting in its entirety. The official version accepted her as "reliable" and credited her with watching the initial confrontation between Tippit and his murderer, peeping fearfully through her fingers as the murderer loped away and thus being able to identify Oswald at a police line-up. Yet this "reliable" witness made more nonsensical statements than can reasonably be catalogued here. She said she talked to Tippit and he understood her until he was loaded into an ambulance. All the medical evidence, and other witnesses, say Tippit died instantly from the head wound. A witness who also saw the shooting—from his pick-up truck—and then got out to help the policeman, put it graphically: "He was lying there and he had—looked like a big clot of blood coming out of his head, and his eyes were sunk back in his head. . . . The policeman, I believe, was dead when he hit the ground." Mrs. Markham said it was twenty minutes before others gathered at the scene of the crime. That is clearly nonsense. Within minutes men were in Tippit's car calling for help on the police radio, and a small crowd was there when the ambulance arrived three minutes later, at 1:10 P.M. Mrs. Markham is credited with recognizing Oswald within three hours at the police station. It turns out that she was so hysterical at the police station that only after ammonia was administered could she go into the line-up room. When she appeared before the Commission, Mrs. Markham repeatedly said she had been unable to recognize anyone at the line-up and changed her tune only after pressure from counsel. The star witness in the Tippit shooting was best summed up by Joseph Ball. Senior Counsel to the Warren Commission itself. In 1964 he referred in a public debate to her testimony as being "full of mistakes" and to Mrs. Markham as an "utter screwball." He dismissed her as "utterly unreliable," the exact opposite of the Report's verdict.

Controversy has swirled around the other witnesses who identified Oswald as the man who ran from the shooting.[30] There is no doubt that at least one of the three police line-ups was unfairly conducted. Oswald himself complained so noisily about being the only adult among a group of teenage boys that one witness said, "You could have picked him [Oswald] out without identifying him just by listening to him bawling at the policemen." Oswald was also the only man at that line-up wearing a white T-shirt. The risk quickly arose that people attending police line-ups had seen Oswald's face already, plastered across newspapers and on television.

It was hard forensic evidence that was used to link Oswald most firmly to the Tippit murder. Four revolver cartridge cases were produced as evidence recovered at the scene after the shooting, and a .38 Smith & Wesson revolver was found on Oswald when he was arrested. In questioning later, he admitted owning the gun and gave a feeble excuse for carrying it when he was captured: "You know how boys do when they have a gun. They just carry it." The revolver and the cartridge cases seemed to pin the Tippit murder on Oswald. Firearms experts are unanimous in saying that all four cartridge cases had been fired in Oswald's gun. Since four bullets were recovered form Tippit's body, since the cartridges were found at the scene, and since Oswald was arrested not far away with the revolver, common sense suggested he indeed fired the fatal shots. Yet, ironically, these same ballistic clues have led to a degree of doubt.

Firearms experts are unable to say for sure that the four bullets were fired from Oswald's weapon. That in itself is not unusual, but the bullets present a difficulty of their own. Three of the four were of "Western-Winchester" make, and one was "Remington-Peters." Of the four cartridges found, only two were "Western" ammunition, and two were "Remington-Peters." The Warren Report got around the discrepancy by offering alternative guesses. One was that the killer fired *five* bullets—three "Westerns" and two "Remington-Peters." One "Remington-Peters" bullet missed Tippit and was never found. Similarly, one "Western" cartridge was lost. A second hypothesis was that Oswald perhaps fired only four shots—three "Westerns" and one "Remington-Peters" but already had used "Remington" cartridges in his gun which was ejected along with the other four shells. One of the "Western" shells was not found. In 1978 the Assassinations Committee firearms panel suggested similar options but in the end pointed out that it was not their business to speculate. Efforts to explain these discrepancies have failed to quell suspicions that, in their zeal to pin the murder of a fellow officer on Oswald, Dallas police tampered with the evidence. These dark thoughts arise from what was, at best, messy police work.

Only *one* bullet was handed over to the FBI the day after the policeman's murder, and Dallas police at first indicated that it was the only one recovered from Tippit's body. Not until four months later, under pressure by the Warren Commission, did the police produce three more bullets. Still more troubling was the possibility that the cartridge cases presented in evidence were not those found at the scene of the crime. One witness, Domingo Benavides, picked up two shells and handed them to a policeman, Officer J. M. Poe. Poe was ordered by a senior officer to mark the shells with an identifying mark, a routine procedure to record the "chain of evidence" in gunshot cases. Although Poe later told the FBI he had indeed marked the cases with his initials, "JMP," the marks could not be found when the cases were examined six months later. While it is possible that Poe forgot to initial the cases, it would have been highly unusual. The lack of identifying marks has bred suspicion that Oswald—at a subsequent stage of the Tippit investigation—was framed, a suspicion encouraged by the way the police produced the cartridge cases.

In a police list of evidence, compiled on the day of the assassination, there was no mention of the Tippit cartridge cases. Other known ballistics evidence was catalogued when it was handed over to the FBI the next day, but the Tippit cartridges were still curiously absent. The same applied to a police property clerk's list on November 26. It was only on November 28, nearly a week after the assassination, that the four cartridge cases were handed over to the FBI as a separate package. There has been speculation that the cases originally found were of a different ammunition type to those later produced in evidence.

The gun taken from Oswald when he was arrested was a .38 revolver, not an automatic. At 1:36 P.M., however, a policeman at the scene of the Tippit shooting radioed a description: "I got an eyeball witness to the getaway man—that suspect in this shooting. He is a white male . . . apparently armed with a .32, dark finish, *automatic* pistol. . . . " This description was gleaned from a passer-by, and yet, a few minutes later, another police officer sent a message which should have been reliable: "The shells at the scene indicate that the suspect is armed with an *automatic* .38 rather than a pistol." This categorical message, pointing to a gun other than the one found on Oswald, came from Sargent Gerald Hill, the same officer who reportedly ordered Officer Poe to mark the cartridge cases. In 1963 Detective Hill had years of army experience and police work behind him, a background which gave him a certain expertise. Sergeant Hill may have made his snap judgment on the basis of certain marks which appeared typical of an automatic mechanism, or the position of the cases on the ground may have suggested automatic ejection. Hill's deliberate message, "The shells at the scene indicate . . . an automatic rather than a pistol," suggests that he had noted such characteristics. Yet the shells eventually produced by the police, six days later and minus Officer Poe's initials, matched Oswald's *non*-automatic weapon. With the bullets retrieved from Tippit's body too mangled for identification, the shells were the only firm link with the pistol found on Oswald. These weak spots in the evidence have nourished the theory that either Oswald did not shoot Tippit at all, or that he had an accomplice. It is a notion encouraged by the evidence of two eyewitnesses to the shooting, neither of whom were heard by the Commission or even included in FBI reports.

Mrs. Acquilla Clemons, who was in a house close to the spot where Tippit was killed, told independent investigators she saw *two* men near the policeman's car just before the shooting. She said she ran out after the shots and saw a man with a gun. But she described him as "kind of chunky . . . kind of heavy," a description which does not fit Oswald at all. Much more disturbing, this was not the only man she saw. Here is part of a filmed interview with Mrs. Clemons:

INTERVIEWER: Was there another man there?
MRS. CLEMONS: Yes, there was one, other side of the street. All I know is, he tells him to go on.
INTERVIEWER: Mrs. Clemons, the man who had the gun. Did he make any motion at all to the other man across the street?
MRS. CLEMONS: No more than tell him to go.
INTERVIEWER: He waved his hand and said "Go on."
MRS. CLEMONS: Yes, said, "Go on."

Mrs. Clemons said the man with a gun went off in one direction and the second man in another. She described the man with the gun as "short and kind of heavy" and wearing "khaki and a white shirt"—a description which does not fit Oswald at all. The second man, she said, was "thin" and tall rather than short, a description which could refer to Oswald. Obviously, Mrs. Clemons should have been questioned more thoroughly than in a television interview. She said she had been visited by the FBI, who decided not to take a statement because of her poor health. Mrs. Clemons was a diabetic, hardly a condition to deter efficient investigators from taking a statement. According to two reporters, who visited Mrs. Clemons several years after the assassination, she and her family still spoke with conviction of seeing two men at the scene of the Tippit shooting. Mrs. Clemons' story finds corroboration from another witness, and he too was ignored.

Frank Wright lived along the street from the spot where Tippit was killed and heard the shots as he sat in his living room. While his wife telephoned for help, Wright went straight to his front door. He later told researchers: "I was the first person out" and caught sight of Tippit in time to see him roll over once and then lie still. Wright also said, "I saw a man standing in front of the car. He was looking toward the man on the ground. I couldn't tell who the man was on the ground. The man who was standing in front of him was about medium height. He had on a long coat. It ended just above his hands. I didn't see any gun. He ran around on the passenger side of the police car. He ran as fast as he could go, and he got into his car. His car was a little gray old coupé. It was about a 1950–1951, maybe a Plymouth. It was a gray car, parked on the same side of the street as the police car but beyond it from me. It was heading away from me. He got in that car and he drove away as fast as you could see. . . . After that a whole lot of police came up. I tried to tell two or three people what I saw. They didn't pay any attention. I've seen what came out on television and in the newspaper but I know that's not what happened. I know a man drove off in a gray car. Nothing in the world's going to change my opinion."[31]

Mr. Wright was interviewed by two researchers from Columbia University, New York, less than a year after the assassination, and his story never received national publicity. The researchers did not jump to hasty conclusions but emphasized that the evidence of witnesses like Mrs. Clemons and Frank Wright had never been officially taken, let alone investigated. The authorities could have found Wright and his wife easily enough—Mrs. Wright telephoned the emergency services after the Tippit shooting. Proper inquiry at the time could—for example—have established the time of her call and helped fix the time of the shooting. It is the time factor which prompts the next nagging doubt about Oswald's role in the affair.

The official inquiry decided Officer Tippit was shot at about 1:15 P.M.—and even on that basis was unable to explain satisfactorily how Oswald could have reached the scene of the murder in time to commit the crime. By any account Oswald did not leave his roominghouse until four minutes past one o'clock. By 1:15 P.M., the official report claims, he could have covered the nine tenths of a mile to the scene of the Tippit shooting. This glosses over the tightness of that timetable by saying Oswald left home "shortly after 1:00 P.M." and by guessing that he walked at "a brisk pace." In fact, assuming a good walking speed of four miles per hour, the distance would have taken the alleged assassin more than twelve minutes. Add twelve minutes to Oswald's departure time of 1:04 P.M., and we have him arriving at 1:16 P.M., by which time the murder was already being reported over the patrol-car radio. If Oswald had gone at a trot, he might have arrived in time, but house-to-house inquires of dozens of inquisitive housewives—in quiet streets—failed to produce anyone who had seen a hurrying young man. More important, the official schedule for Oswald can work only *if* Tippit was really murdered as late as 1:15 P.M. Strong evidence, ignored by the official inquiry, indicates Tippit was murdered earlier than that.

T. F. Bewley came upon Tippit's body in the street while on his way to pick up his wife. As he got out to help, Bewley looked at his watch, which read 1:10 P.M. For once, Mrs. Markham may supply real data, because when Tippit was shot she was *on the way* to catch her regular 1:12 P.M. bus to work. Domingo Benavides, who was credited with reporting the shooting over the police radio at 1:16, said he had by then already crouched terrified in his truck for "a few minutes" after the murder, afraid the gunman might reappear. On all of this evidence, even allowing for Bewley's watch being a little slow, it is reasonable to conclude that Tippit was shot by 1:12 P.M. at the latest. On that basis, Oswald could not, as a pedestrian, have reached the scene of the crime in time to be Tippit's murderer. Not surprisingly, the official inquiry balked at such a conclusion. They dwelt not at all on the final conundrum in the Tippit murder, the conflict over which way the alleged assassin was walking when Tippit pulled up beside him.

Mrs. Markham gave the inquiry the information on which it

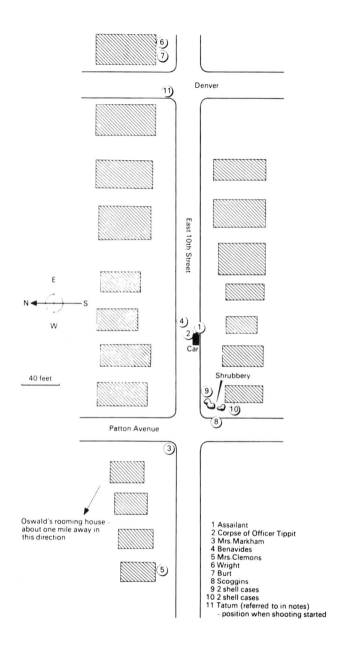

Scene of Officer Tippit shooting

depended, that Oswald was walking east when the policeman stopped. East is the logical way Oswald would be going if he had walked from his lodgings (*see street plan, preceding page*), and that is the way the official Report flatly recorded it. To do so was to ignore the statements of at least two other witnesses, neither of whom were prone to Mrs. Markham's troubling inconsistency.

William Scoggins, the cab driver, said on the day of the assassination, "The officer got out of his car and evidently said something to a man who was walking *west* on Tenth." One might expect a professional cab driver to get his directions right, and Scoggins is backed up by another witness. Moments before the Tippit shooting Jim Burt, a soldier on leave, was talking with a friend in front of his house, just a block away from the scene of Tippit's murder. He first noticed a man walk past him "going *west* on the sidewalk" directly in front of him. Immediately afterward he saw the same man talking to Officer Tippit, then heard gunfire, and last saw the man running away. Burt was later interviewed by the police, and they believed the version he and Scoggins told. Police reports on the Tippit shooting consistently refer to a "suspect who was walking west" before he shot Tippit. So do Secret Service reports written two weeks later, after a reconstruction exercise on the basis of eyewitness testimony. So did Assistant District Attorney William Alexander, who led the initial local inquiry. The Warren Report, without explanation, omitted all of this, preferring to rely on the confused testimony of Mrs. Markham. Congress' Assassination Committee did discover a witness who also believed Tippit's killer had been walking east just before the shooting.[32] The Committee report, however, failed to weigh this statement against those of other witnesses. It side-stepped the problem of direction by ignoring it altogether.

If Oswald was walking west the official theory of his route to the murder scene, already undetermined by the problems with the time factor, collapses. Walking east would have Oswald coming back *toward* his rented room, from a point he could not have reached on foot in the known time period. There are only two ways to resolve that contradiction. Either Oswald had traveled to a point beyond the Tippit scene by some form of transport, or, conceivably, Tippit's killer was not Oswald.

Oswald was last seen by his landlady waiting by a stop on a bus route that would have taken him back toward downtown Dallas, a highly improbable destination. There was no public transport at that hour which could have delivered Oswald beyond the scene of the Tippit shooting. Since Oswald had neither car nor driving license, and there is no evidence that he turned hitchhiker, the evidence encourages an option the original report rejected—that Oswald had an accomplice. This is not the lonely speculation of wild conspiracy theorists. In 1978 I found that the very conservative official who directed the immediate investigation of the Tippit shooting, William Alexander, still believes Oswald may have had help. As assistant district attorney in 1963, Alexander recommended that Oswald be charged with both the Kennedy and Tippit murders. He still believes Oswald played the leading part in the Tippit murder, on the strength of the ballistics evidence, but doubts he acted alone: "One of the questions that I would like to have answered is why Oswald was where he was when he shot Tippit. . . . Along with the police, we measured the route, all the conceivable routes he could have taken to that place; we interrogated bus drivers, we checked the cab-company records, but we still do not know how he got to where he was, or why he was where he was. I feel like if we could ever find out why he was there, then maybe some of the other mysteries would be solved. Was he supposed to meet someone? Was he trying to make a getaway? Did he miss a connection? Was there a connection? If you look at Oswald's behavior, he made very few nonpurposeful motions, very seldom did he do anything that did not serve a purpose to him. People who've studied his behavior feel there was a purpose in his being where he was. I, for one, would like to know what that was."

In 1978, as he drove me around the route Oswald is supposed to have taken to the Tippit murder, the former district attorney slapped the dashboard and repeated, "Oswald's movements did not add up then, and they don't add up now. No way. Certainly he may have had accomplices."[33] A few months later, Congress' Assassinations Committee skipped over the Tippit murder in little more than a page of its report and dodged the question of accomplices altogether. Its published research rightly scotched rumors that Oswald and Tippit had been associates before the assassination. Yet there was no sign that the Committee's investigation even tried to deal with the rickety chain of evidence in the Tippit ballistics area, or considered testimony suggesting that more than one man was involved in the policeman's killing. The Tippit section of the report, as did other areas, smacked of an approach shaped before the Committee's late decision that more than one assassin had been at work in Dealey Plaza. Of course, once the probability of conspiracy is accepted—and the Committee did come to accept that—it follows that accomplices may well have been involved at other stages.*

In passing acknowledgement of that thought, the Committee commented on how one witness described a gunman at the Tippit scene finishing off the policeman with a point-blank shot to the head. In contradiction of its own thesis about Oswald, the Committee said this was "more indicative of an execution than an act of defense intended to allow escape." The Committee noted pointedly that this was typical of "gangland murders." In the context of the report, this is clearly a reference to the Committee's strong feeling that elements of the Mafia had a hand in the President's murder. On the Tippit killing, the Committee was certainly stretching the evidence, but may not have been far off the mark.

Long after the Kennedy assassination, a Mafia associate called John Martino said in a private conversation that he had knowledge of what happened after the President's assassination. Martino said of Oswald's movements before his arrest, "Oswald was to meet his contact at the Texas Theater [the theater where Oswald was arrested]. They were to meet Oswald in the theater, and get him out of the country, then eliminate him. Oswald made a mistake. . . . There was no way we could get to him. They had Ruby kill him."

"They" referred to "the anti-Castro people," who, said Martino, "put Oswald together." Martino, who in 1963 was himself deeply involved in Cuban exile operations, was part of both the world of organized crime and that of the CIA. Long before 1963

---

*Since this book's first publication, there have been fresh developments in the Tippit case. See Aftermath chapter.

the Mafia and American intelligence had become involved in the anti-Castro crusade, in parallel with an extraordinary relationship with each other. Martino, whose role will be discussed in detail elsewhere, said Oswald "didn't know who he was working for—he was just ignorant of who was really putting him together."

Martino was well placed to learn the information he claimed. Whether he did know or not, he seems to have been on the mark in his analysis of Oswald. As this book will show, the alleged assassins was involved in a weird world of intrigue. He had blundered into a quicksand of intelligence agents, Cuban exile plotters, and thugs, and the likelihood is that he was in over his head.

One day in the Seventies CBS television interviewed former Warren Commission counsel David Belin. Belin, an inveterate champion of the Warren Commission, declared, "I don't happen to believe that Oswald was part of any conspiracy, and as a matter of fact, the very fact that twelve years have passed and there really is no concrete evidence of conspiracy is in itself evidence of the fact there was no conspiracy." "Or," came the dry reply from CBS reporter Dan Schorr, "that it was a very good one." That was in 1975. In 1979 came the considered opinion of Congress' Assassinations Committee that the Warren commission "failed to investigate adequately the possibility of a conspiracy . . . " and that President Kennedy was probably killed as a result of a conspiracy. The record suggests that the Committee was right and that the conspiracy was, indeed, a rather good one. In large part, the conspirators have Lee Oswald to thank for that.

CHAPTER 7

A Sphinx for Texas

Constitutional scrutiny of intelligence services is largely an illusory concept. If they're good, they fool the outsiders— and if they're bad they fool themselves.

—John le Carré

Fifteen years on, standing in the sixth-floor window of the Texas School Book Depository, Jesse Curry stared out over Dealey Plaza and remembered the oddest prisoner he ever had: "One would think Oswald had been trained in interrogation techniques and resisting interrogation techniques," said the retired Dallas police chief, recalling Lee Oswald's performance under questioning. Curry's puzzlement was echoed by Assistant District Attorney Alexander, who told me, "I was amazed that a person so young would have had the self-control he had. It was almost as if he had been rehearsed, or programed, to meet the situation that he found himself in. . . . " "Rehearsed? Rehearsed by whom?" I asked Alexander. He could only shake his head and answer, "Who knows?"

Lee Oswald was an enigma, and not only for Texas law-enforcement officials. The learned worthies on the Warren Commission never could ascribe to Oswald that basic ingredient any investigator seeks in any crime—a motive. Their report admitted, "No one will ever know what passed through Oswald's mind during the week before November 22, 1963" and fell back with little conviction on guesses about "hostility to environment" and "hatred for American society" and the like. There has never been any serious suggestion that the alleged assassin was mad, nor is there any evidence of insanity. In 1979 Congress' Assassinations

Committee dug into the same old bag for an explanation and came up only with talk about Oswald's "conception of political action, rooted in his twisted ideological view of himself and the world around him." If the same conclusion was drawn about all young people of Oswald's addled left-wing politics, we should expect a President to be assassinated every day. The Committee admitted that it picked on that explanation only "in the absence of other more compelling evidence"—a phrase perhaps suggesting that its section on motivation was conceived before science forced the conclusion that there had been more than one assassin. The Committee went some way from the old blinkered official position, but it did not—apparently—give any houseroom to the notion that Oswald was framed. Where the Committee identified sinister hands behind the assassination, they were of the right—the Mafia or anti-Castro activists. It avoided the question of how Oswald's left-wing stance fitted into that, and dwelt hardly at all on the possibility that—*because* of that very stance—he may have seemed ripe for a set-up. Whatever the truth about that, Oswald's lack of motive has always mitigated in his favor. In his police questioning, indeed, the alleged assassin gave his captors one clear impression: Lee Oswald rather *liked* President Kennedy.

"I am not a malcontent; nothing irritated me about the President," replied Oswald mildly when asked what he thought of John Kennedy. He also said, "I have no views on the President. My wife and I like the President's family. They are interesting people. I have my own views on the President's national policy." In this instance, Oswald's version was corroborated unanimously by those who knew him. Even the accused's wife, Marina, whose testimony was to damn him in so many other ways, has told of Oswald's enthusiasm for Kennedy. She has said of her husband, "He always spoke very complimentary about the President. He was very happy when John Kennedy was elected. . . . Whatever he said about President Kennedy, it was only good, always." Kennedy was voted into office while the Oswalds were living in Russia, and Marina says of Lee, "He was very proud of the new President of his country." She says that Oswald called Kennedy "a good leader" and that he usually gave the impression that "he liked him very well." Acquaintances and relatives told the official inquiry much the same thing, and Oswald's attitude apparently remained consistent in the months before the assassination. In August, when the Oswalds were in New Orleans, the American press was full of the latest Kennedy family tragedy, when the President's newborn son died two days after birth. Then, like many people in America, Oswald followed bulletins on the baby's progress with concern. He hoped the child would survive and was anxious when its condition went downhill. More dispassionate was the opinion of a New Orleans policeman who interviewed Oswald at that very same period, following a street incident between Oswald and anti-Castro exiles. Lieutenant Francis Martello formed the impression that Oswald liked President Kennedy. Martello described Oswald as: "Not in any way, shape or form violent . . . as far as ever dreaming or thinking that Oswald would do what it is alleged that he has done, I would set my head on a chopping block that he wouldn't do it."

It frequently occurs, of course, that people commit crimes that appear totally out of character to those who have known them. Nevertheless, it must be borne in mind that nobody, anywhere, heard Oswald speak ill of the President. The only hint of anything amiss before the assassination lies in Marina's account of a conversation with her husband on the eve of the murder. She says she tried to bring up the subject of the President's impending visit, but her husband avoided talking about it. That does not seem so strange in the knowledge that—according to Marina—Oswald was preoccupied that night with personal worries. He was pressing Marina to live with him once again, and talked repeatedly of making a fresh start by moving the family into an apartment together. In that sense, it was hardly the talk of a man planning a crime that might, as it indeed turned out, spell his own imminent death.

Apart from his "frantic" denials of murdering the President and his shout to the press of "I'm just a patsy!" Oswald did drop a hint in custody that he would have more to tell. He would say none of it, though, till he obtained legal advice. When visited in custody by the president of the Dallas Bar Association, Oswald spoke of finding a lawyer "who believes in anything I believe in, and believes as I believe, and believes in my innocence as much as he can,

I might let him represent me." Oswald tried to get in touch with a specific lawyer, John Abt of New York. A Secret Service inspector was present when Oswald asked help in contacting Abt and his report may throw light on Oswald's thinking: ". . . he wanted to contact a Mr. Abt, a New York lawyer whom he did not know but who had defended the Smith Act 'victims' in 1949 or 1950 in connection with a conspiracy against the government." John Abt was away from his home during the weekend of the assassination, and Oswald never managed to contact him. If the alleged assassin knew of a "conspiracy," he kept it to himself.

Oswald was a mystery, and he knew it. When his brother Robert visited him in custody, Oswald warned him: "Do not form any opinion on this so-called evidence." Robert wrote later in his diary: ". . . I searched his eyes for any sign of guilt or whatever you call it. There was nothing there—no guilt, no shame, no nothing. Lee finally aware of my looking into his eyes, he stated: 'You will not find anything there.' " The years of endless investigation, of groping toward an understanding of Oswald's real role, have given us no firm answers. But we now have fragments of a picture of Oswald denied to the public in the wake of the assassination. Ironically, it was President Johnson—the man who succeeded John Kennedy and appointed the Warren Commission—who eventually dropped the heaviest official hint that Lee Oswald was more than he appeared to be. In a 1969 interview for CBS Television, Johnson remarked: "I don't think that they [the Warren Commission] or me or anyone else is always absolutely sure of everything that might have motivated Oswald or others that could have been involved. But he was quite a mysterious fellow, and he did have connections that bore examination." That was quite an understatement, but the former President felt he had said too much. He asked CBS to withhold that section of the interview on grounds of "national security." CBS obliged and suppressed Johnson's remarks until 1975.

It was that word "security" again. Chief Justice Warren had used it in 1964 in answer to a general question on whether Warren Commission documentation would be made public. Warren had replied, "Yes, there will come a time. But it might not be in your lifetime. I am not referring to anything especially, but there may

be some things that would involve security. This would be preserved but not made public." Protestations about national security
may have seemed hard to square with the original official verdict
that President Kennedy was killed by one misguided Texas boy,
acting entirely alone. It seems even harder to swallow now that the
Assassinations Committee had concluded that, even if he was
involved, he was *not* acting alone. Some explain that an intelligence agency must protect its information-gathering systems and
the identity of its personnel. While the protection of 1963 operations may no longer seem valid in 1981, it remains a sort of
justification. What does feed suspicion is that even today the
intelligence agencies of the Untied States continue to treat their
Oswald files like state secrets. The Central Intelligence Agency
has refused to release assassination documents except under intense legal pressure, or sometimes at the insistence of Congressional and Senate committees. Such releases are often censored
virtually out of existence. Some scholars are now certain that only
a fraction of the CIA records connected with the assassination
were seen even by the Warren Commission. After all these years,
those who specialize in prizing documents out of the intelligence
agencies do not doubt that hundreds of CIA assassination documents are classified in whole or in part. Senior staff members of
Congress' Assassinations Committee, empowered to investigate
the President's murder by the full authority of the House of
Representatives, ended their inquiry still feeling stymied by the
procrastination, evasiveness, and obstinacy of the CIA. In 1977,
the FBI went through the public motions of releasing 100,000
pages from its Kennedy assassination files. The press uttered an
uncritical cheer and seemed either uninterested or ill-equipped to
ask probing questions at the press conference to celebrate the
event. For the European visitor, indeed, that occasion was a
troubling spectacle of the American media at work. I found myself
virtually alone in pressing the FBI spokesman into the admission
that "up to ten percent of the [Kennedy] file will not be released."
One reason for keeping the records secret, he said, was to protect
individuals' privacy. The other reason seemed less justifiable. It
was the perennial one—"national security."

Some of the documents that are pried out of the records

themselves present new mysteries or simply affront the intelligence of the public. Take page 66 of Warren Commission Document 206, finally declassified in 1976. This is a page from an FBI report, showing that on the day after the assassination a telephone call was intercepted in Dallas in which a "male voice was heard to say that he felt sure Lee Harvey Oswald had killed the President but did not feel Oswald was responsible, and further stated, We both know who is responsible.' " This document failed to state that the tapped telephone numbers were those of Michael Paine and his wife, Ruth Paine, the woman who was playing host to Marina Oswald at the time of the assassination. It is not clear whether anybody ever asked the couple about this conversation between Mrs. Paine's house and Mr. Paine's office. There is no record of the full telephone conversation, nor of what happened to the original recording. Whatever the meaning of Document 206, it is typical of official gestures to the public's right to know.

Much of this book will be given over to assembling pieces of the jigsaw that have slipped through the net of "national security" restrictions. Sometimes the emerging picture will seem to point to sinister Communist conspiracy—a specter which President Johnson, just after the assassination, feared "could conceivably lead the country into a war which could cost forty million lives." Marina, the Soviet wife Oswald brought back from Russia, remains a mystery in her own right. The questions about her continue to multiply.

Why did Russian authorities issue her with new documents just before she left for the United States? Well before the assassination, the CIA pondered whether she might be a Soviet plant, sent to the United States with a phony identity. Afterward, the Agency asked a series of questions about Mrs. Oswald's documentation but never received satisfactory answers.

Why, once in the United States, did Marina receive a letter from the address in the Soviet Union of a man suspected by the CIA of being an agent of the First Chief Directorate of the KGB, Soviet intelligence? In 1964, the Warren Commission considered the possibility that Marina might be a "Soviet agent"—almost humorously. Senator Russell commented, "That will blow the lid if she testifies to that." She did not, of course, but there is little sign that anyone on the Commission really wanted to peer under the lid. Some suggestive leads, which raised awkward questions for American intelligence agencies, were left unpursued.

One of Oswald's Dallas acquaintances, Teofil Meller, told police after the assassination that in 1962 he had taken precautions before plunging into a relationship with a former defector. He said he had "checked with the FBI, and they told him that Oswald was all right." What exactly did that mean?

Another Dallas resident, George de Mohrenschildt, befriended Oswald after his return from Russia. Like Meller, he later claimed he had felt the need to check up on Oswald, in his case by seeing an agent of the CIA's Domestic Contact Service, J. Walton Moore. According to de Mohrenschildt, the agent replied without hesitation: "Yes, he is okay. He is just a harmless lunatic." What would a CIA man in Dallas know about Oswald, as early as 1962, to be able to give assurances without even checking CIA files? (The de Mohrenschildt connection will be discussed, later in this book.)

Then there is Warren Commission Document 1133. In 1975 a distinguished Washington newspaper correspondent, Seth Kantor, discovered that the FBI was continuing to suppress "1133" and was bemused to find that the document was a record of his own phone calls from Dallas on the afternoon of the assassination. The journalist found that the official reason for turning his calls into a state secret was that public disclosure "might reveal the identity of confidential sources of information. . . . " Kantor began an intensive effort to get the document released and cross-checked with his own notes of that afternoon which he had kept. In the end he was given the document, which appeared to contain the less than world-shaking information that Kantor had placed phone calls from Dallas City Hall, Parkland Hospital, and the airport at Love Field. The FBI passed off the delay in releasing the document as a bureaucratic blunder, but Kantor's notes finally revealed that one of the calls Kantor made from City Hall was to a Florida number, Coral Gables MO 5-6473. This was the number of Hal Hendrix, a Miami journalist, also working for Kantor's newspaper group, who was offering information on Oswald. Hendrix, on the afternoon of the assassination, was able to give Kantor details of Oswald's past, his defection to Russia, and his pro-Castro activities on his return—information that would become common knowledge soon enough, but the Hendrix call has a special significance. He is no ordinary journalist.

Hendrix had won a Pulitzer Prize earlier in 1963 for his coverage of the Cuban missile crisis in October 1962, but it was in autumn 1963 that he really showed his brilliance. On September 24 he described and justified the coup that ousted the pro-Kennedy President Bosch of the Dominican Republic. The remarkable thing, Kantor relates, was that Hendrix reported the coup twenty-four hours *before* it happened. A key advantage Hendrix had, reportedly, was a CIA source at Homestead Airforce base, south of Miami. In the months and years to come, Hendrix became known as The Spook to his Washington Colleagues because of his phenomenal relations with American intelligence. Years were to pass before Hendrix' intimate association was made fully public. In 1976 he pleaded guilty to withholding information from a Senate committee investigating links between multinational corporations and the CIA. He had lied to the committee with the collusion of the CIA and had concealed his access to CIA information. This was the man who knew so much about Lee Oswald on the afternoon of November 22, 1963, and whose identity the FBI tried to protect for twelve years.

As we have already seen in the context of Oswald's "Hidell" alias, U.S. Army intelligence had a file on Oswald before the assassination. As a result, a colonel in intelligence was feeding information to the FBI within an hour of Oswald's arrival at the police station. It would be nice to be sure that this was just an example of how efficient Army intelligence was in watching what the colonel now calls "a possible counter-intelligence threat." That, however, became impossible when the Army applied the ultimate censorship to its Kennedy files. I spoke to Congressman Richardson Preyer soon after the Assassinations Committee learned those records had been destroyed. He said bluntly, "There have been instances of files being, I guess you could say, maliciously withheld or even destroyed. . . . We don't know what the motive is and it's the kind of problem we run into. The Pentagon had destroyed its Kennedy assassination files, the Army file on the Kennedy assassination has been destroyed, and we don't know why it was done."

For some, the conduct of the American intelligence agencies raises the specter that they played a direct role in the assassination of the President, that his murder was nothing less than a *coup d'état*. It is, however, highly improbable that any agency—or agency leadership as a group—had any part in the assassination. In 1979 Congress' Assassinations Committee concluded bluntly that neither the Secret Service, nor the FBI, nor the CIA were involved as organizations. It made no reference, in its list of main findings, to the military. The Committee did, on the other hand, consider evidence indicating that individual members of the agencies might have had prior covert associations with Oswald and even played a role in the assassination. One particularly serious allegation[34] remains, as the Committee's Chief Counsel carefully put it, "undiscredited." Yet the shifty behavior of the intelligence organizations as a whole may conceal—apart from inefficiency—an embarrassing truth less heinous than actual involvement in the assassination.

The Warren Report stated, "Close scrutiny of the records of the Federal agencies involved and the testimony of the responsible officials of the U.S. Government establish that there was absolutely no type of informant or undercover relationship between an agency of the U.S. Government and Lee Harvey Oswald at any time." Today, in the wake of Watergate and a stream of CIA scandals, such all-embracing trust sounds quaint. The Warren Commission staff did not see all the records, and some of the "responsible officials" consulted have been exposed as very irresponsible officials indeed. In 1979 Congress' Assassinations Committee was careful to make no such sweeping statement.

The transcript of one Warren Commission executive session, released only in 1974, throws an interesting light on the CIA's attitude to the ethics of public disclosure. Commission member Allen Dulles, himself a former director of the CIA, told his colleagues how a CIA official would deal with inquiries about an agent he had recruited.

DULLES: . . . he wouldn't tell.
CHIEF JUSTICE WARREN: Wouldn't he tell it under oath?
DULLES: I wouldn't think he would tell it under oath, no.
CHAIRMAN: Why?

DULLES: He ought not to tell it under oath. Maybe not tell it to his own government, but wouldn't tell it any other way. (Sic)
CHAIRMAN: Wouldn't he tell it to his own chief?
DULLES: He might or he might not. . . .

Whatever Lee Oswald might eventually have revealed about himself and U.S. intelligence was lost to history forever two days after his arrest. In the late morning of November 24 the Dallas police chief decided to move his prisoner to the county jail. In the basement of City Hall, as Oswald was being led to a police car, a bystander with a revolver lunged forward to fire a single lethal bullet into Oswald's stomach. Jack Ruby, a local club owner with Mafia connections, had silenced Oswald once and for all. The last words the accused assassin had heard before being shot were a newsman's shouted question: "Have you anything to say in your defense?"

Lee Oswald was conscious for a few minutes after being shot. Police officers laid him down on the floor of a nearby office, and one tried to talk to him. In 1978 Detective Billy Combest told me of Oswald's dying response to questioning abut the assassination: "At that time I thought he was seriously injured, so I got right down on the floor with him, just literally on my hands and knees. And I asked him if he would like to make any confession, any statement in connection with the assassination of the President. . . . Several times he responded to me by shaking his head in a definite manner. . . . It wasn't from the pain or anything —he had just decided he wasn't going to correspond with me, he wasn't going to say anything."[35]

Before Oswald was carried to an ambulance somebody applied artificial respiration—the worst possible treatment for an abdominal wound because it multiplies the chances of severe internal bleeding. At Parkland Hospital the doctors who two days earlier had tried to save the President's life now worked in vain over Oswald.

The corpse was taken to a mortuary, where an FBI team photographed Oswald and took his fingerprints for the last time. Late on November 25, the same afternoon that President Kennedy was laid to rest in Washington, the alleged assassin was buried in a cemetery outside Dallas. He lies today in a moleskin-covered coffin, within a sealed concrete vault, beneath a black slab bearing one word, "OSWALD." There are no details, not even dates of birth and death.

During his interrogation by Dallas police, Lee Oswald is reported to have responded once by exclaiming.: "Everybody will know who I am now." Today we have still had only glimpses of who he really was.

II

OSWALD

Maverick or Puppet?

CHAPTER 8

Red Faces

Ask me, and I will tell you I fight for communism. . . .
—Lee Oswald, in a letter from Russia, 1959

The reaction in Dallas to the capture of Oswald could aptly be described as having been Pavlovian. The moment local officials realized their prisoner had been in Russia, and discovered armfuls of Communist propaganda amongst his belongings, they began babbling about an "international Communist conspiracy" to kill the President. Far away in Washington and Moscow, a different breed of official reacted with more sophistication. Officers of the CIA and the KGB knew full well the questions that would soon be asked: Was Oswald an agent? Was he one of ours or one of theirs? These questions still await satisfactory answers, and those that have been given are riddles in the sand.

In a recently released memorandum an anonymous CIA official makes much of how, in November 1963, he scurried to the files because "we were extremely concerned at the time that Oswald, as an American returning from the USSR, might have been routinely debriefed by D.C.D.* The CIA man reports that none of the subsequent "traces" revealed any agency contact with Oswald.

In February 1964 a Soviet intelligence officer defected to the United States and gave a glib account of Moscow's reaction to the assassination. This was Yuri Nosenko, and he claimed that within hours of the news he had himself been ordered to investigate the Soviet end of the Oswald case. According to him a special plane was dispatched to Minsk, where Oswald had lived, to collect all

* Domestic Contacts Division.

official papers on the alleged assassin's stay in Russia. The results, Nosenko insisted, were negative. He claimed that after Oswald came to Russia, the KGB "decided that Oswald was of no interest" and declared, "I can unhesitatingly sign off to the fact that the Soviet Union cannot be tied into this in any way."

In 1975 neither CIA nor Soviet disclaimers convinced the Senate Intelligence Committee when it looked into the performance of the intelligence agencies at the time of the Kennedy assassination. Senator Richard Schweiker, who was prominent in that inquiry and had access to many classified U.S. intelligence files, told me in 1978 the facts indicated that "Either we trained and sent him to Russia, and they went along and pretended they didn't know to fake us out, or in fact, they inculcated him and sent him back here and were trying to fake us out that way." It is, then, not only fireside amateurs who suspect Oswald had some sort of intelligence role. He did move in a mysterious way, a multiple shadow on the face of the later Cold War years. Yet, in the effort to bring that shadow into focus, the outsider labors under an enormous handicap. His main sources are men for whom untruth is a way of life—officials of the self-styled intelligence community.

In 1978 one of the most long-serving writers about the Kennedy assassination, Edward Epstein, caused a stir with a book suggesting that Oswald may indeed have been recruited by the KGB, though not with assassination in mind. Epstein drew heavily on interviews with former CIA Chief of Counterintelligence James Angleton. In 1975, at one Senate Intelligence Committee hearing, this same Angleton was asked to verify a quotation of something he was reported to have said earlier. Angleton replied in characteristically opaque style, "Well, if it is accurate, it should not have been said." As I discovered when I interviewed him, Angleton is indeed a master of deception and disinformation. By the same token he is unquestionably a brilliant intelligence analyst, long unrivaled as an interpreter of Soviet skullduggery. Any probe into the foggy world of the Oswald who went to Russia must be ever sensitive to the double and triple public postures of officials like Angleton. For initial simplicity, our look at that world at first follows the proposal that Oswald, the youthful Marine, was recruited by the Communists. He may also have been the tool of others, with the opposite allegiance, and that thesis will be considered in due course.

The fledgling Oswald was a contradiction from the start. At the age of sixteen in New Orleans, he was reportedly devouring Communist literature from the library and apparently writing off to the Socialist Party of America for information.[36] According to one high-school friend, he started spouting about Socialism, declaring that he was "looking for a Communist cell in town" and that "Communism was the only way of life for the worker." Another contemporary friend said that reports that the young Oswald was "studying Communism" were nonsense—a detail which will gain significance much later in his story. Oswald had a funny way of showing that Communism was the only course for him, for he was trying at the same time to join the U.S. Marine Corps, one of the most potent symbols of American imperialism— for those on Oswald's professed side of the political fence. Oswald tried to cheat his way into the Marines while still under enlistment age and—when he failed—began devouring his elder brother's Marine Corps manual as avidly as he had reportedly been studying Marxist tracts. According to his mother, Oswald learned the handbook till he "knew it by heart" and finally did succeed in joining up—six days after his seventeenth birthday. Like the possible inspiration of his Socialist bent, the possible human cause of his enthusiasm for the Marines will loom up as we plunge deeper into the historical fog of Oswald's story.

During his basic training, Oswald the recruit declared an interest in Aircraft Maintenance and Repair, and spring 1957 saw him learning radar and air traffic control. These, and further assignments, required a security check, and Oswald passed it. He was, says the official record, granted clearance at a "confidential" level. Over these months, Oswald emerged as a loner who kept apart from his Marine buddies. He did not always run with the pack when the unit was allowed out of camp, and, with hindsight, some of his actions seem a little mysterious. While at Keesler Air Force Base, friends thought Oswald used his weekend passes to go "home" to New Orleans, a hundred miles away. Yet, as we now know, his mother had moved to Texas, and other relatives in New Orleans say Oswald did not visit them.

Marine Oswald did rather well. He finished seventh in a class of thirty and qualified as an Aviation Electronics Operator—an assignment designed for those credited with above-average intelligence. It was this that led directly to a foreign posting with MACS-1, Marine Air Control Squadron One at Atsugi in Japan. In 1957 Atsugi was the home of the now famous U-2 spy plane, and Oswald was entering a world of military secrets. In the controversy over the alleged assassin's true colors, this period is pivotal.

Atsugi air base, a few miles southeast of Tokyo, had been inherited by the Americans from Japan's World War II Air Force. When Oswald arrived it had become a jump-off point for marine jet fighters and Navy Constellations equipped for detecting enemy radar. Atsugi was also the site of a radar "bubble" responsible for surveillance of a vast sector of air space. Its function, according to the Warren Report, was "to direct aircraft to their targets by radar, communicating with the pilots by radio." The squadron also scouted for incoming foreign aircraft, mostly Russian or Chinese planes which had strayed. It was in the radar bubble that Oswald worked, gazing for hours at a time at the blips on the screen and plotting aircraft courses. The newcomer proved so good at his job that one officer wrote, "I would desire to have him work for me at any time. . . . He minds his business and he does his job well." Sometimes, as the senior enlisted man, he served as crew chief. One of the leading Marines in Oswald's group says of him, "He had the sort of intelligence where you could show him how to do something once and he'd know how to do it, even if it was pretty complicated."

While Oswald worked in the radar room he witnessed a phenomenon that mystified everybody. Sometimes, out of the ether, a pilot's voice would request weather information for an altitude of ninety thousand feet, and no one, in 1957, had heard of a plane that flew that high. The mystery lasted only till the Marines discovered they were living at close quarters with a newfangled aircraft called the U-2. The officers called it a "utility plane," but the U-2 was a spy in the sky, perhaps the West's most important single military intelligence asset.

As the weeks passed Oswald and his friends saw the U-2 in action as it was wheeled out of a special hangar, as it rocketed aloft at astonishing speed, and as it returned from distant missions.

Long and pencil-thin, the U-2 looked to the young Marines like something out of science fiction. There were no spy satellites then, and it was invaluable to the United States for penetrating Soviet and Chinese air space to return laden with telltale photographs. Army and air bases, seaports and factories, all were vulnerable to the high-altitude eyes of the U-2. Today the U-2 is credited with having gathered almost *all* contemporary intelligence on Soviet military activity. The beauty of it, for Western intelligence, was that the Communists were powerless to stop the U-2. The new superplane flew so high that no ground-to-air missiles or conventional aircraft could touch it. Its precise operational altitudes were top secret, as was any technical data that would teach the Russians how to knock the U-2 out of the sky. Oswald and his friends were left in no doubt about the secrecy. The hangar where the planes were kept was ringed by guards with submachine guns, and the Marines were ordered not to discuss what they did see and hear on the airfield and in the radar room.

It is probable that Atsugi also held another secret, almost as sensitive as the U-2 project—a stockpile of nuclear weapons. According to the American agreement with Japan, no nuclear armament should have been stored on American bases, but personnel at Atsugi suspected the pact was violated. One officer, Lieutenant Charles Rhodes, has recently recalled being taken by a colonel to a vast underground complex "at least three stories below ground." On either side of a central thoroughfare, in deep alcoves, Rhodes observed huge armaments which he identified as bombs. The colonel did not say what they were and did not invite questions.

The aura of military secrecy at Atsugi was fascinating for everyone, down to the lowliest Marine, and some suggest that for Oswald it was more than that. Lieutenant Charles Donovan, the officer in charge of Oswald's radar team, says he clearly remembers a day when Oswald discussed the U-2's radar blips with him. One Marine friend recalls Oswald wandering about Atsugi with a camera, taking pictures. If his photographs were of radar installations or of the U-2 in action, they would have been manna from heaven for Soviet intelligence. Some believe Oswald made sinister contacts who were just that—spies.

Just as he had once gone off alone on trips to New Orleans,

Oswald now went on two-day trips to Tokyo. He confided to a friend that he was having an affair with a Japanese nightclub hostess. That on its own would have been normal enough, but Oswald seemed to be loving above his station. The hostess worked at the "Queen Bee," then one of the smartest clubs in the city. Its clientele were American officers rather than enlisted men, and a night with one of the girls cost more than Oswald earned in a month. He and his lady friend were sometimes seen together, and Oswald's mates were amazed that a girl of her style and beauty would have time for Oswald. Perhaps they simply underestimated Oswald's talents with women, but some suspect the girl from the Queen Bee was pumping Oswald for classified information. Loose talk in the Tokyo clubs, like soldiers' bar talk anywhere, was known to cause security leaks, and the use of sex as bait for intelligence information is as old as spying itself.

Whatever the nature of his glamorous liaison, Oswald reacted miserably to the news that his unit was to be transferred to the Philippines. It was now, in October 1957, that his early image as a model Marine began to look tarnished. According to the record, Oswald shot himself in the arm, inflicting a minor wound, before his unit was due to leave Atsugi. He did so, allegedly, with a pistol he had purchased privately and kept in his locker. For possession of an unregistered weapon, against service regulations, Oswald was later fined and sentenced to twenty days' hard labor. If he had been trying to dodge transfer to the Philippines, he failed. Oswald was discharged from the hospital in time to leave Japan with his unit and did not return to Atsugi for several months. When he did get back he was soon in trouble again, this time apparently because he picked a quarrel at a party. A second court-martial acquitted him of deliberately pouring a drink over a sergeant but found him guilty of using "provoking words." This time Oswald had to serve his sentence and spent eighteen days in the cells. From now on, say his former friends, Oswald spoke bitterly against the Marine Corps and reinforced his reputation as a loner. He avoided Marine acquaintances and was again seen with Japanese acquaintances, both male and female.

In autumn 1958 Oswald's radar unit moved to Taiwan, during a crisis sparked off by fighting between Communist and Nationalist

Chinese forces. Oswald reportedly went with them[37] and again drew attention to himself. While alone on guard duty at night he loosed off four or five shots into the darkness and then claimed he had fired at "men in the woods" who failed to answer a challenge. Whatever the truth of that, Oswald declared that he could not stand doing sentry duty. Shortly afterwards he was apparently transferred back to Atsugi, where he was once again seen consorting with a striking woman, this time a Eurasian. Oswald told a friend she was half Russian.

Soon Oswald's tour of duty in the Pacific ended, and he was transferred to El Toro base at Santa Ana in California. The function of his unit there, according to Lieutenant Donovan, one of Oswald's officers was "to surveil for aircraft, but basically to train both enlisted men and officers for later assignment overseas." Like other officers, Donovan found Oswald "a good crew chief," "very competent," and "brighter than most people." The lieutenant took Oswald on at chess and found him "very good" at the game. He also noted that the young Marine "was particularly capable in the field of world affairs." In that area, Oswald had a special interest. It quickly became clear that he was now preoccupied with things Russian.

At the El Toro base, Oswald applied to take a Marine proficiency examination in written and spoken Russian. This he failed but did show a knowledge of the basics of the language. In the weeks to come Oswald was observed laboring hour after hour with his Russian books, and he began taking a Russian-language periodical. He played Russian records so loudly they could be heard outside the barrack block and began addressing people in Russian whether they understood it or not. Oswald even had his name written in Russian on one of his jackets. Marine friends nicknamed him "Comrade Oswaldskovich," and young Lee thought it just as funny as they did. One Marine friend, Kerry Thornley, noted later, "He often joked about Communism. I remember one time a master sergeant got up on the tailgate of a truck for a lecture of some type. Oswald remarked in a Russian accent, "Ah! Another collectivist farm lecture. . . ."

Oswald openly showed himself interested in Socialist ideology and in Soviet politics in particular. He again subscribed to the

People's World, the Socialist newspaper he had first read as a youth in New Orleans. Marine Thornley, who discussed politics with Oswald, gained the impression that Oswald thought, "The Marxist morality was the most rational morality to follow" and Communism "the best system in the world." With another Marine, Nelson Delgado from Puerto Rico, Oswald held animated discussions about Cuba, where Fidel Castro had just seized power. Both young men said they supported the Castro revolution and discussed going to Havana together one day. Delgado suggested that Oswald should write to the Cuban Embassy in Washington, and Oswald later said he had made contact with Cuban diplomats. Delgado noticed that his friend began getting more letters than usual, and on some of them he noticed the Cuban official seal. On trips into Los Angeles with Delgado he would say he was on his way to "visit the Cuban consulate." One night Oswald was allowed to stand down from guard duty when an outsider asked for him at the camp entrance. An hour later Delgado saw Oswald at the gate deep in conversation with a man wearing an overcoat and concluded that the stranger was a Cuban. Oswald and his visitor talked for about two hours.

Years later this incident was raised in a CIA memorandum, which declared, "Delgado's testimony has the cast of credibility . . . says a lot more of possible operational significance than is reflected by the language of the Warren Report, and its implications do not appear to have been run down or developed by investigation." The memorandum says that after the Kennedy assassination, Soviet and Cuban cooperation with the American inquiry was minimal, "designed to cover up an admission of knowledge of, or connection with, Oswald." Of the stranger at the gate, the CIA officer asked, "Who was it, and was there reporting from Los Angeles to Washington and Havana that could, in effect, represent the opening of a Cuban file on Oswald?"

Shortly before the end of his Marine service, Oswald asked Delgado to take a duffel bag to a bus-station locker in Los Angeles. According to Delgado and another Marine, it contained, along with personal property, photographs showing a fighter aircraft from various angles. Oswald could have obtained the pictures legitimately during training, but Delgado wondered why he had kept them. Meanwhile, Oswald, whatever his allegiance, was getting ready for a dramatic move.

Already, in spring 1959, Oswald had applied to study philosophy at the Albert Schweitzer College in Switzerland, and the college had accepted him. Then, in a letter home to his brother, Oswald had written mysteriously, "Pretty soon I'll be getting out of the Corps and I know what I want to be and how I'm going to be it . . ." Now, in August, Oswald behaved as if he was impatient to leave the Marines. He then achieved that by asking for an early release on the ground that his injured mother needed his support. This was a fabrication, for Mrs. Oswald had been only slightly hurt, many months before, and was now perfectly all right. Nevertheless, Oswald got her to provide evidence to support his plea and promptly obtained the discharge. He simultaneously applied for a passport, openly stating in his application that he intended to travel to Russia and Cuba. Although this hardly squared with his pretense of going home to look after mother, there is no sign that the Marine Corps raised any query. In Oswald's unit, the rapidity of his discharge came as a surprise. The passport, however, was quickly granted, and within days Oswald was out of the Marines and on his way to Texas.

In 1979, in a superficial review of Oswald's service record, Congress' Assassinations Committee said it found nothing very out of the ordinary. If Oswald was being manipulated by a competent intelligence unit, one surely should not expect to find obvious discrepancies. There is no sign that the Committee talked extensively with Oswald's barrack colleagues. Nor, apparently, did it ponder the Marines' remarkable tolerance to Oswald's blatant Russophilia or the calm acceptance of his planned trip to Russia.

Oswald did not delay long in Texas. Once there, he told his brother he was going straight to New Orleans to "work for an export firm." That was as bogus as the story about caring for his ailing mother. When Oswald reached New Orleans he boarded a ship bound for Europe and disembarked at the British port of Southampton on October 9. By midnight next day he was checking into a hotel in the Finnish capital of Helsinki. Lee Oswald was on the last lap of his journey to Moscow, and things continued to go smoothly for him. Within two days, after no known advance notice at all, the Soviet consul in Helsinki granted Oswald a six-day tourist visa to enter the Soviet Union. Oswald's easy access had encouraged the belief that the Soviets were expecting him. The suspicion is bolstered by a claim that Swedish intelligence detected a flying visit by Oswald to Stockholm, where he may have visited the Soviet Embassy.[38] CIA and State Department studies show that it was normal to keep visa applicants waiting for two weeks and at least for five days. The Soviet consul in Helsinki was, however, a suspected KGB officer, and American intelligence had learned he could give a visa in a matter of minutes if convinced the would-be-traveler was "all right." Oswald, apparently, came up to scratch. On October 16 he arrived in Moscow by train, was met by an Intourist representative, and shepherded to the Hotel Berlin. There he registered as a student.

After two weeks and a series of contacts with Soviet officials, Oswald walked into the American Embassy in Moscow. There, according to consular officials who received him, Oswald announced that he wished to renounce his American citizenship. To hammer home his intention he slapped his passport down on the table, along with a formal letter ending with the sentence, "I affirm that my allegiance is to the Union of Soviet Socialist Republics." For good measure, Oswald declared that he had "voluntarily told Soviet officials that he would make known to them all information concerning the Marine Corps and his speciality therein, radar operation, as he possessed." He added, too, "that he might know something of special interest." On the face of it, Oswald was now an authentic defector and a traitor to his country. But was it as simple as that? One of the American consular officials, John McVickar, noticed something puzzling about Oswald, and felt ". . . he was following a pattern of behavior in which he had been tutored by a person or persons unknown . . . seemed to be using words he had learned, but did not fully understand . . . in short, it seemed to me there was a possibility that he had been in contact with others before or during his Marine Corps tour who had guided him and encouraged him in his actions."

McVickar's reaction was identical with that of the Dallas officials who would one day interview Oswald on suspicion of assassinating President Kennedy. In 1978 the former consul told me he still had the same nagging feeling, that Oswald's performance at the Embassy was not spontaneous. But if McVicar was right, what "person or persons unknown" had coached Oswald?

On a first assessment of young Oswald's behavior, the easy answer is that he had been in contact with Communist agents in Japan or the United States, and that he perhaps defected at their urging. After the assassination, Oswald was reported as saying he had known Communists in Tokyo.[39] Perhaps so, but the person who reported this later turned out himself to have links with *American* intelligence. If Oswald was in touch with Communist agents, they may not have been his only connection with the secret world. Take a second look, and the picture blurs.

CHAPTER 9

Cracks in the Canvas

We have not been told the truth about Oswald.

—Senator Richard Russell, former Warren Commission
member, in 1970

Back on the Marine Air Control base in California, Oswald's
roommate had been puzzled. Nelson Delgado had heard his friend
talk of being in contact with Cuban officials, and now he was
receiving a Russian newspaper. Years later he recalled asking
Oswald incredulously. "They let you get away with this in the
Marine Corps, in a site like this?"

It was a good question. There was Oswald openly dabbling
with revolution while working in a sensitive area on an American
military base at the height of the Cold War. The nearest anyone
came to blowing the whistle was when mailroom workers reported
the "leftist" nature of Oswald's mail. An officer, Captain Block,
raised the matter briefly with Oswald, who reportedly explained
that he was "trying to indoctrinate himself in Russian theory in
conformance with Marine Corps policy." That was as far as it
went, and Oswald went on merrily playing Russian records, reading Russian books, and generally flaunting his preoccupation with
things Soviet. It failed, apparently, to cause any official concern.

Today another Oswald acquaintance at the California base,
Kerry Thornley, cannot accept that. Thornley, too, was doing his
share of youthful talking about Communism; he says now, "Looking back, I feel that both Oswald and I must have been put under
surveillance by the Office of Naval Intelligence during our periods
of active duty in the Marine Corps. The Cold War was raging then.
He was widely regarded as a Communist. . . ." Thornley has a
valid point; it is odd that Oswald's indiscretions do not crop up in

any naval file—at least none that the public has been permitted to see. In the study of historical mysteries, the omissions from official records sometimes turn out to be more significant than the inclusions. Should we apply the inefficiency theory of history to Oswald, explaining all the contradictions as being just the result of human error or laziness? Perhaps nobody was sufficiently alert to bother with Oswald's Socialist protestations; or maybe Naval Intelligence heard about Oswald but did not take the information seriously. Perhaps, but if so it was the start of an extraordinary chain of inconsistencies and official oversights. It is a chain which lasted, virtually without interruption, until the day of the assassination. It is so protracted and so unlikely that, to a number of naturally cautious and scholarly researchers, it has led to a startling conclusion. They believe that, somewhere along the line, Oswald the youthful Socialist became a tiny cog in the machinery of American intelligence.

This thesis is at the heart of the continuing inquiry into the assassination of President Kennedy. It involves fumbling in the historical dark, endless perusal of the documentary record, and obstinate demand for the release of classified official documents. Also, contrary to the image of the blinkered "critic" so readily drawn by the more prejudiced media, those at the serious core of the critical community do have open minds. They falter, with each new development, between theories within theories. In the end, though, they are left with these questions. Was Oswald wholly diverted from his Marxist course and henceforth used for what some intelligence department construed as patriotic duty? Was he simply identified as a left-winger and then unwittingly exploited by American intelligence? Was Oswald recruited by Soviet or Cuban intelligence? Or was he, as the official reports have insisted, just the confused disciple of the left he appeared to be, controlled by nobody and no country, a scrap of flotsam on the swirling political tide? The evidence may suggest that the conventional version has been wrong, that Oswald was some sort of pawn on the intelligence chessboard. The logical point for the game to have begun was during his military service, and it was then that the inconsistencies began. They justify a more skeptical look at Oswald the Marine, beginning with his avid study of Russian.

The official report on the assassination skates quickly over the details of Oswald's progress in learning Russian, saying only that he rated "poor" in all parts of a test he took after being transferred from Japan to California. In fact, Oswald scored "4 +" in Russian reading, which means he got four more answers right than wrong. He scored "+3" in written Russian, and "−5"—a very low result—in understanding spoken in Russian. Although "poor," these results show that Oswald had grasped the basic principles. It indicates that he had been working on his Russian before leaving Japan, yet none of his friends there noticed him doing so. The only evidence that he was trying to pick up Russian at that stage comes from Marine Dan Powers, who had seen Oswald outside the base in the company of a Eurasian woman. From the little Oswald said about her, Powers understood she was half Russian and was teaching Oswald the language. We know nothing more about the mysterious Eurasian, and it would be wrong to assume that she was a Communist agent. What is significant, and what the Warren Report skipped quickly past, is that Oswald suddenly made remarkable progress in Russian between late February 1959, when he failed the Marine test, and the summer of the same year. That summer a Marine friend, knowing of Oswald's interest in Russian, arranged for him to meet his aunt, who was studying Russian for a State Department examination. The aunt, Rosaleen Quinn, had supper with Oswald in Santa Ana, and they talked together in Russian for two hours. According to Quinn, Oswald spoke Russian better, and with much more assurance, than she did after working with a teacher for more than a year. Oswald explained the excellent progress by saying he had been listening to Radio Moscow. This was the man who only months earlier had achieved a miserable "−5" in understanding spoken Russian, let alone speaking it himself. Anyone who has learned a foreign language knows that only practice in conversation leads to fluency—books are merely a basis for picking up grammar and elementary language structures. This is especially true of Russian, which is one of the hardest languages for an Anglo-Saxon to tackle. It was as though Oswald had had some sort of crash course. The official report skipped past this little inconsistency, but there is now evidence that may explain it and open a Pandora's box of nagging questions.

Two months after the assassination, at a closed executive session of the Warren Commission, Chief Counsel Lee Rankin outlined areas of the case which required further investigation. He did so armed with initial reports from the military and the various agencies which had already supplied information on Oswald. In the midst of a prolonged exposition, he said, ". . . we are trying to run that down, *to find out what he studied at the Monterey School of the Army in the way of languages. . . .*" The "Monterey School" in California, now the Defense Language Institute, has long provided highly sophisticated crash courses in languages ranging from routine European languages to the most obscure dialects. It was and is used by U.S. Government and military agencies to familiarize staff with languages ranging from Swahili to Mandarin Chinese.

The Monterey School was functioning and active in 1959, while Oswald was based in California. The official record makes no mention of Oswald ever receiving instruction in Russian, or any language, during his Marine service. Yet the reference in Rankin's briefing—". . . we must run that down to find out *what he studied* at the Monterey School of the Army"—seems to imply knowledge that Oswald had attended a language course. The transcript of the executive session in which this appears was classified "Top Secret" and only released in 1974 after prolonged litigation by a private researcher. Some other episodes during Oswald's Marine service deserve a new look, without prejudice.

There may be something strange about that incident at Atsugi, when Oswald is said to have shot himself in the arm. One of the Marines present at the time, Thomas Bagshaw, says today that the bullet hit the ceiling and missed Oswald altogether. A second, Pete Connor, says the same thing. Other Marines recall that Oswald was slightly wounded. None of the three unit doctors who would have been involved have any recollection of a Marine with a self-inflicted wound in the arm. The years have, of course, blurred memories, but it is a little odd that such a bizarre little incident has faded totally for all three.

There are inconsistencies in accounts of Oswald's movements while serving in the Far East and specifically when his unit was stationed on Taiwan in autumn 1958. The Department of Defense told Congress' Assassinations Committee in 1978 that, while the main unit did go to Taiwan, Oswald stayed with a "rear echelon" at the Atsugi base. It appears, though, that Oswald himself claimed to have served in Taiwan, a claim supported by the recollection of one of his officers. Lieutenant Charles Rhodes recalls that Oswald did make the trip with the main unit but on October 6 was abruptly flown by military aircraft to Atsugi—the base for CIA operations in the Far East. The official explanation given to Rhodes was that Oswald was being transferred for "medical treatment." The record defines Oswald's complaint at this time, and it raises another question mark.

Oswald had urethritis, a mild venereal ailment incurred—as Marine files comically tell us—"in line of duty, not due to own misconduct." When I talked to one of the doctors who treated Oswald he did not recall the episode and explained that the notation was most probably a routine device to avoid jeopardizing Oswald's pay. (A similar description had been made about Oswald's supposed shooting incident.) The doctor's explanation is perfectly credible. What does seem strange is the urethritis, the mildest of the venereal illnesses, should have been judged sufficient cause to fly Oswald to another base far across the China Sea. Urethritis can be a nuisance, but thousands suffer from it while going on with their everyday lives.

Given the imponderables of the Oswald story, and given the saga yet to come, we may here indulge in some very cautious speculation. The bullet wound the doctors cannot remember, and the ailment which required transoceanic travel, could conceivably have been excuses to get Oswald out of circulation for another purpose. If so, Oswald's case is by no means unique. While doing research for another book I puzzled for a long time over a contradiction between the official record and the personal reports—released later—of a British naval officer in World War I. The contemporary record had him in a Navy hospital on the island of Malta when his reports and later recollections had him running around bursting with health on the Russian mainland. I later discovered the officer was at the time one of the top British Naval Intelligence officers in South Russia. The hospital record was just a cover to conceal his part in a secret and sensitive operation.

The sickness ploy, it turns out, is a standard intelligence technique. Without for a moment comparing young Oswald with a top World War I agent, it is not impossible that he too had illnesses of expediency.

From his arrival in Japan, Oswald lived literally in the shadow of American intelligence operations. At Atsugi, where he witnessed the U-2 spy flights, a cluster of some two dozen buildings bore innocent-looking signboards reading, "Joint Technical Advisory Group." This was the euphemistic title for one of the CIA's largest bases in the world, overseeing the U-2 program and other covert operations in Asia. The official account asserts only that Oswald, like other Marines working in the Atsugi radar room, had a "Confidential" clearance. However, Lieutenant Donovan, who commanded Oswald's radar team in California, said that by that time Oswald had a higher rating. Donovan insisted, "He must have had 'Secret' clearance to work in the radar center, because that was a minimum requirement for all of us." Oswald's fellow Marine, Nelson Delgado, said, "We all had access to classified information. I believe it was classified 'Secret.' " In 1979 Congress' Assassinations Committee noted that, while Lieutenant Donovan did have a "Secret" clearance, several other enlisted men who served with Oswald were given only a "Confidential" rating. One of Oswald's closest Marine associates, however, thought Oswald—and specifically Oswald—was an exception.

Kerry Thornley, who served with Oswald in California, testified that "Oswald, I believe had *a higher clearance*. . . . I believe that he at one time worked in the security files; it is the S and C files, somewhere at LTA or at El Toro . . . probably a 'Secret' clearance would be required." Asked about this, Thornley recalled hearing it as a "rumor" about Oswald, a detail suggesting that something about Oswald's status attracted the curiosity of his fellows.

After the assassination the Marine Corps Director of Personnel wrote a report on Oswald's clearance which exceeded even the military reputation for contorted semantics. The report seems to say that Oswald may have had "Secret" clearance while doing certain secret duties; and simply leaves it at that. Whatever Oswald's precise status, there is no sign that the Marine command lost faith in him after two court-martial offenses. Nor was Oswald's clearance removed once he began openly flaunting Marxist convictions and Russophilia.

The next puzzle is a financial one. Could Oswald, a lowly enlisted man, really have saved enough money from his Marine pay to make that roundabout trip to Moscow?[40] The written record suggests he did not, for his sole bank account, which he emptied on leaving, contained only a paltry $203.

Further doubt surrounds Oswald's ability to cover his considerable expenses in the years to come, after his return to the United States. That area is too complex, and in the end too speculative, for full treatment here, but the official position on Oswald's finances only encourages speculation that he received other funds. In 1978, fifteen years after the murder of President Kennedy, the alleged assassin's Internal Revenue record for 1962 was still closed to the public.[41] By contrast, that of his killer Jack Ruby appears in the Warren Commission volumes.

Then there are the logistical hiccups in the conventional account of Oswald's journey to Moscow. One seems to have floored the Commission staff altogether, because the report falls back on blatant misrepresentation of the facts. It states that Oswald arrived in England on October 9, 1959, and, "on the same day, flew to Helsinki, Finland, where he registered at the Torni Hotel." This ignores the evidence of the British date stamp in Oswald's passport, which indicates that, although Oswald indeed arrived at Southampton on October 9, he did not leave until the *next* day. The record of exit, stamped by an immigration officer at London Airport, reads, "Embarked *10* Oct 1959." This raises a real snag, for the only direct flight from London to Helsinki on October 10 did not reach the Finnish capital in time for Oswald to check in at the hour recorded in the registration book of the Torni Hotel. Finnair Flight 852 did not get on to the ground at Helsinki until 11:33 P.M. Experience in Helsinki demonstrates that Oswald could not have reached his hotel in time to check in by midnight.

The contradiction has led some to suggest that Oswald traveled from London to Helsinki by military aircraft. That seems unlikely, as London Airport is not normally used by military aircraft, and if Oswald was on some covert assignment, he would hardly have gone through the charade of an Atlantic sea crossing only to finish his journey under a dangerously transparent cover. Congress' Assassinations Committee, after intensive research, declared itself "unable to determine the circumstances regarding Oswald's trip from London to Helsinki." The problem remains unresolved, but the inconsistency of the passport date stamp invites speculation. Once in Helsinki, Oswald's movements were rather odd. The day after arriving he checked out of the Hotel Torni and into the Hotel Klaus Kurki. Both hotels are in the downtown area, and both—a real exception for Oswald—were first-class hotels.

After the assassination Oswald's highly emotional mother, Marguerite, quickly offered one explanation of what was being covered up. She declared her belief that her son had been "an intelligence agent of the U.S. government." Mrs. Oswald is a colorful lady with a reputation for overreaction, but today she is no longer alone in her claim that Oswald was linked to American intelligence. The most serious specific allegation, which came recently from a former CIA employee, has served only to muddy the waters.

In 1978 a former CIA finance officer, James Wilcott, *offered* a sensational story to Congress' Committee on Assassinations. He asserted that Oswald had indeed been "recruited from the military for the express purpose of becoming a double agent assignment to the USSR." Wilcott, who had served with the CIA in Tokyo, said he had learned this from a CIA case officer shortly after President Kennedy's assassination. He claimed that—according to what he was told—Oswald had been handled under a specific "cryptonym," or code designation. Wilcott said the cryptonym in question was familiar to him at the time, and he gathered that he had himself unwittingly handled funding for the Oswald project. He learned, he said, that it had been "a stupid project," that Oswald was a poor subject for a deep cover operation, and had failed to convince the Russians. He added that the CIA apparently had some kind of special "handle" on Oswald, perhaps because the Agency had discovered he had "murdered someone or committed some serious crime, during a routine lie detector test."

James Wilcott's revelations did not cause a major sensation in the United States, partly because of national weariness with stories about the CIA and the Kennedy assassination. The claims were, nevertheless, given prominence in the *New York Times* and a serious hearing by the Assassinations Committee. The Committee's staff followed up with the research and was unimpressed. Wilcott could not identity the specific case officer who had first told him of Oswald's CIA connection, and other officers he named denied all knowledge. One CIA man, mentioned as taking part in a conversation about Oswald, had not been in Tokyo in November 1963. Finally, Wilcott has joined the ranks of those who are committed to a virulent campaign against the CIA. Shortly after making his Oswald allegations, he attended an international meeting in Havana, side by side with Philip Agee, the former CIA officer who reaped success as an author by giving away Agency secrets. He did work for the CIA for years, and just as most of Agee's allegations are accepted as authentic, there may be some nugget of fact within the story he has told. It is possible, too, to postulate that Wilcott has retained his CIA allegiance, and has told his Oswald story for a CIA purpose. The intelligence world delights in the use of disinformation, and it is conceivable that this unconvincing tale was designed to be so—for the express purpose of deflecting Congressional interest. It should certainly not deter continuing inquiry into Oswald's background. As it turns out, the general gist of Wilcott's allegation remains quite plausible.

It is worth pausing to consider Wilcott's speculation that American intelligence may have had "some kind of special 'handle' on him [Oswald]. Perhaps . . . they had discovered he had murdered someone or committed some other serious crime. . . ." A Marine did die in suspicious circumstances on the same base as Oswald, in the Philippines. One night a patroling guard, Martin Schrand, was found shot dead with his own weapon, and the inquest never established how it happened. The nature of the wound—Schrand had been shot under the right arm—and the fact that the gun was found lying some distance behind him seemed to rule out suicide. In the end the death was written off as accidental. Several Marines suspected foul play at the time, and one said— after the Kennedy assassination—that he had "heard a rumor to the effect that Oswald had been in some way responsible for the death."

There is no hard evidence that Lee Oswald really was involved in the death of Marine Schrand, but the incident may take on significance in the light of Wilcott's allegation about a CIA "handle" on Oswald. What it suggests about CIA recruiting methods is at least consistent with remarks made during an executive session of the Warren Commission. Speaking of the CIA and FBI, Chief Justice Warren said, "They and all other agencies do employ undercover men who are of terrible character." Former CIA Director Allen Dulles agreed. "Terribly bad characters," he said.

The CIA, of course, has always denied that it had anything to do with Oswald. In 1964 its then director, Kennedy appointee John McCone, said in testimony, "My examination has resulted in the conclusion that Lee Harvey Oswald was not an agent, employee, or informant of the Central Intelligence Agency. The Agency never contacted him, interviewed him, talked with him, or received or solicited any reports or information from him, or communicated with him directly or in any other manner." In 1979 the Assassinations Committee received similar assurances from CIA chiefs, including Richard Helms, who in 1963 was Deputy Director for Plans and responsible for CIA activities involving agents and informers. Helms had sworn, as early as 1964, that there was "no material in the Central Intelligence Agency, either in the records or in the mind of any of the individuals, that there was any contact had or even contemplated with him [Oswald]." He also assured the Commission that a member of its staff had been welcomed at CIA headquarters and given access to "the entire file." Today those assurances ring rather hollow.

In 1975 the Senate Intelligence Committee investigated CIA plots to murder a foreign head of state, Fidel Castro. Pressed on why he had not told even Director McCone about the plots, Richard Helms said lamely, "I guess I must have thought to myself, well this is going to look peculiar to him . . . this was, you know, not a very savory effort." Another witness was more forthright. He suggested that Helms kept quiet because he knew McCone opposed such assassination schemes on principle. When McCone gave his 1964 assurances about Oswald he had relied, for a key briefing, on Deputy Director Helms.

A document recently released makes nonsense of Helm's bland assertion that CIA files proved nobody at the Agency ever

considered contacting Oswald. In fact, one Soviet research department contemplated doing exactly that. The partially censored
memorandum, written three days after the Kennedy assassination,
says of Oswald, "Sometime in the summer of 1960 . . . we showed
intelligence interest."[42] The writer adds that he discussed "the
laying on of interviews through the Domestic Contacts Division or
other suitable channels. . . . I do not know what action developed
thereafter." As the Deputy Director responsible, Helms should
have known about this document when he made his assurances to
the Warren Commission.

Perhaps the most charitable interpretation of Helms' attitude
to Government inquiries came from Helms himself, in this 1975
exchange with a member of the Senate Intelligence Committee:

> SENATOR MORGAN: . . . you were charged with furnishing the
> Warren Commission information from the CIA, information
> that you thought relevant?
> HELMS: No, sir, I was instructed to reply to inquiries from the
> Warren Commission for information from the Agency. I was
> not asked to initiate any particular thing.
> SENATOR MORGAN: . . . in other words, if you weren't asked
> for it, you didn't give it.
> HELMS: That's right, sir.

A few years later Helms was pressed by Congress' Assassinations
Committee to explain why the Warren Commission was not told
about efforts to murder Fidel Castro. This time Helms shrugged
off the vital omission, saying merely, "I am sorry. It is an untidy
world." By that time some of Helms' "untidiness" had caught up
with him. In 1977 he pleaded *nolo contendere* to charges concerning testimony to another Senate committee. For making misleading statements on oath about the CIA's operations against President Allende of Chile, Helms was fined and given a suspended
sentence of two years. He professed to have been obeying the
higher authority of his intelligence loyalty oath. Helms has been
quoted as saying of himself and CIA colleagues, "We are honorable men. You simply have to trust us."

James Angleton, who was CIA Chief of Counterintelligence,

has come into this story before. Documents released in 1976 reveal that he once contacted FBI Assistant Director William Sullivan with some advice on how to deal with the Warren Commission. Angleton warned that the Commission was likely to put the same questions to both the CIA and the FBI to see whether it would receive conflicting answers. Two questions Angleton foresaw were:

"1) Was Oswald ever an agent of the CIA?" and

"2) Does the CIA have any evidence showing that a conspiracy existed to assassinate President Kennedy?"

Unlike his colleague Helms, Angleton's proposed replies were at least concise. As the "replies that will be given," he offered:

"1) No," and

"2) No."

James Angelton was at one stage responsible for CIA dealings with the Warren Commission. He testified recently that during the Commission's work he "informally" discussed the assassination with one of the Commissioners—naturally enough identified as Allen Dulles, the former CIA chief. It turns out that Commissioner Allen Dulles was in close touch with CIA officials throughout, perhaps too close for propriety. Another censored document, pried out of the CIA under the Freedom of Information Act, reveals that Dulles privately coached CIA officers on how best to field the question of whether Oswald had been an agent. According to an internal memorandum, Dulles "thought language which made it clear that Lee Harvey Oswald was never an employee or agent of CIA would suffice." The unidentified writer had no argument with that and commented, "I agreed with him that a *carefully phrased denial* of the charges of involvement with Oswald seemed most appropriate" (author's italics). A carefully phrased denial is what the Warren Commission got, and that is what was offered to the public. But did the Agency have every need to be careful with its phrasing?

The CIA readily admits that it holds a "201" file on Lee Oswald and that this is the "principal repository" for documents on the alleged assassin. For a while the very fact of this file's existence caused misplaced public excitement, on the supposition that a "201" file is assigned only to a CIA agent. Sadly for assassinologists determined to prove that Oswald was an agent, that simply is not true. Inquiries to independent specialists as well as former Agency officials confirm that a "201" file is one opened on any person in whom the CIA takes an interest. The fact that the Agency has one on Oswald does not mean that he was an agent, nor does it—necessarily—mean he was not. Today it is the fine detail of the CIA's handling of its Oswald "201" file which deserves attention. The CIA says it has 1,196 documents on Oswald, some of them many hundreds of pages long. It says the "201" file is "the principal repository" for all these documents. Two hundred and sixty of them are still classified, and those that are released are in some cases severely censored. It may be, however, that what is not in the file is more interesting than what is.

The existing Oswald "201" file was opened on December 9, 1960. The CIA has stated that this was done in response to five documents originated by other agencies—the FBI, the State Department, and the Navy—in the light of Oswald's queries about returning to the United States from the Soviet Union. This, however, was inconsistent with the fact that the file contains several State Department documents dated earlier, in 1959 and summer 1960. It is the delay in opening the file, over a year after Oswald's defection, which has seemed most odd to researchers. They insist that the Agency would have been sure to take an active interest in Oswald from the moment he arrived in Moscow announcing his intention of passing radar information of "special interest" to the Russians. It would have been logical to conclude that he was referring to information gleaned from his experience at Atsugi in Japan. Atsugi, of course, was a base for U-2 spy flights, and that was a most jealously guarded CIA secret. In 1979 Congress' Assassinations Committee concluded that the "201" file had in fact been opened following a request from the State Department for information regarding American defectors in general, an inquiry that came in only at the end of 1960. The opening of Oswald's file did coincide with the opening of files on several other defectors, and the Committee found that "201" files were often not opened until long after an individual's actual date of defection. Not all defectors, however, *announce* that they are offering radar secrets to a hostile foreign power. The current explanation remains unsatisfactory to many who suspect a relationship between Oswald and American intelligence. Nor will such doubts be dissipated by a further vacuum found in CIA files.

One obvious way for the CIA to have monitored Oswald's activities would have been by reading his mail. In 1976, during a study of CIA activity unrelated to the Kennedy assassination, the Senate Intelligence Committee established that—for years—the CIA intercepted and photographed letters passing between the Soviet Union and the United States. The mail-intercept program was in operation, specifically, during the months Lee Oswald was in the Soviet Union. Therefore, one might assume, CIA records should contain photocopies of mail sent and received by a defector who had offered secrets to his Soviet hosts. The reality is not that simple. Assassinations Committee staff were shown two index cards for Oswald in the records of the mail-intercept program, both stamped "Secret Eyes Only." The first, dated within two weeks of Oswald's first appearance at the American Embassy in Moscow, placed staff on the lookout for Oswald's mail. A note on the card, dated November 20, 1959, indicates that a name trace for Oswald in CIA files that day proved negative. It should, however, have reflected telegrams sent several weeks earlier in the wake of Oswald's defection. The really remarkable thing, though, is that the CIA's mail-intercept file contains only one solitary document as a result of all the vigilance—a letter sent to Oswald by his mother in 1961. Unfortunately for the CIA, we know—from copies kept by his family and so on—that Oswald sent or received more than *fifty* communications during his time in Russia. Why, then, does the CIA file contain only one? The Agency told the Assassinations Committee that its intercept program "only operated four days a week, and even then proceeded on a sampling basis." That is not the impression gleaned from the Senate Intelligence Committee study, which indicates a comprehensive spying operation. The Oswald intercept file is not plausible, and the Assassinations Committee report refers caustically only to what it "ostensibly" contains.

Those who believe Oswald was sent to the Soviet Union by some branch of American intelligence point out that Consul Richard Snyder, the official who interviewed Oswald at the American

Embassy in Moscow, was not the simple diplomat his title suggests. The left-wing publication *Who's Who in CIA* refers to him, quite independently of the Kennedy case, as having worked for the CIA since 1951. The implication is that he was a CIA officer, under diplomatic cover, during Oswald's stay in the Soviet Union. The CIA, and Snyder himself, say he worked for them for only a year in 1949. Congress' Assassinations Committee found, however, that Snyder's CIA file had been 'red-flagged" because of a "DCI [Director of Central Intelligence] statement and a matter of cover. . . ." The CIA explains this partially as a reference to statements on the Oswald case by Richard Helms, who later became CIA director; it cannot, however, explain the reference to "cover." The Assassinations Committee did not find this CIA explanation satisfactory and described it as "extremely troubling."

American embassies around the world are peppered with CIA men, just as Soviet embassies are filled with "Secretaries" and "Attachés" who are really KGB officers. If, as suspected, "Consul" Snyder was a CIA employee, it seems even more certain that Oswald's threatened treachery over radar secrets would have caused documented concern in CIA files. A likely answer is that there was such documentation but in some other fashion or under some other guise. Oswald's "201" file could be just a front, one which, among other things, can be produced publicly, without embarrassment, as The File on Oswald. Intelligence analysts point out that men on undercover assignments are rarely, if ever, linked with those projects under their real name. It is important to understand that intelligence covers are originally designed as just that, not to fool an avid public years later but to protect intelligence operations from detection at the time. Intelligence agencies indulge in a daily game of documentary deception, in which false names are used to mislead enemy agents who have penetrated the organization and even to protect one department's secrets from its colleague department down the corridor. Sometimes the name on the file may be real but the contents false, to divert attention from the subject's real activity. Whatever the truth about Oswald's "201" file, intelligence officials must be highly amused at the spectacle of busy assassination researchers squirreling away, hoping to learn some elusive truth from a "201" file. Another recently released document suggests only too clearly just how futile such efforts may be. It concerns a chilling CIA project code-named "ZR/RIFLE" and known within the CIA as "Executive Action."

In 1975, Intelligence Committee member Senator Walter Mondale, later Vice President of the United States, confirmed that "Executive Action" was conceived specifically to establish a "capability to perform assassinations." Some CIA officials—including Richard Helms—have claimed the plan was never activated, and the known evidence suggests it existed for operations against foreign targets. There is no evidence that "ZR/RIFLE" has anything to do with the assassination of President Kennedy, although it provides disturbing proof of CIA links with professional assassins. One of them, identified only by the code name "QJ/W/N," was—according to the Senate Intelligence Committee—"a foreign citizen with a criminal background recruited in Europe." Former CIA chief Richard Helms has said, "If you need somebody to carry out murder, I guess you had [this] man who might be prepared to carry it out."

In terms of CIA methods, some recently released papers from "ZR/RIFLE" files have a direct relevance to any study of Oswald and the CIA. These take the form of handwritten notes written by William Harvey, senior CIA officer. Discussing the sort of assassins the CIA would use, Harvey wrote, "Cover: planning should include provision for eliminating Sovs or Czechs in case of blow. . . . Use *nobody* who has dealt with criminals; others will just be aware of pitfalls or [illegible] factors such as freedom to travel, wanted lists, etc. . . . *Should have phoney 201 in files to backstop this, documents therein forged and backdated. . . .*" (author's italics).

Harvey writes so casually about the creation of phoney "201" files that there is no reason to suppose he was proposing anything out of the ordinary in CIA terms. The significance of Harvey's reference to "phoney 201" files is obvious. If Lee Oswald was anything other than the misguided young man of the official version, his "201" file may not be worth the paper it is written on. A former senior officer whose business it was to work with such files has no doubt there was monkey business with the record on Oswald. He is Colonel Fletcher Prouty, who as "focal point officer" between the Pentagon and the CIA at the very period of Oswald's Marine service and defection to Russia. He has, moreover, a special knowledge of U-2 spy-plane operations and the Atsugi air base where Oswald served while in Japan.

Colonel Prouty told me in 1979, "The whole idea of 'cover' and 'cover arrangements' is so foreign to most people that it is very hard to unscramble. This is all very basic to Agency work. . . . First of all, Oswald enlisted as a Marine, then he went to the super-secret Marine unit at Atsugi. This put him into the CIA organization. Usually some men would be needed and they would be selected by the CIA. Then, if they volunteered for duty, they would be brought into the Agency—a rather detailed process." At that point, the colonel explained, the record of a CIA volunteer enters a many-layered world of make-believe. He revealed that it "would give the man a Marine file, in other words his regular file, because he would have told his friends, etc., that he was in the Marine Corps. They would have to keep that file up—it would have to show promotions and duty assignment changes like a regular Marine. However, since he was a member of the CIA he would also get a CIA "201" file. This would be the file of all of his work in the Agency, and this would include all of his duty in the station at Atsugi. There he was really a CIA man under the cover of a Marine. So he has two files. Then on top of that he might need a civilian file to account for things he did, or may have done, as a civilian, so that when he went back to civilian life, for the Agency, he would have a file which he could use to account for the continuity of his life. In a sense all three files would require some fabrication. . . . This triple file system permits the Agency to use a surprising amount of flexibility with certain agents. My office kept such files either with the CIA—agreeing with their entries, etc.— or independently. For example, when a man came out of the CIA tour of duty, we had to make his records appear to show that he had a normal tour of duty without the CIA period in his records. It is complicated, but it works. . . ."

Colonel Prouty says flatly, "Lee Oswald was not an ordinary Marine. He was a Marine on a cover assignment. . . . It is obvious that much of the material in the Oswald cover file is wrong. It could be human error, though I doubt it, or it could be some kind of obfuscation. There are thousands of people who have had such files—that is, life records—done, and it is all mixed up. . . . "With the Oswald case in mind, Congress' Assassinations Committee found it "disturbing" to learn that CIA Executive Action officers contemplated the use of faked "201" files and forged documents. The Committee noted that "Agency files would not always indicate whether an individual was affiliated with the Agency in any capacity. . . ." The Committee hoped it would have picked up any inconsistencies by comparing the file record with replies from CIA interviewees. Nevertheless, in the light of the documentary maze conjured up by Colonel Prouty, it is quite possible that the CIA Oswald file is a fiction.

In 1964, during a Warren Commission executive session, this exchange took place between Congressman Hale Boggs and former CIA Director Allen Dulles:

DULLES: There is a hard thing to disprove, you know. How do you disprove a fellow was not your agent? How do you disprove it?

BOGGS: You could disprove it, couldn't you?

DULLES: No . . . I never knew how to disprove it.

BOGGS: Did you have agents about whom you had no record whatsoever?

DULLES: The record may not be on paper. But *on paper would have hieroglyphics that only two people know what they meant, and nobody outside of the agency would know*; and you could say this meant the agent and somebody else could say it meant another agent. (Author's italics)

Dulles added another possibility to his comments on the inscrutability of CIA records. Asked whether, if Oswald was an agent, a CIA chief would know who had hired him, the former director replied obliquely, "Someone might have done it *without authority*. . . ." Dulles opens the door to the notion that Oswald could have been hired at low level and without formal backing, in a way that left no identifiable trace in the record. In 1978 a CIA officer told the Assassinations Committee there was indeed a "remote possibility that an individual could have been run by someone as part of a vest pocket [private or personal] operation without other Agency officials knowing about it." The former deputy chief of the Agency's Soviet Russia clandestine activities section, on the other hand, said Oswald was never part of any such operation. Looking for Oswald at the CIA must, nevertheless, be compared to a probe in a black hole in space. On the Assassinations Committee, which had this unenviable mission as an official task, some staff never ceased to feel that the CIA was stubbornly clinging to information on Oswald and the facts surrounding the President's murder. That said, America's obsession with the sins of the CIA may have diverted attention from a different focus on Oswald's function.

When CIA Director McCone denied any CIA connection with Oswald, he ended by saying, "When I use the term 'Agency,' I mean the Central Intelligence Agency, of course." Although somebody in the CIA would most probably have known about it, Lee Oswald may have been used by a quite separate intelligence agency. Colonel Prouty, with his Pentagon background, has explained how recruitment by one agency can result in the fudging of records in several diverse places. The Assassinations Committee noted that, with the destruction of his Army intelligence file, "the question of Oswald's possible affiliation with military intelligence could not be fully resolved." The hint of this other option was raised in the testimony of none other than former CIA chief Richard Helms.

In an appearance before the Assassinations Committee Helms was pressed on whether the CIA would not have asked the Defense Department how much potential damage Oswald could cause by his defection. He replied, "I would have thought the feeling would be that that was the Navy Department's responsibility. . . ." Helms hammered home this point about the Navy's responsibility; it was not an inadvertent remark. As a member of the Marine Corps, Lee Oswald was a Navy man, and there are oddities in the record of the Navy's handling of the case. Inquiry to the Navy three days after his appearance at the U.S. Embassy in Moscow evoked an interesting reply. An FBI report states that "No derogatory information was contained in the USMC [Marine Corps] files concerning Oswald," which suggests that the corps, synonymous around the world with red-blooded American patriotism, had made no note of Oswald's self-avowed Marxism and his study of the Russian language.

In Moscow, when Oswald told the Embassy he was in touch with Soviet officials about giving away radar secrets, the official reaction was astonishingly relaxed. There is no indication that Consul Snyder, the official who received Oswald, made any effort to dissuade the young defector from his treacherous intention. Back in the United States, the FBI learned from the Office of Naval Intelligence that "no action against him was contemplated in this matter." Surely, even if Oswald was out of its reach, the Navy would have had action very much in mind, against the day it could lay hands on the defector.[43] Oswald was, by his own admission, a would-be traitor to his country.

While at one level the Navy appeared blithely unconcerned, at another it seems to have gone through the motions of concerned reaction.[44] In California, where Oswald last served, aircraft call signs, codes, radio and radar frequencies were changed within weeks. Oswald's former associates remember being questioned about him by visiting officials in civilian clothes. It looked as though the defection was being taken seriously, but once again there is an apparent inconsistency. According to the former head of counterintelligence at the Defense Intelligence Agency, Colonel Thomas Fox, "A net damage assessment, indicating the possible access Oswald had to classified information, would have to be undertaken. . . ." Although this was standard procedure, and although Oswald had worked on highly secret bases, the Navy now admits that no "formal damage assessment was conducted."

In his incisive analysis of Oswald's defection, Edward Epstein states that until that defection, only two other enlisted men had defected from the American armed forces to a Communist country. As with Oswald, there were reasons for suspicion that both had been in contact with Soviet or East German intelligence. A net damage assessment was conducted after both defections. In 1960, after Oswald's defection, damage assessments were also made in the cases of at least two other low-ranking military defectors. The Navy has not explained why the Oswald affair was treated differently.

For a long time after Oswald's defection the Navy bureaucracy continued to act as though Oswald was still without blemish—or at least so the known record suggests. It was only in September 1960, a whole year later, that the Marine Corps Reserve gave him an "undesirable discharge." To add to the confusion, Oswald's "201" file at the CIA shows Oswald's occupation as "Radar Operator, U.S. Marine Corps, as of 1960," even though Oswald had signed out of active service in autumn 1959. All this may reflect nothing more than the slip-ups of a creaky military bureaucracy. If so, the Oswald case has more than its fair share.

In 1978 I interviewed Gerry Hamming,[45] a former Marine sergeant who served in radar control at Atsugi air base shortly before Oswald. Hemming claims that he was himself recruited by Naval Intelligence at the end of his own time in the Marines and that he met Oswald in January 1959 at the Cuban consulate on the outskirts of Los Angeles. The time fits the start of Oswald's stay at the Santa Ana base, near Los Angeles, which followed his unexpected and unexplained lone transfer home from Japan. The place of the alleged encounter, the Cuban consulate, fits with Oswald's interest in Cuba as expressed in talks with his barrack mate Delgado and specifically with Oswald's claim that he was in touch with Cuban officials. The year 1959 was a turning point in Cuba's relationship with the United States. Fidel Castro's revolution, a year earlier, had initially been welcomed by Washington as a change for the democratic better. It was only later, as the regime showed its true Marxist colors, that relations first soured and then turned to open hostility. Gerry Hemming was to become well known in the Sixties for his links with CIA-backed anti-Castro exiles; but in January 1959, as American policy hung in the balance, he was still working with Castro's people. This is how Hemming describes his encounter with Oswald: "He was attempting to get in with the representatives of Castro's new government, the consular officials in Los Angeles. And at that point in time I felt that he was a threat to me and to those Castro people, that he was an informant or some type of agent working for somebody. He was rather young, but I feel that he was too knowledgeable in certain things not to be an agent of law enforcement or of Military Intelligence, or Naval Intelligence." Hemming says he gained his impression "because of the questions he was asking and by his obvious knowledge of *my* background. At a first meeting, not thirty minutes after we first met, he automatically not assumed but stated that *I'm* a radar operator and named the outfit *he* was attached to and details not every Marine would know—the crypto, the abbreviation of the outfit he was attached to. He obviously stated it knowing my background. Somebody had briefed him; somebody told him to approach me." Hemming explained that he believed Oswald's service at the Atsugi base made him a likely recruit for intelligence: "As a radar operator, living in a highly restricted area, he would have been fraternizing with CIA contract employees. Sooner or later he would fraternize with a case officer, one or more, that handled these contract employees. He would be a prime candidate for recruitment because of job skills, and expertise, and the fact that they could personally vouch for him and give him a security clearance. . . ."

Hemming offers only his personal opinion, based on a gut feeling at the time, that Oswald was involved with one of the intelligence services when he met him in 1959. Beyond the curiosities and inconsistencies we have already identified, there is no way to pin down the nature of Oswald's role when he departed for Moscow. One former senior CIA officer, however, not only finds it plausible that Oswald worked for a branch of American intelligence but says it fits his own knowledge of efforts to infiltrate Russia at the relevant period.

Victor Marchetti resigned from the CIA in 1969, disillusioned with the Agency after fourteen years' service. As a staff officer in the Office of the Director, and an executive assistant to the Deputy Director, he is one of the few who speaks not only scathingly but with knowledge of how the Agency worked in the late Fifties and the Sixties. Marchetti has written a book, regarded as highly authoritative, which the CIA went to great lengths to prevent being published. The Agency's opposition did achieve the dubious success of making it the first book in American history to be censored before publication, and the publishers accordingly left the final text sprinkled with gaps where CIA scissors had been at work. The censorship is in itself ironic testimony to its author's qualifications. Marchetti's explanation of the relationship between the CIA and the military intelligence agencies—such as the Office of Naval Intelligence—helps the outsider understand the infrastructure in which the Oswald case may be enmeshed. Marchetti writes: "Although the CIA has had since its creation exclusive responsibility for carrying out overseas espionage operations for the collection of national intelligence, the various military intelligence agencies and the intelligence units of American forces stationed abroad have retained the right to seek out tactical information for their own departmental requirements. . . . The military intelligence agencies have consistently sought to acquire information through their own secret agents." Marchetti's exposition may also explain how, if Oswald was some sort of agent, the CIA was able to deny accurately that he had anything to do with the Agency. He writes: "To avoid duplication and proliferation of agents, all of these espionage missions are supposed to be coordinated with the CIA. But the military often fail to do this because they know the CIA would not give its approval, or because an arrangement has been previously worked out to the effect that as long as the military stay out of CIA's areas of interest, they can operate on their own. . . . The tribalism that plagues the intelligence community is at its worst in the military intelligence agencies. . . ."

Marchetti wrote this several years ago, in a general context quite separate from the subject of Lee Harvey Oswald or his possible use as a "fake" defector. I contacted Marchetti in 1978 when I became aware that he had specialist knowledge of Soviet affairs. He was recruited into the CIA from university, where he had majored in Soviet studies and history, and at the time of Oswald's defection he held a post in the Agency team analyzing Soviet military activities. In this capacity he was aware officially, and sometimes from private contacts, of Naval Intelligence operations. I asked Marchetti specifically about independent Naval Intelligence espionage operations against the Soviet Union, and his answer was startling. He said, "At the time, in 1959, the United States was having real difficulty in acquiring information out of the Soviet Union; the technical systems had, of course, not developed to the point that they are at today, and we were resorting to all sorts of activities. One of these activities was an ONI [Office of Naval Intelligence] program which involved three dozen, maybe forty, young men who were made to appear disenchanted, poor, American youths who had become turned off and wanted to see what communism was all about. Some of these people lasted only a few weeks. They were sent into the Soviet Union, or into eastern Europe, with the specific intention the Soviets would pick them up and 'double' them if they suspected them of being U.S. agents, or recruit them as KGB agents. They were trained at various naval installations both here and abroad, but the operation was being run out of Nag's Head, North Carolina."

No other former American intelligence officer of Marchetti's background has talked publicly about such a plan to put false defectors into Russia. It fits the Oswald case so well one might suspect Marchetti had dreamed up the project to fit the characteristics of the alleged assassin. On the other hand it could just be that Oswald was spotted as a candidate tailor-made for the ONI operation and turned around to a point where he was prepared to take part. Marchetti, who also served for a while with CIA's Clandestine Services department, finds that notion quite plausible. He drew my attention to an incident that followed Oswald's arrest, one he thinks bears out his suspicion and does remain unexplained.

On November 22, 1963, once Oswald was safely installed in a cell on the fifth floor of the Dallas City Hall, Police Chief Curry gave instructions that the prisoner should be allowed all the usual rights and privileges. According to routine Dallas police reports, Oswald asked to use the telephone on Saturday, the day after the assassination. The police record shows that he was allowed to do so at least twice, at about 4:00 P.M. and 8:00 P.M. Apparently he twice reached Ruth Paine, the woman who owned the house where Oswald's wife, Marina, was living, and talked to her about his search for legal assistance. He also "failed to complete" another call. According to one of the switchboard operators, he also tried to make a call later that night. The operator, Mrs. Troon, remembers the incident because of the unusual circumstances. She says that her colleague, Mrs. Swinney, had been forewarned that law-enforcement officers—she thinks it may have been Secret

Servicemen—would be coming to listen in on an Oswald call. Sure enough two men arrived, showed identification, and were shown into a room next to the switchboard. At about 10:45 P.M. a red light blinked on the panel, showing that someone was placing a call from the jail telephone booth. Both telephone operators rushed to plug in, and in the event Mrs. Swinney handled the call, with Mrs. Troon listening in avidly. According to Mrs. Troon, a curious thing then occurred. Operator Swinney spoke to the two officers eavesdropping in the next room and told them Oswald was placing the expected call. As Mrs. Troon tells it: "I was dumbfounded at what happened next. Mrs. Swinney opened the key to Oswald and told him, 'I'm sorry, the number doesn't answer.' She then unplugged and disconnected Oswald without ever really trying to put the call through. A few moments later Mrs. Swinney tore the page off her notation pad and threw it into the wastepaper basket." Mrs. Troon says she later retrieved the note referring to the Oswald call, and kept a copy as a souvenir. Recent research, including inquiries by Congress' Assassinations Committee, indicates that—assuming Mrs. Troon's record is accurate, Oswald intended to call a man named "Hurt" in Raleigh, North Carolina. The note lists two alternative numbers, which do relate to listed subscribers of that name. Both men, contacted today, deny all knowledge of the Oswald call. There has been concern, however, because one of the two—John D. Hurt—served in U.S. Military Intelligence during World War II. The Chief Counsel of Congress' Assassinations Committee, Professor Blakey, says, "It was an outgoing call, and therefore I consider it very troublesome material. The direction in which it went was deeply disturbing."*

Former CIA officer Victor Marchetti observes that the Oswald call was directed at a number in the same general area as the North Carolina base where—says Marchetti—U.S. Naval Intelligence once planned infiltration missions into the Soviet Union. For all the mass of minute detail about Oswald's life, and although we have his address book. Oswald had no known contacts in North Carolina. Unless further research resolves the mystery, this Oswald call remains yet another loose end in the assassination story.

---

* Some theorize that the aborted call was incoming; not an attempt by Oswald to call out.

In the face of a serious claim that U.S. intelligence was engaged in a scheme to get agents into Russia, the record of American defections deserves scrutiny. State Department documents, coupled with fresh Assassinations Committee research, do indeed provide food for thought. It is reported that, in all the fourteen years between 1945 and 1959, only two American enlisted men defected to the Soviet Union or Eastern Europe. In the eighteen months up to 1960, however, a good number of the known defectors either went over direct from the military or had sensitive backgrounds. In a sudden rash of turncoats, no less than five were Army men stationed in West Germany,[46] and two were former Naval men and employees of the National Security Agency—the top-secret department charged with breaking foreign codes and ciphers. Of the civilians who went to the Soviet Union, one was a former official of the Office of Strategic Services (the forerunner of the CIA), another was a former Air Force major, and a third a former Navy enlisted man currently working for the Rand Development Corporation. Then of course there was Lee Oswald, fresh out of the Marines. It is not known for sure what eventually became of all these individuals. Two are believed to have died in the Soviet Union, and the CIA regards the two National Security Agency cases as "too sensitive" to impart to Congress' Assassinations Committee. It may be significant that of the remaining seven, four are known to have returned to the United States after a few years.

An assessment of the claim that U.S. intelligence was sending out false defectors must take account of the sudden increase in the number of Americans with Government or Defense Department backgrounds who went to Russia just before or after Oswald. There has been insufficient investigation into the cases of the five Army men who chose to cross the border. For the outsider, research in this area is extremely difficult—not least because genuine defectors who return home, let alone possible spies, have understandably stayed out of the public eye. It might be especially useful, however, to locate the Rand Development Corporation employee who went over in 1959.

The Rand employee was Robert Webster, a young plastics expert who failed to join colleagues returning to the United States after working at an American exhibition in Moscow. He had been, at the time, employed by the Rand Development Corporation, one of the first American companies to negotiate with the Soviet Union for the purchase of technical products and information. Rand Development was, on the face of the evidence, quite separate from the better known Rand Corporation, the CIA-funded organization for which Daniel Ellsberg was working when he copied the "Pentagon Papers."* Nevertheless, there is some mystery about Rand Development. Research in the Seventies established that the company's former New York City address was just across Lexington Avenue from the Rand Corporation offices, a factor which may or may not be mere coincidence. A Congressional Expense Inquiry shows that Rand Development held several CIA contracts. The president of Rand Development, Henry Rand, has been identified as a senior veteran of the Office of Strategic Services—or OSS—the forerunner of the CIA. So too was another top official of the company, George Bookbinder. Rand Development's onetime Washington representative, Christopher Bird, was a CIA agent. At the time of Robert Webster's defection, both Rand and Bookbinder, in the company of U.S. Consul Snyder, met with Webster in Moscow when he declared his intention of remaining in Russia. There are some intriguing parallels between the Soviet odysseys of Webster and Oswald.

Webster told American officials of his intention to defect less than two weeks before Oswald did the same thing. Webster, a former Navy man as was Oswald, was put to work by the Russians in the trade in which he specialized. Webster did not actually marry a Soviet wife; he already had a wife in the United States. He did, however, take a Soviet common-law wife, and the couple had a child born in the Soviet Union. It is believed that the Soviet woman was an agent for the KGB. Webster finally left the Soviet Union, apparently disillusioned with the Socialist paradise, a fortnight before Oswald.

Lee Oswald either actually met Webster or learned something about him. Years later in America, Oswald's Russian wife Marina told an acquaintance that her husband had defected to the Soviet

* Rand Development Corporation was formed by the Rand family. The name "Rand Corporation" is a title made from the contraction of the words "Research and Development."

Union after working at an American exhibition in Moscow. That was the Webster scenario, not the Oswald story. In 1961, while arranging his own return to the United States, Oswald made an intriguing inquiry. According to a recent report, he "asked about the fate of a young man called Webster who had come to the Soviet Union shortly before he did. . . ." Webster is said to have told American officials on his return that he never had any contact with Oswald. Whether or not there is a connection between the two apparent defectors, Webster's account of his encounters with Soviet and American intelligence would be invaluable. If there was a project to place temporary agents as "defectors" in Russia to gather further information, it is of course possible some may never have turned up in the published official record. A recently obtained CIA document reveals the existence of one other American who was in Russia at the same time as Oswald.

The subject of the document—an internal memorandum—is an American citizen and his "Possible Connection to Investigation of Lee Harvey and Marina Oswald." I shall call the man "X," as his name and file number are everywhere blanked out in the released document. The memorandum says that "X" was in Russia in 1958 and 1959 and spent several months of both years in the city of Minsk, where Oswald was later to live while in the Soviet Union. He had clearly left the Soviet Union by 1961, when he was "interviewed" by a CIA officer in the Danish capital of Copenhagen. According to the document, "X" claimed to have been something of an oddity in Minsk since he was the only American residing there at the time. As such, he claimed to have attracted to himself a group of young Soviets who displayed a great curiosity about the standard of living in the United States and Western Europe. Those interests centered around girls, cars, having a good time, and listening to jazz music on the Voice of America. Among these young Soviets, according to "X," was a young man named Igor (LNU),* whose father was a Soviet army general." It is interesting that Oswald also reportedly considered himself to be an oddity as the only American residing in Minsk, and attracted more or less the same type young Soviets as did

* Last Name Unknown.

'X.' " It should be noted that Oswald listed among his close friends in Minsk a young Soviet named Pavel Golovachev, whose father ostensibly was a Soviet army general.

Much of the last part of this memorandum is censored, possibly to protect the address of "X," by now back in the United States. However, yet another tantalizing sentence does survive. It reads: "Both Oswald and 'X' had served as enlisted men and technicians in the United States Marine Corps."

The city of Minsk, where both Oswald and "X" spent many months, was a major industrial city filled with economic targets of great interest to Western intelligence. Given the Marine background of both men, the timing of their presence in the Soviet Union, and the still unexplained inconsistencies in the official Oswald story, there can be no out-of-hand rejection of the claim that U.S. Naval Intelligence was running a fake defector program. Oswald may have been part of it, or a tool of some other branch of American intelligence. The main objection to this theory is a fair one: surely a twenty-year-old was a poor candidate for a mission behind the Iron Curtain? It is perhaps not sufficient to counter that youth and apparent inexperience provided a good cover. I would, however, hazard a personal speculation. While Oswald may have been poor material for spying in the usual sense, he might have been used simply to gather information on how the Soviets handled young military defectors. At a time of increasing concern about defections this would have answered an intelligence need. If that notion is accepted, a second vital question arises. Was Oswald perhaps an unwitting tool, a genuine left-wing defector whose movements were observed and monitored from the very beginning? Or was he consciously an agent, on a limited mission which an Oswald could, in spite of his youth, be expected to handle? Certainly, the idea that Oswald was somebody's agent has not been the private preserve of Kennedy conspiracy theorists.

Otto Otepka, the controversial former Chief Security Officer of the State Department, says that in 1963 his office engaged in a study of American "defectors," because neither the CIA nor military agencies such as Naval Intelligence would reveal which were authentic and which were intelligence plants. One of the cases being studied was that of Lee Harvey Oswald, Only five months before the Kennedy assassination, according to Otepka, the State Department was still uncertain whether Oswald was or had been "one of ours or one of theirs."

While the inconsistencies and contradictions in the Oswald case remain unexplained, the suspicion remains that, in some sense, Oswald was "one of ours." As we shall see, it is a suspicion borne out above all by new evidence of his later activities and connections in the months preceding the assassination.

Of course, when the Warren Commission asked the CIA and FBI whether they had links with Oswald, both replied in the negative. The Defense Department, which covered military and naval intelligence, also affirmed that Oswald "was never an informant or agent of any intelligence agency" in the Department's jurisdiction. Notably, however, the department failed to respond adequately to a specific Commission request that all records on Oswald should be handed over. The Warren Commission was never supplied with the Army Intelligence file on Oswald. This was in spite of the fact that—as we saw earlier in connection with the "Hidell" alias—one definitely did exist. That is the file which, as the Assassinations Committee discovered to its great concern, has since been destroyed. This leaves a major area of doubt, not least because a military agency was the most likely to have first spotted Marine Oswald, radar technician.[47]

From the moment of his arrival in the Soviet Union, whether or not he set off as the lone renegade of the official version, Oswald became an obvious focus of interest for both Soviet and American intelligence. The denials, by both sides, are highly unconvincing.

CHAPTER 10

Mischief from Moscow

*A Communist must be prepared to . . . resort to all
sorts of schemes and stratagems, employ illegitimate
methods, conceal the truth. . . .*

—Lenin

Oct. 21

Eve. 6:00 Recive word from police offial. I must leave
country tonight at 8.0 p.m. as visa expirs. I am shocked!! My
dreams! I retire to my room. I have $100 left. I have waited for
2 year to be accepted. My fondes dreams are shattered because
of a petty official; because of bad planning I planned to much!
7.0 p.m. I decide to end it. Soak rist in cold water to numb
the pain. Than slash my left wrist. Then plaug wrist into bath-
tub of hot water. I think 'when Rimma comes at 8. to find me
dead it will be a great shock. somewhere a violin plays, as I
wacth my life whirl away. . . .

This is supposedly Oswald's own account—complete with
spelling disability—of a suicide attempt he made in his Moscow
hotel after learning that the Russians did not want to accept him. It
is taken from an "Historic Diary," found years later among Oswald's effects in Dallas, which purports to be his own memoir of
his time in Russia. The "Diary," along with Soviet hospital records, relates that Oswald was rescued in the nick of time by
"Rimma"—apparently Rimma Shirokova, Oswald's Intourist
guide—was rushed to the Botkin Hospital, and spent a week
recovering there. It was after this that Oswald was to march into

the American Embassy to hand in his passport and was followed by Soviet officials to stay on in Russia. The Soviet Government has refused United States requests to interview Russian citizens with knowledge of Oswald. It provided only fifteen documents as the ostensible record of his stay in the Soviet Union.[48] These, along with the Oswald "Diary" and statements by his widow, Marina, represent the record of a period likely to remain obscure forever. The Soviet papers and the "Diary" are themselves dubious documents.

It is not the chronically poor spelling which raises problems with the "Diary." Oswald does seem to have *suffered* from a dyslexia-type spelling disability, although his various writings show intelligence and sometimes considerable insight. It is the narrative itself which raises suspicions. The dramatic opening about suicide, to a violin accompaniment, is peppered with inconsistencies, and these may be the first clues to Oswald's real treatment by his Soviet hosts.

Oswald's account says he was not found, bleeding, in his room until eight in the evening. Botkin Hospital records—some of the few documents on Oswald's Soviet interlude released by the Russian authorities—have Oswald's Soviet interlude released by the Russian authoriities—have Oswald being admitted hours earlier, at 4:00 P.M. The hospital version says: "The patient does not speak Russian. One could judge only by his gestures and facial expression that he had no complaints." This hardly sounds like the Oswald who, months earlier in California, was able to talk for two hours in passable Russian. After the assassination a scar was noticed on Oswald's left wrist, but the CIA were doubtful whether it really represented a suicide attempt. A document released in 1976 shows the Agency was so suspicious that it actually recommended exhuming Oswald's body to take another look. In his "Diary," Oswald writes disparagingly about an "elderly American" he supposedly encountered in the hospital. When they had talked together, the other American was allegedly distrustful of Oswald because he had not registered as a tourist at the American Embassy and because he was evasive about his reasons for being in Moscow. Sadly for the author or authors of the Oswald journal, it proved possible to check this reference because so few Americans passed through Moscow hospitals in those days. After the assassination, FBI inquiries did trace an elderly American who had been admitted to Botkin Hospital at the time. He was a New York businessman, and when questioned he was quite sure he had *not* encountered Lee Oswald or any other American during his stay in the hospital.

Oswald was not the only American defector to spend time in the hospital after his arrival in the Soviet Union. For others hospitalization has been a convenient excuse for a time in which the KGB, the main Soviet intelligence organization, conducted interrogations. It is very possible that this was the method used to process Oswald, the latest arrival in a minor torrent of defectors. After the assassination, predictably enough, a Soviet source insisted to American intelligence that the KGB had done no such thing. The source was Yuri Nosenko, the KGB officer who himself defected to the United States just two months after the assassination, claiming that he had personally monitored the Oswald defection case.[49] He told CIA interrogators that the KGB had not even taken the trouble to question Oswald in depth because its officers considered him "unstable." Nosenko's story is full of holes; it will be considered in more detail later. Oswald himself, when he visited the Embassy before returning to the United States, also declared that the Russians had never grilled him about his knowledge of U.S. radar or any other military secrets. None of this can be taken seriously. CIA officials are unanimous in saying that the Russians would have been interested in Oswald simply because he was a Marine, even if he had not been offering to peddle radar secrets. Former CIA career officer Harry Rositzke, who specialized in studying Soviet intelligence methods, writes, "The favored KGB targets are junior employees of the U.S. government, both male and female: code clerks, secretaries and *Marine guards in the embassies, enlisted men in the armed forces*. There are, in the Soviet view, not only 'second-class citizens' but politically unsophisticated and lonely." (Author's italics.) Rositzke makes it clear that Soviet agents go to great lengths to contact such U.S. personnel around the world. The notion that they would not bother to question a Marine like Oswald on their own doorstep and with his experience on a U-2 base, is untenable. Oswald's "Historic Diary" looks very much as though there was a Soviet hand at the writer's elbow. As a recent analysis points out, there is a major question mark over when and why it was written.

Tests by hand-writing experts, including document examination performed by Congress' Assassinations Committee, reveal that the "Diary" is written almost entirely on the same paper and in writing which appear continuous. It seems that, instead of being written in installments, it was written in one or two sittings. Author Edward Epstein has noted that in a reference to Oswald's visit to the Embassy with his passport on October 31, 1959, the journal mentions that John McVickar had taken over from Richard Snyder as "head consul." That change did not take place till nearly two years later, when Oswald was about to leave Russia. Elsewhere the account refers to Oswald's pay during his Russian employment in new rubles. The ruble was not revalued until a year *after* the date referred to in the entry. These and other details show that the "Diary" was almost certainly written long after the events described.[50] Why?

The purpose of the "Diary" may have been to sketch in Oswald's Russian episode in the barest terms, omitting any intelligence involvement by the Soviet authorities.

By his own account, Oswald's first Soviet contacts were his Intourist guides and interpreters, who then, as now, are known to be KGB agents or informers. There are no details of where the Russians kept Oswald for a period of at least six weeks, beginning around the end of November 1959, when it was noted that he had left his hotel room.[51] During this early period Oswald was most probably interviewed by KGB officials, repeatedly and in depth. His Soviet interrogators would have labored not only to extract any useful information Oswald could give them; they also had to assess why Oswald had come over and whether they were being given good information. As events were to show, in Oswald's case these questions were central to discovering Oswald's real role— and this is one still unanswered today: was Oswald a genuine defector blabbing what he knew from his military experience, or was he a tool, perhaps unwitting, of U.S. intelligence?

Whatever the Soviets concluded, they decided to move Oswald out of Moscow in January 1960. He was issued with an

identity card for a stateless person—although he was technically
still an American citizen—and eventually moved to the city of
Minsk, 450 miles away. To cover his expenses Oswald was given
5,000 rubles by the "Red Cross," which in Russia is simply a
euphemism for a post of the MVD, the internal security organization. In what may be a clue to an awareness of his real function,
Oswald was to write after leaving the Soviet Union: ". . . after a
certain time, after the Russians had assured themselves that I was
really the naive American and believed in Communism, they
arranged for me to receive a certain amount of money each
month." In Minsk, Oswald was launched into the most luxurious
and enjoyable stage of his whole life. Both from Oswald's "Diary"
and from photographs brought home to the United States, we
know that Oswald was given the sort of accommodation which,
certainly in 1960, was beyond an ordinary worker's wildest
dreams. He had a roomy apartment with balconies overlooking
the river, fully equipped with what Soviet citizens would regard as
luxuries. He was given work as an "assembler" by the Byelo-
russian Radio and Television factory, and the combination of his
wages and the continuing "Red Cross" allowance provided Oswald with more money than he could spend. Oswald himself wrote
about affairs with five local girls, and he spent evening after
evening, a girl on his arm, going to the movies, the theater, or the
opera. As Oswald himself wrote in his "Diary," he was "living
big."

There may also have been a more serious side to Oswald's life
in Minsk. FBI Director J. Edgar Hoover was one day to wonder
aloud to the Warren Commission about the rumored existence of
"an espionage training school outside of Minsk." In fact, the CIA
had been told there was a spy school in Minsk as long ago as 1947,
and information since the Kennedy assassination has confirmed
the existence of a training school with one-way windows protected
by a high wall. This establishment was located close to the Minsk
Foreign Language Institute, and in one of his sets of notes Oswald
seems to have gone out of his way to obscure the fact that he had
been to the language school.[52] But nothing in Oswald's Russian
odyssey has attracted such durable concern as his marriage to
Marina, the girl he met in Minsk and eventually brought home to
America.

After the assassination, Marina Oswald gave the Warren commission the following sketch of her life. She said she was a war baby who had never known her father and lost her mother while still a young student. In 1959, she said, she qualified as a pharmacist but left work after only one day. In the wake of her mother's death, she moved to Minsk to live with her mother's brother and his wife and took a job at the Third Clinical Hospital. She lived an active social life, had male friends, and went out a great deal—to the opera and to dances. According to Marina and to Oswald's written account, her meeting with the young American defector was a chance encounter at a trade-union dance in Minsk. It happened in mid-March 1961—that much is agreed—but Marina's memory is remarkably foggy on other points a woman could be expected to remember. Take, for example, the question of who introduced her to Oswald at that first meeting. Warren Commissioner staff, working on a combination of Marina's early testimony and Oswald's "Historic Diary," decided the Soviet Cupid was one Yuri Mereginsky, a lecturer's son who knew both Oswald and Marina already. Marina's ghosted biography says he was a medical student. With KGB manipulation in mind, Congress' Assassinations Committee thought his identity an important detail and asked Marina about it on several occasions.[53] The first time Marina said she did not remember anybody called Mereginsky. The second time she said she did remember the name, that she met him again subsequently, and that Lee used to mention his name "occasionally." Finally, at a public hearing just a few weeks later, Marina's memory had gone wholly blank. Asked if she remembered who had introduced them, she replied flatly, 'No, I don't." One might imagine, investigatory interest apart, that Marina would recall vividly—perhaps with resentment—the person whose introduction caused such a drastic change in her life. It may be that Mr. Mereginsky has been a fiction all along, or that detail about him would stir a hornet's nest of information.

Marina says Oswald spoke Russian so well at their first meeting that, although he had an accent, she thought he merely came from another part of the Soviet Union. That first meeting lasted about three hours, and there was a further meeting at another dance. Then, when Oswald went into the hospital to have his adenoids out, Marina supposedly visited him regularly. According to her, the antiseptic atmosphere had the curious effect of sparking an instant urge in Oswald to marry her. On this most feminine subject, Marina's tale is once again cockeyed. She has said Oswald asked her to be his "fiancée" while he was still in the hospital and popped the question seriously just one month after their first meeting. She told the Assassinations Committee, though, that the proposal came "a month and a half" before the actual wedding. That is odd indeed—it would mean that Oswald asked for Marina's hand the very moment he met her. The couple were married on April 30, just six weeks after their alleged first meeting. In the context of such a whirlwind courtship, it does not seem too much to expect the bride to remember—within a week or so—when she said "Yes."

Within a month or so of the marriage, according to Marina's story, Oswald announced that he wanted to return to the United States. After correspondence with the American Embassy in Moscow, he was to retrieve the passport he had left there after his defection. Marina, for her part, met little Soviet opposition in getting permission to leave for the United States, although she says she was severely criticized at her place of work. In February 1962 she gave birth to her first child, a daughter, and on June 2 the brand-new Oswald family left the Soviet Union for good.

That was the story the Warren Commission was given and was obliged to accept. We now know that the Commission had problems with Oswald's written account of his life in Russia, with Marina's tale, and with the whole touching story of courtship and marriage. Chief Counsel Rankin told Commission members in a secret executive session, ". . . there are manifold problems about the fact that the way he lived, the additional income he received under the name of the Red Cross . . . she said he had never been to Leningrad. He said he had . . . and members of her family are a curious thing. She was apparently a child with a father unknown at the time she was born, and yet she acquired a name of a father in some of the registrations under the Soviet system . . . Then the fact of her uncle and what his status was apparently a part of the Interior government . . . it would appear that he was much more than just a person of the Interior government like she had said. . . . And then this period that he [Oswald] belonged to a gun club, and there is no explanation by her of that[54] . . . that entire period is just full of possibilities for training, for working with the Soviets, and its agents, and unusual compared with the experience of most Americans. . . ."

Marina never did satisfy the Warren Commission on all these points, although in the end she provided some of the most damning evidence against her dead husband. Even in that she was vacillating and inconsistent. At first she won public sympathy for her comment in broken English, "Lee good man. Lee not shoot anyone." As the weeks passed, she moved from saying Oswald had been a good husband to saying he had been violent toward her. She once identified the Mannlicher-Carcano rifle as "the fateful rifle of Lee Harvey Oswald" and later she said she was not sure it was in fact her husband's gun. She alleged that Oswald wanted to kill two other political figures in the months before the Kennedy assassination. First, she said, her husband had been the would-be assassin who fired at and missed General Edwin Walker, a right-wing extremist, in spring 1963. It was an allegation the Warren Commission rightly took seriously, but—as we shall see— it is by no means certain Oswald really was the lone culprit. Marina also alleged that her husband once announced that former Vice President Nixon was coming to town, put his pistol in his belt, and told her he was going to "have a look." Marina's clear implication was that her husband, catholic in his killing tastes, intended to take a shot at Nixon. She said she stopped him by locking him in the bathroom. That allegation crumbled when inquiry revealed that the bathroom door could only be locked from the inside. In any case, Nixon was not even in Dallas at the relevant time.

Marina Oswald's reaction to difficult questions tended, as Senator Russell commented, to be along the lines, "Don't understand what you're talking about." At one stage of the Warren inquiry a Commission counsel expressed skepticism about the "public image of Marina Oswald as a simple, devoted housewife. . . ." The lawyer felt she was probably "a very *different* person— cold, calculating, avaricious, scornful of generosity, and capable of an extreme lack of sympathy in personal relationships." Marina had been caught out in so many inconsistencies that the lawyer formally recorded his concern that she had "repeatedly lied" on vital points. Yet it was not so much Marina's evidence about the assassination that worried the CIA. In the Agency probe of Marina's background, officials were more and more worried by her shadowy origins and activities back in the Soviet Union.

According to Oswald's wife, in early versions of her story, she was born Marina Nikolaevna Prusakova, in Russia's Arctic north, in 1941. The middle name was a patronymic taken from her father's name, Nikolai, and Prusakova was her mother's maiden name. Marina said she had never known her father and took her mother's name. This explanation altered somewhat in 1977, when her biography was published. It was now reported that Marina had assumed for a long time that she was the child of her mother's second husband, until she discovered she had actually been born illegitimately. When she challenged her mother's second husband, he told her that her father had really been Nikolai Didenko, a traitor who had been killed during the war. While this new version may be true, there is no good reason why she should not have provided it to the Warren Commission. The CIA was more worried by a detail in Marina's birth certificate, which identified her place of birth as "Severodvinsk." The problem was that the town now called Severodvinsk had not been so named until 1957, when Marina was already sixteen. Edward Epstein has drawn attention to the nagging fact that, although Marina needed a birth certificate to get married in April 1961, the certificate she needed for travel to the United States was dated June 19 that year. This led to suspicion that Marina had been issued new papers, and perhaps false ones, when she left for the United States. It was just a suspicion, but the CIA doubts did not arise in a vacuum. Marina had intriguing relatives. There was Alexander Medvedev, her mother's second husband; he was supposed to be a skilled electrical technician, accomplished enough to have been transferred to a responsible post in Leningrad. Why, then, wondered the CIA investigators, were Medvedev's letters to Marina "nearly illiterate?" Then there was Marina's uncle in Minsk, the relative who supposedly gave family approval for her marriage to Oswald. This was Ilya Prusakov, an engineer who also happened to be a lieutenant colonel in the MVD, Russia's Ministry of the Interior. Prusakov was one of the leading citizens in Minsk and a member of the Communist Party. Marina herself was a member of the Komsomol, the Communist Party youth movement, although she denied it on her departure to the United States. These were only details, but they multiplied. The CIA was worried by the information that, fresh out of her training as a pharmacist, Marina had quit her first job after one day and then supposedly taken several months' holiday. In the Soviet Union such behavior would be considered delinquent and invite retribution. A CIA study concluded, ". . . it is almost impossible for her to have quit and gone on vacation so easily. . . . She would have been in trouble immediately with the Komsomol and her trade-union." There was no evidence of any such trouble, but the CIA analysts did notice a disturbing coincidence. The months of Marina's "holiday" happened to be just before Oswald's arrival in Moscow as an apparent defector from the United States. Was there more to all this than Marina had admitted? Had Marina been groomed to make contact with a defector from abroad? CIA counterintelligence analysts were never satisfied on this point, and a secret CIA document, only released in 1976 after a Freedom of Information Act suit, goes a long way to explaining why not. It concerns another month's holiday which Marina admitted taking at a government "Rest Home" near Leningrad in autumn 1960.

CIA experts, who had a copy of Marina Oswald's address book, noted in it the name Lev Prizentsev, next to a Leningrad address. According to an FBI report, Marina claimed this was a man she had met at the "Rest Home." As a matter of routine, the CIA analysts fed the name "Prizentsev" into the computer and came up with a blank. Then they tried the address: "Kondrat'yevskiy Prospkt 63, Apt. 7., Leningrad" (or No. 7, Apt. 63—the note in the address book did not specify which way around the numbers should read). This time the computer did react and in a startling way. The CIA analyst noted dryly:

> Robert E. Webster, who renounced his U.S. citizenship in 1959 when he defected to the U.S.S.R. and who returned to the U.S. as an alien under the Sov quota in May, 1962, claimed to have resided in a three-room apartment at Kondrat'yevskiy Prospekt 63, Apt. 18, Leningrad, during his stay in the U.S S.R.

There he was again, Robert Webster, the former Navy man who declared his defection before Oswald, who returned to the United

States at the same time as Oswald, and whom Oswald asked about when he visited the American Embassy in Moscow. The CIA officer must have paused for a long moment when the computer spewed out this latest coincidence—Marina Prusakova in touch with someone in the building that housed the American defector next in chronological line to Oswald. Leningrad is a large city, and this time, surely, the man of coincidence seemed a little too long. For some time the CIA had been watching with concern and keen interest the way suspect Americans in Russia tended to return home with Soviet wives in tow. Robert Webster himself, the defector whose path crisscrosses that of Oswald and Marina, had a child by a Soviet woman believed to have been a KGB agent. James Mintkenbaugh, a defector who later admitted being trained as a Soviet spy, reported that his mentors urged him to marry a Soviet woman. The intention was to send her home with Mintkenbaugh and plant her as a Soviet agent in the United States. Just after the Kennedy assassination, a CIA official recalled in a memorandum that he had been interested in Marina Prusakova Oswald before she left the Soviet Union. He wrote:

> . . . at the time I was becoming increasingly interested in watching develop a pattern that we had discovered in the course of our bio [biographical] and research work: the number of Soviet women marrying foreigners, being permitted to leave the USSR, then eventually divorcing their spouses and settling down abroad without returning "home." The [name deleted] case was among the first of these, and we eventually turned up something like two dozen similar cases. [Deletion] became interested in the developing trend we had come across. It was out of curiosity to learn if Oswald's wife would actually accompany him to our country, partly out of Oswald's own experiences in the USSR, that we showed [deleted] intelligence interest in the Harvey [sic] story.

Of course, the Soviet authorities did permit Marina Oswald to leave. It was a point that initially worried Warren Commission Chief Counsel Rankin. He told an executive session, ". . . the fact that she was allowed to leave the country the way she was is not adequately explained by her testimony, her statements or any-thing." The Commission eventually declared itself satisfied that Marina's Soviet exit permit was granted in much the same way as previous cases, after a delay of some five and a half months. (In fact the permit came through in *four* months.) Counterintelligence experts at the CIA did not share the Commissioner's equanimity. Sources at the Agency point out that if Marina really was steered into her relationship with Oswald, then the Soviet authorities would have orchestrated her exit only after a *show* of caution. At all events, American intelligence had cause for continued concern even after the Oswalds returned to the United States.

First, in July 1962, Marina wrote what seemed a routine letter to the Soviet Embassy in Washington, informing the authorities there of her new American address. The note was intercepted in an FBI operation designed to monitor mail received at Communist embassies; it might have seemed innocuous were it not that the addressee was not the simple "Second Secretary" he appeared. He was Vitaliy Gerasimov, identified in CIA records as being "known to have participated in clandestine meetings in this country and to have made payments for intelligence information of value to the Soviets." Even so, Gerasimov was also performing routine consul-ar functions, so this contact on its own would have been no great reason for American intelligence to worry about Marina. It was a letter sent from the Soviet Union later that year which had set the CIA analysts fretting anew about the wife of Lee Harvey Oswald. Once again it meant work for the computer.

In 1962 the office of James Angleton, Chief of Counterin-telligence, was running a massive domestic surveillance program that involved opening and photographing mail and maintaining files on as many as ten thousand American citizens. It was all quite illegal and has since been the cause of a major scandal in the United States. But in summer 1962 the operation netted a letter sent to Marina Oswald from Leningrad. It was apparently from a friend called Ella Soboleva, and the contents read like just that—a letter from a girlfriend back home. Yet according to Edward Epstein, who interviewed Angleton, when CIA officials ran a computer check on the address of the sender, which appeared on the envelope, they came up with yet another of those nagging coincidences. The address was that of one Igor Sobolev, a Soviet citizen already on file at the CIA and thought to be an agent of the First Chief Directorate—the senior intelligence branch of the KGB. Perhaps, of course, "Ella" was Sobolev's wife or daughter, with a perfectly innocent connection with Marina. Perhaps, but the coincidences were really piling up.

We should reject the notion that Marina Oswald was some kind of Mata Hari.[55] Like her husband, she was surely too young and inexperienced for such a role. Yet Marina may have been steered toward Oswald, not with a view to spying in the cloak-and-dagger sense but simply to gather information on Oswald's true role and personality. Intelligence sources consider this theory viable and believe Marina may not even have fully understood how she was being used. Whatever the truth, the festering suspicion at the CIA was heightened immeasurably after the assassination by a dramatic development, an intelligence puzzle which has never been resolved. This arose in early 1964, when Yuri Nosenko, a senior KGB officer, defected to the United States, positively brimming over with implausible assurances that his people had never had the remotest interest in Oswald. Was Nosenko a real defector, or was he sent by Moscow as a messenger boy? And what message was so important that it justified sending a senior officer out of Russia forever?

A Fairy Story from the KGB

Exactly two months after the President's assassination, CIA headquarters in Virginia received a coded message from Yuri Nosenko, a KGB officer accompanying the Soviet delegation to the latest stage of disarmament talks in Geneva. Nosenko had made contact with the CIA on his own initiative during a previous visit to Switzerland, and he was regarded as an important catch. At thirty-six he was in the prime of a career in Soviet intelligence which had taken him from postwar naval intelligence to a senior rank in the KGB's Second Chief Directorate, the department handling counterintelligence within the Soviet Union. In Moscow Nosenko had for years specialized in operations aimed at compromising and blackmailing foreigners, and he had particular responsibility for

American and British targets. The CIA was nurturing high hopes that this KGB contact would become a prime source of information at the heart of Soviet intelligence. Then, in January 1964, at a secret meeting hastily convened in Geneva, their recruit dashed CIA expectations and produced a package of surprises.

Nosenko led off by declaring that he wished to defect to the West at once, abandoning his KGB career and the wife and children he said he had left behind in Moscow. This was completely unexpected, for at a previous meeting Nosenko had said he would never leave Russia. It was also unwelcome, and for the next few days the CIA tried to persuade Nosenko to stay in Moscow as an active and productive contact. It was then that Nosenko presented the Americans with a development that left little room for argument. He claimed he had received a cable from KGB headquarters ordering him to fly home to Moscow within five days. Nosenko feared this meant his treachery had been discovered and insisted that the CIA do the honorable thing and get him to the United States as quickly as possible. The Agency realized it had no choice, and—on the very day he said he was due to fly back to Moscow—Nosenko was spirited out of Switzerland. Meanwhile, CIA analysts were trying to assess some remarkable information Nosenko had brought to Geneva as his last intelligence offering from behind the Iron Curtain. This was that he, Nosenko, had personally handled the case of Lee Harvey Oswald during his stay in the Soviet Union.

Nosenko said that, as Deputy Chief of the Second Directorate's American-British section, it had fallen naturally to him to supervise Oswald's case when he arrived in Russia in late 1959. According to him, the KGB knew nothing about Oswald until, already in Moscow, he requested permission to stay in the country. At this stage they did not even know about Oswald's Marine Corps background, and—Nosenko claimed—they would not have been interested anyway. He was dismissive about Oswald, alleging that the KGB found him not very intelligent, even "mentally unstable." What interest they did have waned when Oswald attempted suicide rather than accept Soviet demand that he leave the country. Nosenko claimed that Oswald later threatened suicide a second time, and the KGB then "washed its hands of Oswald."

Nobody from Soviet intelligence ever debriefed the young American on his military background, and no one considered using him as an agent. It was some other government department, not the KGB, that allowed Oswald to stay in the Soviet Union and sent him off to live in Minsk. Nosenko conceded that in Minsk KGB agents were ordered to "maintain a discreet check" on Oswald, in the light of the possibility that Oswald might be a " 'sleeper agent' for American intelligence." But, insisted the Russian, "the interest of KGB headquarters in Oswald was practically nil." There was little concern, and no opposition, when Oswald decided to return to the United States, taking a Russian wife with him. Of Marina, Nosenko said scornfully, "She was not too smart anyway. . . . The Soviets were glad to get rid of them both." That was virtually the end of the episode, said Nosenko, except that some months before the assassination, Oswald had requested a visa to return to the Soviet Union. It had been refused. When news of the assassination came through in November, the KGB reacted with concern. The head of the Second Chief Directorate, General Gribanov, personally coordinated an urgent check on Oswald's activities and associations in the Soviet Union. On his orders Oswald's file was flown from Minsk to Moscow on a special military flight and thoroughly examined. Nosenko has said that no less than two suitcases filled with documents on Oswald arrived at KGB headquarters. If there is any truth to this, it makes a mockery of the mere fifteen documents supplied by the Soviets to the Warren Commission. Nosenko, however, said the only evidence of any attempt to influence Oswald was that Marina's uncle, the MVD colonel, had suggested that Oswald "not be too critical of the Soviet Union when he returned to the United States." Nosenko knew all this, he said, because—once again—he was personally assigned to the Oswald case after the Kennedy assassination. He had personally seen the KGB official file and had received the reports of a special investigation team sent to double-check the facts in Minsk. The file, which exonerated Soviet intelligence from any malice involvement with Oswald, was eventually forwarded to Prime Minister Khruschchev himself.

All in all, Nosenko left the KGB bathing in an aura of almost angelic innocence and respectability. And that, in the Soviet

Russia Division of the CIA, was just the first of the problems with the Nosenko story. With the defector himself flown to the United States for intensive debriefing, there began a controversy within the intelligence community which was to last more than ten years.

CIA suspicions about Nosenko and his tale turned out to be more than justified. There had been reservations about Nosenko even before the assassination. He had, for example, volunteered his services to the CIA—and then accepted a paltry $300 as down payment for services rendered. That had seemed odd for a man who claimed to be a lieutenant colonel in the KGB. Now, as CIA analysts probed the facade of Nosenko's story, it gradually crumbled. A key breakthrough concerned the Russian's claim that, while trying to defect in Geneva, he had received a telegram from Moscow instructing him to fly home. A team of American code-breakers, with access to every cable sent between Moscow and Geneva at the relevant time, established that no message had been sent to any member of the Soviet delegation on the day Nosenko said he got the cable. After persistent interrogation, Nosenko confessed that he had made up the whole thing. He maintained, though, that he had done so on his own initiative, to force the United States to accept him. Meanwhile, the very foundation of Nosenko's story was being undermined, as CIA counterintelligence threw doubt on his own account of his career in Soviet intelligence. Another KGB defector, Major Anatoli Golitsin, told the CIA that Nosenko had indeed been in the organization but had not held the positions he claimed. Golitsin had been in close touch with the departments Nosenko had named but had never come across him. Then the CIA questioners began to probe Nosenko's claim that he had enjoyed a meteoric rise in rank—from captain to lieutenant colonel in less than four years. The defector failed to account for this and then caved in. He had exaggerated his rank, he said, to make himself more attractive to the CIA. So far, Nosenko's lies could conceivably be explained as desperate ploys to ingratiate himself, but his story continued to collapse. It did so in a way that persuaded senior CIA officers that they were dealing with a Soviet plant.

Nosenko made mistakes that could not be put down to poor memory. Alerted by his vague account of a case he claimed to have handled in the early Fifties involving an American military attaché, CIA questioners asked him to describe the end of the attaché's tour of duty. Nosenko's answer showed that he was not even aware the officer in question had been expelled from the Soviet Union, something he was bound to know if he had really been in charge of the case. From then on, Nosenko walked into trap after trap. He claimed intimate knowledge of the Penkovsky case, so named after the Soviet officer who spied for the United States until he was caught and executed in 1963. Yet the events he said he had learned from daily reports in early 1961 did not, in fact, occur till much later, when Nosenko was, by his own account, in another KGB department. On top of this, the defector showed himself sadly ignorant of simple facts about the American establishment in Moscow, facts he should certainly have known if he had been, as he claimed, a top officer in the American Department of the KGB's Second Directorate. In light of all this, it comes as no surprise to learn that Nosenko also failed two CIA lie-detector tests he was given in the three years following the assassination; and when the CIA took a harder look at "good" information he had supplied, officials came away less than impressed. Nosenko had been credited with identifying William Vassall, the British Admiralty clerk who passed top-secret material to the Russians for seven years. He was also responsible for the arrest of an American Army soldier, Sergeant Robert Johnston, also believed to have been leaking classified information. Fresh analysis of both these cases suggested to the CIA analysts that the KGB had every reason to think both these sources of intelligence had already been compromised by the time Nosenko pointed the finger at them. In the brutal world of intelligence, Vassall and Johnson had already become disposable assets. Very probably Nosenko had used their names merely to bolster his credentials with his American contacts. The CIA team groped its way across this minefield of Soviet falsehood and bluff and looked in vain for a definite motive. They still did not know why the KGB would be prepared to jettison an important career officer like Yuri Nosenko. One theory, championed by Chief of Counterintelligence Angleton, was that Nosenko was putting up a smokescreen designed to conceal treachery in American intelligence. As Angleton saw it, many of Nosenko's apparent confidences provided convenient explanations for the failure or exposure of important American operations inside the Soviet Union. Nosenko's mission might be to ally suspicion in Washington that a highly placed Soviet agent was active within American intelligence. None of this dealt with the immediate problem in the wake of the Kennedy assassination. Why was Nosenko spinning his story about the KGB handling of Lee Harvey Oswald? The problem became submerged in feuding within the American intelligence community. It has never been resolved.

Soon after Nosenko's arrival in the United States, he reportedly became a subject of dispute between the CIA and the FBI under Director J. Edgar Hoover. To Director Hoover the Russian defector may have seemed a godsend. With his claims that Oswald had no links with Soviet intelligence, Nosenko was helping to squash allegations that the great Federal Bureau of Investigation had failed to expose a dangerous Communist agent. Today, the FBI says merely that—subject to his bona fides being established—Nosenko's information was the best available indication of Soviet innocence in the assassination. However, at the height of CIA concern, a full scale "hostile interrogation" was ordered. Now, and for nearly four years afterward, Nosenko was to be treated more like a prisoner of war than a welcome American protégé. For a long period he was totally cut off from the world, confined in a single room in a specially constructed CIA building which has been compared to a bank vault. He was watched twenty-four hours a day and, at one stage, denied reading material and forbidden to lie down during the daytime. When Nosenko's CIA guards watched television they did so with earphones for the sound so that their prisoner could not overhear. Once, apparently, Nosenko became so desperate to read that he resorted to studying the blurb on his toothpaste. This too was then taken away from him. At another point, in an effort to keep track of time, Nosenko tried to mark the days by tearing strips of material from his clothing.

This extraordinary treatment caused Congressional outrage when it was revealed to the Assassinations Committee in 1978. It had reportedly been modeled on an interrogation technique practiced by Soviet intelligence, a detail which only caused greater dismay in the House of Representatives. While the shock of American politicians is understandable, Nosenko's ordeal is here relevant only in terms of what information it extracted on Oswald's relationship with the Soviet authorities. The answer, ironically, is that it resolved nothing. For some at the CIA, the interrogation did confirm suspicions that Nosenko was lying—on a whole range of matters. In the opinion of the Assassinations Committee, "The fashion in which Nosenko was treated by the Agency—his interrogation and confinement—virtually ruined him as a valid source of information. . . ." As for the object of all this fuss, he never did crack.

Nosenko was still stalling when the Warren Commission wound up its investigation, and the Commissioners had to choose between a general lack of concern about Nosenko at the FBI, and continuing CIA suspicion that Nosenko might be a Soviet plant bearing false information. The Commission dodged the issue and left Nosenko out of its report altogether. Meanwhile, Nosenko stayed on in prison conditions, and his case festered on as a cause of internal wrangling at a high level within the CIA. It was not until four years after the Kennedy assassination that the director of the CIA moved to take the heat out of the Nosenko affair. The Soviet prisoner was then treated in a more friendly fashion, and officers newly appointed to the case wrote reports papering over the cracks in his story. Soon after, Nosenko was freed altogether and provided with a new home and American citizenship. Today—incredibly—he enjoys a post as a CIA consultant. Almost all the top CIA officers who most doubted him are retired. Those who defend the former KGB man maintain that if he lied it was only to boost his importance in CIA eyes and that most of his unfortunate "mistakes" can be put down to poor memory.

In 1978, when Nosenko appeared at a secret session of Congress' Assassinations Committee, he was caught out in more apparent inconsistencies. He ended up refusing to answer any questions dealing with past CIA interviews, on the grounds that his statements then were "the result of hostile interrogations." Nosenko claimed he had simply been confused. His excuses, and those of his defenders, ignore the most sinister clue of all—that the supposed defector was aided and abetted by the KGB in creating his cover story. For example, when he confessed that he had inflated his rank merely to impress his American contacts, Nosenko failed to account for a glaring discrepancy. Detailed KGB documents, brought with him, referred to him as a lieutenant colonel, the senior rank Nosenko admitted he did not really hold. Pressed to explain that, Nosenko could only suggest lamely that some KGB bureaucrat had blundered. CIA analysts, familiar with the minutiae of KGB procedures, could not accept this. To them the papers strongly supported the belief that Nosenko had been put up to his masquerade by the KGB. It was a theory encouraged by a development that implicated the Soviets even more.

When FBI Director Hoover committed himself to accepting Nosenko, he reportedly did so after consultation with another secret Soviet source. This was a Russian diplomat at the United Nations in New York, actually a KGB agent, who had, for some time, been feeding information to the Americans. The FBI, which code-named their source "Fedora," consulted him after Nosenko's defection. Fedora obligingly spoke up for Nosenko's bona fides and supported the false claim that the defector had been a lieutenant colonel in the KGB. He also said he knew—from the Moscow end—that KGB headquarters had indeed sent Nosenko a cable in Switzerland just before his defection, ordering him home. It was this, though, that emerged as glaring evidence of KGB deception. CIA codebreakers proved the cable had never existed, and Nosenko himself admitted it was a total fabrication. The last, and perhaps the most obvious, giveaway is the way the Soviets themselves have promoted "defector" Nosenko.

In the Seventies, while researching his book *Legend*, the author Edward Epstein had a meeting with the press officer of the Soviet Embassy in Washington. His questions were about Oswald's time in Russia, and the Russian diplomat knew Epstein was planning a major book. To Epstein's astonishment he suddenly confided that there was, in the United States, a former KGB officer who "knew as much about Oswald as anyone in the Soviet Union." The Soviet representative was, of course, recommending Nosenko, a traitor to his country. Similarly, some years ago, a Soviet journalist offered photographs of Nosenko's family to the

French magazine *Paris Match*. CIA veterans find all this explicable only if the Soviets wanted Nosenko's stories to gain currency. It is hard to escape the conclusion that Yuri Nosenko was indeed a Soviet plant, sent to the United States with false information. What then was the meaning and purpose of the tale about Oswald which featured so prominently in the Nosenko repertoire?

There have been allegations, backed by no credible evidence, that the Soviets were behind the assassination of President Kennedy and that the KGB put Oswald's finger on the trigger. All responsible analysts, including the CIA officers who most doubted Nosenko, reject such notions as wholly implausible. So did Congress' Assassinations Committee, in a formal finding in 1979. There is no reason to suppose that the Soviet Union would ever have considered such folly, nor indeed that the removal of President Kennedy served Russian political ends. Why, though, did Moscow go to a great deal of trouble to disseminate a story about Lee Oswald which defies belief? The CIA's counterintelligence people simply could not accept Nosenko's blithe assertion that the KGB had not questioned Oswald on his military background. They had learned from other returning defectors that it was routine KGB practice to grill American newcomers intensively for every scrap of information. In was inconceivable that Oswald—a radar operator fresh out of the Marines—should have been an exception to the rule.

The former chief of the CIA section responsible for counterintelligence against the KGB, Newton Miler, said in a recent interview that Soviet intelligence would have been interested in Oswald whatever his experience. According to Miller, "Marines have been prime KGB targets since they started guarding American embassies. The First Chief Directorate would have had an interest even after he was discharged . . . in fact it is known that the KGB screening process for tourists called special attention to ex-servicemen." CIA analysts were unimpressed by the fact that Oswald's "Diary" account made no mention of KGB interrogation, for the "Diary" bore all the marks of fabrication anyway. The former Deputy Chief of the CIA's Soviet Bloc Division told the Assassinations Committee that the possibility Oswald was not questioned by the KGB is "absolutely unthinkable . . . unthinkable for anyone who knows the automatic procedures of the Soviet Union—there is no way he could have evaded this action." Another senior CIA veteran told the Committee that he found the Soviets' professed attitude to Oswald "implausible." It was, he said, inconsistent with "the experience of any of us who had anything to do with Soviet operations." In its final report, the Committee concluded it was "certain Nosenko lied about Oswald. . . ."

The KGB would, then, have taken an interest in Oswald anyway. A KGB grilling would have been automatic, and it would have been no great interviewing feat to extract the information that the ex-Marine had served at Atsugi in Japan. Once the Soviets had an inkling that Oswald had some knowledge of the U-2 spy plane program—and they already had a general idea of operations at Atusgi—Oswald's interrogation would have been intensive. Indeed, Soviet secrecy over Oswald's time in Russia is most probably linked inextricably with the U-2 and with the major international crisis in precipitated.

On May 1, 1960, six months after Oswald's arrival in Moscow, a U-2 spy plane under CIA control crashed near the Soviet city of Sverdlovsk. It was the first and only U-2 ever to come down over Russia, and the incident occurred two weeks before a planned summit meeting between President Eisenhower and Soviet Prime Minister Khrushchev—a long-planned and sensitively prepared conference which many hoped would lead to a dramatic improvement in relations between East and West. The wreck of the U-2 shattered all that. Gary Powers, the pilot of the spy plane, was captured alive by the Russians. Equipment and film from the wrecked aircraft left no doubt that the U-2's mission had been espionage. Unaware just what evidence had survived, the United States pretended for days that the plane had been on an innocent weather research mission and had strayed into Russian air space by mistake. When Khrushchev finally produced the damning evidence and said the U-2 had been brought down by Soviet missiles, Eisenhower was forced to admit the truth and took personal responsibility. Although the summit meeting did take place, the U-2 affair effectively destroyed it as a forum for any real progress toward peace.

In the domestic furor that followed in the United States a key question was raised: How had the Russians managed to bring down the U-2 in the first place? The whole U-2 operation was geared to the fact that the spy plane flew higher than any other known aircraft and beyond the effective range of any missile. Short of a chance hit, the Americans believed the Russians incapable of shooting it down. The U-2 program had been going on for years, and for all that time the Russians had been powerless to do anything to stop the plane they called "The Black Lady of Espionage." Clearly the Soviets had been avid for new technology that would make the U-2 vulnerable. The crash of Gary Powers' aircraft implied either that the Russians had developed a better missile system, or the U-2 in question had not been flying at its normal operational altitude. There has been some speculation that the Russians were able to shoot down the U-2 because they had learned vital new information about it, information provided by Lee Harvey Oswald. It is a suspicion expressed by the pilot of the U-2 himself, Gary Powers, who was later released by the Russians and wrote a book about the affair.

Powers noted that Oswald openly told the American Embassy in Moscow that he intended to give the Russians "all information" he possessed from his military experience and intimated that he might "know something of a special interest." He also said he had already offered his information to "a Soviet official." There is no doubt that, aside from more routine code and radar information, Oswald's experience at Atsugi and elsewhere could have given him knowledge of the U-2's actual operational altitude and the radar techniques used during its flights.[56] Powers inferred that if Oswald indeed gave certain data of this sort to Soviet intelligence, the Russians may have learned how to target their missiles accurately at a far greater height and thus shoot down the U-2. The former pilot pointed out darkly that his plane came down just a few months after Oswald's arrival in Russia, a period during which there had been only one other flight over Soviet territory.

There are, however, indications that if the Russians did shoot down the plane, they did so when it was at a low altitude. Moscow later claimed, with apparent precision, that its rockets had hit the U-2 at 65,000 feet, far below the operating altitude of the U-2. In their persistent questioning of Powers, the Soviets seemed genuinely uncertain what the operating altitude actually was. If they knew, and if they had really hit the U-2 at 90,000 feet or over, why the questions? Colonel Fletcher Prouty was Focal Point Officer between the CIA, which supervised the U-2 program, and the Air Force, which provided equipment and pilots like Gary Powers. Clandestine operations such as the U-2 flights were his special responsibility, and he had detailed firsthand experience of how the U-2 functioned technically and of the chain of command which directed the operations. Prouty maintains, "It is preposterous to assume that information given to the Russians by Lee Harvey Oswald would have made it possible for them to shoot it down. Even if he gave them the U-2's operating altitude and radar defense system, the information would have been irrelevant. The Russian's simply had nothing that could touch a plane flying that high." Colonel Prouty's reading of the technical evidence is that—for some reason never revealed—the Powers U-2 was flying below its operational altitude when it was brought down. Some suspect the cause was sabotage at the U-2's base of origin in Pakistan.

The full truth about the U-2 affair is presumably known in the inner councils of American and Soviet intelligence but may never be revealed publicly. Powers, who might have shed more light on the subject than appeared in his CIA-authorized biography, cannot now be questioned. He died in a helicopter crash in 1977. Meanwhile, the enigma of Oswald's possible role is heightened by a couple of tantalizing clues he himself left behind.

First there is a letter home written just after the Russians released Gary Powers. In this Oswald wrote of the American pilot, "He seemed to be a nice bright American-type fellow when I saw him in Moscow." That is all, a single casual remark—the only reference Oswald ever made to the U-2 incident. Oswald's suspect "Diary" has him far from Moscow on the day Powers was shot down—at a May Day party in Minsk. Yet, after his return to the United States, Oswald mentioned to a colleague at work that he had been in Moscow on May Day. After the assassination Dennis Ofstein reported that "Oswald mentioned that he was in Moscow for the May Day parade at one time." Ofstein also recalled Oswald saying that the only time he saw jet aircraft in Russia was "in

Moscow on May Day." Of Oswald's three May Days spent in the Soviet Union, the only one unaccounted for is May 1, 1960, when the U-2 incident occurred. Nowhere in the "Diary" is there any mention of the U-2 affair, curious considering that it was a major Soviet news story and one of special interest to Oswald, who had seen the U-2 at Atsugi. It may be significant too that after May 1 the "Diary" contains no entries at all for the rest of the month, the period during which the captured American pilot was being questioned in Moscow. Gary Powers was later to write of a peephole through which he was observed during his incarceration in Lubyanka Prison. It is tempting to speculate that Oswald was one of those who secretly watched and listened. The pilot was questioned intensively about the U-2 operations from Atsugi in Japan, although that was not the point of departure for his own ill-fated flight. It would have been logical enough for the Russians to bring in Oswald, the only available American with knowledge of the U-2, to comment on Powers' responses and even to suggest further questioning. Powers, who was debriefed by the CIA after his release, subsequently had no doubts about Oswald's qualifications for the role. He told one interviewer that Oswald had "had access to all our equipment. He knew the altitudes we flew at, how long we stayed out on any mission, and in which direction we went."

The fact that, whatever Oswald's true loyalties, nobody can seriously doubt that the Russians grilled him intensively on U-2 operations and on anything else he could tell of his work in the U.S. Marine Corps. If, as has been suggested, he was a fake defector sent to the Soviet Union with American approval, he presumably gave misleading or only innocuous information. If he was a genuine turncoat, he may indeed have given the Russians valuable secrets. Either way, Nosenko's insistence that Oswald was not questioned at all is transparent nonsense. While we can still only speculate at Moscow's reasons for priming Nosenko with a phony Oswald story, embarrassment in the wake of the Kennedy assassination is an inadequate explanation. Perhaps the Russians feared that a probe of Oswald's past could lead to new revelations about the U-2 affair, an episode from which the Russians had so far emerged with propaganda advantage. They may have surmised rightly that there were those in the United States who also had reason to keep the U-2 case closed.

Congress' Assassinations Committee said that, over Nosenko, the CIA "failed to capitalize on a potential source of critical evidence . . . lost an opportunity to elicit information that might have shed light on Oswald, his wife Marina, and a possible KGB connection to them." It is possible that—for some at the CIA—the Oswald defection and the U-2 affair were twin cans of worms best left undisturbed. Ironically, too, Nosenko may have been sent to head off public exposure of a continuing chess game being played by the intelligence agencies of Washington and Moscow, using "defectors" as pawns. If that was the KGB's motive, and if indeed Oswald had been a tool of American intelligence, the feeling in Washington must have been mutual. Certainly, at the time it mattered most, the Nosenko story was quietly shoved into the background of assassination inquires. It proved such a hot potato that it was not even mentioned in the Warren Report and henceforth became a state secret. The essence of Nosenko's message, proclaiming Soviet innocence of any connection with Oswald, was echoed in the report. Meanwhile, to the public at large, a whole world of intelligence stayed the way its masters wished—through the looking glass.

CHAPTER 11

The Man Who Was Perfectly All Right

*Intelligence-gathering activities . . . have a special and
secret character. . . . These activities have their own
rules and methods of concealment which seek to mislead
and obscure. . . .*

—President Dwight D. Eisenhower, 1960

Standing hatless and coatless in the biting cold, the first American
President born in the twentieth century took the oath of office in
Washington. He uttered the stirring words that today ring hollow,
"Let the word go forth from this time and place, to friend and foe
alike, that the torch has been passed to a new generation of
Americans . . . unwilling to witness or permit the slow undoing of
those human rights to which this nation has always been committed, and to which we are committed today at home and around the
world." The new President spoke fervently of peace, but with a
clear message for the Kremlin. "We dare not tempt them with
weakness. For only when our arms are sufficient beyond doubt can
we be certain beyond doubt that they will never be employed." It
was January 20, 1961, and John Kennedy had begun his thousand
days as President. Across the world, in the Soviet city of Minsk, a
young American was involved in moves which would inexorably
link Kennedy's savage fate and his own. It was time for Lee
Oswald to go home.

According to the public record, nobody in the United States
had heard from Oswald in more than a year. Now, in the first week
of February, he sat down to write to the American Embassy in
Moscow, "I desire to return to the United States. . . ." In his letter
Oswald referred to an earlier letter, on the same lines, which he

claimed he had sent in December. The Embassy, in the shape of Consul Snyder, replied, claiming that it had not received the earlier letter. However, the timing of events at this juncture is replete with coincidence. On February 1, the State Department had asked the Moscow Embassy to inquire about Oswald's whereabouts, following concern expressed by his mother. The CIA was informed of her anxiety. Then, right on cue, Oswald chose to write saying he had had enough of the Soviet Union and wanted American cooperation in getting home.[57] He was launched on more than a year of bureaucratic exchanges that culminated in American and Soviet approval for his departure to the United States with a Russian wife. On July 10 Oswald's passport was returned to him at the Embassy by Consul Snyder, the official with a CIA background who had seen him at the time of his defection. This followed, first, correspondence in which Oswald had requested guarantees that he would not be prosecuted on his return to the United States and, later, notification that he wished to take a Soviet wife with him to the United States. On this point, at Consul Snyder's request, Oswald, with Marina, had made a visit to Moscow. According to an Embassy report, he "stated frankly that he had learned a hard lesson the hard way and been completely relieved of his illusions about the Soviet Union." The Embassy then returned Oswald's passport, valid only for travel to the United States, and recommended that Washington agree to Marina's application for a visa. Although all this at first sight seems normal and proper procedure, the bureaucratic record contains another of those inconsistencies that permeate the Oswald story. Theoretically, the Passport Office should have posted a "lookout card" on Oswald after his defection, a procedure which would alert officials at once if he applied for documentation at any American Embassy in the world. Again, when he was loaned repatriation money, a lookout card would normally have been mandatory until the loan was repaid. No such card was ever placed in the file—a phenomenon the State Department later explained as repeated human error. More astonishing, Oswald was to be issued a passport within twenty-four hours as late as 1963, when he applied for a new passport for yet more travel to Communist countries. All this might seem a happy expression of American *laissez-faire* if such laxness were characteristic. In fact, during the period of Oswald's adventures, the FBI and the State Department collaborated to keep tabs on American travelers with supposed Communist sympathies, and caught the most innocuous people in their net. Oswald, of course, was noticed—even without a lookout card—during the conclusion of the Russian episode. The mystery is how, with all his accumulated sins, he would accidentally escape the system when he applied for a repeat performance in 1963. But then accident seemed to play a permanent role in the Oswald saga.

In August 1961 Oswald stood beside a British-registered car in a public square in Minsk, the city where he lived in the Soviet Union. As he did so, two American camera shutters clicked. The resulting photographs (*see illustration 10*) turned up after President Kennedy's assassination, were noted by the Warren Commission, and then virtually forgotten. All the Warren Report said of them was that they had been "taken by American tourists in Minsk . . . the tourists did not know Oswald, nor did they speak with him; they remembered only that several men gathered near their car." That was not accurate, even on the evidence of the inquiry's own files. Background documents, obtained since by researchers, filled some of the gaps in that bald statement. They indicated that three American women, passing through Minsk on a motoring tour, had encountered Oswald briefly while on an evening picture-taking excursion in Minsk's Central Square. He did talk with them for a few moments but apparently had little to say beyond small talk about their trip. The published record says he just happened to be caught by the tourists' cameras when they took photographs of the Palace of Culture. According to the CIA, the tourists were contacted "on a one-time basis, following their return"—purely in line with a then common Agency procedure of contacting Americans fresh home from Iron Curtain countries. The CIA borrowed more than 150 photographs taken by the tourists and copied five for filing in its "Graphics Register." Supposedly it was only after the President's assassination, during a search of the register, that CIA staff realized a man in the photograph was none other than Lee Oswald. A second picture was, allegedly, obtained from another of the three tourists. That was the official story, and for obvious reasons it has caused incredulity among independent researchers. They have found it almost impossible to believe that, of all the millions of people in Russia, genuine tourists took photographs of Oswald purely by chance. It has seemed even less probable that the CIA merely chanced to include a picture of Oswald among the five it selected from twelve dozen photographs borrowed from the tourists. In 1979 Congress' Assassinations Report referred briefly to the photographs, but only in considering whether the CIA maintained concealed files on Oswald. It asked its readers to believe the pictures were indeed taken by chance and to take their pick of alternative CIA explanations for having picked an Oswald photograph long before the assassination. One employee said the picture was interesting because "it depicted a Soviet Intourist guide"; another said it was because "it showed a crane in the background." The Committee's documents on this matter are listed as "classified," and—whether the Committee knew it or not—its Report certainly fails to tell the whole story. As this book went to press, I succeeded in contacting one of the three tourists, Rita Naman. The account she supplies changes the entire scenario for the Oswald photographs in Minsk.

Naman, who is of British origin, confirms that she and a friend, Monica Kramer, traveled through the Soviet Union by car in late summer 1961. They were in a sense tourist pioneers, as few Westerners had then yet ventured across the Communist nations by road. Naman insists, however—and I find her credible—that they were genuine tourists, not in touch with any branch of American intelligence before setting out on their adventure. The first surprise in her account, though, involved their stay not in Minsk but in the Soviet capital. At the beginning of August, Naman recalls, they were taken by their Intourist guide to visit the site of the Moscow film festival, which had opened the previous month. There, just as they were leaving, they were approached by a young man who—unlike most Russians they met—spoke English with an American accent. Although he merely passed the time of day and said nothing about who he was or what he was doing in Russia, the two tourists noticed that their Soviet guide became agitated and pressed them to drive on. As they sat in the car the young man delayed the women by talking through the open window, until finally the guide virtually ordered them to leave. That, says Naman, was an incident they might have forgotten—except that the identical young man turned up again ten days later. It was he who approached them in the main square at Minsk, exchanged small talk once again, and was then caught for posterity by Kramer's camera. As we now know, the friendly young man was Lee Oswald. Naman's account puts the Oswald encounter in an entirely new light and raises a new question. Can we now believe that, purely by chance, Oswald just happened to talk to the same tourists, after an interval of ten days, in the streets of cities more than four hundred miles apart?

A check reveals that, according to his own suspect written account, Oswald was in Moscow that summer—several weeks before the tourists had their first encounter with him. The "Diary" tells of visiting Consul Snyder to discuss repatriation plans and of summoning Marina to join him for a few days in the capital. That is all very well—except that the "Diary" records Oswald's return to Minsk on July 14, nearly three weeks *before* the tourists apparently encountered him in Moscow at the film festival site. On August 1, the day of the Moscow meeting, Oswald's writings place him back in Minsk. This all appears to confirm suspicion that Oswald's written journal is bogus but does nothing to answer the fundamental question about his encounters with the Americans. Even supposing Oswald made a second trip to Moscow—a journey mentioned nowhere in his written record—the two meetings with the Americans must surely have been by design. Rita Naman now supplies further clues, which increase the smell of intrigue and only deepen the mystery.

First, Naman reveals that the Soviet authorities became extremely perturbed about their activities—for reasons which were and remain obscure. As soon as the tourists arrived in Minsk from Moscow, but before the second Oswald encounter, Naman was summoned to the hotel manager's office. There she was intensively questioned by an official in plain clothes who wanted to know the true purpose of the visit to Russia. He accused her of spreading anti-Soviet progaganda—in Moscow the women had given a copy of *Newsweek* magazine to a man who said he was a student and was probably in fact a Soviet provocateur. Naman responded that they were simply tourists, and the confrontation ended. It was an hour later that the tourists had their Minsk encounter with Oswald. Naman says that this time—still shaken as she was by her grilling at the hotel—she made a point of not getting into conversation with him. The tourists' troubles, however, were not over. Naman recalls that they were again interrogated—by the same official—on crossing the Soviet border into Poland. Their car, says Naman, was "virtually taken apart" in a thorough search, and the tourists gained the impression the Russians were looking for documents.

In 1979 the Assassinations Committee Report referred to only two tourists involved in the Minsk photograph episode, but the record long ago revealed that there were three. The identity and precise role of the third now demands further investigation. She is Mrs. Marie Hyde,[58] an elderly American woman who struck up an acquaintance with Naman and Kramer at their Moscow hotel. As Naman remembers it, Hyde told them she had become separated from her tour group and asked to accompany them on their trip through Minsk to Poland and the West. They agreed, and thus it was that Hyde came to be with them when the Minsk pictures were taken. It appears, indeed, that the photograph session in the square was undertaken at Mrs. Hyde's initiative. Hyde took one picture with Kramer's camera, then got Naman to take a second shot of the same scene using Hyde's own camera. These are the two photographs in which Oswald appeared.

Hyde herself confirmed most of this account, after reference to notes, when the FBI questioned her after the assassination. She omitted to mention, though, an episode which occurred in Warsaw, after the trio crossed the Soviet frontier. In Warsaw, says Naman, Hyde was interrogated alone and at length by Polish officials. The reason why never became clear to the other two women, but they had wondered about their new companion ever since meeting her in Moscow. Hyde, they thought, seemed very familiar with Russia, knew her way around the Moscow subway, and generally gave the impression of being a "very sharp cookie." Kramer, apparently, was so struck by this that she told Naman— perhaps not too seriously—that their elderly friend might be some sort of American agent. Little is known of Hyde's background, beyond the fact that her husband was a captain in the merchant marine. One detail in the story of her trip to the Soviet Union is certainly strange—her causal account of joining up with Naman and Kramer because she "had become separated from her tourist group." As anybody knows who visited the Soviet Union at that period, or nowadays for that matter, casual changes in itinerary are rare and difficult in the Soviet Union. The Intourist system is designed to monitor the activity of all foreigners, and a sudden change of the kind described sounds very unusual. Perhaps that alone sufficed to attract the unwelcome official attention the party eventually received. After the assassination, however, a CIA employee who visited Naman told her he thought "the contact with Oswald was the reason for the trouble at Minsk."

It could be that the episode involved some sort of provocation involving KGB use of Oswald to confront the same American tourists in both Moscow and Minsk. The possibility remains, however, that Naman and Kramer drove unwittingly into a covert contact operation inspired by American intelligence. Congress' Assassinations Committee noted that in 1961 the CIA was running what it called its "American visitors program." This project "sought the cooperation, for limited purposes, of carefully selected persons traveling in the Soviet Union." Former CIA Soviet specialist Harry Rositzke has pinpointed this period as a time when "not only were more and more outside tourists briefed to look and report, but individual Westerners, mainly Americans, were recruited by the CIA to go to the Soviet Union on a prearranged itinerary and report in depth on the key target installations. . . ." According to Rositzke the Agency's drive for information paid off handsomely. The "tourists" and "visitors" managed to snatch thousands of pictures of missile support facilities, factories, and even missile sites. They also brought home a stream of information about Soviet industry and technology. With such machinations now established fact, it does not seem impossible that American intelligence tried to contact, or at least observe and photograph, Lee Oswald.

It is also, perhaps, possible that the conventional version is correct, that Oswald just happened to bump into some American visitors and just happened to get photographed. We cannot credit that, however, while key questions remain unanswered. How did

Oswald, an alien with limited travel privileges, encounter the same people in places far apart and within a matter of days? Why has that fact not emerged in official reports? Kramer and Naman appeared to have been genuine tourists, but was Mrs. Hyde? Finally, can we really believe it was pure chance that, of five photographs selected from a multitude of others, the CIA chose and filed a picture of Lee Oswald? If these questions have been answered in the classified research of the Assassinations Committee, the explanations should be made public. If not, there should be fresh official research.

Following the Minsk photograph episode, Oswald continued to plan his return to the United States. Eventually, the State Department advanced him the necessary cash, and forcefully cleared the way for Marina's entry to the U.S.A.

Just before the Oswalds left the Soviet Union, they visited the American Embassy. There, both Lee and Marina talked with Captain Alexis Davison, the Embassy doctor who doubled as Assistant Air Attaché. Later, Davison was involved in a major intelligence scandal. He had acted as contact man for U.S. intelligence in operations involving Penkovsky, the Soviet colonel who spied for the CIA and Britain's M16.

On June 1, 1962, the Oswalds and their daughter left the Soviet Union by train, bound for Holland. The record of their journey is shot through with nagging inconsistencies. It has been supposed that the couple entered the West through Helmstedt, one of the most strictly monitored checkpoints on the East German border. Yet, while Marina's passport was stamped at Helmstedt, Oswald's was not. State Department and West German sources are emphatic that it would have been stamped. A clue to Oswald's true movements, paid scant attention by the Warren Commission, lies on a page of his address book used for notes relating to his travel from Russia. As a reader of the first edition of this book has pointed out, the page bears a hand-drawn map covering Berlin. Prominently marked on the map is the train station which is the main access point to West Berlin for travelers leaving cross-country trains on Oswald's East-West route. The evidence indicates strongly that Oswald did stop over in West

Berlin—without Marina—and subsequently continued his journey west by some other means. Why? Oswald had no known reason for the diversion. West Berlin, however, has long served as an intelligence crossroads, and as a haven for operatives coming in from the cold.

When the Oswalds arrived in Amsterdam they stayed not in a hotel but at an establishment recommended by the U.S. Embassy in Moscow. Marina has since described it variously as a "private apartment" and as a "boardinghouse." The documentary record of the Oswalds' journey shows a stay in Holland of only one night. Marina, however, stated after the assassination that they stayed for three days. She reacted with confusion when questioned about this episode by Congress' Assassinations Committee. It is of interest, however, that she believes advance arrangements had been made for their accommodation and that their hosts spoke English. Some researchers suspect that Oswald was debriefed by American intelligence in Holland. Certainly the Dutch stopover worried the Chief Counsel of the Warren Commission, who said at an executive session, ". . . it is unexplained why they happened to go there and stay, and got a place to live, some little apartment, and what they were doing in the interim. . . ." The Commission learned little from Marina to clear up such problems. As the Chief Counsel commented dryly, ". . . whenever she gets to these areas that might be enlightening for us, she is unable. . . ."

The Warren Report made no mention of a Marina account of the journey from the Soviet Union which is totally at odds with the evidence. In one of her earliest interviews after the assassination— with the Secret Service—Marina was recorded as saying that she and Lee "went to Moscow, where the transportation was supplied by the American consulate." She said they "then arrived in New York *by air* . . . stayed in some hotel in New York City for one day and then went *by train* to Texas." (Author's italics.) This version is radically different from the account which eventually appeared in the official inquiry. It could conceivably be explained as a bizarre double error in translation—yet Marina spoke in the presence of two qualified interpreters. Was this an early lapse in a poorly rehearsed cover story? At all events, it remains an unexplained oddity.

The official inquiry concluded, on the basis of documentary and other evidence, that the Oswalds in fact crossed the Atlantic by sea, aboard the S.S. *Maasdam*. That, indeed, is what Marina eventually said herself when testifying to the Warren Commission in 1964. The Commission, however, never did locate any witnesses who remembered them on the ship, even though Oswald and his poorly dressed Russian wife, with their baby swaddled Russian-style, made an unusual couple. On arrival in New York, the defector and would-be traitor was supposedly met by neither FBI nor CIA agents. The couple were met and helped, though, by Spas Raikin, described in the Warren Report as "a representative of the Traveler's Aid Society, which had been contacted by the Department of State." In fact, Raikin was also secretary-general of the "American Friends of the Anti-Bolshevik Bloc of Nations," an emigré group in direct touch with the FBI and U.S. military intelligence. It also had contacts with anti-Communist activists in New Orleans, headquartered in the very building where, in months to come, Oswald's name was to be linked with CIA-backed anti-Castro activists. Raikin has since said that Oswald told him he had been one of the guards at the American Embassy in Moscow. The Traveler's Aid man has also recalled that the chief immigration officer at the dock, normally helpful to him when he had to meet people, seemed surly and reluctant to help in the case of the Oswalds. The Immigration Service, of course, had recently been overruled by the State Department when it raised objections to granting Marina Oswald an entry permit. The State Department, on the other hand, had gone out of its way to smooth the Oswalds' passage.

The prodigal's return had been additionally cushioned in advance by State Department approaches to the Department of Health, Education, and Welfare—HEW. It had been agreed that the defector would be eligible for aid—even if this meant bending the rules. This was a remarkable concession towards a supposed defector who was very possibly a traitor too.

HEW records in Dallas state that Oswald went to Russia "with State Department approval" to work as a radar specialist. Other records establish a chain of communication on Oswald with HEW in New York and Washington, and show that the Washington office had been briefed by—the State Department. There is not a word in the Warren Report about Oswald having gone to Russia with State Department approval.

The Oswalds, it seems, flew to Texas the day after their arrival in the United States. As they were preparing to leave, one of the officials helping them noticed something that was to recur— the Oswalds had two suitcases fewer than the seven they had been carrying when they arrived. Oswald said he had sent them ahead by rail, but the baggage was to shrink even more before the family reached Texas. When Oswald's brother met them at Dallas airport, he observed that there were only two suitcases. The Warren Commission seems to have taken little interest in this oddity, and the phenomenon remains unexplained. However, it may fit in with another strange detail about the last stage of Oswald's odyssey. Although there were direct routes available, the flight chosen to bring the Oswalds home—Delta 821—made a stop in Atlanta. Coincidentally, an Atlanta name and address were found in Oswald's address book after the assassination. It was that of Natasha Davison, the mother of Captain Davison, the American attaché with intelligence connections who had talked to the Oswalds at the Moscow Embassy.

After the assassination, Captain Davison first told the Secret Service he did not recall meeting the Oswalds in Moscow; but he did remember when the FBI interviewed him. Recently, in testimony to Congress' Assassinations Committee, Davison admitted receiving "some superficial intelligence training" and acknowledged his part in the Penkovsky spy operation. He said he had been involved in no other covert work and specifically denied any secret connection to Oswald. A review of Davison's record turned up nothing further, and the Assassinations Committee concluded merely that there was "insufficient evidence for concluding that Davison was an intelligence contact for Oswald in Moscow." There never has been an adequate explanation for the Oswalds' travel home through Davison's home city of Atlanta, a route they had no known reason to take.[59]

Oswald and his wife began the difficult process of adjusting to life in American society. Oswald was home but he was visibly uncomfortable, especially when his mother tried to manage his affairs. Within a few weeks he had found a place to live, a rented wooden bungalow in Fort Worth, and there Oswald, Marina, and their daughter made a very simple home. Oswald also found a job, as a manual worker with a local metal factory, and began working long hours. It seemed he needed to, for Oswald owed more than six hundred dollars, most of it to the Government for bringing him home from Russia, plus two hundred to his brother, who had paid the fare from New York City. For a misfit, Oswald seemed to be facing up to his responsibilities. The curious thing was the way the American military and intelligence authorities treated his return or claim they did.

In the first place, there was no sign whatsoever that the Marine Corps ever considered the possibility of prosecuting Oswald, a reservist who had bragged about offering electronic secrets to the Soviets. On leaving active duty Oswald had signed a form which listed the penalties for revealing classified information and specified that personnel "can be recalled to duty . . . for trial by court-martial for unlawful disclosure of information. . . ." Oswald's defection, and his threats about handing over secrets, had supposedly caused the American military to order important changes in its secret codes. Yet, on his return from Moscow, the Marine Corps showed no interest in even seeing the prodigal, let alone putting him on trial. Oswald—very possibly guilty of serious treason—just went quietly home.

When Oswald returned to Texas, FBI agents seemed somewhat ignorant about his case and slow to react. Oswald's name had not been placed on the list of those thousands of people categorized by the Bureau as being potentially disloyal. But the FBI had opened a "security case" on Oswald after his defection, and local FBI agents did interview him some weeks after he returned home. They asked Oswald whether he had been approached by Soviet intelligence while in the Soviet Union. Oswald said he had not and declined to take a lie detector test. And that, effectively, was that—the Oswald "security case" was closed shortly afterward. There were to be other contacts between Oswald and the FBI during the period leading up to the assassination, but the nature of that relationship is, as we shall see, clouded with doubt.

As late as 1976, CIA Director William Colby insisted in a

television interview that his agency never contacted or debriefed Oswald following his return from Russia. The statements in the interview reflected a staff briefing Colby had been given in advance which said that Oswald, "if he came to DCD [Domestic Contacts Division] notice at all, would easily have been bypassed, because he simply did not possess the type of information the DCD was seeking at that time." The briefing paper added that by 1962 so many people were traveling to and from Communist countries that the CIA was "incapable of talking to all of them." We are asked to believe that American intelligence, capable of scooping up an "accidental" picture of Oswald taken in Minsk by tourists, did not have time to bother questioning a defector who had bragged about offering radar secrets to Soviet intelligence. Of all CIA claims in the wake of the Kennedy assassination, this remains the one unanimously rejected by even the most conservative observers.

As early as November 1959, within a week of Oswald's visit to the American Embassy in Moscow to announce his defection, a naval message went out requesting other agencies to report any developments "in view of *continuing interest* of HQ, Marine Corps and U.S. intelligence agencies." The Oswald case was, as the same document specifically stated in capital letters, an "INTELLIGENCE MATTER." In March 1961, as soon as Oswald showed signs of a desire to return to the United States, a senior State Department official wrote that any risk involved in returning Oswald's passport "would be more than offset by the opportunity provided the United States to obtain information from Mr. Oswald concerning his activities in the Soviet Union."

Skepticism about the claim that Oswald was not fully debriefed extends to the intelligence community itself. Thomas Fox, former Chief of Counterintelligence for the Defense Intelligence Agency, recently told an interviewer that he found it "inconceivable" that American intelligence would not have wanted to ask Oswald how he had been handled by the KGB.

In 1979 Congress' Assassinations Committee concluded that the CIA did not debrief returnees "as a matter of standard operating procedure." It did, on the other hand, reveal that several defectors were interviewed by the CIA at some stage. One of these was Libero Ricciardelli, a World War II Air Force hero who came home from Russia with his family in 1963. Another was Bruce Davis, a soldier who had deserted from the U.S. Army in Germany. A third was Robert Webster, the Rand Development Corporation employee who defected at the same time as Oswald and whose case contains intriguing parallels to that of Oswald. Webster, who returned to the United States only a few weeks before Oswald, was debriefed in great depth by CIA staff working in conjunction with Air Force representatives. After initial questioning, Webster was brought to Washington and interrogated for two weeks. Given Oswald's background, it would seem almost obvious that U.S. intelligence would have found a way to debrief him too. The Committee stumbled across a tantalizing lead which strongly suggested that this had occurred.

As we noted earlier, one CIA memorandum reveals that there was at one point at least discussion by Agency officials about "the laying on of interviews" with Oswald. The writer of the document was interviewed by the Committee but said he knew of no interview actually being conducted. However, the officer's memorandum emphasized a particular area of Oswald's experience which was of interest to the CIA. He wrote:

> We were particularly interested in the [deleted] Oswald might provide on the Minsk factory in which he had been employed, on certain sections of the city itself, and of course we sought the usual [deleted] that might help develop personality dossiers. . . .

It was another former CIA officer who seemed to set the Assassinations Committee on the road to establishing that Oswald had indeed been debriefed. He recalled collecting information on the Minsk plant where Oswald had worked, and he added a specific detail. He claimed that in summer 1962 he "reviewed a contact report from representatives of a CIA field office who had interviewed a former marine who had worked at the Minsk radio plant following his defection to the U.S.S.R." The CIA officer said the returnee in question had been living with his family in Minsk and believed he could have been Oswald. It is hard to imagine who else the description could fit, yet the Assassinations Committee met another CIA deadend. A search of the files, including the dossier on the Minsk factory mentioned by the former officer, proved fruitless. The Committee had to leave it at that, but there is some sort of trail to follow.[60]

Both the earlier CIA memorandum and the Committee's new witness referred to the way an Oswald debriefing would have been handled, with their respective references to the Domestic Contacts Division and "a CIA field office." The logical place to have debriefed Oswald was in the Dallas area, where he lived on returning home. The CIA was represented there by J. Walton Moore of the Domestic Contacts Division. Moore, as we shall see, denies contact with Oswald. Consider, though, one more clue. The CIA memorandum about "interviews" with Oswald included this passage:

> I remember that Oswald's unusual behavior in the USSR had struck me from the moment I read the first [deleted] dispatch on him, and I told my subordinates something amounting to "*Don't push too hard to get the information we need*, because this individual looks odd."

The writer of this document, who may not even have known of earlier contacts between Oswald and U.S. intelligence, was advising his colleagues that a hard, hostile interrogation was the wrong way to handle Lee Oswald. What was needed was somebody who could extract information in the guise of friendly conversation. Very probably, that is how a debriefing did happen. Today we can even make a guess at who the gentle inquisitor may have been.

Oswald and the Baron

Less than a week after arriving in Texas Oswald made a call to Peter Gregory, an exiled Russian working in the Texas oil business. All Oswald wanted, according to Gregory, was a letter of reference vouching for his competence in spoken Russian, and this Gregory provided. The meeting was an entrée to the social life of the local Russian exile community, and in the weeks that followed the young Oswald couple were made welcome by a bevy of Russian and East European emigrés. They seemed shabby and incongruous in the smart drawing rooms of their affluent new friends, but the exiles listened avidly to the fresh reminiscences about everyday life in the Soviet Union. It was in this improbable atmosphere that Lee Oswald met the man who openly became his mentor and friend and may have had specific and secret reasons for doing so. This was George de Mohrenschildt, an oil geologist and, apparently, much more.

Even the Warren Commission could not wholly ignore George de Mohrenschildt. It reported conducting an "intensive investigation" and concluded that this "developed no sign of subversive or disloyal conduct" on his part. In a remarkable understatement, the Report concluded that de Mohrenschildt was "a highly individualistic person of varied interests." That he certainly was. The man who would one day patronize the Marxist defector was—at least according to him—born shortly before World War I into a Russian aristocratic family; technically he had the right to call himself a Baron. He said his father, Sergei von Mohrenschildt, had been a Marshal of Nobility in the province of Minsk, where years later Oswald was to spend most of his time in Russia. Supposedly the father spoke out publicly against the Bolshevik revolution, was imprisoned for his pains, and finally made a narrow escape—taking his wife and son with him. George recalled growing up on the family estate in Poland, training at the elite Polish cavalry academy, and finishing his education at university in Belgium. He traveled to the United States at the age of twenty-seven, a dashing, cultured, romantic figure—ready-made for the role of professional exile. In the years before World War II he was welcomed, like so many others of this type, into American East Coast society. By curious coincidence he became acquainted with the wealthy Bouvier family, including the parents of a girl named Jacqueline, one day to become the wife of President Kennedy. He was to marry four times, on the first three occasions into wealthy American families and then to another Russian exile. In the hurly-burly of his privileged first few years in the United States, a regular job was not a priority for George—in that he was the archetypical white Russian refugee. During the Forties he picked up a Master's degree in petroleum geology at the University of Texas, a qualification which launched him on the career in the oil business which was to take de Mohrenschildt around the world for twenty years. Meanwhile, along with the glitter, the exiled Baron had ventured into the world of intelligence.

After the Kennedy assassination de Mohrenschildt was to tell the Warren Commission flatly, "I have never been an agent of any government, never been in the pay of any government, except the American government, the International Co-operation Administration." That connection, which came about in the Fifties, is itself fascinating, but de Mohrenschildt was involved in international intrigue long before then. That much is clear from what we know of de Mohrenschildt's activities during World War II. There has been speculation, based largely on FBI reports, that de Mohrenschildt did undercover work in the United States for Nazi Germany. This arises partly from an incident early in the war when de Mohrenschildt was found cheerfully sketching a Texas coastal scene which happened to include a naval installation. In 1942 he was deported from Mexico in a cloud of dark allegations about espionage on behalf of the Germans—apparently arising from his relationship with a Mexican woman. As a result of all this de Mohrenschildt's passport file was specially marked for review "to determine if the person posed a security threat. . . ." In New York, there was suspicion about de Mohrenschildt's involvement with his cousin, Baron Konstantin Maydell, a controversial White Russian who did apparently have pro-German sympathies. De Mohrenschildt appears to have done little worse for Maydell than help produce a film about the Polish resistance movement, and other factors may indicate that his true allegiance was to the Allied side.

A letter from Maydell to de Mohrenschildt reminded his relative to get the "necessary letters of credit from Nelson Rockefeller," and when arrested in Mexico de Mohrenschildt was carrying letters of credit worth $6,000 issued by Chase Manhattan—the Rockefeller bank. During the war Nelson Rockefeller was closely linked with Allied intelligence through the famous BSC—British Security Co-Ordination—and had set up his own operation to prevent oil supplies from reaching Germany from Latin America. The apparent official caution over de Mohrenschildt's passport may mask a different reality. There is no evidence that his case ever was seriously reviewed, and de Mohrenschildt continued to receive a series of passports without difficulty. According to de Mohrenschildt himself, the war had swamped Europe just as he was about to answer a Polish Army call-up for the fight against Germany. Instead, he said, he worked for French intelligence in the United States—"collecting facts on people involved in pro-German activity." The documents make it clear he did travel and recruit at least one individual on behalf of the Allies. In late 1942 de Mohrenschildt lived in Washington at the same house as a British intelligence officer and a senior American naval officer. That same year, according to CIA records, he expressed a desire to work for the Office of Strategic Services, the forerunner of the CIA. He was rejected then, according to a CIA memorandum written years later, because of the allegations that he was involved with the Germans. Yet if precautions were deemed necessary in wartime, American intelligence overcame its scruples in the years to come.

As de Mohrenschildt pursued distinction and fortune through the Fifties, he made intriguing friendships. At New York's exclusive Racquet Club he was seen frequently with Jake Cogswell, reported later to have been a CIA operative in Cuba. De Mohrenschildt visited Cuba during this period. He also traveled to West Africa, quietly gathering data on possible oil projects. In 1957 de Mohrenschildt spent many months in Yugoslavia on a geological field survey, and the link with American intelligence was clear-cut. It was now that he worked for the American Co-operation Administration, since identified as a CIA funded subsidiary of AID—the now notorious Agency for International Development.[61] While in Yugoslavia he was accused by the authorities of making drawings of military fortifications. When de Mohrenschildt returned to the United States he was debriefed by the CIA, in Washington and at home in Dallas, Texas. A CIA report says of the Dallas contacts, "in the course of several meetings the CIA representative obtained foreign intelligence which was promptly disseminated to other federal agencies in ten separate reports." From late 1960 till autumn 1961 de Mohrenschildt was in Central America and the Caribbean along with his fourth wife, Jeanne. He and his wife have insisted that this protracted trip was purely for pleasure, although de Mohrenschildt did later write to the State Department offering his written record of the journey. A photograph taken during the Central American phase of the trip shows de Mohrenschildt with the American ambassador to Costa Rica. The couple were in Guatemala—a major jumping-off point for CIA-backed Cuban exiles—during the Bay of Pigs invasion.

One of de Mohrenschildt's Dallas acquaintances told the Warren Commission, "George repeatedly hinted that he was doing some service for the State Department." De Mohrenschildt's Dallas lawyer, Patrick Russell, also knew his client as a close personal friend. In 1978 he told me, "I personally have always felt that George was a CIA agent. . . . He did have among his acquaintances people belonging to foreign governments as well as to the American government who were members of the military or in political or quasi-political positions. . . ." As will become clear, de Mohrenschildt did indeed become involved in matters involving American military intelligence. His lawyer, Patrick Russell, confirms that his client "traveled abroad regularly, frequently without his wife. And each time upon his return to the States he would undergo debriefing. It has always seemed most plausible to me that he was an agent, that he did have an assignment, that his association with Lee Harvey Oswald went a little deeper than friendship." In 1979, an Assassinations Committee source, who had specialized in studying de Mohrenschildt, observed that—while his name is not on file as an agent—"he had contacts with intelligence again and again. We could certainly give him no clean slate as far as intelligence was concerned."

When Oswald and his Soviet wife came to Texas in 1962, Russian emigré de Mohrenschildt was in the area and available, an excellent candidate if someone was needed to pump Oswald on his Russian adventure. He and his wife have always claimed they encountered Oswald by chance, in autumn that year, following a casual introduction by friends in the Russian community. Over the years, however, the participants have differed as to how precisely it came about. One early version was that they were taken to see Oswald by a Dallas businessman of Russian descent, Colonel Lawrence Orlov. Orlov, though, told a recent interviewer than when that meeting took place it was obvious the Oswalds and the de Mohrenschildts had met before. De Mohrenschildt told the FBI after the assassination that they had been introduced by the doyen of the affluent Russian colony in Dallas, George Bouhe. Bouhe said it did not happen that way. Jeanne de Mohrenschildt says simply, "My husband and I heard from the Russian community of an American Marine that defected to Russia and returned bringing a young wife and daughter. . . . He needed a job and she needed help with the child. So we decided to take them under our wing." Under pressure, however, George de Mohrenschildt was to inject a quite different element into the story—that he was cleared to associate with Oswald by a CIA agent based in Dallas, J. Walton Moore.[62]

Moore exists; he was the Domestic Contacts Division agent who debriefed de Mohrenschildt after the Yugoslavia trip in 1957. His job, as defined in 1979 by Congress' Assassinations Committee, was "to contact persons traveling abroad for the purpose of eliciting information they might obtain." Moore's own correspondence with CIA headquarters reveals that, in the two years following the Yugoslavia debriefing, he saw de Mohrenschildt several times. They discussed their mutual interest in China, and in 1961 Moore viewed films made by de Mohrenschildt during his Central American travels.

It was in the wake of the assassination that de Mohrenschildt first implied that CIA agent Moore had special knowledge of Oswald. He told the FBI that, after meeting Oswald, he asked Moore whether it was "safe" to associate with him. Moore, according to de Mohrenschildt, responded by saying, "Yes, he is okay. He is just a harmless lunatic." Jeanne de Mohrenschildt says she was present during the conversation and that "Moore seemed to be aware of Oswald. He knew who we were talking about. He said the CIA had absolutely no trace on him, that he was perfectly all right and clear. The CIA had nothing on him in the records." If the wife's version is accurate, George de Mohrenschildt's CIA friend was behaving very strangely. CIA files did contain material on Oswald and his activities in Russia. But an even more discordant note is struck by Jeanne's allegation that Moore was at once familiar with the Oswald case when the subject was brought up—

as she claims—out of the blue, over dinner. If the CIA had nothing on Oswald, how was its Dallas representative qualified to comment on Oswald without even checking? And did de Mohrenschildt really consult his local CIA contact *after* meeting Oswald, or did he start to cultivate Oswald at the suggestion of the CIA?

The CIA was and remains embarrassed by de Mohrenschildt's revelations about the Agency man in Dallas. De Mohrenschildt claimed that an FBI agent who visited him after the assassination, James Wood, tried to pressure him into withdrawing the story of the Moore meeting. The documentary record reflects that pressure and de Mohrenschildt's humiliating (and implausible) recantation. Moore himself, who still lives in Dallas, fobbed off one reporter in 1976 by claiming airily, "To the best of my recollection, I hadn't seen de Mohrenschildt for a couple of years before the assassination. I don't know where George got the idea that I cleared Oswald for him. I never met Oswald. I never heard his name before the assassination." On the matter of when he had last seen de Mohrenschildt, Moore was more careful about his "best recollection" when questioned by the Assassinations Committee. Its report says that—while still denying he ever discussed Oswald—Moore indicated that from 1957 on he "had 'periodic' contact with de Mohrenschildt for 'debriefing' purposes over the years. . . ." Jeanne de Mohrenschildt responds to even that statement with rather credible feminine scorn. She says that at the relevant period, Moore was so close an associate that he and his wife were dining once a fortnight with the de Mohrenschildts.

As Dallas representative of the CIA's Domestic Contacts Division, and given his established rapport with de Mohrenschildt, Moore was well placed to arrange a discreet debriefing of Oswald on his return from the Soviet Union. In his last interview on the subject, in 1977, a weary George de Mohrenschildt came up with what may well have been the truth. He said that CIA agent Moore encouraged him to see Oswald, that he would not have seen Oswald at all without Moore's encouragement. There can now be little doubt that whether he knew it or not, Oswald was monitored by the Central Intelligence Agency as soon as he returned to the United States. There is no doubt at all that George de Mohrenschildt had a direct effect on Oswald's life.

George swiftly established a man-to-man relationship with Lee, and they made a strange pair. De Mohrenschildt was thirty years older than Oswald, swashbuckling and sophisticated, a hanger-on of a well-to-do social group which Gerald Ford, a former member of the Warren Commission, has described as "conservative, anti-Communist." Oswald, in contrast, seemed introverted, consumed with idealistic notions, and grindingly poor. Yet just as in the war George de Mohrenschildt may have played the Germanophile, infuriating friends with "Heil Hitler" salutes while privately working for the Allies, so now he was well equipped to cultivate Oswald. De Mohrenschildt was a maverick among his Dallas friends, an articulate champion of minority causes and a liberal who loved to flout convention. He had no trouble building a bridge to Lee Harvey Oswald and seems genuinely to have liked him. Years later de Mohrenschildt would say, "Lee Harvey Oswald was a delightful guy. They make a moron out of him, but he was smart as hell. Ahead of his time really, a kind of hippie of those days. . . ." Apart from the Soviet episode, the Baron and the "hippie" covered a lot of ground together. In a rough manuscript written after the assassination, de Mohrenschildt portrays Oswald as a young man with ideas which today would raise few eyebrows. For example, he shared with de Mohrenschildt a sense of outrage over racial discrimination in the United States and spoke admiringly of Martin Luther King. Most poignant of all today are Lee Oswald's statements about President Kennedy. As reported by de Mohrenschildt, Oswald repeatedly praised the President for his efforts to improve the racial situation and to reach an understanding with the Communist world. De Mohrenschildt quotes Oswald, who within a year would be accused of killing John Kennedy, as saying of the President, "How handsome he looks, what open and sincere features he has! How different he looks from the other politicians! . . . If he succeeds he will be the greatest President in the history of this country."

If de Mohrenschildt's main purpose was to extract information about the Russian episode, Oswald was a walkover. The two new friends talked hour after hour about Oswald's experiences in the Soviet Union, and de Mohrenschildt received one unexpected bonus. When Oswald arrived in the United States he had started collecting notes and comments on his stay in Russia and spoke briefly of getting them published. Then he seems to have had second thoughts, for he did not respond at all when a persistent local reporter tried to discuss them with him. Now, though, Oswald handed over his detailed notes to de Mohrenschildt and respectfully asked for his opinion. Possibly the papers were promptly copied and passed to de Mohrenschildt's friend in the local CIA, Jim Moore. De Mohrenschildt's son-in-law, Gary Taylor, was to tell the Warren Commission that Oswald became putty in de Mohrenschildt's hands, "Whatever his suggestions were, Lee grabbed them and took them, whether it was what time to go to bed or where to stay." In October 1962 Oswald followed his older friend's advice in a way that changed the direction of his life.

On October 7 a group of Russians, including the de Mohrenschildts with their daughter and son-in-law, visited the Oswalds at their rundown apartment in Fort Worth. Oswald announced that he had lost his job at a nearby metal factory, a claim that was not true, and thus sparked a discussion as to what he should do next. It was George de Mohrenschildt who volunteered what seemed a ready-made plan. He suggested that Oswald would have a better chance of finding work in Dallas, thirty miles away, and that Marina would be better off staying awhile with one of the emigré families. Everyone present had been aware of tension between Oswald and Marina, and some believed Oswald had been beating his wife. De Mohrenschildt's proposals seemed reasonable and were accepted. Much later, some of those present would remember that George de Mohrenschildt was overdoing things a bit, that he seemed strangely clear about Oswald's job prospects in Dallas. He even gave the impression that he was personally supplying Oswald with funds. Perhaps significantly, Oswald—for all his apparent poverty—had just finished repaying the $200 his brother had lent him to help with the travel from New York. The day after the meeting at his apartment, Oswald followed de Mohrenschildt's advice to the letter. He walked out of his perfectly good job in Forth Worth, without notice or explanation, and traveled to Dallas. Apart from a few days at the city YMCA, it is not known where Oswald stayed for the best part of the next month.

He rented a post-office box, a system which—assuming no

official surveillance—ensured the receipt of mail with absolute privacy. Oswald used a post-office box wherever he went from now on. Four days after arriving in Dallas he also secured a new job—one which paid, within a few cents, exactly the same as his old job in Forth Worth. Although technically the work was found for Oswald by the Texas Employment Commission, George de Mohrenschildt's wife and daughter both say de Mohrenschildt organized it. Instead of factory chores the job involved photography, a skill Oswald was keen to learn. It was to be an odd setting for a young man who had sullied his name by defecting to the Soviet Union and offering to give away military secrets.

Oswald's new employment was with a graphics-arts company called Jaggars-Chiles-Stovall. The firm not only prepared advertisements for newspapers and trade catalogues but also handled contracts for the U.S. Army Map Service. Much of the Army work involved material obtained by the very U-2 planes Oswald had once watched in Japan, and only employees with a special security clearance were supposed to see it. In practice everybody—including Oswald—worked in cramped conditions which made secrecy impossible. He worked side by side with a young man named Dennis Ofstein who had previously worked in the Army Security Agency. Oswald was closemouthed about his background, but loosened up a little when he found Ofstein knew some Russian. Ofstein later recalled the curiously professional way his new colleague discussed matters of military interest he had observed in the Soviet Union. Oswald mentioned "the dispersement of military units, saying they didn't intermingle their armored divisions and infantry divisions and various units the way we do in the United States, and they would have all of their aircraft in one geographical location and their infantry in another. . . ." Once, when Ofstein helped Oswald enlarge a picture, he said it had been taken in Russia and showed "some military headquarters and that the guards stationed there were armed with weapons and ammunition and had orders to shoot any trespassers." Over a period of six months at Jaggars-Chiles-Stovall, Oswald became acquainted with sophisticated camera techniques. He also acquired items of photographic equipment which seemed unlikely possessions for a youngster living on a pittance. When police seized Oswald's effects in

November 1963, after the assassination, they found a Minox camera—the sort usually referred to as a "spy camera." This fact remained obscure until very recently.

Dallas police detective Gus Rose says he found the Minox camera in Oswald's old Marine seabag. It was listed with other confiscated possessions in Dallas police headquarters and kept there until the FBI took over the inquiry and carried off all evidence, including the camera, to Washington. Two months later the FBI contacted the Dallas police and tried unsuccessfully to have the manifest of Oswald's possessions changed. They now claimed that the equipment found had not been a camera at all, but a Minox *light meter*. The police declined to change the manifest, and today Detective Rose remains adamant that it was indeed a Minox camera he found. He is emphatically supported by Assistant District Attorney Bill Alexander, who saw the Minox camera just after its seizure. He scoffs at FBI attempts to say the camera never existed, recalling that he personally worked the mechanism on Oswald's Minox. As a professional investigator, Alexander is familiar with the workings of the Minox camera and owns one to this day. He regards the FBI behavior over the camera as further indication that before the assassination, Oswald had some connection with a government agency. Warren deBrueys, the FBI agent who took Oswald's possessions to Washington and monitored his activities during part of 1963, today says he "cannot remember" the Minox camera. Now retired from the Bureau, deBrueys adds, however, that there are "limitations as to what I can say. . . . I have signed the secrecy agreement before leaving the Bureau." In the recent proceedings of Congress' Assassinations Committee, a staff lawyer made it clear that the item seized was indeed a Minox camera.

Along with the camera, police confiscated a whole array of other equipment after the assassination, including rolls of exposed Minox film. In 1978, after a legal suit under the Freedom of Information Act, the FBI released twenty-five pictures developed from the Minox cassettes. The majority show scenes shot in Europe, and five show military scenes apparently ' ʰotographed in Asia or Latin America. Apart from the Minox material, the police also seized three other cameras, a 15-power telescope, two pairs of fieldglasses, a compass, and even a pedometer. None of those who knew Oswald in the two years before the assassination have remembered him as a cross-country hiking enthusiast. The total cost of all this equipment must have been hundreds of dollars.

Oswald's address book, also confiscated after the assassination, contained the words "micro dots," written alongside the entry for the firm of Jaggars-Chiles-Stovall.[63] The microdot technique is used to store and transmit intelligence information. By a system of photographic reduction a mass of written material can be transferred to a tiny spot like a punctuation mark and then concealed in an apparently innocent document, such as a letter. It is a technique that has little use outside espionage. Taken together, Oswald's activities, possessions, and associations all jar with his public image of a hard-up workingman. There is no avoiding the strong suspicion that he was, in reality, something else.

In the weeks before Christmas 1962, Lee and Marina appeared to lurch from crisis to crisis in their married life. For a while they were separated again—and the Russian exile colony buzzed with rumors of Lee's cruelty toward his wife. Oswald, for his part, complained that Marina had her faults—not least a weakness for gossiping to others about their sex life. Many of the local Russians, who had at first befriended the Oswalds, swiftly backed away from the marital strife. George de Mohrenschildt, however, did not. He continued to spend time with Oswald, talking politics with him—largely in English, a language Marina still had trouble following.

As the fateful year of 1963 began, Oswald moved into a new phase. Ostensibly he plunged once again into a lonely obsession with left-wing causes, this time with a tragic spiral into violence. The conventional wisdom for a long time was that Oswald was now set on a course which would lead him—and him alone—to Dealey Plaza, as the assassin of President Kennedy. Today, with the Assassinations Committee finding that at least two gunmen were involved, the signposts point in new directions. So far as the role of triggerman is concerned, Oswald may even have been the fall guy he claimed to be.

CHAPTER 12

"Hunter of the Fascists"

Not even Marina knows why I came home.

—Lee Harvey Oswald, on his return from Russia

The New Year card for 1963 arrived early at the Soviet Embassy in Washington, wishing all the employees "health, success, and all the best," The signature read "Marina and Lee Oswald." Greeting cards do not, it seems, escape the eyes of the U.S. Government mail-intercept service, and Oswald the Marxist was at it again. He had never really stopped. In spite of the disappointment he had expressed about life in the Soviet Union, Oswald had been sending off for Socialist literature since soon after his return to the United States. He subscribed both to *The Worker*, the newspaper of the American Communist Party, and to *The Militant*, a news sheet produced by the Socialist Workers' Party. According to those who knew him, he was reading Marx and Lenin, and in the first weeks of 1963 Oswald fired off more letters to left-wing publishers, requesting propaganda. He even requested an English translation of the Socialist anthem, "The Internationale." At the same time, however, he was also reading H.G. Wells, along with biographies of Hitler, Nikita Khrushchev—and President Kennedy. Oswald was also taking that openly capitalist publication, *Time* magazine.

At about this time, according to Marina, married life became intolerable for both her and Lee, and her husband came up with his idea of a solution—that Marina and the child should return to the Soviet Union. In February, Marina actually wrote to the Soviet Embassy asking for assistance to return to Russia. Meanwhile, she became pregnant for the second time, news which apparently delighted Oswald. It was at this point, according to the documen-

tary record, that Oswald began playing with fire. He started buying guns.

It was in March 1963, according to the mail-order forms and
company records recovered after the assassination, that Oswald
purchased a Mannlicher-Carcano 6.5-mm. rifle and a Smith &
Wesson .38 revolver. The rifle was the weapon that would be
found in the Texas School Book Depository after the President's
murder, and the revolver was the gun linked to the shooting of
Officer J.D. Tippit, allegedly shot by Oswald after the assassination. The rifle cost only $21.45, including postage, the revolver
$29.95. These were the weapons ordered in the name of
"Hidell"—the nickname given to one of Oswald's fellows in the
Marine Corps. Apart from its use in the purchase of the guns,
Oswald is not known to have used the name as an alias at any other
time. Yet, as we have seen, a top Army Intelligence officer now
says his unit had a "Hidell" file before the assassination, apparently because it was an Oswald alias. On the basis of the known
record, it is hard to see any explanation for that—other than that
military intelligence was aware of Oswald's gun purchases at the
time he made them.* That Oswald was involved in buying the
guns, though, has never been seriously doubted. They were sent to
his post-office box number in Dallas, and the handwriting on the
order forms was firmly identified by document examiners as Oswald's. What, though, did Oswald do with the guns?

The Warren Commission concluded that, seven months before the Kennedy assassination, Oswald used his rifle in an attempt
to kill Major General Edwin Walker, a former U.S. Army officer
living in Dallas. In 1979 Congress' Assassinations Committee also
found that the evidence strongly suggested Oswald's involvement,
and both inquiries said the Walker shooting was a damaging indication of Oswald's "disposition to take human life." Whether or
not that is right, the attempt on General Walker is an important
and neglected part of the assassination saga. As the Warren Report tells the story, this is how it came about.

General Walker was, by 1963, a notorious leader of the ultra-
conservative right wing, opposed to accommodation with the Sovi-

*See Chapter 5, "Finding a Fugitive."

et Union, opposed to racial desegregation, opposed to anything at
all that smacked remotely of liberalism. Two years earlier, as
commander of the 24th Division of the U.S. Army in West Germany, he had caused a national scandal by using his position to
foist right-wing propaganda on his men. Rather than obey orders
to stop doing so, Walker had been relieved of his command. Then
he resigned from the Army in high dudgeon. Back in civilian life,
he launched himself into politics, at one stage running for the
Texas governorship on an extreme right wing platform. In late
1962 he again erupted into the headlines when President Kennedy
ordered the enforcement of desegregation at the University of
Mississippi.

General Walker played a leading role in events which led to a
racist mob trying to prevent a black man from enrolling as a
student. The resulting confrontation with marshals and federal
troops caused two deaths and many injuries. Afterward General
Walker was temporarily detained in a mental institution on orders
from the President's brother, Attorney General Robert Kennedy.
In early 1963 he was back in Dallas, where he had become a
leading light of the local John Birch Society. General Walker was
certainly the sort of person President Kennedy had had in mind at
the end of his first year in office when he declared, "The discordant voices of extremism are once again heard in the land. . . .
They object quite rightly to politics intruding on the military—but
they are very anxious for the military to engage in their kind of
politics."

Living in the Dallas area as he did, Lee Oswald could not fail
to be aware of the outrageous general; and for Oswald, in his role
as Marxist and liberal idealist, Walker was an obvious political
bogeyman.

It seems clear from the testimony of several witnesses that
Oswald discussed right wing extremism on several occasions. Not
surprisingly it came up in his political debates with George de
Mohrenschildt, and General Walker himself was discussed in the
course of a conversation in early 1963. At a Dallas party in February, Oswald talked for a long time with a visiting German oilman
who, according to de Mohrenschildt, described Walker as "the
most dangerous man in the country" and compared him to Adolf

Hitler. On the way home from that party de Mohrenschildt allegedly held forth about the sins of the right wing, of "fascists," and the John Birch Society in particular. De Mohrenschildt liked to make dirty jokes and bad puns, and to him Walker was Nazi General "Fokker" Walker. If Oswald was not already interested in the general the message had now been rammed home. On the very next day the newspapers announced that Walker was about to make a nationwide speaking tour. For what happened next the official report relied mainly on the testimony of Marina and on persuasive evidence found among Oswald's effects.

The couple moved to a new and larger apartment, and Oswald turned one room into a study, where he could write and work on his photographic hobby—a hobby with an apparently murderous purpose. Months later the police were to seize five photographs, taken with a camera they linked to Oswald, all showing the rear of General Walker's home or railway tracks in the vicinity. This, the Warren Commission believed, was the reconnaissance stage of a carefully laid plan to shoot General Walker. Details in one of the photographs make it possible to date it to March 10, just two days before mail orders were sent off for Oswald's revolver and the Mannlicher-Carcano rifle.[64] Both weapons were shipped to Dallas on March 20. According to his wife's testimony, Oswald had the rifle at home shortly after this and told her he was going to use it for hunting. She once observed him leaving the house with the gun and several times saw him cleaning it. Allegedly, at the end of March, Oswald asked his wife to take photographs of him holding the rifle in one hand, two Socialist newspapers in the other, and the revolver on his hip. (These are the controversial pictures dismissed by some photographic experts as fakes. While this author believes they are probably genuine pictures of Oswald, his purpose in posing for them remains mysterious.)*

In the first week of April, Oswald stopped working at Jaggars-Chiles-Stovall, supposedly fired because of unsatisfactory work. That rings a little strange because the company used Oswald more and more in his last weeks with them, giving him many hours of overtime. At any rate, Oswald now started spending whole days

---

*Controversy treated in full in Chapter 5, "Finding a Fugitive."

away from home, never fully explaining what he was doing with his time. On April 12, according to Marina, he stayed out very late. That was the night somebody tried to shoot General Walker.

At nine o'clock that evening, says the general, he was working at his desk in a downstairs room, near an uncurtained window. There was a single loud bang, and a bullet smashed into the wall, missing Walker's head by inches. Although he summoned the police, nobody was ever caught. The case remained unsolved until after the Kennedy assassination, when the Warren Commission decided that Oswald—and Oswald alone—had been the culprit.

The ballistics evidence in the Walker shooting has since been questioned. A bullet was recovered from General Walker's house, but it was severely damaged by its impact on a window frame and a wall. The Assassinations Committee firearms panel could not say whether or not it had been fired from the rifle found after the President's assassination. Neutron activation analysis, however, indicated that it very likely was a 6.5-mm. Mannlicher-Carcano bullet. Some confusion has been caused by early statements about the bullet. Immediately after the shooting press reports quoted the police as having identified the bullet as *30.06* caliber, not 6.5-mm. A contemporary police report described the bullet as "steel-jacketed, of unknown caliber."[65] If the evidence of the bullet is not wholly conclusive, however, other evidence has strongly suggested that Oswald was at least involved.

According to Marina, Oswald, when he went out on the night of the attack on Walker, left a note for her. She "thinks" she found the note before he came home. It finally turned up inside a book among Oswald's effects, ten days after the Kennedy assassination, and was identified as being in Oswald's handwriting. It reads, as the Warren Commission noted, like the work "of a man expecting to be killed, or imprisoned, or to disappear," telling Marina how to dispose of his clothes and possessions and how to reach the city jail "if I am alive and taken prisoner." The note also asked her to inform "the Embassy"—presumably the Soviet Embassy—what had happened. Marina said that at 11:30 P.M., after she found this sinister note, Oswald rushed home in a state of panic. He blurted out to his wife that he had just used his rifle to fire at General Walker but did not know if he had killed him.

Later, said his wife, he showed her the reconnaissance photographs and notes he had made while planning the shooting. Supposedly at Marina's insistence, he then destroyed everything except the photographs and the incriminating note. Marina said she was shocked at what her husband had done but decided to keep quiet about it because he had failed. According to Marina, Oswald left his rifle buried near the scene of the Walker shooting, then went back a few days later to retrieve it. She said he promised her he would never do such a thing again, and for a few days it seemed he had got away scot-free. Then something astonishing happened.

The weekend after the incident, the Oswalds had unexpected visitors—their friends, the de Mohrenschildts. Soon after arriving George de Mohrenschildt allegedly made a shattering remark. He asked Oswald. "How is it that you missed General Walker?" There was shocked silence, and according to de Mohrenschildt himself, Oswald "sort of shriveled . . . made a peculiar face . . . changed the expression on his face." Marina said much the same thing. Oswald "became almost speechless," and then somebody changed the subject. One odd aspect of this story is the nature of Oswald's alleged reaction. It suggests Oswald was thrown visibly off balance by de Mohrenschildt's remark and was even more agitated a few nights earlier when he arrived home after the Walker attempt. Yet months later, when challenged by a policeman within moments of allegedly killing President Kennedy, Oswald was to behave very differently. According to Officer Baker and another witness, he seemed normal, calm, and collected and did not change his expression at all—just a minute or two after supposedly seeing his bullet explode in the President's head. This, however, is only one of the contradictions in the story told by Marina and the de Mohrenschildts.

Marina's evidence suggested Jeanne de Mohrenschildt had first observed the rifle, in a cupboard, while being shown around the apartment a few days before the Walker shooting.[66] Yet Jeanne said she saw the rifle for the first time during the visit *after* the shooting, mentioned it within minutes to her husband, and this led directly to his—"with his sense of humor"—making the extraordinary remark suggesting Oswald had been the Walker gunman. Is it possible that after the shooting, at a time when she and her husband were supposedly doing all they could to cover up the crime, Marina readily opened a cupboard door permitting Jeanne to see the rifle? That improbability aside, Marina and the de Mohrenschildts have come up with conflicting dates for the occasion Jeanne de Mohrenschildt saw the rifle. After the assassination, in an interview with State Department officials, the de Mohrenschildts claimed the gun incident had occurred as early as autumn the previous *year*. If another, Jeanne de Mohrenschildt, version is right, then she saw the rifle in the cupboard on a day it was supposedly still buried somewhere near General Walker's house. If the Walker case had ever come to court a defense counsel would have made great play of these flaws in the testimony. He would also have used a whole armoury of other inconsistencies.

After the Kennedy assassination, Marina's statement about her husband's use of his rifle were ludicrously inconsistent. Two weeks after the tragedy she told the FBI she "had never seen Oswald practice with his rifle or any other firearm and he had never told her that he was going to practice." This she repeated four times in a series of different interviews, adding that she had never seen Oswald practicing with the rifle in Dallas or anywhere else. Months later she changed her story, saying he had trained with the rifle. She referred to an occasion in *January* 1963 when she had seen him cleaning the rifle, and he had mentioned he had been practicing that day. That was a bad slip—the rifle was not even ordered till two months later! By 1978, when she gave sworn testimony to Congress' Assassinations Committee, Marina was saying that Oswald used to clean his gun "once a week" and went out quite often to practice.

According to the de Mohrenschildts, describing their visit after the Walker incident, both Oswald and his wife were just bursting to tell them how he liked going target shooting. Jeanne de Mohrenschildt quoted Marina as saying of Oswald's outings with the baby that "he goes in the park and shoots at leaves and things like that." Not surprisingly, the official report left out that gem. Nor was there any mention of that fact that, just as no ammunition was found among Oswald's effects, nor were any pull-through cords or other weapon-cleaning equipment.

In April 1967, more than three years after the Kennedy assassination, George de Mohrenschildt declared he had come into possession of some fresh and "very interesting information" about Oswald. On returning from abroad, he claimed, he had sorted through luggage he had left in storage and discovered a photograph of Oswald. The photograph was a copy of the now famous picture of Oswald holding his guns and Socialist magazines supposedly taken before the Walker shooting. On the back were two inscriptions (*see insert to illustration 8*). One, which Assassinations Committee examiners found to be Oswald's handwriting, read, "To my friend George from Lee Oswald," along with a date—"5/IV/63."[67] The date, one would think from circumstances, is meant to indicate 5 April 1963, but it is written in the style and order that Europeans write the date. An American, like Oswald, would normally wrote the month first and the day second, thus 4/5/63. A researcher's check of the dozens of letters and documents written by Oswald has produced not one example of a date written like the one of the back of the photograph.[68]

The second inscription on the back of the picture, written in Russian Cyrillic script, translates as "Hunter of fascists ha-ha-ha!!!" Expert testimony to the Assassinations Committee was that this ironic slogan—clearly directed at Oswald—had been written and then rewritten in pencil. Most important of all, it could not be identified with the writing of either Oswald, his wife Marina, or George de Mohrenschildt. There remains the question as to whether it was written by Jeanne de Mohrenschildt—but a further detail seems to rule that out. The Assassinations Committee expert considered that the top layer of pencil writing had been done by "somebody who was apparently not conversant with the Cyrillic alphabet." That seems to rule out both Oswalds and both de Mohrenschildts, all of whom either grew up using Russian or had extensive practice. What fifth person, unversed in Russian, wrote note a on the photograph which serves only to make it more compromising to Oswald? The question remains open.

Marina Oswald has behaved strangely over the photograph, even allowing for her supposedly poor memory. She has said she does not remember writing the "Hunter of fascists" slogan. Leaving aside the expert evidence that indeed she did not—surely that is something even Marina would remember one way or the other. Recently, in front of the Assassinations Committee, she seemed to provide some sort of a breakthrough on the subject. Speaking of the photograph and her husband, she blurted out, "What strikes me, I think I was surprised *that he showed pictures to George de Mohrenschildt* because I thought the rifle and the gun, first of all I was always against it so, if in my memory I remember being surprised at him showing pictures like that to George, so apparently I saw them at the apartment . . . something strikes my memory that: how dare he show pictures like that to a friend?"

An Assassinations Committee lawyer evidently realized at once the significance of what Marina had appeared to let slip. When he tried to pursue the question of the Oswald rifle picture and George de Mohrenschildt's first sight of it, Marina backed away from "casting shadows on somebody that is maybe innocent. . . ." Then she pleaded failing memory and finally asked to be excused from questioning for a while. When testimony resumed, the familiar curtain of forgetfulness came down again on the whole episode of the photographs. Nevertheless, if Marina's brief burst of memory was true, she has taken the case a small but significant step forward. It means that George de Mohrenschildt, a man with known connections in the world of intelligence, saw Oswald pictured in a left-wing militant pose—and four or five months before the President's assassination.

The de Mohrenschildts have come up with their own dubious account of how and when they first set eyes on the photograph of Oswald with the rifle. According to them it turned up, wrapped in brown paper inside a stack of records, among effects stored in a Dallas warehouse during the de Mohrenschildts' absence abroad. Nobody has satisfactorily explained how it got there. How odd. According to the de Mohrenschildt story, they discovered the photograph only in January or February 1967. This was when they did indeed return from several years abroad. It was also, however, a time when the Warren Report was under increasingly effective critical attack. Specifically, it was being suggested that the picture of Oswald with the rifle was in some way bogus. De Mohrenschildt's production of a new copy of the photograph, apparently signed by Oswald, encouraged the belief that it was genuine. How timely.

One last point, concerning the purchase of the rifle and the revolver, went unquestioned in the Warren inquiry. Oswald's known finances for the period have been carefully documented, and all who knew him agree he was living at poverty level, just scraping by. When he returned from the Soviet Union he owed large sums—$200 to his brother and $435 to the State Department. During the last part of 1962, he repaid the latter, as one might expect of a man in his humble economic position, by dribs and drabs, ten dollars at a time. Then, quite suddenly, Oswald was able to pay off the entire remaining State Department debt of $396 in less than seven weeks—a period during which he earned only $490. At the risk of wearying the reader with arithmetic, we must pose a serious question. How did he pay the rent and keep his family for those seven weeks on a balance of just $94? The rent alone paid in that period took $68, leaving Oswald the princely sum of less than *four dollars* a week to provide for his family and pay the bills. That is clearly nonsense. Once can only conclude that Oswald received funds from another source. His sudden unexplained affluence happens to coincide precisely with his supposed decision to spend even more money—on firearms. The State Department mailed Oswald a receipt indicating that his debt was cleared on Saturday, March 9—and the record shows that the money order for the Mannlicher-Carcano rifle was bought at a Dallas post office on Tuesday, March 12. It was purchased early in the morning, yet Oswald's time sheet shows that he had clocked in by 8:00 A.M. that day.[69] The post office did not open *until* eight o'clock. These facts raise nagging questions. From what source did Oswald receive a sudden influx of funds, enabling him to pay off his debts, just before the weapons were purchased? And was it Oswald or somebody else who bought the money order which paid for the famous rifle?

As for the Walker shooting, there was from the beginning evidence suggesting that more than one person had been involved. The Warren Commission found it convenient to ignore the matter, but Congress' Assassinations Committee took the evidence seriously.

General Walker was not the only person startled by the loud report of the shot which nearly killed him. Walter Coleman, a fourteen-year-old boy, was standing in a doorway of a nearby house when he heard the shot. He at once peered over the fence to see what was going on—in time to see a suspicious scene involving at least *two* men. The Assassination Committee report recalls that young Coleman "saw some men speeding down the alley in a light green or light blue Ford, either a 1959 or 1960 model. He said he also saw another car, a 1958 Chevrolet, black with white down the side, in a church parking lot adjacent to Walker's house. The car door was open, and a man was bending over the back seat as though he placing something on the floor of the car."[70]

When the Walker case was reopened after the Kennedy assassination, Coleman was questioned again. He said he had got a look at these men. Neither resembled Oswald. Oswald did not own a car and was only learning to drive many months later.

In 1963, as a man constantly in the public eye for his controversial right-wing views, General Walker was aware that he might be in danger. Then, as now, he made a point of having aides with him wherever he went, and part of their work was to guard his home. Four nights before the shooting incident one of the aides, Robert Surrey, had spotted two men prowling around the house, "peeking in windows and so forth." He reported it to General Walker, who was concerned enough to report the matter to the police the next morning. Another of the general's aides, Max Claunch, says that while on watch for prowlers a few days before the incident, he noticed a "Cuban or dark-complected man in a 1957 Chevrolet" drive slowly around the general's house on several occasions. Suspicious activity was also observed weeks after the Walker shooting incident—but this reference to a car leads directly to a troubling example of apparent cover-up in the assassination investigation.

One of the photographs found among Oswald's possessions showed a view of the rear of General Walker's house, and parked outside is a car—a 1957 Chevrolet. When produced by the Warren Commission as an official exhibit, this photograph had one intriguing characteristic. A hole had been cut in the picture where the car's number plate should be (*see illustration 9*). The two Dallas policemen who found the photograph said the picture was already mutilated when they found it and "surmised that Oswald had evidently taken the license-plate number area out of the photo-

graph to keep anyone from identifying the owner of that automobile." Marina Oswald, however, told a different story. Questioned intensively about the photograph, she repeated several
times that there had been no hole—neither when she first saw it in
Oswald's possession nor when she was shown it by the FBI. She
insisted, "I remember very distinctly that there was a license plate
on this car. . . . There was no hole in the original when they
showed it to me—I'm positive of it." Marina's testimony, of
course, is notoriously unreliable, but this time she was, it seems,
right.

Six years after the assassination the former Dallas police
chief, Jesse Curry, wrote a memoir on his experiences at the time
of the President's murder. He published a number of police photographs for the first time, and among them is one showing Oswald's
possession after seizure by the police. In the bottom left-hand
corner is the photograph of Walker's house, partially obscured,
but it looks as though the portion containing the number plate is
intact (*illustration 9*). Unfortunately, because it is in this case a
small part of a much larger picture, the number plate—though
visible—is illegible to the human eye. It may not have been illegible in the original print. Did somebody tamper with vital evidence
after the assassination? If so, why?

In 1979, Congress' Assassinations Committee reported that it
had conducted only a "limited" and abortive investigation into the
evidence that accomplices were involved in the shooting attempt
against General Walker. It abandoned that line of inquiry but
apparently regretted doing so when scientific evidence indicated
that more than one gunman took part in the President's murder. In
the context of the Walker episode, the Committee referred to
Marina Oswald in a manner which many reflect its opinion of her
veracity. The report states, ". . . it is not necessary to believe all of
what Marina said about the incident, nor to believe that Oswald
told her all there was to know, since either of them might have
been concealing the involvement of others." The Committee,
which was committed to the belief that Oswald was one of those
who fired at President Kennedy, eventually said of the Walker
shooting, ". . . it is possible that associates of Oswald in the
Kennedy assassination had been involved with him in earlier activ-

ities. . . ." The Committee speculated, "If it could be shown that Oswald had associates in the attempt on General Walker, they would be likely candidates as the grassy knoll gunman." Today, it seems clear, the Walker shooting merits more investigative effort than the Committee could give it. A starting point might be expert study of the photograph of the 1957 Chevrolet parked behind General Walker's house and its number plate.

In another of the coincidences that run through this case, a 1957 Chevrolet was being sought by Dallas police on the day of the Kennedy assassination. Police radio transcripts show that two hours after the President had been killed, when Oswald was already in custody, headquarters put out the description of a 1957 Chevrolet sedan. If found, said the message, the occupants should be checked for concealed weapons. The car's last known position was near the scene of the shooting of Officer Tippit, the Dallas policeman killed shortly after the assassination. The record tells us nothing more. The case of the 1957 Chevrolet behind General Walker's house becomes another elusive dead end. It may, though, yield one clue to the nature of the Walker shooting—the remark by the general's watchman that the cruising Chevrolet was driven by a "Cuban or dark-complected man." Cuba and Cuban politics were of paramount importance to both Lee Oswald and General Walker. The Cuban issue, moreover, is central to the disentangling of the Kennedy assassination.

Apart from the race issue, Cuba was the general's favorite rabble-rousing topic in 1963. In his speeches and actions throughout the year Walker was, in his own words, "raising holy hell with the government over Castro and the Communists." In Walker's circles Cuba had become another reason for vilifying President Kennedy. In the opinion of the extreme right wing the President was personally to blame for the failure of efforts to topple Fidel Castro, using small armies of CIA-trained anti-Castro exiles. He was a traitor to the cause of freedom, they cried, and that made him a Communist too. Rabid though it all sounds now, General Walker's jingoism in those days found a significant following, and powerful friends. President Kennedy himself took the outcry seriously. In 1962 *Seven Days in May* had been published, a fictional story of how a group of right wing generals plot to overthrow an American President because of his "appeasement of the Communists." When President Kennedy heard that a film was to be made of the book he offered the White House as a shooting location. According to his former Special Assistant, Arthur Schlesinger, the President believed the film would be a warning to the nation." It was General Walker's aide and partner, Robert Surrey, who produced the "Wanted for Treason" leaflet aimed at President Kennedy and distributed in Dallas before the assassination. In those leaflets the President was accused of "betraying" Cuba. In the months before the assassination General Walker had been at meetings of exiles, in the words of one witness, "trying to arouse the feelings of the Cuban refugees in Dallas against the Kennedy administration." Walker's words of wisdom fell on the somewhat unlikely ears of a young man who called himself a Marxist, Lee Harvey Oswald.

Oswald was probably there in early October 1963 when General Walker attended a fund-raising meeting held by an exile group called the Directorio Revolucionario Estudiantil. According to a witness who also attended, Oswald sat at the back of the room, "spoke to no one, but merely listened and then left." By his own admission, Oswald was at a Dallas meeting a few days later when General Walker addressed a crowd of more than a thousand people. General Walker's address and phone number were listed in Oswald's address book. What was Oswald's purpose in assiduous attendance at Walker meetings just a month before the assassination, more than six months after he is supposed to have tried to shoot the general? Was this the lingering obsession of a would-be murderer, or did Oswald have some other purpose? How can we reconcile Oswald's supposed hatred for a right-wing extremist with his alleged murder of the President the right-wing abhorred? One Dallas associate, a sophisticated man from a political family, felt, as a result of talks with Oswald before the assassination, that Oswald was no Communist. For all his left-wing talk, it all somehow seemed insubstantial. George de Mohrenschildt, Oswald's friend with intelligence connections, had a way of explaining things. Years later he said Oswald had been "an actor in real life."

According to George de Mohrenschildt, he left Dallas nine days after the attempt on General Walker's life. De Mohrenschildt testified to the Warren Commission that he spent his time at this period getting ready for the work on the Caribbean island of Haiti which was to occupy him for the next several years. That work, he said, involved a highly lucrative oil surveying contract with the Haitian government and an interest in a sisal plantation. For this last project, he maintained, he established an association with the president of the Banque Commerciale of Haiti, Clemard Charles. De Mohrenschildt claimed his interests in Haiti were purely in the line of business, with no other "purpose or intent." Before leaving for Haiti, he stated, he spent time in Washington "preparing for the eventuality of the project, checking with the people, Bureau of Mines, and so forth." The Warren Commission took his word for it. In reality, de Mohrenschildt's schedule confirms his involvement in undercover political intrigue. What we now know is the result of fascinating research by Assassinations Committee staff.

A CIA Office of Security memorandum, written eleven years later, notes that—ten days after his departure from Dallas—a CIA officer "requested an expedite check on George de Mohrenschildt." The same document notes that de Mohrenschildt failed to account fully for what he did in Washington before leaving for Haiti and adds:

> It is interesting that [name deleted] interest in de Mohrenschildt coincided with the earlier portion of this trip and the info would suggest that possibly [name deleted] and de Mohrenschildt were possibly in the same environment in Washington D.C., circa April 26, 1963.

One of de Mohrenschildt's appointments in the capital has now been established. His CIA file reveals that in the first week of May a CIA employee called the office of the Army Chief of Staff for Intelligence—specifically to discuss de Mohrenschildt and his Haitian associate Clemard Charles. The Assistance Director of Army Intelligence has acknowledged meeting Charles that month. Also present were Tony Czaikowski of the CIA, who was introduced as a professor from Georgetown University—and George de Mohrenschildt. De Mohrenschildt brought his wife with him. The former Army Intelligence executive told the Committee she "did not know what role de Mohrenschildt was serving" but felt that he "dominated" his Haitian companion in some way. She said the Haitian had no military information of value to offer, and she did not recall any discussion of arms sales. Other evidence now available indicates that in coming months Charles was involved in a series of arms deals involving the United States. The Assistant Director from Army Intelligence said the meeting had been suggested by Colonel Sam Kail, an Army Intelligence officer, because of Charles's relationship to the President of Haiti and "Haiti's strategic position relative to Castro's Cuba." Colonel Kail specialized in Cuban intelligence operations involving Army Intelligence and the CIA. In that context his name will appear later in these pages.

The Army Intelligence representative at the Washington meeting has an apt comment on de Mohrenschildt's presence that day. "I knew," she said dryly, "the Texan wasn't there to sell hemp." Nor is it likely that, once in Haiti, de Mohrenschildt was wholly preoccupied with sisal plantations and oil surveying. An Assassinations Committee source who knew him there said de Mohrenschildt's behavior was "strange" and included "following people in his car." The source noted that he and his friend the bank president associated with a woman who ran an establishment "frequented by many American intelligence personnel from the American Embassy. . . ."[71] According to one source with CIA links, de Mohrenschildt was involved in an abortive CIA plot to overthrow the Haitian dictator, President "Papa Doc" Duvalier.

Something of the true role of Oswald's friend George de Mohrenschildt has now emerged. It seems that, with the departure for Haiti, his connection with the alleged assassin was over. Apart from a change-of-address postcard from Oswald, the improbable relationship ended as abruptly as it had begun. Oswald sent the card from New Orleans, the city where he spent the entire summer of 1963.

In 1979, when it announced its conspiracy findings, the Assassinations Committee suggested that anti-Castro exiles and elements of the Mafia may have been involved in President Kennedy's murder. Oswald's time in New Orleans is central to such a thesis. It was from that point on that, in public, Oswald became known for left-wing posturing in support of Fidel Castro. In private, his name was used by somebody presenting himself as an *anti*-Castro activist.

Who was Oswald, and who was playing what game? For in a scenario where much is obscure, there certainly was a game. The backdrop was Cuba.

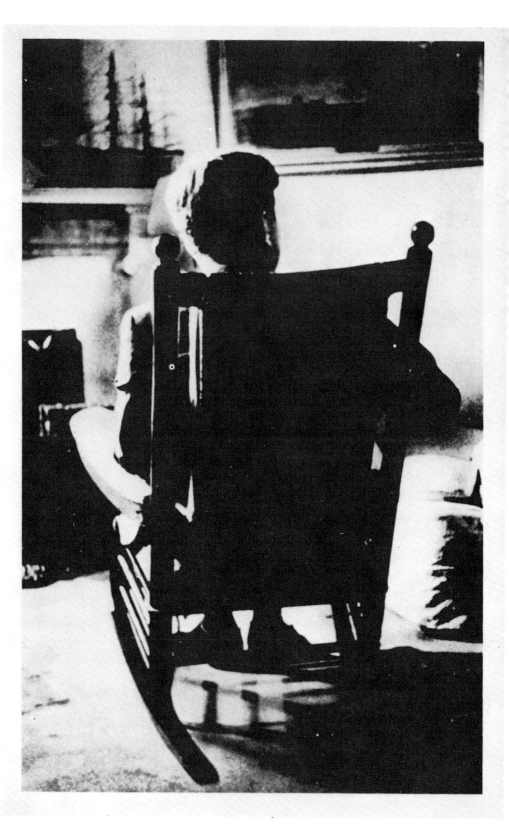

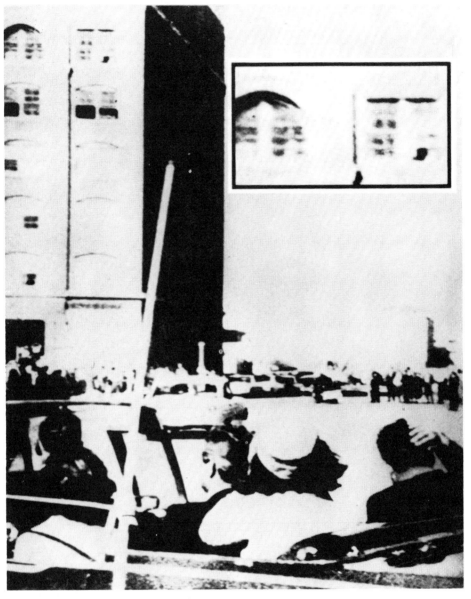

1. Seconds before the shooting started. At about this moment, the Governor's wife remarked to the President, "Mr. Kennedy, you can't say Dallas doesn't love you."

2. Was there one gunman, or two, behind the sixth-floor windows (*inset*)?

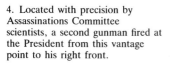

3. The ambush. Beyond the stricken President is the area of the stockade fence where acoustics scientists now place a second gunman. Private researchers have long suspected that one of the objects (*see box*) may be a man's head. Congressional photographic experts have recommended sophisticated analysis. (Much damaged polaroid photograph.)

4. Located with precision by Assassinations Committee scientists, a second gunman fired at the President from this vantage point to his right front.

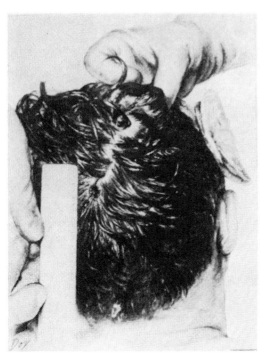

5. A botched autopsy: one of the medical drawings published in 1979 by Congress' Assassinations Committee. The medical panel, working from an original photograph, concluded that the early doctors made a four-inch error in placing an entrance wound in the President's head. (Medical illustration drawn from photograph.)

5a. **Best evidence?** Some of the autopsy photographs have now been seen by the public, some not. The result is further confusion. No damage to the rear of the President's head is seen in this photograph, though Dallas doctors described a massive wound. The explanation, one surgeon says, is that the scalp is merely being held in place for the photographer, thus covering a gaping hole. Meanwhile, some claim complex forgery of photographs and X-rays. Now that some of this horrific material has leaked, it would be as well to make all of it public. This would assist serious scholars, and perhaps dispel some of the suspicion.

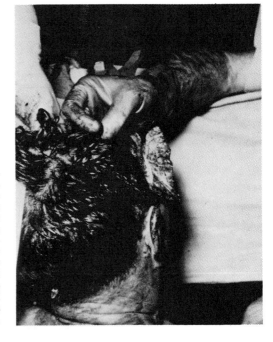

6. The rifle at the scene: ordered in the name "Hidell" (*see below*), it led straight to Oswald. But who knew he used that name? Was Oswald's finger on the trigger on the day of the assassination? Did the almost intact bullet (*right*) cause both the President's first wound and the Governor's multiple injuries?

7. Lee Oswald, at the time of his arrival in the Soviet Union, 1959.

8. A contentious photograph. Supposedly taken in spring 1963, this appears to show Oswald holding the rifle later retrieved at the scene of the assassination. Some still insist it shows signs of forgery. One copy, which turned up years later, bore an apparently authentic Oswald dedication, and the legend, in Russian, "Hunter of fascists ha-ha-ha!!!" (*inset*) The author of that curious phrase remains unidentified. The writing is not Oswald's.

9. Tampering with evidence? Oswald allegedly took this photograph of General Walker's house, before trying to shoot the general. It was long claimed that the number-plate on the car was obliterated by Oswald, before police recovered the photograph. In fact, it appears from a picture of Oswald's collected possessions (*below*) that the picture was unblemished until *after* the assassination. What would have been the motive for concealing the plate?

10. Surveillance by chance? Lee Oswald (*arrowed, right*), photographed in 1961 in the Soviet city of Minsk. The picture, taken by American tourists, soon reached CIA files.

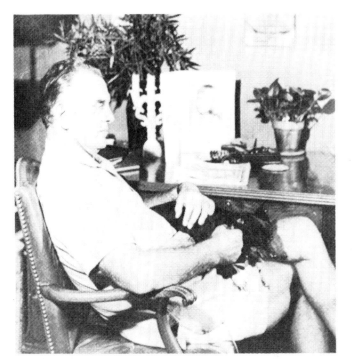

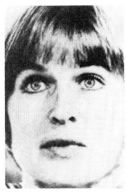

12. Marina, Oswald's Soviet wife. How spontaneous was their whirlwind courtship, and what could she tell about Oswald's activities in 1963? Her forgetfulness has frustrated successive official investigations.

11. The friend with a line to American intelligence. George de Mohrenschildt, who spent much time with Oswald in Dallas, has been linked to the CIA and to U.S. Military Intelligence. He said the CIA encouraged him to see Oswald, but shot himself on the eve of congressional questioning.

13. Senator Richard Russell, member of the Warren Commission: "We have not been told the truth about Oswald."

14. Congressman Hale Boggs, House Majority Leader and member of the Warren Commission: "Hoover lied his eyes out to the Commission—on Oswald, on Ruby, on their friends . . . you name it."

15. Senator Richard Schweiker, Senate Intelligence Committee: "I believe Oswald had a special relationship with one of the intelligence agencies . . ."

16. Congressman Richardson Preyer, Select Committee on Assassinations: "The Pentagon has destroyed its Kennedy assassination file . . ."

17. Richard Helms, CIA Deputy Director for Plans in 1963: "We are honorable men. You simply have to trust us." Helms failed to tell the Warren Commission about the Castro murder plots.

18. Allen Dulles, former CIA Director, actually served on the Warren Commission. He too knew of CIA-Mafia plots against Castro, but never told his Commission colleagues.

19. James Hosty, FBI agent who investigated Oswald in 1963, says he was ordered to destroy evidence after the assassination.

20. William Sullivan, Assistant Director of the FBI, told a congressional committee: "I think there may be something" on a special relationship between Oswald and American intelligence. He died in a shooting incident in 1978.

THE MAFIA.

21. Carlos Marcello, reported to have talked of "setting up a nut to take the blame" for the President's murder. Key figures in the investigation had links to his organization.

22. Santos Trafficante, alleged to have forecast that the President was "going to be hit." Oswald's killer knew several Trafficante associates, and may have met Trafficante personally.

23. Friends of the CIA: gangsters John Roselli (*left*) and Sam Giancana (*below left*) were used by the CIA in plots to assassinate Fidel Castro. Giancana, the Chicago crime boss, patronized "party girl" Judith Exner (*below right*), who also had a relationship with President Kennedy. Giancana and Roselli were brutally murdered in the 1970s, when both were expected to face congressional questions about the Kennedy assassination.

24. A personal feud: Teamsters Union leader Jimmy Hoffa (*above*) had bitter confrontations with Robert Kennedy long before his brother became President. In 1962 Hoffa's aide Edward Partin (*below right*) reported Hoffa plans to shoot or bomb the younger Kennedy, who was by then Attorney General. Federal investigator, later Judge, "Hawk" Daniels (*below left*) listened in on a Hoffa telephone conversation in which explosives were discussed. Partin and Daniels agree that Hoffa also posed a threat to President Kennedy.

FPCC
544 CAMP ST.
NEW ORLEANS, LA

The Crime Against Cuba

25. A crossroads for conspirators? The shabby
building at 544 Camp Street, New Orleans,
housed Guy Banister (*top right*) and David
Ferrie (*top left*), both right-wing extremists with
reported links to U.S. intelligence and to the
Mafia. Yet apparent left-winger Lee Oswald
(*above*) distributed *pro*-Castro leaflets stamped
with that address. Banister's employee Delphine
Roberts (*left*) says that Oswald used the office,
with Banister's connivance.

26. The heart of the matter? This artist's impression (*top left*) was issued in 1978 by Congress' Assassinations Committee in an effort to identify a U.S. intelligence officer who operated under the name of "Maurice Bishop." The source of the description, anti-Castro leader Antonio Veciana (*photographed with the author, below*), says "Bishop" met Oswald before the assassination and tried to fabricate evidence linking Oswald to Cuban diplomats in Mexico City. The Assassinations Committee, considering whether former Mexico CIA officer David Phillips (*top right*) was "Bishop," was not satisfied by his denials, nor by Veciana's. The search for "Bishop" continues.

27. Spying on the spies: Cuban intelligence identify the building (*left*) as the vantage point from which CIA cameras and sound devices monitored the Cuban embassy in Mexico City. Cuban photographers in turn watched Albert Rodriguez Gallego (*right*), said to have been the CIA agent manning the observation post. The CIA admits the surveillance, but claims it has no pictures of Oswald visiting the consulate. It says sound tapes of Oswald were destroyed. Why?

28. The reconnaissance. As early as the night of the assassination, Jack Ruby was at Dallas police station with his gun. This picture, taken from moving footage, shows him (*arrowed*) at a crowded press conference.

29. The end of the interrogation.

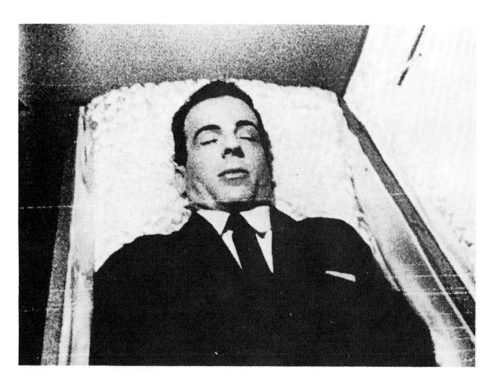

30. Lee Oswald in death: a previously unknown photograph, taken by a police intelligence officer.

III

CUBA

The Key to the Crime

CHAPTER 13

The Company and the Crooks

Anti-Castro activists and organizations . . . acquired the means, motive and opportunity to assassinate the President.

—Staff report to Congress' Assassinations Committee, 1979

Cuba was President Kennedy's albatross, but it had hung in the rigging of the American ship of state for decades. Washington had perceived it as just another poverty-stricken island in the sun, an American puppet which would hopefully stay that way. So it had, mostly under the rule of a former army sergeant named Fulgencia Batista, an old-fashioned dictator with a priority interest in lining his own pockets. He was able to do so above all because of the patronage of American organized-crime bosses, and they turned Havana into a mecca for gambling and prostitution. It was fine for everyone but the vast majority of the Cuban people, who remained miserably poor. On New Year's Day 1959 Cuba rallied to the liberation call of an unknown named Fidel Castro, and Batista fled. In Washington, as in America's citadels of organized crime, the government of President Eisenhower watched and waited to see what sort of revolution Castro had wrought. Few in the outside world suspected its true Marxist colors, but the Central Intelligence Agency had for many years been watching Castro with foreboding. Within months of his coming to power it became clear that Cuba was to be a Communist state, raising the specter of a Soviet outpost on America's doorstep. The United States reacted with instinctive outrage and nowhere more strongly than at the CIA and in the Eisenhower White House.

The Agency began eagerly encouraging the activities of the many thousands of anti-Castro exiles who had flooded into the

United States, mostly to Florida and the Southern coasts. Under the direction of a CIA officer called Howard Hunt, later to become notorious for his role in the Watergate affair, the refugee leaders formed a united front, eventually to become the Cuban Revolutionary Council. With the active assistance of the CIA, known colloquially as "The Company," young Cubans were recruited for armed struggle against Castro. At camps in Florida and Panama, and later in Guatemala and Nicaragua, U.S. Army officers trained the exiles for an invasion of their homeland. The unscrupulous nature of American intentions was summed up by Hunt, who recommended: "Assassinate Castro *before* or coincident with the invasion (a task for Cuban patriots). Discard any thought of a popular uprising against Castro until the issue has already been militarily decided."

In the White House, Richard Nixon was Vice President. With President Eisenhower in poor health and seeing out the last days of his administration, Nixon had a more active role than most deputy leaders. He was close to many of those wealthy Americans and Cubans who had most interest in the fall of Castro and was by his own account the "strongest and most persistent advocate" of efforts to bring it about. Nixon thus willingly became the White House action man on the Cuban project, reportedly favoring the extreme right-wingers among the Cuban exiles. It is a role he would apparently prefer forgotten, as he revealed years later. On one of the tapes which exposed his perfidy as President, Nixon brooded fearfully about what could still come out about the Cuban affair: "You open that scab, there's a hell of a lot of things and we just felt it would be very detrimental to have this thing go any further. . . . If it gets out that this is all involved, the Cuban thing, it would be a fiasco. . . ."

In November 1960, at the height of preparations for an exile invasion of Cuba, John Kennedy was elected President. The plans he inherited from the CIA and the Eisenhower administration led him into worse than fiasco. Kennedy disciples and their opponents still argue about where the fault lay for what occurred on April 17, 1961, when a force of Cuban exiles were put ashore on the south coast of Cuba, at the now infamous Bay of Pigs. It seems, sifting through the multiple accounts, that the new and inexperienced

President was inadequately briefed by the CIA and given bad military advice. The idea was that the exiles would establish a beachhead, then capture and hold an area which would be claimed as the territory of the provisional government. It was blithely hoped, against all the evidence, that there would then be a general uprising against Castro, leading to his fall from power. In fact the motley band of fifteen hundred Cuban exiles went ashore on a true Mission Impossible, into country bristling with well-prepared Castro defenders. The attackers floundered around in treacherous salt marshes, ran out of ammunition when their supply ships were sunk by Castro's aircraft, and were then ignominiously defeated. Many were killed and more than a thousand rounded up and marched off to prison. In public, President Kennedy accepted full responsibility, but the Bay of Pigs disaster was to be the cause of lasting acrimony.

In the CIA and some military circles the President was accused of vacillation at the moment of crisis. He had refused permission for air strikes, and for intervention by United States armed forces, on the ground that such action was diplomatically indefensible. Howard Hunt, the CIA officer who had helped prepare for intervention in Cuba, told me how, as news of the debacle came in, he and his colleagues reacted with dismay and scorn: "At CIA headquarters, in our war-room, while the invasion force was being churned up on the beaches, there was a sense of confusion, a spirit of desperation . . . we thought, as the indications came in, that the administration would feel more and more an obligation to unleash some United States power to equalize the situation. We kept receiving the administration's refusals with incredulity. I felt a sense of hollowness. It seemed totally unbelievable to me that the administration, having set this operation in motion, could abandon it and permit those fine men to be destroyed on the beachhead . . . somewhere along the way we lost a good part of our national will to prevail." Of President Kennedy, Hunt says: "I think it was a failure of nerves."

This CIA reaction suggests strongly that the Agency knew in advance, the Bay of Pigs operation could not succeed without U.S. military support, and that it had banked on being able to pressure the President into direct intervention. In the aftermath, John

Kennedy and his brother realized that the Agency had led them up the garden path. Worst of all, perhaps, CIA Director Dulles had encouraged the President to believe the landing would be followed by a mass popular uprising—a prospect CIA intelligence reports indicated was wholly improbable. There were also clear indications that the CIA had become a law unto itself. Contrary to the President's express orders, CIA officers had landed on the beach with the exiles. CIA agents had earlier told their Cuban protégés that they should go ahead with the invasion even if the President called off the landing at the last moment. This, as Robert Kennedy later commented, was "virtually treason." The President, understandably furious, said privately that he would like "to splinter the CIA into a thousand pieces and scatter it to the winds." He did not do quite that, but the ensuing shake-up led to the resignation of the Deputy Director responsible for the Bay of Pigs planning, Richard Bissell, and of the Director himself, Allen Dulles. Dulles, ironically, would later serve on the Warren Commission inquiry into the President's assassination—the Commission which so glibly glossed over the failings of American intelligence agencies. In the lower ranks of the CIA, the President had stirred lasting anger and resentment in many officers. For them, involvement with the Cuban exile movement had become a passionate crusade against Communism.

The President's brother, Attorney General Robert Kennedy, raised hackles at the Agency when he personally took over the responsibility of overseeing Cuban affairs. Howard Hunt thought him "an abrasive little man" whose presence became objectionable to CIA colleagues. Hunt recalls one significant clash between Robert Kennedy and William Harvey, the swashbuckling CIA agent who played a leading role in Cuban exile affairs after the Bay of Pigs. It was Harvey who was appointed to establish and manage the CIA's infamous "Executive Action" capability for the removal of foreign leaders, if necessary by assassination. Harvey liked to display, behind his desk, a lurid poster with the legend "The tree of liberty is watered with the blood of patriots," in this case a not so subtle reference to the Bay of Pigs fiasco. Robert Kennedy found this and its owner objectionable, and Harvey was eventually moved sideways. But if the Kennedys were alienating many officers at the CIA, they had roused even stronger passions among the hot-blooded Latin exiles themselves. Hunt says, "The failure of the Bay of Pigs had a disastrous effect on the morale of the exiles. First of all, they were outraged that a country so powerful as the United States, only ninety miles away from their homeland, could have permitted a disaster such as the Bay of Pigs to have taken place. . . . It provoked a crisis of faith among the Cuban exiles. . . . The more knowledgeable, the more sophisticated people in the Cuban community did blame the President personally."

For many exiles the catchword for the Bay of Pigs was "betrayal." The Cuban who had led the exiles onto the beaches, Pepe San Roman, recalls that when it was over, "I hated the United States, and I felt that I had been betrayed. Every day it became worse and then I was getting madder and madder and I wanted to get a rifle and come and fight against the U.S. . . . Our hopes were crushed. For me, the government of the United States was the utmost of everything—bigger than my father, than my mother, than God. And to me it was so low, so low a blow to us with so many plans and so many hopes. . . . And they knew before they sent us, in my mind, that they were not going to go ahead with it."

To some exile extremists, San Roman's comments were too kind. They looked for somebody to blame and not unnaturally placed the burden of guilt firmly on the American leadership. Mario Kohly, whose family played a vociferous part in exile politics, is specific about the author of the "treachery." He quotes his father, who claimed the Cuban presidency in exile, as saying, "John Kennedy sold out the American people. John Kennedy was a traitor . . . he was a Communist." The President had made enemies early in his administration, and the confusion and ambiguity of America's Cuba policy over the next two years only increased the distrust. Kennedy's handling of Cuba was a sorry story of misconception and brinkmanship, and it may in the end have proved personally fatal for him. The young President spoke at his inauguration of welcoming the responsibility of "defending freedom in its maximum hour of danger." In the months after uttering those brave words Kennedy was to learn many lessons and belated prudence. The light may have dawned too late.

The Bay of Pigs at first stiffened the President's determination to put the debacle behind him and resolve the Cuban problem aggressively. He went boldly along with the precept articulated by his advisers, that "There can be no long-term living with Castro as a neighbor," and allowed them to take action accordingly. The CIA, theoretically more tightly controlled under the eye of the Attorney General, set up an extraordinary new center of operations. Code-named "JM/WAVE," and situated in Miami, it was, in effect, the headquarters for a very public "secret war" against Cuba. This was the most ambitious CIA project ever, and came to involve seven hundred CIA and co-opted Army officers recruiting, training, and supplying thousands of Cuban exiles. The aim this time was to wage a war of attrition against Castro, harassing him with hit-and-run raids against industrial and military targets and inciting guerrilla warfare by anti-Castro groups operating inside Cuba. There were contradictions from the start—even within the family. The President urged that "all actions should be kept at a low key,' while his brother Robert urged rather vaguely that "no time, money, effort—or manpower—be spared." He threw himself with boundless Kennedy energy into the excitement of the fray. At the CIA there was no shortage of armchair cowboys eager to do just that, offering their resources as warrior father figures to the Cuban exiles.

The nerve center of the new struggle was set up in Miami, where the vast majority of the exiles were concentrated. There, in woods on the campus of the University of Miami, the CIA established a front operation in the shape of an electronics company called Zenith Technological Services. In 1962, at the height of its activity, the "JM/WAVE" station controlled as many as 600 Americans, mostly CIA case officers, and up to 3000 contract agents. It spawned front operations—boat shops, detective and travel agencies, and gun stores—all of them to provide flimsy cover for the Cuban crusade. There were also literally hundreds of "safe houses" for clandestine meetings and accommodation—ranging from apartments to opulent townhouses.

There were by now nearly a quarter of a million Cuban refugees in the United States, many of them content to settle into new lives in the United States, others obsessed with the idea of defeating Castro. The diehards, backed by many brave young men, clutched at the new straw of hope offered by the Americans. Night after night high-powered launches slipped out of the Florida waterways on missions of sabotage and propaganda. The exiles built up huge arms caches concealed in the Florida "safe houses" provided by the CIA. They trained in secret camps with CIA facilities and U.S. military instructors. Few, however, seem to have given serious thought to the main flaw in the master plan, that in Cuba Fidel Castro remained a popular leader. The exile operations achieved little in the long run, but they did everything to confirm Castro's accusations that the United States was guilty of criminal aggression.

Meanwhile, the President and his brother had become committed to rescuing the hundreds of Cuban commandos who had been so ignominiously captured at the Bay of Pigs. In a rush of sincere emotion and determination, they determined to get the men home by Christmas 1962. After protracted negotiations with Castro a ransom was agreed, and just before the New Year the last of the Bay of Pigs captives flew home. President Kennedy greeted them at a massive rally in a Miami sports stadium. Deeply moved, he plunged into a stirring speech, railing not only against Castro and Communism but seeming to promise much more. The President declared: "Castro and his fellow dictators may rule nations, but they do not rule people. They may imprison bodies, but they do not imprison spirits. They may destroy the exercise of liberty, but they cannot eliminate the determination to be free." Then, holding in his hands the banner of the exile brigade which had landed at the Bay of Pigs, Kennedy made a promise the thousands of dispossessed Cubans in the audience wanted to hear: "I can assure you," cried Kennedy, pausing for effect, "that this flag will be returned to this brigade in a free Havana." The applause was rapturous, but Kennedy's advisers were worried. Kennedy's last remarks had not been in the script, and they implied a commitment to the exile cause which was simply not there any more. A great deal had changed in the past eighteen months.

Kennedy accepted the cheers in the Miami stadium only weeks after the final conclusion of the missile crisis. Through the month of October the world had trembled as the leaders of the

United States and Russia traded threats of war. The immediate cause had been the arrival in Cuba of Soviet missiles capable of bombarding the United States, and the outcome—to Castro's noisy fury—had been a Soviet agreement to withdraw them. The United States, for its part, had given indirect assurances that there would be no invasion of Cuba by the United States. It was a commitment, the President knew, which would earn him no honors among his political opponents. The Republicans would say, he reflected, that "we had a chance to get rid of Castro, and, instead of doing so, ended up by guaranteeing him." That, certainly, was what many in the CIA and the Cuban exile community thought. A measure of the gulf between Kennedy and such critics is the fact that to this day many of them claim the Soviet missiles never were removed from Cuba. Howard Hunt, the senior CIA political officer who is still a rare American hero to the exiles, told me, "It has never been established that any missiles were ever removed from the island. Mr. Khrushchev agreed that photo surveillance could be conducted of the departing Soviet ships, but there have been no satellite scanners or aircraft cameras developed yet that can peer inside a wooden crate or through a tarpaulin. [The President] did not insist upon on-site inspection or on boarding the Soviet ships as they departed. Hopefully the missiles were taken out, but nobody dare say that they were." One Cuban exile I talked to in 1978 still spoke bitterly of the missile crisis, which he described as "a beautifully planned theatrical hoax." Hunt observed President Kennedy's speech to the returning Bay of Pigs veterans with scorn. The Cuban exile leadership did present a flag to the President, but—according to Hunt—"the Brigade feeling against Kennedy was so great that the presentation nearly did not take place at all." Exile distrust of the President was now well founded, for the United States was indeed losing interest in their cause.

President Kennedy—aside from incautious promises at public rallies—was increasingly in touch with reality and in conflict with the wilder elements of the CIA. Robert Kennedy had been appalled, in the midst of the missile crisis, to learn that the CIA was blithely sending commando teams into Cuba at the very moment the world teetered on the brink of nuclear war. The CIA's "Secret War" against Castro was a failure, and in the face of Congressional talk of appeasement, John Kennedy was now prepared to admit it—at least to himself. Notwithstanding his public pledge to the exiles, the President, in fact, began to clamp down firmly on their activities. By the middle of March 1963 he had taken the decision to bring the exiles under control.

Things came to a head in mid-March, after one of the most combative anti-Castro groups, Alpha 66, carried out a series of unauthorized attacks on Soviet ships in Cuban ports. Coming within months of the missile crisis with the Soviet Union,this was dangerously provocative. That, indeed, was the intention—as we shall see when the plot unravels further. President Kennedy acted firmly to dissociate himself and the United States from the raids. On March 31 a newspaper headline ran "U.S. Acts to Stop Raids." The Government announced flatly that it would "take every step necessary to make certain that American soil is not used as a base for refugee raids on Cuban and Soviet shipping." Within two days U.S. authorities matched their words with actions, seizing a commando vessel in Florida and using its influence with the British Government to abort another operation being mounted from the Bahamas. The powerful American apparatus which had previously aided and abetted the exiles now had orders to obstruct them. On the Florida coast the Customs and Immigration authorities, the Coast Guard, the Navy, and the FBI, all began frustrating the efforts of the Cuban hit-and-run raiders. The Justice Department had indicted one of the most notoriously violent exile leaders, Rolando Masferrer, whose enduring reputation was as a crony of the Cuban dictator Batista. On April 12 President Kennedy singled out his name as an example of the sort of man the United States did not wish to see in power in Cuba. At the same press conference he stripped away any lingering illusion that the United States would act militarily against Castro's Cuba. The President said, "There will not, under any conditions, be an intervention in Cuba by United States armed forces, and this government will do everything it possibly can—and I think it can meet its responsibilities—to make sure that there are no Americans involved in any actions inside Cuba. . . . The basic issue in Cuba is not one between the United States and Cuba; it is between the Cubans themselves. And I intend to see that we adhere to that principle. . . ." Kennedy made it clear that the turnabout was at his personal bidding.

Theoretically the President was putting an end only to "freelance" unauthorized exile operations; he was leaving the way open for missions approved by Washington. In fact authorized initiatives against Cuba dwindled to a trickle in 1963. There was a brief flurry of activity in the summer, apparently designed to deter Castro from interference in other Latin American nations. But in the White House the will to overthrow Castro by force had evaporated. CIA officer Howard Hunt recalls bitterly how one disappointed Cuban friend returned from a visit to ask Robert Kennedy for more assistance. He came away realizing "everything was going to be kept very low-key. A certain amount of money, a certain amount of material would be made available to the exiles for morale purposes; as a sop, as a sort of window dressing, so that the Cuban community would think something was being done, when in fact nothing of any significance had ever been done against the Cuban regime since the Bay of Pigs."

Controlling the exiles was easier said than done. One Bay of Pigs veteran, subsequently involved in anti-Castro terrorist activity, has said quite recently, "We use the tactics we learn from the CIA because we were trained to do everything. We were trained to set off a bomb, we were trained to kill." A host of disparate exile groups had been trained and armed to the teeth, and admonitions from the White House only inflamed the determination of many to persist. The most militant groups, those with names like "Alpha 66" and "International Anti-Communist Brigade," had no intention of going out of business. More worryingly, these creatures of the CIA retained the loyalty and moral support of elements within the CIA. It seems that while President Kennedy was apparently winding down the military effort against Cuba, the CIA went on playing soldiers in its Florida commando camps. According to one Army officer seconded to train exiles for the CIA, Captain Bradley Ayers, intensive training continued in great secrecy throughout 1963, and exiles continued to carry out missions against Cuba. The CIA would never admit involvement in such operations, but, says Ayers, "customarily, either by prearrangement through exile operatives or because of their own wish to capitalize on the political impact of such incidents, one of the splinter, independent Cuban exile groups, such as Alpha 66, would publicly take credit for the raids." Was all this sanctioned by President Kennedy, at the very time he was denouncing such operations in public? Ayers says he was briefed by General Victor Krulak, a personal friend of the President and a member of the government committee which authorized Cuban raids. He even claims that twice during the summer of 1963 Robert Kennedy personally visited CIA bases in Florida. The official record, and Kennedy's appointment book, mentions no such visits. Not least because the CIA is still reluctant to discuss its Cuban activities, we cannot be sure of the truth. It may be that Robert Kennedy, frantically busy with other assignments, failed to perceive precisely how the CIA was choosing to interpret official policy—in other words by overstepping it. The distinguished historian Arthur Schlesinger, in a neat turn of phrase, has politely called this the CIA's "distended theory of authorization." The administration was allowing a dangerous vacuum to arise in its handling of Cuban affairs. With the exile militants and their CIA militants straining at the leash, this was perilous indeed.

There can be no doubt that by the spring of 1963 Cuba had led President Kennedy into a confrontation with those who had become purblind to anything but the forceful overthrow of Fidel Castro. By April the President was set firmly on a policy of accommodation which the anti-Castro hardliners could not accept. The clamp-down on the exiles marked the true end of the missile-crisis tension and the start of a new relationship with the Soviet Union. The President announced with satisfaction that thousands of Soviet military "advisers" were being withdrawn from Cuba, a process which was to continue. The new Cuba policy met vociferous opposition within the United States, not least from one Richard Nixon, who in April twice made speeches urging its reversal. He called for decisive action to force the Communist regime out of power and open support for the exile militants.

Above all, the aggressive exiles and their CIA mentors had most cause to resent the President's actions. Many had long since sensed betrayal and by 1963 felt—in the words of CIA officer Howard Hunt—that government assistance to their armed effort was "a fraud, a fraud perpetrated on the Cuban people, and on the American people." Now, as part of the new policy, President Kennedy struck directly at the Cuban Revolutionary Council, the government in exile which had grown out of the anti-Castro front created two years earlier by the CIA in the shape of Hunt. Kennedy ordered an end to CIA financial support for the Council. Its president, Miro Cardona, resigned in fury, accusing Kennedy personally of welshing on a promise to mount a new invasion of Cuba. Passions were running dangerously high.

On April 4, 1963, the head of the police intelligence unit in Miami, Charles Sapp, was worried. Immediately after the clamp-down on exile activities his department had started receiving alarming information from sources in the Cuban refugee colony. What he learned moved Sapp to advise his superiors, "Since President Kennedy made the news release that the U.S. Government would stop all raiding parties going against the Castro government, the Cuban people feel that the U.S. Government has turned against them. . . . Violence hitherto directed toward Castro's Cuba will now be directed toward various governmental agencies in the United States." From then on, Sapp told me in 1978, his unit and the Miami Secret Service considered public officials, and especially the President, to be under real threat from anti-Castro extremists. Apart from the inflamed temper of the exiles themselves, the authorities in Florida saw disturbing signs of danger from the lunatic fringe of the American right. Just after the President's clamp-down on the exiles, a sinister handout appeared in letter boxes around Miami. It advised the exile community that only one development would now make it possible for "Cuban patriots" to return to their homeland: "if an inspired Act of God should place in the White House within weeks a Texan known to be a friend of all Latin Americans." It is hard to interpret this as anything but a call for the death of the President, and his replacement by Lyndon Johnson. The handbill had the hallmarks of the John Birch Society and was signed, "A Texan who resents the Oriental influence that has come to control, to degrade, to pollute and enslave his own people." Although not "within weeks," the writer's wish would soon be granted. As if the sulphurous mix of violent Cubans, recalcitrant CIA operatives, and political extremism were not perilous enough, the President was in 1963 faced with threats from a different quarter. CIA folly, combined with Kennedy zeal, had inflamed another foe—the Mob.

Sixteen weeks before John Kennedy became President, four men, debonair and immaculately suited, chatted over cocktails in the Boom Boom Room of Miami's exclusive Fontainebleau Hotel. They might have been businessmen discussing a deal or politicians planning strategy. In fact two of the distinguished gentlemen were Mafia hoodlums, and they were meeting a CIA representative. The topic on the agenda was assassination, the target Fidel Castro. Their meeting marked the latest and most dangerous in a series of madcap CIA schemes.

The CIA already had a special unit with responsibility for kidnapping and murder, and the galling advent of Fidel Castro was tailor-made for its attentions. Within a year top CIA officers were writing memoranda recommending that "thorough consideration be given to the elimination of Fidel Castro," and by the summer of 1960 it was clear they meant it literally. Cables flashed between Washington headquarters and the Havana CIA station discussing the "removal of top three leaders" and, in the case of Castro's brother Raul, a plan for "an accident to neutralize this leader's influence." The schemes hatched against Castro himself would defy belief were it not that they have been exposed and documented by the Senate Intelligence Committee. As a result we know that the highly paid wizards of the CIA's Technical Services Division at first merely fooled with the notion of impregnating Castro's shoes with chemicals which would cause all his hair to fall out—including the trade-mark beard. Without it, our heroes apparently fantasized, Castro would lose his appeal to the masses. In the CIA world of comic cliché it was a small conceptual step from Castro beard to Castro cigars. The plan was to slip the leader of the revolution a spiked cigar—to make him go berserk during one of his famous speech marathons. Some genius proposed trying for the same result by spraying Castro's broadcasting studio with a form of the drug LSD. The revelation of all this has made the CIA a mockery in the eyes of the American public in recent years and would be merely funny were it not that the custodians of liberty moved from silly schemes to murderous toys and then to the real thing.

By autumn 1960 the Technical Division had prepared cigars treated with a poison so lethal that a smoker—hopefully Castro—would die within moments of placing it in his mouth. In the months to come the CIA was to dream up a fungus-dusted diving suit impregnated with a strain of tuberculosis. There was even an exploding seashell to be planted in Castro's favorite skin-diving spot. Through agents inside Cuba some attempts were even made to deliver the Agency's little surprises. In an Agency prone to such foolishness, it is not wholly surprising that high CIA officials eventually turned to the Mafia. To the old hands, it was not an entirely new idea.

The dalliance between American intelligence and the Mafia had begun in World War II, at a time when anything seemed justifiable if it helped the war effort. In the United States the Office of Naval Intelligence obtained the help of the Mafia's then "don of dons," Lucky Luciano, in preventing German sabotage in American dockyards. Through his close associate Meyer Lansky, Luciano mobilized his network of waterfront thugs accordingly and was rewarded by official leniency for his own past crimes. Organized-crime leaders also cooperated in Europe, where their Sicilian brothers helped Allied operations in the Mediterranean. This improbable alliance has been heavily documented, not least in the official War Report of the Office of Strategic Services, the forerunner of the CIA. The record shows that some intelligence officers had qualms about the long-term propriety of the relationship, but the coming of peace did not end it. The Agency's wartime ally, Meyer Lansky, moved up in the world to become known as the financial wizard of organized crime. The old-fashioned murderous methods were now used to adapt the American gang structure to the modern world, a process which led to what we now know as "organized crime." The rival gangs now operated within a massive syndicate which Lansky himself allegedly described as "bigger than U.S. Steel." The difference, of course, is that the income came, as it still does, from exploitation of human beings and the discipline from torture and killing. The proceeds, meanwhile, were salted away in legal investments almost impossible to trace and identify. It is now clear that a loose working relationship between organized crime and the CIA existed at least until the years of the Vietnam conflict, when mob heroin trafficking and

CIA counterinsurgency found mutually convenient hunting grounds in Southeast Asia. To the old-timers in the CIA, no time can have seemed more propitious for turning to old friends than the 1959 Castro revolution in Cuba. Rarely before or since had there been such a coincidence of interest.

Castro's predecessor, the dictator Batista, had long been a puppet on strings pulled by American intelligence and the mob. In 1944, when the United States feared trouble from the Cuban left, Lansky reportedly persuaded Batista to step down for a while. When he came back in 1952, it was after the current President, Carlos Prio Socarras, was persuaded to resign, a departure reportedly eased by a bribe of a quarter of a million dollars and a major stake in the casino business. It was now that the gambling operation already established in Cuba became a Mafia bonanza. The gangster bosses set up a glittering citadel of casinos and hotels which attracted American spenders like moths to a flame. The cash poured out—on the gaming tables, on prostitution and riotous living—making Havana more lucrative for the syndicate than even Las Vegas. As a bonus there were rich pickings from narcotics, with Havana the crossroads of international trafficking. The figures defy understanding, but estimates suggest the Havana operation netted more than a hundred million dollars a year. This was an investment the mob would defend in every way possible. When the Batista regime began to crumble before a revolution of popular outrage, the mob hedged its political bets by courting Fidel Castro. Many of the guns which helped him to power in 1959 had been provided courtesy of Mafia gunrunners, a policy which did not pay off. Lansky saw the writing on the wall and flew out of Havana the day Castro marched in. For a while the new ruler allowed the casinos to continue operations but under government control. Then he arrested Santos Trafficante, Lansky's associate and the man believed to have been responsible for moving European heroin shipments through Havana to the United States. The casinos were eventually closed once and for all, and in time Trafficante and the last of the casino operators left for Florida. They remained key figures in the criminal hierarchy of the United States, but they brooded mightily over the loss of Havana and dreamed of returning.

In the myopic eyes of the CIA, the mob leaders seemed

perfect co-conspirators for the plots to kill Castro. Information reportedly reached them that Lansky was himself offering a million dollars bounty for Castro's murder. Indeed, it appears the mob was probably already trying to do so by using a girl to slip poison into Castro's food. They may even have come close to succeeding—an Assassinations Committee report notes that Castro suffered a serious "sickness" in the summer of 1960. At all events, the CIA decided it was time to join forces with the mob. There began an extraordinary operation, not to be unraveled until the work of the Senate Intelligence Committee in 1975.

In September 1960 there were top-level CIA conferences on teaming up with the Mafia to kill Castro. At least one of them included the Agency's Director, Allen Dulles—a fact which he wholly concealed when he became a member of the Warren Commission three years later. With his approval and that of Deputy Director Richard Bissell, the CIA's Office of Security went into action. The first step was to appoint a go-between, someone trusted by the CIA but sufficiently independent to protect the Agency in case of exposure. The man chosen was Robert Maheu, a former agent with the FBI in Chicago who had already helped with CIA efforts to compromise a foreign leader with a faked sex film and with interference in Saudi Arabian oil deals. Maheu was now working full time for the billionaire Howard Hughes, who had his own designs on Cuba and readily approved participation in the Castro murder scheme. So it was, in late September 1960, that Maheu came to be sitting down with two top gangsters amidst the tawdry splendor of Miami's Fontainebleau Hotel.

The gangsters used the names of "John Rawlston" and "Sam Gold," but it was a flimsy cover. "Rawlston" was John Roselli, a man who had risen to the top of organized crime in Las Vegas from humble beginnings—running liquor for Al Capone in Chicago. During the Kefauver crime committee hearings he had been firmly identified as a prince among racketeers with close links to Meyer Lansky. His good friend "Sam Gold" at the meeting with the CIA was really Sam Giancana, notable at the time as the crime boss of Chicago and one of the hoodlums specifically targeted for prosecution by Attorney General Robert Kennedy. Giancana had reportedly had an interest in the Cuban rackets, and that, coupled with his seniority in the Mafia pecking order, brought him into the CIA plan. In 1978 I interviewed a fourth man,[72] a Giancana associate, who was present at the Miami meetings, and he explained how the chain of conspiracy worked. As he put it, "Johnny called Sam and told Sam what he needed. You had to have some individual who knew a lot of Cubans and knew the type of Cubans that could be prevailed upon to get into such a plot. They would have to be lawbreakers, but you had to have somebody who really knew the Cubans." Who "really knew the Cubans"? I asked the fourth man. Cautiously, with more than a hint of fear, the contact responded, "Well, the main contact would have been Santos Trafficante." The Senate Intelligence Committee report on Assassination Plots confirms the name. Shortly after the first Fontainebleau meeting, a CIA "Support Chief" met Giancana again, this time accompanied by a man calling himself "Joe Pecora"—in reality the vastly powerful Mafia leader, Santos Trafficante. In 1979 that name remains, as much as ever, synonymous with the brutal exercise of power at the pinnacle of organized crime. It is a name that became a focus of attention for the Congress' Assassinations Committee, which concluded in 1979 that "individual members" of the Mafia may have been involved in President Kennedy's murder.

Santos Trafficante has a suitably dishonorable heritage. His father came to the Untied States at the start of the century and quickly established a Florida power base that nobody ever seriously challenged. As his birthright the young Trafficante took control of the Florida rackets and the Sans Souci Casino in Havana. The extent of his power was recognized in 1957 after the elimination of Albert Anastasis—then known as the most efficient and vicious gang leader in America. Anastasia, who died riddled with bullets while sitting in a barber's chair, had been attempting to move in on the Trafficante interests in Cuba. Although Trafficante was imprisoned by Fidel Castro after the revolution, it was reported to be a strangely luxurious confinement. For some time thereafter, U.S. narcotics agents noticed that the supply of Cuban cocaine to the United States actually increased under Castro's government, and this led to suspicions that the Marxist and the mobster had reached agreement on a mutually profitable *modus operandi*. On the other hand, Trafficante remained close to Meyer

Lansky, who was reportedly offering his million-dollar reward for
the Cuban leader's murder. Whatever the truth, the CIA was
simply out of its depth when it turned for help to Santos Trafficante. He was at the controls of a dictatorship all his own and
served no man but himself. Still, he made obliging noises to the
men from Washington, and they waited eagerly for the results.
Nothing happened.

   The efforts to kill Castro using the Mafia were only a little less
surreal than the clownish schemes that preceded them. Trafficante
introduced the CIA representatives to a "certain leading figure in
the Cuban exile movement," who was supplied with CIA money
and a CIA poison. Reportedly this was Antonio de Varona, a
former Cuban Prime Minister, soon to become Vice President of
the Cuban Revolutionary Council, the exile organization which
President Kennedy abandoned in 1963. Allegedly the CIA—Mafia
murder scheme was that the poison would be slipped into Castro's
food by an employee at his favorite restaurant. It never happened,
supposedly because Castro gave up frequenting the restaurant.
Had it succeeded, Castro would have died at the time of the Bay of
Pigs invasion. It was now April 1961, and President Kennedy was
in the White House. There was a lull for a full year after the
invasion, and then the CIA got busy again—this time with William
Harvey, the notorious gun-toting drunkard, playing a leading role
in coordinating operational efforts with the anti-Castro exiles.
There was another episode involving poison pills and, as the
Senate Intelligence Committee reported, "explosives, detonators,
rifles, handguns, radios and boat radar." All these things were
delivered to the same Cuban contact in a cloak-and-dagger operation in a Miami parking lot. Again nothing happened. Congress'
Assassinations Committee has speculated that—by this stage—the
Mafia bosses had rather given up hope that the Cuban revolution
could be reversed simply by killing Castro. They may, therefore,
have now been simply playing along with the CIA schemes, with
an eye to fending off prosecution for their own offenses in the
United States. In one case, an abortive wiretapping case involving
Same Giancana and his associate Maheu, that hope was justified.
After 1962, so far as is known, CIA attempts to murder Fidel
Castro did not involve the mob.

Since this comedy of errors has become public knowledge in the United States, there has been prolonged polemic over whether the plots against Castro were supported by President Kennedy or whether he even knew about them. The subject certainly came up in the Oval Office, as the Latin American correspondent of the *New York Times*, Tad Szulc, learned during an interview with the President in late 1961. Szulc recalls how—in the middle of a talk about Cuba—Kennedy suddenly leaned forward in his rocking chair and asked, "What would you think if I ordered Castro to be assassinated?" Szulc replied that political assassination was wrong in principle and in any case would do nothing to solve the Cuban problem. Kennedy, says Szulc, "smiled and said that he had been testing me because he was under great pressure from advisers in the intelligence community (whom he did not name) to have Castro killed, but that he himself violently opposed it on the grounds that for moral reasons the United States should never be a party to political assassinations. 'I'm glad you feel the same way,' he said."

It may be that the essence of the President's predicament lies in the remarks he made to Senator George Smathers, himself a passionate opponent of Castro. Smathers says he found the President "horrified" at the idea of assassination and refused to be pushed about his Cuba policy. Smathers adds, "I remember him saying that the CIA frequently did things he didn't know about, and he was unhappy about it. He complained that the CIA was almost autonomous." A number of CIA officials have since said that they assumed the President approved of the assassination plots but that it was simply not done to discuss the subject in front of him. Their assumption of Presidential connivance failed to convince the Senate Intelligence Committee.

There is documentary evidence that the President's brother learned something about the Mafia involvement in the Castro murder plots. In early 1962 Robert Kennedy found that the CIA was trying to protect one of its Mafia contacts, Sam Giancana, from prosecution on another matter. When he insisted on pursuing the matter, Kennedy was finally told about the earlier stages of Giancana's role in the murder plots by a CIA lawyer, Lawrence Houston. According to Houston, the information "upset" Ken-

nedy, who expressed "strong anger" and responded, "I trust that
if you ever try to do business with organized crime again—with
gangsters—you will let the Attorney General know." Houston
testified, "If you have ever seen Mr. Kennedy's eyes get steely and
his jaw set and his voice get low and precise, you get a definite
feeling of unhappiness." Much later, Robert Kennedy discussed
the Castro plots with two aides and claimed, "I stopped it. . . . I
found out that some people were going to try an attempt on
Castro's life and I turned it off." In fact, as an Assassinations
Committee report notes, the CIA failed to tell Kennedy that the
assassination operation had been reactivated *after* the phase he
had learned about. "The implications . . ." of this CIA deception,
says the report, "are serious . . . in direct disobedience to the
Attorney General's personal direction."[73] Meanwhile, having been
told only part of the murky story, Robert Kennedy pursued his
general investigation of Sam Giancana's crimes as vigorously as
ever.

Whatever uncertainties remain about the Kennedy brothers'
policy on Cuba,* their attitude toward organized crime was un-
compromising. Call it vendetta or call it crusade, the mob and the
Kennedys were at war.

---

* Latest analysis tends to support the thesis that the Kennedy brothers did
know of, and perhaps even approved, the earlier Castro assassination
plots. In his penetrating work on the CIA, *The Man Who Kept The
Secrets: Richard Helms and the CIA* (*see bibliography*), Thomas Powers
argues that senior CIA officers have refrained from saying the President
approved—either because they have no proof, or because it is traditional
for a secret service to "take the heat." It seems highly improbable,
however, that President Kennedy would have given the nod to *later* CIA
plots to murder Castro, underway—as a late chapter will show—at a
period in later 1963 when the President was approving active moves to
reach an *accommodation* with the Cuban leader.

CHAPTER 14

The Mob Loses Patience

Mark my word, this man Kennedy is in trouble,
and he will get what is coming to him. . . .
He is going to be hit.

—Mafia leader Santos Trafficante, discussing the President's
future, late 1962

The struggle began a half decade before John Kennedy became President, when he was still a Senator. In 1956, Robert Kennedy, then only thirty-one and counsel for the Senate Subcommittee on Investigations, began turning up evidence that leading gangsters had penetrated the American labor movement. As he delved further it emerged that some unions were already literally controlled by the mob. Frightened informants told of massive sums in union funds being diverted into private bank accounts, of known gangsters acting as union officials, and of murder and torture inflicted on those who complained or tried to resist. Typical of the horror encountered was this story, told later in Kennedy's own account of the inquiry: "There was the union organizer from Los Angeles who had traveled to San Diego to organize jukebox operators. He was told to stay out of San Diego or he would be killed. But he returned to San Diego. He was knocked unconscious. When he regained consciousness the next morning he was covered with blood and had terrible pains in his stomach. The pains were so intense he was unable to drive back to him home in Los Angeles and stopped at a hospital. There was an emergency operation. The doctors removed from his backside a large cucumber. Later he was told that if he ever returned to San Diego it would be a watermelon. He never went back." The victim in question was comparatively lucky. Kennedy's investigation was to turn up scores of killings—by multiple shooting in the face, by electrocution, by slow, excruciating torture.

At an early stage the Kennedy inquiry led straight to the leadership of America's largest and most powerful union, the International Brotherhood of Teamsters. With a vast membership across the country, the Teamsters controlled the nation's truck drivers and warehousemen and exercised a direct influence on almost every industrial enterprise. Earl Warren, who would one day lead the inquiry into John Kennedy's assassination, had declared his "admiration" for the union, calling it "not only something great of itself, but splendidly representative of the entire labor movement." That is not what Robert Kennedy found. The union was riddled with corruption, starting with its then president, Dave Beck. As the evidence piled up, a special Senate committee—with Senator John Kennedy as a member and his brother as chief counsel—was assembled. As a result of its revelations, Beck was destroyed as a public figure and eventually convicted and imprisoned for larceny and income-tax evasion. But it was his successor, James Hoffa, who was to become the enduring focus of Kennedy prosecution and a dangerously vicious enemy.

Long before he became union president by rigging his own election, Hoffa's crimes were being unrelentingly probed by Robert Kennedy. The personal feud between the two men began in earnest after Kennedy caught Hoffa red-handed giving a bribe to a Senate lawyer.

In 1958 Hoffa was indicted on two other charges—perjury and wiretapping. He wriggled out of all three cases, and there was never any secret about how he did it. Hoffa told Kennedy, "You never can tell with a jury. Like shooting fish in a barrel." For both men it was only the beginning of a bitter struggle. Certainly Robert Kennedy was obsessed about Jimmy Hoffa, and soon their mutual hatred became a fact of public life. Among Hoffa's more printable descriptions of Kennedy were "vicious bastard," "little monster," and "absolute spoiled brat." In the Senate committee hearings both Kennedy brothers clashed with Hoffa time and again, and one exchange vividly exposed Hoffa's propensity for violence. Leaving one committee session, Hoffa was heard to

mutter, "That S.O.B.—I'll break his back, the little sonofabitch."
Next morning Robert Kennedy picked up the remark:

KENNEDY: While leaving the hearings after these people had
testified regarding this matter, did you say, "That S.O.B.—I'll
break his back"?
HOFFA: Who?
KENNEDY: You.
HOFFA: Say it to who?
KENNEDY: To anyone. Did you make that statement after
these people testified before this committee?
HOFFA: I never talked to either one of them after testifying.
KENNEDY: I'm not talking about "to them." Did you make that
statement here in the hearing room after the testimony was
finished?
HOFFA: Not concerning him as far as I know of.
KENNEDY: Well, who did you make it about?
HOFFA: I don't know. . . . I may have been discussing some-
body in a figure of speech.
KENNEDY: Well . . . whose back were you going to break?
HOFFA: I don't even remember it.
KENNEDY: Now whose back were you going to break, Mr.
Hoffa?
HOFFA: Figure of speech. I don't know what I was talking
about, and I don't know what you're talking about.

Hoffa was escaping conviction, but he was publicly and repeatedly
humiliated by the Kennedys. In the Nixon-Kennedy election campaign, predictably enough, Hoffa threw his powerful union support behind Nixon. In a grim comment as the election approached,
the Teamsters leader told a cheering audience of his members, "If
it is a question, as Kennedy has said, that he will break Hoffa, then
I say to him, he should live so long." John Kennedy, it seems,
shared his younger brother's determination to cripple organized
crime. Once, told that the Senate investigation was likely to implicate a powerful figure in Democratic politics, Kennedy replied,
"Go back and build the best case against him that you can. We

have only one rule around here. If they're crooks, we don't wound 'em, we kill 'em." The brave words aside, there was also action. In late 1959, after strenuous efforts by John Kennedy, a new law governing union elections passed both houses of Congress. It was bitterly attacked by union leaders, including Hoffa. During the build-up to the election, Robert Kennedy revealed, attempts were made to pressure the Kennedys by offering help in the campaign if they would soften their attitude to racketeers and the Teamsters in particular. One such approach was made by a top Hoffa aide, another by a Chicago lawyer who had once worked for Al Capone. Robert Kennedy was increasingly aware—from the minutiae of evidence gathered in painstaking research—that he was up against not only union corruption but also the American Mafia. He put it more carefully than that, referring to gangsters who "work in a highly organized fashion and are far more powerful than at any time in the history of the country. They control political figures and threaten whole communities. They have stretched their tentacles of corruption and fear into industries both large and small. They grow stronger every day." In 1960, just before the election, Kennedy published *The Enemy Within*, his own account of the struggle with Hoffa and the racketeers, and it became a best-seller. At the end of the book he listed some of the hoods who had featured in his inquiry—names like Shorty Feldman, Tony Provenzano, Henry de Roma, and Frank Matula. He wrote, "No group better fits the prototype of the old Al Capone syndicate than Jimmy Hoffa and some of his chief Lieutenants in and out of the union. They have the look of Capone's men. They are sleek, often bilious and fat, or lean and cold and hard. They have the smooth faces and cruel eyes of gangsters; they wear the same rich clothes, the diamond ring, the jeweled watch, the strong, sickly-sweet smelling perfume." Among the names linked to Hoffa were Paul Dorfman and Barney Baker, whom Kennedy called "Hoffa's ambassador of violence." Both, as we shall see, had links with Jack Ruby, the man who silenced Lee Harvey Oswald after the assassination in Dallas. Robert Kennedy also spent months in pursuit of Sam Giancana, the Chicago Mafia leader who would later be involved in the CIA-Mafia plots to kill Castro. He also perceived a chain relationship extending to mob bosses like Meyer Lansky who with Santos Trafficante, had masterminded the mob's gambling empire in Cuba.

In 1961, when John Kennedy became President, he appointed his brother Attorney General. On the steps of the Department of Justice, Robert Kennedy swiftly made his priorities clear. Referring to organized crime, he spoke of "a very serious situation that's facing the country at the present time. And I think a lot of steps can be taken in order to deal with the problem." He was later to define the problem as a "private government of organized crime, resting on a base of human suffering and moral corrosion." Until 1961, with FBI Director Hoover obsessed about the "Communist menace" and virtually denying the existence of the mob, Robert Kennedy had been merely a thorn in the flesh of the private government. Now, as the top law-enforcement officer in the land, he had power. Kennedy used it unrelentingly.

A prime target was, of course, Jimmy Hoffa. Within nine months of the election, thirteen grand juries, sixteen lawyers, and thirty FBI agents were concentrating on bringing the Teamster leaders to justice. Within the Justice Department Kennedy's team worked around the clock unraveling the union's corruption; they became known as the Get Hoffa Squad. Hoffa was indicted for taking payoffs from trucking companies, for conspiracy to defraud the trustees of the Teamsters' pension fund, and for taking illegal payments from an employer in Tennessee. Hoffa, as ever, used every trick he knew to get off the hook.

Years later Hoffa bragged that he had obtained "seamy" information that could have seriously damaged the Kennedys. There have been two main speculations as to what he meant. One is that Hoffa had proof of a relationship between Robert Kennedy and the film star Marilyn Monroe, who committed suicide in the second summer of the Kennedy Presidency. It has been suggested that Hoffa may have had access to tape recordings of compromising telephone conversations between the couple. There is now strong evidence that the President's brother, Robert, was also involved with Monroe, and became as compromised as his brother.* But the two had met more than once, and Monroe had

* See *Goddess*, the 1985 biography of Monroe by this author.

telephoned the Attorney General in Washington. Tapes of such conversations would certainly have been of interest to the devious Hoffa. However, it is far more likely that he learned of a scandalous relationship which certainly did exist and which involved the President in person.

It is now known that for at least a year President Kennedy carried on a liaison with a beautiful West Coast girl twenty years his junior, Judith Exner. In 1975 the Senate Intelligence Committee saw White House phone logs showing that Ms. Exner called some seventy times from just after the President's inauguration until March 1962. Exner has poured out her version of the affair to the press, a heady tale of sexual encounters with the President in hotel rooms and even in the White House itself. Yet, outside the gutter press, it was not the bedroom anecdotes which caused most concern. Although the President was clearly irresponsible in associating with a young woman like Ms. Exner, he was not the first or last politician to indulge that particular human weakness. What has sent tremors of alarmed speculation through Washington is the revelation that throughout the period she knew the President, Judith Exner had another lover and benefactor. He has been firmly identified as none other than Sam Giancana, then the boss of organized crime in Chicago. This instantly raised the disturbing possibility that the Mafia, perceiving Kennedy's weakness for pretty women, deliberately placed one of its own in his path. Ms. Exner, who says she was introduced to both Kennedy and Giancana in Las Vegas by Frank Sinatra, at first seemed to dispel this notion. She placed the Kennedy meeting several months before the Giancana encounter. This is a convenient explanation, but it does not stand scrutiny. Federal investigators and a close associate of Giancana say the Kennedy meeting *followed* the start of the relationship with Giancana. Ms. Exner admitted it is "possible that I was used almost from the beginning."*

What would the Mafia purpose have been? With organized crime being pursued as never before by the Kennedy administration, there was potential advantage in having a spy in the White

---

* In 1988 Exner offered disquieting new revelations, saying she had acted as a courier between the President and Giancana. See Aftermath chapter.

House. It is a theory which becomes even more startling with the knowledge that Giancana was not just any organized crime leader but a key figure in the CIA-Mafia alliance to murder Fidel Castro. Judith Exner claims to have had only "man-woman" conversations with the President. Her memory, however, is oddly vague on a number of points, and her claim does not dispel suspicion about Giancana's real motives. Astonishingly, the Senate committee failed to press Exner on detail and did not call Frank Sinatra. Giancana, who himself reportedly boasted that his organization had placed a girl with the President, is beyond further questioning. He was killed, as we shall see, in a manner and at a time which suggests he could have told much more.

Blackmail is the simplest rationalization for mob interest in placing a mistress in the President's bed. It would explain Jimmy Hoffa's remarks about having "seamy" information on the President. If Hoffa did not learn of the Exner affair direct from Giancana, he was close to several Las Vegas figures who may have shared the secret. Casino owner Morris "Moe" Dalitz, who had underworld connections going back for years, enjoyed a close friendship with Hoffa and also claimed to know Kennedy well. If either Hoffa or Giancana had blackmail in mind, there is not a scrap of evidence it succeeded—rather the contrary. The Exner affair seems to have ended abruptly in March 1962, immediately after FBI Director Hoover—clearly aware what was going on— lunched with the President. During the lunch he briefed Kennedy on Exner's relationship with Giancana, and from that moment on the White House log recorded no more cosy calls from Judith Exner. The Kennedys' pursuit of both Giancana and Hoffa continued unabated.

Giancana and Robert Kennedy had clashed personally when the mobster appeared before the McClellan Committee. Thirty-three times Giancana pleaded the Fifth Amendment, the constitutional clause under which witnesses may refuse to give answers which might incriminate them. At one stage Kennedy asked Giancana, "Would you tell us, if you have opposition from anybody, that you dispose of them by having them stuffed in a trunk? Is that what you do, Mr. Giancana?" Sam Giancana just pleaded the Fifth and giggled. The record shows that brutal murder is precisely the sort of thing Mr. Giancana did. Federal investigators recorded him ordering the killing of opponents as casually as other men might order a cup of coffee. The catalogue of crimes linked to Giancana ranges from the old mob method of dumping victims in rivers, sealed in cement, to hanging a man on a meat hook for days until he succumbed to electric cattle prod, ice pick, and blow torch. By this bloody path, Giancana came to rule his own organized-crime empire, an operation with an annual income reckoned at two billion dollars. As Attorney General, Robert Kennedy is reported to have made Giancana a priority target. By mid-1963 he was the subject of total surveillance. FBI agents in cars sat outside his house twenty-four hours a day, every day. When he went out golfing, the agents went too.

In 1960, before the Kennedy Presidency, there were only thirty five convictions for offenses connected with organized crime. In 1963 there were 288, a figure which doubled within a year as a result of the impetus built up in the dying months of the Kennedy era. Before the Kennedys came to power, Organized Crime Section lawyers spent sixty-one days in court and 660 days making investigations. In the last year of the Kennedy Presidency government lawyers fighting organized crime spent 1,081 days in court and 6,177 days in the field. The former chief investigator of organized crime for New York City, Ralph Salerno, has said, "The end of an era had come, and they recognized it. A tremendous financial empire was being very seriously threatened." Just how much "they," the crime bosses and their lieutenants, felt threatened is strikingly clear in wiretap transcripts resulting from surveillance of Mafia figures. As early as the start of 1962, the Philadelphia organized-crime boss, Angelo Bruno, was tape-recorded while talking with an associate, Willie Weisburg. On the tape, Weisburg is heard to say, "See what Kennedy done. With Kennedy, a guy should take a knife, like one of them other guys, and stab and kill the fucker, where he is now. Somebody should kill the fucker. I mean it. This is true. But I tell you something. I hope I get a week's notice. I'll kill. Right in the fucking White House. Somebody's got to get rid of this fucker." At the time Angelo Bruno responded to this stream of gutter threats with a philosophical anecdote. A year later, though, he was talking about packing his bags and going back to his roots. On another FBI tape, Bruno can be heard saying despondently, "It is all over for us; I am going to Italy, and you should go too. . . ." Some, of course, chose to fight rather than flee.

In the Kennedys, however, the Mafia faced an enemy determined and persistent in a way encountered neither before nor since. When an indictment failed, Attorney General Kennedy would simply order investigators to find new grounds for prosecution. Just a month before his brother's assassination, he asked Congress for greater powers to fight organized crime—an electronic surveillance law and an immunity statute which would compel recalcitrant witnesses to testify. Robert Kennedy, with his brother's backing, was engaged in nothing less than a crusade.

In 1979 one of the Congressmen who had served on the House Assassinations Committee explained why it made sense to suspect a mob role in the Kennedy assassination. Representative Floyd Fithian, who is also a professional historian, said, "Organized crime had a practical motive to seek a quick end to the Kennedy administration . . . the picture for organized crime was very bleak indeed. Bleak enough, in my opinion, for individual members of organized crime to seriously consider killing the President. For if John Kennedy no longer sat in the White House, it would only be a matter of time before his brother would leave the Justice Department. The enmity between Bobby Kennedy and Vice President Lyndon Johnson was well known. . . . Organized crime had the means to kill John Kennedy. It had a motive. And it had the opportunity." The formal findings of the Assassinations Committee echo this assessment precisely. That said, though, is there any evidence that the Mafia actually did it?

In October 1963, a month before the assassination, FBI surveillance microphones in Chicago listened as Sam Giancana shared a joke with three colleagues. This was, of course, a time when Giancana was being tailed by the FBI wherever he went—even on the golf course. The FBI report of the conversation went like this: "They discuss golf. Somebody asks if Bobby Kennedy plays golf; they know that John Kennedy does. Suggest putting a bomb in his golf bag. (They all laugh.)"

For others, the pest in the White House was no longer just a nuisance or a laughing matter. Kennedy justice was catching up with Jimmy Hoffa. He had managed to stay out of prison, but in mid-1963 he was charged with conspiring to fix the jury in the Tennessee case involving taking illegal payments from an employer. A year later the implacable Robert Kennedy would have his obstinacy rewarded. Hoffa was to be jailed for the jury offense and for diverting a million dollars in union funds to his own use. Apparently he was no longer so proficient at "shooting fish in a barrel." But by that time Robert Kennedy may have had little taste for the victory. His brother John was dead. At least one piece of evidence indicates that from 1962 onwards the harassed Hoffa planned to retaliate against the Kennedys with the violence he usually meted out to union opponents. Ironically, the evidence arose directly from the Tennessee investigation which eventually sent Hoffa to jail.

A prime witness in that case was Edward Partin, a Teamster official in Louisiana who gave federal investigators incriminating information on Hoffa. He says that in the summer of 1962, at a meeting in Hoffa's Washington office, the Teamsters leader talked of killing Robert Kennedy. According to Partin, Hoffa said of the Attorney General, "Somebody needs to bump that sonofabitch off. . . . You know I've got a run-down on him . . . his house sits here like this [Hoffa draws with his fingers], and it's not guarded. . . . He drives about in a convertible and swims by himself. I've got a .270 rifle with a high-power scope on it that shoots a long way without dropping any. It would be easy to get him with that. But I'm leery of it; it's too obvious." Hoffa's preference of the moment, according to Partin, was to bomb Robert Kennedy. He said, allegedly, "What I think should be done, if I can get hold of these plastic bombs, is to get somebody to throw one in his house and the place'll burn after it blows up. You know the S.O.B. doesn't stay up too late. . . ."

It has been suggested Partin made up this and other stories to improve his own position with the authorities, but the evidence indicates he was telling the truth. According to Partin, who repeated his account to me in 1978, Hoffa asked him to help in obtaining a suitable "plastic bomb" for the murder plan. Partin alerted a federal investigator, who arranged to listen in while Partin reported back to Hoffa in a telephone call. I interviewed the investigator, Hawk Daniels, who later became a judge in Louisiana. He told me, "Yes, there were two telephone calls, monitored by me. They originated with Partin and terminated with Hoffa on the other end of the line. Partin briefly brought up the subject of the plastic explosives and told Hoffa he had obtained the explosive Hoffa wanted. Hoffa then said, 'We'll talk about that later' and abruptly changed the subject. It was clear from the course of the conversation that he knew very well what Partin was talking about." Judge Daniels took Partin's warning wholly seriously and informed the Justice Department. He says the authorities, including the Secret Service, were aware from then onward that Hoffa posed a real threat. This is confirmed by Ben Bradlee, editor of the *Washington Post* and a personal friend of the Kennedy family. He recalls that in early 1963 President Kennedy himself told him, in all seriousness, that a Hoffa "hoodlum" had been sent to Washington to shoot Robert Kennedy.

Since 1962 the man who first warned of the Hoffa scheme, Edward Partin, has lived in fear of his own life. There have been several attempts to murder him, and Judge Daniels believes they were ordered by a vengeful Hoffa. When I arranged to interview Partin—for television—he failed to show up but sent Teamster colleagues with a note instead. The note read, in part, "I am sorry I cannot keep the appointment with you, but for the safety of my family and myself, especially my family (whom I have had to move out of the state and hide), I just don't think it would be fair to them. . . . Up until now they have known only fear, death, and the threat of death."

The specific Hoffa murder scheme revealed in 1962 concerned only Robert Kennedy. Partin, however, says that as he understood Hoffa, the Teamsters leader "intended the death of the President as well as his brother." Judge Daniels agrees and says, "I think Hoffa fully intended to carry the threats out—I really think he had the capability. It was a question of how and when, not a question of whether he had doubts as to the necessity of eliminating at least Mr. Bobby Kennedy and possibly his brother also." Today evidence exists that Mafia bosses, with even more power and greater expertise than Jimmy Hoffa, shared his murderous intentions. First there is Santos Trafficante.

Trafficante, back in the United States after his expulsion from Cuba, had been deeply involved in the CIA plots to kill Fidel Castro; but Cuba was not the only problem on his mind. The Kennedys had dragged his name into public disrepute even before they came to power. While Trafficante was still in Cuba, Robert Kennedy had pressed for information on him. As a result, the world had heard the Director of the Miami Crime Commission define Trafficante as "the key figure in the Mafia circles of Tampa, Florida." Trafficante's Sicilian family was discussed in the same breath as a score of gangland killings and narcotics operations. Those who know Trafficante say he detests publicity. With John Kennedy in the White House, Trafficante saw his friends Sam Giancana and Jimmy Hoffa being pursued as never before. For Trafficante himself, the writing was on the wall. In 1962, according to evidence gathered by the Assassinations Committee, Trafficante confided his feelings to Jose Aleman, a wealthy Cuban exile living in Miami.[74] The two men had been in contact with each other for some time, and Trafficante had offered to arrange a million-dollar loan for Aleman. The loan, he said, would be coming from the Teamsters Union and had "already been cleared by Jimmy Hoffa himself." It was natural, then, that the conversation turned to Hoffa when Trafficante met Aleman at the Scott-Bryant Hotel in Miami in September 1962. According to Aleman, in an account he confirmed to me at a secret meeting in 1978, Trafficante said of the President, "Have you seen how his brother is hitting Hoffa, a man who is a worker, who is not a millionaire, a friend of the blue collars? He doesn't know that this kind of encounter is very delicate. . . ." Forgetting for a moment, perhaps, that Hoffa was in fact a millionaire, Trafficante said, "It is not right what they are doing to Hoffa. . . . Hoffa is a hard-working man and does not deserve it. . . . Mark my word, this man Kennedy is in trouble, and he will get what is coming to him." When Aleman disagreed with Trafficante and said he thought President Kennedy had been doing a good job and would be re-elected, the Mafia boss replied quietly. He said, according to Aleman, "You don't understand me. Kennedy's not going to make it to the election. He is going to be hit."

Aleman has told investigators that Trafficante "made it clear to him [implicitly] that he was not guessing about the killing; rather he was giving the impression that he knew Kennedy was going to be killed." Aleman said he was "given the distinct impression that Hoffa was to be principally involved in the elimination of Kennedy."

There can be little doubt how Aleman interpreted Trafficante's alleged remark that the President was "going to be hit." He even had a bet with another Trafficante associate as to whether President Kennedy was going to be assassinated. In his talks with investigators and in his interview with me, it was understood that "hit" meant "murder." Yet in 1978, when Aleman was called to testify before a public session of the Congress' Assassinations Committee, his statements were uncharacteristically hesitant and garbled. He suggested, at one point, that "going to be hit" might merely have indicated that the late President was going to be defeated by a Republican majority. Aleman is undoubtedly a frightened man. When I met him I first had to go through a complicated rendezvous routine designed to guarantee his safety. He lives today in virtual seclusion and told the Assassinations Committee, "I have been very much worried, I am very much concerned about my safety. . . . I sold my business. I been in my home because—I mean—Santos Trafficante can try to do anything at any moment." The chairman of the committee expressed respect for Aleman and admiration for his bravery. The chief counsel said, ". . . we have seen manifested in a witness that fear that is all too often characteristic of people called to testify in matters touching on organized crime. A fear that, frankly, must be recognized as justified."

At the time of his alleged conversation with Trafficante about the impending fate of the President, Aleman was an informant for the FBI. He says he promptly reported the conversion to his Bureau contacts, but nobody would listen. During 1963, he says, he continued to meet Trafficante and told the FBI that he thought "something was going to happen. . . . I was telling them to be careful." The FBI, says Aleman, did not take him seriously until it was too late. He says an agent recontacted him only on November 22, 1963, hours after the President had been assassinated. The FBI denies it.

* * * * * * * * *

In New Orleans, a diminutive Sicilian called Carlos Marcello had long had cause to rage against the Kennedys. Known as "The Little Man" because of his 5′ 4″ height, Marcello is—with Trafficante—one of the two or three most sinister figures in the history of organized crime. In 1978 the Director of the New Orleans Crime Commission, Aaron Kohn, described him to me as "the most powerful single organized crime figure in the southern United States . . . the head of the Mafia, or Costa Nostra, in this area." By the year of the Kennedy assassination, the Crime Commission estimated that Marcello's syndicate was raking in the stupendous sum of 1,114,000,000 dollars *annually*. It was, by one estimate, the largest industry—in terms of statistics—in the state of Louisiana, and Marcello has been called its midget Midas. During the Thirties and Forties he fought his way to the summit of the Mafia structure in the southern United States. After an early conviction on narcotics charges, he became notoriously elusive, always placing himself at several removes from crimes committed on his behalf. Unlike Santos Trafficante and Sam Giancana, Marcello did not show up in person at the famous Apalachin convention of organized-crime figures in 1957. He rule his territory without serious challenge and looked abroad for extra pickings. Before the advent of Castro, according to one recent report, he joined with Trafficante and Meyer Lansky in sharing the booty from Batista's Cuba. According to Judge Hawk Daniels of Baton Rouge, Louisiana, he was—just like Santos Trafficante—"closely linked with Jimmy Hoffa, by Hoffa's own admission." It is reliably reported that, at the height of the Kennedy-Nixon campaign, Marcello received Hoffa in New Orleans. An eyewitness to the meeting says, "Marcello had a suitcase filled with $500,000 cash which was going to Nixon. It was a half-million-dollar contribution. The other half [of the million promised] was coming from the mob boys in New Jersey and Florida." Later, Marcello was to be linked with an attempt to bribe the key prosecution witness in the Hoffa jury-tampering case.

Within three months of President Kennedy's inauguration Marcello himself fell victim to the Kennedy campaign against organized crime, in a way more dramatic than any other target of the Justice Department.

Carlos Marcello had been born "Calogero Minacore" in Tunisia, of Sicilian parentage, and although he had spent most of his life in the United States, he knew he faced possible deportation. He therefore arranged forged documentation naming his birthplace as Guatemala—a country likely to receive him kindly and closer to his criminal empire than exile in North Africa or Europe. Nobody, however, really expected it would come to deportation. One must, after all, take account of Marcello's power of patronage. The New Orleans Crime Commission made a sobering list of those who actively sought clemency for Marcello on the only federal offense for which he has been tried and convicted in recent times—assaulting and FBI agent. The roll call comprised—"one sheriff, one former sheriff, one state legislator, two former state legislators, two former state police commanders, one president of a waterfront labor union, one bank president, two bank vice-presidents, one former assistant district attorney, one chief juvenile probation officer, one former revenue agent, three insurance agencies, five realtors, five physicians, one funeral director, and six clergymen." Crime Commission Director Kohn has added that Marcello commanded the corrupt collusion of "justices of the peace, mayors, governors . . . and at least one member of the Congress." Nevertheless, with Robert Kennedy in the Justice Department, Marcello's influence was suddenly ineffective.

On April 4, 1961, Marcello was summarily arrested as he arrived to make a routine appearance at the New Orleans Immigration Department.[75] Reportedly on the personal orders of Bobby Kennedy he was seized, handcuffed, and rushed to the airport, Marcello was flow to Guatemala—a solitary passenger aboard a special government jet. Few thought this would deal with the odious "Little Man" once and for all, and sure enough Marcello was soon back, spirited in illegally either by boat or private plane. Once home in his old stomping ground, with access to his lawyers and purchased privilege, Marcello stayed. Yet from now on he was locked in a protracted legal wrangle with the immigration authorities and the Justice Department, under the direction of Robert Kennedy. Worst of all, Marcello had been publicly humiliated. To one of the world's top Mafia bosses, imbued more than most with traditional Sicilian pride, the experience had been intolerable. According to one compelling report, Marcello vowed revenge.

In autumn 1962, according to one of his former associates,

Marcello met with three men on the mobster's three-thousand-acre estate outside New Orleans. Although he has more than one luxurious home in the area, Marcello preferred on this occasion to talk in a ramshackle building which did occasional service as a hunting lodge. One of those present was Edward Becker, whose background had involved work in the casino business and undercover investigative work for "corporate clients." Becker says he attended the meeting with an oil geologist called Carl Roppolo, who knew Marcello and hoped to bring him in on a business deal. The third man present has not been firmly identified but may have been a Marcello aide called Liverde. Becker is the source of the account which follows, and he says the discussion with Marcello wandered a long way from the planned business conference.

Marcello is renowned for his caution, which has had much to do with his apparent immunity from prosecution. This occasion, however, was apparently an exception. The whisky flowed and so did the talk, which turned to the trials and tribulations of Marcello under the Kennedy onslaught. According to Becker, Marcello became angry as he talked about Robert Kennedy and the deportation episode. He then startled his audience with a traditional Sicilian oath, "*Livarsi na petra di la scarpa!*" Literally translated this means, "Take the stone out of my shoe!" but Marcello left no doubt about his meaning as he talked on in his Sicilian-accented Southern drawl. "Don't worry about that little Bobby son-ofabitch," cried Marcello. "He's going to be taken care of." According to Becker's statement to Congress' Assassinations Committee, Marcello referred to President Kennedy as a dog, with his brother the Attorney General being the tail. He said, "The dog will keep biting you if you only cut off its tail," but that if the dog's head were cut off, the entire dog would die. The meaning of the analogy was clear—with John Kennedy dead, his younger brother would cease to be Attorney General, and harassment of the Mafia would cease. It was, at very least, a chilling prophecy of exactly what did happen after the assassination of President Kennedy one year later. Becker said that, as he listened, he was left in no doubt. A very angry Marcello "clearly stated that he was going to arrange to have President Kennedy murdered in some way." The threat, says Becker, was made in a serious tone and sounded as if Marcello had discussed it previously.

Taken on its own, the Marcello story might seem farfetched. Taken together with the remarks attributed to Marcello's friends Hoffa and Trafficante, it is chilling. The Assassinations Committee was appalled to discover that, although it was told belatedly, the FBI learned about the alleged threat and did nothing about it. In 1967 the Pulitzer Prize-winning author Ed Reid heard the Becker account while researching a major book about the Mafia in general. He told the FBI, and the information reached top officials— including the Director, J. Edgar Hoover. The response was astonishing. The FBI report merely cast aspersion on Reid's professional standards,[76] and on Becker's reliability. The matter was allowed to drop. Noting this in 1979, the Assassinations Committee Chief Counsel called the Bureau's performance "less than vigorous" and "deficient." He found that, by failing to order a proper investigation, Hoover personally violated his promise to the Warren Commission that the Kennedy case would never be treated as closed. FBI correspondence shows that Hoover even went along with deliberate FBI efforts to "discredit" Becker and stop the allegation about Marcello being published. Congress' Assassinations Committee, on the contrary, found that it deserved a serious hearing.

Becker's own history is certainly not lily-white, but one should not expect those who hold meetings with Mafia leaders to be saints. On the credit side, it turns out that Becker had indeed been in Louisiana at the relevant time and does appear to have been in business with his alleged companion Roppolo.* Roppolo's family appears to have been close to Marcello, and a meeting with the Mafia boss is wholly plausible. A former chief investigator for the Los Angeles District Attorney's office recommends Becker as honest and knowledgeable and believes his account of the Marcello threat. Today Becker says, "Among people that came from the old country—Sicilians—and people that practiced the Machiavellian way of politics, it's quite common to talk about assas-

---

* Neither Roppolo nor Liverde, the other associate who allegedly attended the meeting, was interviewed by the Assassinations Committee. They should have been. ("Liverde", says Becker, may have been a member of the Liberto family, one of whose members was suspected of conspiring with Marcello to murder Martin Luther King.)

sination, even of heads of state. I don't think it was beyond
Marcello's grasp [*to have the President killed*]. He had the power.
You know that. You know damn well he doesn't go around making idle statements. If he makes a statement it's got to have some
strength in it. . . . I'm saying he certainly was capable, and he
certainly wanted it to happen. Okay?"

The Director of the New Orleans Crime Commission has said
of Marcello, "In my opinion he's a sociopath. He's a man who
knows how to build up obligations. He's a man who can order
ruthless punishments. He's a man who can order a murder. If you
want to know what kind of man he is, go see *The Godfather.*"

In 1979 the Assassinations Committee weighed the evidence
of the reported threat by Marcello, along with the similar reports
about his friends Hoffa and Trafficante. Knowing Marcello's reputation for prudence and Trafficante's own expertise in avoiding,
the Committee balked at the proposition that the Mafia bosses
would not only have taken the risk of involvement in the President's murder but would also have talked unguardedly about it. In
the case of Jimmy Hoffa, the Committee noted that—not being a
Mafia leader—he might not have possessed an apparatus adequate
to carry out and cover up such a crime. While noting that he hated
the Kennedys, it seemed unlikely that he would himself have
risked active involvement. More cautiously, the Committee said
that, while on the face of it, it seemed unlikely that the mob bosses
would have taken such a grave risk, Trafficante and Marcello
could not be ruled out as suspects. The Committee was alarmed by
the potential implications of the evidence it gathered about both
Mafia leaders—evidence which will continue to unfold in these
pages. Certainly, the Congressmen concluded, both Trafficante
and Marcello had "the motive, means, and opportunity to have
President John F. Kennedy assassinated." The Chief Counsel for
the Committee, Professor Blakey, has flatly expressed his personal
opinion. He has said, "I am now firmly of the opinion that the mob
did it. It is a historical truth." History may not record such a
straightforward verdict, but the professor's conviction of Mafia
involvement is based on a mass of specific evidence surrounding
the assassination.

The Assassinations Committee report provided its own riposte to the argument that Trafficante and Marcello would not have been prepared to put themselves at risk.* Ominously, it noted that "any underworld attempt to assassinate the President would have indicated the use of some kind of cover, a shielding or disguise. . . . An assassination of the President by organized crime could not be allowed to appear to be what it was." There is a further chilling element to the account of Marcello's threat, one which provides a chilling echo to such speculation.

In his very first account, many years before the Committee's speculations, the source of the Marcello allegation included a disturbing detail. Edward Becker has consistently maintained that, during the meeting on Marcello's estate, the Mafia leader spoke of taking out "insurance" for the President's assassination. This he would achieve by "setting up a nut to take the blame." That, says Becker, is "the way they do it all the time in Sicily."

The fiefdom of Carlos Marcello is said to stretch from New Orleans and the cities of the southeast as far inland as Dallas, in the heart of Texas. It was a few months after Marcello's outburst that Lee Harvey Oswald, the man soon to earn infamy as the "lone nut" killer of President Kennedy, arrived in New Orleans.

* For the latest information on Trafficante and Marcello, see Aftermath chapter.

CHAPTER 15

Three Options for History

*My view is that there was in fact a relationship between
the Cuban connection and the assassination. And my
view is that more than one person was involved.*

—Senator Richard Schweiker, after inquiry by Senate
Intelligence Committee, 1976

The assassination of President Kennedy was now seven months
away. The Texan Vice President Lyndon Johnson had just been in
Dallas predicting that the President would visit the state sometime
soon. Now, on the evening of April 24, 1963, amid the clatter of
the Greyhound terminal in downtown Dallas, Lee Oswald
boarded an overnight bus for New Orleans. He was returning to
the city of his birth, and according to the earliest official findings
he would immediately call long-lost relatives and go to stay temporarily at their home. Yet once again there is a minor mystery, a
suggestion of doubt about Oswald's real movements. The relatives
were an uncle and aunt, Charles Murret and his wife Lillian.
Oswald's Aunt Lillian was one day to tell investigators she was
sure it was a Monday when he prodigal nephew called up from the
bus station. Oswald, though, left Dallas on a Wednesday. If Mrs.
Murret was correct, there was a gap of more than four days during
which Oswald's movements are unaccounted for. Perhaps he was
simply whiling away a few days in the fleshpots of New Orleans.
Nevertheless, there is a nagging similarity with the period in Dallas
the previous year, when for almost a month nobody knew where
he was living. Some researchers have long wondered where Oswald was, and what he was up to, during the missing four days.
Others,not unreasonably, have dismissed such concern as needless
quibbling over a detail. Today, however, it is the details of Os-

wald's stay in New Orleans that have become vitally important. The question mark around that one, for example, is now underscored by the revelation that even Oswald's relatives in the city have more than incidental significance. Oswald's uncle, the Assassinations Committee established, had "worked for years in an underworld gambling syndicate affiliated with the Carlos Marcello crime family," That alarming fact, which receives full scrutiny later in this narrative, is typical of the conundrum posed by New Orleans. The investigator, picking his way through a minefield of such clues, must decide time and again whether he is dealing with coincidence or conspiracy.

Oswald's apparent activities and connections in the New Orleans months have a common denominator—Cuba. Yet Oswald's is a shadowy image, now in focus in predictable pro-Castro colors, now flickering into sight in the improbable company of anti-Castro exiles and their supporters from the ranks of both the Mafia and the world of intelligence. This multiple image of the alleged assassin simply will not go away and it leads from New Orleans to the eve of President Kennedy's murder. The inquiring mind must confront a mass of seeming contradictions and it must do so in the knowledge of three main lines of assassination theory.

The first has been mooted repeatedly, but with poor logic and minimal evidence. It is that Oswald was part of a Communist conspiracy, conceived either in Moscow or Havana or both. While Oswald was surely of considerable interest to Soviet intelligence in 1959, when he arrived in Moscow after his Marine service, there is no significant evidence it later used him for any murderous purpose. Congress' Assassinations Committee regretted that the Soviets refuse to this day to cooperate with American inquiries and thought it probable that Moscow had had some intelligence connection with Oswald. Yet, as we have seen, the Committee believed the Soviet Government was innocent so far as the President's death was concerned. Serious scholars do not believe Moscow either desired the death of President Kennedy or would have taken the horrendous risk of directing KGB assassination expertise against him.[77] The Committee also had to deal with the notion that Communist Cuba was behind the tragedy in Dallas—a theory that has received serious attention over the years.

The suggestion has been that Fidel Castro, or the Cuban

intelligence service gone out of control, learned of CIA efforts to eliminate Castro and decided to hit back. It is a thesis which had at least one eminent supporter, Kennedy's successor, President Johnson. Johnson's suspicion arose from his personal discovery while President that the CIA had been trying persistently to kill Fidel Castro. He came to believe Cuba had retaliated with a sort of pre-emptive strike, but it was a belief based more on inspiration than reason. In the mid-Sixties, the CIA continued trying to murder Castro apparently without telling Johnson, just as it very probably concealed its efforts from President Kennedy. In 1979, Congress' Assassinations Committee announced that—for a long list of reasons—it believed the Cuban Government was innocent. Even so, this book will look carefully at allegations that Fidel Castro had a hand in killing the President.* If nothing else, the nature and source of the allegations may reveal much about the real forces behind the assassination.

A second and now respectable conspiracy theory hinges on the belief that Lee Oswald was, all along, the confused left-wing loner he appeared to be—a belief favored in 1979 by the chief counsel of the Congress' Assassinations Committee. Following this theory, the genuinely left-wing Oswald arrives in New Orleans, parades his pro-Castro beliefs, and attracts the malign attention of right-wing anti-Castro militants. Because of the struggle over Cuba, those anti-Castro militants were in 1963 inextricably linked with elements of both the CIA and the Mafia. For these people—goes the theory—the left-wing Oswald is a perfect patsy. Wittingly or unwittingly, perhaps believing that for the first time in his life he has friends and allies, Oswald is drawn into a plot to kill the President. Perhaps hoodwinked into believing himself part of a left-wing operation, perhaps wholly framed, Oswald is finally set up to take solitary blame.

The third proposal, also supported by eminent and qualified observers, is similar to the second but carries even more monstrous implications. It derives from a conviction that, through all the months and years of his left-wing posturing, Lee Oswald was really a low-level agent of American intelligence. Unable to accept

*In Chapter 22, "The First Stone."

Oswald's improbable career as a Marxist Marine, suspicious of the CIA's extraordinary lack of reaction to Oswald's Soviet odyssey, some observers have seen Oswald's left-wing stance as no more than a meticulously cultivated front. Others speculate that Oswald was "turned around" only after he returned disenchanted from Russia, that the link with American intelligence was forged in Dallas. Perhaps, much of the time, Oswald was used by U.S. intelligence without his knowledge. Whichever version is favored, New Orleans is a constant factor in the thesis that Oswald was the tool of some element within American intelligence.

This belief is by no means the unique preserve of paranoid minds who see the hand of the CIA or FBI behind all America's ills. In 1976 Congressman Don Edwards, himself a former FBI agent, concluded from his work as chairman of the Constitutional Rights Sub-Committee that the FBI and the CIA were "somewhere behind this cover-up." Also in 1976, after more than a year of intensive research, two Senators came to alarming conclusions about Lee Oswald. Democratic Gary Hart and Republican Richard Schweiker had been appointed by the Senate Intelligence Committee to conduct a special study of CIA and FBI responses to the Kennedy assassination—a study which evolved into a hard look at Oswald's true role.

Senator Hart, at first reluctant to "fan the flames" of the Kennedy affair, emerged appalled from the experience of privileged access to some classified files and the frustration of Agency stalling over others. In the end he commented bleakly, "I don't think you can see the things I have seen and sit on it . . . knowing what I know—I can't walk away from it." Hart was scathing about the CIA and FBI investigation of Oswald's Cuban connections and rated their work "C-minus." Then, in direct reference to Oswald's time in New Orleans, the Senator raised questions far more disturbing than inefficiency. He called for further investigation into "who Oswald really was—who did he know? What affiliation did he have in the Cuba network? Was his public identification with the left a cover for a connection with the anti-Castro right wing?" Finally Senator Hart declared his considered opinion that Lee Oswald was "sophisticated" enough to have acted as a "double agent." Hart's colleague, Senator Schweiker, was even more positive. In 1978 he told me flatly that "the Warren Commission has collapsed like a house of cards. I believe that the Warren Commission was set up at the time to feed pabulum to the American people for reasons not yet known, and that one of the biggest cover-ups in the history of our country occurred at that time." Of Oswald's role in New Orleans, Schweiker says, "I think that by playing a pro-Castro role on the one hand and associating with anti-Castro Cubans on the other, Oswald was playing out an intelligence role. This gets back to him being an agent or double agent. . . . I personally believe that he had a special relationship with one of the intelligence agencies, which one I'm not certain. But all the fingerprints I found during my eighteen months on the Senate Select Committee on Intelligence point to Oswald as being a product of, and interacting with, the intelligence community."

Senator Schweiker does not stand alone. His inquiry led directly to the establishment by Congress of the Assassinations Committee, which in 1979 startled America with its evidence of conspiracy and a second gunman. Some senior staff members of that committee also ended their two-year investigation convinced that Oswald was indeed a low-level intelligence agent. One investigator, cautious by nature and meticulous in his working methods, firmly believes President Kennedy was killed as the direct result of a plot by an element of American intelligence.

After the assassination the public was burdened with no quandary. Wherever the guilt really lay, the man identified as killing President Kennedy was stamped as a disciple of the extreme left. Rightly or wrongly, the political left was implicitly convicted along with Oswald. Was that verdict just, or were Oswald and his apparent heroes victims of a vicious double-cross by forces of the extreme right? If there is an answer to be found it lies in the evidence of the months which immediately preceded the assassination, much of it omitted or grossly underplayed in the Warren Report. After years of work by private researchers, and controversial investigation by Louisiana public officials in 1967, much of this has at last been placed on the public record by Congress' Assassinations Committee. As its Chief Counsel put it, the Committee provided a road map which indicated New Orleans as the point of departure for further investigation. What we have of the New Orleans evidence is so complex that it may fairly be called the plan of a labyrinth rather than a road map, a maze which ends in Dealey Plaza. At the heart of the labyrinth lies the truth about Lee Oswald. It is an elusive truth.

CHAPTER 16

Viva Fidel?

*The fact that Oswald was a member of this organization
. . . the Fair Play for Cuba Committee . . . is a fact
that can be viewed from many different ways.*

—Wesley Liebeler, Warren Commission lawyer assigned to
Cuban aspects of the assassination

Oswald's involvement with Cuba cropped up years before he went
to New Orleans. There were the discussions he had with his
Marine friend Nelson Delgado about going to join the Castro
revolution. There was the evidence that he made clandestine visits
to the Cuban consulate in Los Angeles; and there was the suspicion, expressed since by a witness who said he met Oswald at the
consulate, that Oswald was not a genuine convert to Castro's
cause. According to Gerry Hemming, then himself involved with
Naval Intelligence, Oswald appeared to be "an informant or some
type of agent working for somebody." That suspicion is at the
heart of the doubt surrounding Oswald's stay in New Orleans.

In the spring of 1963, a few days before leaving for New
Orleans, Lee Oswald wrote a letter. It was to the Fair Play for
Cuba Committee, or FPCC, a pro-Castro organization with headquarters in New York. In his unmistakable scrawl, peppered as it
often was with spelling errors, Oswald reported:

> I stood yesterday for the first time in my life with a placare
> around my neck passing out fair play for Cuba pamplets ect.
> . . . I was cursed as well as praised by some. My homemade
> placard said HANDS OFF CUBA! and VIVA FIDEL! I now ask for
> 40 or 50 more of the fine, basic pamplets.

Months later, two Dallas policemen would remember seeing a man standing on Main Street wearing a pro-Castro sign and passing out leaflets. Reports show that the FBI, which was clearly reading Fair Play for Cuba Committee mail, knew the contents of Oswald's letter to New York three days before he left for New Orleans. A 1962 envelope found among Oswald's possessions shows that he had been receiving correspondence from the FPCC since shortly after his return from Russia. It had seemed a private interest, but now Oswald changed his tactics. Whatever his purpose, he began preparing a very public propaganda campaign and agitation in the streets. In New Orleans Oswald spent a few weeks getting settled in. He took a job as a maintenance man with a coffee production company, found an apartment, and summoned his wife from Dallas to join him. Then, in late May, Oswald embarked in earnest on the pro-Castro posturing that was to occupy the whole summer. In a new letter to the Fair Play for Cuba Committee, he declared his intention of setting up an FPCC branch in New Orleans, where the organization had no representative. Oswald asked for advice on tactics, propaganda material in bulk, and application forms for the members he hoped to recruit. He also confided that he was "thinking about renting a small office at my own expense." Later, that detail will take on a special significance.

The director of the FPCC replied promptly and politely, but he added a word of warning. He pointed out that, not least in right-wing New Orleans, FPCC faced serious opposition. The director warned Oswald against provoking "unnecessary incidents which frighten away prospective supporters." It was advice Oswald would completely ignore. It seems the whole matter was so pressing he could not even wait for a response from New York or for the literature he had requested. Oswald had his own plan and purpose for the FPCC in New Orleans. Within days he was at the Jones Printing Company, just opposite his place of work, ordering a thousand copies of a leaflet in support of Castro. Oswald used the name "Osborne" when placing this order, and again a few days later at Mailer's Service Company when he ordered five hundred application forms for prospective FPCC members, along with three hundred membership cards.

Copies of the pro-Castro handbill were to turn up following leaflet distributions by Oswald in the coming weeks, some bearing his own name and address and, on occasion, bearing Oswald's post-office box number but a different name—"Hidell." The handwritten name "A.J. Hidell" appeared in the space for "President" on one of the New Orleans FPCC cards. According to the authorities, this card was found in Oswald's wallet after the President's assassination—along with two forged military service cards in the same name. As we saw earlier, "Hidell" was the nickname of a Marine called Heindel who served with Oswald at Atsugi, in Japan, the secret base where Oswald worked in the immediate vicinity of American intelligence operations. "Hidell," as we also saw, may have featured in military intelligence files as an alias used by Oswald—even though Oswald never *publicly* masqueraded as "Hidell." The only time he did that was on his application for the rifle credited with killing President Kennedy, a purchase theoretically made in the privacy of the public postal system. Only one person has acknowledged familiarity with Oswald's use of the name "Hidell" in advance of the assassination. That is Oswald's wife, Marina, who eventually said Oswald persuaded her to sign the name in the space for "President" on his New Orleans Fair Play for Cuba card. Handwriting analysis indicates she did indeed do this. The FPCC "chapter" in New Orleans was entirely fictional. Lee Oswald was the sole member of a group which existed only on paper, but it was a role he exploited to the full. He wrote to *The Worker*, the Communist newspaper to which he had long subscribed, and enclosed "honorary membership" cards for Messrs. Hall and Davis, the leaders of the American Communist Party. Then, the day following the date on the "Hidell" membership card, he sallied forth to tout the Castro cause in public.

On June 16 Oswald was seen on the dock at the port of New Orleans, handing out pro-Castro leaflets to sailors from an aircraft carrier, the U.S.S. *Wasp*. Like the last propaganda distribution in Dallas, this little effort quickly fizzled. Alerted by a passing naval officer, a policeman ordered Oswald to leave at once.

After that incident, our Marxist hero abruptly broke off Fair Play for Cuba activities. For nearly two months it was as if the feverish preparations, the accumulation of a mass of propaganda, had all been for nothing, as though Lee Oswald had inexplicably lost interest in Cuba. He did a lot of reading, but books about Communism were in a minority. A FBI check on his library visits reveal that Oswald dabbled in everything from *Everyday Life in Ancient Rome* and *Hornblower and the Hotspur* to James Bond, Aldous Huxley, and science fiction. He also read *Profiles in Courage*, by an author called John F. Kennedy, and a new book about Kennedy himself, *Portrait of a President*. The Kennedy books, however, were just two of twenty-seven books Oswald read that summer. He read no books at all about Cuba.

In July Oswald went with his uncle, Charles Murret, to—of all places—a Jesuit seminary in Mobile, Alabama, where his cousin Eugene was studying. At his cousin's request Oswald gave a talk about his experiences in the Soviet Union and made it clear that in his opinion Soviet-style Communism was a dismal failure. Life in Russia, said Oswald, was not for him; meanwhile, to others, he was asserting exactly the opposite.

Privately, both Oswald and his wife had been keeping up their correspondence with the Soviet Embassy in Washington, supposedly still planning the return to Russia that had first been mooted in Dallas. Both asked for visas, although the correspondence suggests Oswald wanted Marina to go back to Russia while he pursued a plan of his own.

Whether he was indeed on a course of his own or on a mission for others, Oswald the Castro activist had merely been put on ice. In August, three months before the Kennedy assassination, he leapt purposefully into action. From this moment on, nobody could fail to remember Lee Oswald and his loyalty to Fidel Castro. What follows is the conventional account.

On August 5 Oswald allegedly ventured into what was supposedly the enemy camp. He paid a visit to a new Orleans store owned by Carlos Bringuier, a fanatically anti-Castro militant playing an active role in the struggle to remove Castro. According to Bringuier and his companions, Oswald came in unannounced, struck up a conversation, and posed as a friend of the exiles. They allege he presented himself as a Marine veteran with experience in guerrilla warfare, that he was willing to train exiles and even take part himself in the armed struggle against Castro. Next day, goes the story, Oswald was back at the store again, still trumpeting the very opposite of the usual pro-Castro creed. This time he left behind a Marine Corps manual as proof of his qualifications, and departed repeating his desire to fight Castro. Then, just three days later, he turned up in downtown New Orleans, cool as a cucumber and handing out *pro*-Castro leaflets. Carlos Bringuier, supposedly tipped off about this by a friend, searched the city center for Oswald and then angrily accosted him. Bringuier harangued passers-by, telling them how Oswald the Communist had treacherously offered support to the exiles. A crowd gathered, and Bringuier made a great show of losing his temper with Oswald. As things began to turn ugly, the police intervened. Oswald, along with Bringuier and two of his friends, was taken to the police station and charged with disturbing the peace.

However this event is interpreted, it was clearly no accident. Even the officers at the police station sensed something phoney. Their comments are interesting. Lieutenant Francis Martello was to say of Oswald. "He seemed to have them set up to create an incident." Sergeant Horace Austin, for his part, said that Oswald "appeared as though he is being used by these people and is very uninformed." Who, though, was using whom?

A convenient explanation is that Oswald deliberately provoked a dispute as part of a scheme to establish himself even more firmly as a supporter of Fidel Castro. His subsequent actions bear this out. Oswald was now engaged in advertisements for himself.

The day after the clash with the exiles Oswald approached the city editor of the *States-Item* newspaper, cajoling him to give more coverage to the FPCC campaign. Three days later he reportedly went so far as to telephone a prominent New York radio reporter, Long John Nebel, offering to appear on Nebel's radio show at his own expense. Then, exactly a week after the incident involving the exiles, Oswald contrived another scene in the street. On the morning of August 16 he went to the waiting room of a state employment office, offering money to anyone who would help him hand out leaflets, "for a few minutes at noon." For the princely sum of two dollars each he found at least one recruit, a student called Charles Steele. At noon Oswald—accompanied by Steele, and by another man who has never been identified—arrived outside the

International Trade Mart. They passed out pro-Castro leaflets for just a few minutes. In that brief space of time Oswald's demonstration was filmed by a unit from WDSU—the local TV station. The pictures survive to this day—haunting images of a slender, clean-cut young man, a hint of a smile on his lips, diffidently dispensing propaganda to passers-by. Oswald's effort brought the publicity he was courting. Within a day local radio was broadcasting an interview with him about Cuba and the FPCC, and a few days after that he took part in a lengthy broadcast debate about Cuba. This turned out to be a spirited duel with Ed Butler, director of a virulently anti-Communist organization called the Information Council of the Americas, and Carlos Bringuier, the anti-Castro exile who had starred in Oswald's street dispute. Oswald handled himself with verbal aplomb in the face of a fierce onslaught. His opponents, though, had somehow discovered about Oswald's defection to the Soviet Union, and the main thrust of the program was to expose Oswald as a Communist.

Lee Oswald would never again venture out in public support of the Castro regime. He did not need to, for now he was indelibly stamped as a Castro militant. Clearly Oswald had successfully carried out part of a plan. What plan? In the months to come the Warren Commission would offer one rationale. The Commission believed that Oswald was obsessed with the idea of going to Cuba, and his antics in New Orleans were perhaps aimed at acquiring ideological qualifications which would make him acceptable to Havana. On its face, the evidence then available seemed to support that conclusion. Between the New Orleans episode and the assassination, Oswald did, as we shall see, go through the motions of attempting to travel to Cuba. Appearances, in this case, may well deceive. Telltale clues, few of them known to the official inquiry, suggest Oswald may have been part of a covert intelligence scheme involving Cuba and designed to *discredit* supporters of the Castro regime. Consider again the story of Oswald's New Orleans Fair Play for Cuba campaign.

The confrontation with the exiles sounds oddly stagey. By Bringuier's own account, he and his cronies cursed Oswald and threw some of his leaflet up in the air. Oswald's reaction was to smile. Bringuier says he then took off his glasses and prepared to hit Oswald. Oswald went on smiling and said, "O.K., Carlos, if you want to hit me, hit me." There was no fight. Later, after all the participants had been charged with disturbing the peace, the case came up in the municipal court. In a rather puzzling decision the judge fined Oswald ten dollars but dismissed the charges against Bringuier and his friends, the people who had actually started the scene in the street. This scenario is odd but possible. What sticks in the throat is Bringuier's account of Oswald's behavior a couple of days before the incident—that contradictory visit to offer his services as a military instructor to the anti-Castro side. Some suggest this was a deliberate move to draw attention to himself and thus provoke the exiles into attacking the Oswald street demonstration. This is really the only explanation which even begins to resolve the contradiction, but in the end it simply does not bear scrutiny. Oswald could not have known the approach to the exiles would bear fruit, that one of their number would—by astonishing luck— just happen to notice his pro-Castro leafletting and then call reinforcements to cause a fracas. The implausibility of the visit to Bringuier's store, coupled with the fact that Oswald reported the incident to the FPCC before it occurred, suggests the whole affair may have been a charade. If so, what possible purpose did it serve? The conventional explanation—that the whole incident was rigged to give Oswald impressive pro-Castro credentials—may be half the answer. The other half, usually ignored, is that the FPCC incident was a solid propaganda coup for the *anti*-Castro side. First there was the street encounter itself, when Bringuier was able to "expose" Oswald as a "traitor to this country," a man who had tried to double-cross the exiles. With attention once attracted by the arrests and the subsequent court case, there was an excuse for the real propaganda show—on radio and television. Now, before a large audience, the New Orleans representative of the FPCC was dramatically exposed as a Marxist convert who had defected to Russia. Within hours Bringuier, known for his eagerness to resort to Congress' Committee on Un-American Activities, called on his supporters to ask their Congressmen for a full investigation of Lee Oswald and his Communist background.

Oswald's apparent clash with the exiles may have been a staged propaganda operation—the sort of seemingly harmless trick which could be pulled, with variations, all over the country. This is not idle speculation. By 1963 the FBI, the CIA, and U.S. Army Intelligence were engaged in clandestine operations against numerous left-wing organizations. In the case of the FPCC there was a sustained effort, not merely to penetrate and spy on the group but to damage and discredit it. Little was known of this until the Senate Intelligence Committee reported in 1976, and much still remains hidden. One document published by the Committee, a liaison note sent from the CIA to the FBI in September 1963, makes it clear that such operations had been going on almost as long as the FPCC had existed. The anonymous CIA officer writes:

> We have in the past utilized techniques with respect to counter-ing activities of mentioned organization in the U.S. During December 1961 [CIA] New York prepared an anonymous leaf-let which was mailed to selected FPCC members throughout the country for the purpose of disrupting FPCC and causing split between FPCC and its Socialist Workers Party (SWP) supports, which technique was very effective. Also during May 1961, a field survey was completed wherein available public source data of adverse nature regarding officers and leaders of FPCC was compiled and furnished [FBI executive] Mr. De-Loach for use in contacting his sources.

Other documents make it clear that the CIA had penetrated the FPCC with its own agents and that they were supplying the Agen-cy with photographs of documents and correspondence purloined secretly from FPCC files. It is also now certain that not only the CIA but also Army Intelligence had "operational interest" in left-wing groups, including the FPCC. The Intelligence Committee discovered at least one case in which a government informant was "fronting" as a Castro supporter while remaining an approved source of Army Intelligence.

After the assassination the FBI, the CIA, and Army Intel-ligence failed to offer this information to the official inquiry. The role of Army Intelligence demands special scrutiny, not least be-cause of the Assassinations Committee revelation that the Depart-ment of Defense had had a file on "Oswald" and "Hidell" and had destroyed it. The Army claims this unique record was "destroyed routinely in accordance with normal files management." In 1978, when Congressman Preyer told me of that disturbing discovery, he called the destruction "malicious." He also said, ". . . we don't know why it was done. . . . Secretary Laird in 1971, after all the charges *concerning Army spying*, ordered that the spying be stopped and those files be destroyed. . . . Perhaps, as a part of that destruction of files, the Kennedy files were also destroyed at that time. . . . " The eventual report of the Assassinations Committee noted that the Army's extraordinary action made it impossible to resolve from documentary evidence whether Oswald had an "affiliation with military intelligence." It did not, however, say anything about the extent or nature of what the Congressman mentioned to me as "Army spying."

It is now known that in 1963 U.S. military intelligence controlled more agents than even the CIA and had almost as much money to spend as the Agency. It emerged in the Seventies, as Congressman Preyer observed, that the Army had long been conducting surveillance and keeping files on thousands of American private citizens. All this was done in the name of national security, and prime targets were dissident left-wingers of the kind Oswald publicly appeared to be. A few years ago, once this invasion of privacy had been exposed, files hopefully were—as Congressman Preyer surmised—destroyed to protect the rights of the citizens who had been spied upon. Probably, though, the same housecleaning operations also removed traces of how the Army's spy operation had been conducted and who had been doing it. Something of how the system worked did, however, get into the press, even in 1963.

One newspaper article, ironically published in Dallas, Texas, outlined exactly how somebody like Oswald could have been used. It states that in cities across America, military intelligence teams from the Army, the Navy, and the Air Force—working in liaison with the FBI and the police—were assigned to guard against "subversives seeking to harm the nation's security." One way of doing it, the article added, was by penetrating "subversive" groups. This was done by undercover agents who "actually joined these groups to get names, addresses, past activities and future plans, or have established networks of informants to accomplish the same result. . . . Often one small tip from an individual has meant bringing the pieces together for some intelligence agency." The date this information was published was August 5, 1963—the very week that, in New Orleans, Lee Oswald and Carlos Bringuier engaged in that unconvincing fracas over Fair Play for Cuba. Other records make it clear that U.S. military intelligence was deeply involved in monitoring domestic activity involving Cuba. Against that background, and with today's alarming knowledge that Army intelligence has destroyed its "Oswald-Hidell" records, it seems possible that Oswald was part of a military intelligence operation. Was he being spied upon, or was he himself engaged in spying? Today, such speculation about Oswald's little games is wholly justified. Buried in the text of a Congressional report, and hitherto ignored, lies a story and a personality with remarkable similarities to Oswald's.

In November 1963, just four days before the Kennedy assassination, a young man called John Glenn appeared before the House Committee on Un-American Activities. His questioning revealed that he had joined the Fair Play for Cuba Committee in autumn 1962, that he had tried to visit Cuba, at first by traveling through Mexico, and that he eventually succeeded. In summer 1963, at the very time Oswald was becoming active in New Orleans, Glenn did reach Cuba. He outstayed his original visa and then tried to travel on to another citadel of the left, Algeria. The parallels with the Oswald case are numerous. Just as Oswald's fare home from Russia had once been paid by the State Department, so Glenn's was paid from Europe. Like Oswald, Glenn used a post-office box as mailing address and subscribed to *The Militant* newspaper. Like Oswald, he had previously traveled to the Soviet Union and Eastern Europe, in his case supposedly as a guide for an American "travel agency." While it remains possible that Glenn was a genuine supporter of left-wing causes, his background is highly suggestive. Glenn had abruptly interrupted his university career to join the U.S. Air Force, where he became an intelligence operative. He received a "crypto" clearance and studied Russian. His career as a left-wing activist began soon after he left Air Force intelligence. The result of his foray to Cuba was an emotive appearance before the Un-American Activities Committee, one which effectively smeared Fair Play for Cuba as a Communist-front organization. As soon as Oswald had been revealed as a former defector to Russia, the anti-Castro militant Carlos Bringuier issued a shrill call for a Congressional inquiry into *his* activities. While we cannot draw firm conclusions, the striking similarities between Glenn and Oswald demand proper official scrutiny. Meanwhile, several pieces of information about the New Orleans affair—hitherto either unknown or inexplicable—fit neatly into the scenario of deliberate subversion against the FPCC.

Carlos Bringuier, the exile in the New Orleans clash with Oswald, certainly had contact with the CIA. He was New Orleans delegate of the Directorio Revolucionario Estudiantil, the outgrowth of a militant Cuban student group. The group had naturally been deeply involved with the CIA at the time of the Bay of Pigs invasion and continued to receive funds afterward. The Assassinations Committee found that Bringuier had reported his contact with Oswald to his group's headquarters in Miami and that the information had in turn been relayed to the CIA. A document obtained from the Agency reveals that the CIA had "past contact with . . . Carlos Bringuier. . . . Contact was limited to Domestic Service activities." As we noted in the case of George de Mohrenschildt's CIA contacts, the Domestic Contacts Division is best known for its efforts to obtain information from travelers returning from Communist countries. However, CIA spokesmen have in the past confused inquirers by using that title rather than "Domestic Operations Division," the clandestine department which, by 1963, was conducting secret operations within the United States. Carlos Bringuier, as New Orleans head of the DRE, also published a right-wing news sheet backed by the Crusade to Free Cuba Committee. That committee was funded by the CIA. It turns out that the Agency's fingerprints mark every stage of the process by which Oswald was exposed as a Communist. Very little about that, it seems, was spontaneous.

First Carlos Bringuier called William Stuckey, a young reporter who had a weekly radio program on station WDSU. Stuckey went to see Oswald and found him a clean-cut, articulate figure, quite the opposite of the unkempt, wild-looking, left-wing prototype he had anticipated. After recording and broadcasting the initial interview, one which he would later recall as oddly "deliberate," Stuckey then began planning a follow-up debate program. What ensued was a classic case of media manipulation for political profit. Stuckey found himself positively showered with information guaranteed to smear Oswald. First there was a telephone conversation with either the head or the deputy head of the local FBI office, who obligingly read out aloud large extracts from Oswald's file. Thus did Stuckey learn of Oswald's defection to the Soviet Union. Soon the industrious Bringuier popped up again— eager to impress similar information on the reporter. He said he had obtained it by sending an anti-Castro colleague to see Oswald, posing as a Castro sympathizer. Finally, the same day, Stuckey received a phone call from Edward Butler, director of a right-wing propaganda organization called the Information Council of the Americas—or INCA. Butler confided that after telephone calls to Washington he had confirmed Oswald's Soviet connections with "someone at the House Un-American Activities Committee." The very title "Information Council of the Americas" speaks volumes for its origins and allegiances. At the time of the Oswald revelations its manager was a member of the Cuban Revolutionary Council, the anti-Castro government-in-exile created by the CIA.

The outcome of the Oswald radio debate was now a foregone conclusion. Oswald, Communist and traitor, was duly ambushed on the air. After the assassination, the story of the exposé was laid out for the public in the Warren Report—without the details about how Stuckey had been primed and by whom. INCA's man Butler was never called as a witness before the Warren Commission to be asked about that "someone" in Washington. The FBI briefing Stuckey received is mentioned nowhere in the mass of detailed reports on the Bureau's actions over Oswald and the FPCC. On the contrary, FBI records show—incorrectly—that the first Bureau contact with Stuckey about Oswald occurred long *after* the radio debate. This is just one of a series of inconsistencies and disturbing allegations which raise questions about FBI probity. Once again there are signs that American intelligence agencies had some special knowledge which tempered their treatment of Oswald.

First there is the contact between Oswald and the FBI which

occurred after the fracas with Carlos Bringuier. In custody at the New Orleans police station, Oswald asked to see somebody from the FBI, an organization he supposedly detested. August 10, 1963, was a Saturday morning, not the most likely time for an agent to respond speedily to a request by an insignificant prisoner. Nevertheless, Oswald asked and the FBI obliged. For an hour and a half Special Agent John Quigley sat talking with Oswald in the sweltering heat of the New Orleans police station. In his report of the interview Quigley later wrote as though he arrived at the police station unbriefed, with no knowledge of Oswald's history. At one point the report says flatly, "I did not know who this individual was." This is slightly contradictory to what we now know. In 1961, after Oswald's arrival in the Soviet Union, his Navy file had been reviewed by the FBI in New Orleans, the city of his birth. The agent who handled the case then had been—John Quigley. Another Quigley report, released only in 1977, comes closer than other FBI material to saying why Oswald specifically wanted to see an FBI agent after his clash with Bringuier. Quigley reports being contacted by a police intelligence officer who "said that Oswald was desirous of seeing an agent *and supplying to him information with regard to his activities with the FPCC in New Orleans.*" Just what "information" Oswald discussed with Quigley and what his real relationship was with the Bureau—or some other agency to which the Bureau might defer—remains a fuzzy area. The performance of the New Orleans FBI office is, moreover, singularly patchy. As the Senate Intelligence Committee noted with puzzlement in 1976, the FBI failed to reopen its security case on Oswald in late 1962—even though routine mail intercepts had revealed his contacts with *The Worker* newspaper. In FBI terms this was a Communist contact, and it would normally have justified an immediate reopening of the file. The case was eventually reopened several months later at the suggestion of Dallas FBI agent James Hosty, who took the initiative of pointing out the *Worker* contact. Yet in April 1963, when FBI mail intercepts revealed Oswald was in touch with the Fair Play for Cuba Committee, nobody passed on that news to Bureau headquarters. When Oswald made news in August with his New Orleans street activities, FBI headquarters did ask the New Orleans office to investigate and report in full.

Even so, no report was sent until more than two months later, and it was oddly uninformative considering the furor Oswald had been causing. It hardly reflected the intense attention the FBI was, in fact, paying to Oswald according to witnesses I interviewed in 1978. Nina Garner, Oswald's landlady in New Orleans, said FBI agent Milton Kaack questioned her about Oswald within three weeks of his arrival in New Orleans. She later learned that her lodger was under heavy surveillance by "FBI" men in "a car which used to park there at night and watch him and the house, round the corner by the drugstore." After the assassination FBI Director Hoover told the Warren Commission he had obtained affidavits from every agent who had been in contact with Oswald. There is no such affidavit from Milton Kaack, who did indeed investigate Oswald. When I reached Kaack by telephone in 1978, I expected to be referred curtly to the FBI department which deals with press inquiries. Instead, before I asked a single question, I encountered an almost apoplectic response. Kaack cried, "No. No. I'm not talking. You won't get anything out of me" and hung up the telephone. Just as Kaack was excused from providing an affidavit after the assassination, so too was Warren deBrueys, a New Orleans agent with special responsibility for reporting on political groups. Asked by the Assassinations Committee why they had not submitted affidavits for the use of the Warren inquiry, both explained that they had never been asked to do so.

The Assassinations Committee considered various serious allegations that Oswald had some sort of relationship with the FBI while in New Orleans. The most publicized has been the claim by a former FBI security clerk, William Walter, that he saw documents—before the assassination—indicating that Oswald was a Bureau informant. The Committee, after interviews with dozens of Walter's colleagues, decided there was no evidence to support his statement. His credibility was further diminished by another unsupported claim, that the FBI learned in advance of a possible threat to the President's life in Dallas. Then there are the accusations of Orest Pena, a New Orleans bar owner who in 1963 himself supplied occasional information to FBI agent Warren deBrueys. Pena claimed after the assassination that Oswald had been in his bar—one night just before the fracas in the street with Bringuier and the anti-Castro Cubans. Pena, reportedly supported by two associates, talked about an incident in which Oswald supposedly visited the bar accompanied by a Mexican. In front of the Warren Commission, however, Pena vacillated and seemed to withdraw the story. Later, though, he revived the allegation and offered a sinister reason for the temporary retraction.

In 1975 he alleged publicly that he had seen Oswald with FBI agent deBrueys on "numerous occasions" and that deBrueys had threatened him physically before his Warren Commission appearance, warning him to keep quiet about what he had observed.[78] Former agent deBrueys has repeatedly denied Pena's accusation, and the Assassinations Committee believed him. I, too, found him credible but—on also talking to Pena—gained the impression that he produced his FBI accusation to hide some different but relevant truth. He was certainly well placed to know about the Oswald affair in 1963. Pena was active in anti-Castro exile politics and deeply involved with the Cuban Revolutionary Council. Specifically, when Carlos Bringuier was arrested after the incident with Oswald, the man who apparently secured his release was Orest Pena. When I talked to Pena he remained adamant on two points, quite apart from his allegations against deBrueys. He repeated the claim, in which he was after all supported by two others, that Oswald had been in his bar accompanied by a man who seemed to be a Mexican. As we shall see, that is plausible enough. Pena declared too his certain knowledge that Oswald was working "for a government agency" in the summer of 1963. A second New Orleans witness, in my view more responsible than Pena, has provided another account of covert contact with Oswald in New Orleans.

Oswald worked at the William Reily Coffee Company from shortly after his arrival in New Orleans until mid-July, just before he launched into the public phase of his FPCC activities. While he was employed there he made frequent visits next door to a garage managed by an American citizen called Adrian Alba. Alba, whose hobby is gun collecting, often talked to Oswald about firearms and lent him gun magazines. He describes, rather diffidently, helping Oswald fix a sling on his Mannlicher-Carcano rifle. If Alba is telling the truth, that piece of information pales beside the significance of something else he remembers. Alba's was no ordinary garage—he had a contract to look after a number of unmarked cars belonging to the Secret Service and the FBI. One day in early summer 1963, says Alba, a man he thought was an "FBI agent visiting New Orleans from Washington" came to the garage. He showed credentials and was supplied with a green Studebaker from the car pool. A day later Alba observed a strange incident. As he watched from his garage he noticed the same green car drive past and stop outside Oswalds' place of work—just thirty yards away. As it did so, says Alba, "Lee Oswald went across the sidewalk. He bent down as if to look in the window and was handed what appeared to be a good-sized envelope, a white envelope. He turned and bent as if to hold the envelope to his abdomen, and I think he put it under his shirt. Oswald then went back into the building, and the car drove off." According to Alba, Oswald met the car again a couple of days later and talked briefly with the driver. The "agent from Washington" returned the car to the garage a few days later.

Adrian Alba says he was surprised when there was nothing in the Warren Commission about a relationship between Oswald and the FBI. In 1979, when the Assassinations Committee investigated his story, it found no corroborating evidence in the record.* I would hesitate, however, to reject Alba's account. He is a reserved, cautious man with no apparent reason to fabricate. He did, without any doubt, know Oswald when he worked in the adjoining building. Alba has no interest in publicity. He has always refused newspaper and television requests for interviews, despite offers of lucrative fees. Indeed, Alba's allegation was not publicized at all until I talked to him in 1978, although he has discussed it in private for years. While he may be wrong in his surmise that Oswald's contact was from the FBI, Alba's account tends to support suspicions that Oswald had covert links with one of the myriad intelligence agencies.

* The Committee was dubious about this part of Alba's story because he said nothing on these lines to the Warren Commission, and said his later recall was triggered by seeing a T.V. commercial. I was more satisfied with Alba's explanation, not least by his suggestion that—in 1963—he had been fearful of telling the whole story.

Before he left the William Reily Coffee Company, Oswald visited Alba to say goodbye. According to the record, he had been fired for malingering. Yet Oswald seemed pleased, telling Alba he expected to work next at the New Orleans plant of NASA—the National Aeronautics and Space Administration. He never did work there, although four of his colleagues at Reily did move to NASA within weeks of Oswald's departure. At all events Oswald departed, telling Alba, "I have found my pot of gold at the end of the rainbow." It is hard to know what to make of Oswald's stint at the coffee company, although researchers have not failed to discover the ubiquitous New Orleans factor—the Cuban connection. Oswald's boss, William Reily, was a wealthy American backer of the Crusade to Free Cuba Committee, a group formed to raise cash and support for the CIA-backed Cuban government-in-exile, the Cuban Revolutionary Council. Perhaps that was another coincidence.

American intelligence is the common denominator of the anomalies and persistent doubts about the true role of Lee Oswald. Oswald trails behind him, from Japan in 1958 to New Orleans in 1963, the shadow of an undefined connection with the secret world. The interpretation of it all ranges from the reasonable man's skepticism over the apparent lack of intelligence interest in Oswald on his return from Russia, to Orest Pena's shrill accusations against the FBI. Through it all the FBI and the CIA have kept up a chorus of denial and disassociation. The Assassinations Committee found, to its consternation, that the FBI failed—after the President's murder—to use the investigatory resources of its Cuban Section, the department most obviously equipped to analyze Oswald's connections in New Orleans. This, like the FBI's almost nonexistent efforts in the Mafia area, is perhaps attributable to sheer incompetence. FBI and CIA denials about Oswald may indeed have been truthful, at least semantically so. There are many rooms in America's intelligence mansion, and Oswald's tenancy may have been with an agency which has never submitted to exhaustive probing from Presidential commissions and Congressional committees. As the Assassinations Committee has now pointed out, Oswald's "possible affiliation with military intelligence" has not been resolved. It may be, too, that Oswald was—

at least in the months before the assassination—one remove away from the formal structures of the intelligence community. In the world of intelligence many operations are run through "cut-outs," buffer organizations or individuals whose sins can never formally be laid at the door of any agency or government. Thus it may have been with Oswald in New Orleans. In 1978 Congress' Assassinations Committee concentrated last-minute research effort on one clue nobody has ever explained away.

The trail started with a long-discarded document and an address synonymous with subterfuge.

CHAPTER 17

Blind Man's Bluff in New Orleans

*In months leading up to the assassination, I think
Oswald got in over his head. He was no longer quite
sure who he was working for, or why. Somebody was
using him, and they knew exactly how and why.*

–Staff investigator, Congress' Assassinations Committee, 1979

FBI Agent Quigley was carrying a bundle of papers with him when
he wound up his talk with Oswald and left the New Orleans police
station. Whether the agent understood it or not, the young prisoner had been as good as his word when he promised the FBI
information. As Quigley would write later, Oswald had "made
available" several examples of his pro-Castro propaganda. Two
were the yellow leaflets he had been handing out in the street. The
third was a forty-page pamphlet entitled *The Crime Against Cuba.*
At first sight it seemed an unremarkable tract, two years out of
date, a stilted tirade against American policy toward Cuba. Yet
The Crime Against Cuba was an evidential time bomb. Tucked
away inside the back cover, at the very end of the text, was a
rubber-stamped address. It read:

FPCC
544 Camp St.
NEW ORLEANS, LA

To the eye, 544 Camp Street was nondescript. It was a shabby, three-storied relic of the nineteenth century, a peeling facade
looking across a dusty square dominated by a statue of Benjamin
Franklin and frequented by dozing drunks *(see illustration 25).* Yet

the building did not fit in at all with either Fair Play for Cuba or its alleged New Orleans representative, Lee Oswald. Until the summer of 1963 its recent tenants had been the Cuban Revolutionary Council, the umbrella organization of the *anti*-Castro exiles, and Guy Banister Associates, a detective agency which was, in fact, a known meeting place for Cuban exiles and their links to American intelligence. The building was known as a haven for right-wing extremists, and the local FBI knew its habitués very well indeed. When Agent Quigley noticed that address on Oswald's pamphlet, it must have struck him as a total contradiction. Yet he and his FBI colleagues proved incurious.

It was not that the improbable address escaped their attention. A few days after Oswald gave the first pamphlet to Agent Quigley, a second copy arrived in the mail.[79] This one had been sent in by a regular FBI informant who had watched Oswald's demonstration and pocketed a handful of his pro-Castro literature. FBI records show that Quigley lost little time in asking New York for information on the author of this pamphlet, Corliss Lamont. Other details—like a post-office box number Oswald had given— were promptly checked. Nobody, apparently, deemed it necessary or even interesting to investigate what should have been utterly perplexing, the address which did not fit. At some point, perhaps following the assassination, somebody did draw attention to it. The pamphlet sent in by the informant, released to the public only in 1978, bears a scrawled sentence, "Note inside back cover." There the address is circled and the same hand has added what appears to be "ck out"—presumably "check out." A glance at the Warren Report suggests the belated industry by the FBI came to nothing. Buried deep in a chronology of Oswald's life is this sentence: "While the legend 'FPCC, 544 Camp St., New Orleans, LA,' was stamped on some literature that Oswald had in his possession at the time of his arrest in New Orleans, extensive investigation was not able to connect Oswald with that address. . . ." Investigation by the Assassinations Committee, conducted years later on a cold trail, concluded that the FBI's effort was "not thorough." The Committee developed evidence "pointing to a different result." It buttresses suspicion that the alleged assassin was involved in some covert operation. The address at 544 Camp

Street may also—as long surmised—provide the most solid clues to conspiracy in the assassination of President Kennedy.

Three days after the President's death FBI agents followed up on the Camp Street lead with superficial inquiries. They interviewed the owner of the building, Sam Newman, who said he had never rented office space to Fair Play for Cuba and "advised that to the best of his knowledge he had no recollection of seeing Oswald in or around the building." On the basis of a few interviews like this the FBI filed the reports on which the official inquiry relied. Their conclusion was—no FPCC office and no Oswald at Camp Street. Case closed. Nobody drew attention to a singular fact. In addition to the pamphlets recovered in New Orleans, a further twenty were found among Oswald's possessions in Dallas. *Ten* of them were stamped with the 544 Camp Street address. On top of that, the official inquiry dismissed clues in Oswald's own letters of summer 1963. These indicated that he had used an office in New Orleans.

In May 1963, less than a month after his arrival in the city, Oswald wrote to the head of Fair Play for Cuba in New York. "Now that I live in New Orleans I have been thinking about renting a small office at my own expense for the purpose of forming an FPCC branch here. . . ." Although even a humble office would cost about thirty dollars a month, said Oswald, he was intent on finding one. When headquarters warned against rushing into anything Oswald promptly replied, "Against your advice, I have decided to take an office from the very beginning . . ." This sounded very much as though Oswald had already found FPCC premises or was on the brink of doing so. Two months later, he was still writing about it—this time to report its closure. On August 1, having received no reply to his last letter, Oswald wrote, "In regard to my efforts to start a branch office . . . I rented an office as I planned and was promptly closed three days later for some obscure reason by the renters, they said something about remodeling, etc., I'm sure you understand . . ."

Oswald, of course, occasionally adjusted facts to fit his plans. He used untruths for a purpose, and there was clearly a design behind the FPCC caper in New Orleans. The knowledge we now have, that American intelligence was plotting against the FPCC at the very period in 1963, makes it impossible to ignore the pamphlets stamped 544 Camp Street or the repeated references to an office. Take another look at the dates concerned and the oddly vague replies the FBI and Secret Service agents received from the building's landlord, Sam Newman.

Oswald's August 1 letter, saying he had briefly used an office but that it had been closed down, came just before the clash in the street with the anti-Castro exiles. If there is some basis of fact to his story about having had an office, it is a fair guess that he used it sometime during the latter part of July. Newman, the landlord, was to mention several abortive attempts to rent space at 544 in the summer of 1963. These included a very brief rental by a man who "told him that he worked as an electrician by day and desired to teach Spanish by night." The man made an initial rental payment, only to return a week later saying he "had been unable to get enough students to enroll." Money, apparently, was no problem. The man told Newman to keep the deposit money. As Newman told it to the Secret Service, this occurred at exactly the time Oswald indicated he had used an office. The man—described as being in his thirties and olive-skinned—was clearly not Oswald, but the record provides another clue which may explain that. After the assassination the authorities received a tip-off that Ernesto Rodriguez, an anti-Castro militant who "operated a Spanish school . . . had tape recordings of Spanish conversations with Oswald." Rodriguez, to this day, does run a language school, and his father was in the electrical business. Under cursory questioning in 1963, Rodriguez denied having any such tape but admitted that Oswald had contacted him "concerning a Spanish language course." The date, it turns out, fits—sometime soon after July 24. Interviewed again in 1979, Rodriguez admitted that he had indeed met Oswald, but the story about Spanish classes seemed to have slipped his memory. Now, like Carlos Bringuier, he claimed Oswald had visited him to offer his services in training anti-Castro Cuban exiles in guerrilla techniques. Indeed, Rodriguez now says, it was he who sent Oswald to see Bringuier. Further checks reveal that in 1963 Ernesto Rodriguez was a leading activist in the New Orleans campaign against Castro. He was one of those who controlled the funds of the Crusade to Free Cuba Committee, the fund-raising group for the CIA-backed Cuban Revolutionary Council. In that capacity he was almost certainly in touch with William Reily, Oswald's employer in New Orleans and a backer of the Crusade.

Rodriguez also helped manage the Council's affairs in New Orleans—its second most important base in the United States. Although the CRC had theoretically ceased to use 544 Camp Street by the time Oswald got busy in New Orleans, the reality was rather different. The CRC enjoyed a delightfully easygoing business relationship with its landlord, Sam Newman. He had no initial charge for the office space, on the basis that the CRC would pay him if it raised enough money from fund-raising. The fact is that anti-Castro militants were still using 544 Camp Street after Oswald's arrival in New Orleans, and they came and went at will throughout the summer of 1963. The exiles found a warm welcome in the offices of Guy Banister, and he very definitely did maintain offices on the ground floor at 544 Camp Street. From Banister's staff have come the strongest leads to confirm Oswald's use of that unlikely address and perhaps to explain the devious purpose behind the supposed New Orleans campaign on behalf of Castro. The new information now available suggests Banister drew Oswald into an American intelligence scheme, perhaps aimed at compromising the Fair Play for Cuba organization.

Guy Banister was an old-fashioned American hero who had refused to go gracefully. He had been a star agent for the FBI, a tough guy whose long career covered some of the Bureau's most famous cases, including the capture and killing of "Public Enemy Number One," murderer and bank robber John Dillinger. He was commended by FBI Director Hoover and rose to become Special Agent-in-Charge in a key city, Chicago. In World War II—according to his family—he distinguished himself with Naval Intelligence, a connection he reportedly maintained all his life. Banister came to New Orleans in the Fifties, at the request of the mayor, to become Deputy Chief of Police. This was the high point of a flawed career. In 1957, at the age of fifty-eight, Banister was pushed into retirement after an incident in New Orleans' Old Absinthe House, when he allegedly threatened a waiter with a pistol. By all accounts Banister was a choleric man and a heavy drinker. He did not take kindly to humiliation but stayed on in New Orleans to start Guy Banister Associates, nominally a detective agency. In fact, Banister's intelligence background, coupled with a vision of himself as a superpatriot, led him into a personal crusade against Communism. He was a member of the fervently right-wing John Birch Society, of Louisiana's "Committee on Un-American Activities,"of the paramilitary Minutemen, and he published a racist publication called the *Louisiana Intelligence Digest.* He abhorred the United Nations and believed plans for racial integration were part of a Communist plot against the United States. New Orleans Crime Commissioner Aaron Kohn knew Banister well and calls him "a tragic case." Kohn says Banister retired from the FBI suffering from a serious brain disorder which led him increasingly into irrational, erratic conduct. Sane or not, Banister's public persona by 1963 can only be described as that of a right-wing nut. Sadly, there were many Banisters in the explosive political atmosphere of the early Sixties, especially in the American South. After Castro's revolution in Cuba, Banister's concept of the Red Menace was one shared by many, and it was dangerously close to official U.S. policy. He threw himself feverishly into the CIA-backed exile campaign to topple Castro, helping to organize the "Cuban Revolutionary Democratic Front" and "Friends of a Democratic Cuba." In 1961, before the Bay of Pigs invasion, Banister served as a munitions supplier. As late as 1963, say former members of Banister's staff, the offices of the "detective agency" were littered with guns of every distinction. It was no coincidence that the exiles' government in exile, the Cuban Revolutionary Council, made its New Orleans base in the same building as Guy Banister. For Banister and his Cuban protégés the building was well located—close to the local offices of both the CIA and the FBI. American intelligence may have found Banister—with his intelligence background and independent status—a convenient buffer. When the agencies could not openly associate with certain operations, Banister was available as a circuit breaker. Even if his political passions and alcoholism made a dangerously inflammable mix, Banister had his uses. His office had another distinction. It was just around the corner from the William Reily Coffee Company, where Oswald worked in the summer of 1963.

Banister's former FBI colleagues did not seriously investigate him or his office after the Kennedy assassination. He died of a reported heart attack a few months later and never was questioned by the Warren Commission investigators. It is doubtful whether they would have seen any reason to do so. The New Orleans FBI had obscured Banister's address by referring to it as 531 Lafayette Street. That was, in fact, the side door to 544 Camp Street, an address which just might have sparked interest in Washington. A partial investigation of Banister came three years later, when New Orleans District Attorney Jim Garrison began his inquiry into local aspects of the Kennedy assassination.[80] As the world learned from a stream of garish headlines, that inquiry foundered in a storm of allegations about malpractice by Garrison himself. It did, however, bring to light some vital nuggets of good evidence, as the Congress' Assassinations Committee confirmed in 1979.

The first important development came when Assistant District Attorney Andrew Sciambra interviewed Guy Banister's widow. She revealed that after her husband's death she had found among his effects a number of Fair Play for Cuba leaflets. It was odd propaganda to turn up in the possession of the man who had headed the Anti-Communist League of the Caribbean. Banister had kept extensive files at his office, and these were scattered after his death. Some, allegedly, were removed by government agents. Later, however, Louisiana police intelligence retrieved a "half-filled" filing cabinet containing records on "Communist groups and subversive organizations." Not even all that material survived subsequent winnowing of the files, but investigators know something about the contents from an index list and from police interviews. Banister's file titles included: "Central Intelligence Agency," "Ammunition and Arms," "Anti-Soviet Underground," "Civil Rights Program of J.F.K.," and "B-70 Manned Bomber Force." Sandwiched between "Dismantling of U.S. Defenses" and "U.S. Bases—Italy" was a now-familiar name—"Fair Play for Cuba Committee," It was followed by the classification number 23-7. According to a state police officer who saw this file, it contained basic information on Oswald's activities in New Orleans. As Assassinations Committee staff quietly noted, this file has "unfortunately" been destroyed.

It is possible, of course, that Guy Banister merely monitored the activities of an organization and a man he regarded as being in the heart of the Communist camp. Yet the evidence suggests a more sinister connection, redolent of plans conceived in the "dirty tricks" departments of U.S. intelligence. In his continual hunt for Reds under the bed, Banister used to hire young men as inquiry and infiltration agents. To help his Cuban exile contacts, for example, Banister would send young men to mingle with students at New Orleans colleges, primed to report on budding pro-Castro sympathizers. Two such recruits were Allen and Daniel Campbell, both former Marines. I talked to the brothers in 1979, and even their guarded comments proved startling. Daniel Campbell said he was brought into Banister's office initially because "they needed people with small-arms training for sticky situations." On the day Oswald took part in the street scene with Bringuier, however, Campbell was doing humdrum desk work. The incident occurred not far from Banister's office, and Campbell heard about it soon afterward from a friend who had seen it at first hand. As he sat with the friend in Mancuso's restaurant, on the ground floor of 544 Camp Street, she pointed out two men at a nearby table as being among those who had taken part in the street rumpus. Later, when Campbell returned to his office, a young man "with a Marine haircut" came in and used his desk phone for a few minutes. The next time Campbell saw his visitor, he says, was on television after the assassination. It was, Campbell is certain, Lee Oswald. His brother, Allen, also has relevant information.[81] He told the New Orleans authorities, in a 1969 interview, that he was at Camp Street on one of the two occasions that Oswald passed out Fair Play for Cuba leaflets near the International Trade Mart. When somebody in the office mentioned the pro-Castro demonstration, Banister might have been expected to react with characteristic spleen. According to the 1969 interview, Allen Campbell said Banister merely laughed. Other former employees recall, though, something that did make Banister angry—the use of the 544 Camp Street address on some of Oswald's handbills. The personal secretary Banister used at that time, Delphine Roberts, has provided information which goes far toward explaining Banister's behavior. Roberts, described by a former FBI agent and Banister associate as the "No. 1" source on events at Camp Street, asserts that her boss knew Oswald personally. She says Banister encouraged him to mount his FPCC operation from a room at 544. I traced Roberts in 1978, before she had talked to Congress' Assassinations Committee. She had a special role in Banister's operations.

By 1963 Delphine Roberts had made her own mark on extremist politics in New Orleans, one which shows that she and Banister were birds of a political feather. Well born and well educated, she was proud to call herself a Daughter of the American Revolution. Her unashamed allegiance was to the extreme right, and in 1962 she earned brief press interest as a vociferous candidate for a place on the New Orleans Council. Mrs. Roberts declared herself opposed to "anything of a Communistic tinge," which in her terms meant almost anything most people regard as progress. She railed, for example, against "racial integration of any kind, shape or form, because it is an integral part of the International Communist Criminal Conspiracy." She fulminated against what she regarded as federal interference in state affairs and demanded American withdrawal from the United Nations. Guy Banister did not fail to notice, and Mrs. Roberts still remembers fondly how he met and wooed her. The pair became lovers, and Banister brought Mrs. Roberts into his office as personal secretary and researcher. She was with him throughout the summer of 1963 and at the time of the Kennedy assassination. After the assassination, she says, Banister ordered her not to discuss anything with the FBI and kept her out of the office until the immediate uproar had blown over. After Banister's death, she distanced herself from the people she had known at 544 Camp Street and persistently avoided interviews. She stalled questions from the New Orleans District Attorney's office in 1967 and tried to elude Assassinations Committee staff in 1978. When I made contact with her she at first denied repeatedly ever hearing the name Lee Oswald until after the assassination. Then, after an upsetting confrontation with her own lawyer, Mrs. Roberts quietly began talking. One overt surviving sign of extreme political views was her opinion that the American intelligence agencies are today "being destroyed by so much exposure." So much has been revealed, however, that she saw little point in continuing to be secretive herself. If this witness is telling the truth, all the suspicions about Lee Oswald's true role have been justified. She remembers him very well indeed.

According to Delphine Roberts, Lee Oswald walked into her office sometime in 1963 and asked to fill in the forms for accreditation as one of Banister's "agents." Mrs. Roberts says, "Oswald introduced himself by name and said he was seeking an application form. I did not think that was really why he was there. During the course of the conversation I gained the impression that he and Guy Banister already knew each other. After Oswald filled out the application form Guy Banister called him into the office. The door was closed, and a lengthy conversation took place. Then the young man left. I presumed then, and now am certain, that the reason for Oswald being there was that he was required to act undercover." The precise purpose of Oswald's "undercover" role remained obscure to Mrs. Roberts, but she soon learned that it involved Cuba and some sort of charade that required deception. She says, "Oswald came back a number of times. He seemed to be on familiar terms with Banister and with the office. As I understood it he had the use of an office on the second floor, above the main office where we worked. I was not greatly surprised when I learned he was going up and down, back and forth. Then, several times, Mr. Banister brought me upstairs, and in the office above I saw various writings stuck up on the wall pertaining to Cuba. There were various leaflets up there pertaining to Fair Play for Cuba. They were pro-Castro leaflets. Banister just didn't say anything about them one way or the other. But on several occasions, when some people who had been upstairs would bring some of that material down into the main office, Banister was very incensed about it. He did not want that material in his office. "One day, says Mrs. Roberts, she observed the end product of Oswald's preparations upstairs. As she returned to the office in the afternoon, she saw "that young man passing out his pro-Castro leaflets in the street." In what appears to be confirmation of the incident Allen Campbell recalled, she says she mentioned what she had seen to Banister. His reaction was casual, "Don't worry about him. He's a nervous fellow, he's confused. He's with us, he's associated with the office." Nothing Banister said indicated the slightest surprise or anger that somebody from his anti-Castro stable was out in the street openly demonstrating in favor of Fidel Castro. Today Delphine Roberts shrugs off the contradiction, "I knew that such things did take place, and when they did you just didn't question them. I knew there were such things as counterspies, spies and counterspies, and the importance of such things. So I just didn't question them."

It is by no means certain that Delphine Roberts has told the whole truth or revealed all she knows. What she has said was divulged with reluctance, and she has refused to talk at all in the past. Other snippets of information, though, tend to support her account, and David Campbell's claim, that Oswald visited 544 Camp Street. Her own daughter, also called Delphine, used another room upstairs at Camp Street for photographic work. The daughter says today that she and a photographer friend also saw Lee Oswald occasionally. "I knew he had his pamphlets and books and everything in a room along from where we were with our photographic equipment. He was quiet and mostly kept to himself, didn't associate with too many people. He would just tell us 'hello' or 'goodbye' when we saw him. I never saw him talking with Guy Banister, but I knew he worked in his office. I knew they were associated. I saw some other men who looked like Americans coming and going occasionally from the room Oswald used. From his attitude, and from my mother, and what I knew of Banister's work, I got the impression Oswald was doing something to make people believe he was something he wasn't. I am sure Guy Banister knew what Oswald was doing. . . . "That much, indeed, seems certain.

Banister's brother told the Assassinations Committee that Guy "mentioned seeing Oswald hand out Fair Play for Cuba literature." Ivan Nitschke, a business associate of Banister and a fellow former FBI agent, recalls that Banister became "interested in Oswald" in the summer of 1963. Adrian Alba, who ran the garage next door to Oswald's place of work, testified to the Committee that he often saw Oswald in the restaurant on the ground floor of 544 Camp Street. That restaurant had a rear exit leading up to the office section of the building, and Banister was a regular patron.

Mrs. Roberts firmly believes that whatever the nature of

Banister's "interest" in Oswald, it concerned anti-Castro schemes, plans which she feels certain had the support and encouragement of government intelligence agencies. As she puts it, "Mr. Banister had been a special agent for the FBI and was still working for them. There were quite a number of connections which he kept with the FBI and the CIA too. I know he and the FBI traded information due to his former association. . . ." Banister's former employee, Daniel Campbell, also became convinced that his boss was involved with the FBI. An FBI report of an interview with Banister after the assassination indicates that he was asked questions about anti-Castro exiles but none at all about Oswald or use of the 544 Camp Street address on Oswald's leaflets. As for Banister and the CIA, an Assassinations Committee check revealed only that the Agency "considered using Guy Banister Associates for the collection of foreign intelligence" but decided against it. That, however, was in 1960 —three years before the episode of Oswald in New Orleans. Delphine Roberts says, "I think he received funds from the CIA—I know he had access to large funds at various times in 1963." She adds that known intelligence agents and law-enforcement officers frequently visited Banister's office. Sixteen years ago she accepted the comings and going as quite normal, because so far as she was concerned the strangers were involved with her boss in "doing something to try to stop what was taking place, the danger that was facing this country because of Cuba."

The anti-Castro exiles involved with Banister make an intriguing list. There was Sergio Arcacha Smith, an extreme right-winger who had served under Castro's predecessor, the dictator Batista. In 1961 he became New Orleans representative of the Cuban Revolutionary Council and—at Banister's instigation—set up the CRC office at 544 Camp Street. CIA records reveal that Arcacha "maintained extensive relations with the FBI. . . . Two of his regular FBI contacts were (name deleted) and . . . Guy Banister." Significantly Banister, supposedly long retired, is referred to flatly as an active FBI contact. Arcacha, who said privately he was controlled by the CIA, turned 544 Camp Street—in the words of one of his acquaintances—into a sort of "Cuban Grand Central Station" for the exiles. When Arcacha cast around for funds he was offered a "substantial donation" by none other than Carlos Marcello, the New Orleans Mafia boss. By 1963 Arcacha had moved to Texas, removed from his New Orleans CRC job after accusations of misappropriation of funds.[82] Arcacha[83] denies all knowledge of Oswald prior to the assassination, but one of his successors did encounter the alleged assassin. This was CRC delegate Frank Bartes, who turned up with Carlos Bringuier for the court case following the street fracas. On that occasion, he indulged in a noisy argument with Oswald. Bartes said he never visited 544 Camp Street and never had anything else to do with Oswald. Arcacha and the CRC have been firmly linked to at least two other people—apart from Banister—who did cross paths with the alleged assassin. One was Carlos Quiroga, the anti-Castro Cuban who admitted visiting Oswald at home a few days after his street confrontation with Cuban exiles. Quiroga provided some of the information which helped expose Oswald as a Communist on the forthcoming radio debate

The CRC had a friend in a New Orleans advertising man called Ronnie Caire. Caire was a fervent supporter of the exile cause and had been a leading light with Arcacha in yet another anti-Castro organization, the Crusade to Free Cuba. The arm of coincidence was long indeed, it seems, in the New Orleans of 1963. After the assassination Ronnie Caire would say, very carefully, that he "seemed to recall" a visit from Oswald. He said Oswald had been "applying for a job."

Perhaps Caire's memory was better than he thought. In Oswald's address book, on the same page as Carlos Bringuier's address, was the following list of addresses:

117 Camp
107 Decatur
1032 Canal

As written, the entries made no sense. The first was the address of a formal-dress rental shop, and the second did not even exist. Allowing for either a mistake or deliberate secretiveness on Oswald's part, researchers have juggled the numbers. 107 Camp Street, it turns out, was Ronnie Caire's business address. 117

Decatur was the address of Orest Pena, yet another prominent Cuban exile in close touch with the others we have mentioned. Pena had two other distinctions—he had worked closely with Sergio Arcacha Smith and was a regular informant for the FBI. Unfailingly, in any study of Oswald in New Orleans, the connections seem to come full circle. The last and perhaps more important of those connections is the one that links Oswald's name with that of David Ferrie.

David Ferrie, even more than Banister, was a talented misfit. He was a born flier, a skill which had earned him a career as a senior pilot with Eastern Airlines. For Ferrie that was not enough. His was a brilliant but erratic mind, which made for a tragically disordered life. Ferrie dabbled in religion and ended up founding his own church. He dabbled in medicine and began a one-man search for the cause of cancer. He was a homosexual and compromised himself while at work. Eastern Airlines fired him. Ferrie might have remained an unknown eccentric, but then there was Cuba. Ferrie was one of those mavericks who suddenly found a role for themselves in the efforts to topple Fidel Castro. His reputed ability to perform miracles with aircraft finally found an outlet. In 1961, before the Bay of Pigs, Ferrie reportedly flew to Cuba dozens of times, sometimes on bombing missions, sometimes making daring landings to extract anti-Castro resistance fighters. It was Ferrie's brief season as a hero, but it quickly soured. By the summer of 1962, aged forty-five, he was adrift in New Orleans—dividing his time between his passion for young men and an embittered pursuit of extreme right-wing causes. He was by now an outlandish figure, not least because he suffered from alopecia, an ailment which had left him not only bald-headed but without eyebrows or body hair. Ferrie compensated by wearing a red toupée and sometimes grotesquely obvious false eyebrows. He would have been wholly laughable were it not that his quirky intellect still found him listeners in the world of political extremism. As early as 1950, when he joined the Army Reserve, he had been stridently anti-Communist, writing in a letter to the commander of the U.S. 1st Air Force, "There is nothing I would enjoy better than blowing the hell out of every damn Russian, Communist, Red, or what-have-you. . . . We can cook up a crew that will really bomb them to hell. . . . I want to train killers, however bad that sounds. It is what we need."Perhaps, when he came to train anti-Castro Cubans, Ferrie achieved part of his ambition. He was a rabble-rousing public speaker, with his principal subject the festering Cuban confrontation, the principal whipping boy President Kennedy. After the catastrophe at the Bay of Pigs, Ferrie had made a speech on Cuba to the New Orleans chapter of the Military Order of World Wars. His attack on the President had been so offensive that Ferrie was eventually asked to leave the podium. Detestation of the President became, it seems, something of an obsession with him. Some, who heard Ferrie say angrily, "The President ought to be shot," would one day come to believe that in his case it had been no idle oratory. A favorite Ferrie theme was along the lines that ". . . an electorate cannot be depended upon to pick the right man." He was a natural political soul mate for Guy Banister, a man still remembered for an occasion on which he alarmed his companions by pulling out a gun and shouting, "There comes a time when the world's problems can be better solved with the bullet than the ballot." By the summer of 1963 these two were old cronies, and Ferrie was one of the most frequent visitors to 544 Camp Street.

Guy Banister's secretary, Delphine Roberts, remembers Ferrie as "one of the agents. Many time times when he came into the office he used the private office behind Banister's, and I was told he was doing private work. I believed his work was somehow connected with the CIA rather than the FBI . . ." The reporter's mind recoils at the notion that any intelligence service would be misguided enough to hire a David Ferrie, but one qualified source says there was a CIA connection. The former Executive Assistant to the Deputy Director of the CIA, Victor Marchetti, told me that he observed consternation on the part of then CIA Director Richard Helms and other senior officials when Ferrie's name was first publicly linked with the assassination in 1967. Marchetti says he asked a colleague about this and was told that "Ferrie had been a contract agent to the Agency in the early Sixties and had been involved in some of the Cuban activities." As Deputy Director for Plans in 1963, Cuban operations had been at the top of Helms' own priority list. Today Marchetti says he is "absolutely convinced that Ferrie was a CIA contract officer and involved in some rather nefarious activities." In 1979 an Assassinations Committee source, who had investigated Ferrie's background, told me, "We did not find Ferrie named in CIA files as an agent, but in intelligence work that is not unusual . . . Clearly the people he was dealing with had intelligence connections." Certainly David Ferrie was closely associated with Guy Banister and the Cuban exiles in 1963. On the very day Oswald handed out anti-Castro leaflets in New Orleans, Ferrie was leading an anti-Castro demonstration a few blocks away. As with Guy Banister, there have been repeated allegations that he too was involved with Oswald.

After the assassination there was perfunctory inquiry into Oswald's membership, as a youth of nearly sixteen, of the Civil Air Patrol. Oswald was then living with his mother in New Orleans, and joined the Patrol as a cadet in 1955. David Ferrie, an airman of skill and renown, was at that time a leading light of the local Patrol unit. After the assassination one of Banister's employees said he thought he recalled seeing a photograph of Oswald, along with other onetime CAP members, in Ferrie's home. Ferrie was asked about this on a couple of occasions and claimed he could remember nothing about Oswald. He denied ever having any sort of relationship with Oswald. Since he also denied knowing that the Cuban Revolutionary Council and its representative Arcacha ever operated from Camp Street, a fact he certainly did know about, Ferrie's denials should have raised suspicions. The FBI, however, conducted a mockery of an inquiry into Oswald's membership in the Civil Air Patrol, and the matter was dropped. There was no further action when one of Oswald's former schoolmates, Edward Voebel, first stated that he and Oswald had been in the Patrol "with Captain Dave Ferrie," and then—quite suddenly—he "could not recall" the matter. The FBI was unmoved by the fact that Voebel had been scared by a "crank-type telephone call" and a visit to his home by a strange man. Nor was the Bureau strung into action when another former cadet said Ferrie had scurried around to see him—after the assassination—asking whether any old group photographs of Ferrie's squadron featured Oswald. Most of the squadron records, it turned out, had been "stolen in late 1960." Even in 1978, Congress' Assassinations Committee did better.

Investigators established that Ferrie's service with the Air

Patrol fitted in with that of Oswald. They also identified no fewer than six witnesses whose statements tended to confirm that Oswald had been present at Patrol meetings attended by Ferrie. One said flatly, "Oswald and Ferrie were in the unit together. I'm not saying that they may have been there together. I'm saying it's a certainty." Nobody, at this date, can recall any special relationship between the bizarre instructor and the cadet who would one day become infamous. The Assassinations Committee noted, however, that Ferrie's "appeal to several young men may have been related to his taking an extraordinary interest in them. . . . He often gave parties at his residence where liquor flowed freely; and he offered his home as a place for the boys to stay when they were unhappy at home. . . ." Oswald, as we now know, had a miserable home life. His school friend, Edward Voebel, believed Oswald attended a party given by Ferrie after one Patrol qualification ceremony.

Ferrie's homosexuality, and his weakness for young boys in particular, is a matter of record. Over the years it led him repeatedly into trouble and sometimes into police custody. On one occasion he was freed only after the intervention of a familiar figure, Cuban exile leader Sergio Arcacha Smith. Similarly, in the mid-Fifties, Ferrie's misconduct with youths in the Air Patrol led to scandal. There were reports of drunken orgies, of boys capering about in the nude, and in the end it was this that ended Ferrie's tenure with the New Orleans unit. There is not yet any evidence that Oswald was involved in such goings-on, but—at the age of sixteen and on the threshold of an adult sexual life—he was certainly vulnerable to the likes of Ferrie. The Assassinations Committee noted that—homosexuality aside—Ferrie exerted "tremendous influence" through his close associations with his pupils in the Patrol. A Committee analysis adds that he "urged several boys to join the armed forces. . . . Many of Ferrie's cadets became involved in Ferrie's wide spectrum of other activities."

At the age of sixteen, immediately after his brief stint in the Civil Air Patrol, Lee Oswald tried to enlist in the Marines. He failed to do so at first because he was underage and—as we have seen—spent the next year studying the Marine manual until "he knew it by heart." He finally joined up just a few days after his

seventeenth birthday. It was of course at this same period that
Oswald began manifesting an interest in Marxism and the politics
of the left. The conventional view, conveniently ignoring the
stream of anomalies in Oswald's career, has been to regard this as
the start of an authentic lifelong commitment. With his possible
influence on Oswald in mind, consider the ambivalent approach
Ferrie had to politics. He was, in the words of the Assassinations
Committee, "rabidly anti-Communist," yet he sometimes de-
scribed himself as a "liberal." Of his position on Cuba, Delphine
Roberts says, "Well, he had to act a part, of being what many
people would call wishy-washy, *one side and then the opposite side.*
It was important for him to be that way, because he was acting like
a counterspy. He knew both sides. . . ." Consider once again
Oswald's alleged teenage interest in Socialism, which the Warren
Report presented as the foundation stone for a leftist future. The
Report failed to mention another comment by Oswald's former
school friend. Reports that Oswald was already "studying Communism," said Edward Voebel, were "a lot of baloney." The
comment recalls the plethora of incidents which have somehow
rung false. How much of his parroted politics was also "baloney"?
That we cannot know, but the potential influence of David Ferrie,
looming darkly at a seminal point in Oswald's life, is sobering.
Whether or not Ferrie steered the mind and actions of Oswald the
youth, the evidence now suggests they were indeed involved with
each other in the summer of 1963.

If Oswald did frequent 544 Camp Street, he would almost
certainly have encountered David Ferrie. There are several indications of such a link. Dean Andrews, a New Orleans lawyer,
reported after the assassination that Oswald came to his office
several times to ask for help in appealing his undesirable discharge
from the Marine Corps Reserve. Andrews, whose account was
partially corroborated by office staff, says Oswald was accompanied on the first visit by some Mexican "gay kids," one of whom
appeared to be Oswald's companion. Ferrie, the homosexual, had
business connections with Andrews. Other allegations connecting
Oswald with Ferrie are more direct. Jack Martin, a Ferrie associate who also worked for Banister, said after the President's death
that Ferrie once told him about a young man who had witnessed a

sexual act in which Ferrie had taken part, and had then joined the Marie Corps and left New Orleans. Martin also said he suspected Ferrie "had taught Oswald how to purchase a foreign-made firearm. . . ." In 1963, Martin's statements were dismissed by the FBI as those of a disreputable character with a grudge. In 1979, Congress' Assassinations Committee was not so dismissive—and with reason. Banister's secretary, Delphine Roberts, says Ferrie not only met Oswald but took him on at least one visit to an anti-Castro guerrilla training camp outside New Orleans. They went there, according to Mrs. Roberts, "to train with rifles." There is some justifiable doubt about the account of Martin. Some, with less reason, have cast aspersions on the motives of Delphine Roberts. There is other evidence, though, linking Oswald to the extreme right and to David Ferrie, and this is well documented by untainted witnesses. It places Oswald, in early September 1963, in a small town north of New Orleans, in the company of one man who almost certainly was David Ferrie and another who may have been Guy Banister.* True to form, it is a bizarre episode in an odd setting, yet in 1979 the Assassinations Committee found the sources "credible and significant." Just as other events have Oswald posturing as a left-winger on Cuba, this episode connects him with the other great issue of the day—race.

For the United States, 1963 was a critical year in the nationwide campaign to end racial discrimination against the huge black minority. That summer became "the civil-rights summer," with Dr. Martin Luther King at the head of a movement growing ever stronger. The black leaders had found more support in the White House than ever before, and President Kennedy had committed himself personally to the civil-rights bill. Among other things this guaranteed blacks the right to vote, and a major aim of the campaign was to make black citizens more aware of their political rights. Either because of white oppression or their own apathy, tens of thousands of Negroes had never voted or even registered to vote. In cotton country, in the little farming towns of the deep South, the civil-rights campaign was meeting fierce opposition

---

* The date coincides closely with the alleged sighting of Oswald in the company of CIA officer "Maurice Bishop." in Dallas.

from extreme racist groups and from ordinary whites who could not accept that the old days of white domination were numbered.

One such community was Clinton, a township of fifteen hundred people some ninety miles north of New Orleans. Here, at the beginning of September 1963, the Congress of Racial Equality—known as CORE—was organizing the black population to register as voters. The atmosphere was one of tension. Just weeks before a group of blacks had been summarily arrested, merely for writing respectful appeals to the mayor and district attorney. One morning, under the watchful eye of the police, a long line of blacks waited to sign on at the registrar's office—a process which should be quick and simple but which white officials in those days often made tedious and complex. For such a small community, where everybody knew almost everybody else, it was a momentous morning. The policy and local officials, exclusively white, were alert for anything that might constitute a breach of the peace. For their part, black organizers were afraid there would be unfair interference by the police or FBI agents, whom they saw as traditional enemies. This was the setting for a mysterious incident involving Lee Oswald, one which would be consistently reported by black and white witnesses alike.

Their story, pieced together from formal testimony and my own interviews, concerns three white strangers and a distinctive car. The chief witnesses are two CORE organizers, the registrar of voters, and the town marshal.

Sometime after ten o'clock, everyone agrees, a black Cadillac parked near the registrar's office. It was highly conspicuous in the modest main street of a town like Clinton, and almost everyone noticed it. The local chairman of CORE, Corrie Collins, saw it arrive and was immediately suspicious. He and his colleague, William Dunn, thought it was an unwelcome visit from the FBI. There were three men in the car, and one, a slim young white, got out and joined the blacks waiting to register. He apparently waited patiently for several hours, a rare white face in a long line of black ones. After the assassination, witnesses were unanimous in saying this had been Lee Oswald. Most simply recalled his face, but the registrar, Henry Palmer, had more to go on. He had interviewed the applicants in his office and later remembered dealing personally with the young stranger. "I asked him for his identification, and he pulled out a U.S. Navy ID card. . . . I looked at the name on it, and it was Lee H. Oswald with a New Orleans address. According to Palmer, Oswald's story was that he wanted a job at the nearby East Louisiana State Hospital; he believed he had more chance of getting it if he registered as a member of the Clinton electorate. To Palmer it was an odd request, out of context with the black registration drive. He finally told Oswald he had not been in the area long enough to qualify for registration. Oswald thanked him and departed. Meanwhile, out in the street, the black Cadillac had been attracting considerable interest.

The registrar says the car caught his eye when he left his office for a coffee break. He wondered, like CORE campaign workers, what it was doing there and asked the town marshal to check on the occupants. The marshal, John Manchester, did talk to the driver and satisfied himself that there was nothing to worry about. The Cadillac stayed where it was until well into the afternoon, its passengers apparently content just to sit and stare. The policeman, along with other witnesses, later remembered the driver as "a big man, gray-haired, with a ruddy complexion." Two witnesses later remembered the second man, the passenger, for one feature in particular. As CORE chairman Collins, put it, "The most outstanding thing about him was his eyebrows and hair. They didn't seem real, in other words, they were unnatural, didn't seem as if they were real hair." The descriptions of both passengers were strongly suggestive and were later to cause a good deal of controversy.

The New Orleans district attorney, Jim Garrison, used the Clinton evidence in 1967 when he charged Clay Shaw, a prominent businessman and former CIA contact, with conspiring to assassinate President Kennedy. Shaw was indeed tall and gray-haired, and some Clinton witnesses thought he could have been the driver of the mysterious Cadillac. The case against Shaw, however, was extremely weak, and he was acquitted. In the light of all the other evidence, many investigators now favor the theory that the car's driver was in fact Guy Banister. In some respects Banister answered the description better than Shaw, and the description of his companion adds weight to the theory. Not many men have noticeably false hair and eyebrows, and the CORE chairman unhesitatingly identified the Cadillac's passenger as David Ferrie. Ferrie undoubtedly did work frequently with Banister, and both were opposed to operations like the CORE campaign in Clinton. Today, Banister's admirer Delphine Roberts provides a tortured justification. "He and I were against the way they were going about it, which ignored the civil rights of the white person. . . . It was taking away from the whites and giving it all to the Negroes." "They," of course, meant Washington, and Washington meant John Kennedy. Only weeks earlier the President had appealed to the nation to "treat our fellow Americans as we want to be treated. If an American, because his skin is dark . . . cannot vote for the public officials who represent him . . . who among us would then be content with the counsels of patience and delay?" Certainly indefinite delay would have satisfied the men of 544 Camp Street. Guy Banister had openly declared himself in favor of some sort of apartheid. It seems quite plausible that he and Ferrie could have been involved in a nefarious scheme against civil-rights groups. But what sort of scheme, and how was Oswald to be involved? Today we can only guess.

It now seems highly likely that Lee Oswald was in the Clinton area and spent some time preparing the ground for his bid to register as a voter. Several credible witnesses help trace his actions, two of them in the nearby township of Jackson. The town barber, who says it was extremely rare to see any but his local customers, remembers Oswald asking for advice on getting a job as an electrician at the local hospital. He sent him to the State Representative, Reeves Morgan, who confirms that a Lee Oswald did come to see him. Two secretaries at the hospital recall Oswald coming to apply for work, and the vote registration incident seems to have followed shortly afterward. There is no reason to doubt these witnesses, yet it seems highly unlikely that Oswald really wanted either to live or work in Clinton. The possible presence of Banister and Ferrie only adds to the mystery. A plausible explanation is that the incident was connected with some agency operation like the FBI's now infamous Counterintelligence Program, better known as COINTELPRO. In line with other U.S. intelligence schemes against such alleged Communist organizations as Fair Play for Cuba, COINTELPRO was a ruthless long-term operation to disrupt and destroy certain political groups. FBI Director Hoover, implacably hostile to the civil-rights movement, went to extraordinary lengths to discredit its leaders and undermine its effectiveness. By 1963 COINTELPRO was firmly established, and as Arthur Schlesinger has written, "Its weapons were rumor, forgery, denunciation, provocation." When CORE leaders in Clinton spotted the black Cadillac, their immediate suspicion was that the FBI was up to its customary capers. The car stayed in the same spot nearly all day, its passengers impassively watching the comings and goings at the registrar's office. Black campaign workers interpreted it as a crude attempt to scare away local blacks with a threatening "FBI" presence. If Guy Banister was indeed the man behind the wheel, they may have been right. Lee Oswald's role in the episode remains unexplained.[84] The intention may have been to link him with yet another left-wing cause. Perhaps, for motives unknown, the object was to *ensure* that a large number of witnesses would remember Oswald and his behavior. The long-term impression, certainly, is of an Oswald being manipulated by forces representing the precise opposite of his public posture. Those forces had monstrous connections which we have not so far considered. The denizens of Camp Street were linked to the Mafia as well as the CIA.

By the summer of 1963, two summers had passed since the Louisiana Mafia boss, Carlos Marcello, had been unceremoniously deported from the United States by the Kennedy administration. Within months of the deportation he had returned to New Orleans, in defiance of Attorney General Robert Kennedy. The homecoming was secretive, but Marcello was soon seen openly around the city, again in personal control of his organized-crime empire. Yet the battle was by no means over so far as Robert Kennedy was concerned. On his personal order the Justice Department stepped up the pressure against Mafia operations in the South and against Marcello personally. There was now a personal war between the Kennedys and Marcello, just as there was with Marcello's friend Hoffa. In private, like Hoffa and Florida crime boss Santos Trafficante, Marcello reportedly spoke of meting out

Mafia justice to the Kennedys.* In public he was locked in protracted battle with the Government. The charges which had led to Marcello's deportation were revived energetically throughout 1963. Marcello fought back vigorously, and two of those who helped him do so were Guy Banister and David Ferrie.

The Ferrie connection went back a long way, perhaps as early as 1961, when Marcello had sneaked back from exile in Guatemala. Of the several theories as to how exactly the Mafia boss came home, one long favored by investigators, is that he was flown in by private plane. Although Marcello now denies it, a contemporary Border Patrol report identified the pilot of the aircraft as David Ferrie. From early 1962 Ferrie was employed, by his own account, as "investigator and law clerk" in the office of Wray Gill, one of Marcello's posse of lawyers. Ferrie also associated with Dean Andrews, another lawyer who provided his services on Marcello's behalf and who claimed he met Lee Oswald in 1963. In the three months leading up to the assassination, Ferrie was employed specifically to help Marcello fight the Government's case of deportation. This involved at least one fight to Guatemala to gather evidence for the defence, work which one of Ferrie's associates described as that of "research librarian." The research also involved weekend visits to two of Marcello's bases of operation, the Town and Country Motel in New Orleans and his estate outside the city, Churchill Farms. It was reportedly at Churchill Farms that Marcello made his threat against President Kennedy's life a few months earlier. Hatred of the President was, as we have seen, something Ferrie and Marcello had in common. A New Orleans witness who knew both men says, "Marcello thought Ferrie was very intelligent."

The high point of Ferrie's work on behalf of the Mafia leader came at exactly the period in 1963 that Ferrie was also frequenting Guy Banister's office at 544 Camp Street. Banister, it seems, had reversed the zest for hunting gangsters which once brought him distinction in the FBI. He too now lent his expertise to Marcello's cause, as the Assassinations Committee confirmed. In 1979 I

* As discussed in Chapter 14, "The Mob Loses Patience."

traced Mary Brengel, another secretary who worked in Banister's office during the crucial summer and autumn of 1963. She recalls that one day, as she was taking dictation from Banister, he openly referred in a letter to his work in helping Marcello fight deportation. Mrs. Brengel expressed surprise that her employer was involved with organized crime, and Banister responded curtly, "There are principles being violated, and if this goes on it could affect every citizen in the United States." He left no doubt that he was firmly on Marcello's side.

In the closing months of its mandate, Congress' Assassinations Committee broke new ground in an area of research which had been unforgivably neglected. It would seem obvious enough that Oswald's family background demanded intensive inquiry, yet only the Committee has tackled the job seriously. The results are disturbing and show that key members of the Oswald family were touched by organized crime. The connection is to another sort of "family," the Mafia network headed by Carlos Marcello.

A great deal of Oswald's childhood and youth was passed in New Orleans, and many formative years were spent in an environment which should have worried any parent. From the age of fifteen Oswald lived with his mother at 126 Exchange Alley, and it was not an enviable address. Exchange Alley was in the French Quarter, amid the hubbub and razzmatazz synonymous with New Orleans. In the words of New Orleans Crime Commission Director Aaron Kohn, "Exchange Alley, specifically that little block that Oswald lived on, was literally the hub of some of the most notorious underworld joints in the city. . . ." Oswald lived in substandard accommodation above a pool hall, a known hangout for gamblers. Not much is known of his teenage pursuits, but one episode suggests that the atmosphere of lawlessness was infectious. Edward Voebel, Oswald's school friend, remembered having to dissuade his pal from a plan to break into a gun shop and steal a weapon. Boys in bad neighborhoods are especially prone to being rascals, but Oswald was more at risk than we have ever known until now. Oswald, whose father was dead, was brought up by a mother with connections to the world of gangsters.

Another relative once said of Marguerite Oswald. "She's a woman with a lot of character and good morals, and I'm sure that what she was doing for her boys she thought was the best at the time. Now, whether it was or not is something else, I guess." Today the touching portrait of Marguerite the embattled single parent is somewhat tarnished. The Assassinations Committee took a closer look at her known friends. One was Clem Sehrt, a New Orleans attorney. He, the Committee noted, was "associate, lawyer, and financial adviser to a Louisiana banker associated with Carlos Marcello. . . ." He had himself been "long involved in a series of highly questionable undertakings, both business and political." Mrs. Oswald turned to Sehrt when her son Lee was trying to join the Marines, in the wake of his apparent association with the highly suspect David Ferrie. Sehrt was cooperative when she suggested that—since Lee was under age—a false birth certificate might help. After the assassination, according to information which recently reached the New Orleans Crime Commission, Sehrt was asked to represent Oswald. It is not known who asked him to do so. It is interesting, however, that Dean Andrews— another New Orleans attorney, with links to Marcello associate David Ferrie—also said he was asked to represent Oswald after the President's murder. He named the man who called him only by the pseudonym of "Clay Bertrand." He has since said that to reveal the truth about his caller would endanger his life, and my own brief contact with Andrews confirmed that the fear is still with him today.

Marguerite Oswald's friendship with underworld lawyer Sehrt was not a solitary brush with organized crime. She worked for some time for Raoul Sere, a lawyer who went on to become an assistant district attorney for New Orleans. Crime Commission Director Kohn says Sere was strongly suspected of being involved with "The Combine," a group of New Orleans figures who obstructed the course of justice with bribery and corruption. He adds, "The district attorney's office was then under the corrupt influence of the gambling syndicate—Carlos Marcello and others—to a very significant degree." Mrs. Oswald is reluctant to discuss the matter but acknowledges meeting Sere for advice after her son Lee went to the Soviet Union. Finally, the Assassinations Committee found evidence that Mrs. Oswald had been friendly with a man called Sam Termine. Termine, who died recently, was "a Louisiana crime figure who had served as a 'bodyguard' and chauffeur for Carlos Marcello." Investigation of Termine revealed that he was close to Oswald's uncle, Charles Murret. Murret, who was married to Mrs. Oswald's sister Lillian, had a great deal of contact with Lee Oswald. He too, it turns out, tracks back to the Mafia apparatus of Carlos Marcello.

The Assassinations Committee discovered that Charles "Dutz" Murret was much more than the "steamship clerk" he was painted in testimony by his family to the Warren Commission. Murret, who lived beyond the means of a man with that occupation, cropped up as early as 1944—in a survey of vice and corruption in New Orleans. An FBI report named him as being prominent in illegal bookmaking activities—a report which nobody brought to the attention of the Warren Commission. Murret was for years an associate of one Sam Saia, and Saia was a leader of organized crime in New Orleans. The Internal Revenue Service identified him as one of the most powerful gambling figures in Louisiana, and Crime Commission Director Kohn says, "Saia had the reputation of being very close to Carlos Marcello." Marguerite Oswald has said, "Just because Mr. Murret worked for those people, and may have known Marcello, that doesn't mean anything about Lee." That, in the sense that Oswald himself is a highly unlikely candidate for a Mafia role, is partially true. It does nothing to dispel the notion that people in the Marcello network "spotted" Oswald.

For Oswald, whose father died before he was born, Murret was a father figure over many years. At the age of three Oswald actually lived with the Murrets and subsequently went to see them frequently on weekends. He visited them while serving in the Marine Corps—most worrying of all—saw a lot of his Uncle Charles in the New Orleans period before the assassination. He stayed with Murret for a while after he arrived in the city, and Murret lent Oswald money. When Oswald was arrested following his street fracas with Bringuier, he called the Murrets for help in getting bail. When he got through on the telephone, the record tells us, only Murret's daughter was at home. She eventually contacted "a family friend," one Emile Bruneau. Bruneau, says an FBI report, contacted "someone else" who arranged Oswald's release. Bruneau, who has reportedly admitted to the Assassinations Committee that he did indeed help, has been described as "a big-time gambler" by Crime Commission Director Kohn. In 1963 he was, like Oswald's Uncle Charles, an associate of one Nofio Pecora. Pecora, as we shall see, may have received a telephone call from Oswald's killer, Jack Ruby, less than a month before the Kennedy assassination. Pecora is, according to the Assassinations Committee Report, "a long-time Marcello lieutenant."

Most of the underworld figures named in this chapter—the most notable exception being Marcello himself—are now dead. Oswald's mother is today strangely sensitive about her family connections. In one of the last interviews conducted by the Assassinations Committee, she "declined to discuss her past activities at any length, refusing to respond to various questions." Mrs. Oswald would not say if she knew whether her brother-in-law Murret was acquainted with Marcello. It is certain that, if there are to be further official investigations, this will be a key area of inquiry. What it all means is still obscure, but the implications are serious. Nothing about Oswald's adult history suggest he had the remotest sympathy for Mafia criminals—indeed the very contrary is true. Yet his family's connections, his apparent association with Marcello henchman David Ferrie, and the identity of those who arranged bail after the street fracas cannot be ignored. Clearly the mob had every opportunity to become aware of Oswald the posturing left-winger. The latest revelations are all the more ominous in the light of a sinister element in the allegation that Carlos Marcello spoke of planning the President's murder. That was when, reportedly, he talked of "setting up a nut to take the blame."

None of this should detract from suspicion that Lee Oswald was, while in New Orleans, the tool of an anti-Castro intelligence operation. The true nature of the Camp Street connection, and the genesis of the "Hidell" pseudonym, demand further inquiry.[85] The family member closest to him, his wife Marina, may have much to tell. While she has since admitted signing the name "A.J. Hidell" on Oswald's Fair Play for Cuba card, her statements have been inconsistent. Less than a month after the assassination, she said she had no knowledge of her husband having used the name. A

few weeks later she changed her story and said she had heard
Oswald use the name "Hidell" on the radio discussion with anti-
Castro exiles following the street fracas over Oswald's pro-Castro
demonstration. There are full transcripts of that broadcast, and
the name "Hidell" was not mentioned once. Delphine Roberts,
Guy Banister's secretary at 544 Camp Street, has said she believes
Marina Oswald once accompanied her husband on a visit to the
office. Asked about this by the Assassinations Committee, Marina
said she had "no recollection" of going there. She had the same
reply to a question about knowing David Ferrie. As for Charles
Murret, the Oswald relative with Mafia connections whom she met
regularly in New Orleans, Marina said she had forgotten his name.
In 1979 the Assassinations Committee Report went further than
any previous official body to cast doubt on the veracity of Marian
Oswald—the witness who provided so much of the evidence that
damned her husband. The Committee spoke of her "central but
troubling role" and observed tartly, "In its investigation of conspiracy, the Committee's undertaking was not furthered by Marina's testimony, since she professed to know little of Oswald's
associates in New Orleans or Dallas." The Congressmen of the
Assassinations Committee clearly found it trying listening to Oswald's widow. They may, however, have felt she floundered into
reality when pressed about which Castro groups her husband was
involved with. Once she answered, in characteristic style, "I do
not recall whether they were pro-Castro or anti-Castro groups. I
knew it had something to do with Cuba. . . ." Indeed.

When he saw the research information on New Orleans assembled for this book—and the material on 544 Camp Street in
particular—Senator Richard Schweiker described it as a major
breakthrough. Schweiker, whose Intelligence Committee investigation did much of the groundwork for the subsequent inquiry by
Congress, says that "it means that for the first time in the whole
Kennedy assassination investigation we have evidence which
places at 544 Camp Street intelligence agents, Lee Oswald, the
mob, and anti-Castro Cuban exiles. It puts all these elements
together in a way that has never been done before."

By the time New Orleans moved into the humid autumn of
1963, the disparate threads of Kennedy conspiracy did indeed

seem to come together. As the days slipped by toward tragedy in Dallas, the President had given his enemies even greater cause to strike. For the anti-Castro exiles and their hard-line supporters, his latest actions to reduce tension over Cuba irritated a chronic grievance as never before.

CHAPTER 18

The Kennedy Legacy

*Enmities between nations, as between individuals, do
not last forever.*

—President Kennedy, June 10, 1963

The President stood in the open air, bare-headed as always, to
address hundreds of young people. It was graudation day at American University in Washington, D.C. and the speech was the most
significant President Kennedy ever made on foreign policy. The
man at the helm of the United States was announcing a new and
wiser course for his country and indeed for the world. He told his
listeners he intended to address the most important topic on earth,
"world peace," and his words made clear how far he had shifted
from the old policy of head-on confrontation with Communism.
The President said of the Communist countries, "If we cannot now
end our differences, at least we can help make the world safe for
diversity. For, in the final analysis, our most basic link is that we all
inhabit this small planet. We all breathe the same air. We all
cherish our children's future. And we are all mortal. . . ."

John Kennedy, like all thinking men on earth and more than
most, had learned the lesson of the Cuban missile crisis of a few
months earlier. He was now determined that nuclear war must be
made utterly remote and the tensions of the Cold War eased.
From now until his death that was to be the principle behind all his
foreign-policy thinking, and he suited words with actions. In July,
just over a month after the American University speech, United
States and British representatives signed an agreement with the
Soviet Union, banning nuclear bomb tests in the atmosphere,
under water, and in space. The President announced it in an

address to the nation, saying, "Let us, if we can, get back from the shadows of war and seek out the way of peace. . . . Let history record that we, in this land, at this time, took the first step. . . . Now, for the first time in many years, the path of peace may be open." With the hindsight of the years Kennedy's words have lost none of their eloquence and plain sanity. Yet in 1963, to the forces of extreme conservatism in the United States, the words and actions seemed a sudden and dangerous deviation. Many called it appeasement, and where Cuba was concerned it signaled further betrayal of freedom's cause.

The opponents of Castro had been on the road to disillusionment since the missile crisis ended with Havana's Communist regime as firmly ensconced as ever. Yet the diehards had nourished a last hope, even after the President denounced unauthorized raids in April 1963, that the United States would continue to sanction a secret war, albeit one that wholly contradicted the President's public policy statements. As we have seen, there was a short-lived resurgence of hope in June when the Government approved a series of carefully controlled "pinprick" attacks. The record is scanty, but it suggests that these were designed merely to warn Castro against armed interference in the affairs of other Latin countries. If so, this latest veer in policy was dangerously ambivalent and certain to raise false expectations among the Cuban exile militants. Indeed, even before the "pinprick" plans were approved, the exile leadership was jumping the gun with bellicose talk of "a new all-out drive" and "ultimate invasion." Exile groups continued to receive training and funding from the CIA—but something was perilously askew in the chain of command. In the White House, the President was firmly resolved to defuse the smoldering Cuba crisis once and for all. The truth was that Castro had become of minor importance compared to America's global policy and especially compared to peaceful coexistence with the Soviet Union. It is now clear that there developed a tussle of wills, with the Government stamping firmly on renegade military operations and the diehard anti-Castro militants seeing how far they could push their luck. At first, events, were highly confusing.

In the second week of June, even as the Government was

formulating its "pinprick" plan, federal agents in Florida seized an aircraft and explosives intended for use in an exile bombing raid against the Shell Oil refinery in Cuba. Customs agents briefly detained Cuban and American veterans of the CIA secret war and established that they were receiving funds and supplies from an element of Havana's erstwhile gambling fraternity. Within a month it was obvious that whoever had been directing the Florida scheme had no intention of ceasing operations. It was only the location that shifted—to camps near New Orleans, where at that very time Lee Oswald was involved in his own Cuban activities.

Anti-Castro exiles had been training for some time at a camp near Lacombe, just a few miles outside New Orleans. They were being instructed in guerilla warfare techniques, and one of their American instructors, according to a number of reports, was none other than David Ferrie. It was here, some would say later, that he brought Lee Oswald to train with rifles. In mid-July the camp had a fresh influx of guerilla trainees from Florida, and with them came a major consignment of explosives and bomb casings. On July 31 a team of federal agents swooped down on the explosvies dump, at a property controlled by William McLaney. McLaney and his brother, Mike, both of whose names have been linked to reported syndicate operations, had operated out of Havana during the heyday of gambling.* The seizure at the McLaney house included thousand of pounds of dynamite, along with napalm and bomb casings. Immediately after the raid, the training camp nearby ceased operations. Carlos Bringuier, the anti-Castro exile who a few days later was to be involved in the New Orleans confrontation with Oswald, helped coordinate the dispersal of its exile trainees. In coming weeks the Government continued to pounce on others who persisted in mounting anti-Castro raids in defiance

---

* Mike McLaney had owned the International Casino in Havana. In 1973, in sworn testimony to the Senate Sub-Committee on Investigations, a witness stated that Mike McLaney "represents Meyer Lanksy"—the man who has been described as the "finance minister of the mob." The same witness claimed that McLaney had plotted the assassination of Bahamian leader Lynden Pindling. McLaney denied the allegation, and the HSCA found no evidence that the McLaney operation in Louisiana in 1963 was linked to the CIA or the crime syndicate (HSCA X.185).

of Presidential policy. Among those detained or formally cautioned were a number of CIA contract agents and American advisers to the exiles, including members of a group called Interpen—more grandly known as the Intercontinental Penetration Force. They included Alexander Rorke and Frank Sturgis, both of whom had persistently flouted Government orders ever since the missile crisis. Rorke was to die on yet another mission before the Kennedy assassination, Sturgis went on the gain notoriety years later as one of the Watergate burglars controlled by the exiles' CIA hero, Howard Hunt. Sturgis' anti-Castro group, it is reliably reported, received much of its financing from the Mafia. Several of Sturgis' associates arrested after the Kennedy clamp-down are names that would later crop up persistently in the assassination evidence. One of them, Loran Hall, was reportedly detained twice for flouting the ban on unauthorized exile activity. By his own admission, he had previously been in detention in Cuba along with Mafia leader Santos Trafficante. In 1963 he worked with one of the constellation of CIA-backed "Free Cuba" groups. Eladio del Valle, who headed the Free Cuba Committee in Florida, also reportedly had links to Santos Trafficante. Del Valle, in turn, was a close friend and associate of David Ferrie. More than ever, in this labyrinthine tale, the names and the threads of evidence interconnect and merge under the common denominator of American intelligence and the Mafia. In these ranks were the men most stung by the President's clamp-down on anti-Castro operations in the summer months of 1963. In the Seventies, in a masterly understatement, the Senate Intelligence Committee summed up their reaction: "Those individuals sponsoring this activity were angered. . . ." They must have been angriest of all at the message implied by the official jargon explaining the raids and seizures to the public. The raid on the Mafia-backed camp near New Orleans was described as thwarting "an effort to carry out a military operation against a country with which the United States is at peace." The United States at *peace* with Castro's Cuba? That was a notion to stir the exiles and their backers to sheer fury—a reality they were not prepared to accept.

At first it was as though the exile leadership believed it could goad the President into flouting his own policy. Just after the start of the summer clamp-down, with Kennedy engaged in the last sensitive stages of test-ban negotiations with Moscow, the Cuban Revolutionary Council declared it had landed more commandos in Cuba as "the first major step in a war of liberation." Antonio de Varona, the new head of the Council, publicly claimed that the United States had "promised help" if "Russians tried to put down a revolt of the Cuban people." Nothing happened—not least because there were no major new clashes in Cuba, other than in the rhetoric of the exile leaders. Then, as August merged into September, the situation changed. On August 19 Cuba's official newspaper complained that there had been a flurry of air raids against oil installations and factories. From then on, for many weeks, anti-Castro raiders sounded a tattoo of trouble for the Communist regime in Havana. There were more air raids by light planes, more commando landings and sabotage attacks. In his public statements Fidel Castro seemed to inject more vitriol into his routine attacks on the United States, calling President Kennedy "a ruffian . . . a horseman riding from error to error, from folly to folly." Havana continued its daily howl of broadcast outrage against the United States in general and against its armed forces and the CIA in particular. Then, on September 8, Moscow radio referred to the raids in sinister terms. It said there was "a planned campaign of provocation, the aim of which is once more to aggravate the situation in the Caribbean. Ominous reports have appeared in the Western newspapers that bands of Cuban counterrevolutionaries preparing for an attack on Cuba are concentrating in a number of countries of Central America. . . . They do not rely on their own forces, but rely *on drawing the United States into a military conflict with Cuba.*" (Author's italics.) The Soviet broadcast went further, implying that the latest attacks were not occurring because of American national policy but because "certain circles in the United States still cherish plans for the overthrow of Fidel Castro's government by force. . . . Attention should be called to another circumstance. Increasing provocations against Cuba are now being organized at a time when the United States Senate is discussing the Moscow Treaty banning nuclear tests. . . . This cannot be regarded as mere coincidence. The opponents of the Moscow Treaty wish, apparently, to take advantage of an aggravated situation in the Caribbean to prevent, if they can, its ratification." A day later Moscow was again talking darkly of "aggressive forces in the United States" trying to put "the world again on the brink of thermonuclear war."

Was this just another serving of Communist cant? Or is it possible that, in the month President Kennedy was speaking of the test-ban treaty bringing an "atmosphere of rising hope," some faction in the United States was seriously bent on sabotaging it? It is known that the Government's Special Group on Cuba, under the eye of Robert Kennedy, was indeed approving sabotage operations against Cuba—as part of its "pinprick" plans—right up to the assassination and after it. The record shows, however, that the senior officers of state involved, including Kennedy, no longer intended or even hoped that the United States would overthrow Castro. Unfortunately there is disturbing evidence that an element of American intelligence, still intent on doing just that, acted with gross irresponsibility. The results of those actions, indeed, could have destroyed Kennedy's new policy of accommodation.

It was not until 1975, after Senate Intelligence Committee Investigations, that it was learned how and when top CIA officials once again began actively plotting to assassinate Fidel Castro. It was a head-on CIA effort this time, without the dubious cooperation of the Mafia, and it got under way in early September 1963, long after the President's new policy had become clear. The plan envisaged using Rolando Cubela, one of Castro's close colleagues, as Castro's executioner. The CIA code-named him AM/LASH.[86] So far as could be learned from CIA testimony—the only source available to the Senate in 1975—the impetus came from Cubela himself. As the CIA told it, the Agency's relationship with Cubela had existed since 1961, when Cubela became disenchanted with increasing Communist influence and Soviet interference in Cuba. The Cuban spoke of defecting to the United States, but the CIA asked him to stay on in Havana, where he could be a valuable source of information. Then, on September 7, 1973, CIA case officers reported that the assassination of Castro had been discussed at a new meeting with Cubela. A few weeks later, goes the CIA version, Cubela asked for "military supplies" and requested a meeting with Robert Kennedy to give him assurances of American support. The CIA admits that a senior officer, Desmond FitzGerald did meet with Cubela and actually put himself forward as a personal representative of the President's brother. Cubela went on to ask for guns with telescope sights, and some other assassination device. The CIA admits that it eventaully obliged, supplying a poison syringe hidden in a fountain pen—a detail straight out of spy fiction. The plot against Castro—using Cubela—continued, with interruptions, until long after the Kennedy assassination, partially through the intermediary of Manuel Artime, a Cuban exile leader and close associate of Howard Hunt, the CIA officer who had recommended the assassination of Fidel Castro from the very beginning. They finally ceased in 1965 when the CIA decided the operation was insecure.

This version of the Cubela story was dragged out of CIA sources in questioning by the Senate Intelligence Committee. It indicated that CIA staff, with the collusion of officers as senior as Richard Helms, then Deputy Director, went along with plans to kill Castro without seeking authorization. They did not— apparently—tell the President or his brother the Attorney General. They did not even tell their own Director, John McCone, who was Kennedy's appointee following the Bay of Pigs debacle. In 1966 the CIA lied outright, assuring the Secretary of State that "the Agency was not involved with (Cubela) in a plot to assassinate Fidel Castro."

In 1975 the CIA found a way to get itself off the Senate Intelligence Committee hook by admitting the involvement with Cubela but insisting that the initiative for assassination had come entirely from him. Some of the documents provided to the Committee supported that implication. The distinction is more important than it might seem, for it deflects suspicion that in September and October 1963—a crucial moment politically—CIA officers were acting in a way that gravely endangered White House policy.

One witness the Senate Intelligence Committee could not hear was Rolando Cubela himself. Trapped and arrested by Cuban counterintelligence in 1966, he avoided a death sentence only when Castro personally interceded on his behalf. Instead, he was sentenced to thirty years in jail. In late 1978 I traveled to Havana and asked to see Cubela myself. To my surprise the Cuban govern-

ment agreed, and Cubela was brought under escort to take part in
a filmed interview.* I was allowed to talk with him for three hours,
a tall, gaunt figure who bitterly resents his treatment by the CIA.
The story he tells is significantly different from the CIA version.
Cubela insists that it was the CIA, not he, who initiated every
stage of the relationship. He also recalled some fascinating details
which, if true, throw further light on CIA audacity. Cubela says
that the CIA pretended to him not only that Desmond FitzGerald
was Robert Kennedy's representative but also made him out to be
a senior U.S. Senator rather that a mere CIA official. Cubela says
CIA statements that he initiated the request for assassination
weapons are "utterly false" and states rather that for some time he
rebuffed CIA attempts to foist on him James Bond-style murder
devices. His recollection of that episode indicates that the CIA
went to greater lengths than they have admitted. Cubela does
recall being given a poison device but insists that the CIA fountain
pen contained not poison but a "special chamber with a .45-caliber
bullet in it." CIA statements make no mention of this, and one
officer claimed he "could not remember" what Cubela did with the
poison syringe. Cubela says he remembers very well. "I never
accepted either device. I didn't like it, didn't like the idea. . . . I
left them with the CIA officer who tried to give them to me."
Above all, Cubela insists, it was the CIA who brought up the idea
of assassination in the first place—and he who resisted.

Obviously Cubela's statements, spoken as they were in captivity, must be treated with caution. Congress' Assassinations Committee, which also met Cubela in Havana, rightly points this out—
although in another context. However, I found the prisoner consistent and credible in the detailed and spontaneous way he answered my questions. The Cuban authorities allowed me to ask
whatever I wished, for as long as I wanted, and we occasionally
had the chance to talk out of earshot of officials.

While it was true that Cubela's account supports the general
picture of CIA perfidy presented by official Cuban propaganda,
that does not make it untrue. I was confident that in talking with

---

* Cubela, having served thirteen years, was released in late 1979. He is
now believed to be in Spain. (*Miami News*, December 13, 1979.)

me he was honestly relating real experiences. On some points, which a minor falsehood could easily have turned against the Agency, Cubela told me the story as the CIA had done. On balance, I was convinced more by Cubela than by the CIA version. While some of the CIA documents indicate the assassination proposals came from Cubela, there is today no necessity to accept that record as gospel. It is conceivable that the documents were deliberately written that way, especially if the operation involved actions contrary to Presidential policy.

If Cubela's version is accepted as truthful, several CIA officers are exposed as guilty not only of going along with a plan to kill Castro, without authorization, but of actually inciting Cubela to do it; all this at a time when anybody reading the newspapers—let alone officials in the Central Intelligence Agency—knew that President Kennedy was now seeking peaceful solutions to world problems. Although Desmond FitzGerald is dead, former Deputy Director Helms and other officers are still available for further probing as to their motives. Many observers remain unconvinced by their responses to recent Congressional questioning—not least because, in the case of Helms, there is a history of misleading a Senate committee. On the evidence now available, one must conclude that either he and his colleagues were extremely stupid—a possibility not at all to be excluded—or that they deliberately sanctioned actions contrary to Presidential policy and which could, have led to global crisis.* Meanwhile, it remains possible that there was an effort by some intelligence officers to thwart the President's easing of tension with the Soviet Union by any means. Unconscionable though that might once have seemed, there is evidence that one faction was trying to do just that.

In 1978 I talked with Antonio Veciana, a former Cuban exile leader whose evidence is one of the most explosive indications of

---

* The possibility has been raised that Cubela was a double-agent, that Castro learned of the plot against him and responded in kind by ordering the murder of President Kennedy. In 1979 the Congress' Assassinations Committee declared its belief that Havana played no such role. The issue will be dealt with in a later chapter.

conspiracy in the entire case. Veciana was a founder of Alpha 66, one of the most active and militarily effective of the anti-Castro guerrilla groups. In March 1963 he played a leading part in the attacks against Soviet ships in Cuba which precipitated the public Kennedy clamp-down on exile activity. Things came to a head on March 13, after Alpha 66 carried out a lightning raid on a Cuban port, shooting up a Soviet army installation and a Soviet freighter. Coming within months of the missile crisis, this was dangerously provocative. The State Department moved immediately to defuse the situation, declaring the Government's "strong opposition" to such raids. Next day the President personally hammered home the same message—to no avail. Exile commandos promptly attacked another Cuban port. On March 26 "Commando L," an offshoot of Alpha 66, damaged another Soviet ship. Moscow began to protest vehemently, to the accompaniment of shrill outbursts from Fidel Castro, and President Kennedy moved firmly to disassociate himself and the United States from the raids. He had been particularly angered by a press conference which the raiders had held in Washington to boast of their actions and to give the impression they had acted with official sanction. Antonio Veciana and other activists were confined to a small area in Florida and severely restricted. Strict federal action against exile extremists dated from this episode. For years, that seemed to be the sum of the story— recalcitrant exiles being firmly slapped down by the President. It was transformed in 1976, when Veciana was being questioned on other aspects of the case by an investigator for Senator Schweiker of the Senate Intelligence Committee. His revelations identify an element of the CIA, or of one of the tentacles of American intelligence, as being behind the exile outrages—a shadowy presence deliberately trying to sabotage President Kennedy's search for an understanding with the Soviet Union.

Veciana discloses that in March 1963, when his group attacked Soviet ships in Cuban ports, it was on specific instructions from a man he knew as "Maurice Bishop"—the code name for his American intelligence handler. It was at his urging that Veciana and his colleagues bragged about the attack at the Washington press conference which so incurred the President's wrath. It was he who continued to press exile militants to flout Kennedy policy and mount fresh actions. Says Veciana, "It was my case officer, 'Maurice Bishop,' who had the idea to attack the Soviet ships. The intention was to cause trouble between Kennedy and Russia. 'Bishop' believed that Kennedy and Khrushchev had made a secret agreement that the U.S.A. would do nothing more to help in the fight against Castro. 'Bishop' felt—he told me many times— that President Kennedy was a man without experience surrounded by a group of young men who were also inexperienced, with mistaken ideas on how to manage this country. He said you had to put Kennedy against the wall in order to force him to make decisions that would remove Castro's regime. This was why we made the assault on the Soviet ships and then called the press conference in Washington—to try to force Kennedy to take action. My case officer's function in the CIA was to perform 'dirty tricks.' " "Bishop," of course, is not the real name of Veciana's case officer, and Veciana has never assumed it was. He says "Bishop" was "a man who did not leave tracks. He never did like to leave tracks and taught me not to leave a trail." The search for the true identity of "Bishop" caused Congress' Assassinations Committee to commission further research and eventually to issue a national appeal for information. The hunt produced no certainties but uncovered compelling evidence that "Bishop" was no figment of the imagination. Today the hue and cry continues—and rightly so. Veciana's story, which convinced senior Assassinations Committee staff, shows why.

In 1960, when the Communist nature of Castro's revolution became fully apparent, Veciana was an accountant of distinction working in Havana. He was president of the Cuban accountants' association and an employee of a major bank. One day, probably in the middle of 1960, "Bishop" walked into the bank. He introduced himself with a business card for a Belgian construction company, and at first Veciana assumed he was just another customer. Soon, however, it became apparent that this was no ordinary client. "Bishop" took Veciana to lunch on several occasions and quickly moved from political talk to a firm proposal that Veciana should throw himself into the struggle against Castro. From the first, "Bishop" hedged about his precise affiliation. "He told me at the time," Veciana testified, "that he was in no position to let me know for whom he was working or for which agency he was doing this." Nevertheless. Veciana was led to believe that his mentor worked for American intelligence and probably for the CIA. He agreed to work with "Bishop," and thus began a relationship which—according to Veciana—was to last almost thirteen years.

First Veciana was trained, in nightly lectures for one pupil—himself. These were conducted by a man he knew only as "Mr. Melton," in a building which housed the Havana offices of an American mining company. Veciana learned something about guerrilla methods, but the emphasis was on psychological warfare. It was "Bishop's" will that Veciana should become an "organizer," and he did. Taking advantage of his banking expertise, he participated in an effective operation to destabilize the Cuban currency and destroy public confidence in its value. Veciana also planned sabotage operations for one of the anti-Castro groups. Then, in October 1961, Veciana organized an assassination attempt against Fidel Castro—himself—a plot which other sources confirm. Veciana says this was at the instigation of his American mentor, an allegation wholly consistent with the unauthorized murder plots then being hatched by the CIA. The Veciana plot, which called for a bazooka attack on the Presidential palace, was uncovered at the last minute by Cuban intelligence. Forewarned by "Bishop," Veciana escaped from Cuba the day before the attempt was due to take place. He fled to Florida, where "Bishop" urged him to build up what became the Alpha 66 organization.

It was Alpha 66, one of the most pugnacious of the exile groups, which perpetrated—at "Bishop's" direction—the series of outrages designed to ruin President Kennedy's Cuba policy. It is interesting that, in a public statement on behalf of Alpha 66, Veciana said even then that the planning was being done by leaders "I don't even know." Over the years, the mysterious "Bishop" masterminded a series of operations, from assassinations to armed landings on the Cuban coastline. From 1968 on, as the record confirms. Veciana worked as a "banking adviser" in Bolivia. His formal contract was for the U.S. Agency for International Development, the ostensible aid organization which earned disrepute for its part in American subversion against Chile. Veciana's office was in the American Embassy, and his work involved very little banking. In 1971, he says at "Bishop's" behest, Veciana helped mount an abortive attempt to kill Castro during his visit to Chile, then ruled by the Marxist government of President Allende. Two years later, after a falling-out over the methods involved in that operation. "Bishop" had a last meeting with Veciana. At a rendezvous in Miami, attended by two other men, Veciana says "Bishop" made him a severance payment of a quarter of a million dollars. Veciana accepted it as a lump-sum recompense for a dozen years of skullduggery on behalf of U.S. intelligence. He maintains he has not met "Bishop" since that day.

Over the years, says Veciana, he always accepted "Bishop's" meticulously preserved anonymity. It was for intelligence purposes, an accepted operational system. A study of CIA methods shows that false identities, like the use of fake commercial companies such as fronts, is common practice. What is remarkable is that the "Bishop" pseudonym was sustained over so many years, but Veciana says he soon learned not to ask irritating questions. "Bishop" has in fact left some tracks, and the clues to his identity have their place later in this narrative. Now, though, it is time to back-track—to the tumultuous spring of 1963. It was then that "Bishop," in the name of American intelligence, orchestrated the Alpha 66 raids—a deliberate attempt to provoke a new crisis between Kennedy and Khrushchev. Ominously, Veciana says that "Bishop" "considered that the best thing for this country was that people like Kennedy and his advisers should not be running it." A few months after "Bishop" uttered those sentiments, says Veciana, he saw him in the company of Lee Oswald.

It was late August or the first days of September that Veciana recalls being summoned to meet "Bishop" in Dallas, Texas. It was a city where they met often during their long association. Veciana flew to Dallas and on arrival was told to rendezvous with "Bishop" at a skyscraper business building in the downtown area. From the details Veciana has provided, this has been identified as the South-land Center, the headquarters of a major insurance group. It has a public area on the first floor. Veciana arrived a little ahead of schedule, and "Bishop" was not alone. In Veciana's words, "Maurice was accompanied by a young man who gave me the impression of being very quiet, rather strange and preoccupied. The three of us walked to a cafeteria. The young man was with us ten or fifteen minutes, until Maurice told him something like 'All right, see you later,' and dismissed him." After the assassination, when Lee Oswald's face was suddenly plastered over the newspapers and on television, Veciana at once recognized Oswald as the young man he had seen with "Bishop" in Dallas.

Veciana is adamant that there is no mistake. As an Assassinations Committee staff report notes. "There was absolutely no doubt in his mind that the man was Oswald, not just someone who resembled him." Veciana pointed out that he had been trained to remember the physical characteristics of people and that if it was not Oswald it was his "exact double." It is ironical that one of those who trained Veciana was, of course, "Bishop" himself.

Oswald may well have visited Dallas at the time Veciana has mentioned. It was at a time when he was still living in New Orleans, but it also happens to be one of the few periods when his movements are sparsely documented. Oswald was unusually invisible between August 21 and September 17, making only one New Orleans appearance reported by human witnesses. This was on Labor Day, September 2, when he reportedly visited Charles Murret—the uncle with Mafia connections. Otherwise, Oswald's progress is marked by visits to the employment office, the cashing of unemployment checks, and the withdrawal of library books. Even these are not necessarily valid for charting Oswald's movements; the FBI was able to authenticate Oswald's signature on hardly any of the unemployment documents. Of the seventeen firms where Oswald said he applied for work, thirteen denied it, and four did not even exist. Even accepting this doubtful timetable, there is one uninterrupted gap, between September 6 and 9. One hint that Oswald was then indeed out of New Orleans is the fact that three library books returned at the end of this period were overdue—a unique lapse in Oswald's usually meticulous library discipline over many months. Certainly, on the evidence, there is no problem in accepting a possible Oswald excursion to the neighboring state of Texas within the Veciana time frame.

There has been reluctance to accept Veciana's story. When first interviewed by the investigator for Congress' Assassinations

Committee. Veciana had just completed twenty-seven months in a federal prison on a conviction of conspiracy to import narcotics. The key testimony against him had been that of a former business partner—who thus avoided a long prison sentence himself. Veciana has said he believes his prosecution was in some way related to his previous association with CIA officer "Bishop." Privately, he told one of his close associates, a former Cuban government minister, that he thought the CIA framed him because he wanted to go ahead with "another plot to kill Castro." There is nothing inherently implausible in this. The evidence suggests that there was such plotting, and that it did involve Veciana. A former CIA agent, moreover, has stated that one "dirty trick" in which he engaged was to smear Cuban agents with allegations about narcotics. Assassinations Committee checks found that—the one specific case aside—Veciana's record was clean of any narcotics involvement. Finally, on this point, it makes no sense to suggest that Veciana told his "Bishop" story to curry federal favor over his narcotics conviction—he produced it *after* his release from prison.

Congress' Assassinations Committee was perplexed by Veciana's allegations, which it never finished investigating. Its Report reflected a major difference of opinion between the Chief Counsel, who never himself interrogated Veciana, and the staff investigator, who spent many months examining the witness and his claims. In expressing the belief that Veciana had been "less than candid," the Report raised four problems areas. Why had Veciana waited more than ten years before telling his story? Why could he produce no witnesses to his meetings with "Bishop," nor to the encounter with Oswald? Why did he not help the Committee more than he did in its attempts to identify "Bishop"? Veciana had claimed that, at the end of his many years' work for "Bishop," he was paid off with a lump sum of a quarter of a million dollars. Although he specified the precise sum—$253,000—the Committee's Report was skeptical. It said that Veciana had refused to supply proof of the payment, "claiming fear of the Internal Revenue Service." These expressions of doubt—inserted in the Report without even minimal consultation of the staff investigator who handled Veciana for the Committee—are at variance with the facts. They are hard to reconcile with another area of the Report, which indicates that the Committee did believe that "Bishop" existed. Moreover, my own research demonstrates that the negative points, as raised, are distortions of the true picture.

It is not surprising that Veciana said nothing about his relationship with "Bishop," nor about the Oswald sighting, until long after the assassination. He was, in 1963, a prominent anti-Castro leader who believed that his and his people's best hope and support was the United States. Specifically, for Veciana, that meant his connection with U.S. intelligence. His status as an alien also made him vulnerable; he had already crossed United States law enforcement authorities by flouting the government's declared policy on exile raids. Veciana intended, moreover, to continue doing so—with the valued assistance of his American case officer. His over-riding priority was, and remains, the anti-Castro cause. In the immediate aftermath of the assassination, Veciana was unable to determine the full significance of the Oswald encounter he had witnessed. His instinctive response was that his knowledge spelt danger—to the continuance of his covert activity and perhaps indeed to his own life. "Bishop," the linchpin of his American support, could turn against him. Veciana decided to stay close as a clam. Within a few days of the President's murder, says Veciana, he had ample cause to feel apprehensive, and reason to wonder whether he was being tested. What he says happened then may be a vital lead, but it is one of several which the Assassinations Committee failed to pursue.

Veciana states that just after the tragedy in Dallas, he was approached by an American official who asked him whether he "knew anything" about the assassination or Oswald. Veciana, prompted by the feelings described above, said he knew nothing. The official, according to Veciana, was a senior Florida Customs agent called Cesar Diosdado. Diosdado, according to information supplied to the Assassinations Committee, was effectively seconded to the CIA throughout the "Secret War" against Cuba. He was known to anti-Castro exiles as the man who could give clearance for operations launched from the Florida Keys. As such, he was reportedly in constant touch with the CIA officers who supervised exile operations. Diosdado declined to talk to a Committee investigator when contacted by telephone, and the Committee never followed up with a personal visit, or with a subpoena to enforce Diosdado's cooperation. In 1980, when interviewed for this author, Diosdado denied not only that he had asked Veciana about the assassination, but also his connection with the CIA—a connection which was checked with authoritative sources during the Intelligence Committee inquiry. It is disturbing to learn that the Assassinations Committee failed to questions this witness, as it failed in other areas of the Veciana inquiry. It was a typical result of the pressure on the Committee staff to produce a report rather than follow up vital leads in the field. The excuse, that time and funds had run out, is of no comfort to those who believe Veciana's allegations must be pursued, nor can this have encouraged Veciana himself to cooperate further with the Committee.

Veciana says that, after his brush with the Customs agent, almost two months went by until he was again summoned to meet "Bishop." The pre-assassination encounter was conspicuous by its absence from general conversation with "Bishop" about the assassination, and Veciana gained the impression that it was a closed subject. He says today, "I was not going to make the mistake of getting myself involved in something that did not concern me." Veciana adds, "We both understood. I could guess that he knew I was knowledgeable of that. And I had learned that the best way is not to know, not to get to know things that don't concern you; so I respected the rules, and I didn't mention that ever." Veciana adds, and believably, "That was a very difficult situation, because I was afraid."

Veciana was to continue working with "Bishop" until 1973, and—consistent with his initial attitude—he continued to hold his tongue. It was when he was no longer in contact with "Bishop," in 1976, that he at last broke his silence—during questioning on another matter for the Senate Intelligence Committee. He then produced his "Bishop" account, but only on the strict understanding that his anonymity would be protected. Later, however, the Veciana case was handled in a way that would make any professional investigator's hair stand on end, and which came close to wrecking Veciana as a source. After the Senate Intelligence Committee had passed on its Veciana file to the Assassinations Committee, somebody on the Assassinations Committee leaked his identity to the press. Veciana, very reasonably, felt that his trust had been abused, and understandably became less forthcoming. It was, most probably, only his personal confidence in his original Intelligence Committee contact—by now assigned to the Assassinations Committee—which prevented him becoming a total loss. Veciana later took further offense, as a man who has devoted his life to fighting Castro, when he learned that the Assassinations Committee had visited the Cuban leader in Havana. Nevertheless, Veciana did not break contact with the staff investigator he trusted. He did not, as the Committee Report implied, refuse to cooperate when asked for proof that he had received a large payoff from "Bishop" in recent years. Instead, he offered to supply information on the matter either if he was granted immunity from prosecution by the Internal Revenue Service, or in confidence to the Committee's investigator. Today, the investigator says he learned enough to satisfy him that Veciana had indeed received a large sum of money.

As for concern that Veciana could produce no witnesses to his meetings with "Bishop," nor to the specific encounter with Oswald, that provokes snorts of amusement from those familiar with intelligence work. If "Bishop" was the accomplished professional Veciana describes, then it would be routine for him to insulate his contacts. That is an integral part of the craft of intelligence. Veciana points out, for example, that "Bishop" never even phoned him directly, but set up meetings through a third party. (Indeed, this author obtained information that could help to locate that third party. I provided the details to the Assassinations Committee investigator, but on this too the Committee management failed to authorise further research. The explanation, again, was lack of time and funds.)

The investigator who dealt most with Veciana was described to me by one Committee lawyer as "the best man the Committee had in the field." He feels strongly—on the basis of working hundreds of man-hours on the inquiry, many of them spent virtually living with the witness—that Veciana's account of the "Bishop"–Oswald connection is the truth. Another Committee lawyer sums up the outcome of the bungling way in which this potentially vital information was treated. He says:

The information resulted in solid leads which nobody was able to refute. There were enough tie-ins to confirm some of it. It is most unfortunate that the leads were not pursued on the grounds of lack of time and resources . . . The Committee's Chief Counsel, whether because of those pressures or because his own suspicions or instincts lay in other directions, wanted conclusions . . . In the general area of intelligence, we were left with the feeling that we were having to make sweeping generalizations about something we knew nothing about. For congressional investigators, the intelligence world was virgin territory. By the time we had to wind up the work we were learning the ropes, but we left our work incompleted. . . .

In late 1978, when active inquiry into the "Bishop" affair had ground to a halt, Assassinations Committee Chief Counsel Blakey told a public hearing that "the Committee cannot be conclusive, but it can say that Veciana's allegations remain undiscredited . . ." Later, in its final Report, the Committee found it impossible to ignore the Veciana account. As we shall see when we study the clues to "Bishop's" real identity, the Committee uncovered evidence that somebody using that name did exist, and in the ranks of American intelligence. It also established that, although the record was sparse, the CIA did have contact with Veciana in the early Sixties. U.S. Army Intelligence, too, had an "operational interest" because of Veciana's role with Alpha 66. The CIA denied, though, ever appointing a case officer to Veciana—a denial which the Committee could hardly accept. The Report sums up Congressional frustration in a tortured paragraph. It reads, "The Committee found it probable that some agency of the United States assigned a case officer to Veciana, since he was the dominant figure in an extremely active anti-Castro organization. The Committee established that the CIA assigned case officers to Cuban revolutionaries of less importance than Veciana, though it could not draw from that alone an inference of CIA deception of the Committee concerning Veciana, since Bishop could well have been in the employ of one of the military intelligence agencies. . . ." Congressional investigators are privately more blunt. They believe American intelligence, and most probably CIA staff, have concealed the truth. The reader will draw his own conclusion as the story unravels.

If the "Bishop" meeting with Oswald occurred as and when Veciana describes it, the timing has special significance. It came at the height of government closures of anti-Castro training camps and amid new restrictions on the exiles and their American backers. Most importantly, the meeting followed the completion of Oswald's contrived antics over Fair Play for Cuba in New Orleans and immediately preceded the next phase of his Cuba-related activity.

On September 17, just a week or so after the alleged meeting with a senior CIA agent, Oswald walked into the Mexican consulate in New Orleans and applied for a "tourist card," the document necessary for entry to Mexico. He had no difficulty, for he was equipped with a copy of his birth certificate and a brand-new passport—the latest product of Oswald's improbably smooth relationship with the American State Department. He had applied for the passport two months earlier, just before the start of his pro-Castro program in New Orleans. He had specified on the application form—just as he had in 1959—that he intended to travel to the Soviet Union. He had even drawn attention to his inglorious past by noting that his previous passport had been canceled. Oswald's application went to the Passport Office of the State Department in Washington, directed in those days by Frances Knight, a dragon of a bureaucrat famous for her stern restrictions on the movement of American left-wingers. On this occasion, however, the system seemed strangely paralyzed. There was not so much as a query about the intentions of this Marxist defector who had once offered state secrets to the Russians. Nobody was concerned, apparently, about the possibility of a second defection. Oswald had his passport within twenty-four hours. At the Mexican consulate a few weeks later, he was promptly issued Tourist Card No. 824085. In due course, this led to another CIA connection—one which defies explanation as coincidence or as mistaken identity.

After the assassination the FBI, with the cooperation of Mexican authorities, checked on the identities of all other people who had applied for Mexican entry papers on September 17. The resulting list of names was placed on the public record—with the exception of the card-holder next to Oswald on the list, No. 824084. Within eight days of the assassination the FBI had inserted a note on the list saying flatly, "No record of FM 824084 located." It was not true. In 1975, thanks to a bureaucratic blunder during declassication, the name of the holder was revealed. He was William Gaudet, and worked for the CIA. He was, moreover, to travel to Mexico at the same time as Oswald.

In 1978 I found Gaudet, a crumpled old man now, living out his retirement at a seaside home in Mississippi. Pressed to explain how he came to be next to Lee Oswald on the list of applications for travel to Mexico, he said, "It is apparently because we both went into the consulate one after the other. Now why my name was omitted is something I can't tell you. . . . I've got to insist that it was pure coincidence—that I will be strongly emphatic about. It was pure coincidence and er. . . . because I certainly had not discussed it with him, because I hadn't talked to him. . . . I cannot account for why my name was not on that (published) list when it actually should have been on it. Who was responsible I don't know. . . . I have no control over what the CIA did or did not do down in Mexico." When the Assassinations Committee examined Gaudet's CIA file, it found the familiar vacuum. The Agency admitted only that he "provided foreign intelligence information" in the Fifties and mentioned no contact after 1961. Gaudet, however, himself admitted contact with the CIA as late as 1969. He agreed he was "just loaded down with coincidences" and that his appearance on the visa list is astonishing. He said he cannot remember whether his trip to Mexico involved intelligence activity.

Gaudet said that, under cover of running a publication called the *Latin American Newsletter*, he worked for the CIA for more than twenty years. It was a strictly secret connection, one which he confided to nobody—not even his wife. After the President's assassination he was contacted by the FBI but agreed to be interviewed only after a briefing from "Bill," his boss in the New Orleans office of the CIA. The story Gaudet told the FBI was the one he told me—that he is a victim of coincidence and that he did not travel with Oswald to Mexico. He said he used his tourist card to travel to Mexico by air; he could not recall the nature of his business on that occasion. Although now retired, he was angry and suspicious about the way his name was finally revealed. That he did not regard as a coincidence and said, "I've given this a lot of thought. I am now convinced in my own mind that those who are truly behind the conspiracy to kill Mr. Kennedy have done things purposely to draw attention to me. There are too many coincidences that involve me, unless someone was behind all of this."

For a man who declared himself plagued by mere coincidence, William Gaudet was strangely knowledgeable. While denying any involvement in the Oswald visit to Mexico, he made one remarkable admission. He said he had "known" Oswald in New Orleans. This once said, Gaudet quickly adjusted his statement, insisting now that he had merely observed Oswald handing out leaflets in the street, on several occasions, but always fleetingly. Nevertheless, Gaudet talked at length of Oswald's physical appearance and personality, assessing him from personal observation as a "very nervous, frail, weak man. . . . I didn't think he had much strength of character, and when the news came out that he had shot Kennedy it was a complete and total shock to me." Gaudet talked much more as though his first statement had been true, as if he really had met Oswald.

After a few hours with William Gaudet a reporter came away, rightly or wrongly, with an impression of a man who knew more, perhaps only a little more, than he dared discuss on the record. What he did reveal seemed said to protect his own, probably innocent, role and out of indignation that his CIA cover had been blown. Gaudet has since died.

On my second visit to the former agent he did let slip something which at the time meant little but now seems as important as his appearance on the Mexico visa list. It happened when I became openly skeptical that Gaudet could have gained his obvious knowledge of Oswald purely from "coincidental" sightings in the streets of New Orleans. Gaudet suddenly said, "I do know that I saw him one time with a former FBI agent by the name of Guy Banister. Guy of course is now dead. What Guy's role was in all of this was I . . . really don't know." Gaudet had paused briefly, but now he said in a rush, "I did see Oswald discussing various things with

Banister at the time, and I think Banister knew a whole lot of what was going on. . . ."

Gaudet also said, "I suppose you are looking into Ferrie. He was with Oswald. . . ."

He also said, "Another vital person is Sergio Arcacha Smith. I know he knew Oswald and knows more about the Kennedy affair than he ever admitted."

When Gaudet threw out these names I was still new to the Kennedy case. The names "Banister," "Ferrie," and Arcacha" do not appear in the Warren Report. I was little the wiser when Gaudet volunteered that he had seen Oswald with Banister "near my office, which was at Camp Street and Common Street in New Orleans." As it turns out, of course, Gaudet's office was a stone's throw from Banister's office at 544 Camp Street, the mysterious address which has become a major focus of investigation into an assassination conspiracy. The New Orleans connection is pivotal, whether one believes the President's murder was the work of Cuban exiles, the Mafia, some element of American intelligence, or a synthesis of all three. Later, staff who once worked at 544 Camp street would say that Banister did know Gaudet and that Gaudet had on occasion visited the office in summer 1963. Once again in this case, the leads have come full circle.

Where he was short on factual answers, former CIA man Gaudet was forward with opinions. While he quite reasonably balked at the idea that the CIA as an agency had any responsibility for the assassination, he thought there was a tie-in which would embarrass the CIA and says it was "extremely possible" that Oswald was being used by some agency of American intelligence. Gaudet found nothing contradictory in the fact that the CIA has repeatedly denied any connection with Oswald. He said of his own CIA service, "They told me frankly when I did things for them that if something went awry they would never recognize me or admit who I was. If I made a mistake, that was just tough, and I knew it." Gaudet did not believe Oswald killed the President. He said, "I think he was a patsy. I think he was set up on purpose." Asked to explain that statment, Gaudet subsided into silence. He was not prepared to talk about CIA operations in which he played a part but insisted they were nothing to do with the assassination.

On September 16, 1963, just one day before Oswald applied for papers to travel to Mexico, the CIA advised the FBI that it was "giving some consideration to countering the activities of [the Fair Play for Cuba Committee] in foreign countries. . . . CIA is also giving some thought to planting *deceptive information which might embarrass the Committee* in areas where it does have some support. Pursuant to a discussion with the Liaison Agent [name deleted] advised that his Agency will not take action without first consulting the Bureau, bearing in mind that we wish to make certain the CIA activity will not jeopardize any Bureau investigation." (Author's italics.) As we have seen already, American intelligence had long been engaged in "countering activities," penetrating, discrediting, and smearing the Fair Play for Cuba Committee. Mexico City was a place where the FPCC was well supported, a fact which made its local chapter a likely target for the attentions of American agents.

For a few days after obtaining his Mexican visa Oswald busied himself writing a summary of his achievements as a Marxist comrade and in the service of Socialism. The high point of the narrative, after a catalogue of his diligent studies and sojourn in Russia, was the saga of his pro-Castro effort in New Orleans. As he had done in the past when he had urgent personal work to do, Oswald conveniently got rid of his wife for a while. They would never again live together as husband and wife. Marina, burdened with one child and pregnant with a second, left to stay with her friend Ruth Paine in Texas. Oswald was now a free agent, and sometime on the evening of September 24 he slipped away from his New Orleans apartment.

Forty-eight hours later, according to the frontier stamp on his tourist card, Oswald began a week-long visit to Mexico.

IV

ENDGAME

Deception and Tragedy

CHAPTER 19

Exits and Entrances in Mexico City

*The key to the President's assassination lies in Oswald's
movements during the unaccounted for five-day period
after he allegedly tried to get a Cuban visa in Mexico
City.*

—Los Angeles Police Chief William Parker, 1966

Several fellow passengers would remember the young man who
joined Continental Trailways bus No. 5133 in the early hours of
the morning of September 26, somewhere in southern Texas. The
boy was, after all, somewhat unusual. During the journey to the
Mexican border, and afterward on a Mexican bus, he positively
advertised his business. He left his seat to seek out two Australian
girls traveling at the back of the bus and regaled them at length
with stories of his time in the Marines and in the Soviet Union. He
even pulled out his old 1959 passport to prove he really had been
in Russia. He also struck up a conversation with a British couple
from Liverpool, Bryan and Meryl McFarland, and they had good
cause to remember him. The stranger made a point of saying he
had been secretary for the Fair Play for Cuba Committee in New
Orleans and was traveling through Mexico in order to reach Cuba.
He hoped, he confided, to see Fidel Castro. At a time of great
tension over Cuba, when Americans traveling there were liable to
prosecution on their return, this man emphasized that his destination was Havana.

A few weeks later, after the assassination, some of the things
the passengers recalled would seem odd. The Australian girls, for
instance, had noticed that their garrulous companion sat talking to
a much older man who spoke with an English accent. An extensive

search in later months led investigators to a man who had traveled under the name of John Bowen but who was calling himself Albert Osborne when the FBI tracked him down. He denied sitting next to Oswald, but—in a rare flash of skepticism—the Warren Commission concluded that "his denial cannot be credited." Questioned about his use of two identities, Bowen-Osborne said he had been doing so for fifty years. He claimed that he was a "missionary" who traveled extensively and that his most recent trip, begun just before the Kennedy assassination, had included France and Spain. Intensive frontier checks revealed no record of entrance to either country, and Bowen-Osborne did not reveal how his frequent travels were financed. Not surprisingly, there has been speculation that he was in some way connected with intelligence. If so, we may hazard a guess as to which side of the political fence he was on. During World War II Bowen-Osborne was a fanatical supporter of Nazi Germany. It may well be just another coincidence, but the evidence is that Oswald twice called himself "Osborne" when ordering Fair Play for Cuba printed material in New Orleans.

On the final leg of the grueling journey to Mexico City, the young stranger told the two Australian girls he had been there before. According to the record, Oswald had never been to Mexico, apart from a long-ago foray into a border town during leave from a Marine base in California. Guy Banister's secretary, Delphine Roberts, however, told me in 1978 that—on the basis of what Banister told her—she knew Oswald had made more than one trip to Mexico in the summer of 1963. Certainly, on the bus, he talked as though he had been there before, Oswald recommended the Hotel Cuba to the Australian girls as a good place to stay. Strangely, he did not stay there himself. Hotel registration forms show that within an hour of the bus arriving in Mexico City, "Lee Harvey Oswald" checked into Room 18 of the Hotel Comercio.

There can be no serious doubt that the young man on the bus and the man in Room 18 was indeed Lee Oswald. Bus and frontier records, later identification by fellow passengers, and the handwriting in the hotel register together make compelling evidence that Oswald did go to Mexico City.[87] It is also clear that he returned to the United States, again by bus, six days later. His activities during those days, however, remain the subject of continuing controversy and speculation.

The Warren Commission decided that Oswald spent his leisure hours in Mexico alone, going to the movies, perhaps a bullfight, and dining cheaply at a restaurant near his hotel. The Report did not mention the statement by another resident of the Hotel Comercio, who said he observed Oswald in the company of four Cubans, one of whom came from Florida. The hotel, it has since been reported, was a local haunt of anti-Castro Cuban exiles.

The truth behind the Oswald visit to Mexico hinges on Cuba. Somebody, in that crucial period, used the name Oswald a great deal, in a way which would later seem highly compromising. Was it really Lee Oswald, or was he the victim of a sophisticated set-up?

It was Friday, September 27, 1963, in Mexico City. For Sylvia Duran, a young Mexican woman working in the Cuban consul's office, it had been a normal morning of processing visa applications. Then, shortly before lunchtime, in came the young American. Today she remembers him as ungainly, hesitant, and unsure of himself. He asked, "Do you speak English?" and was relieved to find she did. The visitor then explained he was Lee Harvey Oswald, an American citizen, and he wanted a Cuban transit visa. His final destination was the Soviet Union, but he wanted to travel via Cuba. The request was urgent, he wanted to leave in three days' time and stay in Cuba for a couple of weeks. Credentials were no problem—out came the documentary harvest of Oswald's time in the Soviet Union and New Orleans. Sylvia Duran was shown passports, old Soviet documents, and correspondence with the American Communist Party. Then there were the prize exhibits, membership cards for the Fair Play for Cuba Committee, identification as its president in New Orleans, and a newspaper clipping about the demonstration which ended in Oswald's arrest. There was even—says Duran—a photograph of Oswald in custody, a policeman on each arm. Later she was to reflect that it had looked phony, and indeed there is no such known photograph of Oswald. The visitor showed all these things with pride and waited expectantly. The consul's assistant was puzzled and a little suspicious. She found the display of allegiance to the Cuban cause strangely overdone. If the young man was, as he claimed, a member of the Communist Party, why had he not arranged his visa the customary way—by applying in advance to the Communist Party in Cuba? In any case, Sylvia Duran emphasized, her office could not issue a transit visa for Cuba without first knowing the traveler had Soviet clearance for travel to Russia. Looking crestfallen, the visitor departed, promising to come back with the photographs needed for a visa application.

Two or three hours later the young American was back with the photographs. Now Sylvia Duran accepted his visa application and asked him to call in about a week. "Impossible," said the young man. "I can only stay in Mexico three days." The consul's assistant explained all over again how the system worked, and the American left looking perplexed. That evening, says Sylvia Duran, he turned up once more, this time after the consulate had already closed to the public. He talked his way in and rushed into the office visibly agitated. His attitude was peremptory—he said he had been to the Soviet Embassy and knew the Soviet visa would be granted. Now, he insisted, the Cubans should issue him a visa at once. Patiently, says Sylvia Duran, she checked by telephone with the Soviet Embassy and heard a very different story. They knew about Oswald but said Moscow could take as long as four months to decide on his application to go to Russia. At this news the young stranger caused a scene Sylvia Duran would never forget. She told me in 1978, "He didn't want to listen. His face reddened, his eyes flashed, and he shouted, 'Impossible! I can't wait that long!' " The American visitor was now literally raging, and at this point the consul himself, Eusebio Azcue, intervened. He laboriously repeated the formalities, but still the stranger fumed. Now the consul lost patience too, finally telling the American that "a person of his type was harming the Cuban revolution more than helping it." That was still not the end of the saga. There was yet another visit and another row with the consul. Azcue and a colleague were suspicious of a card Oswald produced showing membership in the American Communist Party. It looked strangely new and unused. The officials were justifiably doubtful; Oswald had never joined the Party. According to Azcue, the final straw was when the youngster mocked him and Sylvia Duran as mere "bureaucrats."

At this the consul ordered him out of the building. The man who called himself Lee Harvey Oswald had made an unforgettable impression. Eight weeks later, when the name hit the headlines as the presumed assassin of President Kennedy, both the consul and his secretary instantly remembered their troublesome visitor.

Months later, the Warren Commission investigators pieced together this curious story. They had not only the firsthand account of Sylvia Duran but also secret information provided by the CIA. We know now that in 1963—as it may well do to this day— the Central Intelligence Agency spied on Communist embassies as a matter of routine. In Mexico City, from hiding places across the street from the Cuban and Soviet embassies, CIA agents photographed visitors, bugged diplomats' offices with concealed microphones, and listened in on phone calls. In the case of the Cuban Embassy in Mexico City, Havana's officials say they discovered the extent of the United States' surveillance some time after the assassination. On a research visit to Havana in 1978, I was shown some of the bugging equipment the Cubans claim they found in their Embassy in 1964. According to an electronics technician for Cuban intelligence, every single telephone wall socket in the Mexico Embassy contained a miniature microphone capable of transmitting Cuban conversations to CIA receiver points outside the building. I was even shown a device embedded in the arm of a chair, discovered—say the Cubans—in the ambassador's office. Cuban intelligence says it identified the building across the street where the conversations were monitored, along with the CIA agents who manned it (*see illustration 27*). The CIA is coy about its electronic spying, but recently released documents make it clear that his was the basis for much of the information later used to reconstruct Oswald's visit to Mexico. CIA eavesdropping, and perhaps a human informant as well, indicate that a man calling himself Lee Oswald made repeated visits to the Soviet Embassy pressing for a visa to the Soviet Union. Two of the officials he apparently encountered were identified as KGB officers using diplomatic cover. Piecing together the human testimony and the CIA data, Warren Commission investigators formed a cohesive picture of an Oswald frantic to get to Cuba but rejected by the very Communists he had expected to welcome him with open arms.

That was fine as far as it went, but the lawyers who wrote the Warren Report were at a loss to see how it fitted into the over-all picture of the Kennedy assassination. Had there ever been serious investigation into the possibility that the assassination was not the work of a lone assassin called Oswald, the lawyers might have read different signs in the evidence of New Orleans and Mexico. Today this tale of two cities offers an ominous message. To start with, there is doubt as to whether the man who made the fuss at the Cuban Embassy was really Oswald.

The Cuban consul, Azcue, had been working out the last days of his Mexican tour of duty when the troublesome American made his visits. By the day of the Kennedy assassination he was back in Havana. He at first assumed like everyone else that the Lee Oswald he had met was one and the same as the man arrested in Dallas. Then, two or three weeks after the assassination, Consul Ascue went to the movies. The newsreel included scenes of Oswald under arrest in Dallas and the sensational sequence in which Oswald was shot by Jack Ruby. In this footage Oswald can be seen clearly, in close-up and walking. According to Azcue, the Oswald on the film "in no way resembled" the man who made the scene at the Cuban Embassy less than two months previously. In 1978 he testified as much to the Assassinations Committee in Washington.

The Lee Oswald arrested in Dallas was 5 feet 91/2 inches tall and very slim. He was not yet twenty-four years old at the time of the visit to Mexico. Azcue remembers the man in his office as being "maybe thirty-five years old," "of medium height," with "dark blond" hair and features quite different from those of the authentic Oswald. The film, as Azcue said, shows a young man with a youthful, unlined face. It was, according to the consul, "in radical contrast to the deeply lined face" of the man who came asking for a visa. Shown still photographs of the authentic Oswald, Azcue continued to assert, "My belief is that this gentleman was not, is not, the person or the individual who went to the consulate." Azcue also has a worrying comment on the photograph used on the visa form. He told the Assassinations Committee he could "almost assure" them that the clothing worn in the visa picture was quite different from the clothes worn by the man he met.

Consul Azcue's colleague and successor, Alfredo Mirabal, does not share Azcue's conviction but admits that he saw "Oswald" only briefly when he peered out of his office to see what all the fuss was about. Azcue, on the other hand, had a chance to observe Oswald face to face for a quarter of an hour, because of their row, the consul also had good cause to remember his visitor. Until recently, however, Azcue's assistant Duran has seemed sure enough that she met the real Oswald. Her former boss, a mild-mannered and impressive witness, observes mildly that long experience gave him "better eyes" and he believes he is right about meeting a false Oswald. Is it Azcue who is mistaken?

One important item of evidence does appear to place the real Oswald in the Cuban Embassy—the signature on the visa application form produced by the Cubans. In 1978 experts for Congress' Assassinations Committee declared themselves satisfied that this was the signature of the real Oswald. This opinion must be taken into account, along with the photograph on the application form. That certainly appears to show the real Oswald. As we have seen, the consul's assistant remembered that the Oswald who came to her office arrived without photographs. She recommended a near-by photographic service and off he went, ostensibly to have pictures taken. Yet, after the assassination, intensive research showed that the photographs on Oswald's visa forms came from none of the local establishments. If the man who visited the consulate was deliberately pretending to be Oswald, he would presumably have made it his business to have access to pictures of the real Oswald. Sylvia Duran, the consul's assistant, is no longer clear about when precisely the application forms were handed to the stranger. She told the Assassinations Committee she thought she typed out the forms for Oswald when he returned with the photographs and that he signed them in front of her. Nevertheless, she agreed that she sometimes allowed the forms to leave the building, she concedes that she simply cannot remember the precise sequence of events in the Oswald case. Those who have gone through similar visa applications know that, especially in a Latin atmosphere, consulate routine can be free and easy. As former Consul Azcue admits, "It is conceivable that, while writing down all the information on the application, she might not have checked exactly the picture against the individual who was applying, that, occupied as she was, she most probably proceeded to place the photograph on the application without this check. . . . It is a

mistake that results very often in the course of one's work. . . ." If
the application forms did leave the Embassy for a matter of hours,
and if there was a planned effort to impersonate Oswald, then the
planting of a photograph and the forgery of a signature would have
been at least feasible. At all events, it should be remembered that
the real Oswald almost certainly was in Mexico City at the relevant
time, even if it was somebody else who visited the embassies.
Without knowing how Oswald fitted into whatever plan was afoot,
we cannot tell whether or not he was party to the Cuban visa
application process. The apparently authentic Oswald signature
would seem persuasive evidence that Consul Azcue is mistaken,
that the applicant was indeed the real Oswald. So, too, does the
fact that Sylvia Duran's name and phone number appear in Oswald's address book, seized later in Dallas. Other inconsistencies,
however, serve only to corroborate Azcue's version and to hint at
deception.

Today the consul's assistant, Sylvia Duran, points out sensibly
that the passing of the years has blurred her recollection of Oswald. She emphasizes that, back in 1963, it never occurred to her
that the Dallas Oswald and the Embassy Oswald might be different people. Her former husband, who was with her when the news
of the assassination came through from Dallas, says that the Mexican newspapers carried only a poor wirephoto of the Oswald
under arrest. It was the name, "Lee Oswald," not the photograph
which made his wife think at once of the tiresome person who had
come to her office. Sylvia Duran did see the fleeting television film
of Ruby shooting Oswald and noticed nothing to make her feel the
victim was different from the man she had encountered. Astonishingly, no official investigators have ever asked her to study
either that footage or a longer film of Oswald which has been
readily available ever since the assassination. In 1979 I made
arrangements for Duran to see the filmed interview of Oswald
made in New Orleans a few weeks before the Mexico episode. She
was thus able to see and listen to Oswald addressing the camera for
some minutes. Duran's reaction was disturbing. She said, "I was
not sure if it was Oswald or not . . . the man on the film is not like
the man I saw here in Mexico City." Asked what struck her as
different, Duran replied, "The man on this film speaks strongly

and carries himself with confidence. The man who came to my office in Mexico City was small and weak and spoke in a trembling voice." Sylvia Duran found herself thoroughly confused.

The investigator can build no certainties on Duran's new bouts. Yet she supplies one further detail, and it increases the suspicion that her visitor was bogus. In her notes on the incident, Duran writes that the man at the consulate was a diminutive fellow—at the most about 5 feet 6 inches tall. That is short for a man, the sort of detail a woman might indeed remember. Duran told Assassinations Committee staff that Oswald was "short . . . about my size." Duran is a little woman herself, only 5 feet 3½ inches. This is noticeably shorter than the real Oswald's height of 5 feet 9½ inches.

Duran and her former boss both remember the Oswald at the consulate as being blond haired. She also thinks he had "blue or green eyes." If she is right, neither detail fits with the authentic Oswald. Even so, one might put that down to faulty memory—one might even dismiss the matter of height—were it not for the spontaneous recollection of yet another Mexico City witness.

In 1963 Oscar Contreras was studying to be a lawyer at Mexico City's National University. He belonged to a left-wing student group which supported the Castro revolution and had contacts in the Cuban Embassy. One evening in late September 1963—the time of the Oswald incidents in Mexico—Contreras and three like-minded friends were sitting in a university cafeteria when a man at a table nearby struck up a conversation. He introduced himself curiously, spelling out his entire name—"Lee Harvey Oswald." That made Contreras and his friends laugh, because "Harvey" and "Oswald" were more familiar as names of characters in a popular cartoon about rabbits. Indeed, says Contreras, that was the main reason the name stuck in his mind. With minor variations, "Oswald" gave the students a familiar story. He said he was a painter, had to leave Texas because the FBI was bothering him, and declared that life in the United States was not for him. He wanted to go to Cuba, but for some reason the Cuban consulate was refusing him a visa. Could the students help— through their friends in the Embassy? Contreras and his friends said they would try. That night they talked to their Cuban contacts, including Consul Azcue himself and a Cuban intelligence officer, and were sharply warned to break off contact with "Oswald" at once. The Cuban officials said they were suspicious of Oswald and believed he was trying to infiltrate left-wing groups. When Oswald next came to see them, Contreras and his friends told him bluntly that the Cubans did not trust him and would not give him a visa. "Oswald" continued trying to ingratiate himself and ended up spending the night at their apartment. He left next morning, still begging for help in getting to Cuba, and the next time Contreras heard the name "Oswald" was after the assassination. He made no secret of the recent encounter but did not bother to report it to the American Embassy. Like many ordinary Mexicans, Contreras has little love for the American authorities. His story became known only in 1967, after he mentioned it in conversation with the local U.S. consul.[88] Congress' Assassinations Committee, concluding that neither the CIA nor the FBI had adequately investigated the matter, tried to reach Contreras in 1978. They failed to locate him, but I traced him easily enough in the bustling Mexico town of Tampico. He is today a successful journalist, the editor of the local newspaper, *El Mundo*, and I judged him a good witness. The details he supplied add further to the suspicion that the Oswald who visited the Cuban consulate was an impostor.

Like Azcue, Contreras says the "Oswald" he met looked more than thirty years old. Like Sylvia Duran, he recalls very positively that Oswald was short—he too thinks at most 5 feet 6 inches. Sensibly, he says he would normally be reluctant to be so specific, but his recall on this point is persuasive. Contreras himself in only 5 feet 9 inches tall, and he clearly recalls looking *down* at the man he calls "Oswald the Rabbit."

Contreras adds two further thoughts. Perhaps he is being oversuspicious, he says, but he cannot understand how, of all the thousands of students in Mexico City, the man called Oswald picked on three who really did have contacts in the Cuban Embassy. Contreras remembers that he and his friends were drinking coffee, after a discussion and film show in the Philosophy Department, when the strange American accosted them. Nothing about the evening, or the moment, had anything to do with Cuba. How did the American know that these particular students might indeed be able to help him? Contreras does not believe this was divine inspiration, and he remembers something else the Cuban officials said when they warned him to drop "Oswald." Azcue and the Cuban intelligence officer told Conteras that "Oswald" was "highly suspect as being some sort of provocateur, sent by the United States to go to Cuba with evil intent." The consul's colleague, Alfredo Mirabal, confirms the impression "Oswald" left behind at the consulate. He told Congress' Assassinations Committee in 1978 that his "impression from the very first moment was that it was in fact a provocation." Was this suspicion, first voiced weeks before the assassination, mere paranoia on the part of the Cubans? It may well not have been. A stream of additional clues suggest that American intelligence was to find itself seriously compromised by public revelations of the Oswald incident in Mexico City. Consider this chain of events.

On October 10, 1963, just a week after Oswald visits to the Cuban and Soviet embassies, CIA headquarters issued this teletype for the attention of the FBI, the State Department, and the Navy.

Subject: Lee Henry [*sic*] Oswald.

1) On 1 October 1963 a reliable and sensitive source in Mexico reported that an American male, who identified himself as Lee OSWALD contacted the Soviet Embassy in Mexico City inquiring whether the Embassy had received any news concerning a telegram which had been sent to Washington. The American was described as approximately 35 years old, with an athletic build, about six feet tall, with a receding hairline,
2) It is believed that OSWALD may be identical to Lee Henry [*sic*] OSWALD, born on 18 October 1939 in New Orleans, Louisiana. A former U.S. Marine who defected to the Soviet Union in October 1959 and later made arrangment through the United States Embassy in Moscow to return to the United States with his Russian-born wife, Marian Nikolaevna Pusakova [*sic*], and their child. . . .

This document has been at the heart of a quarter century of struggle between the CIA and assassination investigators, Congressional committees as much as private researchers. All have been justifiably concerned about the American at the Soviet Embassy who "indentified himself as Lee Oswald" but looked totally unlike him—ten years older, much taller and heavier built. No mention was made of the Cuban Embassy. Could this be confirmation of suspicion that somebody was masquerading as Oswald in approaches to at least one of the Communist embassies? Of course not, says the CIA, and offers its explanation.

Agency spokesmen have been at pains to explain that there really is no mystery at all, and certainly no Oswald impostor. Taken together, their stories add up to this. On October 1, when Oswald went to the Soviet Embassy to press for his visa, a "reliable and sensitive source" provided by the CIA with details of the visit and "described" the strange American. The available CIA files suggest it had three different sources of intelligence in connection with the Mexico episode—a human informant inside the Soviet Embassy, hidden microphones (the bugging system described earlier), and surveillance photographs. According to the CIA, the raw data on Oswald's visit was at first associated with a picture of another American—"a person known to frequent the Soviet Embassy" at the relevant time and who had been there three days after the Oswald visit. The second American—the heavily built man of thirty-five—had been photographed by the hidden CIA cameras, and someone in the CIA's Mexico station mistakenly "guessed" that he and Oswald were one and the same. Thus the misleading October report went off to Washington, and headquarters began a laborious process of sorting out the discrepancy between the picture of the thirty-five-year-old and the contradictory file details of the real Oswald, as collected during his visit to Russia. The task was all the harder, the CIA would later claim, because at that time the Agency had no photograph of the real Oswald.

The photograph of the man who visited the Soviet Embassy reached the FBI office in Dallas on the evening of the assassination. It subsequently caused a great deal of confusion, and twelve years later a Director of the CIA, William Colby, was still saying of the American who was not Oswald, "To this day we don't know who he is." Whether or not that is true, the basic CIA story is shaky. It is certainly not good enough to dispel suspicions that U.S. intelligence was linked to the shenanigans in Mexico.

Take the CIA's claim that it had no photograph of the real Oswald to compare with its October 1963 surveillance picture. In 1967, a year of renewed doubt about the assassination, an anonymous CIA official wrote a long analgesic memorandum to CIA lawyer Lawrence Houston. It said cheerily of the general CIA position, "I think our position is very strong, indeed, on the matter" and said specifically of the Mexico episode, "CIA did not have a known photograph of Oswald in its files before the assassination of President Kennedy, either in Washington or abroad." This is almost certainly inaccurate. The CIA apparently did have pictures of the real Oswald at the time of the Mexico affair. The evidence is in its own files.

Less than four months after the assassination the CIA sent the Warren Commission what is called "an exact reproduction of the Agency's official dossier (on Oswald). . . . We are able to make available exact copies of all material in this file up to early October 1963." October 1963, of course, was the precise date of the Mexico Embassy visits, and the CIA memo enclosed as part of the official dossier "four newspaper clippings." The clippings are attached for all to see and turn out to be items in the *Washington Post* and *Washington Evening Star*, reporting Oswald's defection to the Soviet Union in 1959. Two of them feature, prominently, news-agency photographs of the real Oswald. Well before the assassination, therefore, a department of the CIA did have pictures of Oswald. Then there are the two pictures of Oswald we discussed earlier, taken in 1961 in the Soviet Union by American tourists visiting Minsk.* The CIA, of course, maintains that the photographs were taken fortuitously, selected for reasons having nothing to do with Oswald, and that Oswald's presence in the pictures was not noticed until after the assassination. The truth about that episode has yet to be established. In view of Oswald's defection to Russia, it would surely have been natural—in any case—for the CIA to obtain photographs from Marine Corps and Passport Office files. The CIA claims nobody did so until after the Mexico episode, when a picture was requested from the Office of Naval Intelligence. The fact is that the CIA did have news pictures of Oswald before the autumn of 1963, and others were perhaps held

* See Chapter 11 for full discussion.

by some Agency department with a special interest. By indicating otherwise, and by many of its utterances about Mexico, the CIA has floundered even deeper into a mire of inconsistency.

After the assassination the Agency at first indulged in shadow-boxing with the Warren Commission. Asked to provide all its Oswald files, and those on Mexico City in particular, the CIA delayed its replies. Internal memoranda reveal a desire by CIA officials to "wait out" the Commission—in other words, to stall as long as possible. Why? Deputy Director Helms told the Committee that the Agency was afraid full disclosure would compromise its espionage sources and methods. By July 1964, as the Agency fenced with the Warren Commission over how the Mexico affair should be presented to the public, the CIA was saying its surveillance picture—of the man who was not Oswald—was taken on October 4, the day *after* the real Oswald apparently left Mexico City to return to Texas. This must have made him seem irrelevant, diminishing any incentive by the Commission to discover more about the mystery man. It seems the CIA did not reveal he had also been at the Soviet Embassy on October 1, the date of an "Oswald" contact with the Soviets.

Who was the mystery man, anyway? The CIA had referred to him dismissively as the "unidentified man" but appears to hint in the same document that it knows very well who he is. This states that it would be wrong to publish the photograph because "it could be embarrassing to the individual involved, who as far as this Agency is aware has no connection with Lee Harvey Oswald or the assassination of President Kennedy." The CIA's concern about embarrassment may mean the mystery man was somehow linked to an intelligence operation. This begs the key outstanding questions about this whole episode—how and why did the CIA come to associate the unknown stranger with Lee Oswald in the first place? Was it really just a matter of human error, of a CIA operative jumping wrongly to the conclusion that the man identified as Oswald visiting the Soviet Embassy was identical with the heavily-built stranger in the surveillance photograph? On this point, said former Warren Commission counsel Wesley Liebeler, "the CIA was so secretive that it was virtually useless to the Commission."

CIA error or not, it seems it was not the stranger in the

surveillance picture who entered the Cuban consulate as Oswald. Both Consul Azcue and his assistant are sure of that. However, this does not lessen suspicion that *somebody* was impersonating Oswald, nor does it let the CIA off the hook. Take another look at that first CIA message about the mystery man. The implication there is that the Oswald visit was originally "reported" by a human source, and it was he or she who "described" the visitor to the Embassy as "approximately 35 years old, with an athletic build." If this description of the Oswald visitor was provided by a human informant, one can see why the Mexico office thought it tallied with the large man in the surveillance picture. This seems to add a CIA informant to the tally of those who observed the Oswald visiting the embassies as quite different from the real Oswald. The entire puzzle prompts yet another question for the CIA. Even if the unidentified, heavily-built stranger had nothing to do with the case, he was at least clear evidence that the CIA was taking photographs of people visiting Communist embassies. Therefore, should not the Agency have pictures of whoever *did* go to the Soviet and Cuban embassies—on several occasions—calling himself Oswald? If that really was Oswald, then surely the pictures should clear up the matter once and for all. Where are they?

The CIA says it has no pictures of the real Oswald visiting either the Soviet or Cuban embassies, and has come up with contradictory explanations. In 1975 Agency officials claimed that the camera at the Soviet Embassy was not used at weekends and that this explained why there were no pictures of Oswald on the Saturday he supposedly visited the Russians. They also maintained that the camera at the Cuban Embassy happened to break down during Oswald's stay in Mexico. The first Chief Counsel of Congress' assassinations Committee, Richard Sprague, found these CIA stories wholly inadequate. As he told me in 1978, "When I heard all that, I wanted to talk to the CIA camera people. I wanted to find out if it was true. And that's where we got stopped." The greatest weakness in the CIA claim not to have photographed Oswald derives from its own surveillance of the man who was not Oswald. In 1976, it finally emerged that there were at least twelve photographs of him, still frames taken from what was originally moving footage. The dozen pictures, pried out of the

CIA by recent Freedom of Information suits, show the mystery man in various poses and wearing different clothes. One of the pictures was taken at the Soviet Embassy on October 1, and that is one of the days Oswald supposedly went there. In 1978 when I visited Havana, the Cuban authorities gave me a whole file of pictures taken—by their own intelligence people—of American surveillance operations across the street from their Embassy *(see illus. 27)*. The watchers were being watched, and it is apparent that the U.S. operation was extensive. There is every reason to believe there was a similar effort at the Soviet Embassy. Why do we have no American intelligence pictures of Oswald—especially if he was at one of the embassies on a day the cameras were working?

An attempt at a CIA explanation has been provided by a former chief of the Agency's Western Hemisphere Division. This is David Phillips, who had headed the Mexico City CIA unit responsible for distribution of pictures of the man who was not Oswald. In 1977 he claimed he knew why there were no photographs of the real Oswald. He wrote that "A capability for such photographic coverage existed, but it was not a twenty-four-hours-a-day, Saturday and Sunday, capability. (We) spent several days studying literally hundreds of photographs available to the CIA before and during Oswald's trip to Mexico City. He did not appear in any of them." The Phillips account is in conflict with both the evidence and the earlier CIA version. Congress' Assassinations Committee did not accept his explanation. It too noted that, according to the best evidence, photographs were taken "routinely" and that the man called Oswald made at least five visits to the Communist embassies. It was hard to believe that CIA cameras failed to pick him up even once. The Committee dourly stated its belief that "photographs of Oswald might have been taken and subsequently lost or destroyed. . . ." It did not follow up and ask how the CIA could have lost pictures of Oswald—of all people. And why would the Agency *destroy* pictures of Oswald?

If the CIA did have pictures of the real Oswald entering the embassies, and entering them alone, we can be sure it would have been delighted to produce them long ago. The fact that they have not done so encourages the notion that the man who called himself Oswald was filmed entering the embassies but that—just as some witnesses suggest—he was indeed an impostor. The impostor theory is strengthened by the feeble tales the CIA has told about another intelligence-gathering system in Mexico City—the bugging of Communist embassies with hidden microphones. If the embassies were bugged, and if that is how some of the intelligence on the "Oswald" visits was gathered, where are the sound tapes? That question really stumps the Agency.

In 1975 William Colby, then CIA Director, was remarkably vague when asked about the recordings on a television program. He merely said he "thought" there were voice recordings of Oswald from the Embassy contacts. There were indeed; the documents show that the Agency bugged a phone call from the Cuban consulate to the Soviet Embassy by a man calling himself Oswald, a conversation with a guard at the entrance to the Soviet Embassy in which he clearly identified himself as "Lee Oswald," and apparently a conversation in which he named Odessa as the town he wished to visit in the Soviet Union.

We know little about the content of the tapes. There is one important clue in a report about the call from the Cuban consulate to the Soviet Embassy. According to information supplied to the Warren Commission, "The American spoke *in very poor Russian* to the Soviet representative. . . ." This does not sound like the real Oswald, who spoke Russian so well when he met his future wife that, she says, she assumed he was a Soviet citizen from another part of Russia. Even back in the United States, Oswald had impressed the Russian community with his fluency in colloquial Russian. Sylvia Duran, furthermore, insists that "Oswald" took no part in the consultation call she made to the Soviet Embassy about his visa. He spoke no Russian in her presence and did not use the telephone at all. This may be a further indication that Oswald was being impersonated in Mexico City, and obviously the tape deserved careful analysis. If the CIA is to be believed, that is now impossible. The tapes no longer exist.

In 1976, it was once again CIA Mexico veteran David Phillips who offered an explanation. He said that the tapes were no longer available because they had been "routinely destroyed" a week or so after the Oswald visit to Mexico City. He mentioned, though, that a transcript had been made of the tape and that he, as an officer of the CIA Mexico station, had seen it. An investigative journalist from Washington traced the typist and a translator who worked on the transcript. They too recalled the detail Phillips mentioned and added something intriguing. The translator recalled that the Oswald tapes caused his CIA bosses to depart from routine. "Usually," said the translator, "they picked up the transcripts the next day. This they wanted right away." That makes no sense in terms of the CIA's official stance on the Mexico episode. Its officers have maintained that until Oswald's name surfaced after the assassination his visits to embassies in Mexico were merely registered by routine intelligence and passed on to Washington in leisurely fashion. Why, then, did CIA officers react—many weeks before the assassination—as though the Oswald case was a top priority? The alleged destruction of the tape recordings a week or so later becomes even more improbable. Congress' Assassinations Committee had its work further complicated by a top-level report which at first seemed to confirm—unambiguously—that the tapes *were* still in existence at the time of the President's murder.

Within twenty-four hours of the assassination, FBI Director Hoover had compiled a preliminary analysis. It is five pages long and unremarkable except for one paragraph. It reads:

> The Central Intelligence Agency advised that on October 1, 1963, an extremely sensitive source had reported than an individual identifying himself as Lee Oswald contacted the Soviet Embassy in Mexico City inquiring as to any messages. Special agents of this Bureau, who have conversed with Oswald in Dallas, Texas, have observed photographs of the individual referred to above and *have listened to a recording of his voice. These Special Agents are of the opinion that the above-referred-to individual was not Lee Harvey Oswald.*

The message seems crystal-clear. The CIA had sent to Dallas both a picture and a sound recording of the man who had been spotted by its surveillance calling himself Lee Oswald. Neither picture not tape matched the Oswald under arrest. Not surprisingly, this caused alarmed inquiry at FBI headquarters—and an apparent resolution. The FBI Special Agent-in-Charge in Dallas, Gordon Shanklin, informed headquarters that the CIA had delivered only a photograph and *typewritten reports*. Available CIA documents do mention the dispatch to Dallas of a special plane carrying photographs but make no reference to tapes. The FBI agents who interrogated Oswald in Dallas said that, if there was a recording, they never heard it. It may be that no tapes were sent, although it is hard to fathom how such a huge inaccuracy crept into a report on the assassination at FBI Director level. Unfortunately for historical certainty, however, the Committee was also to find—in a separate area—that Shanklin and one of the agents in the Dallas area were involved in the destruction of vital evidence about Oswald. The Committee's report regarded this as an "impeachment of [their] credibility," an indictment which permits us to doubt whether the whole truth has been told about whether the tape reached Dallas. Wearily, the Committee concluded in 1979 that the recording of Oswald never even reached CIA headquarters from Mexico. It failed to resolve, however, what had happened to the tape which clearly did exist, before the assassination, at the CIA in Mexico City.

In the end, the Assassinations Committee found itself faced with an unenviable choice. One pile of evidence suggested imposture, while other material—such as the visa forms bearing the real Oswald's photograph and apparent signature—indicated he really had visited the Cuban consulate. The Committee made its public aware of the conflict and then—citing unspecified "other information provided by the CIA"—concluded that the Oswald who visited the Cuban Embassy was genuine. It made an interesting distinction, though, and said nothing so concrete about the individual who visited the Soviet Embassy. In that case, said the Committee gingerly, "Evidence of a sensitive nature provided. . . . by the CIA *tended to indicate* that the person who contacted the Soviet Embassy" was one and the same as the man at the Cuban consulate. Finally, the Committee confessed itself "unable to determine" whether the CIA did in fact obtain a picture of Oswald during his Embassy visits. This is not a satisfactory conclusion. Even for its key decision as to whether the real Oswald had been at the Cuban consulate, the Committee was forced to fall back on mysterious "CIA" evidence. This could not, apparently, be described because to do so would reveal classified sources and methods. It sounds very much as though national security is being invoked to protect some human source, perhaps an erstwhile spy inside the Cuban Embassy. That might be justifiable, except that—in an apparent reference to the source on another key matter—the Committee judged it to be "in error." On another area of the Mexico inquiry, the Committee spoke tetchily of the CIA's "refusal" to make sources available—even to security-cleared Committee staff. Sixteen years on, it was plain silly for the CIA to make such a mystery out of Mexico—if there was nothing to hide.

What we have of the jigsaw may mean that, perhaps because of an operation against Fair Play for Cuba, one branch of the CIA was isolated from information on Oswald held by another department. This would explain why, in October 1963, one office at CIA headquarters still did not know—according to the record—whether the man in its Mexico surveillance coverage was Oswald. It asked the Navy to supply pictures of the real Oswald, even though CIA files already had photographs of him. Meanwhile, this same office seems to have been curiously out of date on the Oswald case. On October 10, as it initiated inquiries into the Mexico episode, the office stated that its latest information on Oswald was from a 1962 report. Yet the record shows that the FBI sent the CIA three September 1963 reports on Oswald's most recent doings, including one on his latest FPCC activities in New Orleans. Why, then, in a largely automated agency which could process intelligence data at lightning speed, was headquarters so ill-informed? It may have been because of the clandestine operations being conducted against FPCC by a separate intelligence department. In the interest of security, intelligence agencies do often run compartmentalized operations. It might have been undesirable, after the assassination, to reveal what some CIA "dirty tricks" department was up to—against Fair Play for Cuba or simply against Castro's Cuba. Yet there the rationalization ends. If Oswald was part of a covert operation against Havana's interests, he could surely have been sent into the Communist embassies himself. Today the questions remain. Was somebody impersonating Oswald in Mexico City and, if so, why?[89] There are no easy answers, but there are some highly disturbing leads.

In 1976, when former Mexico CIA officer David Phillips offered his account of the surveillance tapes having been destroyed before the assassination, he was reported as making a fresh allegation. According to the *Washington Post*, he indicated knowledge of a transcript of an "Oswald" phone call to the Soviet Embassy, in which "Oswald" had tried to do a deal with the Soviets. The Oswald in the transcript had supposedly said words to the effect, "I have information you would be interested in, and I know you can pay my way [to Russia]." Phillips' reported remarks found apparent corroboration from two CIA employees, the translator and typist who said they worked on the Oswald transcript. The said "Oswald" had indeed offered to give "information" to the Russians. What information? They did not elaborate, and Phillips has since disassociated himself from the reported remarks. But there are two more versions of what "Oswald" supposedly said in Mexico City. Both bear the mark of American intelligence.

One version came in 1975 from Ernesto Rodriguez, who said he was a former CIA contract agent in Mexico City. According to him, "Oswald" told both the Soviets and Cubans that he had information on a new CIA attempt to kill Fidel Castro. Oswald offered more information, said Rodriguez, in exchange for a Cuban entry visa. Rodriguez said "Oswald" not only talked about this on the telephone but openly blabbed about the planned Castro assassination attempt in conversations with Fair Play for Cuba members in Mexico City. Rodriguez also alleged, improbably, that Oswald discussed his calls to the Cubans with local reporters. Rodriguez' story attracted little attention, but a second story has enjoyed a longer life and intense official interest.

In 1967 a British reporter, Comer Clark, claimed he had been to Havana and had secured a sensational impromptu interview with Fidel Castro. He subsequently published a story saying that the Cuban leader had known in advance of an Oswald threat to kill President Kennedy but had done nothing about it. According to Clark, Castro said, "Lee Oswald came to the Cuban Embassy in Mexico City twice. The first time, I was told, he wanted to work for us. He was asked to explain, but he wouldn't. He wouldn't go into details. The second time he said something like: 'Someone ought to shoot that President Kennedy.' Then Oswald said—and this was exactly how it was reported to me—'Maybe I'll try to do it.' This was less than two months before the U.S. President was assassinated. . . . . Yes, I heard of Lee Harvey Oswald's plan to kill President Kennedy. It's possible I could have saved him. I might have been able to—but I didn't. I never believed the plan would be put into effect." According to Clark, Castro simply did not take the Oswald threat seriously and so failed to warn United States authorities.

The Comer Clark story is a real puzzle. In 1978, Castro told members of Congress' Assassinations Committee that he had given no such interview and advised them to check the reporter's background. The Committee found that Clark, now dead, had been an inveterate purveyor of sensational and sometimes dubious stories.* On the other hand, the Committee's chief counsel told a public hearing in 1978, "Even though there may be considerable doubt as to the fact of Clark's interview with President Castro, the committee has been informed that the substance of the Clark article is supported by highly confidential but reliable sources available to the U.S. Government." That sounded impressive until the Committee's report came out. This stated, "However reliable the confidential source may be, the committee found it to be in error in this instance. . . . On balance, the committee did not believe that Oswald voiced a threat to Cuban officials." In other words this mysterious, unnameable source—who sounds very like the source the Committee believed in deciding Oswald had been at the consulate—provided misleading information on what Oswald actually said in the consulate.[90]

"Highly confidential but reliable sources" is a stock euphemism for intelligence information. The main intelligence source for the Assassinations Committee was the CIA. American intel-

---

* Castro's denial is supported by interviews with Clark's wife and assistant. The widow says he never mentioned interviewing Castro. And Clark's assistant, Nina Gadd, says *she* generated the story, without going anywhere near Havana, on the basis of allegations made to her by a Latin American Foreign Minister. (Mrs. Clark and Gadd were contacted after first publication of *Conspiracy*.)

ligence sources, indeed, appear to be behind the various versions of what transpired between "Oswald" and the Cubans—the versions, that is, which incriminate both a leftist Oswald and Castro's Cuba. It is this, the pointing of the finger, that is the common demoninator.

Rodriguez, the CIA contract agent, said Oswald warned the Cubans about an impending CIA assassination attempt. The inference here is that Castro may have responded to the information by launching a pre-emptive strike against President Kennedy. That has become a familiar allegation by Castro's enemies.

The story by the British reporter, about Castro learning of an Oswald threat in advance but failing to act, contains one detail that does sound like the Cuban Leader. According to Clark, Castro said of the "Oswald" episode in Mexico City, "I thought the visits might be something to do with the CIA—whether anything eventually happened or not. . . . Then, too, after such a plot had been found out, we would be blamed—for something we had nothing to do with. It could have been an excuse for another invasion try. In any case, people would have tried to put it at my door. I was not responsible for Kennedy's death, I will tell you that. I think he was killed by U.S. fascists—right-wing elements who disagreed with him."

Was Castro's suspicion unfounded, or was he right in his feeling—reportedly in advance of the assassination—that the Mexico City incidents "might have something to do with the CIA"? Senator Schweiker, the Republican who led the Intelligence Committee inquiry into CIA activity surrounding the assassination, has a similar opinion. He charges that the CIA deliberately concealed the existence of Mexico pictures from his staff, and has expressed the belief that "a CIA cover-up is still going on."

Congress' Assassinations Committee had problems with the CIA evidence on Mexico City, and specifically with the testimony of David Phillips, who was in charge of Cuban operations in Mexico at the time Oswald's name was used at the Cuban Embassy. Richard Sprague, the Committee's first Chief Counsel, told me in 1980, "I did not feel we were being told the absolute truth on Mexico City by the CIA. Specifically, I felt that the narration on Mexico City by David Phillips, given under oath, would not bear

thorough examination. It was contrary to that given by other
sources, and to other facts." The second Chief Counsel of the
Committee, Professor Robert Blakey, observes that "Phillips testified about a variety of subjects, and the Committee was less than
satisfied with his candour."*

David Phillips came to the Committee's attention in a context
other than his accounts of CIA surveillance in Mexico. The Committee gave serious consideration to the possibility that David
Phillips was the man behind the mask of "Maurice Bishop,"[91] the
case officer alleged to have schemed to provoke trouble between
the United States and the Soviet Union over Cuba, and to have
met with Oswald shortly before the assassination. Phillips denied
he was "Bishop," and so did the source of the "Bishop" allegations. Antonio Veciana. Nevertheless, the Committee said in its
Report that it "suspected Veciana was lying" and that Phillips—
referred to on this occasion as "the retired officer"—"aroused the
Committee's suspicion" with the nature of his denial. The question
whether Phillips did use the cover name "Bishop" will be covered
in detail later. At this stage, however, consider one last fragment
of information on Mexico City. It suggest that CIA officer "Bishop" tried to tamper with the evidence so as to link Oswald falsely
with communist officials.

In 1978, exile leader Antonio Veciana added a disturbing
postscript to his account of meeting "Bishop" in Oswald's company shortly before the Mexico episode. After the assassination,
Veciana told me "Bishop" made a strange request. "He asked me
to get in touch with a cousin of mine who worked in the Cuban
Embassy in Mexico City, Guillermo Ruiz. Bishop asked me to see
if Ruiz would, for money, make statements stating that Lee Harvey Oswald had been at the Embassy a few weeks before the
assassination. I asked him whether it was true that Oswald had
been there, and Bishop replied that it did not matter whether he
had or not—what was important was that my cousin, a member of
the Cuban diplomatic service, should confirm that he had been."

Veciana did have a cousin by marriage called Ruiz, and he

* For the latest information on Mexico City and "Bishop," see the
Aftermath Chapter.

worked, fronting as a diplomat in Castro's intelligence service.[92] Veciana says, though, that he could not immediately contact Ruiz following "Bishop's" request. He says that, before he could do so, "Bishop" told him to "forget the whole thing and not to comment or ask any questions about Lee Harvey Oswald."

It must be stressed that, for all the imponderables about the "Bishop" allegation, Committee staff were able to make this report on Veciana's character: "Generally, Veciana's reputation for honesty and integrity was excellent." A former associate who worked with him when Veciana was chief of sabotage for the M.R.P* in Havana said, "Veciana was the straightest, absolutely trustworthy, most honest person I ever met. I would trust him implicitly." That is one estimate of the man who insists " 'Bishop' did work for an intelligence agency of this country, and I am convinced that it was the CIA. . . . The impression I have is that the Mexico City episode was a device. By using it, 'Maurice Bishop' wanted to lay the blame for President Kennedy's death fairly and squarely on Castro and the Cuban government."

If that was indeed the ploy, it would come close to succeeding.

---

* Movimiento Revolucionario del Pueblo.

CHAPTER 20

Double Image In Dallas

Accurate multiple exposures are easily achieved. . . .
—Camera Users' Handbook, Minolta Corporation

The real Lee Oswald made a mundane return to the United States.
His trip home to infamy was another bone-shaking bus journey,
not to New Orleans, but to Dallas, Texas, and a night at the
YMCA. He made a weekend visit to his wife Marina, now awaiting the birth of a second child at the home of her friend Ruth Paine
on the outskirts of the city. It was a contact that would have a total
effect on Oswald's destiny. Ten days after his arrival in Dallas,
Mrs. Paine mentioned to her neighbor, Mrs. Randle, that Oswald
was having trouble finding a job. Mrs. Randle had a bright idea:
there might be an opening at her brother's place of work. Oswald
followed up and two days later began the last job of his life. He
became an order-filler at a warehouse handling the distribution of
educational books. This was the Texas School Book Depository.

Superficially, the last forty days of Oswald's life were unremarkable. After a false start with a temperamental landlady, he
moved into a rented room at 1026 North Beckley. For the first
time in more than a year of renting rooms, Oswald registered
under an assumed name—"O.H. Lee." To the owners of the
house and to his fellow tenants, Oswald seemed quiet and lonely.
He spent almost every evening reading or watching television and
rarely made conversation. He often telephoned his wife[93] and
visited her almost every weekend. October 18 was Oswald's
twenty-fourth birthday, and the girls made quite an occasion of it.
Ruth brought wine, decorated the table, and baked a cake. When
the cake was carried in, glittering with candles, everybody sang,
"Happy Birthday, Lee." Lee was visibly moved, and his eyes filled

with tears. Two days later Marina gave birth to their second child, another daughter, and Oswald rejoiced. In some ways, it seemed, their rickety marriage was recovering a little. Oswald seemed genuinely interested in re-establishing a domestic life and talked of setting up house together again. At work, Oswald's supervisor noticed he "did a good day's work" and thought him an above-average employee. Oswald was doing well at the Texas School Book Depository. He said, according to his wife, that he was saving money. In reality, though, Oswald may have anticipated an early end to his employment.

Around November 1—three weeks before the assassination—Oswald wrote to the Internal Revenue Service. In his letter he stated that he had "worked only six months of the fiscal year 1963." Within days of writing this he supposedly told his wife that "there was another job open, more interesting work. . . . related to photography." There is no knowing what he meant in the letter to the taxman or in the alleged remark to his wife. The Warren Report did not mention the letter indiciating that he expected to cease working; the IRS document did not go on public record until three years later. It merely adds, to the mystery created by the odd official attitude to Oswald's finances. As we saw earlier, the alleged assassins income-tax returns for 1962—the last year of record in his life—remain closed to researchers. No realistic clarification has yet been produced for the reticence about Oswald's income. Meanwhile, during Oswald's last two weeks of life, there came a new and apparently unwelcome development. These were the visits, reported by Marina and her hostess, Ruth Paine, of an FBI agent called James Hosty.

Hosty was the Dallas agent who, so far as one can tell from the record, had proposed the reopening of the Oswald case seven months earlier when routine reports revealed Oswald's subscription to *The Worker,* the newspaper of the Communist Party. Hosty had taken this initiative when, curiously, FBI headquarters seemed to ignore the matter. Now, as a result of routine CIA surveillance reports, the FBI knew that somebody calling himself Lee Oswald had visited the Soviet Embassy in Mexico. In Dallas Agent Hosty learned of this; he also heard from New Orleans that the Oswald family had departed, leaving Ruth Paine's address for forwarding purposes. At New Orleans' request, Hosty checked on the Paine address. On November 1, twenty-two days before the assassination, the FBI agent turned up on Ruth Paine's doorstep. According to Ruth and Marina and by his own account, Hosty said merely that he would like to talk to Oswald sometime and asked how to contact him. The agent was given the address of the Book Depository and left. Four days later he called again but departed on being told the women did not have the address of Oswald's rented room. In fact, the women have said since they did have Oswald's telephone number there. The accounts suggest they were protecting Oswald because they knew he felt the FBI was out to persecute him.

According to Marina, Oswald was plunged into a black mood by news of the Hosty visits. He supposedly reacted—the day after the second one—by making a personal appearance at the FBI's Dallas office. According to a receptionist who talked to him, Oswald's purpose was to see Agent Hosty. When told Hosty was out for lunch, Oswald gave the receptionist an envelope. He said curtly, "Get this to him" and departed. After the assassination the FBI concealed the very existence of the envelope and its contents. What the note contained remains uncertain, and what happened to it stayed a dark secret for twelve long years.

The episode remained hidden until 1975, when a journalist learned about the note from a contact inside the FBI. His subsequent inquiries sparked off a national furor. Eventually the sorry story was pieced together by Congress' Committee on the Judiciary by the Senate Intelligence Committee and by the Assassinations Committee. Former FBI staff, including Agent Hosty, admitted not only that there had been an Oswald note but that it had been deliberately destroyed within hours of Oswald's death. What, the committees wanted to know, had been the contents of the message? Who had ordered its destruction and why? The FBI had no satisfactory answers. The receptionist, Nanny Fenner, made a dramatic claim. She said she had caught a glimpse of the note and that it read:

Let this be a warning. I will blow up the FBI and the Dallas Police Department if you don't stop bothering my wife.

Lee Harvey Oswald

Agent Hosty's public memory was different. He maintained the message read roughly as follows:

> If you have anything you want to learn about me, come talk to me directly. If you don't cease bothering my wife, I will take appropriate action and report this to the proper authorities.

Hosty has privately described the receptionist, Mrs. Fenner, as unreliable; he believes she is excitable. In any case, Hosty maintains, the note was folded in such a way that the receptionist could not have read it in the way she claimed. He insists that the note was nothing out of the ordinary, that he simply placed it in his work tray and forgot about it until after the assassination. Certainly, Mrs. Fenner's version of the note rings false; it is wholly out of character with Oswald's usual actions or words. It is difficult, on the other hand, to take Hosty's account as gospel. If the note was so innocuous, the rest of the story makes little sense. Clearly, after the assassination, something about its connection with Oswald caused dismay and fear at the FBI.

According to Hosty, he was called into the office of his superior, Special Agent-in-Charge Shanklin, within hours of the assassination. Shanklin, visibly "agitated and upset," allegedly asked Hosty to account for the note. Hosty explained his recent contacts with Ruth Paine and Oswald's wife and how the note had subsequently reached him. Then, within hours of Oswald's murder two days later, Hosty was summoned once more. He says Shanklin produced the note from a desk drawer, saying. "Oswald's dead now. There can be no trial. Here—get rid of this." Hosty then tore the note up in Shanklin's presence, but Shanklin cried, "No! Get it out of here. I don't even want it in this office. Get rid of it." Hosty then took the note to the lavatory and—in his words—"flushed it down the drain." A few days later Shanklin asked Hosty for an assurance that he had done as ordered.

Clearly Shanklin had a great deal of explaining to do. In fact his testimony in 1975 merely increased the mystery. He denied outright ever having seen or known about the note and said the first time he ever heard of it was in 1975. This, however, was contradicted by William Sullivan, Assistant Director of the FBI at

the time of the assassination, who said Shanklin had often discussed an "internal problem" over a message from Oswald. Another Dallas supervisor, agent Howe, said that after the assassination he found the note in Hosty's work tray and took it to
Shanklin. He gained the impression that Shanklin "knew what I
had and, for what reason I don't know—he didn't want to discuss it
with me." Howe claimed to know nothing about the destruction of
the note.

In a mass of inconsistent and unsatisfactory FBI statements on
the Oswald note, Shanklin's is the most dubious. In 1979 Congress' Assassinations Committee said it "regarded the incident of
the note as a serious impeachment of Shanklin's and Hosty's
credibility. . . . The Committee noted further the speculative nature of its findings about the note incident. Because the note had
been destroyed, it was not possible to establish with confidence
what its contents were." During his earlier testimony before Congress' Judiciary Committee, Shanklin was warned that he might be
open to prosecution for perjury. There has been no prosecution,
and this, an outrageous and admitted instance of FBI malpractice,
has apparently been consigned to official limbo.[94]

Perhaps, in the numbed aftermath of Watergate, even revelations of FBI deceit and destruction of evidence have seemed too
commonplace to justify firm action. Yet clearly there was deceit,
and clearly the Oswald note was destroyed. The reason why remains wholly pertinent to any serious study of what happened in
Dallas. Some believe the lapse was merely part of a misguided
effort to minimize even an innocent Bureau connection with Oswald. It is suggested that Agent-in-Charge Shanklin, faced with
Director Hoover's fury over the failure to spot Oswald as a potential threat, simply tried to erase evidence of opportunities missed.
Perhaps, though, one is bound to add, somebody in the FBI was
fearful that full exposure of Bureau interest in Oswald would
reveal an element of the case which remains hidden even today.
James Hosty himself has strongly suggested that the original order
to destroy the note came from FBI headquarters and perhaps from
the top. Now retired, with his FBI pension secure, the former
agent has hinted darkly at revelations to come. In late 1978 he said
of Congress' Assassinations Commiteee, "I am the one they are

afraid is going to drop bombs—if they are going to try to contain this like the Senate Intelligence Committee and the Warren Commission, they don't want me there." The Assassinations Committee Chief Counsel subsequently suggested that Hosty had been misreported. That is, however, what he said, and Hosty is currently working privately on aspects of U.S. intelligence treatment of the Oswald case.* Pending the detonation of Hosty's bombs, what further clues might explain the panic at the FBI after the assassination? One may lie in another piece of documentary evidence which only just escaped Agent-in-Charge Shanklin's urge for destruction.

On November 9, while visiting the Paine household, Oswald wrote a very strange letter to the Russian Embassy in Washington. It referred to the visits he had supposedly made to the Soviet Embassy in Mexico and suggested that he and Marina still wanted to return to the Soviet Union. It said he had to curtail his trip to Mexico because renewal of his visa would have involved using his "real name." It informed the Russians that the FBI was no longer interested in Oswald's FPCC activities but that Agent Hosty had warned him against starting them again now he was back in Texas. The letter is a compendium of falsehoods.

Apart from the doubt that the real Oswald ever visited the Soviet Embassy, there was the clear implication that Oswald used a false name in traveling to Mexico. (Actually, the Mexican tourist card had been issued to "Lee, Harvey Oswald.") In addition, everything we know of Oswald's actual attitude suggests that he had no intention of returning to the Soviet Union. As for the comments about the Dallas FBI, they bear no relation to known facts. According to the record, Oswald had not met Hosty, and Hosty had not warned him against doing anything. What happened to the letter is as baffling as its contents. Oswald left the draft of the letter lying on Ruth Paine's desk, as though he wanted her to find it. Indeed she did, and found it alarming enough to make a copy, apparently with a view to giving it to Hosty if he called again. After the assassination she lost no time in supply the

---

* In late 1980 Hosty claimed that documents on Oswald in Mexico had been secretly removed from the FBI's Dallas file after the assassination.

letter to Hosty, who in turn showed it to his superior, Gordon Shanklin. Hosty said Shanklin "became highly upset and highly incensed" and ordered Hosty to destroy the note. Today Hosty thinks Shanklin may have been confusing the Russian Embassy letter with the Oswald note to the FBI. At all events, Hosty and a colleague decided on their own initiative to ignore orders and preserve the letter. In fact it would have survived in any case because a routine FBI mail intercept turned up a copy Oswald actually mailed to the Soviet Embassy.

The contents of the letter remain puzzling. If Oswald had no intention of returning to the Soviet Union, what was its purpose? A possible answer is that, right up to the assassination, Oswald was engaged in the sort of *anti*-Communist schemes that seemed likely in New Orleans and Mexico City. While Hosty may have been, and probably was, ignorant of such an involvement, some other part of the intelligence apparatus may have been informed— at least—of what was going on.

On November 1, the very day of Hosty's first visit to the Paine household, Oswald reverted to an old practice and rented a post-office box in downtown Dallas. On the rental form he authorized two non-profit organizations to receive mail at the box. One, not surprisingly, was the Fair Play for Cuba Committee, and the second was the ACLU—the American Civil Liberties Union. This last was a new departure for Oswald. The ACLU, unlike the FPCC, existed for no political purpose but simply to champion civil liberties—free speech, the right to fair trial, and other rights of the individual. A few days later Oswald joined the ACLU and asked its national headquarters how he could get in touch with "ACLU groups in my area." Yet neither the new membership nor the inquiry make any sense. Only ten days earlier Oswald had been to a local ACLU meeting along with Michael Paine, Ruth's husband. Oswald had himself spoken briefly at the gathering and afterward chatted with several people; both Michael and Ruth Paine were members. So Oswald had no innocent need what-soever to write to the other end of the country for information on ACLU activities in Dallas. As for joining the ACLU himself, he had specifically told Paine he would never join such a group because it was too apolitical. The same day Oswald opened his post-office he wrote to the Communist Party of the United States, showing he knew perfectly well where and when ACLU meetings were held in Dallas; he also asked for advice on how to heighten "progressive tendencies" in the local branch of the ACLU. Was Oswald launching off on some dark scheme involving a fake branch of the ACLU, similar to those odd FPCC activities in New Orleans? Whatever his purpose, one further clue throws a glimmer of light on Oswald's last days. It links Oswald, once again, with New Orleans.

Before leaving for Dallas via Mexico, Oswald had himself arranged for the post office to forward his mail to Ruth Paine's house. Yet, in the second week of October, somebody in New Orleans filed a second change-of-address card, duplicating Oswald's original request. The handwriting on the card was not Oswald's. When this was brought to the attention of the Warren Commission by a postal inspector, a Commission lawyer saw the problem at once. He said, "Let me come bluntly to the point. My problem is this: Oswald wasn't in New Orleans on October 11. He was in Dallas." The postal inspector admitted there was no simple explanation. He offered the improbable suggestion that someone had perhaps telephoned the change-of-address to the sub-post-office in New Orleans and that the writing was that of a post-office clerk. The matter was not investigated further. The Commission lawyer simply passed on, with the weary comment, "Well, in any event, we will add this to the pile." Even if the postal inspector's guess was right, it changes nothing. Oswald was in Dallas and had already organized his mail transfer. Somebody else, identity unknown, was apparently taking the trouble to look after Oswald's business in Louisiana. The New Orleans connection had not ceased with Oswald's departure.

Meanwhile, as the authorities learned to their chagrin after the assassination, Texas was being graced with a phenomenon assassinologists would one day dub "The Second Oswald."

After any crime which makes news, anywhere in the world, police are flooded with reports by people claiming to have seen the chief suspect. Some of them are genuine cases of mistaken identity, and other stories are mischievous. Predictably the Kennedy assassination sparked off literally hundreds of "Oswald" sightings, and most would eventually be discounted. Others, however, were strikingly different—both because of the obvious integrity of the witness reporting and because of the credible detail they provided. These cases worried official investigators but eventually were discarded like jigsaw pieces that get into the wrong box. Later, when private researchers snatched the pieces up again, they suspected that somebody might have been impersonating Oswald in the weeks leading up to the assassination. The sightings of a "second Oswald" joined the confusing pile of conspiracy evidence. The concept is so bizarre that—like the harried lawyers on the Warren Commission—I wanted to reject it. Yet some of the sightings are not only credible but fit the pattern of events in New Orleans and Mexico City. Reluctantly, I have reached the conclusion that somebody may possibly have been impersonating Oswald, either to incriminate him or to confuse later investigation—or both. Consider first the manifestations of the second Oswald.

On September 25, 1963, a young man calling himself Harvey Oswald walked into the offices of the Selective Service System— the American military draft organization—in Austin, the capital city of Texas. He introduced himself to Mrs. Lee Dannelly, the assistant chief of the administrative division, and explained a problem. He had, he said, been discharged from the Marine Corps under "other than honorable conditions," and this was making it hard to get a job. He now hoped to get the discharge upgraded on the basis of two years' subsequent good conduct. Could Mrs. Dannelly help? In the event she could not, because there was no "Harvey Oswald" in her files. Since the visitor said he was living in Fort Worth, Mrs. Dannelly suggested he check with the offices there. "Oswald" thanked her politely and left. The next time Mrs. Dannelly heard the name "Oswald" was on November 22, when it was mentioned in broadcasts about the assassination. She then reported her experience, as did two others who believed they had seen Oswald in Austin that day.

There was one little problem with Mrs. Dannelly's story. On September 25, the date she specified, Oswald was just setting off from New Orleans. He was Mexico-bound, on a route that would taken him nowhere near Austin, Texas. Yet of course the real Oswald did have an undesirable discharge from the Marine Reserve, and he had once lived in Fort Worth. Was someone trying to impersonate him?

Exactly two weeks before the assassination "Harvey Oswald" made another appearance. The proprietor of a supermarket, Leonard Hutchinson, came forward to say that he had been asked to cash a check for $189 made out in the name of "Harvey Oswald"—the same name that had been used in the Austin appearance. Hutchinson had turned down the request, he said, but recalled that the man visited the store several times, sometimes accompanied by two women. Hutchinson's supermarket was in Irving, Texas, the Dallas suburb where Marina Oswald lived with Ruth Paine. The Warren Commission rejected Hutchinson's evidence on the grounds that Oswald had not been in Irving at the specific time mentioned. This ignored the evidence of a barber who had a shop near Hutchinson's. He said he had cut the hair of a man who looked like Oswald and that he had seen him entering Hutchinson's supermarket. The man had mentioned visiting his wife. Who had Hutchinson and the barber seen, and what was he trying to achieve? A further "Oswald" appearance, one of the best documented, suggests a man who was trying to draw attention to himself.

Twenty-four hours after the assassination, the FBI received a report that a man calling himself "Lee Oswald" had visited a Dallas car showroom on November 9, had discussed the purchase of a used car, and—on a demonstration drive—rattled a car salesman by driving at speeds of up to eighty miles per hour. The salesman, Albert Bogard, remembered "Oswald" saying he did not have money to buy a car quite yet but would receive "a lot of money in the next two or three weeks." Bogard's account was corroborated on important points by two of his colleagues, one of whom remembered that "Oswald" said that in view of the high prices he might have to go "back to Russia where they treat workers like men." One salesman said "Oswald" came back on a second visit, just days before the assassination. The car showroom in question was very near to the Texas School Book Depository, where the real Oswald worked. The Warren Commission spurned the evidence—in spite of the three witnesses—on the usual ground that other evidence placed the real Oswald elsewhere. Yet the list of strange appearances, reported by credible citizens, goes on.

There was the night manager of Western Union in Dallas, a Mr. Hamblen. After the assassination, he told his superior he was sure Oswald was a customer who had collected money orders several times and who had sent a telegram during the second week of November. He said that one of the money orders had been delivered to the YMCA and that the customer had identified himself with a "Navy ID card and a library card." Although neither money orders nor telegram ever were traced in the name of Oswald, Hamblen was supported on these details by a second Western Union employee, Aubrey Lewis. The real Oswald, of course, was a former Marine and did carry a library card. Who was the visitor, and why could no messages be found in the name of Oswald?

Then there was Hubert Morrow, the manager of Allright Parking Systems at the Southland Hotel in downtown Dallas. He recalled that a man, identifying himself as Oswald, inquired about a job as a parking attendant two weeks before the assassination. When Morrow at first wrote the man's name down as "Lee Harvey Osborn," the applicant corrected it to "Oswald." Morrow's evidence is interesting for two reasons. The real Oswald did not usually spell out his full name but called himself simply "Lee Oswald." And, according to Morrow, this man asked a strange question. He asked how high the Southland building was and whether it commanded a good view of Dallas. That detail, of course, later took on an obvious sinister significance. So did a number of other incidents, which are usually discussed out of context. Assembled in chronological order, they assume a disturbingly logical pattern—a sequence which seems almost beyond coincidence. This involves an Oswald linked firmly, by a whole gaggle of witnesses, to guns, ammunition, and target practice.

On November 1 a young man drew attention to himself while buying rifle ammunition at Morgan's Gunshop in Fort Worth. He was "rude and impertinent" and boasted about having been in the Marines. Three witnesses who had been in the shop at the time remembered the incident after the assassination and thought the man had looked like Oswald. The real Oswald was busily occupied in Dallas on the day mentioned.

The next incident belies the notion that all these witnesses were notoriety seekers who hurried forward with their information. It was revealed, only by chance, when a London *Evening Standard* reporter canvassed all the gun shops in the suburb where Marina lived with Ruth Paine. Seeing the sign "Guns" outside a furniture store, she went in to ask questions and found herself the second person to make that mistake in the past few weeks. After explaining that the premises had previously housed a gunsmith, the manager recalled an early November visit by a man she thought looked exactly like Oswald. He had been accompanied by a wife and two children, one of them an infant. The wife had not uttered a word, although the husband spoke to her in a foreign language. The manager, whose account was corroborated in detail by a second witness, said this "Oswald" asked where he could get the firing pin on his rifle repaired. She thought she had directed him to the nearby Irving Sports Shop—and that was strange indeed.

Two days after the assassination, an anonymous caller told the Dallas police that the alleged assassin had had a rifle sighted at Irving Sports Shop. The staff there did not remember an Oswald visit but produced something more tangible than a memory. Dial Ryder, an employee in the shop, found a customer's ticket for work on a rifle between November 4 and 8. It bore the name the customer had given, just "Oswald." Intensive inquiry turned up no other Oswald in the area who had had a gun repaired.

While neither Ryder nor his boss could remember much about their mysterious client, both did remember something about the gun. According to the ticket, the work done involved drilling holes for a telescopic sight mounting. The weapon found in the Book Depository required only two holes. There were other technical differences, and the sum of the evidence pointed in one direction. Somebody who was not Oswald had commissioned alterations for a gun—not Oswald's—in Oswald's name. From that date on, right up to the assassination eve, there are reports of an "Oswald" seen at a local shooting range.

The sightings at the Sports Drome Rifle Range begin on

November 9, the day after the rifle was probably retrieved from the Irving Shop. A number of witnesses later described a man who had drawn attention to himself by being loud and obnoxious. He was variously described as being both an excellent shot and yet a man who infuriated another sportsman by shooting at his neighbor's target. The Warren Commission dismissed some of these reports as the wishful thinking of witnesses who wanted to get in on the act. Some, indeed, seemed to be describing a man who did not even look like Oswald. Yet the original account, of a sighting on November 16, should not have been included in this bracket. In 1978 Dr. Homer Wood, who had been at the range that day with his young son, told me just why he felt obliged to report what he had seen. Dr. Wood said, "On November 22, in the afternoon, I was watching the television at home. As soon as I saw Oswald on TV I said to my wife, 'He looks like the man who was sitting in the next booth to our son, out at the rifle range.' . . . When my son came home from school I purposely didn't say anything to him. Well, he also looked at the television and he spoke to me quickly, saying, 'Daddy that looks just like that man we saw at the range, when we were sighting in our rifles.' " Dr. Wood was so struck by the double identification that he called the FBI. Wood's thirteen-year-old son had a better memory for detail than his father and was a gun enthusiast in his own right. He well remembered talking to the man in the next booth, who was an excellent shot. The man volunteered that the gun he was using was a 6.5-mm Italian rifle with a four-power scope. It emitted a "ball of fire" when fired. The FBI later tried persistently to get young Wood to change his very specific story, but he stuck to his guns. Today, now a successful doctor, he still thinks the man he saw at the range was Oswald. It is not wholly impossible—Oswald's movements on the weekend before the assassination are poorly accounted for. Yet the young Wood, like the gun-shop staff, remembered a gun with a scope different from the one on the weapon linked to the assassination. And he recalled that when the marksman left, he was accompanied by "a man in a newer model car." We now have a chronologically logical pattern of the Second Oswald appearances, a man who—besides sightings at which he provided details matching those of the real Oswald—bought ammunition, had a gun fixed, and then got himself remembered for accurate shooting and ownership of a 6.5-mm Italian rifle. The important point here is that the rifle was unusual enough to be remembered as 6.5-mm and Italian, like the real Oswald's weapon, but differed in such details as the scope. This brings us to a last sighting involving a weapon, one which may be the most revealing.

In October, when the real Oswald had just returned from Mexico, three men were disturbed while firing a rifle on private property just outside Dallas. The owner of the land, a schoolteacher named Mrs. Lovell Penn, asked them to leave. After the assassination she, like other witnesses, remembered that one of the men had looked like Oswald. But once again it was a tangible piece of evidence which made that incident significant. Mrs. Penn reportedly found a 6.5-mm Mannlicher-Carcano cartridge case on her land and handed it over to the FBI. Laboratory tests showed it had not been fired from the Carcano found in the Book Depository. If the sightings of a Second Oswald with a gun do have significance, this one—and the dropping of the unusual make of shell—may have been unintentional. Witnesses at the rifle range say the marksman there carefully collected his cartridge cases before leaving. The schoolteacher also added one last clue; she remembered that at least one of the threesome on her land was "Latin, perhaps Cuban." This, it turns out, was a feature of several of the other reports—made spontaneously at a time when there was no public suspicion involving Cubans.

One of the witnesses at the Western Union office, where an ex-Navy "Oswald" drew attention to himself, described his visitor as being accompanied by a second man who looked "Spanish." A witness at the Sports Drome range made a similar comment. Ms. Dannelly, the very reputable witness at the Selective Service office, recalled that her "Oswald" responded to an awkward question by saying he was registered as a serviceman in Florida. While the real Oswald registered as a Marine in California and had no reason to lie on this point, Florida was the state where the vast majority of anti-Castro activity took place.

On October 13, a Dallas citizen would report after the assassination, a man described as "identical" with Oswald attended a local meeting of the DRE, one of the radical anti-Castro groups.

The name "Oswald" appears on an equipment purchase form filled—in 1961—by New Orleans representatives of the anti-Castro group "Friends of Democratic Cuba"

Also present, it happens, was the extreme right-wing General Walker, whom the real Oswald had allegedly tried to kill several months previously.

Five days before the assassination a citizen of Abilene, two hundred miles west of Dallas, picked up a note left for one of his neighbors. It was an urgent request to call one of two Dallas telephone numbers, and the signature read "Lee Oswald." After the assassination the citizen, Harold Reynolds, twice tried and failed to arouse FBI interest. The neighbor, it turns out, was Pedro Gonzalez, president of a local anti-Castro group called the Cuban Liberation Committee. Gonzalez became noticeably nervous when he was handed the note and minutes later was seen phoning from a public telephone. Reynolds says he had previously seen a man who closely resembled Oswald attending a meeting at Gonzalez' apartment along with a second and older American from New Orleans. Gonzalez is remembered for extreme anti-Kennedy sentiments and was known as a friend of Antonio de Varona, leader of the CIA-backed Cuban Revolutionary Council.[95] He left Abilene soon after the assassination and was last heard of in Venezuela.

Although all these incidents are from credible witnesses and

```
Date:        June 3, 1960

To:          Office of Security
             Department of State

From.:       John Edgar Hoover, Director

Subject:     LEE HARVEY OSWALD
             INTERNAL SECURITY - R
```

```
             Since there is a possibility that an imposter is
using Oswald's birth certificate, any current information the
Department of State may have concerning subject will be
appreciated.
1 - Director of Naval Intelligence                    39. 6-981
```

The shadow of Oswald. Three years before the assassination, FBI Director Hoover expressed concern that somebody else might be using Oswald's name

mostly well documented, they are slender threads. Some, perhaps, would not have taken the investigation forward. Stronger evidence, though, links "Oswald" with Cuban activities—long before the assassination and when the real Oswald was far away. Again it comes from New Orleans.

In 1975 the Senate Intelligence Committee, investigating American intelligence agencies in connection with the assassination, heard testimony from a former New Orleans immigration inspector. While protecting the inspector's identity, the Committee published his story in its formal report. The inspector "testified before the Committee that he is absolutely certain that he interviewed Lee Harvey Oswald in a New Orleans jail cell sometime shortly before April 1, 1963. Although the inspector is not now certain whether Oswald was using that particular name at that time, he is certain that Oswald was claiming to be a Cuban alien. He quickly ascertained that Oswald was not a Cuban alien, at which point he would have left Oswald in his jail cell." This witness was an immigration inspector, specifically trained to note faces and details. Yet the time he describes—and he had excellent reasons for believing it was before April 1963—predates the real Oswald's descent on New Orleans. There is one further clue as to

what was going on, one that gives the Second Oswald an even
longer history.

Immediately after the assassination the FBI was contacted by
the manager of a Ford Motors franchise in New Orleans, Oscar
Deslatte. The name Oswald had struck a chord with him, and he
had checked back in his order files. Deslatte found a docket
showing that a prospective purchaser named Oswald had nego-
tiated to buy Ford trucks *two years* previously. The FBI expressed
interest and took possession of the old docket, carefully enclosed
in a fingerprint cover (*see next page*). Deslatte's Oswald, an American accompanied by a swarthy Cuban, had tried to purchase ten
trucks on January 20, 1961, during the build-up to the Bay of Pigs
invasion mounted by the CIA. It was a time when thinly veiled
American intelligence officers and their Cuban protégés were buying supplies and equipment for the invasion—mostly for shipment
via the invasion bases in Central American countries. This would-
be purchaser asked Deslatte to "give a good price because we're
doing this for the good of the country." Deslatte also recalled that
the American first identified himself as "Joseph Moore" but asked
that the name "Oswald" should go on the purchase documents.
"Oswald," he said, was handling the money for his anti-Castro
organization and would pay for the trucks if the deal went through.
The Ford manager could not identify his visitor from 1963 photographs of Lee Oswald, and that was hardly surprising. In early
1961 the real Oswald was on the other side of the world, in the
Soviet Union.

Most intriguing of all, Deslatte's carbon copy of the old purchase form—released by the FBI only in 1979—contained more
than just the name Oswald, which is not after all the most unusual
name in the world. It recorded the name of the anti-Castro group
that intended buying the trucks, "Friends of Democratic Cuba."
In 1961 a leading light of that organization was Guy Banister—
former top FBI agent still engaged in undercover work, and the
man identified as using the real Oswald in the suspect Fair Play for
Cuba operation of summer 1963. Once again the evidence comes
full circle, with the implication that the anti-Castro movement may
have been using Oswald's identity as far back as 1961. The notion
of Oswald imposture before the assassination takes on a more
credible perspective. It was a possibility raised as early as 1960 by
none other than the Director of the FBI.

On June 3, 1960, an FBI memorandum, issued over Hoover's name, warned the State Department that "there is a possibility that an impostor is using Oswald's birth certificate." (*see top of page.*) The context was Oswald's visit to Russia, and Hoover's evident concern was that the Russians might make use of Oswald's identity documents. Yet the phrasing is strange. What led to the feeling that "there is a possibility" of imposture? It could have been routine caution in a Bureau trained by Hoover to be constantly alert to Communist perfidy. Yet in March 1961, just weeks after the Oswald incident at the truck company, the deputy chief of the U.S. Passport Office expressed continued concern because "it has been stated that there is an impostor using Oswald's identification data." In the wake of the assassination an intriguing piece of information was provided by, of all things, the Retail Merchants' Credit Association of Fort Worth, Texas. A spokesman revealed that—within two weeks of the truck-purchasing incident—the FBI twice inquired whether the association knew of business dealings by Oswald. The FBI has explained only that "the purpose of these contacts was to obtain background data for leads concerning Oswald." Yet the inquiries immediately preceded Passport Office concern that "there is an impostor using Oswald's identification data."

While Oswald was in Russia, his mother told the FBI that he had taken his birth certificate with him when he left home. When he returned, however, he told the Bureau he had not taken his birth certificate with him and did not know where it was. The original birth certificate is one document that never has turned up, and Oswald did spend time in New Orleans before traveling to the Soviet Union. It was conceivably then that, perhaps unwittingly, he provided a convenient alias for someone involved in covert operations during his absence. It is possible the FBI knew something of such activity. In 1975 the State Department official who served as liaison with the FBI during the investigation, Richard Frank, commented that it seemed possible that "when the Oswald file suddenly became the object of the most intensive research and review. Mr. Hoover and his friends in the security operation at State simply made it disappear."

Former Warren Commission counsel David Slawson, known for his caution in commenting on the case, learned of the impostor correspondence in 1975. He then declared himself in favor of reopening the assassination inquiry, saying, "I don't know where the impostor notion would have led us, perhaps nowhere, like a lot of other leads. But the point is, we didn't know about it. And why not?" Slawson added, "It conceivably could have been something related to the CIA. I can only speculate now, but a general CIA effort to take out everything that reflected on them may have covered this up."

The last and most important sighting of a Second Oswald was one which official investigators have found most credible of all, and it occurred just weeks before the Kennedy assassination. If ever an Oswald impostor was really used it was on that occasion. This time there is an indubitable link to the anti-Castro movement, to CIA operatives, and to New Orleans.

The Odio Incident—the Strongest Human Evidence

It was evening in Dallas, late in September, when the doorbell rang at Apartment A, Crestwood Apartments. Inside, Silvia and Annie Odio were not expecting visitors. Annie went to answer the door and then called her elder sister. The door was still held on the night chain, and through the crack Silvia could see three strange men—two Latins and an American. What they said gave her enough confidence not to turn them away, and thus began an enduring conundrum for any serious student of the Kennedy assassination. The Odio incident has been called, with reason, "the proof of the plot."

Silvia and Annie Odio came from a distinguished and wealthy Cuban family, prominent in revolutionary politics. Their father, although upper-class, had supported Fidel Castro in the underground fight to overthrow Batista; but he had wanted democracy, not Communism, and soon began working against the new regime. By 1963 he was a political prisoner in the notorious Isle of Pines, and his family was scattered in exile. Silvia, twenty-six years old, and Annie, seventeen, had joined the growing exile community in Dallas. There, following in her father's footsteps, she had become active in exile politics. A few months earlier, in Puerto Rico, Silvia had helped form Junta Revolucionaria, or JURE. This group, although against Castro and Communism, was well to the left in exile politics. Its members thought of themselves as social democrats, while many in the exile movement considered them dangerously left-wing, offering "Castroism without Castro." The men who called on Silvia Odio in late September said they were fellow members of JURE, and that is why she agreed to talk to them. Although Odio has told her story repeatedly to the authorities, she had never given press interviews. In 1978 I talked with her on two occasions, and once again she relived the frightening episode of fifteen years earlier.

As they talked that evening, it soon became clear that one of the two Latins was the group's leader. He was tall, looked about forty, and said his "war name" was "Leopoldo." Silvia Odio thinks the second Latin, who was shorter and wore glasses, was called "Angelo" or "Angel." Like Leopoldo, he had an olive complexion and could have been either Cuban or Mexican. The third man, who was much younger, was an American. As Leopoldo began to explain why they had come, the American stood quietly by, saying almost nothing at all. Like the others, he looked weary, rather unkempt, and he had not shaved.

Leopoldo said the three of them were on a trip and had just come from New Orleans. He claimed they were working with the blessing of the government in exile, the Cuban Revolutionary Council, as well as being members of JURE. As for the affiliation with JURE, Silvia Odio was impressed by the fact they knew her father's underground name and came up with a number of details about events in Cuba which only an insider would be likely to know. They were clearly familiar with recent plots to kill Fidel Castro. Leopoldo said his group was trying to raise funds for anti-Castro operations and wanted her help. Specifically, they wanted her to translate into English a number of fund-raising letters addressed to American businessmen. Something made Silvia Odio feel uneasy. Her father had warned her to take the utmost care in the Byzantine intrigues of exile politics, and she was leery of dealing with strangers. She told her visitors she wanted no part in a campaign of violence. The meeting did not last long and broke up inconclusively. The men left, in their red car, supposedly about to embark on another long journey.

All the time they had been at the apartment, the young American had said hardly a word. He had just stood watching and listening, in Odio's words, "sort of looking at me to see what my reaction was, like somebody who is evaluating the situation." Eight weeks later, both Silvia and her sister Annie would react with fear and bewilderment when they saw pictures of the man arrested for shooting President Kennedy. Silvia had a special reason for shock. When the three strangers had visited her, the American in the group had been introduced as "Oswald"—"Leon Oswald." For Silvia, moreover, there was an even more jolting reason to remember him.

Leopoldo, who had introduced Oswald, telephoned Silvia Odio within forty-eight hours of the visit. He brought up the request for help again, but he also seemed keen to discuss something else. "what did you think of the American?" he asked. Odio, thinking how quiet the American had been, said she had not really formed an opinion. Then Leopoldo made a number of remarks which—even at the time—Odio found chilling. He said of Oswald, "Well, you know, he's a Marine, an ex-Marine, and an expert marksman. He would be a tremendous asset to anyone, except that you never know how to take him." Listening to this, Silvia Odio wondered what she was expected to say. She knew even less when Leopoldo went on. "He's kind of loco, kind of nuts. He could go either way. He could do anything—like getting underground in Cuba, like killing Castro." And then Leopoldo added, "The American says we Cubans don't have any guts. He says we should have shot President Kennedy after the Bay of Pigs. He says we should do something like that."

That was all. Leopoldo seemed to have little else to say. The conversation ended, and Silvia Odio never heard from him again. She says today that she felt even then that there was something wrong, something sinister and deliberate about the phone call. "Immediately," she recalls, "I suspected there was some sort of scheme or plot . . ."

When the President was killed in the same city, just weeks later, Silvia was sure. She heard the news at work, and her head filled with a kaleidoscope of frightening thoughts. When news broadcasts confirmed that the President had died, her boss decided all the staff could go home. Silvia was prone to fainting fits, and she passed out now—on her way to the parking lot. She was taken to a hospital. Across the city, Annie Odio had watched the President drive past on his way to his death. An hour or so later, as soon as she saw Oswald's picture on the television, her first thought was "My God, I know this guy and I don't know from where. . . . Where have I seen this guy?" Soon, on being told her sister Silvia had been taken ill, Annie visited her in the hospital. She at once told Silvia she had seen Oswald somewhere before but could not quite place him. Silvia, who had started crying, reminded her of the three men who had visited the house. She also told Annie about the disturbing call from Leopoldo. There was a television in the hospital room, and now Silvia saw the pictures of Oswald for the first time. As she recalls, "Annie and I looked at one another and sort of gasped. She said, 'Do you recognize him?' She said, 'It is the same guy, isn't it?' I said, 'Yes, but do not say anything.' "

The sisters were frightened, and worried that their experience had somehow placed them in danger. Their parents were imprisoned far away in Cuba, and they felt very much alone. The decided to say nothing to the authorities. Silvia's extreme reaction and distress, and their not at first reporting anything, does not impeach their credibility. Silvia then suffered from a physical condition which frequently caused blackouts when she was under stress[96]; Annie was a scared girl of seventeen. If they had had their way, the story might never have come out at all. As it turned out, it became known purely by chance. Silvia had another sister, and she casually told an American friend. A series of casual conversations finally brought the incident to the attention of an FBI agent. At first there was only cursory interest; the matter was not pursued with any vigor until the following summer, when the Warren Commission was well into its work. It then emerged that there was every reason to believe Silvia Odio's account. A key new factor was the discovery that she had discussed the visit of the three men with another witness *before* the assassination. She also had documentary proof that she had reported it—again well in advance—in a letter to her father in Cuba. All this, coupled with the fact that Annie Odio clearly recalled the visit and also said the mysterious American had looked like Oswald, finally attracted some attention. A senior Warren Commission lawyer wrote, "Mrs. Odio

(Silvia) has checked out thoroughly, . . . The evidence is unanimously favorable. . . . (Mrs. Odio) is the most significant witness linking Oswald to the anti-Castro Cubans.''

There was a problem, one which the Warren Commission found it preferable to deem intractable. Odio placed the visit to her apartment between September 24 and 29—most probably in the middle of that time frame. This was a period when Oswald was ending his stay in New Orleans, a time not precisely determined, and setting off on his trip to Mexico. By any account of his movements, he could not have been at Odio's apartment unless he was flitting around the country at great speed. There was no evidence Oswald had traveled by commercial airline. Nevertheless, the Odio evidence remained troubling. In the dying days of the Commission, Chief Counsel Lee Rankin wrote to FBI Director Hoover, ''It is a matter of some importance to the Commission that Mrs. Odio's allegations either be proved or disproved.'' On September 21, 1964, just as the Warren Report was being finalized, Hoover reported that his agents had traced a man called Loran Hall, a ''participant in numerous anti-Castro activities,'' who said he had been in Dallas at the relevant time and had visited Silvia Odio along with two colleagues. Hall said one of his friends looked like Oswald, and Hoover seemed satisfied that this had led to all the fuss. The Warren Commission looked no further. It published a finding that implied acceptance of the Hall story and a firm conclusion that Oswald could not have been at Odio's apartment because of the known evidence on his movements. That finding was wholly unjustified, and Congress' Assassinations Committee said so in 1979.

Loran Hall's story, trotted out right on cue to explain away the Odio incident, collapsed even before the Warren Commission heard about it. FBI agents traced the two other men Hall had named as his companions at Odio's apartment. Both said the story was untrue; they had made no such visit. Faced with that, Hall retracted his story. Meanwhile, all unknowing of this development, the Warren Commission had already written it into history. The Commission cannot be forgiven, however, for its claim that Oswald could not have been in Dallas at the relevant time. In doing so, it twisted Odio's statements and the available evidence. The Commission had simply balked at what the evidence did imply. In 1979, Congress' Assassinations Committee did not. It accepted that, to have been at Odio's apartment in the known time frame, "Oswald had to have had private transportation. . . ." Oswald had no transport of his own. If he traveled from New Orleans by car—or conceivably by private plane—he must have done so with help. It was, as an Assassinations Committee report stated, "a situation that indicates possible conspiratorial involvement." What sort of conspiracy?

The Committee faced a further obvious problem. If Oswald was a genuine pro-Castro leftist—as the Committee thought—what was he doing in the company of anti-Castro militants? It speculated that perhaps Oswald, as part of a left-wing assassination plot, was associating with the exiles in order to implicate the anti-Castro side in the President's murder. On this the Committee speculated with little conviction and ended up with only one firm conclusion. This was that it believed Silvia and Annie Odio and accepted that they had met a man who at least *looked like* Oswald and was introduced as Leon Oswald. There can be no innocent explanation.

A reasonable interpretation is that the mysterious "Leopoldo"—an anti-Castro plotter—was deliberately using the name of the real Oswald to set him up as a fall guy. Why else tell Odio he was an ex-Marine who urged the killing of the President? A second, and subtler, rider to that theory is that this was—simultaneously—a deliberate ploy to link JURE, a left-wing exile group, with the assassination. Odio's visitors posed as JURE members, and the Odio family supported its aims. In prison in Cuba, Silvia Odio's father reacted with alarm when he received his daughter's letter about the visit. He wrote back, "Tell me who this is who says he is my friend—be careful. I do not have any friend who might be here, through Dallas, so reject his friendship until you give me his name." Today, released from his long imprisonment in Cuba, Sr. Odio says he is certain the visitors were in no way connected with him. The leaders of JURE in the United States were equally nonplussed. The diverse anti-Castro political groupings were only nominally unified and were regularly at logger heads. To the rightist, JURE supporters were little better than Communists, and they may have been the target of a set-up. Who, though, might have been trying to frame the left and Oswald in particular? The known interconnections point in a familiar direction.

Consider, above all, Loran Hall, whose "explanation"—however short-lived—helped relegate the Odio incident to the Warren Commission's pile of trivia. He turned up again in 1967, when the New Orleans area of the case was being reopened, and again muddied the waters with information that led in useless directions. In 1977, Hall was highly reluctant to give evidence to the Assassinations Committee. When he eventually did so, on a basis that assured him against prosecution arising from his testimony, Hall maintained he had never claimed to have visited Silvia Odio. In its final report, however, the Assassinations Committee called his original tale "an admitted fabrication."

Loran Hall has cropped up in this story before—in connection with his detention for unauthorized military activity and for running guns for the anti-Castro side. Other reports place him in perturbing proximity to others with roles in the mystery. He was a leading member of "Interpen," a obstinate anti-Castro force made up of exiles and CIA contract agents. As such, he worked with Gerry Hemming, the Marine veteran who reports meeting Marine Oswald and identifying him, as early as 1959, as a low-level intelligence operative. Hall, along with Hemming—his comrade in the International Anti-Communist Brigade—reportedly trained Cuban exiles at a camp on Lake Pontchartrain outside New Orleans. There was such a camp, and it was there that Oswald allegedly went with David Ferrie. David Ferrie, his anti-Castro activities aside, was also unquestionably linked to Mafia boss Carlos Marcello. As for Loran Hall, it seems possible that he had some connection to the other Mafia leader alleged to have forecast the President's murder, Santos Trafficante. By his own admission, Hall was in detention for a time with Trafficante. He was freed on the same day as Trafficante and is reported to have left Cuba with him and another released prisoner. Trafficante, of course, was a key CIA contact man in assassination plots—against Castro.

Early on the morning after the assassination, a Dallas police detective wrote a brief report on a lead he had received from an informant. It was that "Oswald" had attended meetings of an anti-Castro movement at an address in Dallas. The same informant reported that the Cubans in the group had left that address in the past few days. It is now known that the house in question had been a local headquarters for Alpha 66, the exile group which—earlier in 1963—launched guerrilla attacks against Presidential policy and at the direct urging of CIA officer "Maurice Bishop." Could this "Oswald" be linked to the Odio incident? One further strand in the Odio story suggest he may have been and makes the whole Odio affair loom more sinister than ever.

Silvia Odio's father had been imprisoned in Cuba because he had helped and harbored an anti-Castro plotter called Reinaldo Gonzalez. Gonzalez's offense was that he had taken part in a plot to kill Fidel Castro. His co-conspirator had been none other than Antonio Veciana, the leader of Alpha 66 who operated under the control of the U.S. case officer he knew as "Maurice Bishop." It was in Dallas, very shortly before Odio met "Oswald," that Veciana saw the man he believed to be Oswald in the company of "Bishop." The CIA man's expertise and training, according to Veciana, was in the area of propaganda, deception, and "dirty tricks."

Today, when asked what haunts her most about her experience fifteen years ago, Silvia Odio replies, "It is the thought that perhaps, somehow, I could have prevented the assassination."

In September 1963, at the very moment "Oswald" was seen by Odio and with "Bishop," President Kennedy was involved in moves which offered the anti-Castro movement a stronger motive then ever before to do away with him. The moves were top secret, theoretically shared only by a trusted few among the President's advisers. It is very likely there was a leak, with American intelligence the recipient.

CHAPTER 21

Countdown to Conspiracy

*There is no doubt in my mind. If there had been no
assassination we probably would have moved into
negotiations leading to a normalization of relations with
Cuba.*

—Ambassador William Attwood

On September 17, 1963, an American and an African met over
coffee at United Nations headquarters in New York. The African
was a little-known diplomat, but what he had to discuss could have
changed the course of modern history. Ambassador Seydou Diallo, Guinean envoy to Cuba, brought word from Havana. As his
American contact he had selected Ambassador William Attwood,
Special Adviser to the United States delegation at the UN. Diallo
knew and trusted Attwood as a former American ambassador to
Guinea, but there was more to the choice than that. Not only had
Atwood met and talked with Fidel Castro since the revolution, but
he was on close personal terms with President Kennedy and his
most important advisers. Now, seated in a corner of the Delegates'
Lounge at the United Nations, Attwood listened while the Afrian
ambassador talked carefully. The burden of his message was that,
after more than three years of confrontation, Fidel Castro wanted
to reach some sort of understanding with the United States.

According to Diallo, Castro was especially unhappy about the
way Cuba was becoming tied to the Soviet Union and was looking
for a way out while there was still time. Castro was at odds with
international Communists in the Cuban leadership, such as Che
Guervara, and hoped to redress the balance by finding an accommodation with the United States. The stalemate between the two

countries had lasted long enough, and it was time to break it. "Castro," said Ambassador Diallo, "is salvageable." In practical terms, the African suggested, it would not go amiss if Attwood found a way to talk to the Cuban delegate at the United Nations, Carlos Lechuga.

The African had spoken like a strictly unofficial intermediary, carefully but with deliberation. Ambassador Attwood knew well that, in the world of diplomacy, conversations over coffee are often less casual than they seem. In recent weeks other sources had given Attwood the same impression—that after more than three years of confrontation, Castro wanted talks about talks. In 1963 terms this had a potential for breakthrough as momentous as the first tentative contacts between Egypt and Israel in the Seventies. Attwood reported what was in the air to his immediate boss, United States Ambassador to the United Nations Adlai Stevenson. He also briefed Averell Harriman, Under Secretary of State for Political Affairs. Both men reacted with keen interest, and Stevenson promptly called the White House to discuss the new development with the President himself. Should Attwood go ahead and meet a Castro representative?

In terms of American public policy, any sort of dialogue with Castro would be a startling change of course. To many, including top officials at the CIA and the State Department, the very idea was heresy. Castro was to be overthrown, not wooed. President Kennedy was wary, but he had an open mind. Nine months ago his Presidential adviser on foreign affairs, McGeorge Bundy, had proposed finding some way to talk to Castro; in April American negotiator James Donovan, back from talks in Havana about prisoner exchanges, had reported that Castro was concerned about Soviet domination. Castro had asked how Havana and Washington could go about resuming diplomatic relations, and Donovan had replied, "The way porcupines make love—very carefully." Now, Kennedy felt, the time had perhaps come to start that interesting experiment. The idea was, after all, wholly in line with the President's search for peaceful alternatives.

Three weeks earlier, the "hot line" telephone link between the White House and the Kremlin had been opened—itself a symbol of determination to bring the United States and Russia into closer touch on sensitive issues. In the coming month Kennedy and Khrushchev would sign the nuclear test-ban treaty. The President publicly projected the return of a thousand troops from Vietnam, the first stage of a withdrawal program that was to bring all American personnel home within two years. On Vietnam, the President knew, he was in direct conflict with a strong body of opinion within the CIA, which was virtually running the war. The CIA was generally against withdrawal and looked sourly on the President's policy of global disengagement. Publicly the President was trying to conceal these fundamental disagreements. Privately he was seriously concerned. One of his last acts was to commission a task force to review United States intelligence activities. Meanwhile, Kennedy intended to grasp opportunities for peace when they presented themselves. In June, the President's advisory group on Cuba had agreed it would be a good thing in theory to start a dialogue with Havana. Now the opening was there.

In his September telephone call with Adlai Stevenson, John Kennedy made a snap decision. Attwood was to go ahead and meet Carlos Lechuga, the Cuban delegate to the UN, as soon as he liked but on two conditions. On no account must it appear the United States was soliciting the discussions. The contact was to be informal and top secret. "Secret" meant not telling the State Department bureaucracy or the CIA.

In New York, Ambassador Attwood received the news with satisfaction. He was personally eager for an end to the Cuban deadlock, and he had a ready-made device for the delicate contact with Lechuga. A television correspondent, Lisa Howard of the American Broadcasting Company, had recently been to Havana and secured a scoop interview with Castro. He had expressed satisfaction over the Kennedy crackdown on exile raiding parties, and Howard too had returned with the feeling that Castro was ready to talk. She was already in touch with Atttwood and on good terms with Cuban officials at the United Nations. Attwood took her into his confidence, swearing her to secrecy, on the understanding that if the talks came to anything she would have an exclusive story. For her part, Lisa Howard was to give a small cocktail party.

On September 23, at nine o'clock, a dozen carefully selected guests gathered in Howard's Manhattan apartment. Ambassador Attwood was there, and so was Castro's man at the UN, Carlos Lechuga. Attwood broke the ice by recalling how he had enjoyed talking to Castro in 1959, and Lechuga responded by saying—not so casually—that he believed Castro still liked talking. Sitting at a discreet distance from the other guests, the two diplomats chatted cautiously for half an hour. Lechuga said that Castro had appreciated Kennedy's recent moves to ease Cold War tensions and had particularly like the President's June speech on making the world "safe for diversity." As for a next step, Attwood said he would be glad to talk to Castro if the invitation came from Havana and if the White House approved. As Attwood told me when I interviewed him in 1978, "I left the party with the clear impression the Cubans were seriously interested in talking. We agreed to keep in touch." He then moved fast.

The next morning saw him on an early shuttle to Washington and a meeting with the President's brother. Attorney General Robert Kennedy thought an Attwood visit to Cuba might appear to commit the United States too much and wondered if a Castro meeting could be arranged on neutral territory, perhaps in Mexico. As a first step, it might be best if Attwood met a Castro emissary in New York. Two days later Attwood met Lechuga again at the United Nations. Almost apologetically, the Cuban said he would shortly be making an obligatory anti-American speech in the United Nations Assembly, just as Kennedy had done a few days earlier against the Havana regime. The White House, said Lechuga, should not read too much into it. Meanwhile, he would ask Havana whether they favored sending someone for talks to New York. The wheels of state were turning, slowly and secretly. The secrecy side of things bothered Robert Kennedy a lot. It was, he had told Attwood, "bound to leak." Meanwhile, far away, some strange things had been happening.

It had been public knowledge for weeks that the President would shortly be visiting Dallas. On September 26, one week after Kennedy had given his approval to tentative talks with the Cubans, the date of November 22 had been announced. At exactly this time the "Second Oswald" began to make appearances in Texas.

On September 25, when Attwood had his second meeting with Lechuga, "Harvey Oswald" walked into the Selective Service office in Austin to say how upset he was about his undesirable discharge from the Marines. Within forty-eight hours, in Dallas, an anti-Castro militant was introducing Silvia Odio to "Leon Oswald," ex-Marine, and saying Oswald felt President Kennedy should have been assassinated long ago. On September 27, in Mexico City, the man calling himself Lee Oswald demanded a Cuban visa and caused a memorable scene when he was not immediately given one. As an "Oswald" made visit after visit to the Cuban and Soviet embassies, CIA cameras and tape recorders were turning.

At exactly this time, the CIA made its first contact in nearly a year with Rolando Cubela, the traitor in Castro's inner circle. Without the knowledge of either the Kennedys or their own director, a small group of CIA officers prepared to use Cubela to "remove" Castro. In Washington, ignorant of this, President Kennedy and his aides proceeded quietly with plans for friendly contact with the man their own intelligence agency was trying to kill.

Through October, as the days ticked by to tragedy in Dallas, the White House began asking Ambassador Attwood what progress he was making. The answer was that the Cuban bureaucracy was racing at Latin speed—very slowly. Havana's foreign ministry, it seemed, was not giving the matter high priority. Attwood, by now personally committed to the peace effort, began to take some initiatives of his own. He angled for ways of ensuring that Castro personally understood the new feeling in the White House. In early October he learned that the eminent French journalist, Jean Daniel of *L'Express*, was in the United States on his way to Havana. As Attwood noted in his dairy. Daniel too felt that Cuba was "ripe for bold diplomacy." Together with Ben Bradlee, then Washington Bureau Chief of *Newsweek*, Attwood urged President Kennedy to see the Frenchman. At first the President did not respond, but he changed his mind promptly on learning that Daniel might soon be seeing Castro. At an interview in mid-October, Kennedy expounded his thoughts on Cuba. The essence of the problem he told Daniel, was that Castro had betrayed the revolution by becoming "a Soviet agent in Latin America" and that it was his actions which had brought the world to the brink of nuclear war in the missile crisis. As President Kennedy said, he could not tolerate continued Communist subversion in Latin America. On the other hand, the President surprised Daniel by vigorous approval for the principle of Cuba's own revolution. He said the United States must take most of the blame for the evils of the old Batista regime. "I have," said Kennedy, "understood the Cubans." He asked Daniel to come and see him again on his return from Havana, to report on Castro's attitude. Daniel, and Castro in his turn some weeks later, understood that Daniel was to be an "unofficial envoy."

Meanwhile, in New York, Ambassador Attwood had been receiving inquiries from the White House about his progress with official contacts. In late October he decided to bypass the Cuban foreign ministry and get a message through to Castro personally. Attwood did so by using the television journalist Lisa Howard to telephone Dr. Rene Vallejo, Castro's personal doctor and trusted aide. A string of telephone calls went out to Cuba from Howard's Manhattan apartment. On October 29 there was movement. Vallejo tentatively brought up the idea that an American official—it was agreed this would be Attwood—should fly to meet Castro at Veradero, a resort on Cuba's north coast. Ambassador Attwood briefed Adlai Stevenson at the United Nations and then shuttled to Washington to brief the White House. On his return he was able to note in his diary, "President more in favor of pushing this than State Department." Kennedy was personally keen to press for an opening with Cuba, to take Castro "out of the Soviet fold and perhaps wiping out the Bay of Pigs and getting back to normal." However, the President would at this stage prefer a Cuban—perhaps Vallejo—to come to the United Nations for preliminary talks. Ambassador Attwood decided it was time to call Castro's aide himself and began a series of calls from Lisa Howard's apartment. Even getting through to Vallejo involved hours of wrestling with the telephone. Meanwhile, the President seized a new opportunity to make his feelings heard in Havana. On November 18, four days before the assassination, he made an important speech in Miami, the city with the largest Cuban exile population in the United States.

Kennedy said little to raise the hopes of the exiles but much to interest listeners in Havana, just 200 miles across the water. He declared, "It is important to restate what divides Cuba from my country. . . . It is the fact that a small band of conspirators has stripped the Cuban people of their freedom and handed over the independence and sovereignty of the Cuban nation to forces beyond the hemisphere. They have made Cuba a victim of foreign imperialism, an instrument of the policy of others, a weapon in an effort dictated by external powers to subvert the other American republics. This, and this alone, divides us. As long as this is true, nothing is possible. Without it, everything is possible. . . . Once Cuban sovereignty has been restored we will extend the hand of friendship and assistance. . . ."

In 1978 the historian Arthur Schlesinger, former special assistant to President Kennedy, explained the background and purpose of this speech. It had been written by the President's closest foreign-policy advisers, including McGeorge Bundy, the aide most concerned with the Attwood negotiations. It was meant to reinforce what the President had said to Jean Daniel, that good relations were possible if Cuba ceased its interference in Latin American countries. Months earlier, Castro's aide Vallejo had taken a visiting American aside to explain that a rift had developed between the Cuban leader and some of his Communist colleagues. Now, Kennedy's phrase about "a small band of conspirators" was a thinly veiled reference to those hard-liners, and the speech as a whole was designed to encourage Castro to stand firm against them. Above all, says Schlesinger, it was to help Ambassador Attwood gain Fidel Castro's confidence. The President of the United States wanted to find a way to reopen relations—yet behind his back the CIA twisted his words into a very different message.

CIA officials had been continuing their contacts with Castro's disaffected aide, Rolando Cubela. As the Senate Intelligence Committee learned in 1975, they had started discussing Castro's assassination with him and promised him lethal equipment—all without the authority of the Government. At the end of October the head of the CIA's Cuba unit, Desmond FitzGerald, masquerading as an American Senator, had told Cubela that a coup against

Castro would have the full backing of the United States Government. A month after both Kennedys had given their personal support to peace feelers, the CIA "Senator" had told Cubela he came as Robert Kennedy's personal representative. After the Miami speech a CIA officer compounded the untruth. He told Cubela that the"Senator" had helped write the speech, which he had not; and he claimed the speech was meant "as an indication that the President supported a coup."

As Arthur Schlesinger told me in 1978. "The whole Cubela thing raises even deeper questions. The CIA was reviving the assassination plots at the very time President Kennedy was considering the possibility of normalization of relations with Cuba—an extraordinary action. If it was not total incompetence—which in the case of the CIA cannot be excluded—it was a studied attempt to subvert national policy." Schelsinger suggests the most sinister explanation for such perfidy. Both he and Ambassador Attwood today believe it likely that, just as the President and his brother had feared, the exchanges between Washington and Havana had leaked.

Attwood had been instructed to maintain extreme secrecy over the whole matter. On the President's orders, only half a dozen senior officials of state had been in the know. The CIA, specifically, had not been told. With hindsight, though, there were two glaring security loopholes. The CIA had long penetrated the Cuban mission at the United Nations with anti-Castro agents. The National Security Agency intercepted calls to Havana, and U.S. intelligence agencies reaped the harvest of information.[97] From late October, and probably earlier, Attwood's intermediary, Lisa Howard, made a series of phone calls to Castro's closest confidant. In at least one of these she told Havana of the President's personal commitment to the Attwood efforts. Arthur Schlesinger says now, "I think the CIA must have known about this initiative. They must certainly have realized that Bill Attwood and the Cuban representative to the UN were doing more than exchanging daiquiri recipes when they met. They had all of the wires tapped at the Cuban delegation to the United Nations." Ambassador Attwood now realizes the telephone calls were insecure and is nagged by a sinister possibility. He says, "If the CIA did find out what we were doing this would have trickled down to the lower echelon of activists, and Cuban exiles and the more gung-ho CIA people who had been involved since the Bay of Pigs. If word of a possible normalization of relations with Cuba leaked to these people, I can understand why they would have reacted violently. This was the end of their dreams of returning to Cuba, and they might have been impelled to take violent action. Such as assassinating the President."

Arthur Schlesinger agrees. He told me, "Undoubtedly if word leaked of President Kennedy's efforts, that might have been exactly the kind of thing to trigger some explosion of fanatical violence. It seems to me as possibility not to be excluded."

Far away, and unbeknownst to those around President Kennedy, the prelude to tragedy had been unfolding. As the fateful month of November proceeded, the strange "Oswald" manifestations had taken their course in Dallas. Somebody using that still insignificant name had made himself notice—trying to pass a check, test-driving a car at high speed, receiving money orders, and applying for work in a high building. Those who encountered him would later remember those unmistakable references—the Marine background, the Navy ID, the talk about a visit to the Soviet Union. In logical order, "Oswald" was also making his most compromising appearances—buying ammunition, getting a telescopic sight fixed, and making a nuisance of himself at a rifle range. Through the strange appearances, too, ran the repeated association of "Oswald" with Cubans or "Latins." An unknown exile called Silvia Odio had by now written to her father about that frightening visit by two anti-Castro militants accompanied by an "Oswald" who thought the President "should have been assassinated."

In October, at a house in the Dallas suburb of Farmers Branch, the local John Birch Society hosted three venomously anti-Kennedy exiles. A member of the audience taped what was said and later provided the recording to a senior officer in the Dallas police. It remained a secret until 1978, when the policeman gave me a copy. On the tape a Bay of Pigs veteran called Nestor Castellanos reviles the President: "Get him out! Get him out! The quicker, the sooner the better. He's *doing all kinds of deals. . . .*

Mr. Kennedy is kissing Mr. Khrushchev. I wouldn't be surprised if he had kissed Castro, too. I wouldn't even call him *President* Kennedy. He stinks." (Author's italics.)

Castellanos had something else to say. He confided to this audience, "We are waiting for Kennedy the 22nd (November), buddy. We are going to see him, in one way or the other. We're going to give him the works when he gets in Dallas." There were no recorded demonstrations by anti-Castro exiles on the day of the assassination, nor is there evidence to link this speaker to the murder. The chilling timing aside, however, the speech reveals the passionate feelings against the President in anti-Castro circles.

Before going to Dallas, the President was due to visit Chicago, on November 2, and Miami, on the 18th. In Chicago, three days before the President was to arrive, the Secret Service learned of a potential threat to his life. After a brief surveillance operation, police arrested a former Marine with a history of mental illness. The man, Thomas Vallee, was found to be in possession of an M-1 rifle and three thousand rounds of ammunition. Vallee, who was a member of the John Birch Society an outspoken opponent of the Kennedy administration, had arranged to take time off from his job on the day of the President's visit.

According to the claims of former Secret Service agent, Abraham Bolden, Chicago Secret Service agents were also alerted to another threat—this one involving a four-man team armed with high-powered rifles. One of the men, according Bolden, had a Latin name. He says that two of the suspects were detained on the eve of the President's arrival and that two others eluded a surveillance operation. Although one other agent recalls a threat at that time. Congress' Assassinations Committee found nothing on the record on this threat.[98]. It noted, however, that President Kennedy's visit to Chicago—an important political event—was abruptly canceled when crowds were already gathering to greet him. It is unclear whether the cancellation was becasue of a crisis in Vietnam following the assassination of President Diem, because the President was feeling unwell, or because of a threat in Chicago. If there was no sensitive cause for the dramatic change of plan, it is surely odd that a Congressional committee cannot establish the reason today.

The Committee did establish, however, that information on the known Chicago threat was never passed on to the authorities preparing security for the President's visit to Texas. Meanwhile, the man involved, Thomas Vallee, was released.

On November 6, at the Dallas office of the FBI, the real Oswald left his note, the one that Bureau officials would see fit to destroy after the assassination. Elsewhere, there was another serious security alert.

On November 9, in Miami, the head of police intelligence sat listening intently to a fuzzy tape recording of a conversation between a known right-wing extremist and a trusted police informant. Later that day the tape was transcribed. It ran as follows:

> INFORMANT: I think Kennedy is coming here on the 18th, or something like that to make some kind of speech. . . .
>
> EXTREMIST: You can bet your bottom dollar he is going to have a lot to say about the Cubans. There are so many of them here.
>
> INFORMANT: Yeah. Well, he will have a thousand bodyguards, don't worry about that.
>
> EXTREMIST: The more bodyguards he has the easier it is to get him.
>
> INFORMANT: Well, how in the hell do you figure would be the best way to get him?
>
> EXTREMIST: From an office building with a high-powered rifle. . . . He knows he's a marked man. . . .
>
> INFORMANT: They are really going to try to kill him?
>
> EXTREMIST: Oh yeah, it is in the working. . . .
>
> INFORMANT: Boy, if that Kennedy gets shot, we have got to know where we are at. Because you know that will be a real shake if they do that.
>
> EXTREMIST: They wouldn't leave any stone unturned there, no way. They will pick somebody up within hours afterwards, if anything like that would happen. Just to throw the public off.

Captain Charles Sapp, head of Miami's Police Intelligence Bureau, and his team of a dozen specialized detectives had "done security" on President Kennedy twice before when he had visited

Miami. They worked closely with the local Secret Service and the FBI, providing back-up intelligence and support on the ground. Miami was a major security headache because of its teeming population of well over a hundred thousand Cuban exiles. It was Captain Sapp who, seven months earlier, had warned his chief of police of a growing danger from the anti-Castro movement. His information then was that, as a reaction to the President's crackdown on raids, "violence hitherto directed against Castro's Cuba would now be directed toward various governmental agencies in the United States." Now, listening to the taped conversation with the Miami extremist, Sapp feared there might be an attempt on the President's life when he arrived on his November 18 visit to Miami.

The extremist on the tape was Joseph Milteer, a wealthy agitator. He belonged to a galaxy of ultra-right-wing and racist groups, including the Congress Of Freedom, the White Citizens' Council of Atlanta, and the National States Rights Party. This last organization had close links with the anti-Castro movement. Apart from informing his chief of police, Captain Sapp made sure a warning went to the FBI and the Secret Service, noting especially Milteer's remark that the President's assassination was "in the working." The Secret Service did check on Milteer's whereabouts, but he was not even questioned, let alone arrested. The agents responsible for the President's safety in Miami were, however, briefed on the matter. While the Assassinations Committee found no reference in the documentary record, it has been reported that there was a last-minute change in the Miami program. Captain Sapp recalls that a planned motorcade was canceled—for fear of trouble from the anti-Castro movement. On arriving at Miami Airport late in the day, the President flew by helicopter to and from his speech-making at the Americana Hotel. As in the case of Chicago, the Secret Service failed to mentioned the Miami scare to the agents responsible for advance planning in Texas. Dallas was now four days away.

As the President flew home from Miami,[99] Ambassador Attwood was on his way to yet another tussle with the telephone in Lisa Howard's apartment. Still trying to nail down an acceptable formula for talks, the Ambassador and Vallejo had been thwarted by telephone delays and broken connections. At last, in the early morning hours of November 19, they did have a proper conversation. Although Attwood did not know it at the time, Vallejo was relaying Castro's immediate personal reactions; the Cuban leader was sitting beside him throughout the conversation. Clearly, Castro wanted to handle the whole matter personally; he was still insisting that the American representative should find a way to come to Cuba. Castro, after all, could not come to the United States. In accordance with American wishes, though, the Cubans would submit an agenda through their office at the United Nations. Castro given an assurance that Che Guevara, one of the hard-line Communists and an apostle of global revolution would not take part in the meeting. Attwood noted that the voice at the Cuban end of the telephone sounded "very eager" about the proposed talks. Within twenty-four hours Castro would finally meet with French journalist Jean Daniel. Since arriving in Havana, fresh from his White House talk with President Kennedy, he had waited in vain for an interview. Now, in a talk that lasted till dawn, Castro made Daniel repeat time and again what Kennedy had said about his personal approval of the revolution—and his criticism of Castro's foreign policies. Castro defended his role in the missile crisis and said he could not, for now, discuss the future of Cuba's links with the Soviet Union. Yet he did see hope for a breakthrough with the United States—in the person of President Kennedy.

Castro said of the President, "He still has the possibility of becoming, in the eye of history, the greatest President of the United States, the leader who may at last understand that there can be coexistence between capitalist and socialists, even in the Americas. He would then be an even greater President than Lincoln I know, for example, that for Khrushchev, Kennedy is a man you can talk with. Other leaders have assured me that to attain this goal, we must first await his re-election. Personally, I consider him responsible for everything, but I will say this: he has come to understand many things over the past few months; and what's more, in the last analysis, I'm convinced that anyone else would be worse." Then, with a grin, Castro added. "If you see him again, you can tell him that I'm willing to declare Goldwater my friend if that will guarantee Kennedy's re-election! . . .Since you are going to see Kennedy again, be an emissary of peace."

Early in the morning of November 19, still weary from his marathon telephone stint during the night. Ambassador Attwood placed a call from New York to the White House. He briefed McGeorge Bundy, the President's adviser on foreign affairs, on the latest contact with Castro. The President, as Robert Kennedy would later relate, had given "the go-ahead." Attwood was to go to Havana and "see what could be done to effect a normalization of relationship." Bundy told Attwood the President would want to brief him as soon as the Cubans came up with an agenda. Kennedy would not be leaving Washington, said Bundy, except for a brief visit to Texas.

Texas was Dallas, and the President came back in a coffin.

CHAPTER 22

The First Stone

Time's glory is to calm contending kings, To unmask falsehood, and bring truth to light.

—William Shakespeare

Four days after John Kennedy's funeral, President Lyndon Johnson brusquely summoned the Chief Justice of the United States to the White House. He told Earl Warren, in melodramatic terms, that it was his national duty to head the commission of inquiry into the murder of John Kennedy. If certain rumors were not stopped, said Johnson, they could lead the United States "into a war which could cost forty million lives." He was more specific than that. Johnson said, "If the public became aroused against Castro and Khrushchev, there might be war." Ten months later, the Warren Commission reported that no foreign government played any role in the assassination.

So far as Cuba was concerned, if public statements meant anything, this had been clear within hours. Havana's ambassador to the United Nations, the man who had been helping arrange a dialogue between Washington and Havana, said "Despite the antagonisms existing between the government of the United States and the Cuban revolution, we have received with profound displeasure the news of the tragic death of President Kennedy." In Cuba, the French journalist Jean Daniel had actually been with Castro when the news of the shooting came through. Castro, Daniel would later recall, was utterly shocked. Slumped in his chair, he said, *"Es una mala noticia"*—"This is bad news." He repeated that three times, and then—since the first bulletin had said only that the President was wounded—expressed hope that the President would recover and automatically be re-elected. When the death was confirmed Castro remarked, "Everything is changed. Everything is going to change. . . . The Cold War, relations with Russia, Latin America, Cuba, the Negro question . . . all will have to be rethought. I'll tell you one thing: at least Kennedy was an enemy to whom we had become accustomed. This is a serious matter, an extremely serious matter." Later, as the American radio station announced that the assassin was a member of Fair Play for Cuba and an admirer of Fidel Castro, the Cuban leader declared, "If they had had proof, they would have said he was an agent, an accomplice, a hired killer. In saying simply that he was an admirer, this is just to try and make an association in people's minds between the name of Castro and the emotion awakened by the assassination. This is a publicity method, a propaganda device. This is terrible. . . ." Then, as the radio began calling Oswald a "pro-Castro Marxist," Castro called off his engagements. The Cuban government was in fear of a swift revenge strike by the armed forces of the United States. No such thing happened, but Castro had been right about the reflex action of many in the United States. In Dallas, Assistant District Attorney Alexander talked of charging Oswald with murdering the President "as part of an international Communist conspiracy." Newspaper editorials spoke darkly of "The Enemy Without," and a Gallup Poll revealed that a large number of Americans thought Russia, Cuba, or "the Communists" were involved.

In 1967, when suspicions of a right-wing conspiracy began receiving serious attention for the first time, Chief Justice Earl Warren was alerted to an alarming story. The source, a Washington lawyer, reported that one of his clients had sensational information. It was that Fidel Castro, learning of the American plots against his own life, had retaliated by having President Kennedy murdered. In March 1967, the allegation came to the attention of President Johnson, and he ordered an FBI inquiry. Agents interviewed the lawyer, who said his client had learned from "feedback furnished by sources close to Castro" that the Cuban leader had "employed teams of individuals who were dispatched to the United States for the purpose of assassinating President Kennedy." The investigation failed to come up with hard facts or names, but

President Johnson was clearly impressed. He later confided to one newsman, "I will tell you something that will rock you. Kennedy was trying to get Castro, but Castro got him first."*

The lawyer's client who sparked off the new Castro rumor, unidentified publicly until 1976, was none other than John Roselli, the Mafia gangster who had helped the CIA in its plots to kill Castro. Congress' Assassinations Committee, noting that Roselli's revelations—which he revived several years later—corresponded with his own efforts to escape prosecution and avoid deportation, found it quite plausible that Roselli "manipulated public perception of the plots, then tried to get the CIA to intervene in his legal problems as the price for his agreeing to make no further disclosures." Whatever Roselli's precise purpose, the witch hunt he started proved durable.

In 1977, after hearing evidence from Roselli and others, the Senate Intelligence Committee devoted great attention to the possibility of Castro involvement. One of its members, Senator Robert Morgan, went so far as to say, "I believe that the circumstances in this case are so strong that they convince me beyond every reasonable doubt that the assassination of our President was an act of retaliation for what we had tried to do in eliminating Castro." For a career lawyer, Morgan was being rash. The only reason for believing Fidel Castro ever considered retaliation against President Kennedy is a statement he reportedly made two months before the assassination. On the night of September 7, 1963, Castro appeared at a Brazilian Embassy reception in Havana. There, to the chagrin of his hosts, he spent a long time giving a rare and lengthy interview to the Associated Press correspondent, Daniel Harker. According to Harker's subsequent report, which appeared in leading American newspapers, he excoriated President Kennedy in terms extreme even by Cuban propaganda standards. Castro called the President "a cretin . . . the Batista of his times . . . the most opportunistic American President of all time."

---

* Soon after the assassination President Johnson—prone, apparently, to theorizing about his predecessor's murder—reportedly expressed the view that Kennedy had been killed in retribution for the murder three weeks earlier of President Diem of South Vietnam. (Thomas Powers, *op. cit.*, p. 121).

He bitterly denounced recent exile raids and then said, according to Harker, "We are prepared to fight them and answer in kind. United States leaders should think that if they are aiding terrorist plans to eliminate Cuban leaders, they themselves will not be safe."

This, not surprisingly, has proved a great long-term embarrassment in Havana. As late as 1975 a CIA official, hinting darkly at links between Oswald and the Cubans, called it "an act of singular irresponsibility and under no circumstances excusable as retorsion [sic] for what the Cuban emigres were doing during the summer of 1963." Castro's remark has been widely interpreted as a threat against the President, especially in the light of its timing. On the very day Castro saw Harker, the CIA in Washington learned that Castro's colleague Rolando Cubela had discussed killing the Cuban leader with his CIA case officer. Was Cubela a double agent, faithfully reporting the CIA's machinations back to his master? And was Castro issuing a serious warning that he knew about the threats and would hit back?

In 1978, when I talked to Rolando Cubela in captivity, he argued passionately that he was not a double agent. Cubela pointed out that, after his arrest by Cuban intelligence in 1965, he did not reveal his involvement with the CIA in assassination plots. In a country where the regime seizes every opportunity to accuse the CIA, nothing of the sort came up at Cubela's trial. It emerged only in 1975, thanks to the revelations of the Senate Intelligence Committee. Most compelling of all is the fact that Cubela was given a harsh prison sentence—hardly a likely reward for a double agent with an ultimate loyalty to Castro. Yet the question remains—did Castro plot to assassinate Kennedy—with or without information from Cubela?

The Cuban leader has denied it repeatedly, most recently to Congress' Assassinations Committee. In 1978 he welcomed Committee members to Havana, and they later played a recording of his statements to a hushed public hearing. His voice booming around the caucus room, Castro was heard to say, "Who here could have planned something so delicate as the death of the United States President? That would have been insanity. From the ideological point of view it was insane. And from the political

point of view, it was tremendous insanity. . . . The leaders of the
Cuban revolution have never made that sort of madness." Castro
has told other interviewers that "our Marxist policy leaves no
room for liquidation of leaders of any social system through terrorist acts. . . . We were fighting against reactionary ideas, not
against men." On this, as an Assassinations Committee study
agrees, Castro is convincing. During Cuba's own revolution his
guerrillas did not even try to kill the hated Batista, and it is the
exiles, not Castro's regime, who to this day commit outrages on
United States territory. From the political point of view, too, a
Castro role in the assassination is nonsensical. If he planned to kill
Kennedy, Castro would hardly have been negotiating for normalization of relations on the very eve of the assassination; had this
merely been duplicity, the huge risk of American retaliation could
never have justified the negligible reward. In any case, as Castro
has himself said, any successor to President Kennedy was likely to
be even tougher toward Cuba.

As for the "threat" reported by Harker, Castro admits to the
interview but does not remember specifically what he said. He told
the House Assassinations Committee that he probably meant to
warn Washington that he knew of the plots against his own life and
that it was "a very bad precedent" which might "boomerang"
against its authors. He insists that he never intended his words to
be taken as a physical threat against individuals in the United
States. He has pointed out that such actions by Cuba would have
been suicidal in view of the power of the United States to hit back.
The most persuasive argument in Castro's favor, though, is one he
did not put forward himself. If Castro had really intended harm to
President Kennedy, he would hardly have announced it to the
press two months in advance.

As it turns out, there is room for some doubt about the way
Castro's remarks were reported. Many American newspapers did
not use the offending passage, and I came across an allegation that
Harker—himself a Latin despite the English-sounding name—left
Havana under a cloud. In 1978 Cuban officials I interviewed
claimed that during his stay in Havana, Harker had been reported
for using his journalistic privileges "to send information unrelated
to his work as a reporter." This should be taken with a sizable

pinch of salt—few honest reporters long avoid the wrath of regimes whose own press is fettered. Nevertheless, the Harker report should be reviewed carefully at least in the light of recent revelations about use of journalists by the CIA.* If the "threat" section of Harker's report was anything but factual reporting, the implications would be sinister indeed.

In 1978 the Assassinations Committee considered the possibility that Oswald, perhaps having read the Harker interview with Castro, convinced himself that he could become himself a revolutionary hero by killing the President. In fact, New Orleans, where Oswald was at the time, was one American city where the controversial passage was published. The Warren Commission, too, wondered whether Oswald had been influenced by the virtual torrent of polemic which Castro poured out against the United States and its President.

The theory failed to square with the consistent evidence of Oswald's attitude toward President Kennedy. In custody after the assassination, Oswald was specifically asked if he thought Cuba would be better off now that the President had been murdered. In the words of the police officer in charge of the case, he replied that "since the President was killed someone would take his place, perhaps Vice President Johnson, and that his views would probably be largely the same as those of President Kennedy." This hardly sounds like a man who had killed the President to change America's Cuba policy. Oswald's statements before the assassination, of course, carry more weight, but they leave the same impression. In the heat of the radio debate in New Orleans, Oswald was asked whether he agreed with remarks by Fidel Castro that President Kennedy was a "ruffian and a thief." Oswald did not agree and said merely that he thought the State Department and the CIA had made "monumental mistakes" in their actions toward Cuba. With hindsight, that attitude seems mild enough. Oswald was even more positive about President Kennedy when he talked

---

* There is no question, for example, about the later CIA associations of Hal Hendrix, the Miami-based reporter who—as we have seen—was bursting with information about Oswald so oddly early on the day of the assassination (pages 104–105).

to an officer of New Orleans' police intelligence unit after the fracas caused by one of his FPCC demonstrations. Lieutenant Francis Martello later said Oswald "seemed to favor President Kennedy" rather than the Soviet leader, Khrushchev. Martello said Oswald "in no way demonstrated any animosity or ill-feeling toward President Kennedy." On the contrary, "he showed in his manner of speaking that he liked the President. . . ." As we saw earlier, nobody has ever made the flimsiest allegation that the authentic Lee Oswald had anything but good to say about John Kennedy.

In the face of all this the Warren Commission did not try to make a serious case for Oswald killing the President as an expression of his loyalty to Fidel Castro. On the contrary, they pointed out that Oswald's "unhappy experience with the Cuban consul seems to have reduced his enthusiasm for the Castro regime and his desire to go to Cuba." As for the suspicion of an actual involvement on the part of the Castro regime, Congress' Assassinations Committee tried in 1979 to lay the question to rest once and for all. After exhaustive inquiry and two visits to both Havana and Mexico, it declared a formal finding that there was no evidence that the Cuban government had anything to do with the Kennedy assassination.

Today the allegations against Castro have an importance quite distinct from the redundant question of whether Havana actually had a hand in the murder. In several interviews Castro himself has pondered whether the accusations were an expression of something more sinister than American political paranoia. He wondered aloud, "What secrets surround the Kennedy assassination? . . . It is very intriguing that this man Oswald traveled to Mexico a few months prior to the assassination and applied for a permit at the Cuban Embassy to travel to Cuba. . . . You would have to have good doses of naïveté to think that he was the one who planned the trip to Cuba. . . . Now, imagine that by coincidence he had been granted this permit, that he had visited Cuba for a few days, then returned to the United States and killed Kennedy. That would have served as provocation. . . . Sometimes we ask ourselves if someone did not wish to involve Cuba in this. Because I am under the impression that Kennedy's assassination was organized by some reactionaries in the United States."

Obligatory anti-American verbiage aside, Castro may have been right. There are signs of a deliberate effort to paint a track of guilt leading straight to Havana. Identification of the painters may in turn point to the real culprits in the assassination.

At noon on November 25, the day after the real Oswald had been silenced forever, a young Nicaraguan calling himself Gilberto Alvarado walked into the American Embassy in Mexico City.[100] What he had to say was so important, he said, that he needed to see the ambassador himself. Soon he was pouring out a story that could be interpreted only one way. He claimed that in mid-September, during a visit to the Cuban consulate, he had eavesdropped on a conversation between Lee Oswald and two men. At first, he said, he saw "Oswald" talking alone on a patio in the company of a thin black man. They were then joined for a moment by a tall Cuban who passed money to the black man. He then heard the black man remark to "Oswald" in English, "I want to kill the man." "Oswald" replied, "You're not man enough—I can do it." His black companion then said in Spanish, "I can't go with you. I have a lot to do." "Oswald" replied, "The people are waiting for me back there." The black man, supposedly, then handed "Oswald" $6,500 in large-denomination notes, adding apologetically, "This isn't much." And so the meeting ended.

This story caused a major stir at the American Embassy and set the wires humming between Mexico City and Washington. From its surveillance coverage, CIA staff already knew that an "Oswald" had visited the Cuban consulate, so Alvarado's story seemed plausible. Above all, it had found an eager listener in Ambassador Thomas Mann, a hard-boiled career diplomat with strong feelings about the advance of world Communism. He had formally expressed suspicion of the Cubans within hours of the assassination and now encouraged his staff to treat Alvarado's tale with attention. They were duly shocked by the Nicaraguan's claim that before the assassination he had tried to warn the Embassy but that some official had told him to stop wasting the Embassy's time. Now, in the wake of the assassination, the CIA in Mexico gave Alvarado priority treatment. The story was flashed to Washington for the attention of the FBI, the State Department—and the White

House. It thus became one of the first pieces of "evidence" to sow the idea of Cuban conspiracy in the mind of President Johnson. Twenty-four hours later the CIA sent a further message, reporting information "from a sensitive and reliable source" which tended to confirm Alvarado's story. On the same day Ambassador Mann cabled the State Department expressing his opinion that Cuba had indeed had a hand in the assassination. As he was to explain in detail in a later message, "In reading Oswald's rather complete dossier . . . I did not get an impression of a man who would kill a person he had never met for a cause, without offers from the apparatus to which he apparently belonged, when there was nothing in it for him. I therefore had a feeling—subjective and unproven to be sure—that either in Mexico or the United States someone had given him an assignment and money." The ambassador dismissed the notion that the Russians would use Oswald, but he did point the finger firmly at Havana. Mann told Washington, "Castro is the kind of person who would avenge himself in this way. He is the Latin type of extremist who reacts viscerally rather than intellectually and apparently without much regard for risks. His whole life story shows this. And the unprofessional, almost lackadaisical way in which the money is alleged by Alvarado to have been passed to Oswald fits with the way Cubans would be expected to act if the Russians were not guiding them." The ambassador also drew Washington's attention to a familiar story—Daniel Harker's report of a Castro "threat." He wrote, "This supposition has been strengthened by my recollection of an AP story with a Havana dateline, attributing to Castro threats against United States officials in reprisal for alleged CIA-sponsored raids on the Cuban coast." On November 27 the Embassy's legal attaché relayed a press statement by a "former Cuban diplomat"—clearly a prominent exile—which went even further than the ambassador an took a major liberty with Harker's "threat" story. This alleged that Castro had "accused CIA and President Kennedy of planning an attempt against Castro and that Castro stated 'Let Kennedy and his brother Robert take care of themselves since they too can be the victims of an attempt which will cause their death.' " The messages from Mexico were fanning the flames of suspicion in Washington that Castro was behind the assassination.

Washington—to its credit—reacted to all this with extreme caution. Indeed, it responded in a way that upset and angered Ambassador Mann. An FBI supervisor, flown down to Mexico on November 27, went out of his way to play down any suggestion of conspiracy. He seemed much more concerned to impress on the ambassador what has been the FBI position ever since, that Oswald—and Oswald alone—killed the President. The State Department in Washington sent Ambassador Mann a telegram he has never forgotten. When I interviewed Mann in 1978 he was still irritated by what he called "an instruction from Washington to cease investigation." In fact, even as the ambassador fumed, it was becoming apparent that there was something very odd indeed about Alvarado's story.

Under questioning by the Mexican authorities, the young Nicaraguan at first admitted that he had made up his entire story. He said he had never seen Oswald anywhere and knew of no money changing hands at the Cuban Embassy. He had never tried to warn the American Embassy before the assassination. Then, when American officials showed continuing interest, Alvarado reverted to his old story, claiming that the Mexicans had pressured him into the retraction. He agreed to submit to a lie-detector test. The polygraph, however, indicated that Alvarado might be lying. Faced with that information, and with inconsistencies in his story, the Nicaraguan began to crumble. He now said he "must be mistaken," was no longer certain about the date of the incident, and now talked only of having seen "someone who looked like Oswald." In Washington, American authorities were to conclude that the man had simply concocted his story. In Mexico City, though, Ambassador Mann remained unpacified. He felt, and still feels, that Alvarado should have been flown to the United States for intensive questioning. In that the ambassador was right. The fact that the Nicaraguan was lying made him no less relevant to the inquiry into who killed John Kennedy. The nature of his story, and above all his background, strongly suggests that this was no spur-of-the-moment impulse to tie Castro to the assassination. First, there is the conspiratorial conversation Alvarado claimed to recall.

In the conspiratorial conversation Alvarado said he overheard, he claimed Oswald told his companion, "You're not man enough [to kill the man]. I can do it." This is almost a carbon copy of what Silvia Odio was told by her mysterious visitor "Leopoldo." He too confided that "Oswald" had said "We *Cubans don't have any guts*. He says we should have shot President Kennedy after the Bay of Pigs." The two accounts could have come from the same bad film script—but by what scriptwriter. The Americans concluded the Alvarado was a Nicaraguan intelligence agent—a fact he admitted. His cover story, to explain his presence at the Cuban Embassy, was that he had been sent to Mexico to try to get to Cuba on an infiltration mission. In response to American inquiries, the Nicaraguan secret service disowned Alvarado and denied sending him on any mission. They suggested, on the contrary, that he was a known Communist. This was a wholly implausible label for a man who was tying to implicate Communists in the Kennedy assassination, and the Americans did not believe it. They concluded that Alvarado was—just as he claimed—a Nicaraguan agent. Yet there, astonishingly, the matter was allowed to rest. Alvarado and his story were allowed to fade into obscurity, with no serious inquiry into the origins of his misinformation mission. The implications of the Nicaraguan connection are, in fact, familiar and potentially significant.

The then Nicaraguan dictator, Anastasio Somoza, was always an avid supporter of the anti-Castro movement—a natural role for Central America's version of Cuba's own former dictator Batista. In 1961 his country served as one of the main assembly points for the Bay of Pigs invasion, and the connection continued long afterward. Nicaragua remained open house for the CIA and its Cuban protégés—until after the Kennedy assassination. In particular, it played host and helper to Manuel Artime, the anti-Castro leader dubbed the CIA's "golden boy," who was to play a key role in plots to kill Castro using Rolando Cubela. At the time of the President's murder, Artime had two bases in Nicaragua, an armed force in the area of three hundred men, and a huge arsenal of equipment. Artime's best friend and close associate was Howard Hunt, the CIA propaganda expert and political officer who was one of the first to recommend Castro's assassination. (He is now, of course, internationally notorious for his role in the Watergate scandal.) According to the respected correspondent Tad Szulc, Hunt was serving in Mexico City at the time of Oswald's supposed visit to the Cuban Embassy. Hunt denies this. Szulc assured me in 1979 that he remains "fully satisfied of the credibility and accuracy" of his original allegation concerning Hunt.

The Alvarado story died hard in Mexico City. According to an FBI supervisor sent down from Washington, the CIA denied his repeated requests to see the Nicaraguan agent. The Alvarado case remained a live issue for some time and came to the personal attention of President Johnson at least three times. Even the Warren Commission was to find itself obliged to note what one member, Gerald Ford, has called "the strong personal feelings of the then U.S. Ambassador to Mexico . . . that Castro was somehow involved in a plot to assassinate President Kennedy. . . ." If the Alvarado story had been designed to cause a flap in high places, it succeeded. Even as that anti-Castro allegation lost its first head of steam, other rumors proliferated.

On December 2 a new Mexico City witness came up with a variation on the theme originated by Alvarado. Pedro Gutierrez, a credit investigator, wrote to President Johnson that he too had seen "Oswald" at the Cuban Embassy. Like Alvarado, he said he had seen a large wad of money passed to "Oswald." As in the Alvarado case, Gutierrez' story caused extensive investigation which led nowhere. Gutierrez, it turned out, was a zealous anti-Communist who had played a leading part in at least one major political clash while working in the Mexican prison service.

Within a day of the Gutierrez allegation, a "sensitive source" told the CIA that on the night of the assassination a Cubana Airlines flight had been delayed for hours at Mexico City Airport, awaiting a mysterious passenger. He finally arrived in a private aircraft and allegedly traveled to Havana hidden in the pilot's cabin. A check reveals that the Cuban aircraft actually left for Havana before the alleged arrival of the second plane. Congress' Assassinations Committee dismissed the whole thing.

Also in December another CIA "source" had caused a flap about the "suspicious" travels of a Cuban called Gilberto Lopez. Lopez crossed the Texas border to Mexico the day after the assassination and four days later flew to Havana. He was reportedly the only person on board that Cuban flight. The Assassinations Committee found that, although the matter had been inadequately investigated, Lopez had plausible personal reasons for his return to Cuba. This story was especially inflammatory because—like Oswald—Lopez was affiliated with the Fair Play for Cuba Committee. He had also, supposedly, stopped by at the Cuban Embassy in Mexico City. Well he might, if he was headed for Havana, but then the Cuban Embassy was under intensive propaganda fire.

Meanwhile, in the United States, rumors linking Oswald to Castro were propagated energetically by every sort of anti-Castro oddball. Many of these were simply the work of hopeful opportunists, but others—like the Mexico allegations—had the ring of calculated black propaganda.

What follows is an account an Assassinations Committee report cautiously called "allegations [which], although related to certain facts, cannot be substantiated. . . ." Late on the night of the assassination, goes the story, the telephone rang in the New York apartment of Henry Luce, the wealthy publisher and editor-in-chief of *Time* and *Life*. The call was for his wife, Clare Booth Luce, and was from a Cuban exile she knew well. Like other wealthy Americans, Mrs. Luce had long supported the anti-Castro movement and says she funded one of the motorboats used by exile commandos on their raids against Cuba. The man calling her now was one of her protégés, and he was calling from New Orleans. His story, says Mrs. Luce, was that he and two comrades had met Oswald during the summer and that he tried to infiltrate their Free Cuba cell. Oswald offered his services to help kill Castro, but the exiles had not trusted him. They eventually discovered he was a "Communist" and a member of Fair Play for Cuba. They took pictures of his street actions and made tape recordings of Oswald talking about Cuba within his "Communist cell." Mrs. Luce quotes her caller as saying Oswald made "several" trips to Mexico City and then suddenly had an ample supply of money. Then, she says, the voice from New Orleans launched into a familiar litany, saying Oswald had boasted he was "a crack marksman and could shoot anybody—including the President or the Secretary of the Navy." Finally, says Mrs. Luce, her caller told her, "There is a Cuban Communist assassination team at large, and Oswald was their hired gun."

Mrs. Luce, whom I interviewed in 1978, asserts that she instructed her caller to give his information to the FBI. She says she recontacted him in 1967, when serious allegations of an anti-Castro part in the assassination were being investigated in New Orleans. This time she was told by her Cuban exile contact that FBI agents in New Orleans had merely seized the "Oswald" tapes and pictures and told the exiles not to repeat their story. She says she later learned that one of the three-man team she sponsored had been murdered and a second deported. She also told me that the third, whom she reached through an intermediary, still fears for his life if he were to talk openly. In 1978, therefore, she said she declined to give the Cuban's name to the Assassinations Committee.

The Committee ran into a dead end when it tried to investigate Mrs. Luce's account. It found that Mrs. Luce had given some help to the DRE, the exile group represented in New Orleans by Carlos Bringuier, Oswald's opponent in the street fracas over Fair Play for Cuba. The Committee contacted Bringuier and several other DRE veterans, and all denied making the call to Mrs. Luce. Nevertheless, Mrs. Luce, a former diplomat and a distinguished public figure in her own right, insists she did receive the alarming telephone call. Her interpretation of events following the assassination—based, she says, on her own high-level contacts—is that President Johnson and top American officials "received sufficient information to make them strongly suspect a Castro involvement but decided to say nothing about it since even to raise the suspicion might have risked plunging us into a war against Cuba. . . . The mood of the country was such that this could easily have been the result." Whether or not Mrs. Luce is right about that, her story fits a well-used mold. Here, yet again, is the scenario of a Communist Oswald, bragging about his marksmanship and talking of killing the President and the Secretary of the Navy.* Shades of the Odio incident and the Mexico allegations.

---

* Governor of Texas John Connally, who was wounded in the fusillade which killed the President, had been Secretary of the Navy in 1961. When Oswald wrote to the Secretary asking for a reversal of his undesirable discharge, Fred Korth had become Secretary. Korth, as it happens, had been a lawyer in the divorce of Oswald's mother, Marguerite.

The most important and ominous detail in the Luce episode is the reference by her caller to Oswald's travel to Mexico City. Mrs. Luce is certain she received the call late on the night of the assassination; she remembers the phone ringing while she and her husband were watching television coverage of the tragedy. Yet Oswald's visit to Mexico did not become public knowledge until forty-eight hours *later*. On the night of November 22 Oswald's visit to Mexico was theoretically known only to Oswald himself, perhaps his wife Marina—and *American intelligence*. If the Luce call was another fable aimed at incriminating Castro's Cuba, as seems likely, this is a significant and incriminating giveaway. Mrs. Luce quotes her caller as saying he belonged to the Free Cuba group in New Orleans, which places him at the epicenter of the anti-Castro intrigue that swirled around Oswald in the late summer of 1963. The incident is suggestive of collaboration between the exile movement and an element of American intelligence. It joins the pattern of incidents that preceded and followed the assassination, a mosaic of disinformation that was never properly investigated.

In 1963, this came closest to exposure in Miami, the main base for the CIA-backed exile movement. There, it appears, the false trail was being laid *before* President Kennedy was killed.

After the assassination an employee of Parrot Jungle, a bird sanctuary, reported a conversation she had had three weeks earlier with a Cuban customer. He had told her the old tale—about an American acquaintance called Lee who was a former serviceman, a Marxist, spoke Russian, and was in Texas or Mexico. "Lee" was, as usual, a brilliant marksman, and there was talk of President Kennedy and "shooting between the eyes." Weeks later the Cuban was identified as an exile called Jorge Martinez, who had been brought to the United States by Mike McLaney, one of the old Havana gambling bosses. The McLaney family has appeared in these pages before. It was William McLaney, Mike's brother, who controlled the property near New Orleans where, in July 1963, federal agents seized a large ammunition dump. This and a nearby training camp were being maintained in defiance of Presidential policy. It is that camp that Oswald allegedly attended in the company of David Ferrie. The FBI did not catch up with Mike McLaney's friend Martinez until months after the assassination;

predictably, he denied spreading the tale about the Marxist "Lee" who was a crack shot. Another Miami fiction was harder to deny and impossible for the authorities to ignore.

On November 26, while in Mexico the Nicaraguan was spinning his fable about Oswald and the Cubans, a Florida newspaper splashed a major story. This alleged that Oswald had been in Miami in November 1962 and credited him with doing exactly as he had supposedly done in New Orleans. Oswald, said the report, had contacted "Miami-based supporters of Fidel Castro," had tried to infiltrate an anti-Castro group, had passed out his Fair Play for Cuba leaflets, and had got into a fight with anti-Castro militants. On top of that, "Oswald had telephone conversations with the Cuban government G-2 Intelligence Service. . . ." Faced with this sort of publicity, the Miami FBI at once tried to discover its origin. That proved a frustrating task. The article had named Frank Sturgis, a leading member of the International Anti-Communist Brigade, the group "Oswald" had allegedly tried to infiltrate. Sturgis would one day become infamous as one of the Watergate burglars, operating under the orders of that familiar figure, Howard Hunt. During the Watergate scandal, in a memorandum to the White House, the Director of the FBI quoted sources as saying that Sturgis was "now associated with organized crime activities . . ." Back in 1959, before Castro closed the mob's gambling activities, Sturgis had acted as a government overseer at the Tropicana, then managed by Lewis McWillie, a close friend of Oswald's executioner, Jack Ruby. After leaving Cuba, Sturgis took part in dozens of CIA-backed anti-Castro operations and was in trouble shortly before the assassination for flouting Kennedy's ban on raids. Questioned repeatedly about the Miami article on Oswald, Sturgis denied any connection with it. This was flatly contradicted by the author of the article, James Buchanan, who said it was Sturgis who gave him the story about Oswald having had contacts with Castro's intelligence service. By this time the FBI had also tracked down Buchanan's brother, Jerry, who—like Sturgis—had been detained because of Kennedy's clamp-down on exile activities. He maintained that there had indeed been a fight with Fair Play for Cuba supporters and that Oswald had been present. The Miami FBI soon concluded there was not a scrap of real evidence that there had ever been any FPCC demonstration or any scuffle, let alone one in which Oswald participated.[101] Yet—and this is almost the end of this particular labyrinth—they had received information about it from another source, one John Martino. His involvement has significant implications and—in the end—a disturbing sequel.

John Martino was a Mafia figure, of Italian origin, who worked for the mob in Havana's casinos before the revolution. Shortly before the Castro takeover he was staying at the Deauville Hotel, then operated by Santos Trafficante, and had planned to open a brothel nearby. An FBI report written before the assassination described him as a "close friend" of Santos Trafficante. Martino quickly joined the struggle to topple the new Cuban regime, but his initial role was short-lived. Martino was arrested for entering Cuba illegally, and was incarcerated in one of Castro's jails. There he languished until late 1962, when he was released with a batch of Bay of Pigs prisoners. In the United States he gained brief publicity with a book about his experiences, called *I Was Castro's Prisoner*. Martino quickly plunged back into the clandestine war against Cuba, and in spring of 1963 he played a leading role in one of the strangest episodes of the entire shambolic campaign. He joined an operation which, like "Maurice Bishop's" raids against Soviet shipping, was designed to scuttle President Kennedy's understanding with the Soviet Union. This was the "Bayo-Pawley Affair," a madcap mission that remained secret until 1976.

In the spring of 1963, an exile leader called Eduardo "Bayo" Perez began spreading word that the Russians still had missiles in Cuba, in direct violation of President Kennedy's agreement with Khrushchev. That is a theory still propagated by diehard exiles and such worthies as Howard Hunt, the CIA's former Cuban expert. In 1963 it was widely believed; if it could have been proved it would have dealt a crippling blow to Kennedy's prestige and provoked a new crisis. Bayo claimed to have the proof. He said his guerrilla contacts in Cuba were holding two Soviet army colonels who had defected. If they could be brought to the United States, he said, they would tell all about the missiles. It all sounds outlandish, and it was. Bayo was a renegade to even the most extreme exile groups, and he found little support from even the leaders of

Alpha 66 and its offshoot "Commandos L," themselves working actively to stir up trouble. He found powerful support, however, through the good offices of his Mafia contact, John Martino. In Miami, Martino helped forge a strange alliance of the CIA, *Life* magazine, and a former American diplomat called William Pawley. *Life*, which was nominally in on the deal for the scoop value, had itself been running shrill editorials about the continuing reports of missiles in Cuba. William Pawley was a hugely wealthy adventurer with an extraordinary career behind him. After founding the Flying Tigers in Asia during the Second World War, he had held ambassadorial posts in Latin America and had achieved high office in the Defense and State departments. A staunch Republican conservative and a friend of CIA Director Allen Dulles, he had a hand in the CIA's overthrow of the Communist-orientated government in Guatemala. Pawley had a special interest in Cuba, where he had once owned an airline and the Havana bus system. He struggled hard and long to keep Batista in power and then pressured President Eisenhower to give American support to the first anti-Castro exiles.* Now, in the summer of 1963, Pawley lent his prestige and his practical help to "proving" that the Russians had kept missiles in Cuba. On June 7 a CIA plane and Pawley's own launch combined to ferry a band of exile guerrillas to a landing point on the coast of Cuba. John Martino organized the exiles, who set off for the shore in small boats under cover of darkness. Pawley, along with three CIA agents, a *Life* photographer, and John Martino, waited for the raiders to return with their prize—the two Russian defectors. They never did come back. After a prolonged search by the CIA aircraft, it was assumed they had been either killed or captured. The latest and most misguided effort to provoke trouble between Washington and Moscow had failed miserably. If this operation had been intended merely to

---

* It was Pawley who had persuaded Clare Boothe Luce to finance anti-Castro guerrilla operations (see p. 420). As wife of the chairman of Time Inc., Luce was influential. *Life Magazine*, then part of the Time empire reportedly cooperated with the CIA in many instances—notably is inflating the importance of anti-Castro groups like Alpha 66, at the center of the allegations linking CIA officer "Maurice Bishop" to alleged assassin Oswald.

make tendentious publicity, it failed in that too. Without their Russian colonels, *Life* dropped the story altogether. The key organizer, John Martino, was unabashed. He quickly resumed his shadowy role in the anti-Castro movement.

Although little is known about Martino's involvement in the weeks leading up to the assassination, he did make one intriguing appearance. In September he turned up in Dallas to address an anti-Castro meeting. While there he mentioned that he knew Amador Odio, a wealthy Cuban then imprisoned by Castro, and that he knew one of Odio's daughters was living in exile in Dallas. This of course was Silvia Odio, the witness whose meeting with "Oswald" remains the firmest evidence of a deliberate attempt to frame the alleged assassin. Like Martino, the Cuban who brought "Oswald" to her house professed detailed knowledge of the senior Odio's activities. Martino's next known appearance was after the assassination, spreading false information about Oswald in Miami.

So far as the FBI investigation could determine, Martino was a prime source, and very probably the originator, of the story that Oswald had fought with anti-Castro supporters in Miami. In one interview he claimed to have received a personal tip-off about Castro' alleged threat against President Kennedy—as reported in the Cuban leader's interview with Associated Press correspondent Daniel Harker. Martino also claimed that Oswald had been paid by Fidel Castro to kill the President. Pressed by the FBI to reveal his source, Martino named him as Oscar Ortiz, a member of an anti-Castro group "too sensitive to name." He said "Ortiz" was "known in Washington, D.C., and could even be a double agent." The FBI could locate no "Ortiz," and there the matter ended— almost.

In the years after the assassination, Martino flourished as a businessman in Miami. The nature of his business, however, was never wholly clear. At the time of his questioning by federal agents Martino described his occupation as "manufacturer of electronics products in Miami."* By the Seventies he was selling, among other things, bullet proof vests and traveling frequently in Latin

---

* The CIA used a bogus electronics company. "Zenith Technological Services," as the front for its anti-Castro operations center in Miami.

America. Martino's business led to a long association with a Texas businessman, Fred Claasen, and ultimately to a remarkable conversation. Martino told Claasen he had been a CIA contract agent and in 1975, during one of his daily telephone calls, confided that he had personal knowledge of the conspiracy behind the Kennedy assassination. It was then that, as reported in the part of this book dealing with the shooting of Officer Tippit (Chapter 6), Martino told Claasen:

> The anti-Castro people put Oswald together. Oswald didn't know who he was working for—he was just ignorant of who was really putting him together. Oswald was to meet his contact at the Texas Theater [the movie house where Oswald was arrested]. They were to meet Oswald in the theater, and get him out of the country, then eliminate him. Oswald made a mistake. . . . There was no way we could get to him. They had Ruby kill him.

That startling fragment is all that survives. John Martino died soon after talking to Claasen. According to his widow, "the Company* or the government" picked up his body to establish the cause of death, which was determined to have been a heart attack. In 1978 Claasen gave his information to a Texas journalist and contacted Congress' Assassinations Committee. He has now left his former business, and Committee staff were frustrated in their attempts to interview him. It is not possible to say whether Martino was referring to matters he knew of at first hand. In 1978, when a Congressional investigator searched his private papers, they showed he did have links to known figures in both intelligence and organized crime. Most ominous among these connections is the FBI's report of Martino's close friendship with Santos Trafficante. In terms of his dubious associations, Martino had all the right qualifications. There is no doubt that, in the wake of the assassination, he played a leading part in a disinformation campaign to blame the President's murder on Castro's Cuba. That campaign,

---

* Jargon for the CIA.

against the background of the mysterious events before the crime, was surely no accident.

In 1978 I interviewed the son of the late Mario Kohly, extreme right-wing Cuban leader and self-styled President-in-exile, who by 1963 had long since broken with the mainstream exile movement. Kohly too was bitterly opposed to President Kennedy and convinced that Soviet missiles were still in Cuba. The younger Kohly recalled opening a bottle of champagne at the news of President Kennedy's death and then calling his father. According to Kohly, "My father seemed elated and quite relieved; he seemed more pleased, I would say, than surprised. I am sure he had knowledge of what really happened in Dealey Plaza. But, if you recall, everyone that has had knowledge ended up dead." When I asked Kohly who he believed killed Kennedy, he said he would rather not comment. "Let's just say it is very possible the assassination was done by the anti-Castro movement in the hopes of making it look like Castro had done it. If they could blame the assassination of President Kennedy on Fidel Castro and arouse enough indignation among the American people, this would have helped the movement to get the support we needed to regain our country. In other words, they either would have supported a new invasion against Castro or might have invaded Cuba themselves. We wanted the first alternative—we wanted to do it ourselves."

It never happened, of course. As the months went by it became apparent that the American Government had written off Cuba. Yet, even as the exiles were consigned to the political trash can, so too were President Kennedy's hopes of reaching an understanding with Fidel Castro. Three days after the assassination Ambassador Attwood received formal confirmation that Havana wished to proceed with talks. President Johnson was briefed on what had been happening and wanted none of it. Already he had reversed Kennedy's policy of disengagement from Vietnam, and—with an election coming up—he had no intention of appearing "soft" on anything, least of all Cuba. Today Ambassador Attwood reflects sadly, "The word came back that this was to be put on ice for the time being, and the time being has been ever since. . . ."

The Kennedy era was over, its promise vanishing into mythology as surely as the flame on the President's grave flickered and vanished on the wind. With Lee Oswald dead, the Warren Commission glossed over the inconsistencies of the case—the Odio incident and the string of false "Oswalds," the odd scenario in Mexico City. No scientists were assigned to analyse the tell-tale sound recording—the hard evidence that would one day establish that there had been at least two gunmen at work in Dealey Plaza. Late in the inquiry, faced with the imponderables of the Odio evidence, Chief Counsel Rankin spoke volumes when he said irritably, "We are supposed to be closing doors, not opening them."

Behind one of the doors stood the surviving principal in the case, Jack Ruby. That door, too, was better left closed.

CHAPTER 23

The Good Ole Boy

The pattern of contacts did show that individuals who had the motive to kill the President also had knowledge of a man who could be used to get access to Oswald in the custody of the Dallas police.

—Congress' Assassinations Committee Report, 1979

Seven months after the assassination, in a nondescript room at Dallas County Jail, the Chief Justice of the United States presided over a vital interrogation. Earl Warren, accompanied by Congressman Gerald Ford and a pack of lawyers, was going through the motions of questioning Jack Ruby.[102] The man who had so effectively silenced Lee Oswald sat shifting uneasily, chewing nervously at his lower lip, and occasionally drying up altogether. If he was afraid the Warren Commission would prove hard to handle, Ruby worried unnecessarily. The interrogators listened with equanimity to the well-rehearsed story of why he murdered the accused assassin. Ruby testified: "No one . . . requested me to do anything. I never spoke to anyone about attempting to do anything. . . . No underworld person made any effort to contact me. It all happened that Sunday morning. . . . The last thing I read was that Mrs. Kennedy may have to come back to Dallas for a trial for Lee Harvey Oswald and I don't know what bug got hold of me. . . . Suddenly the feeling, the emotional feeling came within me that someone owed this debt to our beloved President to save her the ordeal of coming back. I had the gun in my right hip pocket, and impulsively, if that is the correct word here, I saw him [Oswald] and that is all I can say. . . . I think I used the words, 'You killed my President, you rat.' The next thing I was down on the floor."

Ruby had presented himself as the misguided exponent of his own brand of schmaltzy patriotism, and the Warren Commission saw no need to probe further. The Ruby questioning was just one ineffectual scene in an inquiry that had been doomed for weeks. A month earlier the two lawyers charged with the Ruby investigation, Leon Hubert and Burt Griffin, had fired off a long memorandum to Chief Counsel Rankin. It laid out, in precise detail, areas they felt had been inadequately investigated; they emphasized that the Commission had yet to disprove that "Ruby killed Oswald at the suggestion of others." The lawyers got little thanks for their concern. Their recommendations were followed up in a half-hearted sort of way, but—as Griffin puts it today—"They were in a different ball game than we were. They thought ours was psychotic. They really thought that ours was crazy and that we were incompetent." Eventually Hubert resigned—but on the understanding that he would be present at the forthcoming interview with Ruby. That promise was not kept. Warren, Ford, and Rankin departed for Dallas without informing Hubert. The Commission's own specialists on Ruby, the two men most qualified for the job, were excluded from questioning the man who perhaps held the key to vital unsolved areas of the assassination.

The Commission members who did talk to Ruby found it a tedious chore. Apart from parroting his story about shooting Oswald to save Jackie Kennedy the trauma of attending a trial, Ruby rambled on for hours. He went on and on, often irrelevantly, about his activities before the murder; and he seemed to show signs of mental disturbance, prattling about his own Jewish origins and how the Jews would be killed in vast numbers because of what he had done. Ruby seemed tense and frightened, so much so that Chief Justice Warren apparently dismissed him as a psychiatric case. That was insufficient justification for what happened before the interview ended.

Ruby had been doodling on a notepad. Suddenly he threw it down and cried, "Gentlemen, unless you get me to Washington, you can't get a fair shake out of me. . . . Unless you get me to Washington, and I am not a crackpot, I have all my senses—I don't want to avoid any crime I am guilty of." Repeatedly, eight times in all, Oswald's murderer begged the Chief Justice of the

United States to arrange his transfer to Washington for further questioning and lie-detector tests. Warren, who could easily have arranged such a move, told Ruby it could not be done. He was unimpressed when Ruby insisted, "Gentlemen, my life is in danger here." That must have seemed further confirmation of paranoia. Ruby stayed in Dallas, and the eminent inquisitors traipsed back to Washington. In the Warren Report, issued a few months later, they would discuss Ruby as merely "moody and unstable," one lone nut who killed another. The Warren Commission said Ruby's background and activities "yielded no evidence that Ruby conspired with anyone in planning or executing the killing of Lee Harvey Oswald."

Fifteen years later, even with Ruby long dead and beyond further questioning, Congress' Assassinations Committee replaced the Commission's certainty with a positive cobweb of suspicion. Along with its finding that the evidence in the assassination pointed to conspiracy, the Committee portrayed in awesome panorama a Ruby who had for years been involved with the people most motivated to kill the President. They found that vital aspects of the case had been glossed over in the original inquiry and that Ruby probably received "assistance" in gaining access to the jail basement where he shot Oswald. This last point was a diplomatic way of pointing to complicity on the part of somebody in the Dallas police force. It may be that Jack Ruby had reason to fear talking openly so long as he stayed in Texas. Yet the most startling revelations about Oswald's killer concern his involvement with organized crime and with Cuba. The original inquiry declared there was "no significant link between Ruby and organized crime" and dismissed what it called "rumors linking Ruby with pro- or anti-Castro activities." Given the material they possessed even then, it is difficult to believe that the authors of the Warren Report expected to be taken seriously. Ruby's life story is the dossier of a sort of gangsters' groupie—an acolyte on the petty fringe of organized crime. It started in Chicago.

Jacob Rubenstein—for that was Ruby's original name—came into the world in 1911, the fifth of eight children born to Polish immigrants. His childhood was made miserable by constant feuding between a drunkard father and an illiterate, slightly crazed mother. All eight offspring ended up in foster homes. Jacob regularly missed school and never made it past the eighth grade. By the age of sixteen he was "Sparky" to his pals, a tough street-smart kid roaming Chicago's West Side. There he became one of a group of boys who earned an occasional dollar by running errands. Thus, early on, Ruby earned dubious distinction. The errands were for a boss whose name is synonymous with violent crime—Al Capone. Jacob could not take to regular work, and his early record was an apprenticeship in petty crime—ticket scalper, race-track tip-sheet vendor, illicit dealer in contraband music sheets, and nightclub bouncer. In the course of it all he had a few minor brushes with the law and earned the reputation for senseless violence which would stay with him all his life. Then, in 1937, he did take a real job of sorts—as what he later liked to call "union organizer" and "secretary" for a local branch of the Scrap Iron and Junk Handlers Union. For Ruby it was a debut in a special sort of criminal milieu. The union leadership was taken over by stooges for Chicago's leading racketeers, and Ruby became a "bagman" for the new president, John Martin. According to one report, Ruby once pulled a gun while trying to recruit members in a scrap-paper plant. Then, in 1939, Ruby gained notoriety for the first time—in connection with a shooting. His union boss, Martin, shot down his predecessor, and Ruby was pulled in for questioning. There is no evidence that he personally played any part in the murder, but it was a milestone. After the killing the union was taken over by one Paul Dorfman. Years later, it would be Robert Kennedy who wrote that Dorfman "was a big operator—a major operator in the Chicago underworld . . . closely linked with such underworld figures as Tony Accardo, who became head of the Chicago syndicate after the death of Al Capone." Dorfman, as Kennedy also pointed out, was to become a key ally and henchman of Jimmy Hoffa, the Teamsters Union leader reported to have threatened the lives of both Kennedy brothers. At twenty-eight, Ruby was working in the shadow of some of the worst criminals in Chicago. Years later the Warren Commission would accept his claim to have "left the union when I found out the notorious organization had moved in there." In fact, Ruby stayed on for some time under the new regime. The Warren Commission ignored, too, an FBI interview with a Chicago crime figure who recalled that Ruby "was accepted and to a certain extent his business operations controlled by the syndicate." After an uneventful wartime spell in the U.S. Air Force, followed by an abortive business venture with his brothers, Ruby left Chicago for Dallas and the nightclub business. According to him the move was at the direction of his mob associates.

In 1978 I talked to Giles Miller, a Dallas businessman who knew Ruby well. He recalled, "Jack Ruby would sit at the table where I was seated and discuss how he was sent down here by 'them'—he always referred to 'them'—meaning the syndicate in Chicago. He always complained that if he had to be exiled, why couldn't he have been exiled to California or to Florida? Why to this hellhole Dallas? I heard him say it many times." Ruby reportedly said much the same thing on a more formal basis, in statements to the staff of the Kefauver Committee, the 1950 Senate inquiry into organized crime. According to a former staff lawyer on the Committee, Luis Kutner, the staff learned that Ruby was "a syndicate lieutenant who had been sent to Dallas to serve as a liaison for Chicago mobsters." Ruby, of course, liked to inflate his own importance. Yet his name has been associated with a major Mafia effort to extend its power in Dallas. It occurred just after Ruby settled in the city.

In 1946 an emissary of the Chicago mob, Paul Jones, tried to make a deal with the Dallas district attorney and the sheriff.[103] He promised them a thousand dollars a week each, or a major share in the profits, if they would permit the syndicate to operate in Dallas under "complete protection." As part of the scheme, the mob planned to open a flashy restaurant and nightclub as a front for a gambling operation. Sadly for the gangsters, however, this attempt to suborn public officials failed. Jones, the advance man for the underworld, had walked into a police trap. The conversations had been tape-recorded, and Jones ended up facing bribery charges. Years later, when Ruby shot Oswald, former Sheriff Steve Guthrie came forward to say that the man named by Jones to run the proposed front operation had been—Jack Ruby. The Warren Commission failed to talk to Guthrie and relied instead on the policeman who made the recordings of the conversations with Jones, Lieutenant George Butler. Butler, who had at first also been reported as saying Ruby was involved in the bribery attempt, eventually said he did not recall it. Ruby's name did not come up on any of the surviving recordings; yet two of the recordings of Jones' meeting with Sheriff Guthrie were missing—a fact that the Warren Commission learned but failed to pursue adequately. Lieutenant Butler, it turns out, was years later involved in the basement security operation just before Ruby shot Oswald.

Paul Jones, the Mafia envoy to Dallas, was in sporadic contact with Ruby and his family from the late Forties on—right up to November 1963. The names of Ruby or his immediate relatives cropped up twice in investigations on Jones—in connection with narcotics smuggling and with a bootleg whisky operation. When Ruby opened his first Dallas club, the Silver Spur, Jones and his cohorts became regulars in the bar. Years later Jones would admit that he had been introduced to Ruby in Chicago by syndicate contacts. They gave him assurances that their friend Jack was "all right" so far as the mob was concerned. The contacts in question, "Needle-nose" Labriola and Jimmy Weinberg, were later eliminated in a particularly barbaric gangland killing. They had been close associates of the man who then ran organized crime in Chicago, Sam Giancana. Giancana, of course, played a prominent role in the CIA-Mafia plots to kill Fidel Castro. First a link to Hoffa's Teamsters cronies, now to Giancana henchmen; Ruby's connections, with organized-crime figures prominent in the Kennedy assassination inquiry today, went back a long way.

As the years went by Ruby continued to make a sort of career for himself as proprietor of a series of shady night spots. He did not get rich; indeed he regularly plunged deeply into debt. The clubs gained notoriety for after-hours drinking and violent brawling. Yet, from his own twisted viewpoint, these were the very episodes that made Ruby feel he was a man to reckon with. He welcomed the slightest excuse for fisting his way out of trouble. He beat up those who crossed him; yet none of Ruby's outrages earned him severe retribution, not least because he had assiduously cultivated members of the Dallas police department. After the assassination Ruby's police pals would deny it in droves, but research leaves no doubt that, as a nightclub owner, Ruby dispensed favors to the police and received them in return. In the

Fifties Ruby was arrested twice for carrying a concealed gun, three times for offenses against the licensing laws, once for assault, and once for traffic violations. The only offense he was penalized for was the traffic summons. Some FBI documents quote Dallas underworld sources as claiming Ruby was "the pay-off man for the Dallas Police Department," a man who "had the fix with the county authorities." Meanwhile, while based in Dallas, Ruby apparently played more dangerous games further afield.

In 1965 Ruby was named by an FBI informant as the man who "gave the okay to operate" in part of a major drug-smuggling scheme. From now on, too, his name was linked with activities the Warren Commission preferred to sidestep. Enter Ruby the Cuban gunrunner and Ruby the wheeler-dealer, reportedly trying to extricate prisoners from Castro's Cuba. Reports about Ruby's Cuba connection linked him—although the CIA did not mention it to the Warren Commission—with a minor Agency operative and with Mafia leader Santos Trafficante. Ruby's apparent connections led to the very core of the most enduring suspicions as to who really killed Kennedy. Yet some were withheld from the Warren Commission by the CIA and the FBI. The rest were ignored or given minimal weight in the official Report. These were indefensible omissions.

So far as can now be established, Jack Ruby's interest in Cuba began six years before the assassination. According to a former associate, James Beard, Ruby stored guns and ammunition at a house on the southern Texas coast, prior to ferrying the equipment into Cuba. Beard says he "personally saw many boxes of new guns, including automatic rifles and handguns," loaded aboard a military-surplus boat. He claimed that "each time the boat left with guns and ammunition, Jack Ruby was on it." The shipments, said Beard, were destined for the followers of Fidel Castro, then still fighting Batista. In the years before the revolution, Castro was indeed supplied and supported from the United States, not least by the leaders of organized crime. The Mafia hoped thus to insure future good relations with a victorious Castro. In view of Ruby's criminal connections, the allegations of gunrunning activity are not implausible. There were several other such reports.[104]

One informant told the FBI that Ruby was "active in arranging illegal flights of weapons from Miami to Castro forces in Cuba," and this report suggests a potentially significant connection. The informant named the pilot in the operation as Eddie Browder. Browder, a Florida arms dealer, was engaged in gun smuggling with a Havana mobster called Norman "Roughhouse" Rothman. Rothman, in turn, was one of Santos Trafficante's close associates. He managed the Mafia boss's Sans Souci Casino and controlled the slot machines at the Tropicana. Other evidence suggests that a year later, after Castro came to power in Cuba, Ruby was not only still engaged in nefarious Cuban activities but may have been in direct contact with Santos Trafficante.

In 1959, probably in late spring, Ruby apparently got in touch with convicted Texas gunrunner Robert McKeown, who had previously ferried munitions to Castro.[105] McKeown, whom I interviewed, quotes Ruby as saying he was "in with the Mafia and had a whole lot of jeeps he wanted to get to Castro." According to McKeown, who becomes extremely nervous when discussing this area, one of the Mafia contacts was Santos Trafficante. Ruby also told McKeown, without naming names, that he "wanted to talk about getting some people out of Cuba" on behalf of "a man in Las Vegas." He offered McKeown a large sum of money for a letter of introduction to Castro, a letter he hoped would help secure the release of unnamed friends detained in Havana. Although Ruby never followed through on the offer of money, he did make unexplained visits to Cuba that year. In 1963 Ruby avoided telling the truth about why he went to Cuba or how often, a lapse that can only be explained rationally in terms of the connections which risked exposure. At this point in Ruby's story there looms a suspected direct association with Santos Trafficante, the Mafia chieftain who would later be reported as prophesying that the President was "going to be hit."

After the assassination, when it emerged that Ruby had been in Havana in 1959, he said he had merely been there on an eight-day August vacation at the invitation of a man called McWillie.[106] That name, and its associations, should have alerted the early investigators. Ruby considered Lewis McWillie, who had run gambling establishments in Texas, one of his closest friends. By 1959 he was in Havana as manager of the Tropicana nightclub, then owned by Norman Rothman, the Trafficante associate whose name has already come up in connection with alleged Ruby gun-running. According to a contemporary FBI report, Ruby's good friend McWillie had "consolidated his syndicate connections through his associations in Havana, Cuba, with Santos Trafficante, well-known syndicate member. . . ." Like Ruby, McWillie has spoken of only one Ruby visit to Cuba, a trip organized and paid for by McWillie in an effort to drum up publicity for the Tropicana through one of Ruby's friends in the press. McWillie says Ruby stayed for about a week, that he made himself rather a nuisance, and that he saw him off at the airport when he left. Ruby himself mentioned only one visit, giving the impression that he had rather a dull time, much of it spent hanging around the gambling tables waiting for his friend McWillie. Other information, however, suggests more than one visit and activities which fit not at all with the old tale about a freeloading summer holiday in the Caribbean.

In May 1959 a woman called Elaine Mynier, a mutual friend of both Ruby and McWillie, traveled alone to Cuba. As she was boarding her flight at Dallas, Ruby asked her to "tell McWillie 'Sparky' from Chicago is coming." He also gave her "five letters and numbers which was a coded message." In Havana, Mynier dutifully passed on the message to McWillie. He supposedly reacted dismissively, saying of Ruby, "He's nuts." Today McWillie denies Mynier was used as any sort of courier and claims he and Ruby would have spoken on the telephone had there been anything to discuss. Contradictorily, though, McWillie also says he would not have called Ruby on a sensitive matter because "every call was monitored in Havana. . . ." Whatever the truth about the Mynier message, the written record demolishes the story Ruby and McWillie told about Ruby making a single trip to Cuba that summer, a vacation lasting just a few days.

Cuban airport files show that Ruby arrived in Havana on August 8, 1959, flying in by Delta Airlines from New Orleans. A New Orleans ticket agent, who knew Ruby from previous flights, recalled him leaving for Cuba that summer. Far from staying in Havana for just a few days, the evidence is that Ruby was in Cuba a full month after his initial arrival. Three witnesses—two attorneys and an architect—later remembered meeting Ruby at the

Tropicana Casino during Labor Day weekend, in the first week of September. Their testimony is corroborated by a postcard Ruby sent on September 8 from Havana to a female friend in Dallas, mentioning in passing that "Mac"—almost certainly McWillie— "says hello." A Cuban exit card shows that Ruby flew out of Havana three days later, on September 11. His travels, however, were not over.

American and Cuban documents show that within twenty-four hours of leaving Cuba, Ruby flew back to Havana from Miami. They show, too, that he stayed for only one night before leaving once again for the United States. His home run this time was to New Orleans and marked the apparent end of his Cuban travels. The evidence so far, then, is that far from spending one week-long vacation in Havana, Ruby made at least two trips. The first, lasting more than a month, was promptly followed by a two-day journey in the space of forty-eight hours, a shuttle that can hardly have been part of the pleasure trip claimed by Ruby and McWillie. There were, almost certainly, even more comings and goings.

Elaine Mynier, who played messenger before Ruby's Cuban episode, worked at the Dallas airport. She has said that she "frequently saw Ruby and McWillie . . . coming and going on their frequent trips." The Delta agent at New Orleans spoke of Ruby's "numerous flights." Other records place Ruby at home in Dallas on four occasions when the travel document's suggest he was in Cuba. On August 10, two days after his first arrival in Havana, a Dallas police report has Ruby in Dallas—being interviewed about traffic violations. That might be dismissed as bureaucratic error, yet bank records for the next week again show Ruby in Dallas, visiting his safe-deposit box. The next occasion he surfaces is part of a separate controversy, of great potential significance, to be dealt with elsewhere in this chapter. This was August 31, when Ruby was apparently in Dallas meeting with an FBI agent, Charles Flynn. Four days later Ruby was still in town, visiting his safe-deposit box again. From all of this, Congress' Assassinations Committee concluded in 1979 that Ruby must have made at least three trips to Cuba——perhaps more. There was also evidence that hinted strongly at what Ruby's true role was. During what appears to have been the same period, he turned up in Miami for a few days. It was a stay noted by a man he knew well, Meyer Panitz. Panitz had learned Ruby was in town from McWillie, who told him so in a telephone call from Havana. Panitz then met Ruby at a well-known restaurant in Miami. The establishment had been frequented by Santos Trafficante and his associates and by the notorious Hoffa strong-arm man Barney Baker. The Assassinations Committee concluded that Ruby "most likely was serving as a courier for gambling interests."

Whatever the precise object of Ruby's Cuban travels four years before the assassination, it may have been then that he made a fateful connection. There is no doubt that in Cuba he was closely in touch with Lewis McWillie, who knew Trafficante. Today there is evidence that Ruby met Trafficante himself.

In the summer of 1959 Trafficante was languishing in one of Castro's detention centers, a prominent victim of the Cuban clamp-down on Mafia gambling and narcotics operations. He was held at the Trescornia camp, on the outskirts of Havana, an easy-going institution that allowed inmates to receive frequent visitors. Among those confined in the same camp was a detainee of English origin called John Wilson. In 1963 Wilson—by then in London—contacted the American Embassy promptly when it became known that Oswald had been murdered by Jack Ruby.[107] He reported that, at Trescornia camp in 1959, he "met an American gangster called Santos. . . . Santos was visited several times by an American gangster type named Ruby." Wilson, now dead, lived a checkered career as sometime journalist and political activist in Latin America. Press accounts published long before the assassination confirm that he had indeed been picked up—along with several confederates—on charges of planning a bomb attack on Nicaragua. In 1963, when he produced his information about Ruby and "Santos," he could not have known from public sources that Ruby had been in Cuba in 1959. Other details in the Wilson account suggest that he was well qualified to offer it and that the "Santos" mentioned was in fact Santos Trafficante. One of those detained with Wilson was apparently involved in gun smuggling with Eddie Browder, who had been working with one of Trafficante's close associates and who has been linked to earlier arms deals involving Jack Ruby. In 1978, in an interview in Cuba, the former detention-camp superintendent recalled the "English journalist"—apparently John Wilson—and confirmed that he was held in the same area as Santos Trafficante. In 1963 Wilson recalled that four years earlier Ruby "would come to prison with person bringing food." Two witnesses, one of them the camp superintendent, have confirmed that Trafficante and his companions did receive special meals brought in daily from one of the Havana hotels. During his stay in Havana Ruby stayed—according to his travel documents—at the Capri Hotel. Trafficante had a major interest in the casino at that hotel. In 1978, when McWillie and Trafficante himself were grilled by Congress' Assassinations Committee, their answers on Ruby and his visit to Cuba were a model of equivocation. McWillie said he had twice been to see friends at Trescornia camp and that he "probably said hello" to Trafficante once. He said, "Jack Ruby could have been out there one time with me. I don't think he was. . . . I don't know if he was there at that time or not. If he was, I could have taken him out there with me, yes. . . ." Trafficante said carefully, "I never remember meeting Jack Ruby. . . . I don't remember him visiting me either. . . . I never had no contact with him. I don't see why he was going to come and visit me." To the Assassinations Committee, McWillie even acted at one point as though he did not even recognize the name "Trafficante." In the end he claimed he did know Trafficante slightly but saw him only to "say hello to him, and he would say hello to me." While Trafficante claimed he had no business dealings with McWillie, he said he saw him "around Havana a lot." He admitted meeting McWillie at his home since leaving Cuba. As for the reported meeting between Trafficante and Ruby, the Assassinations Committee concluded, "There was considerable evidence that it did take place." It stated flatly that Ruby had been connected with three other Trafficante associates.

One of these connections was with Russell Matthews, another old Cuba hand. He had worked in the casino at Havana's Deauville Hotel when it was operated by Santos Trafficante. Like Trafficante, he was allegedly involved in one of the CIA's plots to assassinate Fidel Castro. Since then, following his return to the United States, Matthews has been described by one of his own lawyers as "a local godfather" and "probably the closest thing to the Mafia we've ever seen in Dallas." Two years before the assassination, the Dallas chief of police named Matthews as "an undesirable citizen."

Another Ruby contact was James Dolan, who has been described as "one of the most notorious hoodlums" in Dallas. In the period before the assassination, Dolan had not only committed acts of violence on Trafficante's behalf, but official reports linked him—just months before the President's murder—with the Marcello network in New Orleans. The evidence also shows that Ruby fraternized with Jack Todd, a Dallas resident described in the Assassinations Committee report as yet another "Trafficante associate." His telephone number was found in Ruby's car after the murder of Oswald.

In some areas, the Committee's intensive probing came fifteen years too late. John Wilson, the former detainee who told of Ruby visiting "Santos" in Cuba, was never questioned for the Warren Commission. Although the CIA and the FBI were both fully informed about the alleged Ruby—Trafficante link, neither agency passed on the lead to the official inquiry. Their reticence remains unexplained. There are, however, ominous indications that Ruby may have had intelligence connections as well as dealings with the criminal underworld. The first concerns the meeting with an FBI agent in Dallas in the midst of Ruby's Cuban travels. It was, we now know, one of a series of contacts which ran through that spring and summer; it ended soon after the last of the trips to Cuba.

The FBI concedes that, beginning in March 1959, Dallas agent Charles Flynn had meetings with Ruby as a "potential criminal informant." The Bureau says its interest was confined to possible information Ruby, as a nightclub owner, might pick up in the course of his work. Ruby's behavior at this time, however, suggests he was involved in sophisticated activity with a definite purpose. After the first FBI contact Ruby went on an electronic shopping spree. He purchased a great deal of modern eavesdropping gadgetry—including a wrist watch with a built-in microphone, a telephone bug, a wire tie clip and bugged attaché case. This represented an outlay of more than five hundred dollars and provided Ruby with some of the most advanced spy equipment then available. It is unclear who his intended target was, but suspicion remains that the contact with the FBI was somehow related to the spate of travel to Havana. Ruby's airline acquaintance at the New Orleans airport overheard Ruby talking on the telephone before taking off on one of his flights. He listened as Ruby instructed one of his employees not to disclose his whereabouts "unless it were to the police or some other official agency." This hardly sounds like the Ruby whose usual life was spent on the borderline of crime. The one "other agency" known to have been in close touch with Ruby at that period was the FBI. Flynn, the agent dealing with Ruby, has admitted that Ruby told him about one of his Cuban trips. He insists, however, that he can remember nothing concrete about his dealings with Ruby. The FBI line remains that interest in Ruby was confined to information he might provide on common crime in Dallas. The Bureau also says that, in spite of nine 1959 meetings between Ruby and FBI Agent Flynn, no useful information ever was obtained. As a result, says the FBI, all contact with Ruby ceased in October that year. Some observers find all this highly improbable, and they include former FBI agents. They have said that no FBI agent would meet a potential informant nine times unless he was getting positive results. In 1975 Congressman Don Edwards, himself a former agent, was chairman of the Constitutional Rights Sub-Committee. Following hearings into FBI aspects of the Kennedy case, Edwards told fellow Congressmen, "There's not much question that both the FBI and CIA are somewhere behind this cover-up. I hate to think what it is they are covering up—or who they are covering for." Even the ubiquitous CIA crops up in the Ruby story and in a way that may be pertinent to the Cuban connection.

In 1963, three days after Ruby killed Oswald, the authorities in New Orleans received a tip about Jack Ruby's past activities. The information proved true, although seemingly innocuous. It was that, in the summer of 1959, Ruby had purchased paintings while passing through New Orleans. Ruby had indeed been in the city, in August that year, on his way to Havana. The informant's identity, however, is more intriguing than the information. He was, according to the official report of his telephoned tip, one

William George Gaudet. Gaudet was the CIA operative whose name turned up beside Lee Oswald's on the visa list covering the alleged assassin's visit to Mexico. Gaudet, while professing ignorance of the Mexican episode, admitted seeing Oswald in New Orleans with Guy Banister. Banister, the reader may wearily recall, was the former top FBI officer who ran anti-Communist operations from 544 Camp Street, where Oswald was sighted during his stay in New Orleans.

Former CIA operative Gaudet claimed he had been "set up," just as he said Oswald was set up. Yet the record states flatly that it was Gaudet who reported Ruby's passage through New Orleans four years before the assassination. This bizarre detail, complex as it is, begs a simple question. Why would a CIA operative in New Orleans have been interested, as early as 1959, in the mundane activities of a Dallas huckster called Jack Ruby?

Gaudet, in his CIA work, specialized in Latin American affairs. Jack Ruby was reportedly involved in Cuban gunrunning and had associates in the Mafia. The CIA had long had an interest in the arms trafficking and would before long enlist the Mafia in plots to kill Fidel Castro. Of the top Mafia chieftains who were to help the CIA, one was Santos Trafficante. Ruby, allegedly, was in touch with Trafficante in Cuba as early as 1959. That is the extent to which we can now bring together these strands of intrigue long past. Yet, somewhere in this skein of evidence may lie the key to why Ruby killed Oswald in 1963. Ruby's own statements, coupled with his Cuban activities, suggest strongly that he laid himself open to underworld pressure.

The Warren Commission received information that, some two years after Castro's takeover, Ruby took part in gunrunning to the anti-Castro side. One of his former employees testified that her boss had been involved in plans to ferry British rifles for the exiles. From then on, indeed, Ruby paraded anti-Castro sentiments. Another associate reported, as the dainty language of an FBI report rendered it, that he had "heard Ruby speak of Castro in such a derogatory manner that it was obvious he did not like him and was not in sympathy with the Castro government in Cuba." If Ruby was dutifully taking the lead from his underworld contacts, this is just as one might expect. The crime bosses switched their support to the anti-Castro cause when they realized their day in Cuba was over. It was then, of course, that some organized-crime leaders— including Santos Trafficante—began assisting CIA plans to murder Castro. Ruby, however, may at some stage have failed to play the Cuban game according to the new rules and thus crossed his underworld idols.

In jail, long after shooting Oswald, Ruby manifested an obsessive fear. One prison visitor related, ". . . one time he was shook he said . . . 'now they're going to find out about Cuba, they're going to find out about the guns, find out about New Orleans, find out about everything.' " One of Ruby's lawyers noted that Ruby was afraid "his patriotism might have come under a cloud . . . because he had tried to arrange some sort of a deal with Cuba after Fidel Castro overthrew the Batista regime." In a letter from jail, Ruby tried to backtrack on something he felt he had given away to a guard in a moment of weakness. He wrote, "The guard knew I was vulnerable to almost anything. I came to where he has sitting and broke down and said that I had sent guns to Cuba, which I had incriminated myself innocently. . . ." Then, in a series of typically confused and implausible sentences, Ruby maintained that, in fact, he had been referring not to gunrunning but merely to some handguns he had supposedly sent to Trafficante associate Lewis McWillie. A psychiatrist who visited Ruby in prison reported, "There is considerable guilt about the fact that he sent guns to Cuba; he feels he helped the enemy and incriminated himself. . . ." Ruby also told the psychiatrist that the assassination was "an act of overthrowing the government" and that he knew "who had President Kennedy killed." Most significant of all, he said he had been "framed into killing Oswald."

"They," Ruby confided, "got what they wanted on me." He never did say who "they" were.

In his letter from jail, Ruby told his correspondent, "Don't believe the Warren Report, that was put out to make me look innocent, in that it would throw the Americans and all the European countries off guard." His first lawyer quickly confided to the press that poor Ruby's mind simply went blank at the moment of shooting Oswald. It was, the lawyer said, a case of "temporary insanity."

Insanity or conspiracy? Ruby's behavior before the Oswald
shooting provides some clues to that.

For a man judged by the Warren Commission to have "no significant link" with organized crime, 1963 caught Jack Ruby in a hail of
coincidences. In early June a number of Chicago racketeers gathered in Dallas for a series of meetings aimed at coordinating
syndicate control of local prostitution and gambling. The plan was
to introduce hired guns to frighten independent operators out of
business. Within days of this Mafia mini-convention, police intelligence noted that the gangsters were meeting in the Carousel
Club, one of Ruby's two dives. Telephone company records show
that Ruby twice called a restaurant near Dallas where the hoods
also held meetings. It is the record of Ruby's phone calls which has
thrown most light on Ruby's associations in the weeks and days
leading up to the assassination weekend. Congress' Assassinations
Committee studied these in far greater depth than the Warren
Commission, using a computer to analyze Ruby's own telephone
records, seized after his arrest, and those of other key individuals.
After so much time had passed, the study would not be complete,
but it is at least hard fact. It makes nonsense of early official
assurances that Ruby's connections before the Oswald shooting
were innocuous. Many of the calls were perhaps harmless, but
others were suspicious. What is not in doubt, as the Committee
says, is that Ruby had a whole series of conversations with individuals "affiliated, directly or indirectly, with organized crime."[108]
The calls establish that—at the crucial period—men with the motive to kill President Kennedy had knowledge of Ruby and his
"possible availability."

In September Ruby was in touch with his old friend McWillie,
Trafficante's casino contact from the Havana days. McWillie was
now established in the gambling business in Las Vegas—another
Mafia citadel. In early October, just after the first firm public
announcement of President Kennedy's forthcoming Dallas visit, a
call went from Ruby's telephone at the Carousel to a Louisiana
number listed under the name of the ex-wife of Russell Matthews,
another Trafficante associate from the Cuba days. Late in October
Ruby made a call to Irwin Weiner, a Chicago insurance man—and

much else besides. Weiner was in a very special sort of insurance business. He was, as one press report described him, "the mob's favored front man." Weiner was a professional bondsman who specialized in getting jailed gangsters out of bail. He headed the insurance company that underwrote the pension fund of the Teamsters Union, led by Jimmy Hoffa. He was one of Hoffa's financial advisers and would later be charged with helping to defraud the Teamsters Pension Fund of one and a half million dollars. Weiner was found not guilty after the Government's chief witness was shot dead by masked men just before the trial. Weiner also knew Sam Giancana and Santos Trafficante—and this last relationship was still current as late as 1977.

Just two weeks before the Kennedy assassination, Ruby received a call from one of Hoffa's top hoodlums. This was Robert "Barney" Baker, Hoffa's personal strong-arm man. Robert Kennedy, in his protracted duel with Hoffa and his criminal associates, had described Baker to his face as being involved with "underworld lice . . . the scum of the United States." More specifically, Kennedy called him Hoffa's "roving ambassador of violence." The day after the call from Baker Ruby called another Hoffa lieutenant, Murray "Dusty" Miller, in Miami. Then, half an hour later, he called Baker again.[109]

Jack Ruby was a keep-fit enthusiast who drank little and smoked hardly at all. In the autumn of 1963, however, he was taking a stimulant drug. It is perhaps a coincidence that, in the wake of the conversations with these vicious individuals, Ruby asked his doctor for pills to calm him down. It was a prescription he would renew a few days later.

At exactly this time Ruby had a series of meetings with two interesting visitors. The first, Alex Gruber, was an ex-convict whose associates included one of Hoffa's key officials. Gruber would later tell the FBI that he simply decided to drop in on Ruby "since Dallas, Texas, was about 100 miles" out of his way. Dallas was actually 400 miles from Gruber's previous stop. After the President's murder he told the FBI conflicting stories about how long he stayed in Dallas and how often he met Ruby. Ruby's other visitor at this time was Paul Jones, onetime emissary of the Chicago mob. Jones had been in and out of Dallas for many years, ever since his thwarted attempt to engineer a Dallas protection racket by bribing local officials. He appears to have arrived in town the same day Ruby called the home of the girlfriend of Mickey Cohen, another racketeer who had been under attack by Robert Kennedy.

This chain of events deserved meticulous investigation. Instead, the first official inquiry treated it with all the intensity of a treasure hunt on a rainy weekend. Ruby's questioning, in the absence of the Warren Commission's Ruby specialists, was amateur and incomplete. Ruby, and some of those who had been in contact with him, explained the calls away as part of an effort by Ruby to solve problems he was having with AGVA, the entertainers' union. In 1979, the Assassinations Committee was not so easily satisfied. It accepted that Ruby had labor problems at his clubs and that many of Ruby's calls may have been on that subject, but it was alarmed by several ominous factors.

Weiner, the Chicago front man for organized crime, had refused to discuss his Ruby call when the FBI questioned him after the President's murder. In 1978, though, he told a reporter that the conversation had had nothing to do with labor troubles. Then, in testimony to the Assassinations Committee, he said that he had lied to the journalist and that he had discussed the union problem with Ruby. As for Hoffa's henchman, Barney Baker, he told the FBI he had received only one call from Ruby. The Committee established that there had been two conversations, the second just two weeks before the assassination. He too said that Ruby had discussed his union problems.[110] Why, though, would Jimmy Hoffa's strong-arm man take time out to help with Ruby's petty worries? Hoffa's son, James Hoffa Jr., has said recently, "I think my dad knew Jack Ruby, but from what I understand, he [Ruby] was the kind of guy everybody knew. So what?"

In fact, of course, the potential significance of such a connection is immense. The Ruby-Baker calls came at a time when Hoffa was under increasing attack from Kennedy's Justice Department. Hoffa as we saw earlier, was on record as not only hating both Kennedy brothers but as actually threatening their lives. Hoffa was much favored by Mafia boss Santos Trafficante, associate of several of Ruby's friends and author of the reported prophecy that

President Kennedy was "going to be hit." The other calls aside, Assassinations Committee staff were especially shaken by the result of their probe into a call Ruby made—three weeks before the assassination—to New Orleans number, CH 2-5431.

That call, which lasted only one minute, went to the Tropical Court Tourist Park and specifically to the office of its operator, Nofio Pecora. Pecora is, as we noted earlier, a lieutenant of New Orleans Mafia boss Carlos Marcello. There is no question about the connection. The director of the New Orleans Crime Commission has noted that "Pecora and Marcello used to be street thugs together a long time ago when they were both in the narcotics traffic. Both Mr. and Mrs. Pecora are still considered very active members of the Marcello organization." In 1963, long since risen to dizzy heights of underworld power, Pecora and Marcello remained close. Marcello, a man who uses the telephone only with extreme caution, had himself placed a call, in midsummer 1963, to the same Pecora number that Ruby called before the assassination. That was at a time when Lee Oswald was embarking on his dubious Fair Play for Cuba activities in New Orleans. Oswald's uncle, Charles Murret, was an associate of Nofio Pecora. When Oswald was arrested in August, following the street fracas over his Fair Play for Cuba activity, he was bailed out thanks to the intervention of Emile Bruneau—an associate of Nofio Pecora. At that time less than a year had passed since Pecora's patron and friend, Marcello, reportedly talked of having the President murdered and "setting up a nut to take the blame."

In 1978, when Assassinations Committee investigators asked Pecora about the phone call from Ruby, he "declined to respond." Later he did agree to talk but said he "did not recall" speaking to Ruby and did not know him. He suggested that he might have taken a message for somebody else in his trailer park but did not believe he had done so. Ruby, it turns out, did have an associate who lived on Pecora's property. This was Harold Tannenbaum, a New Orleans club manager who had been in regular contact with Ruby during the summer of 1963. They had apparently discussed going into business together, and indeed Tannenbaum called Ruby an hour after the call to Pecora's number. Tannenbaum, who is now dead, ran several New Orleans clubs within Marcello's fiefdom. The director of the New Orleans Crime Commission today suggests a greater connection between Ruby and New Orleans than was previously established. He says, "Ruby was in the strip business and he had girls working down on Bourbon Street. And the owners of those places were always in contact with each other about booking girls. Marcello's brother, Peter Marcello, ran one of the bigger places. . . . Two other men close to the Marcello organization ran five of the biggest money-making strip joints on Bourbon Street. And Ruby would know these men, and Harold Tannenbaum managed for these men. . . . Ruby also used to come up here to New Orleans to visit."

In its formal report, the Assassinations Committee declared itself "dissatisfied" with the Pecora statements on the Ruby call. While the matter has not yet been resolved, it underlines even further the potential significance of Ruby's remark in jail that "they're going to find out about New Orleans, find out about everything."

The early investigators knew nothing about another, more mundane development, one which may be highly significant. In 1963, Jack Ruby was in dire financial straits. At the start of the year he borrowed more than a thousand dollars from the bank; and two weeks later he was still being pursued for an even greater sum in rent arrears for his club premises. In March the Internal Revenue Service was after him for nearly twenty-one thousand dollars in unpaid taxes. By midsummer his debt to the Government had risen to nearly twice that figure. Come the autumn, he was advertising a nightclub for sale in the local newspaper, and in early October he was still engaged in painful negotiations with the IRS. Yet suddenly, in the very last days before the assassination, Ruby began behaving as though he expected his financial affairs to take a dramatic change for the better. On November 15, Ruby began using a safe and discussed plans to embed it in concrete in his office. This was a change for Ruby, who had long lived out of his hip pocket or left his money littered around his apartment. Then, on November 19, just three days before the assassination, Ruby told his tax lawyer that he now had a "connection" who could supply him with money to settle his tax debts. He also did something that, for him, was unprecedented. Ruby signed a form giving his lawyer power of attorney to control his financial dealings with the Government. That day, according to Ruby's bank record, there was a mere $246 in his Carousel Club account. On the afternoon of November 22, though, three hours after the President's death, Ruby visited his bank and talked to an official who regularly dealt with his affairs. According to the official, Ruby was then carrying the huge cash sum of $7,000. The money was in large bills, stuffed in his pockets. Ruby deposited none of the money, and almost half of it had vanished by the time he was arrested two days later.[111] The Warren Commission knew nothing about this incident. In 1979, the Assassinations Committee considered Ruby's situation before the President's murder in the context of its discoveries about his criminal contacts at that time. It concluded that, in Jack Ruby, those with the motive to commit the murder "had knowledge of a man who had exhibited a violent nature and who was in serious financial trouble." Did the mob take up its option?

The Weekend of the Killings

It is possible that Ruby's disturbing contacts before the assassination involved nefarious goings-on unconnected with a conspiracy to kill the President; yet disturbing contacts continued into the early-morning hours of the day of the crime itself. On the eve of the assassination Ruby appears to have gone about his usual club business until the late evening. Shortly before 10:00 P.M. he went out to dinner with an old crony, Ralph Paul. Paul ran a local drive-in restaurant. He had long been putting money into Ruby's projects, apparently without ever seeing any of it back. The two men dined at the Egyptian Restaurant, a meal uneventful except—according to Ruby—for a brief conversation with a salesman for the *Dallas Morning News* named "Connors." No person of that name worked at the *News* in 1963. The owner of the restaurant where Ruby dined is himself interesting. He is Joseph Campisi, whose description in official records range from "definite" organized-crime member to "suspected" or "negative." He and Ruby shared mutual acquaintances. Both knew associates of Santos Trafficante. Both knew Joseph Civello, who reportedly ran Dallas operations for Carlos Marcello, and Campisi acknowledges a long-standing personal relationship with the New Orleans Mafia leader. Campisi may have contradicted himself on the extent of his friendship with Ruby and on his knowledge of Ruby's business affairs. He told the FBI after the assassination that he knew nothing about Ruby's background—yet he did know Ruby well enough to visit him in jail.

After Ruby's dinner at Campisi's restaurant his nocturnal movements became fascinating. Earlier that night, at his Carousel Club, he had met with Lawrence Meyers, a friend from Chicago who was in town for a business convention. Meyers, who had known Ruby for years, had visited the Carousel the previous month. Now, on the night before the assassination, Meyers spoke briefly with Ruby and invited him back to his hotel for a drink.[112] Ruby did go to the hotel and, according to Meyers, talked for just a few minutes before saying he had to return to his club. Yet, it seems, Ruby did not merely occupy himself with his business. As late as 2:30 A.M., according to one of his employees, he telephoned—as before—from the Cabana. What he was actually doing remains uncertain, but the Cabana was that night providing lodging for an intriguing and undesirable guest. This was Eugene Brading.

Brading, who had recently changed his name to Jim Braden, was known to police forces throughout the country for his record of offenses involving burglary, gambling, and the black market. His involvement in crime covered a period of more than twenty years. In 1963 he was dabbling in the oil business with Victor Pereira, with whom—nine years earlier—he had been convicted of offenses under the mail fraud and stolen property laws. An Assassinations Committee staff report noted that in 1951, while going under the name of "James Bradley Lee," Brading had been observed in the company of James Dolan. (Dolan, as we noted earlier, knew Jack Ruby well, and is described in the Assassinations Committee Report as "reportedly an acquaintance of both Carlos Marcello and Santos Trafficante.") Now, in November 1963, Brading was out of prison and had received permission from his parole officer for travel to Texas on oil business. He arrived in Dallas on November 21 and checked into Suite 301 of the Cabana Motel along with one Morgan Brown. There is no knowing whether it was in fact Brading whom Ruby visited late that night at the Cabana, but Brading certainly made his mark the next day. He was detained for questioning, at a building overlooking the scene of the assassination, shortly after President Kennedy's assassination.

The President was shot at 12:30 P.M. Some fifteen minutes later Brading was noticed by the elevator man in the Daltex building, an edifice in Dealey Plaza. The observant elevator man noticed Brading as a stranger and ran to fetch a policeman. Out on the sidewalk, Brading was detained for "acting suspiciously" and escorted to the sheriff's office for questioning. There, and again later, he said he was "walking down Elm Street trying to get a cab" when he heard people saying the President had been shot. Brading said it was only then that he entered the Daltex building and took the freight elevator to the third floor to find a telephone. The explanation was accepted, and Brading was released. Back at the Cabana Motel, his colleague, Morgan Brown, had departed abruptly at 2:00 P.M., apparently while Brading was still at the sheriff's office.

Brading might not have been released so swiftly had the police known they were dealing with a convicted criminal. He had, however, identified himself with a credit card in the name of "Jim Braden"—the name he had started to use a few months earlier.

Brading has said that, moments before the assassination, he was at the federal courthouse, two blocks from the scene of the crime. His purpose there, he said, was to inform his Dallas parole officer that he was about to leave the city. Brading said he noticed another officer, a "Mr. Flowers," enter the courthouse just after the President's motorcade passed by. No officer of that name worked at the parole office in November of 1963.

Today researchers have noted a further reason for pursuing information on Brading's activities. The lead concerns a familiar figure in the story of Oswald in New Orleans—David Ferrie.

In 1963, Ferrie, the former CIA operative reported to have

been in contact with Lee Oswald,* was working for Carlos Marcello, the Mafia boss who reportedly said he planned to use "a nut" in a plan to murder President Kennedy. In his work for Marcello, Ferrie worked out of an office in New Orleans' Père Marquette Building. This was designated Room 1706, which was incorrect, but he did have his mail sent to Room 1701. A check of federal records shows that Eugene Brading gave that same building, and the same floor, as his New Orleans address. He told parole authorities he used Room 1701. Both rooms were just along the corridor from the office used by David Ferrie. This strangest of coincidences may not be the only one linking Ferrie to the denizens of the Cabana Motel, Dallas, on the assassination eve. A check of Ferrie's telephone records reveals that eight weeks earlier he made a call to Chicago number WH4-4970. This, it turns out, was the number of an apartment building which in 1963 housed one Jean West.[113] On the night before the President's murder, Jean West was staying at the Cabana Motel as the companion of Lawrence Meyers, the friend Jack Ruby visited that midnight. All this, one must add wearily, may be coincidence. Yet Ferrie, as we shall see later, did move through Texas in a mysterious way in the days after the President's assassination. He would produce an alibi, though, for the moment of the ambush itself. So too would Jack Ruby.

On the morning of the assassination Ruby dallied for hours in the offices of the *Dallas Morning News*. He was there for breakfast, and he made himself obvious to a number of employees during the morning. In the half hour before the President's death he was in the advertising department chattering about publicity for his clubs. Ruby was known at the newspaper as a customer tardy in submitting advertising copy for his clubs and erratic about paying the bills. November 22, though, was an exception. Ruby turned up on time with his publicity material and with cash in hand. He was in the advertising department until 12:25, and he was noticed there again minutes after the shots rang out in Dealey Plaza, just a few blocks away. His presence gave Ruby a viable alibi and more. Even before news of the attack on the President flashed through

---

* See Chapter 17, "Blind Man's Bluff in New Orleans."

the newspaper offices, Ruby launched into the first act of a prolonged pantomime. Seated at a desk with a copy of the morning
paper, he held forth angrily about the notorious black-bordered
advertisement "welcoming" President Kennedy to Dallas. As people gathered around a television in reaction to news of the shooting, Ruby appeared "obviously shaken and an ashen color—just
very pale . . . and sat for a while with a dazed expression in his
eyes." That did not last long. Soon he was beginning a telephone
marathon that would last for days. Ruby quickly called his club,
declaring that he might decide to close up. Then he made a big
show of a call to his sister, handing the telephone to a newspaper
employee so that he could hear the sister cry out, "My God, what
do they want?" Ruby himself would say later that he was in tears
as he left the newspaper building. Twenty minutes later he drew
attention to himself again—this time in the throng at Parkland
Hospital, where reporters were waiting for news of the President's
condition. Ruby tugged the sleeve of White House correspondent
Seth Kantor, who had known him during a previous stint of
newspaper work in Dallas. Kantor turned and recognized Ruby,
who had called him by his first name.[114] Ruby looked miserable and
said what a terrible thing the shooting was. "Should he close his
clubs?" he wanted to know. Kantor muttered that it would be a
good idea and hurried on up the stairs. Moments later the President's death was confirmed.

The grief-stricken Jack Ruby next turned up at his Carousel
Club, giving orders to close for business until further notice. He
then launched into a spate of phone calls to relatives, friends, and
business people. Later they would remember him sounding upset,
very "broken up." He made some of the calls from his sister's
apartment, and she would remember him saying, "I never felt so
bad in my life, even when Ma or Pa died." Certainly Ruby was
overreacting—but was it genuine or feigned? Was it just a show
calculated to build up the image of the Ruby who would soon
claim to have shot Oswald in a fit of uncontrolled emotion?

That night Ruby was to show up at a local synagogue for a
special service in memory of the dead President. He made his
appearance, though, only at the every end; the rabbi, who talked
to him, noticed that Ruby said nothing at all about the assassina-

tion. Later still, on a visit to a local radio station, Ruby seemed preoccupied with excitement rather than grief. A *Dallas Morning News* journalist, Hugh Ainsworth, would later tell the FBI what he though of Ruby's reaction to news of the attack on the President. Ainsworth said Ruby "feigned surprise at this announcement and gave some show of emotion." Whether his skepticism was right or not, Ainsworth made another good point. Ruby knew the President was in town, and the *Dallas Morning News* offices were only two minutes' walk away from where the motorcade passed through Dealey Plaza. Why, if Ruby had the overblown devotion to the President he claimed, had he not bothered to go and see him pass by?

One of the earliest calls Ruby made, once the President was known to be dead, was to a contact in Los Angeles. This was Alex Gruber, the long-lost friend with a criminal record who had met with Ruby ten days before the assassination. Ruby also made two calls to his old Dallas crony Ralph Paul. Paul would later say that Ruby phoned merely to say he was closing his clubs. Gruber would say that Ruby called him to discuss a potential car-wash business—and his intention to send Gruber a pet dog. That evening Jack Ruby was seen repeatedly—over a period of nearly five hours—at the police station where Oswald was being held prisoner.

At about 7:00 P.M. that Friday night, according to a police reporter who recognized him, Ruby emerged from an elevator on the crowded floor where Oswald was being questioned. He was hunched over, walking between two journalists and writing something on a piece of paper. He was observed in an area where there were three detectives he knew; then he was seen hanging around outside the Homicide Office, where Oswald was being interrogated. According to the reporter who saw him, Ruby "walked up to the door of Captain Fritz's office and put his hand on the knob and started to open it. He had the door open a few inches and began to step into the room." Two officers on duty at the door then stopped him, saying, "You can't go in there, Jack." On this occasion the fact that he knew so many policeman had hindered rather than helped Jack Ruby. After breaking off for his trip to the synagogue, Ruby returned to the police station, this time armed with a supply of corned-beef sandwiches for his uniformed friends.

Ruby was still there after midnight, when Oswald was brought briefly into the midst of a mob of pushing, shouting reporters (*see illustration* 28). A few minutes later, when the district attorney told the press that Oswald belonged to the Free Cuba Committee, Ruby piped up and showed a rare knowledge of the minutiae of Cuban affairs. He pointed out that the DA had meant Fair Play for Cuba, the pro-Castro group. It was an important distinction. The Free Cuba Committee, after all, was on the *anti*-Castro side—the cause Ruby had been helping of late.

Ruby may well have hoped to kill Oswald that very first night at the police station. He was to admit, in one statement, that he had his .38-caliber revolver with him as he mingled with the journalists and policemen on the third floor. It was an admission that made Oswald's murder seem premeditated, and Ruby later withdrew it.

Ruby's night of drama did not end even when some of the exhausted pressmen went off to snatch a few hours' sleep. He dropped into a nearby radio station, where one staffer remembered that he "looked rather pale as he talked to me and kept looking at the floor." And then, in the small hours of the morning, Ruby spent at least an hour talking in a car with an off-duty policeman. This was Harry Olsen, who was accompanied by one of Ruby's nightclub girls.[115] Olsen and the girl would later say that Ruby cursed Oswald during the conversation. Ruby, for his part, would belatedly quote Olsen as telling him that "they should cut this guy [Oswald] inch by inch into ribbons." Olsen was further connected to the case by two odd coincidences. he had rented an apartment from Bertha Cheek, the sister of Oswald's rooming-house manager. Mrs. Cheek had met Ruby four days before the assassination, apparently to discuss business.[116] Also, on the afternoon of the assassination, Olsen was not far away from the spot where Tippet was murdered. He said later that he was moonlighting at the time by doing guard duty at a vacant estate. Unfortunately Olsen could not remember exactly where the estate was. He left Dallas for good less than a month after the President's death, and was last hear of in Las Vegas.

After the meeting with Olsen, Ruby went to the other Dallas newspaper, the *Times-Herald*, and made more people aware of how upset he was about the assassination. At 4:30 A.M. he went home at last, but not to sleep. Ruby rousted a roommate and an employee out of bed and dragged them off on a bizarre dawn expedition. He drove to a large signboard bearing a political poster aimed against the Chief Justice of the United States, and instructed his employee to take photographs. Ruby's bemused companions could not make out whether he thought the poster was the work of communists, the John Birch Society, or a combination of both. Then at last, having added irrationality to his sustained show of grief, Jack Ruby went home to bed.

Next day at noon, in the police station, senior officers began to discuss moving Oswald to the County Jail. There was some talk of doing it that same afternoon. Within an hour Jack Ruby was busily trying to find out more details. He made two calls to a local newsman, asking when Oswald was to be moved. At four o'clock, which had been the first time considered for the transfer, Ruby was back at the police station. Nothing happened. Some time later, Police Chief Curry advised the press to return next morning at 10:00 A.M. An hour after Curry's statement Ruby called Lawrence Meyers, the Chicago contact he had visited at the Cabana Motel the night before the assassination. Then he began a series of calls which have never been satisfactorily explained. A study of Ruby's telephone records shows that his use of the phone increased vastly just before the assassination. Now, on the night before the elimination of Oswald, Ruby indulged in a flurry of apparently urgent messages.

At 10:44 P.M. a call went from Ruby's sister's apartment to The Bullpen, a restaurant owned by his long-time backer Ralph Paul. Later, in one account of his activity that evening, Paul said he had left the restaurant by that time. A waitress, however, said she remembered Ruby calling. She also said she heard Paul, in responding, say something about a gun. At 11:00 P.M. Ruby was at his club and starting a frenzied chain of long-distance calls to Galveston, in southeastern Texas. The purpose, apparently, was to speak to Breck Wall, a friend of Ruby's who was on his way to Galveston from Dallas. When Ruby found that Wall had yet to arrive he quickly called Paul again and spoke to his home number for several minutes. Half an hour later he talked to Paul's number yet again, and then—twenty minutes before midnight—Ruby finally got through to Wall in Galveston. The business that had been so pressing took only two minutes to conclude. Then, pausing just long enough to get the dial tone back again, Ruby made yet another brief call to Paul's home number.

Ralph Paul did not mention these late-night calls at all when FBI agents questioned him soon after Oswald's murder.[117] Later, Paul said Ruby had called merely to say other clubs in town were doing poor business. Breck Wall, who now lives in Las Vegas, has said that Ruby called only to discuss union business—the same excuse offered to explain Ruby's call eleven days earlier to Barney Baker, aide to Teamsters leader Jimmy Hoffa. Ruby, as even the Warren Report pointed out, "has not provided details" of this series of strange calls. The Report did not mention, however, that somebody else had arrived in Galveston within minutes of Breck Wall. This was David Ferrie, former CIA operative and employee of Mafia boss Carlos Marcello.

From the moment of the assassination, Ferrie had been behaving very strangely indeed. He was later to provide an ironic alibi for the actual moment of the assassination. It was that he had been in court in New Orleans, where his boss Marcello was being cleared of the charges which had led to his earlier deportation by Robert Kennedy. After that, however, Ferrie began to act very oddly. In the company of two young friends, he drove 350 miles through the night to Houston, Texas. After resting briefly at a motel, Ferrie visited the Winterland Skating Rink, and there, he would claim later, went ice skating. That was not quite how the rink manager remembered it. He said Ferrie had not been skating at all but had spent a great deal of time at a pay telephone, making and receiving calls. Then, in the evening of the day after the assassination—and in spite of the hundreds of miles he had already driven in recent hours—Ferrie decided to go to Galveston. He checked into a motel there at about 10:30 P.M. and then immediately went out again until the early hours of the morning. Ferrie had arrived in Galveston just before the arrival in town of Ruby's friend Breck Wall and just before the phone call to Galveston that Ruby found it so vital to make that night. Ferrie left Galveston before nine o'clock next morning and headed back toward his home base in New Orleans. Ferrie never did explain his purpose in visiting Galveston.

While all this was going on Oswald was spending his second night in police custody. It was to be his last.

There is uncertainty about Jack Ruby's movements on the morning of Sunday, November 24. He and his roommate, George Senator, claimed later that Ruby stayed in his apartment till nearly eleven o'clock. Senator, however, behaved oddly when he heard Oswald had been shot. He went straight to a telephone and called one of Ruby's lawyers, *before* Ruby was publicly identified as Oswald's killer. Then, for days afterward, Senator behaved like a man "overwhelmed with fear," as one associate described him. He refused to sleep at home and soon left Dallas altogether. It may have been Senator, not Ruby, who took a phone call from Ruby's cleaning lady some time after eight o'clock that Sunday morning. She later testified that the voice on the phone sounded so strange that she could not be sure it was really Ruby. Other evidence suggests Ruby was out and about early that morning and in ominously familiar territory. Three television technicians said later that they saw him by their outside broadcast van near the police station. A church minister said he traveled with Ruby in the police-station elevator at 9:30 A.M. and that Ruby's destination was the floor where Oswald then was. At all events, Ruby was at home about an hour later, when one of his strippers called to ask for money. He promised to wire her some cash at a nearby town, but she noticed how abrupt and hurried Ruby sounded. It was as though he could not wait to get off the line. The money for the girl, and what motivated Ruby next, are central to understanding the events that led to Oswald's murder. For Oswald now had just one hour to live.

Ruby left his apartment shortly before eleven o'clock, his pockets stuffed with more than two thousand dollars in cash—and with his gun. He parked his car downtown and then walked to the Western Union office, along the street from the police station. There he arranged to send twenty-five dollars, as promised, to the girl who had called earlier. The time stamp on the form recording the transaction read 11:17 A.M. Although the authorities acknowledge the possibility that the actual transaction may have been slightly earlier, the Western Union visit was important to Ruby. It was to suggest that his actions a few minutes later were those of a crime of passion, not a planned execution.

It was no distance to the police station, and Jack Ruby was in its heavily guarded basement within minutes. He had penetrated an area peopled only by policemen and the reporters waiting to cover Lee Oswald's transfer to the County Jail. Two minutes later Oswald, handcuffed to a detective, was brought down to the basement in the elevator. At that very moment a lawyer, Tom Howard, peered into the basement jail office and said, "That's all I wanted to see." Then he walked away. Seconds later Oswald was led out of the office and into the blinding glare of television lights. The car he was to travel in was several paces away, and he never reached it.

A police officer, Detective Combest, saw Ruby stride swiftly forward. "He was bootlegging the pistol like a quarterback with a football. . . . I knew what he was going to do . . . but I couldn't get at him." Ruby fired one destructive bullet into Oswald's abdomen. It ruptured two main veins carrying blood to the heart, and tore through the spleen, the pancreas, the liver, and the right kidney. Oswald never spoke another word. He died soon afterward at Parkland Hospital. Jack Ruby had silenced the man who, perhaps, could have unraveled some of the mysteries of the Kennedy assassination. One of the first officers to talk to Ruby under arrest quoted him as saying. "Well, I intended to shoot him three times."

Less than three hours later Ruby was visited by the man who was to be his first lawyer. It was Tom Howard, the man who had looked through the jail-office window seconds before Oswald was shot. Howard, a maverick local lawyer with a police record of his own, had six minutes with Ruby that afternoon. Months later, during his trial for murder, Jack Ruby would explain how he came up with his tale about shooting Oswald to save the President's widow the grief of coming back to give evidence in court. In a private note to another lawyer, Ruby wrote, "It was not my idea to say I shot Oswald to keep Jackie Kennedy from coming back here to testify. I did it because Tom Howard told me to [say so]. . . ."

The world would never know for sure why Ruby really killed Oswald. Nor have we learned yet how—with split-second timing—

he managed to get into position to do it. A police report written soon afterward said he did so because of a "series of unfortunate coincidences which caused a momentary breakdown in the security measures. . . ." The Warren Commission decided he was just plain lucky. As Congress' Assassinations Committee concluded in 1979, that verdict was naïve and almost certainly wrong.

The first official inquiry encouraged the belief that Ruby got into the basement by slipping past a policeman guarding the car ramp that led into the building from Main Street. It suggested that the officer concerned, Roy Vaughn, was distracted by a police car leaving the basement just before the shooting. Ruby almost certainly used that moment, said the Warren Report, to slip past Vaughn. This ignored not only Vaughn but also the testimony of several credible witnesses. Vaughn, who knew Ruby, said nobody could have got past him without being noticed. All three of the senior policemen in the car, two of whom also knew Ruby, were also sure nobody had been on the way in when they were on the way out. Another officer, Sergeant Flusche, was standing beside his car opposite the ramp entrance at the relevant time. He says he knows "beyond any doubt in his mind that Jack Ruby, whom he had known for many years, did not walk down Main Street anywhere near the ramp." Corroboration came from a cab driver, who was watching the ramp with special attention because he had been hired to pick up an enterprising journalist to follow the Oswald transfer car. Another reporter, who had stationed himself in the middle of the ramp inside the basement, said much the same. He was sure nobody had walked past him in the five minutes before Oswald was killed. The Warren inquiry passed over all these witnesses, just as it passed over compelling evidence of how Ruby might really have got in.

The first authoritative questioning of Ruby was done by a veteran Secret Service agent, Forrest Sorrels. According to his careful notes, Ruby said nothing at all about how he had got into the basement. Later, Ruby was interrogated by FBI agent Ray Hall. Hall, who had twenty years' experience behind him, also made detailed notes. He was to say categorically that Ruby "did not wish to say how he got into the basement or at what time he entered." Ruby continued to refuse to reveal how he got in at three subsequent interviews over twelve days. Only a month after the Oswald shooting did he state firmly that he had come in down the ramp from Main Street, just as a police car was coming out.

Soon after murdering Oswald, Ruby had a chance to speak with his lawyer, Tom Howard, and a number of police officers. One of these was Sergeant Patrick Dean, who had known Ruby for years and had been in charge of securing the basement against intruders. Dean, along with three other officers, was to claim that Ruby had offered the Main Street ramp version from the very beginning. Their claim has been seriously questioned.

The day after Oswald's death, Dean wrote a report. It claimed that Ruby "stated to me *in the presence of Mr. Sorrels* that he had entered the basement through the ramp entering on Main Street." That, to be sure, later astonished Secret Serviceman Sorrels, who was certain Ruby had said no such thing. Dean's version received apparent corroboration from three other policemen, Detectives McMillon, Clardy, and Archer, who had been present at various stages of the Ruby interview with Sorrels and FBI agent Hall. Yet, although Ruby's means of entry was an immediate and central issue, not one of the officers mentioned the Main Street ramp story in reports filed on the day of the shooting. McMillon, who had worked under Dean as a patrolman, produced that version the day afterward. Clardy and Archer did not come up with their claims until a week after the Oswald murder. McMillon and Clardy, both of whom had supposedly heard Ruby say he came in down the ramp, were present when Ruby refused to tell FBI agent Hall how he had got in. It seems improbable that they would not, at that point, have told the FBI agent what Ruby had allegedly already said.[118] Like Sergeant Dean, Clardy and McMillon had known Jack Ruby for years.

Warren Commission Counsel Burt Griffin, the lawyer at first charged with sorting out all this malarkey, quickly became skeptical. He says today, "I always thought all along about the Dallas police that anything that would get them into trouble or embarrass them, they would lie to us. No question about that." He was so frustrated during his questioning of one Dallas officer that he called him a "damned liar" to his face. In the case of Dean, Griffin was so sure he was lying about the Main Street ramp story that he broke off in the middle of taking the sergeant's testimony and sent the stenographer out of the room. Then, in private, he told Dean flatly that he did not believe he was telling the truth on some points and appealed to him to reconsider. Dean reacted with righteous indignation, complained to all and sundry, and the story leaked to the press. Griffin was recalled from Dallas, and the Warren Commission ended up using Dean's account.

In this book I have so far made little mention of lie-detector tests, which are frequently more confusing than useful. It is worth noting, though, that officer Vaughn—the policeman who supposedly let Ruby slip past him on the ramp—did pass a test on the issue. Sergeant Dean, who was allowed to write the questions for his own test, admitted that he failed it. Dean said, "That particular day I was nervous and hypertensive, so I flunked it. Or rather it was inconclusive." Research in 1979 revealed that the written record of Dean's lie-detector test was nowhere to be found. A former Warren Commission lawyer has said, "You have to suspect the possibility that Dean at a minimum had seen Ruby enter the basement and had failed to do his duty." It is that statement which begs the final question. If certain policemen were lying, were they doing so merely to cover up bungled security? Or were they covering up a more sinister truth, that one or more policemen had actively conspired with Ruby in the murder of Oswald?

Nobody now doubts that Jack Ruby knew dozens of Dallas policemen, some of them very well indeed. Even a Dallas police inquiry concluded that he knew up to fifty officers personally, and independent estimates have placed the figure in the hundreds. Sergeant Dean, indeed, conceded that he knew Ruby for ten years before the assassination and saw Ruby several times each night he was on duty. Ruby, who ran his Carousel Club on a legal tightrope, knew how to look after the local police. Dean, again, admitted that he and other favored officers would receive bottles of whisky from Ruby at Christmas. On special occasions, too, Ruby offered the favors of his girls in much the same spirit that he doled out free liquor. It seems more than possible that this calculated generosity finally paid off the day Ruby needed to get at Oswald to kill him. The report of an interview with Ruby, a week after the shooting, states that he "became very emotional and was almost to the point of hysteria in his efforts to protect any police officer from being implicated in his entrance into the basement of City Hall." Apart from the controversy about precisely how Ruby got in, the kernel of suspicion is the timing of his entry to the basement. Was it extraordinary luck that he arrived right on cue? Or did somebody tip Ruby off? If, as the evidence suggests, Ruby had been stalking Oswald for thirty-six hours, why did he not show up at 10:00 A.M. on Sunday morning? That was the time the police chief had suggested, the night before, that the transfer of Oswald was likely to take place. How did Ruby, sitting at home, know that the transfer was to be delayed? Yet he did not show up at 10:00 A.M. and thus did not run the risk of ejection from the basement during the hour and a half he would have had to idle around until Oswald actually appeared. The suspicion is that somebody in the know kept Ruby closely in touch with Oswald's changing timetable.

It was at 9:00 A.M. on Sunday morning that senior officers began issuing detailed orders for Oswald's transfer. From that moment on it was clear that—while the 10:00 A.M. move was off— Oswald was definitely going to be transferred within hours. It was also known, for the first time, that Oswald would be taken out through the basement. If he was going to be hit, it would have to be at that moment. Of the officers who learned this key information, three names have come under greatest scrutiny.

There was William "Blackie" Harrison, who was on duty in the basement that day. Television videotape, examined after the event, showed Ruby apparently sheltering behind the ample form of Officer Harrison just before he dashed forward to shoot Oswald. Harrison denied having any contact with Ruby that morning, but his possible involvement was intensively probed during the internal Dallas police inquiry into Oswald's murder. Lieutenant Jack Revill, a supervisor in Criminal Intelligence, was astonished by Ruby's violent reaction when asked about Harrison. According to Revill, Ruby "got real angry at me and cussed me, and told me I was a hatchet-man. . . ." At Revill's insistence, Harrison submitted to a lie-detector test. On the day of the test, according to reports noted by the Secret Service, Harrison took tranquilizers to help him keep his composure. The results, reportedly, were "not conclusive."[119] Lieutenant Revill later told the Warren Commission, "I have never been satisfied personally with

Harrison's statement." There the matter was allowed to rest. Harrison's movements that morning had been reconstructed by Seth Kantor, the respected Washington correspondent and specialist on the Ruby case. He argues that it may have been Harrison, the man whose shoulders shielded Ruby just before the shooting, who kept Ruby in touch with events before the Oswald shooting.

Officer Harrison had known Ruby for eleven years. He was twice away from his colleagues that morning, and in a position to telephone Ruby at crucial moments. First, when word was passed to set up the basement operation, Harrison and Detective L. D. Miller were summoned back to headquarters by a phone call to the Deluxe Diner, where they were taking a coffee break. When questioned later, Kantor suggests, Miller behaved more like a suspect than a policeman. At first he refused point-blank to give a sworn deposition. Warren Commission lawyer Griffin noted Miller's "lack of memory and his original reluctance to testify at all." When he did finally testify, Miller said that at the Deluxe Diner, "Officer Harrison received a telephone call from an unknown person." When Harrison himself testified he brought a lawyer with him. As Griffin recalled, Harrison was "somewhat slow in revealing the coffee break he had taken with Miller. . . . He had to be prodded to talk about the telephone call he received there." Harrison claimed the call had been the one summoning him and his colleagues back to police headquarters. That, though, makes little sense of Miller's comment that the call was from "an unknown person." Kantor postulates that, from the Deluxe Diner, Harrison made an initial call to Jack Ruby. He says so in the knowledge that Harrison was missing at a vital moment later that morning. When members of Harrison's unit trooped down to the basement at 11:10 A.M., they encountered Harrison coming up from the sub-basement. He later said he had gone down there to get cigars. Yet, it seems, that chore took him well over ten minutes. On his way to the cigar machine, Kantor points out, Harrison had access to four telephones. He theorizes that it was now, with Oswald's departure imminent, that Ruby was given the go-ahead to make for the police basement. Officer Harrison is dead and will answer no more questions.

Lieutenant George Butler was another officer detailed to take part in the basement operation. Butler has also known Ruby for a long time. It was he who, many years earlier, had handled the exposure and prosecution of Ruby's friend Paul Jones when he tried to bribe Dallas officials into giving the Mafia free rein in Dallas. After the assassination it was Butler who, in contradiction of the former sheriff, declared that Ruby had been innocent of involvement in the Mafia operation. Just before the Oswald shooting Butler was sought out in the basement by a reporter who had found him especially reliable and controlled in the hectic hours since the assassination. Now, however, the reporter testified later, Butler's poise "appeared to have deserted him completely. . . . He was an extremely nervous man, so nervous that . . . I noticed his lips trembling." Today, Butler concedes that he had the jitters but says that it was because he was concerned that arrangements for Oswald's transfer were poorly organized.

Finally, there was Sergeant Dean himself, who was actually in charge of the group ordered to search and seal the basement. Apart from his suspect claims about Ruby's means of entry, it has since been reported that Dean had a connection with a known organized-crime figure. Years earlier he had been on good terms with Joe Civello, the Dallas Mafia figure widely acknowledged to have been Texas representative for Carlos Marcello, the New Orleans crime boss alleged to have spoken of plans to murder the President.

As we saw earlier, and as the Assassinations Committee established, Ruby was a personal acquaintance of Civello. Nobody wanted to know about that, though, after he killed Oswald. One witness, having seen a television broadcast saying Ruby had no significant Mafia connections, came forward to tell the FBI that Ruby "was a frequent visitor and associate of Civello. . . ." The witness was apparently well qualified—he was a former employee, at separate dates, of both Ruby and Civello—but his statement sparked no interest. Nor was there any response when the known Ruby associate and organized-crime front man, Paul Jones, stated that Civello would know of underworld plans to protect Ruby in prison. This same Civello had invited Sergeant Dean to dinner as far back as 1957, not long after Civello's arrest at the famous

Apalachin meeting of organized-crime figures. In the circumstances, it is a highly disturbing association to find in the background of Dean, the policeman in charge of securing the basement against intruders before the Oswald transfer.

In 1979, the Assassinations Committee rejected the old theory that Ruby got in down the ramp from the street. Following its own research on the spot, it plumped instead for a brand-new hypothesis. The Committee found that Ruby could have got into the basement by slipping down an alleyway at the side of the police station. In the middle of the alley is a door opening onto the ground floor of the building which houses the police station, and from there Ruby could have reached the basement. It was a far less conspicuous means of entry than the ramp route and therefore a better choice for a premeditated approach. The Committee had to consider whether, if he indeed took this route, Ruby would have been stopped by a locked internal door leading to the basement. On this point, it once again encountered the ubiquitous voice of Sergeant Dean.[120] It turned out that he had vacillated in his statements as to whether the door could be opened from the outside. On one occasion he had not answered the question and then said he had been assured by a maintenance man that the door was secure from both sides. Two maintenance men and a porter had said the opposite. They asserted it could be opened, without using a key, from the direction Ruby would have entered.

An Assassinations Committee report notes that, in 1978, Dean refused to answer a written questionnaire in the form of a sworn affidavit. It proved impossible to arrange a "convenient" date to take his deposition. The final Committee Report says it is improbable that "Ruby entered the police basement without assistance, even though the assistance may have been provided with no knowledge of Ruby's intentions." Its investigators' report observed that Dean was "a key figure." Dean himself, in retirement, said he feared he was being "set up" and that he would be "hearing from the Justice Department." He has since died.

Jack Ruby himself succumbed to cancer in 1967, just as New Orleans District Attorney Jim Garrison was reopening the Kennedy case. Ruby did not die, however, without dropping a number of hints. To the Warren Commission worthies, who refused to listen to his pleas to be removed from Dallas, he had said darkly, "I have been used for a purpose." There was, too, the interview with a psychiatrist, in which Ruby claimed he "was framed into killing Oswald;" and once, as Ruby was being moved from jail to court, he spoke—according to a reporter's notes—of "complete conspiracy. . . . If you knew the truth you would be amazed." Many believe these were the ramblings of a shattered mind. Today, it is true, any analysis of the actual Ruby shooting must fall back to some extent on speculation. Yet, in the wider context of the assassination, Ruby's Mafia links and Cuban activities seem beyond coincidence. The connections are undeniable. It is clear, moreover, that in this area the Warren Commission was ill-served—perhaps even obstructed—by some officials in the FBI and the CIA. The reasons remain mysterious.

A former FBI agent, Arthur Murtaugh, has alleged there was a disturbing episode during the original inquiry into the Ruby aspects of the assassination. Murtaugh claimed that a colleague in Atlanta, Daniel Doyle, found a number of significant links between Jack Ruby and the anti-Castro movement. According to Murtaugh, these leads were "washing out" of the reports finally assembled for consumption in Washington. Agent Doyle resigned soon afterward, reportedly disillusioned by his experiences in the service of the FBI.

Whatever the validity of Murtaugh's allegations, a check of the Atlanta files today does identify the area that keenly interested Agent Doyle. It was the claim that Ruby had engaged in gunrunning with smuggler Eddie Browder.[121] The FBI never followed up, despite the fact that it held a file on Browder more than a thousand pages thick. A little diligent work might have led to rich investigative rewards. Certainly it would have drawn attention to the fact that Browder was aligned with Trafficante associate Norman Rothman.

Even as a result of what they did learn, Warren Commission lawyers Griffin and Hubert quickly became concerned about Ruby's links with organized crime and with Cuba. In March 1964, therefore, the CIA was asked to provide the Commission with any information it could obtain on ties between Ruby and a whole range of individuals and groups who had come up during inquiries.

The CIA did not produce a written answer for many weeks, and when it came it was not illuminating. It stated bluntly that "an examination of Central Intelligence Agency files has produced no information of Jack Ruby or his activities."

Neither the CIA nor the FBI volunteered information on a point that puzzled Warren investigators. The Commission staff had been stymied by a laconic statement by Ruby that he had been involved with an anti-Castro gunrunner he identified only as "Davis." Ruby's first lawyer had asked him to specify anything that might damage his defense. Ruby responded promptly that there would be a problem if Davis' name should come up. The FBI not only did not locate Davis for the Commission; it did not even put a first name on him. He was identified only years later, after research by Seth Kantor, the former White House correspondent and specialist on the Ruby case. Ruby's contact, it turns out, was in Texas FBI files all the time. He was a former bank robber named Thomas Davis, an American criminal not unknown to the CIA. Davis, who had met Ruby at one of his Dallas clubs, had friends—not least, apparently, in American intelligence circles.

At the time of the Kennedy assassination Davis was in North Africa. Less than a month later he was in jail in Tangier, being held in connection with the President's murder. According to correspondence between FBI Director Hoover and the State Department, Moroccan security police thought it necessary to detain Davis "because of a letter in his handwriting which referred in passing to Oswald and the Kennedy assassination." The letter was addressed to a lawyer in New York. Reporter Seth Kantor has learned from sources that—soon afterward—Davis was sprung from the Moroccan prison thanks to the intervention of a CIA operative called QJ/WIN.[122] To students of CIA clandestine activity, that name opens a Pandora's box of CIA worms.

The Senate Intelligence Committee established in 1975 that QJ/WIN was a key agent in the CIA's "Executive Action" program, formed to plan assassinations of foreign leaders. The CIA declined to identify QJ/WIN to Senate investigators, revealing only that he was a "foreign citizen with a criminal background, recruited in Europe." His boss in the CIA's assassination department was William Harvey. Harvey's specialty was in the Agency's Cuban operations, and, specifically, he was involved in assassination plots against Fidel Castro. Harvey was in personal touch with John Roselli, the gangster used as liaison man in the CIA-Mafia murder plot assisted by Santos Trafficante. The connections are complex, yet—out of the millions of Americans with whom Ruby might have crossed paths—the association with apparent CIA protégé Thomas Davis cannot yet be written off as coincidence.[123]

Davis himself will never be questioned about his link to Jack Ruby or his association with the CIA. He was killed in 1973, electrocuted while cutting a power line, apparently in the course of a robbery. In the summer of 1963, however, he appears to have been involved in recruiting mercenaries for a planned coup in Haiti. Davis' wife said her husband had worked as a "soldier of fortune" in Indochina, Indonesia, Algeria, and Cuba—always on the "Western side." She has said recently that he also "probably worked with the Mafia or something." Congress' Assassinations Committee learned about Thomas Davis, but too late. It did not have time to make a full investigation of his reported connections with Jack Ruby and the CIA.

In perhaps their most glaring omission in the Ruby case, neither the CIA nor the FBI told the official inquiry what both agencies knew of the report that Ruby had once visited Mafia boss Santos Trafficante in Cuba. Trafficante, of course, was deeply involved with the CIA in its Castro murder plots, a fact that CIA Deputy Director Richard Helms kept secret from his own Director, let alone the Warren Commission.

John Roselli, gangster and key contact man in the CIA-Mafia assassination plots against Castro, talked about Ruby before he himself was murdered.[124] Allowing for the self-interest implicit in his main allegations, which implicate Castro in the Kennedy assassination, his comments on Oswald's killer are interesting. Washington columnist Jack Anderson reported Roselli as telling him: "When Oswald was picked up, the underworld conspirators feared he would crack and disclose information that might lead to them. This almost certainly would have brought a massive U.S. crackdown on the Mafia. So Jack Ruby was ordered to eliminate Oswald. . . ." Roselli did not, apparently, expound on what Oswald might also have revealed about American intelligence.

As for Ruby, he left behind him a little-known verbal testament. In 1978, as I was searching through old videotapes in Texas, I found a fragment of a rare television interview with Ruby, one that had never been shown on national television. Slumped in a chair during a recess in his interminable and inconclusive series of court appearances, Ruby had this to say:

> The only thing I can say is—everything pertaining to what's happened has never come to the surface. The world will never know the true facts of what occurred—my motive, in other words. I am the only person in the background to know the truth pertaining to everything relating to my circumstances.

At this point the interviewer asked Ruby if he thought the truth would ever come out. He replied:

> No. Because unfortunately these people, who have so much to gain and have such an ulterior motive to put me in the position I'm in, will never let the true facts come aboveboard to the world.

In those sentences, for all their tortured syntax, Jack Ruby may have given us more than an epitaph for himself. He may have uttered the ultimate truism about the sad, shoddy saga of the Kennedy assassination.

CHAPTER 24

Aftermath

*. . . so far as the FBI is concerned, the case will be
continued in an open classification for all time.*

—FBI Director J. Edgar Hoover

Since 1979, when Congress' Assassinations Committee reported,
the Kennedy case has seemed to have been abandoned by the
mainstream media, except when the anniversary comes around
each year. The Committee's conclusion, that both the President
and Martin Luther King were killed as a result of conspiracies,
drew sarcastic comment from the press. One editorial opined that
the Committee had done no service to history and should never
have convened at all if the best it could do was to prolong public
confusion. Meanwhile, one Justice Department official was reported as saying the latest official inquiry "offered nary a clue" as to
who, other than Oswald, might have taken part in the assassination. Another declared that the Justice Department had better
things to do than to "chase ghosts." Ignorant bluster like this did
not bode well for the further study the Committee recommended.
In the decade that followed, the Justice Department has been
predictably delinquent. Still, year by year, independent research
has broken new ground. In its earliest editions, this chapter charted the date of key figures in the case, and the status of key issues.
It is now brought up to date.

The acoustics evidence, credited by the Committee as proving
there were four shots, and therefore more than one gunman, has
had a rough ride since 1979. From the start, there were signs that
the press simply did not want to believe it. One eminent commen-
tator "declined to accept" the evidence for a second gunman, yet
admitted that he wrote without close study of the Committee's

volumes of evidence. "It would have taken too long, and I had a deadline," he told me. From a writer of such stature, it was a sorry admission.

On the other hand, the Committee was wrong to rely on its acoustics conclusion so heavily. Dissenting expert opinion was bound to come, and soon.

First there was the FBI, with a skimpy report declaring the two-gunman theory "invalid." Even a lay reading reveals this critique to be hopelessly flawed, and it deserves no public airing here. Former Assassinations Committee Chief Counsel Blakey called it "a public relations gimmick designed to avoid carrying the investigation forward." He respected today's FBI for its general competence, but said that "on the Kennedy case they seem institutionally incapable of thinking or acting positively. It is a failure that began within a day of the assassination, when the FBI decided there was no conspiracy, and it has blocked open-minded handling of the case ever since."

The serious blow to the acoustical evidence came in a 1982 report by the National Academy of Sciences. A panel of distinguished scientists concluded that the Committee's studies "do not demonstrate that there was a grassy knoll shot." At the core of the finding lay, not some abstruse scientist's deduction, but the curiosity of a rock drummer in Ohio, Steve Barber.

Barber came to the controversy thanks to a girlie magazine. In the summer of 1979 *Gallery* offered its readers, amongst the nudes, a record of the section of the police Dictabelt that includes the noises said to be gunshots. He played it again and again, and detected something the experts had missed. What had been thought to be unintelligible "crosstalk"—conversation coming in from another radio channel—Barber's ear identified as the voice of Sheriff Bill Decker, in the lead car of the motorcade. The Sheriff's voice occurs at the same point on the recording as the sound impulses that the Committee's experts said were gunshots. What he is saying is, "Move all men available out of my department back into the railroad yards there . . . to try to determine just what and where it happened down there. And hold everything secure until the homicide and other investigators can get there." Clearly Decker did not issue his orders till *after* the shooting, so

Barber's discovery triggered an onslaught on the acoustics evidence. Because of the timing, the Academy of Sciences was to conclude, the sounds on the recording had to be something other than gunshots, static perhaps, but not gunshots.

Dr. James Barger, chief acoustical scientist for Bolt, Beranek and Newman, whose expertise was used in court in connection with the infamous gap in the Watergate tapes, and after the Kent State shootings, was one of the experts who told the Assassinations Committee that sounds on the dictabelt were gunshots. Barger is unrepentant, in spite of the Academy's decision. "We used an entirely different method of identifying the time at which the recording was made," he says, "Our method involved noting what time the police dispatcher said it was. We think our method was much more straightforward, and much less subject to error by some extraneous artefact than was the Academy's method. Our method is more robust."

While Sheriff Decker's orders obviously came a minute or so after the shooting, Dr. Barger insists that this could have been caused in several ways. The Dictabelt needle could have jumped back—as sometimes occurred with that old-fashioned system—or the illusion of "crosstalk" may have been caused during copying of the original police recording.

Dr. Barger stands by his original findings, "The number of detections we made in our tests, and the speed of the detections—the odds that that could happen by chance are about one in twenty. That's just as plain as the nose on your face."

Physicist Paul Hoch, a veteran student of the assassination as well as a scientist, does not entirely share Barger's confidence. But he thinks the Academy of Sciences, having determined that there was a problem with the Sheriff's "crosstalk," should have gone on to study the Dictabelt's history. "Was there indeed a possibility that copying, or needle-jump was involved?" Hoch asks, "Did the Committee's experts detect real shots which were somehow made to overlap with the spoken words? There are reasons, independent of the acoustical analysis, for questioning the genealogy of the recordings. . . ."

The Committee's Chief Counsel, Professor Blakey, admits himself shaken by the Academy's conclusion, but annoyed that such a respected body failed to do a complete study. "What they did," Blakey says, "was to make an observation that does not contradict what we did, but shows up an inconsistency. And they've simply bought the inconsistency and quit. Another way of looking at it is to say that our study is inconsistent with theirs, therefore theirs is wrong. They didn't say we were wrong, if you look at it carefully. They didn't say there weren't four events on that tape. They made no effort to explain how those four random events would have fit so hand in glove with the film and eyewitness testimony, as well as the ballistics and everything else. They didn't go far enough. They should have gone forward and done some of the other studies we recommended. What would have happened if the other studies had *confirmed* our version? In the end, what do you have to believe that our experts made a mistake? Nothing really, except the inconvenience that flows from two shooters . . ."

"On balance," says Blakey, "I say there were two shooters in the Plaza, and not just because of the acoustics. And indeed it's the existence of the other testimony that makes me think the acoustics is right." Professor Blakey is referring not least to the large number of people—sixty-one by one count (see page 23)—that shooting came from in front of the President. (The very "crosstalk" by Sheriff Decker, which has disturbed the seeming certainty of the acoustics evidence, suggests that the Sheriff's own reaction was that the shooting came from the front—from the area of "the railroad yards" in front of the President.) As things stand, only more thorough investigation could vindicate or demolish the Assassinations Committee's reliance on its acoustics evidence. And even if the Dictabelt sounds were shown conclusively not to be gunshots, the case for conspiracy would not go away. It would simply lose what, in 1978, seemed to be brave new support from Science.

There is another branch of science, of course, that could have answered many of the key questions within hours of the assassination—had the autopsy been performed by forensic experts in Dallas, as the law required. Had the procedure been done by qualified personnel at the Naval Hospital in Washington, the questions might still have been answered. As it was, all agree that the Washington autopsy was a desperately bungled affair, performed by men with virtually no experience of gunshot wounds.

The best evidence, the President's wounded body, was squandered. In the past decade, however, that evidence has continued to cause every bit as much controversy as the wrangling over the acoustics.

The case of two coffins is one many view with distaste, none have satisfactorily explained, but that refuses to go away. It arises from the book *Best Evidence*, a massive investigative work by David Lifton, which in 1981 became a durable bestseller. In 1988 he produced a new edition, containing new surprises.

Lifton, a former computer engineer, has been fascinated by the Kennedy case since 1964, when stories of cover-up and "grassy knoll" gunmen first circulated. He is a man addicted to detail, and he first spent years analyzing the medical evidence and confronting the riddles that left him, as they have so many others, (*see Chapter 3*) disconcerted.

Was the entrance wound in the President's back just finger-deep, as appeared to be the case at the autopsy? Or was there really a bullet path leading to a point of exit in the throat for a bullet that had gone on to injure Governor Connally, as the official inquiries would have it? After many years, Lifton traced former Navy laboratory technician James Jenkins, who worked through the night in the autopsy room on November 22, 1963. Jenkins vividly recalled the probing of the back wound.

"What sticks out in my mind," says Jenkins, "is the fact that Commander Humes put his little finger in it, and, you know, said that . . . he could probe the bottom of it with his finger, which would mean to me it was very shallow." Later, when the surgeons opened the President's chest, Jenkins watched as the doctors probed again. "I remember looking inside the chest cavity and I could see the probe . . . through the pleura (*the lining of the chest cavity*). . . . You could actually see where it was making an indentation . . . where it was pushing the skin up. . . . There was no entry into the chest cavity. . . . No way that that could have exited in the front because it was then low in the chest cavity . . . somewhere around the junction of the descending aorta (the main artery carrying blood from the heart) or the bronchus in the lungs. . . ."

Jenkins' graphic account is compelling support for those who reject the magic bullet theory. Lifton's suspicions are aroused further by the fact that, while autopsy surgeon James Humes and the autopsy photographer say pictures were taken of the interior chest, no such photographs survived. This seemed relevant because all original testimony on the throat wound, by numerous Dallas doctors and nurses who saw it before a tracheotomy was performed, described it as a very small entry wound—no bigger than a pencil. Indeed, some of the Dallas doctors initially thought the bullet that entered there had lodged in the chest. At autopsy, Humes found a bloody bruise at the top of the right lung, but no bullet. Chest photographs were taken—both Humes and the autopsy photographer say so—yet no such photographs survived.

Was there fudging of the medical evidence, destruction of photographs that failed to support the notion of a bullet penetrating from the rear and exiting through the throat? Lifton's darker suspicion is that the missing pictures provide evidence that a bullet had in fact lodged in the chest but that—after it had been removed before the formal autopsy—the fact of its existence was suppressed.

Once again, failure to track the wound at autopsy, and the absence of either bullet or obvious rear exit, make the matter unresolvable. The wound may have been caused not by a missile, but by a bone fragment from the President's massive head injuries. The fact remains that, if the back wound did not exit—as Jenkins' testimony strongly suggests—the single bullet theory is invalid. In which case, (*see page 37*) more than one gunman fired at the President.

The President died, of course, from the terrible wounds to his head, and author Lifton exhaustively studied the evidence regarding the head. He pointed out that the Dallas and Bethesda doctors gave conflicting descriptions of the head wounds, that the Dallas doctors thought the wound they observed—at the right rear—was a wound of exit. None of the Dallas doctors reported the small wound at the back of the head, identified by the autopsy doctors as being a point of exit. While Lifton's work examines every minute detail and its potential meaning, I believe it may be in vain. So poorly were the wounds reported by the autopsy surgeons, so confusing has the reporting been since then of the medical photographs and X-rays, (*see p. 97*) so shoddy was the handling of the brain and the collection of bullet fragments, that it is probably impossible for anyone—however expert—to say the evidence proves the President was shot in the head from the rear, from in front, or perhaps from both directions at virtually the same instant. I make this remark carefully, after a prolonged re-reading of all the evidence.

Most recently, Lifton gave his attention to photographs of the President's body, taken at autopsy, which had previously been seen only by the original autopsy doctors, Assassinations Committee experts, and a few doctors permitted access by the Kennedy family. In 1979, however, some photographs began to circulate, apparently having been "liberated" by someone working for the Assassinations Committee. Another set, Lifton says, was provided by James Fox, a former photographer for the Secret Service. Horrific though they are, the photographs have now been shown on television—notably on Walter Cronkite's PBS television special in 1988—and published in two books, including the latest edition of Lifton's *Best Evidence*. Two of them (*frontispiece and Illustration No. 5a*) are published in this edition. The former, a moving photograph of a President familiar even in death, shows the controversial throat injuries. The second, showing the rear of the head, has caused fresh controversy.

Illustration 5a shows a large flap of scalp and bone laid open, like a hatchcover, beside a terrible hole, directly above the dead man's right ear. There is no sign at all of the massive damage to the occipital area, the back of the skull, that was described by the Dallas medical staff. The rear of the President's head looks virtually undamaged, and this has greatly puzzled many people.

Dr. Robert McClelland, the general surgeon who helped perform the tracheotomy, is one of those best qualified to describe the President's head wounds from memory. "I took the position at the head of the table," he told the Warren Commission, "I was in such a position that I could very closely examine the head wound, and I noted that the right posterior portion of the skull had been blasted. It had been shattered, apparently, by the force of the shot so that the parietal bone was protruded up through the scalp and seen to

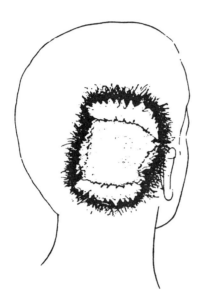

be fractured almost along its posterior half, as well as some of the occipital bone being fractured in its lateral half, and this sprung open the bones that I mentioned, in such a way that you could actually look down into the skull cavity itself and see that probably a third or so, at least, of the brain tissue, posterior cerebral tissue and some of the cerebellar tissue had been blasted out." The wound McClelland described would look like the drawing above, a drawing that he approved for publication during the Sixties. No such damage can be seen in Illustration 5a.

The only neurosurgeon present at the President's deathbed, Dr. Kemp Clark, described the wound as a "large, gaping loss of tissue" located at the "back of the head . . . towards the right side." No less than eleven other Parkland doctors, and four nurses—including the supervising nurse—have described this gaping wound at the back of the head. A large bone fragment later found in Dealey Plaza was identified at the time as coming from the back of the skull.

The Secret Serviceman who climbed into the President's limousine as the shooting ended, Clint Hill, said, "I noticed a portion of the President's head on the right rear side was missing. . . . Part of his brain was gone. I saw a part of his skull with hair on it lying in the seat. . . . The right rear portion of his head was missing. It was lying in the rear seat of the car."

Jacqueline Kennedy came to one of the doctors in the emergency room, her hands cupped one over the other. She was holding her husband's brain matter in her hands. "From the front there was nothing," she later said of the wounds. "But from the back you could see, you know, you were trying to hold his hair and his skull on."

Author David Lifton traced the technicians who X-rayed the President's body in Washington, Edward Reed and Jerrol Custer. They too recalled a posterior wound, and Custer said it was enormous. "I could put both my hands in the wound."

The eyewitness testimony seems incontrovertible. The back of the President's head was shattered. After studying Illustration 5a, which shows the rear of the President's head virtually unmarked, several of the Dallas medical staff expressed consternation. One, Dr. Bashour, insisted the photograph was wrong. "Why do they cover it up?" he repeated several times, "This is not the way it was!"

In 1966 David Lifton pounced on an unnoticed paragraph in an FBI report that seemed to offer an explanation for the medical anomalies. Two agents, James Sibert and Francis O'Neill, were present at the Washington autopsy. ". . . it was ascertained," their report says of the doctors' initial examination ". . . that a tracheotomy had been performed, *as well as surgery of the head area*, namely, in the top of the skull." (author's italics) Years later Agent Sibert told this author that this was a direct quote—"exactly what the doctor said."

For David Lifton, this report was a telltale clue that went to the heart of the matter. Unable to believe that numerous doctors lied, yet unable to reconcile the differences between the Dallas wound descriptions and those made in Washington, he decided that "the body lied to the doctors. . . . During the six hour period between the Dallas assassination and the Bethesda autopsy, President Kennedy's body was intercepted and altered."

It sounds utterly preposterous. Lifton's theory supposes a complex operation, for which hardly any time was available, and which would surely have become known to too many people to remain secret long. Yet there is no denying Lifton the remarkable testimony that resulted from his decades of research. Consider first his evidence for more than one coffin.

Lifton tracked down the undertaker who placed President Kennedy in the coffin in Dallas. Aubrey Rike, now a police sergeant, told how the body was wrapped in sheets, then laid on a plastic sheet—to keep the blood away from the satin lining of an expensive casket. This was the one millions later saw on television, arriving in Washington aboard Air Force One. It was heavy, bronze, a ceremonial affair. Three witnesses from Bethesda Naval Hospital in Washington, however, say the President arrived there in a totally different casket.

Dennis David, who retired from the Navy as a Lieutenant Commander in the Medical Service Corps, was a Petty Officer on November 22, 1963. He was medical "Chief of the Day" when he learned that the President's body was coming to Bethesda. David was there when the coffin that now bore the President's body was unloaded at the rear of the hospital—from "a black unmarked ambulance." The casket was a plain, grey box, a metal box," says David, "Anybody who's ever been in Vietnam will know what I'm talking about. We shipped hundreds of bodies out of there in the same kind of casket. It was just a plain, shipping casket."

Paul O'Connor, one of two medical technicians who prepared the body for autopsy, was in the morgue when the casket came in. O'Connor, who worked in a funeral home as a youth, is a retired police officer. His memory of the casket that bore the President is also quite clear—it was "a grey metal casket . . . a typical pinkish-grey shipping casket . . . a plain casket, a cheap casket." Former Petty Officer Donald Rebentisch, and Floyd Reibe, assistant to the autopsy photographer, also says it was "not a viewing casket," not at all like the "very nice expensive" panelled casket in which the President left the Dallas Hospital, and which was seen being unloaded at the airport in Washington.

The coffin problem does not end here. Not only the Dallas undertaker, Rike, but also three nurses and a hospital orderly, say the bleeding body was laid out on a plastic sheet in the bronze casket. Paul O'Connor recalls opening the casket to see "a grey body bag, zipped shut. We unzipped the body bag, and the President's body was lifted out. . . ." Asked whether he could be mistaken, whether the President could have left the Dallas Hospital in a body bag, Rike says, "No way. . . . I remember picking him up. I'm the one that had blood and everything on my shirt from the body."

A mass of evidence indicates that at least two ambulances were used in a very odd arrival procedure at the Naval Hospital that night, a black ambulance and a regular grey Navy ambulance. James Felder, a former Army sergeant on the security guard awaiting the President's body, says, "There were two ambulances. One was supposed to be the decoy." A Navy man on the same detail, Hubert Clark, also speaks of a decoy. So did Bethesda Chief of the Day Layton Ledbetter. So again, did Donald Rebentisch and others. Richard Lipsey, former aide to the general commanding the Military District of Washington, explains it as "strictly a security measure."

The notion of a security measure, designed to protect the President's body in a potentially unruly crowd, at first seems plausible. But it leaves serious questions unanswered. Two witnesses, Dennis David and Jerrol Custer, recall seeing Mrs. Kennedy arrive in the grey Navy ambulance—the one carrying the Dallas casket—and enter the hospital by the front door. The problem is that, by that time, the President's body had *already been unloaded*—from the unmarked black ambulance at the rear. Indeed, it had been there long enough for X-ray pictures to have been taken. Jerrol Custer, the X-ray technician, was on the way through the lobby on his second or third trip with those pictures, when he met Mrs. Kennedy "coming in through the main entrance."

The only way to construe this testimony is that the coffin that arrived at the airport from Dallas, to be taken nonstop to Bethesda, was empty. Yet witness after witness insists that, while there may have been decoy *ambulances*, the President's body was never disturbed between Dallas and Washington. The evidence of two totally different coffins, and of a military-style body bag in

Washington where there had been none at Dallas, suggests otherwise.

Author Lifton believes it all supports his theory that the body was a medical forgery, that the President's head wounds were altered to conceal the fact that he had been shot from the front, and that there was thus a conspiracy. In one of the available autopsy pictures, he points out "what appears to be a clip or device inside the head." Lifton wonders whether this is evidence of the reconstruction of the head which, he believes, followed surgical alteration—before arrival at Bethesda. The "clip" picture, however, like so much else in the medical evidence, is not clear enough for certainty. Lifton's theory remains just that, a theory.

Today Lifton suspects, and the authors of *High Treason*, a 1989 book by Harrison Livingstone and Robert Groden—formerly a photographic consultant to Congress' Assassinations Committee—believe totally, that there was forgery of autopsy photographs and X-rays. They do so in spite of a firm conclusion by the rest of the Committee's experts that the photographs are authentic, a finding supported in 1981 by a panel of photo-optics experts and a radiologist retained by the *Boston Globe*.*

Meanwhile, in 1988, four of the Dallas hospital doctors, acting as consultants for PBS Television's *Nova* program, were permitted to view the autopsy pictures and X-rays held at the National Archives. Doctors Dulany, Jenkins, Peters, and McClelland now saw this evidence for the first time. All had previously said that on November 22, 1963, they observed a massive wound at the rear of the President's head. Now, though, they emerged from the viewing room saying that they had seen no evidence that wounds had been altered. How then to explain Illustration 5a which shows a head unmarked where the Dallas doctors placed a gaping wound?

I interviewed Dr. McClelland in 1989. He explained that, when he saw the President in the emergency room, a great flap of scalp and hair had been "split and thrown backwards, so we had looked down into the hole." In Illustration 5a, however, McClelland believes the scalp is being pulled forward, back to its

* See Ben Bradlee Jr. in *Boston Globe*, June 21, 1981, and Steve Parks in *Baltimore Sun*, November 18, 1979.

normal position, to show what looks like a small entrance wound near the top of the skull. This is not visible in Illustration 5a. "I don't think they were trying to cover up the fact that there was a large hole," said McClelland, "but that's what they were doing . . . they were covering up that great defect in the back and lateral part of the head by pulling that loose scalp flap up. You can see the hand pulling the scalp forward."*

Dr. McClelland says the "great defect in the back" *is* visible on some photographs amongst the *full* set of some fifty pictures he saw at the National Archives—pictures in which the torn scalp has been allowed to fall back on the President's neck, pictures the public has never seen. His explanation goes a long way to explain the apparent discrepancy. None of the other doctors who have inspected the autopsy evidence, however, have referred to such photographs. Dr. McClelland's observation certainly demonstrates that no outside researcher should form judgments on the basis of the incomplete set of photographs that is as yet in circulation. That said, other questions about the autopsy record remain unresolved even for Dr. McClelland, who of course has seen the materials at the National Archives. As this edition went to press, the doctor who attended the dying President added his own doubts to those of laymen who question the authenticity of the autopsy X-rays. *Inside Edition*, the nationally syndicated television program, reported in 1989 that McClelland "says the X-rays do not show the same injuries to the President's head that he saw in the emergency room."

Interviewed on the program, Dr. McClelland said, "There is an inconsistency. Some of the skull X-rays show only the back part of the head missing, with a fracture of the anterior part of the skull on the right. Others, on the other hand, show what appears to be the entire right side of the skull gone, with a portion of the orbit— that's the skull around the eye—missing too. That to me is an inconsistent finding. I don't understand that, unless there has been some attempt to cover up the nature of the wound."

---

* Dr. McClelland's statement is supported by the autopsy surgeons' report of January 26, 1967, reprinted in Harold Weisberg's *Post Mortem*, p. 577-579.

Dr. McClelland, still a senior surgeon in Dallas, is astonishingly forthright about how the President was hit. "I think he was shot from the front. . . . I think that the rifle bullet hit him in the side of the head and blew out the back of his head. . . . I certainly think that's what happened, and that probably somewhere in the front part of the head, in the front part of the scalp, there probably was an entry wound, which—amongst all the blood and the laceration there and everything, was not seen, by us or anybody else perhaps, and it blew out the back part of his head." Dr. McClelland was one of the doctors who appeared on a heavily researched 1988 documentary made by Sylvia Chase and Stanhope Gould. Both are veteran journalists, respected across the United States. Gould is the winner of four Emmy awards for investigative journalism. It was his program on Watergate that did most to bring Watergate to national attention. Chase and Gould followed up on David Lifton's work, and re-interviewed the witnesses. Both came away impressed and troubled.

The Lifton evidence is, in Gould's judgement, "what amounts to courtroom evidence that the President's body left Dallas in one coffin and arrived at Bethesda in another. With that, and with the discrepancy between the autopsy photos and the recollection of several eyewitnesses as to the location of the head wounds . . . it seems clear that—whether or not there was a conspiracy to murder JFK—there was a conspiracy to cover up essential facts."

"Somebody is concealing the whole plot," Dr. McClelland said in late 1988, "There was somebody on the grassy knoll who shot at the President and blew his head off." Coming as it does, at this time, from Dr. McClelland, this is a remarkable statement. It is likely to reverberate for a long time.

On all the evidence—and there is far too much to lay out here—it is *impossible* to say flatly that shots came only from the rear. To say that is to bend the available facts. Those same facts leave a good possibility that the President was hit from the front, and perhaps, at almost the same moment, from both front and rear. The historical verdict, in the end, will surely be that there may have hits from both directions, but that there can be no certainty on this vital issue.

* * * * * * * * * *

Officer J. D. Tippit has till now been little more than a cipher in the assassination story. Within hours of the assassination, he became simply the "poor dumb cop," the fellow Oswald drew attention to himself by shooting, before getting arrested in a nearby movie theater. As we have seen, (*in Chapter 6*) the evidence that Oswald—and Oswald alone—shot Tippit, is shaky. The Tippit angle was never thoroughly investigated, either by the Warren Commission or Congress' Assassinations Committee. Today, after work by independent researchers, it is clear that it should have been.

For Officer Tippit, it now appears, November 22 1963 began as a day of marital drama, a sad suburban soap opera that became by chance a sideshow of national tragedy. A Dallas citizen, Larry Harris—along with a friend in law enforcement, Ken Holmes Jr.— has spent much time investigating the background of the dead policeman. He discovered that Tippit, a married man with three children, had been having a long affair with a blonde waitress at Austin's Barbecue Drive-In, where he moonlighted as a security man on weekends. The waitress, too, was married, and—for legal reasons—neither she nor her husband will be named here.

Harris and Holmes traced Tippit's former mistress, who admitted that she and the policeman were lovers for some two years. She has offered two different dates for the end of the affair, summer 1963 and early fall 1963. The dates are significant, for the woman may have been pregnant with Tippit's child.

According to the mistress' husband, whom she divorced in August 1963, Tippit's murder led directly to their reconciliation. He and his former wife went together, he says, to view the policeman's body at the funeral home, before the widow and her family arrived. The experience greatly upset the mistress, and she confessed that she was pregnant by Tippit. A child was indeed born seven months later. Tippit's mistress, though, claims it was her former husband's child, and that it was reared accordingly. After the President's assassination—and Officer Tippit's murder—the couple stayed together for several years, then parted finally in 1968. But there is more.

According to one source, Tippit's wife visited a neighbor on the morning of November 22, in tears because "on that morning Officer Tippit has told her he wanted a divorce to marry someone else." By the mistress' account, her husband—though a drinker and womanizer himself—had been greatly upset by her affair with Tippit. Several times he had followed her and Tippit late at night, trailing them in his car. Could the death of Officer Tippit have been a crime of passion? Or was it more complex? There have long been suggestions that Tippit was somehow linked with organized crime, or with right-wing politics. Why was Tippit off his regular beat when he was killed? Shortly before his death, several witnesses reported, Tippit spent some ten minutes sitting in his patrol car at a service station not far from where he would be killed. He then drove off at high speed. Just ten minutes before he was murdered, it was learned from fresh interviews in 1982, Tippit hurried into a record shop near the site of the killing. He hastily used the store's telephone to dial a number, then rushed out again. Assassinations Committee counsel Andrew Purdy offers a conspiratorial hypothesis. "It may be," he said in 1988, "that Officer Tippit, by himself or with others, was involved in a conspiracy to silence Oswald. And that when the attempt to kill Oswald by Tippit failed, then Jack Ruby was a fallback."

The murder of Officer Tippit has been called the Rosetta Stone of the Kennedy case, the key to the mystery, because it led so directly to Oswald's arrest. Yet all we know for sure about the Tippit angle is that we do not know enough. It was never properly investigated.

* * * * * * * * * *

Much has been made of the fact that many important witnesses died violently, or strangely, in the wake of the Kennedy assassination.[125]

Yet time does pass, and men do die; it would be wrong to read too much into their deaths. All the same, it is interesting to record what has happened to some of the principals in the crime of the century.

Guy Banister, former FBI agent and intelligence operative, helper of Mafia chief Carlos Marcello, died in 1964 of a heart attack. Banister, who had told his secretary not to talk to the FBI about Oswald, died without giving evidence to the Warren Commission.

David Ferrie, aide in Carlos Marcello's apparatus, and alleged CIA operative, attracted brief official attention less than forty-eight hours after the assassination. Just hours before Ruby killed Oswald, and while Ferrie was still away on his peculiar marathon around Texas, a disaffected member of Banister's staff called New Orleans authorities to say he suspected Ferrie of involvement in the President's murder. This was Jack Martin, a Banister investigator, and he voiced suspicion that Ferrie had been in contact with Oswald. Within hours of the assassination, Martin had been involved in a dispute with Banister—a confrontation that may have occurred when Banister caught Martin trying to examine confidential files. For whatever reason, Banister injured Martin by hitting him on the head with a revolver butt. It was the day after this, following a visit to the hospital, that Martin raised the alarm over Ferrie. A hue and cry began, but Ferrie—as we have seen—was away in Texas. His associates, questioned in his absence, proved uninformative. One did, however, relate a strange incident. He said that a lawyer had already been to Ferrie's home, promising to act on Ferrie's behalf as soon as he returned. The lawyer, said Ferrie's friend, had remarked that "when Lee Harvey Oswald was arrested by the Dallas police, Oswald was carrying a library card with Ferrie's name on it." The lawyer, C. Wray Gill, was one of Carlos Marcello's attorneys. Ferrie spoke with Gill by telephone, on the evening of the day Ruby killed Oswald, but did not immediately report to the authorities. When he finally did so next day, Ferrie turned up accompanied by the Marcello lawyer. He denied knowing anything about Oswald or the assassination. Martin, the informant who had started the chase after Ferrie, was dismissed as a crank with a grudge. Ferrie was released. His accuser, Jack Martin, is indeed an odd character—a fact for which Ferrie may have been most grateful. As this story has shown, there was good reason to suspect him. A case in point is the reported concern by Marcello's lawyer about a library card.

Nothing in the record reflects the finding in Oswald's possession of any document relating to Ferrie. Yet the Secret Service did ask Ferrie whether he had loaned Oswald his library card. Ferrie denied it, but the statements of two witnesses suggest he was panic-stricken over just that. One of Oswald's former neighbors in New Orleans would later tell investigators that Ferrie visited her after the assassination—asking about Oswald's library card. Oswald's own landlady says the same—and adds a disturbing factor. She recalls Ferrie turning up to ask about the card within hours of the assassination—*before* he set off on his Texas trip. This bizarre episode, which may be of key significance, remains unexplained.[126] In the event Ferrie went free, largely because the authorities accepted his alibi—that he had been in a New Orleans court at the actual moment of the assassination. The case he supposedly attended was—irony of ironies—the latest stage in Carlos Marcello's fight against Kennedy efforts to have him deported. Marcello won that legal bout and was in court for his victory. Both he and his lawyer Gill vouched for Ferrie's alibi, but their stories were inconsistent. Marcello said Ferrie had been at the courthouse at the crucial time, while Gill's information was that Ferrie had been at his office till shortly after noon, when he departed. Ferrie did not come back to the office and later claimed that he spent the rest of the day of the President's murder "celebrating" Marcello's court victory. Ferrie's ties with Marcello were to last till the end of his life, but—three years after the assassination—he had no cause to celebrate.

In late 1966 he was questioned by New Orleans District Attorney Jim Garrison, who had opened a local investigation into the Kennedy assassination. Garrison discovered that, like Ruby, Ferrie had apparently acquired large sums of money around the time of the President's murder. In the three weeks before the assassination, Ferrie reportedly deposited more than seven thousand dollars in the bank. In pursuit of these and other leads, Garrison planned to arrest Ferrie. It was not to be.

On February 22, 1967, David Ferrie was found dead at home. The coroner's ruling said "natural causes," but the death caused great speculation. Ferrie left behind two ambiguous notes. They suggested suicide, but the text and signature, in each note, was typed. In Ferrie's last known conversation, which was with a reporter, he apparently discussed Jimmy Hoffa and the Teamsters Union. The Garrison inquiry fizzled out in a blaze of adverse publicity—an episode in which concern about Mafia links was conspicuously absent. In 1979 an Assassination Committee report noted that the New Orleans District Attorney met John Roselli—a key figure in the Mafia's relationship with the CIA—no more than a month after Ferrie's death. The report quoted a CIA Inspector General's report, as finding this meeting, coming at the height of the New Orleans investigation, "particularly disturbing." Within hours of Ferrie's death, the corpse of his associate Eladio del Valle was found sprawled in a car in Miami. In his case the cause of death was not in doubt. Del Valle had been shot in the heart at point-blank range, and his skull was split open. Del Valle, a prominent anti-Castro exile, was reportedly an associate of Florida Mafia boss Santos Trafficante. When he died he was being sought for questioning in the New Orleans inquiry.

Jim Braden (né Eugene Brading), who was briefly detained for "acting suspiciously" near the scene of the assassination, is alive. In 1978 he testified to the Assassinations Committee. The assembled information on Braden/Brading was to be considered—along with all other evidence—in the Justice Department's review of the Committee's findings and research.

Loran Hall, the anti-Castro militant who came forward at a convenient moment to explain away the mysterious "Oswald" visit to Silvia Odio's home, it also still alive. In 1977, when first summoned to appear before the Assassinations Committee, he declined to answer when asked whether he was in Dallas on the day of the assassination. Hall later testified in secret session after being given immunity from prosecution arising from his testimony. Elsewhere, Hall has stated that—a month before the assassination—"right-wing radicals," in league with CIA operatives, offered him money to take part in the Kennedy assassination. He has claimed that there have been attempts to kill him and that the FBI distorted his original replies to questions about the Odio episode. Congress' Assassinations Committee, however, has called his original story about visiting Odio "an admitted fabrication." The Odio incident, involving either Oswald or the use of his name before the assassination, remains central to the Kennedy investigation. In a case with a shrinking list of witnesses, it is essential that the full pressure of the law be applied to obtain answers to the obvious questions. Why the fabrication, and what was its inspiration?[127] Hall, it should be noted, was a comrade (in the International Brigade) of Frank Sturgis—who also figures in accounts of deliberate disinformation in the assassination inquiry.

George de Mohrenschildt, the Russian-born Dallas resident who became close to Oswald after his return from the Soviet Union, was found shot dead in March 1977. The coroner's verdict was suicide; the dead man had been shot through the mouth with a 20-gauge shotgun. On the morning of the day he died, an investigator for the Assassinations Committee had called to arrange an interview. De Mohrenschildt received this message with seeming equanimity. Indeed, that same morning, de Mohrenschildt had given one of a series of interviews on the Kennedy assassination to an independent researcher. However, there is evidence that de Mohrenschildt was suffering from severe psychological problems in the months before his death. Earlier, de Mohrenschildt and his wife had prepared a manuscript about Lee Oswald, entitled *I'm a Patsy*. He reportedly said in a 1977 interview that there had been a conspiracy to kill the President and that an element of American intelligence played a part in it. De Mohrenschildt's later statements were confused and ambiguous, but one factor in his life cannot now be ignored. As the Assassinations Committee established, de Mohrenschildt did have connections with both the CIA and U.S. Army Intelligence.[128] Congressman Richardson Preyer, then Chairman of the Assassinations Committee, said on hearing of de Mohrenschildt's death, "He was a crucial witness. . . ."

Carlos Prio, former President of Cuba and friend of top Mafia leaders, has been linked in testimony with both Jack Ruby and anti-Castro militant Frank Sturgis. He was found shot dead in 1977, a week after the death of George de Mohrenschildt. Prio was seated in a chair, with a pistol beside him, outside the garage of his Miami home. The verdict was suicide. He too was on the list of those the Assassinations Committee had hoped to interview.

Jimmy Hoffa, the Teamsters leader who had threatened the lives of both Kennedy brothers, disappeared in July 1975. His body was never found. Government investigators believe that, after being lured to a meeting in Detroit with Anthony Provenzano—a Teamsters official with close links to the Mafia—Hoffa was shot dead. It has been reported that his body was taken away by truck, stuffed into a fifty-gallon drum; it was then, reportedly, consigned to oblivion by being crushed and smelted.

Hoffa was in Miami when President Kennedy was killed. He flew into a rage when he heard that fellow officials in Washington had lowered the flag at Teamsters headquarters to half mast. When a reporter asked him for his reaction to the assassination, Hoffa snapped, "Bobby Kennedy is just another lawyer now."

Shortly afterward the Teamsters boss in Puerto Rico, Frank Chavez, wrote to the President's brother that he was making a collection—to "clean, beautify, and supply with flowers the grave of Lee Harvey Oswald. You can rest assured contributions will be unanimous." Robert Kennedy, who was of course murdered while campaigning for President less than five years after his brother, suspected Hoffa's hand in the tragedy at Dallas. His friend and biographer, Arthur Schlesinger, told me in 1978, "Robert Kennedy had very serious reservations about the Warren Commission Report. He developed serious doubts and was open to the possibility of a conspiracy."

In the context of the web of intrigue surrounding the assassination, one recent allegation has potentially explosive implications. According to a Government informant described by veteran investigators as "absolutely reliable," Jimmy Hoffa was the "original liaison" between the CIA and the Mafia in their Castro murder plots. The informant, a former Chicago contract killer called Charles Crimaldi, claims Hoffa was killed to protect the secrets of those plots and all that stemmed from them. The record encourages the belief that Crimaldi is right.

Salvatore Granello and James Plumeri, both of whose names have been linked with those of Hoffa and Santos Trafficante, reportedly played minor roles in the Castro assassination plots. Granello was found murdered in late 1970. He had been shot four times in the head, and his corpse was left in the trunk of a car. Plumeri was executed a few months later.

Dave Yaras, Hoffa henchman and old friend of Jack Ruby, was murdered in 1974. He had been deeply involved in affairs in Cuba.

Charles Nicoletti, who had reportedly also been involved in the Castro conspiracies, was murdered in 1977. He was discovered in a Chicago parking lot, slumped over the wheel of his car with three bullet wounds in the back of the head. Nicoletti's dead foot was jammed against the accelerator, so that the engine—apparently still running after his death—overheated. The car was severely damaged by fire, obliterating possible fingerprints and other evidence. The day before Nicoletti died, Assassinations Committee staff had reportedly begun trying to contact him for an interview.

Irwin Weiner, the Chicago bondsman who specialized in getting jailed gangsters out on bail, is alive. Weiner, who received a call from Jack Ruby just weeks before the Kennedy assassination, did not satisfy Congress' Assassinations Committee with his explanations. The Committee did not accept that Ruby would have turned to Weiner, in far-off Chicago, for legal help with his union problems in Dallas. The Congressmen noted that Weiner had admitted lying about the Ruby call on one recent occasion, and also remarked on something else. Earl Ruby, Jack's surviving brother, alleged that Weiner made a "business proposition" to him—the day before Ruby's brother was due to testify before the Committee. Weiner denied it, and the Committee was "not able to resolve the difference between the two witnesses."

Sam Giancana, the Chicago Mafia boss who took part in the CIA's attempts to kill Fidel Castro, was murdered in June 1975. He was found at home, lying face up in a pool of blood. Giancana had been shot once in the back of the head and six times—in a neatly stitched circle—around the mouth. When he died the Senate Intelligence Committee was preparing to question him about the CIA plots to kill Fidel Castro. The one clue in the Giancana killing was a sawed-off .22-caliber pistol, which police traced to a gun shop in Florida. In 1978 I talked to an authoritative witness who was involved in the original Castro plots and who knew Giancana well. He remarked, "When the Senate Intelligence Committee was formed, the headlines in Chicago said, 'Giancana Hired to Kill Castro.' So a few days later, before Sam can come here to testify, he's dead. There's a gun found a few days later. The gun originally was purchased in Miami. Now when do you get a hit man in Chicago going all the way to Miami to buy a gun, when in Chicago you can get a gun on any corner? Somebody didn't want Sam to testify, and all Sam was going to say was 'I did a contract for Santos—period.'" "Santos Trafficante?" I asked. "That would have been the headline," replied my contact.

Charles Crimaldi, the Government informant who also claims knowledge of the Hoffa murder, agrees that Giancana was executed to stop him talking about the CIA-Mafia plots.

Leo Moceri, an Ohio syndicate figure, also told a Government agent that this was the reason for the murders of both Giancana and Hoffa. After his second meeting with the agent, Moceri vanished. His car was found abandoned.

John Roselli, the Las Vegas gangster who also took a leading part in the CIA assassination plots, disappeared in July 1976 after leaving his Florida home to play golf. His car was found empty at the Miami airport. Ten days later, Roselli's decomposing body was found floating in Miami's Dumfoundling Bay, rammed into an oil drum. The drum was weighted with chains and punctured with holes, apparently intended to ensure that the gases from the corpse escaped and did not bring it to the surface. Police found that Roselli had been garotted and stabbed. His legs had been sawed off and squashed into the drum along with the torso and head. At the time of his death Roselli had testified to the Senate Intelligence Committee and was due to appear again.

Florida Mafia boss Santos Trafficante had dined with Roselli about two weeks before he vanished. "Authorities believe," the *New York Times* reported, "it was a member of the Trafficante organization who was able to lure Mr. Roselli to his death." According to one report, Roselli was last seen alive on a boat owned by an associate of Trafficante. During the Senate Intelligence Committee inquiry, Trafficante was out of reach in Costa Rica.

Before he died, Roselli had reportedly informed the Government that he believed his former associates in the Castro assassination plots had gone on to murder President Kennedy. Within weeks of his death, the House of Representatives voted by a huge majority to reopen the Kennedy assassination case. It was this decision that led to the formation of the Assassinations Committee.

Robert Maheu, the former FBI agent who became the CIA emissary first charged with recruiting the Mafia to kill Castro, is alive and available for further questioning.

James Hosty, the Dallas FBI agent who handled the Oswald case before the assassination, has now retired. Although his personal performance before the assassination appears to have been efficient, he was one of several FBI officers disciplined after the assassination. Hosty maintains this was unjustified and says privately that much remains to be uncovered about the case.

Gordon Shanklin, the top Dallas agent who—says Hosty—ordered the destruction of the note delivered to the FBI by Oswald, has died.

Regis Kennedy, a senior agent who played a key role in the New Orleans investigation, now emerges in—at the very least—a shabby role. His attitude to organized crime was wholly inconsistent with his post. When David Ferrie needed an alibi after the assassination, it was Regis Kennedy who lined up with Carlos Marcello himself, and with Marcello's lawyer, to provide the inconsistent alibi. If Kennedy did see Ferrie that fateful noontime, it was right to say so. However, this FBI officer's attitude to the Mafia, and to

Marcello in particular, seems indefensible. Contrary to all other authorities, he insisted to the Assassinations Committee that Marcello was indeed a mere "tomato salesman and real estate investor." Regis Kennedy declared blithely that he "did not believe Marcello was a significant organized-crime figure" and singled out the 1963 period as one of Marcello's innocent years. A report by the chief counsel of the Assassinations Committee found that the FBI's "limited work on the Marcello case may have been attributable to a disturbing attitude on the part of the senior agent who supervised the case, Regis Kennedy." Regis Kennedy directed much of the New Orleans inquiry after the assassination and was one of those assigned to investigate the original allegation that Marcello had uttered threats against the President's life. He died in 1978, shortly after talking to the Assassinations Committee. Two of the most senior FBI executives, who gave orders from Washington during the Kennedy inquiry, are also beyond further questioning. Bureau Director J. Edgar Hoover is dead.

William Sullivan, one of Hoover's top aides, would have been questioned by the Assassinations Committee in 1978. Before that could take place, however, Sullivan was found shot dead—the victim of an apparent hunting accident at daybreak. Sullivan had been head of the FBI's Division Five, which handled much of the Kennedy and King investigations. He was also deeply involved with the notorious COINTELPRO operation which Hoover used to infiltrate and smear the political left. In 1975 Sullivan responded in opaque fashion to a question from a Congressional committee about Oswald. Asked whether he had seen anything in the files to indicate a relationship between Oswald and the CIA, Sullivan replied, "No . . . I think there may be something on that, but you asked me if I had seen anything. I don't recall having seen anything like that, but I think there is something on that point. . . . It rings a bell in my head." Sullivan's fatal accident occurred before the Assassinations Committee could ask him to be more specific about the source of that bell in his mind.

Desmond FitzGerald, the CIA officer who played a leading role in the CIA's plotting against Fidel Castro and reportedly masqueraded as a U.S. Senator when meeting the Cuban traitor Cubela, is also dead.

William Pawley, former American diplomat, shot himself in 1977, at the height of Congressional inquiry into the Kennedy assassination. In June 1963 Pawley had collaborated with Mafia figure John Martino in the bizarre, CIA-aided operation to prove that Soviet missiles were still in Cuba. It was Martino who, before his own death in 1976, said privately that an anti-Castro conspiracy was behind the Kennedy assassination.

Howard Hunt, the former CIA officer who was among the first to recommend the assassination of Castro, is still alive. In 1954, like Pawley, he was instrumental in the ruthless overthrow of the Communist-oriented regime in Guatemala. Guy Banister, who reportedly manipulated Lee Oswald in the summer of 1963, has also been linked with the Guatemala operation. The report persists that Hunt was in Mexico City in late September 1963, at the time of Oswald's visit to Mexico.[129] Hunt denies this, as he has denied allegations that he was in Dallas on the day of the assassination.

Frank Sturgis (né Fiorino),[130] Howard Hunt's associate in the Watergate burglary, was one of those who helped spread the story that Oswald was affiliated to Castro's intelligence service. He is still alive. Hunt says he did not meet Sturgis until 1972, while Sturgis has said he met Hunt two years before the Kennedy assassination. Sturgis has denied to say where he was on the day the President was killed.

In 1979 an Assassinations Committee report stated that Sturgis took part in an anti-Castro operation called "Cellula Fantasma." This involved dropping leaflets from the skies over Cuba, and Sturgis—who was a pilot—was involved. The importance of the detail is that Sturgis has been connected to the operation by a Cuban who attended its planning stages. The Cuban is Antonio Veciana, and his reason for mentioning the scheme to Congressional investigators was the identity of a CIA officer who took a personal interest in it. The officer, says Veciana, was "Maurice Bishop."

Antonio Veciana was the victim of a murder attempt in late 1979—
an ambush while he was on the way home from work. Four shots
were fired, and a fragment of one bullet lodged in Veciana's head.
He recovered—in what police and doctors consider a freak escape.
Publicly the veteran anti-Castro fighter has blamed the attack on
Castro agents, but privately he has also expressed concern that it
may have been linked to his allegations about CIA case officer
"Maurice Bishop," who—says Veciana—met Oswald shortly before the Kennedy assassination and later urged the fabrication of a
false story about Oswald and Cuban diplomats in Mexico City.
More on this vital area follows in the next chapter.

* * * * * * * * * *

Final Targets

The Kennedy case has not been dead in the water since 1980. The
pages that follow include new developments and fresh information, the fruits of the labors of those researchers who have continued to press ahead in the face of official apathy. First, what has
become of the two Mafia chieftains targeted by Congress' Assassinations Committee as prime suspects?

Santos Trafficante, the Florida Mafia chieftain suspected by the
Assassinations Committee of involvement in the Kennedy assassination, died in 1987, following heart surgery. About two hundred people attended the funeral, including one fellow in a black
suit, black shirt and white tie, with a red carnation in his lapel.
Trafficante's body was placed in a marble mausoleum at the La
Uniana Italiana Cemetery in a shabby part of Tampa. He was 72.

Ten years earlier, Trafficante had been forced by subpoena to
appear before Congress's Assassinations Committee. He turned
up, suave and sprightly, and solemnly swore to tell the truth.
Among the questions the Committee asked Trafficante were these
three:

> "Did you ever discuss with any individual plans to assassinate
> President Kennedy?"

"Prior to November 22, 1963, did you know Jack Ruby?"
"While you were in prison in Cuba, were you visited by Jack Ruby?"

In response to all three questions Trafficante intoned, "I respectfully refuse to answer pursuant to my constitutional rights under the First, Fourth, Fifth, and Fourteenth Amendments." "Pleading the Fifth" on the principal that no person can be forced to give evidence that may be incriminating to himself, is a traditional recourse of organized-crime figures. Later, Trafficante appeared again, after being granted immunity from prosecution arising from his own evidence. After testifying on that basis once in secret, Trafficante was called before a public hearing in late 1978. He denied saying in advance that President Kennedy was "going to be hit." Asked whether he was aware of threats made against the President by Carlos Marcello, Trafficante replied, "No, sir; no, no chance, no way."

It can now be reported that the Assassinations Committee was provided with an FBI surveillance tape of Trafficante, recorded following the murder of Sam Giancana. "Now only two people are alive," Trafficante was heard to say, "who know who killed Kennedy. And they aren't talking."

Carlos Marcello, also once a towering Mafia figure, is now a sick old man, aged 79. Late in life, he discovered that he was not—as his long career had allowed him to believe—beyond the reach of the law. In 1981, as a result of a brilliant FBI undercover operation in New Orleans, Marcello was found guilty of racketeering, mail and wire fraud. Soon after came another guilty verdict, in California, on charges of conspiracy to bribe a federal judge. Since April 1983 Marcello has been in jail, with little likelihood of release till 1994. He is incarcerated at Texarkana, a high security prison in Texas, and my well die there.

Ironically, it was Professor Robert Blakey, the former Chief Counsel of the Assassinations Committee, who drafted the law under which Marcello faced his most serious charges. It was Blakey who, in 1978, summoned Marcello before his Committee because, like Santos Trafficante, he had allegedly once spoken of killing President Kennedy. Marcello told the Congressmen that his business in life was selling and distributing tomatoes—a service he apparently also extended to the Defense Department. Comic dialogue aside, Marcello gave his answers to allegations that he schemed to murder the President. He acknowledged that David Ferrie had worked on his deportation case and for one of his lawyers. He denied, however, that Ferrie actually worked for him. Asked if he had ever spoken of murdering the President, Marcello replied, "Positively not, never said anything like that."

Marcello and Trafficante on occasion used the same lawyer, just as Trafficante once used the same lawyer as Jimmy Hoffa. As long ago as 1967 one of these lawyers—apparently acting with Trafficante's approval—went to the FBI to volunteer that Trafficante felt he would soon be the victim of a "frame-up" by federal authorities anxious to put him behind bars. In particular, the lawyer told an odd anecdote about a remark made while Marcello and Trafficante were travelling together by car. Santos Trafficante, said his lawyer, had turned to his friend Marcello and said, "Carlos, the next thing you know, they will be blaming the President's assassination on us."

In 1979 Congress' Assassinations Committee announced that "extensive investigation led it to conclude that the most likely family bosses of organized crime to had participated in such a unilateral assassination plan were Carlos Marcello and Santos Trafficante." The Committee found—as we have noted—that both Mafia leaders had "motive, means and opportunity." It observed dryly that "it was unable to establish direct evidence of Marcello's complicity."

The emphasis, as the reader knows from this book, should be on the word "direct". A great mass of information ties key characters in the assassination to Marcello or his organization. And in 1988 the case for suspecting the Mafia boss was bolstered by publication of *Mafia Kingfish** by John Davis, an impressive work of investigative non-fiction. Davis brought to light two important leads—clues overlooked by both official enquiries.

---

* *Mafia Kingfish: Carlos Marcello and The Assassinaton of John F. Kennedy*, by John Davis, McGraw-Hill, New York, 1988.

The first lead is a statement made to the FBI by Eugene De Laparra a young man who, in spring 1963, had worked at a New Orleans restaurant owned by a Marcello associate, Bernard Tregle. One day in April, De Laparra reported, he observed Tregle and two friends looking at an advertisement for a cheap foreign-made rifle. Tregle, according to De Laparra, spoke of it as a suitable rifle "to get the President." "There is a price on the President's head, and other members of the Kennedy family," he added, ". . . Somebody will kill Kennedy when he comes down south."

De Laparra worked part-time for one of Marcello's brothers, Vincent. In a later statement, not to the FBI, he said that another Marcello brother, Anthony, first said, "The word is out to get the Kennedy family." Afterwards, Tregle repeated the remark to others.

The second lead comes from Gene Sumner, a respected businessman who later became the mayor of Darien, in Georgia. In spring 1963, either March or April, he went with a colleague to the Town and Country Restaurant in New Orleans. A young couple came in, and sat down at a nearby table. The restaurant boss joined the couple, then took a wad of money from his pocket and passed it to the young man under the table. The man and his companion then got up and left.

When, after the assassination, Sumner saw pictures of Oswald, he thought he was the same young man he had seen accepting money in the restaurant. The curious incident took on a new significance, and he reported it to the police. His story, today, is heavy with possible meaning. The Town and Country Motel and Restaurant was owned by the Marcello family, and Marcello himself ran his operations from a building on the property. The restaurant manager, Joseph Poretto, was a top figure in the Marcello organization.

According to FBI records, the Bureau learned of the Sumner and De Laparra leads within a week of the assassination. Marcello's men were briefly questioned and offered bland denials. Ben Tregle maintained he had never said the President would be killed when he came south. Poretto and Anthony Marcello denied that Oswald had been at the Town and Country in the spring of 1963.

And there the FBI dropped the matter, for no defensible reason. The times fitted and the association was plausible. It was in April that Oswald returned to his native New Orleans from Dallas. For a while, after his arrival, he stayed with his uncle, Charles Murret, the surrogate father of his youth and, in 1963, a prosperous bookmaker in Marcello's gambling network. That aside, the two leads fit into a pattern that linked Oswald, Ruby, and others in the assassination scenario, time and again to the world of Carlos Marcello. Yet the FBI, and J. Edgar Hoover personally—for he received all the relevant reports—did nothing. There was no serious investigation of Marcello, nor of Oswald in New Orleans, until fifteen years after the assassination, when the Assassinations Committee began work.

The FBI that at last put Marcello behind bars, in the Eighties, is a very different organization from Hoover's Bureau. As a result of its undercover operations against Marcello, we now have some further fragmentary knowledge. Joseph Hauser, a controversial key witness at the Marcello trial in New Orleans, claims he managed to lure Marcello into discussing the assassination.

According to Hauser, an FBI plant, the conversations took place in the spring and summer of 1979. They arose from discussion with Marcello of New Orleans press stories about the assassination—including coverage of the Assassinations Committee Report. According to Hauser, Marcello readily admitted knowing Oswald and his uncle Charles Murrett. He said Oswald had worked as a runner in his betting operation during 1963.

Later, in 1980, Hauser reported to the FBI something Marcello's brother Joseph had said. Senator Edward Kennedy's presidential campaign was under way, and Hauser deliberately raised the subject of the "rough time" the elder Kennedys had given Marcello in the early sixties. "Don't worry," said Joseph Marcello, "We took care of them, didn't we?"

Author John Davis is now suing for the release of three surveillance tapes that were not admitted into evidence at Marcello's trials. These contained conversations between Carlos Marcello, FBI undercover agents, and others, about the assassination of President Kennedy and the Assassinations Committee investigation. The tapes remained sealed, but former Chief Counsel

Blakey had been briefed on their content. On one, an FBI bug was operating in the spring of 1979, when a visitor to the Town and Country asked Marcello how he would respond to the Committee's suspicions of him. Marcello simply told the man to shut up. Then there was the sound of a chair being pushed back, and of the two men walking out of the room. The last words picked up by the microphone had Marcello telling his visitor that this was something to be discussed outside, away from possible surveillance.

This sort of thing is tantalizing, but it is not evidence. Professor Blakey remains bitterly disappointed in the Justice Department's failure to exploit its surveillance of Marcello to obtain real information on the Kennedy case. "They had that surveillance in during our investigation," he points out. "One of the things they could have done was to stimulate that wire by provoking conversations about the assassination, hopefully inducing those people to talk about it. But they didn't, not really."

In summary, there is compelling circumstantial evidence indicating Marcello's possible involvement in the Kennedy assassination. To say otherwise is to reject no less than eighteen witnesses and informants as fabricators, and to reject the web of interconnections between the Marcello apparatus and Oswald and Ruby. Yet that, in 1963 and in 1988, is what the Justice Department has done. Today, with Trafficante dead and Marcello sliding into senility, Justice has missed its chance.

David Phillips, the former CIA officer who was Chief of Cuban Operations in Mexico City at the time of the Kennedy assassination died of cancer in 1988.

Antonio Veciana, who was at the center of speculation that Phillips—using the code-name "Maurice Bishop"—had been his CIA case officer, was the victim of a murder attempt in late 1979. He was ambushed on the way home from work, and four shots were fired. A fragment of one bullet lodged in Veciana's head. He recovered in what police and doctors considered a freak escape. Publicly the veteran anti-Castro fighter blamed the attack on Castro agents. Privately he expressed concern that the attempt was linked to his allegations about the CIA's "Maurice Bishop", who, according to Veciana, met Oswald in Dallas shortly before the Kennedy assassination. Since the attempt to kill him, Veciana prefers not to discuss the Kennedy assassination.

Was it David Phillips who used the cover name "Bishop"? Was it he who met Oswald in Dallas? Was it Phillips who, after the assassination—again behind the mask of "Bishop"—tried to arrange the fabrication of a false story linking Oswald to Cuban diplomats in Mexico City? In life, Phillips riposted furiously to such suggestions. In death, he remains the focus of intense suspicion and continued research.

Assassinations Committee investigators, working on Veciana's description, built up a picture of their quarry. "Bishop", who would now be in his late sixties, was 6′2″ tall, of athletic build, and weighed more than 200 pounds. The eyes were gray-blue, the hair light brown going gray, the complexion fair.

"Bishop's" face was usually tanned and he had 'sunspots' under his eyes. He was meticulous about his dress, and—in the Seventies—was wearing glasses for reading. Veciana gained the impression he was either from the American South or, more likely, from Texas. In 1978 the Assassinations Committee issued an artist's impression of "Bishop" and made a nationwide appeal for assistance in tracking him down (see illustration 26, top). That proved unrewarding, but the investigators did make considerable progress in the information desert and disinformation jungle that they encountered at the CIA.

Veciana recalled that "Bishop"—as his spymaster in Havana—suggested he seek assistance from a number of officials, working in the U.S. Embassy. One was an unnamed CIA officer, a second was Wayne Smith, and the third was Sam Kail. Smith, who was third secretary at the Havana Embassy, has not been questioned—just one example of the failure by the Assassinations Committee management to follow up relevant leads in the Veciana affair. Colonel Sam Kail, however, a Texan who was a military intelligence officer at the Embassy, was contacted. He said he saw so many Cuban visitors that he could not remember Veciana. Nor, he said, could he recall the name "Maurice Bishop". It was Kail, who in summer 1963, proposed the meeting with Army Intelligence that was attended by Oswald's Dallas mentor, George de

Mohrenschildt. So far, the Kail lead has been unproductive apart from that connection, but the Committee found encouragement elsewhere. Several CIA officials have said they did indeed know of a "Maurice Bishop."

First there is the former Director of the CIA, Kennedy appointee John McCone. During his disposition, this conversation took place:

QUESTION: Do you, or did you, know Maurice Bishop?
ANSWER: Yes.
QUESTION: Was he an Agency employee?
ANSWER: I believe so.

Former Director McCone said he could no longer remember what "Bishop" actually did for the Agency. The Committee also interviewed a former CIA agent described publicly merely as "B.H." Asked if he knew Bishop, "B.H." replied that "Mr. Bishop was in the organization, but I had no personal day-to-day open relationship with him. . . . He said vaguely that Bishop had been a senior officer and that he had met him "two or three times" at CIA headquarters. In Miami, Assassinations Committee investigator Gaeton Fonzi stumbled on a more informative witness. He had formerly been a CIA case officer at JM/WAVE, the headquarters in Florida for the CIA's Secret War against Castro. This officer, whom the Committee quoted under the pseudonym "Ron Cross", had handled one of the most active anti-Castro groups and was potentially well placed to have known "Bishop".

Committee investigators threw not one, but three names at "Cross". The first was "Bishop," another was "Knight", and the third was the real name of an officer who had worked out of Havana. "Cross" duly pointed out the fact that the third name was the true name of somebody he had encountered in Havana. "Knight," as he recalled it, was a name occasionally used by Howard Hunt. And "Bishop," "Cross" believed, was the name used by David Phillips. He said this promptly and spontaneously.

For investigator Fonzi, this was an extraordinary moment. Phillips' name had come up much earlier, when Veciana's Bishop story was first considered, by the Senate Intelligence Committee.

Then, Fonzi had a police artist draw a composite sketch of "Bishop", based on Veciana's description. Senator Schweiker was shown the sketch, and astonished his colleagues by saying he thought he recognized it as David Phillips, who had recently testified before his Committee. (Later, the sketch was also recognized by Phillips' own family.)

As a result of the Senator's hunch, Fonzi and another investigator brought Veciana to a luncheon for retired intelligence officers, in Virginia. In the crowded hallway, after lunch, Fonzi introduced Phillips to Veciana by name. Veciana at once launched into a number of questions in Spanish, asking Phillips if he remembered the names of prominent anti-Castro Cubans from Havana in 1960. Phillips did remember some names, then asked, "What was your name again?" Told—three times—it was Antonio Veciana, he repeated the name, appeared to think about it, then said "Veciana' was not a name he knew. Told that Veciana was helping in the Kennedy investigation, Phillips abruptly excused himself. He appeared visibly nervous, and said he would answer further questions "only in Congress".

Asked after the lunch if Phillips was "Bishop", Veciana said, "Not, it's not him. . . . But he knows." Asked what he meant, Veciana merely repeated, "He knows."

For investigator Fonzi, therefore, it was a revelatory moment when, eighteen months later, CIA veteran "Cross" said he thought "Bishop" had been a cover name used by David Phillips. Later he declared himself "almost certain". "Cross" was qualified to know, for Phillips had sometimes visited the CIA station in Miami. In addition, "Cross" now coupled "Bishop" to the first name "Maurice"—a name the Committee investigators had not so far mentioned.

Fonzi decided to pursue the statement by "Cross" that Phillips and Howard Hunt had operated under the names "Bishop" and "Knight" respectively, using what appears to be a chess analogy. It found a sort of corroboration, which also contains a contradiction. Hunt, who has written several novels and a non-fiction work about the Bay of Pigs, has used pseudonyms in his books. For example, although Hunt claims he did not meet Frank Fiorini/Sturgis until the Seventies, a character very like him appears under

the name Hank Sturgis in a novel written as early as 1949. The
fictional character is an ex-Marine turned gambler and soldier-of-
fortune, a career that sounds similar to that of the real-life individual who legally took the name Frank Sturgis in 1952. In his book
about the Bay of Pigs, Hunt refers to his old associate Phillips,
then propaganda chief for the operation, as "Knight." In his 1977
memoirs, for his part, Phillips makes much of this identification,
commenting that "Bestowing the name of Knight was the ultimate
accolade—people who have worked in CIA will recall that pseudonym belonged to one of the Agency's most senior officers, a man
Hunt idolized. . . ." The man Hunt idolized, it turns out, was
Richard Helms, the controversial former Director of the CIA. The
recent authoritative book on Helms, *The Man Who Kept the
Secrets*, states flatly that "Knight" was Helms' codename in the
CIA. Hunt's literary back-patting of Phillips, however, does not
necessarily correspond with the use of cover names in real-life
operations in the early Sixties. If Hunt indeed idolized Helms, it
seems plausible that—as former case officer "Cross" recalls—he
would have dubbed himself "Knight" during anti-Castro operations. "Cross," of course, suggests it was Phillips who borrowed
the other name from the chessboard, "Bishop." He said the reason he was "almost positive" Phillips actually used that name was
because of conversations he recalled with Phillips' assistant, Doug
Gupton. Gupton, says "Cross" would often say something like,
"Well I guess Mr. Bishop will have to talk with him," and "Cross"
would know he was referring to his boss, David Phillips. At this
point, however, the Assassinations Committee inquiry faltered.

The Committee traced Gupton, who confirmed that he was in
daily contact with "Cross." However, he said he "did not recall
whether either Hunt or Phillips used the cover name "Knight"
nor did he remember Phillips using the name "Maurice Bishop."
Faced with "Cross," recollection of his having referred frequently
to Phillips by the name "Bishop," Gupton said, "Well maybe I
did, I don't remember." He said he did not recognize the artist's
impression of "Bishop" drawn from the description by Veciana.
He did say, however, that Phillips "used many of his old contacts
from Havana in his personal operations."

Undeterred, investigator Fonzi delved deep into David Phillips' background. He was a Texan, born near Fort Worth, who had originally wanted to become an actor. After a false start in the theater, he moved to Chile and tried his hand at publishing a small English-language newspaper. It was there that he attracted the attention of local CIA officers, who launched him on his long career in U.S. intelligence—a career that spanned some of the Agency's most infamous operations to topple foreign governments (*see illustration 26, right*). In 1954, in association with a CIA team including Howard Hunt as Political Action Officer, Phillips played a leading part in the overthrow of the anti-American, left-leaning Arbenz government in Guatemala. It was a remarkably cunning operation, in which Arbenz was panicked into resignation as much by propaganda as by actual force of arms. Phillips, a propaganda expert, ran the clandestine Voice of Liberation radio— broadcasting false reports about imaginary rebel forces and about battles that never took place. When American-backed forces took over, Phillips spent some time in Guatemala studying the documents of the defeated regime. It was he who noted the recent activities in Guatemala of an obscure young revolutionary called Che Guevara, and opened a CIA file on him.

Six years later, in 1960, Phillips was in at the very start when President Eisenhower approved the earliest plans to reverse Castro's revolution in Cuba. He attended the first CIA executive meeting on the subject, and later became propaganda chief of the Bay of Pigs operation. He was Chief of Station in the Dominican Republic during 1965, the year American troops invaded the country.

At the peak of a career in which he rose to become Chief of the Western Hemisphere Division, Phillips was to the fore in American meddling in Chilean affairs. He was chief of the Chile Task Force established to try to prevent Salvador Allende assuming the presidency to which he had been legally elected. Phillips, for all that, insisted he was a man of progressive sympathies.

The Assassinations Committee inquiry, faced with the suggestion that Phillips was "Bishop," took into account certain coincidences between Phillips' career and "Bishop" as described by Veciana. Phillips was a Texan, and Veciana had from the first expressed the belief that "Bishop" was most likely from Texas.

Phillips had served in relevant places at times consistent with Veciana's account of "Bishop's" activities. In 1960, when Veciana said he was recruited by "Bishop" in Havana, Phillips was serving there as a covert operative. Veciana says "Bishop" initially introduced himself as a representative of a construction firm headquartered in Belgium. He also used a false Belgian passport. Phillips, in a biography not yet published when Veciana first made his allegations, states that by 1959, following the Castro revolution, he was running a public relations firm as a front for CIA operations. One overt function of the company was to represent "foreign industrialists." There is evidence that the CIA has indeed used Belgian identity papers for secret operations abroad.

When Veciana was first recruited, "Bishop" instructed him, he says, to attend a series of night lectures, as preparation for his role as a guerrilla leader. Veciana recalled two signs on the building, that of a mining company and that of the Berlitz School of Languages. The Assassinations Committee asked Phillips what clients he had had for his Havana public relations firm. Phillips could recall only one—the Berlitz School of Languages.

The CIA's liaison in the Castro regime was one of Veciana's closest associates, and Phillips knew him. Veciana says it was "Bishop" who incited him to take part in a plot to murder Fidel Castro, while Phillips said he knew nothing of CIA assassination plots. He did, however, admit that—in Cuba—he took part in other anti-Castro activity very similar to that ascribed to "Bishop." Phillips, writing before the Veciana allegations became known, said he contacted one of a group of Cubans who were planning an early coup attempt against Castro. His CIA instructions, Phillips wrote, were to introduce himself as "an American anxious to assist," perhaps "using a false identity." The plan leaked, and several of the Cubans involved were arrested. Much the same happened when Veciana's plot to kill Castro was discovered.

Veciana has claimed that "Bishop" was involved in a much later plot to assassinate Castro, in 1971 in Chile. He also says that "Bishop" played an important role in efforts to remove the then Chilean President, Salvador Allende. Allende fell in 1973—the year Veciana says he was finally paid off by "Bishop" with a lump sum of more than a quarter of a million dollars. Phillips, who played a leading role in CIA operations against Allende, said that, as chief of CIA Latin American operations in 1973, he knows that no such CIA payment was made to Veciana. He insisted that such a sum could have been paid only with his own approval or that of the Director of the CIA. It is known, however, that CIA operatives in Latin America, including Phillips as a key executive, disposed of thirteen million dollars on covert action operations between 1963 and 1974. Congressional Oversight Committees have yet to be told how much of that vast sum was spent. Millions, however, went to fund manipulation of radio stations and newspapers for propaganda purposes, an area that has been Phillips' speciality since the Fifties. None of this, of course, proves that the CIA, let alone Phillips, made the payment to Veciana. Funds were available, however, and they are so far fuzzily accounted for.

Phillips said he hoped to produce documentation showing he was at CIA headquarters near Washington during at least part of the day "Bishop" allegedly paid off Veciana in Miami. He never did. Phillips made no such appeal to the record over his whereabouts at the time of the incident at the heart of the "Bishop" furor, the alleged autumn 1963 meeting with Oswald in Dallas, Texas. Phillips admitted he was in Texas "around that time", visiting relatives thirty miles from Dallas.

When David Phillips testified under oath to the Assassinations Committee, he denied ever having used the name "Bishop", and said he had never heard the name used by a CIA employee. His testimony did not convince his audience. Phillips reacted to unexpected questions by lighting a second cigarette moments after his first and, on one occasion, lit a third while the first two smouldered in the ashtray. Most seriously, Phillips gave contradictory and inaccurate testimony.

On Mexico City, where Phillips' CIA staff had been personally concerned with the "Oswald" visits to Communist embassies, Phillips got himself in a serious muddle. He claimed he was there at the time, while investigation revealed he was not even in the country. He said all sound surveillance transcripts were transcribed word-for-word, which they were not. And he said all transcripts were routed to him, yet the Committee saw none that were. As we have seen (page 366), two Chief Counsels of the Committee deplored Phillips' testimony—Professor Blakey saying drily that he was "less than satisfied with his candor".

It was worse than that. Phillips lied to the Committee about the luncheon confrontation with Antonio Veciana, at which he not only failed to recognize the Cuban's face, but even his name. Later, in his testimony, Phillips falsely claimed that no one has mentioned Veciana's name to him, that he had merely been introduced as "the driver". Investigator Fonzi believes this lie was a desperate measure, designed to cover the glaring mistake Phillips had made—caught by surprise at the luncheon—in claiming not to know the name of Antonio Veciana. It would have been ludicrous for the CIA's former Chief of Cuban Operations not to know the name of the founder of Alpha 66, the largest and most active anti-Castro group with which the CIA had been closely involved.

The Committee's Chief Counsel, Robert Blakey, was urged by his staff to bring perjury charges against David Phillips, but declined. Depending which staff member one talks to, this was either because of the opposition of the Justice Department, or for fear of upsetting what Blakey called the Committee's "delicate working relationship" with the CIA.

In the end the Assassinations Committee was not satisfied with the responses of either Veciana or Phillips. Its Report said that the Committee "suspected Veciana was lying when he denied that (Phillips) was Bishop. . . ."[131] The Report said of Phillips, "For his part, [he] aroused the Committee's suspicion when he told the Committee he did not recognize Veciana as the founder of Alpha 66, especially since [Phillips] had once been deeply involved in Agency anti-Castro operations. . . ."

The Committee left the "Bishop"/Phillips issue painfully unresolved. Its inquiries had been stymied by the confusing responses by the CIA and its former employees. Once the Agency declared it could find no reference to "Bishop" in its files, onetime Director McCone said he must have been mistaken when he told the Committee he *did* remember "Bishop". "B.H.", the former covert operative believed by Committee staff to have been used on assignments involving violence, stuck to his vague story of having met "Bishop" at CIA headqaurters. Investigator Fonzi thinks the

"B.H." angle may have been a red herring designed to confuse the trail, and subsequent developments support that suspicion.

"B.H.", a short, dark man of Cuban origin, is belligerent— not least about the way the CIA has been treated by Congress. He told the Committee that Phillips was "a personal friend," an officer he worked with on a "day-to-day" basis between 1960 and 1964. Interviewed by the Washington *Post* in 1980, "B.H." stated that after Phillips testified to the Committee, but before he himself was formally interviewed, he discussed the Committee inquiry with Phillips. In his Committee interview "B.H." was asked simply whether he had known anybody named Maurice Bishop. After replying that he had, "B.H." responded to Committee questioning, "Mr. Bishop was in the organization but I had no personal day-to-day open relationship with him. Phillips, yes; Bishop, no. I knew them both." "B.H." appeared in his replies to be stressing that he remembered "Bishop" as being somebody other than Phillips. There are notable discrepancies between what "B.H." told the Committee and what he said to the *Post*. He told the Committee he encountered "Bishop" "two or three times." He told the *Post* he met him only once. He told the Committee that he encountered "Bishop" between 1960 and 1964. In his *Post* interview, he said it was probably after 1964—after the time most relevant to the Veciana allegations. "B.H." told the Committee he worked closely with Phillips between 1960 and 1964. In the conversation with the *Post*, he claimed he did not work with Phillips until after 1964. "B.H." accounts for these differences by claiming that his comments were "wrongly recorded."

Suspicions about "B.H.'s" possible collusion with Phillips might have been resolved had the Committee management given the "Bishop" case the attention it deserved. Sadly, it did not. While Phillips did testify, the Committee failed to take testimony on oath from "Cross," "B.H.," or "Gupton." "Cross," who told two investigators he believed "Bishop" was Phillips, was not even subjected to a formal interview. There were no systematic interrogations of relevant CIA officers who might have further confirmed the use of the name "Bishop." The Committee failed to follow up on a key lead provided by Veciana—the identity of a prominent Cuban who may have originally proposed Veciana to

"Bishop" as a promising candidate for CIA recruitment. The Cuban's name was known to the Committee, and is known to this author. Other leads received cursory treatment.

The Committee never tried to trace a vital witness whose name was provided by Veciana months before the Committee wound up its inquiry. Veciana had spoken, from the start, of a go-between whom he used during his association with "Bishop." He explained that, in line with intelligence tradecraft, "Bishop" had always initiated their clandestine meetings, either by telephoning direct, or through a third person who always knew where to reach Veciana. Veciana was long reluctant to identify this third party, but finally did so—providing an old, invalid address in Puerto Rico. In 1980 I did follow up the lead, and traced down the Veciana-"Bishop" go-between. This proved to be the first independent corroboration that Veciana really was in touch with somebody called "Bishop."

The person who helped arrange meetings between "Bishop" and Veciana is a woman, a prim grandmother in her sixties, who works as a minor functionary in a U.S. government administrative department. She requested anonymity, and will be identified here only as "Fabiola," a Cuban exile who left Havana in autumn 1961. She worked until that year as Veciana's secretary at the Banco Financiero, and was there at the time Veciana claims he was recruited by "Bishop." While she said Veciana never mentioned a CIA contact, Fabiola recalled details that fit his story. She recalled a time when Veciana started going to "language courses" in the evenings. Veciana, as we have seen, spoke of attending nightly U.S. intelligence briefings in an office building that housed, on the first floor, the Berlitz School of Languages, the only client Phillips could recall from his undercover days as a businessman in Havana. Fabiola said she did become aware that Veciana was involved in subversive activities. He once produced the huge sum of half a million dollars, which he asked her to safeguard until he retrieved it. Veciana has always said he worked with "Bishop" on a "program that resulted in the destabilization of the Cuban currency." In Cuba, Fabiola decided not to ask Veciana awkward questions. Politically, she sympathized with him, and later, in exile, collaborated actively when Veciana became leader of Alpha 66. He asked her to act as an answering service for him when he was travelling, and in the months to come, Fabiola became familiar with the name of a caller from the mainland United States. The name was "Bishop."

When I interviewed Fabiola I threw out a number of names, including that of "Bishop." "Bishop" was the only name to which she responded, and it stirred in her the memory of another name. "Bishop" is firmly linked in Fabiola's mind with a second person— "Prewett." For her, the two names are so definitely associated that at first she had difficulty remembering which was which. Fabiola said both individuals telephoned Veciana over the same period, and she understood that they were associated with one another. She believed both "Bishop" and "Prewett" were connected with an American news publication, based on the East Coast. Finally, she recalled that "Prewett" was female.

A check of American press directories turned up Virginia Prewett, a Washington journalist who specialized in Latin American affairs all her life. She wrote extensively about the struggle between Fidel Castro, whom she characterized as a "betrayer," and the Cuban exiles, whom she described as "patriots." In summer 1963 Prewett attended a conference on Cuba co-sponsored by Freedom House and the Citizen's Committee for a Free Cuba. Her report on the conference, later inserted in the Congressional record, began by quoting a call by Freedom House "to remove both Fidel Castro and the Soviet presence from Cuba without delay." For many years, Prewett wrote for the North American Newspaper Alliance (NANA), a syndication organization founded by Prewett's friend Ernest Cuneo, also a member of the Committee for a Free Cuba. It was Cuneo, a veteran of the CIA's forerunner, the Office of Strategic Services, who arranged for Prewett to work for NANA. In 1963 NANA was severely criticized in a Senate Committee Report, for syndicating pro-Chiang Kai-shek propaganda written by a paid American lobbyist.

In spring 1963, seven months before the Kennedy assassination, Prewett was assailing the administration for its opposition to the raids mounted against Cuba by Antonio Veciana's Alpha 66 guerillas. On April 2, in the Washington *Daily News*, Prewett lambasted a Kennedy spokesman who had "called the daring and

gallant Alpha 66 raids on Cuba irresponsible acts." Prewett called
this "an all-time low in pronouncement of U.S. foreign policy,"
and mocked the notion that "unless we stop the Alpha 66 raids
against Communist Cuba, there'll be nuclear conflict." Three
weeks later, after President Kennedy ordered strong measures
against would-be exile raiders, Prewett rushed to support the exile
leadership and berated the Kennedy White House for assuming it
had "carte blanche to create a foreign policy outside the nation's
popular consent." These Prewett articles were read into the Congressional Record.

The Alpha 66 raids, which so embarrassed President Kennedy
and which pleased Virginia Prewett, were the very attacks that—
according to Alpha 66 leader Veciana—were carried out on specific instructions from CIA officer "Maurice Bishop." As Veciana
tells it, "Bishop's" intention was to cause further trouble between
Kennedy and Russia—within months of the Missile Crisis that had
brought the world to the brink of nuclear war. His purpose was "to
put Kennedy against the wall in order to force him to make
decisions that will remove Castro's regime."

In the company of a Washington *Post* reporter, I talked to
Virginia Prewett in 1980. She agreed that she had contact with
Alpha 66 in the early sixties, and accepted that Alpha 66 was
"probably" backed by the CIA, even if its leaders were not formally told so. Prewett made it clear she was once familiar with the
work of the group's leader, Veciana, and asked, "Where is he
now?" Later in the interview, however, she said she had never met
Veciana. Veciana, for his part says he did know Prewett, and
refers to her as "Virginia." He asserts he met her at her hotel in
Puerto Rico more than once, and "probably in Washington."
When the name "Bishop" was first raised with Prewett, in the
context of the CIA and Cuba, she said, "Well, you had to move
around people like that." When the name came up again, she said,
"I didn't personally know him," and later, in response to a direct
question, she said she did not know "Bishop." Prewett also said
she had never met David Phillips. Phillips, asked about Prewett in
another context, contradicted her. He said he did once know

Prewett quite well, specifically recalling meetings in the Dominican Republic.*

Meanwhile, Phillips talked himself into deeper water. He told reporter David Leigh, on assignment for the Washington *Post*, that former CIA officer "Cross" was a heavy drinker, implying that he was an unreliable source. When Leigh went to see "Cross", he found that Phillips had called him long-distance just before Leigh's arrival. Whatever had passed between them, "Cross" admitted his former heavy drinking, but stood by his assertion that the name "Bishop" had been used in the Miami office, and that he believed it was used to refer to Phillips. "Cross" admitted he had formerly been a heavy drinker, but, as noted earlier, has shown that his recall is accurate on names and details other than "Bishop".

In 1982, in eastern Europe, Washington investigative writer Jim Hougan obtained an interview with Frank Terpil, the former CIA officer now fugitive from a fifty-three year jail sentence for illicit arms deals with Libya—offences for which his partner, Edwin Wilson, is now serving time. Wilson, once an undercover operator for David Phillips, initially supplied the explosive devices used in the 1976 murder of Chile's former ambassador to the United States, Orlando Letelier, by Michael Townley. Townley had been Phillips' CIA liaison with Chilean intelligence, and Phillips' close personal friend. In his 1982 interview, Terpil admitted he had known David Phillips in the sixties, but only under his cover name. What was his cover name? "Bishop", replied Terpil at once, and it was apparent, from the context, that in exile Terpil had learned nothing of the Committee's investigations. He claimed, moreover, that he had seen "Bishop's" name in a file of cover identities at the CIA.

Committee investigator Fonzi points to Veciana's claim that "Bishop" asked him, after the assassination, to incite a Cuban embassy contact to help fabricate a false story about an Oswald link with Cuban diplomats. (see page 377.) It is, for Fonzi, a

* Prewett has since died.

further indication that Phillips and "Bishop" were one and the same. Soon after the assassination, stories began appearing in the newspapers referring to alleged meetings of Oswald with a mysterious Cuban couple in Mexico City. The Cuban wife, Veciana recalls, was supposed to speak fluent English. "Bishop" raised these stories with Veciana, and it was in that context that he asked Veciana to speak to his cousin and Cuban embassy contact, to make up a false story. "Bishop" revealed, in passing, that he knew the contact's wife *spoke excellent English*.

Only a very small number of Americans, even in intelligence, would have known the name of a Castro official in Mexico City, would also have known that his wife spoke such good English, *and* known that he was Veciana's cousin. One who would have known was David Phillips, Chief of Cuban Operations in Mexico.

Finally, there is one more glaring fact. Almost all of the disinformation tales spread about Oswald and the communists are traceable—according to Committee sources—to CIA contacts who were specifically agents manipulated by Phillips, as distinct from CIA contacts used generally by the Mexico station. The disinformation source whose story was produced most promptly, and whose account was persistently brought to the attention of President Johnson, Gilberto Alvarado (page 316), was handled and debriefed by David Phillips. The names of Phillips' disinformation operators are known to former Committee staffers, and to this author.

The late David Phillips never did admit that he once used the cover name "Maurice Bishop". Committee investigator Gaeton Fonzi, for his part, said in 1989, "That Antonio Veciana should produce, in describing the role and character of Maurice Bishop, a figure so specifically identical to David Phillips, and that Phillips' history should have so many relevant and interconnected facets bearing on the Kennedy assassination, breaches the bounds of coincidence."

Before he died, Phillips had several conversations with Kevin Walsh, a former Assassinations Committee staffer now working as a private detective in Washington D.C. He never opened up on specifics, but he did say something about the assassination of

President Kennedy. "My private opinion," said Phillips, "is that JFK was done in by a conspiracy, likely including rogue American intelligence people." Phillips said this in July 1986, and Walsh made a precise note. The remark was astounding, not in itself, but coming as it did from the former Chief of the CIA's Western Hemisphere Division.

There is no evidence that David Phillips had any part in a conspiracy to murder the President. He may well, however, have been "Maurice Bishop", and few—on the evidence in this chapter—can now doubt that there was a "Maurice Bishop", nor that he manipulated Veciana for a U.S. intelligence agency over many years. Phillips' former wife told this author that the one thing she could remember about her husband and the Kennedy assassination was odd only because it was a negative.

On November 22, 1963, David Phillips came home and said . . . nothing at all. He showed neither sadness, nor pleasure, nor interest—he simply had nothing to say. On all the evidence, this author believes it possible that Phillips was involved in manipulating Lee Harvey Oswald, and was knowledgeable about plans to "set up" the young "pro-Castro" American with bogus contacts at the Soviet and Cuban embassies. As a professional expert in disinformation, running exactly that sort of anti-Castro propaganda, there would have been nothing remarkable about such a role for Phillips—had Oswald not be accused of murdering the President.

Did Phillips realize with horror how someone other than he, in U.S. Intelligence, had used the Oswald connection? Did he rush to cover his own, perhaps, innocent, tracks? And did he carry on so running, until his death last year? New revelations about the work of Congress' Assassinations Committee, and what it really found out about Mexico City, may support that thesis.

The Mexico City investigation of the Committee is still classified and beyond the reach of researchers, in a closed section of the National Archives. By a great irony, indeed, the Committee, which was created with the public intention of bringing the mysteries of the assassination into the open, has allowed its own staff work to become secret.

There has been some lobbying in Congress to reverse this silly situation. But, if it does not happen, the intensive staff work on Mexico City—in the form of a 265 page report—will remain sealed at least until the year 2029. The public was fobbed off, when the Committee delivered its conclusions in 1979, with a vacuous seven page section of its Report.

Former Chief Counsel Blakey says the real report must be withheld to protect the CIA's "sources and methods." He agrees that it is "Alice in Wonderland" (his words) that the CIA does not admit publicly that it even has a station in Mexico City, that it does not admit carrying out surveillance work in any foreign country. "There's no way ever," says Blakey, "that the Agency will permit the declassification of such a report. . . . And I don't really disagree with them on that. . . . What you don't have now is how information was gathered, and that's not material anyway. The substance of everything that we did is in the public domain, so that you have sufficient information in our final Report to make a judgement."

Those familiar with the Mexico research disagree with Blakey's claim that the CIA restrictions are justified, or that the Report gave the public a true picture of what the Committee discovered. First, descriptions of the way the CIA worked with Committee staffers—on a matter crucial to the American people—make a litany of evasion and stonewalling.

Theoretically, under a deal struck by Blakey, Committee staffers had the right to see any CIA documents they deemed necessary. In practice the CIA delayed in every way possible, knowing that the Committee's mandated life was severely limited. "They waited us out," says one former staffer, "they gave us misleading information to lead us on wildgoose chases that would take us forever. By the last time we had them in, we had documented every lie they'd told us, from other testimony and other documents that proved they'd been lying constantly. They were toying with us, all along."

The Assassinations Committee did glean information on the Mexico City episode that should have caused uproar in Congress

and the press, had it been published. A key area was the CIA's
story on whether the real Oswald visited the communist embassies
in Mexico, whether the CIA photographed him doing so, and if
not, why not?

Committee investigators discovered that, in 1963, the CIA
had spies in place inside the Cuban embassy. At least some of
them were still active in 1978, during the Committee's inquiry, and
the CIA therefore resisted any approach to them. Committee
Chairman Congressman Stokes appealed directly to then President Carter, and Carter gave the go-ahead. Two of the individuals
concerned were prepared to talk. "They said," says one former
staffer, "that everyone in the Cuban embassy was of the opinion,
that the real Oswald never came inside. They felt, the moment it
occurred, that something weird was going on."

The staffers became doubtful about the statement by the
Cuban consulate secretary, Sylvia Duran, that she believed it was
the real Oswald who applied for a visa. The CIA admitted having
two pre-assassination files on Duran, but refused to let the Committee see them. It also refused to let staffers see verbatim transcripts of Duran's statement on the Oswald matter. After the
assassination, the staffers discovered, the CIA had ordered its
Mexico station to obstruct access by other officials to Sylvia Duran. Duran herself, says one Committee staffer, "ended up scared
to death."

The Committee studied information that Oswald, or someone
like Oswald, attended a party held by a relative of Duran. Perhaps
most significant, "Oswald" was accompanied by two other men. If
he was, who were they? One document in Mexico frontier records
stated that an "Oswald" crossed back into Texas by *car*. The real
Oswald could not drive. So, did an impostor drive back to Texas?
If, rather, the real Oswald was driven across the border by someone else, the Mexico visit must be examined in a fresh light.

The most damning material in the Committee's Mexico report
concerns the CIA's handling of its embassy surveillance material.
The 1978 investigation established beyond question that at least
one former member of the Mexico station—apart from David
Phillips—lied to the Committee under oath. She is a woman, still
alive, not named here. At the heart of the lying was the notion that

no surveillance photograph of Oswald was taken, either because pictures were only taken sporadically, or because there had been a camera breakdown on the relevant day. Committee staffers pored through date and time-stamped surveillance pictures covering a long period and established the locations and schedules of cameras operated by the CIA outside the Cuban consulate. They came away certain that CIA photo coverage *was* working on the day "Oswald" tried to obtain a visa. This conviction is corroborated by a new and stunning piece of information.

The Committee learned that the CIA station chief in Mexico, Winston Scott, became interested in the "Oswald" visit well before the assassination. He was aware then that Oswald's real name was "Lee Harvey" rather than "Lee Henry", as he was referred to in the pre-assassination CIA teletype (*see page 354*). After the assassination, Scott, like Ambassador Mann, was furious about the premature closing down of the Mexico investigation. For his own purposes—perhaps as insurance to protect himself at some future date—Scott prepared a memorandum. He placed it in his safe at home, along with something else, something the CIA has always denied existed—a print of a CIA surveillance photograph of the real Oswald in Mexico City.

The Committee was told this by a former senior officer in the CIA's Mexico office. In addition, the Committee located no less than three former CIA employees who claimed to have seen the photograph themselves in the office at the time and two others who said they knew it existed. The photograph was apparently a right profile shot, taken from a surveillance camera above the subject.

Why has the picture never been produced? One speculation is that the photograph showed another person, or more than one person—perhaps someone connected with the CIA. By the same logic, the person could have been a communist Cuban or a Soviet. At all events, the picture was suppressed. What became of the photograph? It remained in Winston Scott's custody until his death. As soon as he died, the CIA's Chief of Counterintelligence, James Angleton, flew to Mexico to deal personally with the contents of Scott's safe. It was Angleton and his deputy who, in 1964, had handled CIA liaison with the Warren Commission. The CIA does not now have the photograph, or at any rate did not produce it for the Committee in 1978.

This is the saga that lies behind the terse footnote in the Report of the Assassinations Committee that "the Committee believed that photographs of Oswald might have been taken and subsequently lost or destroyed. . . ." There is no justifying such suppression of the facts, and the CIA should, even now, be forced to explain itself to Congress.

A final solution to the mysteries of the assassination may now be impossible. In 1988, however, the FBI failed to pursue a lead that appears, on its face, to be unique, one that might conceivably identify the killers of President Kennedy and perhaps even bring some of them to justice. It is the result of years of dogged research by a California writer, Steve Rivele.

In 1985, Rivele became interested in the CIA's Executive Action program—revealed by the then Senator Walter Mondale following Intelligence Committee inquiries a decade earlier. Executive Action was the detailed planning, in 1961, for the assassination of foreign leaders, and it included the recruiting of a man known only by the code name "QJ/WIN," a foreign citizen with a criminal background recruited in Europe"—as the Intelligence Committee described him. (*See page 143.*)

Rivele's research plunged him deep into the history of the CIA's perilous collaboration with organized crime, at home and abroad. It led to a man called Christian David, a fifty-eight year old Frenchman nearing the end of a heroin trafficking sentence in Leavenworth penitentiary, Kansas. David had been a member of the French Connection network, and the leader of the Corsican network in South America known as the Latin Connection. He had also worked for intelligence services, including the French SAC.

When Rivele interviewed David he was awaiting extradition to France, to stand trial for murdering a policeman, a killing committed in connection with the murder of Mohammed Ben Barka, the Morrocan politician. David told Rivele he had information on the Kennedy assassination. In return for this information, he said, he wanted a deal with the U.S. government that would block his return to France. For his part, he would tell all he knew to a grand jury.

Rivele found David an attorney. A federal judge temporarily halted David's extradition, ordering that he be taken off a plane bound for Paris and held in New York City. Although advised of the Kennedy assassination aspect of the case, the federal government got the judge to lift the stay of extradition and David was hastily flown to Paris. In prison there since 1985, he has been interviewed repeatedly by Rivele, as well as by James Lesar, a Washington attorney.

In May or June 1963, according to David, he was asked by Antoine Guérini, the Corsican Mafia boss in Marseilles, to accept a contract to kill "a highly placed American politician". Guérini made it obvious whom he meant, calling the politician "la plus grosse légume"—the "biggest vegetable." The President was to be killed on U.S. territory. David turned down the contract, on the ground that it was too dangerous.

The contract, said David, was accepted by Lucien Sarti, a Corsican drug trafficker and killer, and two other members of the Marseilles mob, whom he refused to name. They were, he said, "spécialistes de tir"—"sharpshooters." He learned what happened some time after the assassination, at a 1965 meeting in Buenos Aires. Present were Sarti, a drug trafficker called Michèle Nicoli, David, and two others. This is how the assassination was carried out, as David tells it.

Sarti and the other two assassins flew from Marseilles to Mexico City in the fall of 1963. They stayed there several weeks, and were then driven to the United States border, which they crossed at Brownsville, Texas, using Italian passports. They were met at the border by a representative of the Chicago Mafia, who conversed with them in Italian. He drove them to a house in Dallas.

In Dallas, according to David, the assassins took photographs of Dealey Plaza, and made a detailed plan for the killing. The plan was for a cross fire. On November 22, David told Rivele, three gunmen were in position. Two were in buildings to the rear of the President when he was hit—one of them "almost on the horizontal". The third killer, Sarti, dressed in some sort of uniform as a disguise, was "on the little hill to the front, the one with the fence." He had considered shooting from the railroad bridge, directly in front of the President, but found it too exposed and moved to better cover.

Four shots were fired that day, according to David, quoting Sarti and another of the assassins. The first shot, from the rear, struck President Kennedy in the back. The second shot missed, and hit "the other man in the car." The third shot, from Sarti on the hill, struck the President in the head, killing him. Sarti used "an explosive bullet", the only member of the group to use that kind of ammunition. The fourth shot missed the car altogether.

After the assassination, according to David's allegations, the murderers laid low in Dallas for about two weeks. Then—says David—they were then flown out of the country, the last part of the journey by private aircraft, to Montreal.

Asked who could corroborate his story, David suggested that Rivele locate Michèle Nicoli, who had also been with the group in Buenos Aires in 1965, when the assassination was discussed. Rivele made contact with Nicoli, after a lengthy search, with the help of Michael Tobin, a high official in the Drug Enforcement Administration. Nicoli, who testified against French Connection members in 1972, was living under the Witness Protection Program, using a new name. The DEA official vouched for Nicoli's truthfulness in the strongest terms.

Rivele's contacts with Nicoli took place over many months, and he proved extremely reluctant to talk. In the end, however, he told both Rivele and Tobin essentially the same story as had David. So far as could be ascertained, he and David had not been in touch with each other since the early seventies.

Lucien Sarti, the alleged leader of the assassination team, was shot dead by Mexican police in 1972. The identity of his two accomplices remains unclear as of this writing. Apparently they are still alive.

By late 1987, after his own meeting with Nicoli, DEA official Tobin was satisfied—because of Nicoli's proven reliability—that the matter should be pursued. He considered the legalities of the situation and decided that—since in 1963 it was not a federal offense to assassinate the President—the assassination was covered by conspiracy and civil rights statutes. On the basis of those laws, he believed, a federal grand jury could be impaneled and indictments sought through a U.S. attorney in Washington D.C.

In December 1987 Tobin formally notified his superiors that he wanted to conduct an investigation, drawing on Nicoli's statements. DEA officials said the matter was outside his jurisdiction and turned over the information to an Assistant Director of the FBI. In Paris, a U.S. embassy official made contact with the French lawyer acting for Christian David, the witness in jail in France. But that was that. By spring 1989, nothing substantive had been done by the FBI. As ever since 1963, the will was lacking.

For those who wish to see no further progress in the Kennedy case, a much-trumpeted British television program, produced in November 1988 by Central T.V., was a welcome event. Among its many follies, the program named as Gunman Two and Gunman Three two men whose names had come up during Rivele's discussions with David, but who David had since specifically said were innocent. In the wake of the television program, one of the men produced a plausible alibi for November 22, and Rivele's exclusive story suddenly appeared—however unjustifiably—to have been exploded. Rivele's French publishers backed off, and no American publisher had been found as this book went to press. Rivele himself, disgusted with the Central T.V. fiasco, weary from years of non-stop investigation, turned to other work.

In France, meanwhile, Christian David has repeatedly avoided trial by staging "suicide" attempts, and languishes in Paris' La Santé prison. He has given his French lawyer a sealed envelope said to contain a written account of all he knows about the Kennedy assassination, which is allegedly more than he has so far told. Clearly, both he and the second witness, Michèle Nicoli, should be extensively interrogated by the proper U.S. authorities. We should be told why David's deportation was pushed through in haste in 1985, when federal authorities knew he was offering information on the Kennedy case.

As of this writing, the fact remains that two men exist—one of them regarded by officials as a most reliable source—who say they know how President Kennedy was assassinated. From what they say, it may be that two of the assassins—not to mention those who directed them—may still be alive, and could perhaps be brought to justice. There has not been such a situation in the quarter century since the assassination. Perhaps their story is unfounded, but, if the United States is a properly functioning democracy, it should be shown to be bogus. There should be an investigation, and full public disclosure of the results.

A Mafia-CIA link in the Kennedy assassination is, as we have seen, consistent with historical reality. There is now information—arising from the FBI operation that sent Carlos Marcello to prison—that he, like Santos Trafficante, was involved in the CIA-Mafia plots to kill Fidel Castro. In 1988 Judith Exner, the woman who became the mistress of both President Kennedy and Chicago mobster Sam Giancana, claimed she had been used as a courier between the White House and Giancana, and that President Kennedy had gone so far as to meet Sam Giancana. Going far beyond her testimony to the Senate Intelligence Committee, Exner said; "I lied when I said that President Kennedy was unaware of my friendships with mobsters. He knew everything about my dealings with Sam Giancana and Johnny Roselli because I was seeing them *for* him."

For eighteen months in 1960 and 1961, Exner said, she repeatedly carried envelopes from the President to Giancana and Roselli. There were, she calculated, some ten meetings between the President and the Chicago mobster, one of them at the White House. She offered dates, places, and detailed descriptions of the meetings, and—while the political establishment received her statements with a deafening silence—initial research supports some specific detail in her account.

Why would the President engage in such folly? There are three possibilities. One, before he became President, Kennedy may have wittingly relied on the mob to secure votes for the West Virginia primary, as it did in Illinois during the presidential election. Two, as revealed in my book *Goddess*, Roselli intervened in 1961 to remove the President's name as co-respondent in a messy California divorce suit. This likely involved secret contracts, and perhaps exchanges of documents or money. Finally, there is the theory Exner herself espouses. "It finally dawned on me," she says, "that I was probably helping Jack orchestrate the attempted assassination of Fidel Castro with the help of the Mafia."

Whatever his own essential integrity, the President had allowed the mob to believe he was in their debt. Meanwhile, far from turning a blind eye to organized crime, his administration mercilessly pursued the Mafia bosses, bosses who enjoyed close personal relationships with the CIA co-ordinators of the Castro assassination plans. The President and his brother had fashioned for themselves a boomerang, marked with the names of the Mafia and some people in the CIA.

Who planned the assassination? In the closing stages of the Assassinations Committee's mandate, some staff members felt that, while Mafia marksmen may have carried out the assassination, it could only have been orchestrated by someone in American intelligence, someone with special knowledge of Oswald's background. As they pondered this, investigators gave renewed attention to the senior CIA officer who co-ordinated the CIA-Mafia plots against Castro—William Harvey.

William Harvey died in 1976, after a career covered to some extent in this book (*see earlier references*). As far back as 1959, he was one of only three officers privy to plans to send false defectors into the Soviet Union. 1959 was the year of Oswald's suspect defection. Genuine defection or not, Harvey almost certainly knew about it in detail.

Subsequently, Harvey was the man who conceived and planned the CIA's Executive Action program, the contingency plan for foreign assassinations. He was closely in touch with men of the same ilk as Lucien Sarti, and the Corsicans now alleged to have been the gunmen in Dealey Plaza.

Next, as head of Task Force W, Harvey was in direct charge of anti-Castro operations, in personal touch with mobsters Santos Trafficante and John Roselli, inciting them to murder Fidel Castro. He became a close friend to Roselli.

Harvey was a "can-do" operator. During the Castro plots, he personally hired a U-Haul truck to deliver rifles, explosives, and radios to Roselli in a Miami parking lot. He was also an instinctive freelance. Harvey testified to the Senate Intelligence Committee, he was a party to concealing the Castro assassination plans from his own boss, CIA Director John McCone.

Harvey's gung-ho anti-Castro activity not only alarmed his CIA bosses, it drove him into direct confrontation with the Kennedys. According to one former official, Harvey "hated Bobby Kennedy's guts with purple passion." His braggadocio in sending commando teams into Cuba at the height of the 1962 missile crisis—jeopardizing international negotiations—incurred Robert Kennedy's wrath. ("Maurice Bishop", of course, was involved in similarly provocative operations, designed specifically to flout administration policy.)

In spring 1963, as a direct result, Harvey was transferred to a posting in Italy. The intent, according to an authoritative account by David Martin, was to make sure "he would never again be allowed near an operation in which the brothers Kennedy were likely to have an active interest." Yet Harvey was still meeting with Roselli, in the United States, as late as June 1963; and I have learned that he visited anti-Castro camps in Florida, at a time when he was theoretically already in Rome. According to new, unresearched information, initial approaches to hire assassins in Europe were made in Rome—sometime before the recruitment approaches allegedly made to the Corsican Mafia in Marseilles.

Assassinations Committee staff discussed Harvey with former CIA personnel, including a former senior officer from the Mexico City station. "The feeling of some of the CIA people we talked with," says one Committee staffer, "was that Harvey was heavily involved with the organized crime figures. The feeling was that he was out of control and may have worked with organized crime figures to murder JFK. He behaved as if he was all-powerful. . . . He may have been the key in accomplishing the assassination."

* * * * * * * * * *

It is certainly possible that a renegade element in U.S. intelligence manipulated Oswald—whatever his role on November 22,

1963. That same element may have activated pawns in the anti-Castro movement and the Mafia to murder the President and to execute Oswald.

The very suggestion that some of those charged with protecting American security should so betray their trust is clearly abhorrent to modern citizens. Unfortunately there is nothing inherently implausible in the scenario. The revelations of the Seventies showed only too clearly that there were rotten apples in the CIA apparatus and that they included some of those most passionately committed to the elimination of Fidel Castro. In the name of that cause, intelligence officers dabbled in unauthorized operations, including assassination plots that belonged in the purple pages of pulp fiction.

In pursuit of these follies, CIA officials were deeply involved with top members of the Mafia. The mob hated the Kennedy administration, and so did some of those in the CIA whose views clashed with the President's.

The time of the Bay of Pigs, when the President "betrayed" the cause of the anti-Castro movement, coincided with the Kennedy onslaught on the Mafia, including, specifically, the forcible deportation of Carlos Marcello. Over Cuba, the Mafia and the exiles nursed the same resentments as many of the CIA.

There were those in the CIA, steeped in an everyday aura of deception and violent action, who exercised unconscionable power. The signs are that, at least from the time of the unauthorized raids on Soviet shipping after the missile crisis, some intelligence officers encouraged actions designed to sabotage the President's search for peace.

This cannot be dismissed as unfounded speculation. Congress' Assassinations Committee noted that, as early as the Bay of Pigs debacle, a senior CIA officer reportedly incited Cuban exiles to disobey Presidential policy. Before the invasion, the CIA director of operations, working under the cover name of "Frank Bender,"* assembled exile leaders at their Guatemala training camp. According to the authoritative history, "Bender" told the Cubans that

---

* The officer's real name was reportedly "Droller" (Thomas Powers, op. cit. p. 107).

"There were forces in the administration trying to block the invasion, and Frank might be ordered to stop it. If he received such an order, he said he would secretly inform Pepe and Oliva Pepe. [Pepe San Roman, the exile commander] remembers Frank's next words this way: 'If this happens you come here and make some kind of show, as if you were putting us, the advisers, in prison, and you go ahead with the program as we have talked about it, and we will give you the whole plan, even if we are your prisoners.' . . . Frank then laughed and said, 'In the end we will win.' "[132]

William Harvey's desperate folly during the missile crisis, and "Bender's" apparent incitement to mutiny during the Bay of Pigs operation, are both recorded by distinguished chroniclers. The episodes are evidence, if evidence is still needed, that some in the CIA were ready, even eager, to flout the wishes of President Kennedy. While the Assassinations Committee rightly concluded that the CIA as an agency had no part in the assassination, it is wholly possible that mavericks from the intelligence world were involved—as the CIA's David Phillips suggested before he died.

After his brother's death in Dallas, Attorney General Robert Kennedy confided such suspicions to a family friend, then Director of the CIA, John McCone. The younger Kennedy later recalled, "You know, at the time I asked McCone . . . if they had killed my brother, and I asked him in a way that he couldn't lie to me, and they hadn't." As we have seen, Robert Kennedy later developed grave doubts about the official version of the Dallas murder and suspected that organized crime might have had a part in it. As for McCone, he believed at an early stage there had been more than one gunman in Dealey Plaza. It is doubtful, today, that McCone would still feel able to give assurances of American intelligence officers' innocence.

In 1977, in an historic turn around, former Warren Commission counsel Burton Griffin told a BBC colleague and myself, "I feel betrayed. I feel that the CIA lied to us, that we had an agency of Government here which we were depending upon, that we expected to be truthful with us, and to cooperate with us. And they didn't do it. The CIA concealed from us the fact that they were involved in efforts to assassinate Castro which could have been of extreme importance to us. Especially the fact that they were involved in working with the Mafia at that time."

Judge Griffin feels the same about the FBI and says, "What is most disturbing to me is that two agencies of the government, that were supposed to be loyal and faithful to us, deliberately misled us." The judge's rueful conclusions are now not allegations but hard facts, hammered into the record by successive Congressional inquiries.

As for the specific case of the Kennedy killing, the Assassinations Committee declared in 1979 that "the CIA-Mafia-Cuban plots had all the elements necessary for a successful assassination conspiracy—people, motive and means—and the evidence indicated that the participants might well have considered using the resources at their disposal to increase their power and alleviate their problems by assassinating the President. Nevertheless, the Committee was ultimately frustrated in its attempt to determine details of those activities that might have led to the assassination— identification of participants, associations, timing of events, and so on. . . ."

If the Committee was frustrated in its efforts to uncover the precise mechanism of the conspiracy, it did get a glimpse into the abyss. It now seems that the assassination of President Kennedy led to an internal crisis of far greater gravity than was previously known. The government of the Soviet Union, expecting to be blamed for the President's murder, ordered a nuclear alert.

The former Chief Counsel of the Assassinations Committee, Professor Blakey, drawing on his privileged access to closely held information, told me, "The Russians were on alert, and it looked like the beginning, or the possible beginning of world nuclear war." The crisis, Blakey said, ended only when President Johnson, in his first hours in office personally assured the Soviets that the United States had no evidence of Communist involvement, and planned no reprisals. This information makes sense of Johnson's dramatic statement to Chief Justice Earl Warren, four days after President's Kennedy's funeral, when he asked Warren to form a commission of inquiry. When Warren demurred, Johnson insisted that it was his patriotic duty to head the commission. If certain rumors were not stifled, said the new President, they could lead the United States "into a war which could cost forty million lives."

For weeks after the assassination, President Johnson was briefed on the information indicating that Oswald had met with Soviet and Cuban officials in Mexico City, that he had received money from the Cubans, and that assassination had been discussed. Today, the signs are that such evidence was fabricated, and by mouthpieces habitually used by the CIA—the agents of David Phillips.

If fabricated, was this merely a foolhardy effort to turn the assassination to malicious propaganda advantage after the event? Or was it—and this is the terrible possibility—part of an assassination conspiracy intended in advance to do away with President Kennedy and, by linking Oswald to Havana, to provoke American retaliation against Cuba—and thus, potentially, the very real risk of nuclear war? As the evidence stands, such a scenario cannot be excluded.

Asked whether all the testimony taken by the original official enquiry would be made public, Chief Justice Warren replied; "Yes, there will come a time. But it might not be in your lifetime . . . there may be some things that would involve security. This would be preserved but not made public."

Now, in 1989, the records of Congress' Assassinations Committee, ironically the body formed to bring the facts before the public once and for all, remain the subject of bitter dispute. They remain locked up at the National Archives, and could remain so till the year 2029—under a fifty-year rule covering congressional documents. Other classified material, from the CIA and the FBI for example, was returned to those agencies for segregated holding in their files. The Committee's Chief Counsel, Robert Blakey, has said that the Committee "was not able to publish everything it wanted to publish, or which was relevant to the President's assassination, as it ran out of time and appropriations." He has also said, ". . . material ended up restricted in the Archives, and in a sense it's sort of a shame, because the documents are indexed . . . so when the historians come . . . fifty years from now . . . it will be easy to use our documents."

Blakey has his critics, and they think it is more than "sort of a shame" that huge volumes of documents are still suppressed. They say Blakey has opposed efforts to bring in a congressional resolution, routinely used, that would release the material under a special House rule. This would be justified on the grounds of the age of the crime and continuing public interest in a pivotal historical event. As this edition went to press, Blakey maintained there was no reason to make Assassinations Committee material an exception to the usual fifty-year rule, and that nothing of importance had been withheld anyway. Blakey has not explained the apparent contradiction between this and his earlier statements.

Many former Assassinations Committee staff members believe some of the withheld material is vital to the pursuit of truth—not least the suppressed reports on the Mexico City episode. The CIA, Blakey told this author, would never agree to the release of that, because it would reveal CIA sources and methods. Such a revelation, according to Blakey, "would be a matter of international embarrassment today," even though the information involved is now twenty-six years old.

In the opinion of well-informed critics, including this author, it is fatuous to worry about "embarrassment" to the CIA, or to anyone else, when the matter at issue is the assassination of the President of the United States. No less than sixty-four Congressmen have supported resolutions designed to force release of Assassinations Committee material. Seven of them are specially qualified to do so—they themselves served on the Committee.

It seems entirely wrong that any relevant information on the Kennedy assassination should be withheld until we are gone, until our children in turn are old. Then, it will be only the dry bones of history. And will the written record, with all the players long gone from the stage, suffice to convince historians they have the full facts at last?

In a schizophrenic era, the assassination of President Kennedy has reflected the best and worst hallmarks of the American character. The murder itself, enacted on a wide screen of global attention, was somehow intrinsically American, as seminal to the Sixties as the broadcast dramas of Vietnam, the revolution of international youth, and the landing on the moon. The first Kennedy inquiry was bungled, for all the pomp and circumstance with which its conclusions were announced. It was an analgesic, as reality assimilated as the drug culture that was soon to calm and confuse one generation and outrage its parents. In the late Seventies, the reopening of the Kennedy inquiry was a response by the lawmakers to a national doubt that questioned far more than the manner of one man's passing.

America's television father figure, Walter Cronkite, rode out the story from November 22, 1963 to the last anniversary, in 1988. Then, on Public Television, he said he understood why the case has become a "national obsession". "To bring us closer to the truth," he said, "There could be a new rifle test, a new acoustics test, an examination of the brain if it is ever found, an analysis for traces of blood on the single bullet . . ." "The ultimate solution to the mystery," he added, "may lie outside the domain of science."

Edwin Lopez, the Assassinations Committee investigator who spearheaded the investigation into the role of the CIA in Mexico City, says: "It was very obvious, from dealing with people at the CIA for approximately two years, that the CIA was covering something up. We weren't sure whether it had to do with some element of the CIA having assassinated the President, but we knew at the very least that they were covering up something they knew about the Kennedy assassination. I came away feeling that we could not trust our government, that what we had been told all along was a sham. And I thought the American people deserved better."

Gaeton Fonzi was nicknamed "Ahab" by his Committee colleagues because of his persistence in his pursuit of "Maurice Bishop." He was a U.S. Government investigator on the case for three years. "There is no doubt now there was a conspiracy," he has said, "but we aren't sure of anything beyond that. And yet most of us—the polls say and the press reflects it—are not very angry about that. That's history and, Lord knows, there are enough worries today. But you would have been very angry if someone with a gun had stopped you from going into the voting booth, had taken away your freedom to choose. . . . The analogy is obvious: The conspiracy to kill the President of the United State was also a conspiracy against the democratic system—and thus a conspiracy against *you*. . . . I think you should get very angry about that. If not, you might as well let slip the grip on your individual freedom. It will be gone soon enough."

The Assassinations Committee staff may have been divided on the emphasis of the inquiry, but they are all embittered by the official response to their work. The former Chief Counsel said at the end of the inquiry, "The Government, to live up to the meaning of Justice, can do no less than to pursue the course the Committee has charted. Why? Because statutes of limitation do not apply to murder, certainly not the murders of men like John F. Kennedy. . . . Justice demands no less."

Later when he saw how the Committee's work was being mishandled—or downright ignored—Professor Blakey was outraged. "The Justice Department is burying this thing because they want the case to die," he said, "It's almost diabolical. The Justice Department will get out from under this thing entirely, and nothing else is going to be done about it—a conspiracy to kill my President and yours."

And nothing has been done.

It is fitting, perhaps, to close with the words of one who was not yet an American citizen when President Kennedy was assassinated. In 1978, Silvia Odio, the Cuban exile whose chilling testimony about "Oswald" remains the most compelling human evidence of conspiracy, gave me a television interview. I asked her why she was now prepared to talk, after refusing press approaches for so long. She was silent for a long moment, then said, "I guess it is a feeling of frustration after so many years. I feel outraged that we have not discovered the truth for history's sake, for all of us. I think it is because I am very angry about it all—the forces I cannot understand, and the fact that there is nothing I can do against them. That is why. . . ."

Sources and Notes

If not described in full, source books are referred to here under the authors' names and the notation *op. cit.* Full details of these can be found in the bibliography. The following abbreviations are used in reference to citations from official reports.

Warren Commission Report—Report p. -.

Citations referring to the 26 volumes of Hearings and Exhibits accompanying the Warren Report are referred to by volume and page—e.g., XXII.25.

Warren Commission Documents, available at the National Archives, are referred to by abbreviation, document number, and page number within the document—e.g., CD16.5.

Citations from the Report of the House Select Committee on Assassinations (1979) are referred to by page number and the abbreviation—HSCA Report p. -.

Citations from the 12 Kennedy volumes of Hearings and Appendices of the House Select Committee on Assassinations are referred to by volume and page number—e.g., HSCA V.250.

There are many citations from the Interim Report (1975) of the Select Committee to Study Governmental Operations with Respect to Intelligence Activities, United States Senate—*Alleged Assassination Plots Involving Foreign Leaders*. Citations from the above are referred to by page and heading—Sen. Int. Cttee., *Assassination Plots*.

Similarly, sources in the Final Report of the above Select Committee (1976) entitled "The Investigation of the Assassination of President John F. Kennedy: Performance of the Intelligence Agencies" are referred to thus: Sen. Int. Cttee., *Performance of Intelligence Agencies*, plus page number.

All the above are published by the U.S. Government Printing Office and listed in the bibliography to this book.

Preface

Page

xviii Chairman (Downing): Associated Press report, September 17, 1976.

xviii First acoustics expert: Dr. James E. Barger, testified September 11, 1978. HSCA II.17.

Second acoustics experts: Professor Mark Weiss and Mr. Ernest Aschkenasy, testified December 29, 1978. HSCA V.555.

Chief Counsel on two shooters: Blakey interview on DIR radio, New York, August 1979. Full transcript published in *Clandestine America*, Vol. III, No. 3, Jan./Feb. 1980.

Committee Report on "conspiracy": HSCA Report p. 1 and 180.

Marcello and Trafficante: HSCA Report p. 173.

"credible associations": HSCA Report p. 169.

Chief Counsel: Robert Blakey, speaking on television in Dallas, spring 1979.

HSCA members who doubted acoustics evidence: Congressmen Samuel Devine, Robert Edgar, and Harold Sawyer, HSCA Report p. 49.

xix "Three gunmen"?: Congressman Christopher Dodd, HSCA Report p. 483 -.

Committee on Oswald and Ruby: HSCA Report p. 180.

HSCA on intelligence agencies: HSCA Report p. 2.

FBI destruction: HSCA Report p. 196.

Oswald in company of former FBI man: (association with Guy Banister and David Ferrie) HSCA Report p. 142.

CIA file segregated: HSCA Report p. 215.

Refusal of CIA: HSCA Report p. 124.

xxii Close associate: (de Mohrenschildt) HSCA XII.54 and 56; HSCA Report p. 217.

Oswald and intelligence officer: (Oswald and "Maurice Bishop," as reported by Antonio Veciana) HSCA Report p. 135-; HSCA X.37-.

Staff belief: interviews of staff by the author, 1978.

Army Intelligence file: HSCA Report p. 221-.

"Eminent witness" (former Warren Commission General Counsel Rankin): HSCA XI.71.

xxiii Justice Department 1980: *New York Times,* January 6, 1980; (1988) March 28 J.D. letter to Peter Rodino, Chairman, House Judiciary Committee; Blakey, interview May 3, 1989.

1. Ambush

1 Poem: *Poems* by Alan Seeger (Charles Scribner & Sons, 1916).

Kennedy and danger in Dallas: Manchester, *op. cit.* pp. 13, 15, 45.

Dallas notables: General Edwin Walker, Mayor Earle Cabell, H.L. Hunt.

2 Kennedy speeches: Manchester, *op. cit.,* pp. 86, 96.

Advertisement: *Dallas Morning News,* November 22; XVIII.835; inserted by John Birch Society members and rightists.

Kennedy comments: Manchester, *op. cit.,* p. 137; and Bishop, *op. cit.,* p. 25; VII.455—testimony of Kenneth O'Donnell.

Miami scare: CD's 1347/20 and author's interview with former Miami Police Intelligence Captain Charles Sapp, 1978; but see also HSCA Report p. 635 n.44.

3 Spectator comment: Manchester, *op. cit.,* p. 154.

Nellie Connally comment: IV.147 and IV.131.

Officer's remark: Bishop, *op. cit.,* p. 147.

Time: calculated for HSCA—HSCA II.40; and Report p. 48 (Agent Youngblood noticed the clock on the Book Depository).

President's cry: II.73/74.

Note 1: It has been suggested that Agent Kellerman imagined he heard the President speak only because of the possibility his throat wound made speech unfeasible. Doctors differ on this point, but it seems speech may well have been possible (HSCA VII.278/295/305).

Events in car: Mrs. Kennedy's cry—V.179-; Mrs. Connally—IV.148; Governor Connally—IV.133; "buckshot"—HSCA I.54.

4 Doctor breaks news: Manchester, *op. cit.,* p. 215.

2. The Evidence Before You

7   Cartridges found: III.283 (Mooney).
Gun found: III.293 (Boone) and VII.107 (Weitzman); (described)
III.392 (Frazier) IV.260 (Day).
Note 2: There has been controversy over the identification of the
rifle, because it was initially described as a Mauser. Although one
of these descriptions came from one of the officers who found the
weapon (who was familiar with guns), I believe this was simply a
mistake. I do not subscribe to theories that the rifle was subsequently switched for the one supposedly owned by Lee Oswald,
as some have claimed. HSCA experts agree that confusion is the
probable explanation (HSCA VII.372).
Bullet fragments: (listed) HSCA VII.365.
Intact bullet: (found) Report p. 79.
Note 3: The bullet was found by Darrell Tomlinson, the hospital's
chief engineer, when he moved the stretcher. Tomlinson was not
at all convinced that the stretcher was the one that had been used
for Governor Connally. The Warren Commission, however, decided it was that stretcher. The uncertainty has fueled suspicions
that the bullet was perhaps planted as part of a plan to inculpate
Lee Oswald. To this author, that posits too complex a plot and is
improbable. (Report p. 79 and VI.126-.)
Cartridges, bullets, and fragments linked to rifle: Report p. 84-;
HSCA VII.367-.

8   *Note 4:* Admiral Osborne, who attended the Kennedy autopsy,
today says he saw and even handled an intact bullet during the
procedure. He thought it turned up in the body's wrappings,
though he is open to the possibility that it arrived
independently—which may mean he merely saw the famous "single bullet," after its separate transfer from Dallas. However, the
possibility remains that he did see a second mystery bullet, and
full questioning of the other doctors should resolve this (Lifton,
op. cit., chapter 29, & HSCA VII.15). Speculation has also arisen
because FBI agents signed a receipt for a "missile" received from
the autopsy doctors (Lifton, *op. cit.,* & HSCA VII.12). During
the seventies, two private citizens reported finding bullets at the
assassination site (HSCA VII.372 & *Dallas Morning News,* Dec.
23, 1978).
Argument over body: McKinley, *op. cit.* p. 120; "at gunpoint"—
author's interview with Dr. Robert Shaw, 1978.
Helpern: Marshall Houts, *op. cit.,* p. 52.
Baden: HSCA I.298; and see HSCA VII.177.

8   Summary of autopsy: Warren Report p. 86—; HSCA VII.6- and 87-.

Probed: CD7.4 in National Archives: HSCA VII.12-.
Autopsy atmosphere: HSCA VII.13-.
HSCA conclusion: (re Humes) HSCA VII.14.
Finck: HSCA VII.13-; and see State of Louisiana v. Clay Shaw—
Finck testimony, February 24, 1967; (on clothing) HSCA
VII.192.

10 Brain: HSCA VII.17 and 25.
Wecht: *Modern Medicine,* November 27, 1972.
Brain lost, etc.: HSCA VII.25-.
Wecht: *Modern Medicine,* November 27, 1972.

11 Series of re-examinations: HSCA VII.3-.
Autopsy sketch: HSCA VII.89.
Back wound: HSCA VII.85; and see HSCA VII.175-.
Glaring mistake: HSCA VII.104; and see HSCA VII.176.
Debris: HSCA VII.177-.
CIA interference: statement by Congressman Louis Stokes to House
of Representatives, June 28, 1979; *Washington Post,* June 18, 19
and 28, 1979; *New York Times,* June 18, 1979; *Clandestine Amer-
ica,* III.2, p. 4.

13 *Note 5:* In August 1979 a freelance journalist, Harrison Livingstone,
revealed that he had copies of five Kennedy autopsy photographs, and offered them for publication. They were eventually
published in his 1989 book *High Treason,* written with co-author
Robert Groden, a former consultant to Congress' Assassination
Committee. (See *New York Times,* August 19, 1979, and Bibliography.)

13 Zapruder film: Available for viewing at the National Archives,
Washington, D.C.; Penn Jones, PO Box 1140, Midlothian, Texas
76065, can advise researchers on obtaining copies.

14 Recovery of dictabelt: author's research in Dallas, 1978; HSCA
II.16 and 107.
Testimony of Barger: HSCA II.17-; HSCA V.645; author's inter-
view with Barger, November 1978.

15 Testimony of Weiss and Aschkenasy: HSCA V.555; and see HSCA
Vol. VIII.
Objections re acoustics: HSCA V.652 (Report of Anthony Pelicano
summarizes objections); (explained) HSCA V.671, 672.
Unique sound of gunfire: HSCA V.592.
Motorcycle located: HSCA V.679.

16 Acoustics a science: HSCA Report p. 65.
Admitted into evidence: HSCA V.674.
HSCA conclusion: HSCA Report p. 1; (beyond a reasonable doubt)
HSCA V.583.
Academy of Sciences: Ramsey Report, 1982.
Blakey: int. May 3 1989.

3. The Science of Conspiracy

19 Dodd quote: HSCA Report p. 486.

Survey of people on number of shots: HSCA VIII.142.

Acoustics specialists: "Firearms Investigation, Identification and Evidence," Hatcher Jury and Weller, 1957, p. 420—Secret Service memo March 7, 1964 (S.S. Files 221-229).

Rear right outriders: James Chaney and D. L. Jackson.

19 Five in the car: Mrs. Kennedy (V.180); Connallys (IV.132, 145); Agent Kellerman (II.74; XVIII.724; II.61) (he believed there were more than three shots); Agent Greer (II.130).

Rear left outriders: B.J. Martin (VI.292); B. W. Hargis (VI.294); and *New York Daily News*, November 24, 1963.

Moorman: XIX.487; XXII.838; XXIV.217.

Brehm: XII.837.

Hill: VI.206; XIX.479; XXIV.212; XXV.853, 854, 875.

20 Mrs. Newman: XIX.488; XXII.842; XXIV.2; IV.218.

Orr: conversation with Dallas researcher, November 22, 1963, and subsequently. Orr was never interviewed by any official body.

Acoustics: testimonies of Barger (HSCA II) and Weiss/Aschkenasy (HSCA V).

Blakey summary: HSCA V.690.

Time frame: HSCA V.724.

21 Two shots sounded like one: Report p. 87.

Stokes/Weiss: HSCA V.582-.

Blakey and acoustics experts: Interview with DIR radio, New York, August 1979; full transcript published by *Clandestine America*, vol. III, no. 3, Jan./Feb. 1980.

Origin of third shot: HSCA VIII.5.

Origin of knoll shot: HSCA VIII.10.

22 Ford: Article in *Life* magazine, October 2, 1964.

Blakey: int. May 3 1989.

Survey re direction of shots: HSCA Report pp. 87, 90.

Note 6: The first useful survey on shots was *Fifty-one Witnesses: The Grassy Knoll* by Harold Feldman (Idlewild Publishing Company, 1965). I took this, the most perspicacious early work, into account. It agrees, in basic conclusions, with the HSCA findings.

Mrs. Kennedy: V.180.

Governor Connally: IV.132-.

Mrs. Connally: IV.149.

Greer: II.129.

Kellerman: XVIII.724 and II.61.

Left outriders: VI.293 (Hargis) and VI.289 (Martin).

Chaney: unidentified film interview in police station and taped interview for KLIF, Dallas, on record "The Fateful Hours," Capitol Records.

Moorman: XIX.497; XXII.838; XXIV.217.

23 Orr: conversation with Dallas researcher, November 22, 1963, and subsequently.

Brehm: XXII.837.

Hill: VI.206; XIX.479; XXIV.212; XXV.853-, 875.

Newman: XIX.490; XXII.842; XXIV.219.

Book Depository witnesses: manager—William Shelley (VI.328); superintendent—Truly (III.227); TSBD vice-president—O.V. Campbell (XXII.638); vice president publishing company—S. F. Wilson (XXII.685).

Sorrels: XXI.548; (later testimony) VII.347.

Landis: XVIII.758.

Decker: verbatim from police radio traffic recording of November 22, 1963 (as published in *JFK Assassination File* by Jesse Curry, 1969) (see bibliography).

25 Arnold: interviewed by Earl Golz for *Dallas Morning News,* August 27, 1978 (seen by Yarborough—*Dallas Morning News,* December 31, 1978); never interviewed by HSCA—interview of Arnold by Golz, May 23, 1979.

27 Railway supervisor: S. M. Holland—testimony VI.239-.

Woodward and friends: Dallas *Morning News,* November 23, 1963 (Woodward's position indicated in XXIV.520).

Chism and wife: XXIV.204/5.

27 Millican: XIX.486.

Jean Newman: XXIV.218.

Zapruder: CD 87.15566; HSCA Report p. 89.

Holland: (police statement): XXIV.212; (testimony) VI.239; interview of Holland by Mark Lane (on film) taken from transcript of *Rush to Judgment,* transmitted on BBC-TV, January 29, 1967.

28 Eight other witnesses: Frank Reilly—VI.230; Nolan H. Polton—XXII.834; James Simmons—XXII.833; Clemon Johnson—XXII.836; Andrew Miller—VI.225 and XIX.485; Richard Dodd—XXII.835; Walter Winborn—XXII.833; Thomas Murphy—XXII.835 (see also HSCA XII.23).

Bowers: VI.284—testimony of Bowers; and filmed interview by Mark Lane, March 31, 1966; also Lane, *op. cit.,* p. 23-24.

29 Gunpowder (Mrs. Cabell) VII.486-; (Yarborough) Feldman, *op. cit.* (unpaginated); (Roberts) Feldman, *op. cit.* (unpaginated); (Brown) VI.233-; (Baker) VII.510-.

Smith: VII.535; *Texas Observer*, December 13, 1963; two interviews with author, August 1978; XXII.600.

HSCA on photograph by wall (Willis): HSCA VI.121-.

Moorman photograph: HSCA VI.125-; (Groden on Moorman) HSCA VI.296.

31 Zapruder on CBS (Rather error): tape of KRLD, Dallas CBS affiliate—reel 65A.7 (inventory of tapes of Dallas radio stations, National Archives).

Frames reversed (original error): XVIII.70-; "printing error"— Hoover letter to Ray Marcus, December 14, 1965.

31 Riddle: *Ramparts* magazine article entitled "The Case for Three Assassins" by David Lifton and David Welsh, January 1967.

Hargis: VI.293/5; Curry, *op. cit.*, p. 30.

Martin: VI.289.

Harper: CD1269, p. 5; HSCA VII.24.

"covered with brain tissue": HSCA Report p. 40.

HSCA conclusion: HSCA Report p. 1; HSCA V.690-.

32 Neuromuscular reaction: HSCA I.415.

Medical panel agrees on reaction thesis: HSCA VII.174 and 178.

Entrance wound: HSCA VII.176, 107; and HSCA I.250 (brain should have been sectioned); HSCA VII.134; bullet path— HSCA VII.135.

Guinn tests: HSCA I.507; (testimony) HSCA I.491; interviewed by author, November 1978; *Analytical Chemistry*, Vol. 51, p. 484A, April 1979.

33 *Note 7:* Dr. Guinn was unable to test one fragment found in the car, as it was jacketed in copper rather than lead (HSCA I.515). In their analysis, the firearms panel concluded that this was the base of a 6.5 mm. bullet and believe it had been fired through the rifle found at the Depository (HSCA VII.369). This, probably, was the fragment referred to by Congressman Dodd in public session as "not easily identifiable as a result of neutron activation tests" (HSCA V.696).

One of the fragments recovered from the floor of the limousine has vanished since 1963 (HSCA VII.366n). In addition, Guinn reported finding one fragment container empty, a can which had apparently contained particles from the car's damaged windshield. Nor were any samples left from a curb that had reportedly been struck by a bullet. Guinn assumed these had simply been "used up" in earlier FBI tests (HSCA I.196 and letter to author, August 10, 1979). This, at any rate, is the way the HSCA decided to account for the difference in weight and count of fragment material originally listed by the FBI and that handed to Guinn (HSCA Report p. 599n 33). Clearly the fragments were, at one stage, at least poorly catalogued and monitored. Some will suspect a more sinister explanation. See also Note 11 on problems with possible missing fragments in connection with Governor Connally's wrist and the magic bullet (later in this chapter).

Ballistics link fragments to gun: HSCA VII.369-.

Warren conclusion on shot: Report p. 105.

34 *Note 8:* Norman Redlich, Commission lawyer, said on March 23, 1965, "To say that they were hit by separate bullets is synonymous with saying that there were two assassins." (See *Inquest* by E. J. Epstein, p. 55.)

Helpern: Marshall Houts, *op. cit.,* pp. 9 and 59.

Note 9: Helpern was quoting the Warren Commission description of the bullet. The HSCA firearms panel found it to weigh 157.7 grains, however (HSCA VII.368, 372).

36 Wecht: *Modern Medicine,* November 27, 1972; *Forensic Science,* 1974; HSCA I.332-.

Nichols: *Maryland State Medical Journal,* October, 1977.

Shaw: interview with author, 1978; and HSCA I.268, 302.

Boggs: June 11, 1965, interviewed by E. J. Epstein for *Inquest* (p. 148).

Cooper: interview for BBC, produced by author, 1978.

Russell: interviewed by Alfred Goldberg, May 5, 1965, reported in *Inquest* by E.J. Epstein, p. 148; and interviewed in 1970 for *Whitewash IV* by Harold Weisberg, p. 212; see also *New York Times,* November 22, 1966, p. 22.

HSCA on "magic bullet": HSCA Report p. 47.

Forensic panel on "magic bullet": HSCA VII.179.

37 Ballistics reports: HSCA I.411 (tests on bullets); bullet fired in rifle—HSCA VII.368.

Guinn test: HSCA I.533.

Wecht rejection: HSCA VII.199.

38 Baden on "futile" tests and on seeing similar bullets: HSCA I.307.

Note 10: In August 1979, Dr. Baden became the subject of controversy in New York City, where he had been serving as Chief Medical Examiner. The mayor of New York decided not to confirm him in his job, and the city's district attorneys complained that Dr. Baden was responsible for "sloppy record-keeping, poor judgment, and a lack of cooperation." Dr. Baden took strong exception to the criticisms, and the matter had not been finally resolved when this book first went to press. (*New York Times,* August 3, 6, and 8, 1979.)

Operating-room supervisor and policeman: Nurse Audrey Bell, in conversation with author, 1978; and Patrolman Charles Harbison, reported in *Dallas Morning News,* April 3, 1977; interviewed by Earl Golz, September 1977.

Note 11: As cited above, Nurse Audrey Bell, operating-room supervisor at Parkland Hospital in 1963, stated in 1977 that on November 22, 1963, she had seen and handled "four or five bullet fragments" after their removal from the Governor's arm. Bell says she placed these in a "foreign body envelope" and handed it to federal agents. This much seems confirmed by HSCA, VII.156 and Fig. 17, HSCA VII.392. The Warren Commission referred to "two or three fragments" and claimed they could have come from the magic bullet (Report p. 95). Bell, however, has caused concern with her recent remark that "the smallest was the size of the striking end of a match and the largest at least twice that big. I have seen the picture of the magic bullet, and I can't see how it could be the bullet from which the fragments I saw came." (Interview with author, 1978.) Bell has thirty years' nursing experience and has seen hundreds of bullet injuries. In the wake of her 1977 statements came another from Charles Harbison, a patrolman who guarded the Governor's room. He says that on November 25 or 26, when the Governor was being moved, somebody—he thinks a doctor—gave him fragments. Harbison says he gave them to an FBI agent. Since he recalls "more than three," since he and Bell refer to different incidents and since there is still a fragment in the Governor's thigh to this day, it appears there may have been more fragments than the condition of the magic bullet would permit. On the other hand, Bell and Harbison may be confused in their recollections. In 1978, HSCA wound ballistics expert Sturdivan did say he felt more was missing from the magic bullet than is accounted for by the surviving fragments and surmised some had been lost (HSCA I.412). Some fragments have indeed vanished since 1963; see Note 7 on Guinn tests earlier in this chapter. Their loss, without proper accounting, continues to fuel suspicion by some researchers that they were maliciously removed.

Wecht speculation: HSCA I.362.

Ballistics consultant cannot exclude: HSCA I.425.

Wecht objection on head shot; HSCA VII.201; HSCA VII.129 (on shape in brain).

Mark in autopsy photograph: (illustration) HSCA VII.104, 106; (disagreement) HSCA VII.116.

Wecht on possible two head shots: HSCA VII.201.

Baden agrees possible: HSCA Report p. 80 and p. 604n 106.

39 "frangible ammunition": (ballistics denial) HSCA I.401; (doctor's denial) HSCA I.379.

Chairman's question to Wecht: HSCA I.355.

Wecht on four shots: HSCA I.349.

Suggestions of fakery: HSCA VI.298 (Groden); *Clandestine America* II.5 (David Lifton); *Baltimore Sun*, July 9, 1979; *Dallas Morning News*, July 10, 1979.

Note 12: The authenticity of the autopsy photographs and X-rays was most seriously questioned in the book *Best Evidence*, by David Lifton, which appeared in 1981 as this book went to press. (See Bibliography.) His thesis, that the President's body was tampered with surgically between Dallas and the Bethesda autopsy, is dealt with at length in Aftermath, this edition. Lifton's theory seems preposterous, but it is hard to dismiss the testimony of the witnesses he traced and interviewed. He has certainly raised troubling questions about the movement of the President's body. Meanwhile, Harrison Livingstone and Robert Groden (see Bibliography) allege forgery in autopsy pictures and X-rays. The HSCA medical panel and an independent group, however, believed that the autopsy photographs and X-rays are authentic, after exhaustive checks (HSCA VII.37/Report & *Boston Globe* 6.21.81.)

4. Gunmen in the Shadows

41 Curry: Curry, *op. cit.*, p. 61.

Clerks: VI.194 (R. Fischer); and VI.203 (Edwards); and XXIV.207-.

Brennan: III.145; XI.206-.

Euins: II.209; VI.170; VII.349.

Worrell: Warren Report p. 253; II.190.

Mayor's wife and photographers: VII.485-(Mrs. Cabell); II.155 (R. Jackson) and VI.160 (M. Couch).

42 Rowland: II.175; (and FBI) II.183.

Henderson: XXIV.524 (to FBI); interviewed by author, 1978, and by Earl Golz, in *Dallas Morning News*, December 19, 1978. (In

Henderson's FBI statement, which is reported speech, it is not clear if she is discussing the specific sixth-floor window.)

43   Walther: XXIV.522 (to FBI); also interview with author, 1978; and with Earl Golz of *Dallas Morning News,* 1978; recorded interview by Larry Schiller for Capitol Records, "The Controversy," 1967.

Powell: traced and interviewed by Earl Golz for *Dallas Morning News,* December 19, 1978; see same article for suggestion to Warren official re jail.

44   Bronson film: (revealed) *Dallas Morning News,* November 26, 1978; (Groden) HSCA VI.308.

Hughes film: This film was provided to FBI after assassination by bystander Robert Hughes. The FBI reported to Warren Commission that it showed no images that could be interpreted as human movement (XXV.873; Report p. 644; CD205.158).

Still photograph (by Jack Weaver): Josiah Thompson, *op. cit.,* p. 248.

44   Groden: HSCA VI.309.

HSCA photo panel: (boxes moved) HSCA VI.115; (on movies) HSCA VI.109; (Hughes) HSCA VI.115-. (Bronson) HSCA VI.121; (Selzer) *Gallery* magazine, July 1979, pp. 72-16; (HSCA recommendation) HSCA Report p. 7.

Gap between shots 1 and 2: (defined) HSCA V.724; (FBI 1964 and HSCA reaction) HSCA II.105-; (ease over iron sights) HSCA VII.373; (HSCA first test) HSCA II.105-; (second test) HSCA VIII.183; (army spokesman) Warren III.447-9; (the same examination after the assassination revealed that the telescopic sight, whether or not used in the assassination, was defective (Warren Report p. 194); (Dodd) HSCA Report p. 483-.

46   HSCA recommendations: HSCA Report p. 7; and see footnotes 12 and 13 to pp. 486 and 487.

Definition of conspiracy: HSCA Report p. 95.

5. Finding a Fugitive

49   Oswald excuse for leaving scene: Warren Report p. 600.

Secret Serviceman with gun: picture in *The Torch Is Passed* (AP 1964) p. 17; and HSCA Report p. 606n 155.

Willis: HSCA XII.7; (photographs) HSCA VI.121.

Price: XIX.492; interview of Price by Mark Lane, March 27, 1966; HSCA XII.12.

Bowers: VI.284; filmed interview by Mark Lane, March 31, 1966; HSCA XII.12-.

Smith: VII.535; *Texas Observer*. December 13, 1963; interviews with author, August 1978 and subsequently.

50   *Note 13:* The Assassinations Committee was unable to resolve the problem created by Officer Smith's sighting of a man who showed Secret Service credentials. It considered the possibility that he had mistaken an Army Intelligence agent for a Secret Serviceman, given that reliable evidence shows that Army Intelligence officers were in the Dealey Plaza area. The Department of Defense, however, said the record contained nothing about such agents being active in Dallas on November 22. The Committee thought it possible that Dallas police plainclothes detectives might have been taken for Secret Service agents. Officer Smith's experience, however, remains unexplained—especially as he would almost certainly have established a clear contact with a fellow officer (HSCA Report p. 183-).

Arnold: *Dallas Morning News,* August 27, 1978; interviewed by Earl Golz, May 23, 1979.

Hill: interview with author, August 1978; VI.206, XIX.479; XXIV.212; XXV.853, 875; and article *Dallas Morning News,* August 27, 1978; HSCA XII.11 (HSCA staff could not locate Hill, although she still lives in Texas).

51   Curry: interview with author, December 1977.

Tilson: interview with Earl Golz of *Dallas Morning News* and article *Dallas Morning News* August 20, 1978.

Other reports of cars: HSCA XII.13-.

52   Radio calls: XXIII.916—transcript of police radio Channel 1; and Curry, *op. cit.,* p. 43-.

Warren identification: Report p. 144.

Witnesses to "fugitive" from Depository: (dark jacket) XVI.959; (others reviewed) HSCA XII.80-.

Citizen call on radio: XVII.408, transcript of police radio Channel 1; (time) Report p. 165.

53   Suspect description: XXIII.859-, transcript of police radio Channel 1.

Brewer: VII.4.

Ticket seller: VII.10- (J. Postal).

McDonald: interview with author, 1978; III.299.

54   Oswald cry: III.300 (McDonald).

No notes: Report p. 180.

Fritz: R.599 (p. 13 Fritz report).

Interrogation sessions: All information on Oswald statements is from Report, Appendix XI, which contains reports of Captain Fritz, FBI Agents Hosty, Bookhout, Clements, Secret Service Inspector Thomas Kelley, and US Postal Inspector H. D. Holmes.

55 Oswald statements to press: All are taken by the author from contemporary radio and TV tapes.

Cartridges found: III.283 (Mooney).

Gun found: III.293 (Boone) and VII.107 (Weitzman).

Rifle described: III.392 (Frazier) IV.260 (Day).

Palm print: IVH.258 (Day).

Klein's: VII.364 (Waldman) and VII.370 (Scibor).

56 Oswald's writing: VII.420 (Cadigan)/IV.373 (Cole).

Hidell card: VII.58 (Hill).

Fibers: IV.83- (Stombaugh).

Marina on rifle: I.26/52 (Marina Oswald).

Police search: VII.229 (Rose)/VII.548 (Walthers); IV.286.

57 Frazier: II.222 (Buell Frazier).

Frazier sister: II:248 (Linnie Randle).

Bag found: IV.266 (Day).

Prints on bag: R. Appendix X.565-/IV.3 (Latona).

Fibers on bag: IV.77 (Stombaugh).

Photographs found: VII.231- (Officers Adamcik, Moore, Stovall, Rose).

Marina on photographs: I.15 I.117/V.405.

Imperial Reflex: IV.284 (Shaneyfelt).

Marks on "magic bullet": III.429 (Frazier)/III.498 (Nicol): HSCA VII.368.

Tippit ballistics: dealt with extensively in Chapter 6, "An Assassin in Seven-League Boots."

Oswald charged on Tippit count: Report p. 198.

58 Alexander decision: Interview with author, 1978.

Curry account: Curry, *op. cit.,* p. 79.

Note 14: There is considerable doubt whether Oswald was actually arraigned for the President's murder. An FBI report of November 25, 1963, states categorically that "No arraignment on the murder charge in connection with the death of President Kennedy was held, in as much as such arraignment was not necessary in view of the previous charges filed against Oswald and for which he was arraigned" (CD5.400). Homicide Captain Fritz, Police Chief Curry, and Judge Johnston (IV.221; IV.155; XV.507-) said Oswald was charged. The time given is 1:35 A.M. Yet Officer J. B. Hicks was on duty in the relevant office until after 2:00 A.M.

and is certain Oswald was not arraigned at 1:35. Another FBI report, classified until 1975, indicates that Oswald was never arraigned on the presidential charge (CD1084A.11). The author's interview with Assistant District Attorney Bill Alexander suggests the charitable explanation is that officials confused the arraignment on the presidential charge with the earlier one involving Officer Tippit.

Oswald's comments on rifle (and on all points unless indicated): Report, Appendix XI.

Note 15: Nobody at the Dallas post office concerned was ever formally asked whether they recalled handing a hefty package to somebody claiming to be the holder of Box 2915 a few months previously. The way such a package is delivered to a box holder is by leaving an advice note asking him to call at the counter. No postal worker has ever recalled giving Oswald any such package (Meagher, *op. cit.*, p. 50).

60   Warren Report on Hidell: Warren Report p. 313, 644- 292.

Heindel: VIII.318.

"Hidell" card in wallet: VII.58 (Hill) and see discussion in Meagher, *op. cit.*, p. 185.

Oswald identifies himself as "Hidell": VII.228, but see also VII.187-.

60   Public discussion of "Hidell": Meagher, *op. cit.*, p. 188.

Note 16: Some have inferred that the "Hidell" identity card was fabricated by the authorities to link Oswald with the mail order for the rifle. This is impossible to square with Oswald's handwriting on the order form, without assuming a plot to frame Oswald involving law-enforcement officials across the United States. I reject that notion, not because it is inherently implausible that a man would be framed by the authorities but because the deception involved would bring in too many people and be too vulnerable to exposure.

"Hidell" and Military Intelligence: Paul Hoch memo on "Army Intelligence, A. J. Hidell, and the FBI," October 8, 1977; FBI document 10582555 (unrecorded) (original in 62-109060-811); *Dallas Morning News*, March 19, 1978; HSCA Report p. 221.

Both names in Oswald wallet: VII.228.

62   *Note 17:* Oswald does appear to have used the name "Hidell" while in New Orleans but not in a way that could remotely be interpreted as an alias. The signature "A. J. Hidell" appears as "Chapter President" on a Fair Play for Cuba card Oswald showed the police in New Orleans after his arrest following a demonstration over Cuba. The name also appears on an FPCC

leaflet distributed in New Orleans. Handwriting experts are of
the opinion this was signed by Marina Oswald (HSCA VIII.238).
The point here is that Oswald was using "Hidell"—whether he
existed or not—as somebody *other than* himself. The same is
suggested by the discovery in Oswald's effects of an index card
for "Hidell," along with cards for real people (Meagher, *op. cit.*,
p. 197). Oswald was not carrying any Hidell ID when questioned
in New Orleans (X.52-). See full discussion of this episode in this
book, Chapter 17, "Blind Man's Bluff in New Orleans."

62 Shanklin affair: HSCA Report p. 195-; (interviewed by HSCA)
    HSCA Report p. 627; sources 74.

63 Oswald's intelligence: (school record) Texas Attorney General's
    Report, VIII.2965.30d (the record also says Oswald's IQ was "in
    the upper range of bright, normal intelligence"; (intelligence
    noted in Marines) VIII.290, 297, 300.

    Oswald offers garage information: Report p. 603.

    Note 18: Captain Fritz suggests (Report p. 607) that the police had
    the back-yard pictures by 12:35 P.M. on November 23. He ap-
    pears to be in error, according to the versions of policemen who
    found the pictures (VII.193, 231) (HSCA VI.139).

64 Persuasive evidence on pictures; (experts) Warren Report p. 125
    and HSCA VI.161; (Marina) I.117, 16.

    Pickard: interview with author, January 1978; statement used on
    CBC-TV, December 1977.

    Thompson: filmed interview for BBC-TV, January 1978; HSCA
    VI.219-.

65 *Note 19:* One oddity is a difference—to the layman's eye—between
    the two versions of the "rifle picture" printed in the Warren
    volumes (XVI.510-.) (Commission Exhibits 133A, 133B.) In "B"
    Oswald appears to have a ring, clearly visible, on a finger of his
    left hand. In "A" no ring is visible—a curious difference if, as
    Marina testified, she took one picture after another in the space
    of a few moments.

    Assassinations Committee view: HSCA VI.138-; HSCA Report p.
    54.

    Committee expert concedes fakes possible: HSCA II.430; HSCA
    VI.215.

    Letter signed "L.H.": see Newman, *op. cit.*

66 Taking of photographs: (Marina) I.117, 16, and HSCA II.241; (Mar-
    guerite) I.148; (White) HSCA II.321; HSCA VI.141; (fellow
    officer) HSCA VI.153.

    Police re-enactment picture: Warren Commission Exhibit (photo-
    graphs only at LBJ Library, Austin, Texas).

Hester photograph: interviewed by Earl Golz of *Dallas Morning News*, 1978; interviewed and reported by Jim Marrs, *Fort Worth Star-Telegram*, September 20, 1978.

67 Marina: (on burning picture) McMillan, *op. cit.*, p. 441; (on Oswald and rifle) II.415.

Note 20: The Warren Commission based much of its case against Oswald on her testimony—although the very fact that she was Oswald's wife would have disqualified her testimony had her husband come to trial.

Marina "lying": Warren Commission memorandum, Redlich-Rankin, February 28, 1964; HSCA on Marina—HSCA Report p. 55.

Marina lapses of memory: HSCA XII.332.

68 Oswald colleague: X.201—testimony of Dennis Ofstein.

69 *Note 21:* Oswald may have signed one copy of the rifle photograph and given it to his Dallas associate George de Mohrenschildt. This possibility is dealt with in Chapter 12, "Hunter of the Fascists."

Fibers: (FBI) Report p. 124; (Oswald on shirt change) Report pp. 605, 613, 622, 626.

Report produced belatedly: IV.261 (Day).

Note 22: Lieutenant Day of Dallas police did not release the palm print to the FBI till November 26.

Location of print: IV.260 (Day).

71 Shorter package: II.239 (Buell Frazier) and II.248 (L. Randle), IX.475 (Krystinik).

71 Oily gun: XXVI.455.

Inquiry conclusions: (Warren) Report p. 137; (HSCA) HSCA Report p. 57.

Undeliverable package: CD205.148.

No ammunition: VII.226; XXVI.63.

72 *Note 23:* John T. Masen, of Masen's Gunshop (CE 2694 and CD 897.83-), told the FBI he acquired and sold ten boxes of Mannlicher-Carcano ammunition in 1963. Masen had been investigated for violation of the Firearms Act before the assassination (CD 853A.2) and admitted an association with a prominent member of Alpha 66, Manuel Rodriguez. (See index for other references to Alpha 66. At least one of its senior members has a major role in the mystery.)

Dodd theory: HSCA Report p. 484-(*Option one*).

74 Oswald's shooting record: XI.302.

Former Marine on Oswald's shooting expertise: VIII.235 (Nelson Delgado).

75 Oswald statements: Report pp. 600 and 613.

Prints on cartons: (Oswald's) IV.31-Latona; (unidentified print) Report pp. 249 and 566.

Note 24: Astonishingly, not all the employees of the Book Depository were fingerprinted. After the workers known to have handled cartons were checked and ruled out, the Depository superintendent "requested that other employees not be fingerprinted." (XXIV.7). Obligingly, the authorities went along with his request.

Chemical test: IV.275 (Day); CD 5.145/152.

Note 25: Nitrate deposits were found on Oswald's *hands,* which was consistent with his having fired a handgun, like the one he allegedly used to shoot policeman Tippit. Similar deposits could also, however, have resulted from handling printed matter (as Oswald did in his job) or from urine splashes. The nitrate test is today considered outmoded and unreliable.

76 Givens: Report p. 143; (narcotics) Roffman, *op. cit.,* p. 177; XXIII.873; VI.355; (FBI questioning, November 22) VI.355.

Oswald at 11:45 A.M.: III.168 (Williams); VI.337 (Lovelady).

Chicken lunch: III.169- (Williams); III.288 (Mooney); VII.46 (Hill); VII.121 (Boyd); VII.105 (Johnson); VII.146 (Studebaker); VI.330 (Shelley); VI.307 (Brewer); IV.266 (Day).

76 Jarman: III.200- (Jarman).

Norman: III.189 (Norman).

Shelley: VII.390 (Shelley).

Piper: VI.383 (Piper).

Note 26: It appears that Jarman now says that—like Givens—he observed Oswald on the first floor as early as noon (HSCA Report p. 57, referring to an HSCA interview). He did not say this in his Warren Commission testimony (III.201). With Piper, Shelley (and Givens), this makes four witnesses who saw Oswald downstairs at noon.

"going up to eat": XIX.499 (Piper).

Carolyn Arnold: conversations with author, November 1978; also with Earl Golz of *Dallas Morning News,* November 26, 1978; FBI report V.41.

Note 27: Carolyn Arnold has since remarried and has left Dallas.

78 Rowland: II.169/11.183 (Arnold Rowland)/VI.185 and 181 (Barbara Rowland).

Location of motorcade at 12:15 XVII.460/XXI.390/XXI.911.

Mrs. Arnold's leaving time: XXII.635 (Baker)/XXII.656 (Johnson)/ XXII.671 (Rachey)/XXII.645; (Dragoo) XXII.634 (Arnold).

79 Brennan: III.142 (Brennan).

Brennan at line-up: Report p. 145 (see also for both Brennan comments to FBI).

Brennan and "Communists": III.148 (Brennan).

Eyesight: III.147, 157 (Brennan).

Brennan and "no recoil": III.154 (Brennan).

Brennan and "smoke in knoll area": III.211.

Report on Brennan: Report p. 146.

Oswald's brown shirt: XXIII.417; XXVI.445; II.250; III.257; CD 1405; *Life,* October 2, 1964, p. 8; (pictured in color) Model and Groden, *op. cit.,* p. 137.

Oswald's "reddish" shirt: Report pp. 605, 613, 622, 626.

79 Policeman on shirts: III.263, 257 (Baker).

Note 28: Preliminary analysis of the Bronson film (by Robert Groden, reported in *Dallas Morning News,* November 27, 1978) suggested that (at 12:24 P.M.) one of the moving figures on the sixth floor wore "purplish red" upper clothing. Oddly, Oswald claimed during his questioning that he had changed his shirt at his roominghouse after leaving the Depository and before his arrest. He said, according to reports of his interrogation, that the shirt he discarded was "reddish colored" or "red." No such shirt was ever traced. So far as is known, he owned only brown, light brown and blue shirts (XVI.515). What's more, he was remembered as wearing a *tan* shirt by a neighbor who saw him leave for work on the day of the assassination (II.250). Yet Officer Baker's testimony (III.263, 257) does seem to corroborate Oswald's statement that he had changed into a darker shirt. It is not quite clear what color shirt Oswald wore to work that day. While the matter remains unresolved, it clearly was not white or light-colored— and that is the color shirt reported by those observing a window gunman. (The shirt Oswald was wearing when arrested is preserved at the National Archives.)

Rowland on shirt: II.171.

Brennan: III.145.

Clerks: VI.194 (Fischer); VI.203 (Edwards); also XXIV.207/8.

Mrs. Walther: interview with Earl Golz, November 1978; (in line with early statement XXIV.522.)

Baker: III.244- (Baker).

80 *Note 29:* Baker himself initially wrote in his statement (XXVI.3076) that he "saw a man standing in the lunchroom *drinking a Coke.*" He subsequently crossed out "drinking a Coke." One of the details announced by Police Chief Curry was that Oswald was seen by Baker and the building superintendent, Roy Truly, carrying a Coke. (Leo Sauvage in *Commentary*, p. 56.) If that were not so, it is hard to see how such a precise detail arose in the first place. Yet Baker and Truly ended up saying Oswald had nothing in his hand when they met him (Report p. 151). The question is important to the issue of whether Oswald could have got down from the sixth floor to encounter Baker and Truly when he did. Without obtaining a Coke, it would have been a close shave. If Oswald had purchased and started drinking a Coke by the time of the encounter with the policeman, the known time frame is stretched to bursting point—some would say beyond. (Oswald himself, incidentally, told the Chief of Homicide he was "drinking a Coca-Cola when the officer came in.") (Report p. 600.) In this author's opinion, the balance of the evidence suggests he was.

Reconstructions: For extensive discussion, see Roffman, *op. cit.,* p. 201-; Meagher, *op. cit.,* p. 70-; (Assassinations Committee, 1979) HSCA Report p. 601n 123.

President late: Report p. 3; XXII.613- (and see especially 616); Report p. 643.

82   Oswald question: III.201 (Jarman).
Supervisor: III.279 (Mrs. Reid).
Foreman: XXIV.226 (Shelley).
Bus ticket: IV.211 (Fritz); VII.173 (Sims).
Taxi driver: II.260 (Whaley).

6. An Assassin in Seven-League Boots

83   Alexander quoted: interview with author, December 1977.
Roberts: VI.438; VII.439.
Check on cars: XXV.909; XXIV.460.
Oswald name crops up: Report p. 9 (in Hill 1:51 P.M. radio report) XXI.40, 397; (Beckley address discovered after 2:00 P.M.) Report p. 601.
Order to Tippit 12:45: IV.179 (Curry); XXIII.844.
Tippit call 12:54: IV.179, 184 (Curry); VII.75 (Putnam); XXIII.849-.
Call to Tippit 1:00 P.M.: XVII.406 (precise time pinpointed by private study of police tapes).
Tippit call at 1:08: XVII.407.

86   Citizen's call at 1:16: XVII.408.
Report version: Report p. 165 and pp. 6 and 7.

Markham according Report: Report pp. 167, 168.

Markham statements: III.305-, 321-342; VII.499-.

Death instantaneous: Report p. 165; Benavides testimony—
   VI.446-.

87   Crowd: III.336 and 354; VI.448-.

Ammonia: IV.212 (Fritz).

Ball: debate in Beverly Hills, California, December 4, 1964. Lane
   op. cit., p. 161 (*Rush to Judgment*).

Oswald at police line-up: II.261 (Whaley).

Note 30: Attention has been drawn to the fact that one witness in the
   Tippit case, Warren Reynolds, was shot in the head two days
   after telling the FBI he could not identify Oswald. There was no
   apparent cause for the shooting. Reynolds recovered and later
   agreed he thought the fleeing gunman had been Oswald after all.
   Within a week or two of the Reynolds shooting, a key witness in
   that affair was found dead in a police cell, having apparently
   hanged herself. She had herself earlier mentioned an association
   with Jack Ruby and his club. The brother of a Tippit witness was
   shot dead, and many assumed it was a matter of mistaken identity. While these incidents arouse speculation, there is nothing
   evidentiary to link them to the Tippit or Kennedy killings. However, it is clear they were inadequately investigated. [(Injured
   witness) XXV.731; XI.437; XI.435; (dead brother—Eddy Benavides) Meagher, *op. cit.,* p. 299.]

Tippit cartridge cases: Report p. 559-; HSCA Report p. 59; HSCA
   VII.377-.

88   Only one bullet delivered to FBI: III.474 (Cunningham); (three
   more bullets) III.471.

Benavides shells: III.449—testimony of Ronald Simmons (Army
   ballistics expert).

Poe: (ordered to mark) III.49 (Hill); (Poe to FBI) XXIV.415 and
   VII.66.

89   Cases not on list, etc.: (police list) XXIV.260-; (ballistics list for
   FBI) same exhibit p. 131-135; (property clerk's list) same exhibit
   p. 262; (November 28 hand-over) same exhibit p. 117.

Oswald and .38: Report p. 558.

"automatic"—first description: I.36; XXIII.868.

"automatic"—second description: I.40, XXIII, 870 (actual words
   checked on original recording of police messages).

90   Clemons: description and interview—filmed by Mark Lane, March
   23, 1966.

Other Clemons information: interview report by George and Patricia Nash, *New Leader,* October 12, 1964; notes of interviews by Earl Golz and Tom Johnson, 1965.

91 Wright: Nash interview—*New Leader,* October 12, 1964.

Note 31: Other, less specific reports implied a red car was involved (HSCA XII.40).

Tippit shot at 1:15: Report p. 6.

Oswald official schedule on leaving house: Report pp. 163-165.

92 House-to-house inquiries: author's interview of former Assistant District Attorney William Alexander, 1977.

Bewley: XXIV.202.

Markham's bus: CD 630H.

Benavides delay: VI.448—testimony of Benavides.

Markham says "east": III.307 and 313/314—testimony of Markham.

94 Scoggins says "west": III.325; XXIV.225—testimony of Scoggins.

Burt says "west": Dallas researchers' interviews—1967, and with Larry Harris 1978.

Police reports say "west": Tippit homicide report. Police report 54018 (National Archives); Oswald arrest report: CD81b (reprinted in Curry, *op. cit.,* p. 84).

Secret Service reports say "west": CD87.489 and CD87.447—two reports of December 5, 1963.

HSCA "east" witness: HSCA Report p. 59 and HSCA XII.41 (witness is Jack R. Tatum).

Note 32: Tatum, as reported by the HSCA, referred to only one assassin.

95 Alexander: interviews with author, December 1977 and August 1978.

Note 33: Alexander points out that the alleged assassin was close to US Highway 67—R. L. Thornton Freeway—when he supposedly clashed with the policeman and may have been returning from it. Highway 67 is the route to Red Bird Airport, then a field for small aircraft on the outskirts of Dallas. Alexander speculates (interview with author, 1978) that Oswald may have expected to be picked up and taken to the airport, but that something went wrong at the rendezvous, and the getaway failed. Also in 1978 I spoke to Wayne January, who in 1963 ran a plane rental business at Red Bird Airport. He told me that two days before the assassination he was approached by two men and a woman, who inquired about renting an aircraft on Friday, November 22, to go to Mexico. He did not like the look of them and did not rent them a plane. After the assassination, when he saw Oswald on television, he thought he strongly resembled one of the men who had been at the airport. He gave this information to the FBI. (January was first interviewed in 1966 by researcher Jones Harris.)

HSCA on Tippit: HSCA Report p. 59-.

96 Martino: research and interview of Fred Claasen by Earl Golz, *Dallas Morning News*, 1978. (See this book, Chapter 22, "The First Stone.")

97 Belin/Schorr exchange: "Face the Nation," CBS-TV, November 23, 1975.

HSCA conclusion: HSCA Report pp. 1 and 2.

7. A Sphinx for Texas

98 Curry: interview with author, December 1977.

Alexander: interview with author, December 1977.

Oswald motive: Warren Report pp. 421, 423; HSCA Report p. 61-.

99 Oswald on JFK: Report p. 627—report of Secret Service Inspector Kelley; Marina—HSCA II.252, 217, 209; McMillan, *op. cit.,* pp. 194 and 350; HSCA XII.361, 413; (Martello) X.60; (eve of murder) HSCA XII.413, 331.

100 Oswald to president of Bar Association: VII.329 (Nichols).

Abt: report of Secret Service Inspector Kelley—Report p. 627.

101 Robert Oswald: I.468; (diary) XVI.901.

Johnson: *CBS Reports, The American Assassins,* Part II, November 26, 1975.

Warren: *New York Times,* February 5, 1964, p. 19, col. 7.

102 HSCA stymied: author's interviews with HSCA sources, 1978/1979; HSCA Report p. 490 (end of dissent by Congressman Dodd).

FBI spokesman: author's interview of Inspector Hoynden, December 1977.

Telephone intercept: CD 206.66.

103 Johnson: Warren Commission memorandum by lawyer Melvin Eisenberg, February 17, 1964.

Marina Oswald mysteries: see Chapter 10, "Mischief from Moscow."

Russell: Warren Commission Executive Session transcript for January 21, 1964.

Meller: CD950, interview of Meller by Dallas police officers Hellingshausen and Parks, February 17, 1964.

104 Moore: interviews with author of Jeanne de Mohrenschildt, widow of George, in 1978 (she corroborates her husband's version of Moore's remarks); and George de Mohrenschildt interview with Edward Epstein, March 29, 1977, *Legend* p. 186.

Kantor and Hendrix: Kantor, *op. cit.*, p. 198-; (Homestead) "Bayo-Pawley Affair," *Soldier of Fortune*, spring 1976; and see Hendrix references, Thomas Powers, *op. cit.*

104 Army Intelligence: memo attached to FBI document 105-82555 (unrecorded; original in 62-109060-811); *Dallas Morning News*, March 19, 1978, quoting FBI documents; HSCA Report p. 221.

Preyer: interview with author, 1978.

HSCA on intelligence agencies in the assassination: HSCA Report p. 2.

106 *Note 34:* The "serious allegation" referred to is the charge by a former anti-Castro exile leader that he saw his American intelligence case officer—who used the cover name "Maurice Bishop"—with Oswald shortly before the assassination. The same officer allegedly attempted to build up a false story that Oswald had been in touch with the Cuban Embassy in Mexico City. The episode will be dealt with in full later in the book. (See index references to "Bishop.";) Chief counsel's comment that the allegation remained "undiscredited"—HSCA IV.476.

Warren Report on agencies and Oswald: Report p. 327.

Dulles: Warren Commission Executive Session, January 27, 1964.

107 Newsman's question: actuality recording on film.

Combest: interview with author, August 1978.

Note 35: In the 1978 interview Combest also said that Oswald accompanied his headshaking with "a definite clenched-fist salute." This cannot be taken as good evidence of a political gesture, given Oswald's condition at that moment. It may indeed have been an expression of pain. Combest said nothing about the "salute" in his statements on Warren Commission testimony (XII.185 and XIX.350).

Artificial respiration: Manchester *op. cit.*, p. 604.

Oswald prints taken: XVII.308; *Fort Worth Press*, November 25, 1963.

Oswald in interrogation: XXIII.817 (Craig).

8. Red Faces

111 Oswald quote: XVI.817; letter to Robert Oswald, November 26, 1959 (from Moscow).

"Communist conspiracy": William Alexander, Assistant District Attorney, quoted by Manchester, *op. cit.*, p. 326.

CIA document: item 1188-1000, dated September 18, 1975.

Nosenko: *Legend* by Edward Epstein, p. 11.

112 Epstein book: *Legend* (see bibliography).

Angleton: quoted by Seymour Hersh in *New York Times Magazine,* June 25, 1978, from Angleton testimony to Senate Intelligence Committee, 1975 (Book III, 1976).

113 Oswald young Marxist: (statements of mother) interview of Marguerite Oswald in *New York Times,* December 10, 1963; XIX.319; (high-school friend) VII.—William Wulf; (second friend) HSCA IX.109; (writing to Socialist Party) XXV.140.

Note 36: The Oswald letter to the Socialist Party, which included the statement "I am a Marxist and have been studying socialist principles for well over fifteen months, appeared in an unusual way. An FBI report of December 18, 1963, less than a month after the assassination, states that it had turned up that day "during routine processing of inactive files of the Socialist Party of America," stored in the library at Duke University, North Carolina. Although there is no concrete reason to doubt the letter's authenticity, it is odd that this document was discovered among hundreds of other papers, quite by chance, so soon after the assassination. It became the documentary proof that Oswald was a budding left-winger even before his enlistment in the Marine Corps (XXV.140). For further discussion of the origins of Oswald's ostensible Socialism, see Chapter 17, "Blind Man's Bluff in New Orleans."

Interest in Marines: Report p. 384.

"Confidential": XIX.665.

114 Atsugi period dealt with in Warren Report, Appendix XIII.

Officer's comment: Capt. Gajewski, quoted in Epstein's *Legend,* p. 68.

Oswald as crew chief: VIII.291, testimony of Lieutenant J. E. Donovan.

Oswald intelligence: Gator Daniels, interviewed by Edward Epstein, in *Legend,* p. 70.

Role of U-2: primary sources are *Operation Overflight* by Gary Powers; *CIA's Secret Operations* by Harry Rositzke; *The Secret Team* by Fletcher Prouty; *The Trial of the U-2* Trans. Chicago: World Publications, 1960; *The Espionage Establishment* by David Wise and Thomas Ross; Edward Epstein in *Legend* provides the best detail of the U-2 operation at Atsugi, and Oswald's familiarity with it.

115 Donovan talk with Oswald: as reported in Epstein's *Legend,* p. 280, note 2. The conversation took place not at Atsugi but at the Cubi Point base in the Philippines.

Picture-taking: Epstein's *Legend,* p. 69.

Affair with hostess and subsequent liaisons: Epstein's *Legend,* p. 71-.

116 Self-inflicted shooting and scuffle incidents: Report p. 683-.

Taiwan shooting: Epstein in *Legend,* p. 81; (Eurasian) ibid. p. 83 and Report p. 684.

Note 37: In contradiction of personal recollection, the Department of Defense says Oswald was not in Taiwan. For discussion of contradiction, see next chapter and Note 40.

117 Santa Ana and Donovan: VIII.290, 297, 300.

Russian enthusiasm in California: Report p. 685— and related documents; name on jacket—VIII.316.

Thornley: James/Wardlaw, *op. cit.,* p. 5; (on Marxism) Report p. 685.

118 Delgado: VIII.241.

CIA memo: Rocca memorandum to Rockefeller Commission on CIA Activities Within the United States, May 30, 1975.

Oswald in spring 1959: Report p. 688.

119 Mother's injury: Oswald, Robert, *op. cit.,* p. 93; XVI.337.

Speed surprises friend: VIII.257 (Delgado).

HSCA on Marine record and discharge: HSCA Report p. 219-.

Oswald's plans: Robert Oswald, *op. cit.,* p. 95.

Oswald USA-Soviet Union trip: Report p. 690. The Warren Report was in error on details of this journey, discrepancies which left the Assassinations Committee at a loss in 1979. This is covered in the next chapter.

Easy access and Soviets: HSCA Report pp. 212 and 212n21.

120 *Note 38:* The possibility of a Stockholm visit was first raised in a report three days after the assassination (November 25, 1963) in *Dagens Nyheters,* the leading Swedish newspaper. It reported as fact that Oswald "passed through Sweden . . . on his way to the Soviet Union." The article stated that "After an unsuccessful attempt to get a Russian visa in Helsinki, he went to Stockholm, where he rented a hotel room. Two days later he was able to continue his journey to Moscow. That indicates the Russian Embassy gave him a visa." Jones Harris, an independent researcher, reports confirmation, from a CIA source, that Swedish intelligence confirmed the detour to Stockholm. The question arises—if American intelligence did know of this, and knew

within a short time of the assassination, why was nothing said
about it in the Warren Report, or in the HSCA Report in 1979?
Visa studies: XXVI.156, 165, 158; HSCA IV.241.
Moscow arrival: HSCA Report p. 212.
Oswald at American embassy: Report p. 260.
Allegiance letter: Report p. 261.
Oswald on giving Soviets information: Report p. 748; XVIII.908.
McVickar reaction: XVIII.153-.

121 Oswald and Japanese Communists: IX.242—testimony of George
de Mohrenschildt.

Note 39: de Mohrenschildt, a Russian emigré who was to befriend
Oswald in Texas after his return from the Soviet Union, said:
"He [Oswald] told me that he had some contacts with the Communists in Japan, and they—that got him interested to go and see
what goes on in the Soviet Union." Statements by de Mohrenschildt, however, must be read in the light of the evidence about
de Mohrenschildt's background. See Chapter 11, "The Man Who
Was Perfectly All Right."

9. The Cracks in the Canvas

122 Russell quote: conversation with researcher Harold Weisberg, 1970.
Delgado: VIII.242.
Block: interviewed by Epstein for *Legend,* p. 86.
Thornley: affidavit January 8, 1976.

123 Russian language: Report p. 685; VIII.307. XIX.662 (took Russian
test February 25, 1959).

124 Powers: VIII.275/283; Epstein's *Legend,* p. 83.
Quinn episode: VIII.321—Roussell testimony; Quinn XXIV.430;
VIII.293—Donovan testimony; Epstein interview of Quinn, *Leg-
end,* p. 87.
Executive session: transcript of Warren proceedings, January 27,
1964.

125 Self-inflicted shooting: interviews of former Marines Connor, Pitts,
Radtke, and others with Edward Epstein for *Legend,* p. 283.

126 Transfer: HSCA Report p. 220 (citing Department of Defense letter
of June 22, 1978); Folsom DE 1.3; see also "From Dallas to
Watergate" by Peter Dale Scott, *Ramparts,* November 1973;
(Rhodes) quoted by E. J. Epstein in *Legend,* p. 81.
Medical record: IX.603; VIII.313-; XIX.601.
Doctor's comment: author's interview with Dr. Paul Deranian,
1979.

128 "Secret" clearance: VIII.298 (Donovan); VIII.232 (Delgado); HSCA Report p. 219 (HSCA); XI.84 (Thornley).

Marine report on clearance: XXIII.796 (Director of Personnel's report).

Note 40: There may have been hanky-panky with Oswald's pay records. The Warren investigators requested these early in their inquiries, but the documents were not sent to the Commission until a week before the Report was submitted to President Johnson, too late for further probing. At one point, these pay records appear to put Oswald in a different unit from the one mentioned in his personnel file, and show that his pay status changed at the time of his reported transfer back to Atsugi from Taiwan. How they changed is not yet clear, for that part of the pay records was blanked out. As is evident in a recent passage in this chapter, the whole Taiwan episode poses a problem. (Pay records: XXII.180 and XXVI.713-; and commented on by Peter Dale Scott in unpublished ms. "The Dallas Conspiracy," Chapter 2.)

128 Oswald bank account: XXII.180; XXII.180.

Note 41: Oswald's IRS record for 1962 was most recently denied to two private researchers who in 1978 asked to see the record under the Freedom of Information Act. 1962 was the only full-income year for which Oswald filed a return.

Ruby's IRS record: (1962) XXIII.210.

Report on Moscow trip: Report p. 690.

Date stamps: XVIII.162.

Check on flight: XXVI.32.

Committee on Helsinki trip: HSCA Report p. 212.

129 Hotels: Report p. 690.

Marguerite Oswald: XXVI.40 and *A Citizen's Dissent* by Mark Lane (see bibliography) p. 9.

Wilcott: *New York Times,* March 27, 1978; *Clandestine America,* Vol. 2, No. 3; HSCA Report p. 198-.

130 Schrand: Report p. 664; VIII.316; VIII.281; XXV.864; (Marine reactions) Epstein's *Legend,* p. 75; ("rumor") VIII.316, statement of D. P. Camerata. See also HSCA XI.542.

Executive session: transcript of Warren proceedings, January 27, 1964.

131 McCone and Helms: V.120.

CIA assurances to HSCA: HSCA Report p. 198.

Helms and Castro plots: Senate Intelligence Committee Report on Alleged Assassination Plots Involving Foreign Leaders (henceforth called Sen. Int. Cttee. *Assassination Plots*): pp. 101 and 103.

CIA memorandum: HSCA IV.210—internal document, dated November 25, 1963, with name of writer deleted, released 1976; discussed and partially cited in HSCA Report p. 208.

Note 42: It is not wholly clear at what date the writer means he and colleagues discussed interviewing Oswald. He says first "summer of 1960," then later says he does not recall whether this was when Oswald was on the way home or after he arrived in the United States. The latter options would place the discussion in 1961 or 1962.

132 Senator Morgan exchange: Sen. Int. Cttee., *Performance of Intelligence Agencies,* p. 70.

"untidy world": HSCA IV.172.

Helms conviction: *New York Times,* November 5, 1977.

Helms on "trust": quoted in Anson, *op. cit.,* p. 283; but see also Thomas Powers, *op. cit.,* p. 273.

133 Angleton: FBI memorandum Sullivan to Belmont May 13, 1964.

Angleton/Dulles: Sen. Int. Cttee., *Performance of Intelligence Agencies,* p. 69.

Dulles coaching officers: CIA document 657-831, April 13, 1964 (writer and addressee deleted).

"201" file: CIA Information Coordinator letter to the author, February 15, 1979; and to James Tague, August 18, 1977.

"201" defined: HSCA Report p. 200 and independent sources.

134 "201" file opening and handling: HSCA Report p. 200-.

Mail intercepts: Sen. Int. Cttee. Report, 1976, Book III, p. 567.

135 Index cards: HSCA Report p. 206.

Snyder: *Who's Who in CIA* published in book form by Julius Mader, Berlin 1968; (according to CIA and Snyder) HSCA Report p. 214-; see also CIA document 609-786 (p. 2), which says Snyder joined CIA in 1949 and "apparently resigned" in 1950.

136 Mondale: Sen. Int. Cttee. *Assassination Plots,* p. 182.

137 QJ/WIN: *ibid.,* pp. 43 and (Helms) 142.

Harvey notes: released to Congress' Assassinations Committee, 1978; see HSCA Report p. 204.

Prouty: letter to author from Prouty, June 25, 1979.

138 HSCA comment on faked file plan: HSCA Report p. 204.

139 Dulles/Boggs exchange: Warren Commission Executive Session, January 27, 1964.

"vest pocket" possibility: HSCA Report p. 198n5.

140 McCone: V.121.

HSCA on military intelligence possibility: HSCA Report p. 224.

Helms on Navy: HSCA IV.178.

"No derogatory information": XXVI.92- (FBI reply to Warren Commission question).

Note 43: There remains, too, the question of why Oswald went through the charade of his "defection" visit to the Embassy, if it was a charade, if Oswald really was part of a U.S. intelligence operation and if Snyder was himself CIA. Two main factors might explain this. First, it is common practice to run an intelligence operation as tightly as possible. To all except his immediate superiors, therefore, Oswald may indeed have seemed a genuine defector. Second, and perhaps more important, may have been the need to convince the Soviets. Edward Epstein reports (*Legend*, p. 301) that Soviet intelligence had 134 electronic listening devices in the U.S. Embassy in Moscow. The consular section, which Oswald visited, employed Soviet nationals, and it was assumed that they reported back to the KGB. If it was necessary to convince the Soviets that Oswald was a real defector, the visit to the Embassy may have been most effective.

141 Navy reaction: VIII.298, testimony of Lieutenant Donovan.

Note 44: The Assassinations Committee did receive information which suggested that the Marine Corps had taken a hitherto-unknown interest in Oswald *after* the President's death. The Committee was informed by former Marine navigator Larry Huff that—in December 1963 and early 1964—he had taken part in transport operations involving a team of military CID investigators. Huff, who still has personal logs for the period, said the group of about a dozen investigators were flown to Japan, on their way to the Atsugi base where Oswald had once served. Huff said he learned from his passengers that their purpose was to investigate Oswald's activities at Atsugi. When he later picked up the group to take them back to base, they told him something of their investigation and let him take a look at their report. It was, according to Huff, marked "Secret—For Marine Corps Eyes Only." He said the report contained a psychological evaluation of Oswald and concluded that the alleged killer "was incapable of committing the assassination alone." As he held a "Secret" clearance, it was not extraordinary that he had been allowed to scan the report—said Huff. Huff also believed, on the basis of hearsay, that a similar military team had been dispatched to Dallas. The Committee conducted extensive inquiry into these allegations but could find no trace of the supposed report. Late in its research, however—when there was no time left for further inquiry—the Committee obtained confirmation from another crew member that the flights to and from Japan did indeed take place. The Committee left the matter somewhat in the air, and—

now that it is established the flights did take place—a future inquiry should clearly try to establish exactly who the passengers were (HSCA XI.541).

"damage assessment" and defections: *Legend* by Epstein, pp. 102, 366.

Discharge: XIX.665; XVII.663.

Note 45: Gerry Hemming's reliability as a source has on occasion been called into question. I met him in person, saw his service credentials, and spoke to him at length on the meeting he claims to have had with Oswald in Los Angeles. I have included his story because it seems credible in terms of time and place and Hemming's service credentials. (For a further indication of the relevance of Hemming, see Odio episode in Chapter 20, "Double Image in Dallas.")

142 Cuban consulate and Delgado: see Chapter 8, "Red Faces."

143 Marchetti book: see bibliography.

145 Curry instructions: Curry, *op. cit.,* p. 75, and author's interview of Curry, 1977.

Police record: affidavit of Lieutenant Thurber Lord, August 20, 1964 (published in Curry, *op. cit.,* p. 74); see also XXIV.505.

Call to Mrs. Paine: III.85-, testimony of Ruth Paine.

Troon/Swinney episode: statement by Troon to Bernard Fensterwald, Committee to Investigate Assassinations: Raleigh Spectator, 17 & 24 July 1980; *Raleigh News & Observer,* July 17, 1980.

147 Defectors: HSCA XII.437-; and correspondence between Hugh Cumming, Director of Intelligence at State Department, and Richard Bissell (CIA Deputy Director for Plans), October-November 1960, and attachments.

Note 46: The five Army men were a Sergeant Jones, Sergeant Ernie Fletcher, Bruce F. Davis, Sergeant Joseph Dutkanicz, and Specialist 5th Class Vladimir Sloboda. The two National Security Agency employees were William H. Martin and B. Ferguson Mitchell. The former OSS official was Maurice Halperin, the former Air Force major; Libero Ricciardielli; and the Rand Development Corporation employee Robert E. Webster.

148 Webster information: see above sources.

Rand: Canfield/Weberman, *op. cit.,* p. 24-; author's consultation with Professor Peter Dale Scott and the latter's unpublished ms. "The Dallas Conspiracy," II.11.

149 Marina on Oswald defection: CD 5.259 (conversation reported by Dallas friend Katya Ford).

Oswald inquiry about Webster: McMillan, *op. cit.,* p. 107.

"X" document: CIA document 1004-400, released 1976; (Golovachev) mentioned in Oswald's "Historic Diary."
150 Otepka: Otepka interview, 1971, reported in Fensterwald/Ewing, *op. cit.,* p. 230.
Warren Commission questions to Defense Department: XXVI.585-; Warren Chief Counsel letter to Dept. March 11, 1964; (not shown file) HSCA Report p. 223; (destroyed) *ibid.,* p. 224.
151 *Note 47:* In his testimony to the Assassinations Committee in 1977, former Warren Commission staff counsel David Slawson vaguely recollected consulting military intelligence about Oswald. He believed in particular that Naval Intelligence was questioned about Oswald's Marine career (HSCA XI.186).

10. Mischief from Moscow

152 "Historic Diary" excerpt: XVI.94; XXIV.333.
Hospital record: XVIII.450.
Soviet response: XII.452.
153 *Note 48:* Congress' Assassinations Committee noted that the signatures of Soviet officials on documents concerning Oswald were all illegible (HSCA Report p. 100; XII.451-; one of the hospital documents related to Oswald's "suicide attempt" is dated April 25, 1953 (HSCA XII.494).
Oswald reading disability (expert opinion): XXVI.812-.
Scar found: XXIV.7- (autopsy report on Oswald).
CIA and exhumation: CIA release 238, document of February 18, 1964, stating, "We recommend examination of wrist."
"elderly American": "Historic Diary," entry for October 26, 1959; CIA document 1168-432-5 and related documents.
154 Other defector in hospital: *Legend* by Epstein, p. 295.
Note 49: Material on the Nosenko case has been drawn from Warren Commission documents 434 and 451, released in 1975, from related Commission memoranda and from HSCA Report pp. 101-, HSCA XII.475; see also full-length study by Edward Epstein in *Legend* (see bibliography), article by Jack Nelson in *Los Angeles Times,* March 28, 1976, and John Barron, *op. cit.,* p. 452. I have also drawn on my own conversations with James Angleton in 1976 and 1978; additional background is provided in Nosenko presentation of HSCA Chief Counsel Blakey, HSCA II.436 (and attached documents); and HSCA XII.475-.
Oswald claim: XVIII.377.
Rositzke: *op. cit.,* p. 128.

155 *Note 50:* The Warren Commission concluded that Oswald wrote the diary but did not start writing till he arrived in Minsk (Report p. 691). E. J. Epstein (*Legend*) commissioned a handwriting analysis which led him to the conclusion that the diary was fabricated after the dates described. HSCA experts' conclusions, XII.236. Marina Oswald (XII.391) said in 1978 that Oswald would write several days in a row or sometimes skip for a week or so.

Intourist guides: Report p. 260.

Note 51: Oswald was interviewed in his hotel room on November 16 by an American reporter (Report p. 696), and at the end of November the U.S. Embassy informed the State Department (Report p. 750) that he had left the hotel "within the last few days." According to the Soviet record, as presented to the Warren Commission, (XVIII.404), Oswald was in Moscow until January 4. Oswald may have been taken somewhere else before being moved to Minsk. In his own notes about his stay in Russia he says he started work in Minsk in June 1960. This would dovetail with a report by a Soviet citizen who walked into the British Embassy in Moscow after the assassination. The citizen (whose name I withhold) told British and U.S. diplomats that in April-May 1960 he saw Oswald, under KGB control, in the city of Gorky. He also alleged that he knew Marina Oswald to be attached to the KGB. Other, wilder claims by this individual threw doubt on his credibility. But there might be some truth to the Gorky aspect of the story. It has been reliably reported that there was a KGB spy school in Gorky, notably by George Carpozi, the author of *Red Spies in Washington* (Simon and Schuster 1968, p. 12), who states: "Most prospective intelligence agents are sent to the notorious Marx-Engels Institute in Gorky." (For Soviet citizen's report, see XXVI.735-; CD1443; CD1378; for Oswald's time of starting work in Minsk, see XVI.287.)

Oswald account of Soviet payments: XVI.121.

156 Minsk luxury: "Diary," XVI.99, and photographs of life in Russia recovered after assassination.

Hoover on KGB school: V.105—testimony of J. Edgar Hoover.

CIA and KGB school: XXVI.111.

Schools' existence confirmed: in interview of former Minsk citizen with Edward Epstein (*Legend*, p. 299).

Note 52: A Russian book, seized among the Oswalds' effects after the assassination, yielded an odd clue that might suggest intelligence activity dating from Oswald's stay in the Soviet Union. In the novel, *Glaza Kotorye Sprashivayut*, seven separate letters had been excised from the text on page 152. The National Security Agency examined the book, along with other documents, and reported that no conclusion could be drawn from this peculiarity. It is hard, though, to see what innocent purpose could have been served by the removal of letters. The excisions could have been made by either Oswald or his wife, or even by some third party intending thus to impart some coded data (XVI.155).

Marina self-biography: I.84; XXII.740.

157 Meetings at dances: XVI.102—"Historic Diary" entries, March 1961.

Introduction: XVI.102 (entry for March 17, 1961); (biography) McMillan, *op. cit.,* p. 59; I.90-; XXII.745 and 267; HSCA XII.324, 351; HSCA II.208; and Warren I.88.

Note 53: Marina Oswald told the Warren Commission (I.90) that she had been introduced to her future husband by "Yuri Mereginsky," a friend from the medical institute. Without naming the friend, she also told early investigators they were introduced by one of "Sasha P.'s" friends from the institute (XXII.745). Another report relates that she was introduced by the medical student son—presumably Mereginsky—of a woman who had given a lecture on her travels in the U.S.A. before the dance (XXII.750). (And see XXIII.402.)

Subsequent courtship and marriage: Report p. 703; (proposal) XXII.750; XVIII.604; HSCA XII.354.

158 Plan to return to U.S.A.: Report p. 704.

Soviet official permission: Report p. 709.

Criticism at work: Report p. 707.

Rankin doubt: transcript of proceedings of Executive Session of Warren Commission, January 27, 1964.

Note 54: Marina has recently asserted that her husband used a firearm while in Russia (HSCA XII.355-).

Marina on husband's innocence: *Life* magazine, November 29, 1963.

159 "fateful rifle": I.119- (testimony of Marina Oswald).

"not husband's gun": I.119 and V.611- (testimony of Marina Oswald).

Walker allegation: I.16 (testimony of Marina Oswald).

Nixon allegation: V.387 (testimony of Marina Oswald); see also Newman, *op. cit.,* p. 349; Report p. 189.

Russell: proceedings of Executive Session of Warren Commission, January 27, 1964.

Warren lawyer: HSCA XI.126 (reproduction of Warren Commission memo from Redlich to Chief Counsel Rankin, February 28, 1964).

Marina's birth: XXII.740-.

160 Marina's birth (1977 version): McMillan, *op. cit.,* pp. 41, 45, 35, 26.

Marina birth certificate: CD 206.369-.

Medvedev transfer: I.84.

Prusakov: XXII.745 and I.90; (rank) HSCA XII.323.

Komsomol: V.305 (denial mentioned in testimony of McVickar); I.89 and V.607 (admitted by Marina).

Leaving first job: Report p. 703; CIA doubts—Epstein in *Legend,* p. 304.

161 Marina at "Rest Home": XXII.745.

Prizentzev address: CIA document 624-823 (Appendix C).

Webster: see notes and sources for defectors in Chapter 9, "Cracks in the Canvas"; and HSCA XII.449-.

162 Mintkenbaugh: Epstein's *Legend,* p. 305; *Red Spies in Washington* by George Carpozi (Trident Press, New York, 1968), p. 156.

CIA memorandum: addendum to CIA document, November 25, 1963, released 1976.

Rankin: transcript of Executive Session of Warren Commission, January 27, 1964.

Commission and Marina's exit permit: Report, p. 657; see, however, CD 708.3 and XXVI.115.

163 July 1962 letter to Gerasimov: CIA document 296.30.

Soboleva letter: CIA document 296.17.

164 *Note 55:* The background of Marina Oswald, and her version of events, has been documented at greatest length in the book *Marina and Lee* by Priscilla Johnson McMillan (see bibliography). The author of that book was in the Soviet Union when Oswald arrived there and interviewed him for the American press. After the assassination she spent much time with Oswald's widow, and her book is the eventual result. It supports the thesis that Oswald was a lone deranged assassin. Some critics, noting apparent links between McMillan and the U.S. State Department, and the fact that she also wrote a book about Svetlana Stalin after her defection to the United States, have implied that her Marina Oswald book was written in collusion with American intelligence. McMillan has testified that she has never worked for the CIA. However, she applied for work at the CIA in 1952, was debriefed by the Agency in 1962 after a Soviet trip, and has provided "cultural and literary" information to the CIA (HSCA

Report p. 213-). I have avoided, on the whole, using *Marina and Lee* as a major source. As explained in the text of this book, Marina herself has been unreliable on matters of fact. For the same reason, and because her present version of events is now documented by the HSCA, I have not attempted to interview Marina Oswald for this book.

Nosenko material: See Note 49 on Nosenko sourcing.

166 Suitcases: HSCA III.624.

168 Lie-detector tests: HSCA II.453. (Note: Nosenko passed a further test in 1968. For what it is worth, an analysis for the Assassinations Committee found that the second Nosenko lie detector was the most reliable. This test concluded that Nosenko had lied.)

169 Nosenko interrogation: HSCA II.436, 499-, 517, 525; also XII.585-; (HSCA finding on effect of interrogation) HSCA Report p. 102.

Soviets and Nosenko: (press officer) *New York* magazine, February 27, 1978, p. 36; (*Paris Match*) *Legend* by E. J. Epstein, p. 277n4; HSCA XII.590, 630.

172 Soviet Union not involved in assassination: (HSCA finding) HSCA Report p. 108.

172 Miler: interviewed by E. J. Epstein for *Legend*, pp. 30, 278; (deputy chief) HSCA XII.624.

Ex-head of CIA Soviet Russia Section: John Hart (CIA-appointed witness to HSCA), HSCA II.487.

HSCA on Nosenko lies: HSCA Report p. 102.

173 U-2 incident: See sources listed for U-2 reference at p. 144.

174 Oswald threat at Embassy: XVIII.908; (referred to by Powers) Powers, *op. cit.,* p. 358.

Note 56: The former Deputy Chief of CIA's Soviet Bloc Division told the Assassinations Committee (HSCA XII.626) that it had not been proven Oswald knew much about the U-2. It has not been proven, yet this same witness agreed that Oswald worked with radar 500 yards from the U-2 runway, and his radar unit tracked the aircraft. Thus, said the witness, "certain things as to speed and altitude might have come to Oswald's attention." Those were exactly the details the Soviets were interested in at the time.

Prouty on U-2: Prouty, *op. cit.,* and interview with Dick Fontaine and author, 1978; Prouty correspondence with author, 1979.

175 Oswald's letter home: XVI.871—Oswald to brother Robert, February 1962.

May Day party: XVI.100—"Historic Diary."

Oswald reference to Moscow visit: X.203—Ofstein testimony; and CD 205.473.

176 Powers interview: *The Times,* April 20, 1971.
Assassinations Committee on CIA and Nosenko: HSCA Report p. 255.

11. The Man Who Was Perfectly All Right

178 Eisenhower: quoted by Wise and Ross, *op. cit.,* 287.
Previous letter: Report p. 701; HSCA XII.455.
179 State Department inquiry to Moscow Embassy: XXII.102/118; and CIA informed January 26—CIA Archives 2.
Note 57: The CIA opened its "201" file in December 1960. It has been suggested that this relates to the start of Oswald's homecoming operation in February 1961. The HSCA, however, concluded that the "201" file opening related to an inquiry from the State Department about defectors (HSCA Report p. 201).
Passport returned: V.284; XVIII.160-.
Oswald correspondence: XVIII.131; XVI.705.
Embassy comment: XVIII.137.
Embassy recommendation: XVIII.158.
Lookout card: Report p. 750 and p. 722.
1963 passport: Report p. 774.
Strict control by FBI and State: Meagher, *op. cit.,* p. 335.
180 Minsk photographs: Warren Report p. 268 (Kramer Exhibit 1) and XX.474 (Kramer Exhibit 2); (commented on officially) Warren Report p. 267 and HSCA Report p. 206; (background documents) XX.474; XI.212; CIA document 614-261, March 20, 1964; II.212-; CIA 948-927T; CD 859B/ CD 1022; CD 871; (doubt by researchers) *Continuing Inquiry,* December 22, 1976; HSCA XII.639; author's interview of Rita Naman, June 1979; (Oswald's written accounts of Moscow visit) "Diary" in HSCA VIII.290; (HSCA documents classified) HSCA Report p. 630.67; (Hyde) CD 859a; (visitors' program) HSCA Report p. 198 and Rositzke *op. cit.,* p. 58.
183 *Note 58:* It appears, as this book goes to press, that Mrs. Hyde is still alive—perhaps in her eighties.
185 U.S. Government loan: Report p. 770.
Immigration Service and State Department on Marina: Report p. 761-.
Davison meeting: CD 87,SS569; CD 235; CD 409; CD 11; (Oswald mentions Davison in address book) CIA 1281-1024.
Davison in security incident: HSCA Report p. 215; *The Penkovskiy Papers,* Avon Books, New York, 1966, p. 381.

Davison reaction to questioning: CD 87, SS569; CD 235; CD 409.3, CD1115-XIII-103; *Invisible Government* by Wise and Ross, p. 268 (see bibliography).

Train journey: XVI.137, 144.

Helmstedt: XVIII.168; XVI.144 & 47; research contributed by Sidney A. Martin.

186 Apartment: XVIII.615; I.101 (testimonies of U.S. Embassy staff); Marina recently—HSCA II.289 and 310; HSCA XII.369 (Marina has alternately spoken of Amsterdam and Rotterdam).

Executive session: transcript of proceedings of Warren Commission, January 27, 1964.

Inconsistency: XXIII.407—Secret Service report of Marina interviews, November 26-28, 1963.

Maasdam crossing: I.101, testimony of Marina Oswald; Report p. 712.

187 Raikin: Report p. 173.

Raikin's connections: "From Dallas to Watergate" by Peter Dale Scott, *Ramparts*, November 1973.

Oswald and anti-Castro exiles: The reference is to 544 Camp Street, New Orleans. See Chapter 17, "Blind Man's Bluff in New Orleans."

Chief immigration officer: research of independent researcher Jones Harris.

State Department and Department of Health, Education and Welfare: CD75.461-; CD1209, 1211, 1218, 1230.1, 1226, 1230.3, 1241, 903, 882.12.

Suitcases: research of Jones Harris, including report of and interview with HEW official M. L. Lehrman; (two suitcases at Dallas) Robert Oswald, *op. cit.*, p. 117.

188 Atlanta route: XVI.616; XVIII.16.

Address of Davison's mother: XVI.37: XVI.50.

Davison and HSCA: HSCA Report p. 215-.

Note 59: The man who was to be Oswald's mentor in Dallas, George de Mohrenschildt, was to write (in an unpublished manuscript) that Oswald was innocent of the assassination. In this ms. he writes that the Warren Commission failed by insufficient investigation of "Lee's activities in *Atlanta,* New Orleans, and Mexico City" (HSCA XII.250). For a full treatment of de Mohrenschildt's intelligence connection, see later in this chapter.

189 Marine Corps regulations: XIX.680.

Absence from list: XVII.801.

FBI security case: Report p. 434.

Interview on return: Report p. 434.

Refusal to take polygraph test: Dallas FBI office memorandum to HQ, July 10, 1962, revealed in Sen. Int. Cttee., *Performance of Intelligence Agencies,* p. 88.

Oswald case closed: Report p. 435.

Colby TV interview: with Dan Rather of CBS, November 26, 1975, on "The American Assassins," Part II.

Colby briefing: CIA document 1188-1000, September 18, 1975.

190 Naval message: XVIII.116.

State Department memo: XVIII.367, March 31, 1961 memo (White to Hickey).

Fox interviewed: *Legend* by E. J. Epstein, p. 312.

Debriefing: (Fox) *Legend* by E. J. Epstein, p. 312; (HSCA) HSCA Report p. 207- and HSCA XII.463-; (CIA memo) HSCA IV.209 and HSCA Report p. 208; (second former CIA officer) HSCA Report p. 208.

192 *Note 60:* If the Marine in Minsk was not Oswald, who *did* the former CIA employee recall being debriefed on his time at the Minsk radio plant? We have already noted the CIA document referring to another unnamed former Marine living in Minsk for a while, but his stay was in 1958-59, and there is no suggestion he worked at the plant (CIA document 1004-400). Other information may be evidence of a formal debriefing of Oswald. A Washington psychiatrist, formerly used by the CIA, reports being asked by the Agency to meet a young American just back from Russia. The date was mid-1962 and the American had returned from the Soviet Union after marrying a Soviet wife. After the assassination the psychiatrist thought he recognized pictures of Oswald as the man he had questioned for the CIA. It has been suggested that there might be confusion here with Robert Webster, who looked rather like Oswald. Webster, however, did not in fact marry in the U.S.S.R. (CBS evening news, June 30, 1975, and see Epstein's *Legend,* p. 312n14) (and HSCA XII.451).

192 Gregory call: II.337, testimony of Peter Gregory.

de Mohrenschildt: Report p. 282-; (de Mohrenschildt background) IX.166-285—testimony of de Mohrenschildt; FBI file on de Mohrenschildt; HSCA XII.49; HSCA Report p. 217; author's interviews with Jeanne de Mohrenschildt, 1978-9. Except where indicated, material on de Mohrenschildt is taken from these sources.

194 Rockefeller connection: "Who Was George de Mohrenschildt?," article in *Clandestine America,* autumn 1977.

OSS: CIA document 18-522—Helms memo to Warren Commission; (application) CD 531.3; CD 777A.3; CD 533.57.

195 Cogswell: *New York Daily News,* April 12, 1977; see, however,

HSCA XII.60, noting that Cogswell generated information on de Mohrenschildt for HSCA.

AID: "Who Was George de Mohrenschildt?," article in *Clandestine America*, autumn 1977.

Note 61: The role of AID in the 1964 Chilean election was exposed in the *Washington Post* many years later. It quoted a U.S. official as saying "U.S. intervention was blatant and almost obscene." The article, by Laurence Stern, reported that AID cooperated with the CIA in funneling up to $20 million into Chile (Marchetti/ Marks, *op. cit.,* p. 39n).

CIA and de Mohrenschildt as source: CIA document 18-522.

de Mohrenschildt offer to State Department: Report p. 283.

Photograph: seen by author during interview with Jeanne de Mohrenschildt, 1978.

de Mohrenschildt service for State Department: VIII.425 (testimony of Mrs. Igor Voshinin).

196 Orlov interview: with E. J. Epstein for *Legend,* p. 314.

Bouhe: VIII.355 (testimony of Bouhe).

Note 62: de Mohrenschildt discussed his meetings with Moore when visited in Haiti after the assassination by FBI agent James Wood. He documented his "harmless lunatic" quote in a letter to a Dallas associate. Jeanne de Mohrenschildt's version of the de Mohrenschildt/Moore exchange comes from her interviews with the author in 1978. De Mohrenschildt stated in his Warren testimony that he asked Moore and Fort Worth lawyer Max Clark whether it was "safe" to help Oswald (HSCA XII.54).

Moore: (background) HSCA Report p. 217-; HSCA XII.54; (interview in 1976) from "Three Witnesses," article by Dick Russell in *New Times,* June 24, 1977; (de Mohrenschildt last comment) *Dallas Morning News,* March 30, 1978; and see main sources for de Mohrenschildt.

198 Ford: Ford/Stiles, *op. cit.*

199 Oswald "delightful": from "Three Witnesses," article in *New Times,* June 24, 1977.

Reporter: John Tackett of *Fort Worth Press,* interviewed by the author, 1979.

Taylor: IX.96, testimony of Gary Taylor; author's interview, 1978.

200 $200 repaid to brother: Warren Report pp. 741-42.

YMCA and post-office box: Report pp. 719-720.

Jaggars-Chiles-Stovall: Report p. 719 and sources to same.

201 Ofstein: X.202, testimony of Dennis Ofstein.

Minox: *Dallas Morning News,* Earl Golz article, August 7, 1978; (Alexander) interviewed by author, 1978; (HSCA) HSCA XII.390 and 373.

203 Micro dots: XVI.53.

Note 63: Oswald may have used equipment available at Jaggars-Chiles-Stovall to forge the "Hidell" draft card. An FBI expert has said that the forgery involved a very accurate camera "such as are found in photographic laboratory and printing plants." (IV.388)

12. "Hunter of the Fascists"

204 Oswald quote: I.233 (Marguerite Oswald).

New Year greeting and reading material: Report p. 722; (*Time*) CD 1231; XXII.270.

Suggestion Marina return to U.S.S.R.: I.35 (Marina testimony).

Letter to Soviet Embassy: I.35; XVI.10.

205 Mail orders: Report p. 723 and Chapter IV.

Reports on Walker shooting: Warren Report p. 20 and HSCA Report p. 61.

206 JFK on extremism: speech in Los Angeles, November 18, 1961, "Public Papers of the President," 1961 (p. 735), U.S. Government Printing Office.

Oswald conversations on right wing: IX.256—George de Mohrenschildt, *op. cit.,* p. 259, citing Marina; FBI interview with Volkmar Schmidt, in National Archives (unrecorded).

207 Reconnaissance photographs: Report p. 185.

Note 64: The money order for the rifle was purchased on March 12. The mail-order coupon for the revolver was filled in, ostensibly by Oswald, under the date January 27; however, mail-order company records show the revolver was not being processed until March 13, which suggests the coupon for it was sent off at the same time as the order for the rifle, March 12 (see Report p. 174, 119).

Marina on rifle at home: Report pp. 723-24.

Photograph with guns and newspapers: Report pp. 125-28.

Oswald fired: Report p. 724; for unsatisfactory work—CD7.128; CD 6 and 8; XXIII.696; use of Oswald—XIII.529 (time cards); XXII.278 (pay checks).

Walker incident: Report pp. 183-187.

208 Walker ballistics: Warren Report p. 186; HSCA VII.370, I.472; (neutron tests) HSCA I.502; (press reports) *Dallas Morning News,* April 11, 1963, p. 1; and April 12, 1963, p. 5; *New York Times,* April 12, 1963, p. 12; (police report) HSCA Report p. 98n4; Warren XXIV.39.

Note 65: General Walker has added his own note of confusion on the question of the bullet. After seeing the exhibit shown in the Assassinations Committee hearings, the general said it was not the bullet he recovered in his house in 1963. He said the original projectile was so battered it was hardly recognizable as a bullet at all—far less so than the bullet shown in the Committee hearings. While the general has been an irascible eccentric on political matters, he was a soldier of distinction and experience, and he is talking about the bullet that nearly killed him. For the record, a check should be made of the chain of possession. (Walker interviews with the author, 1978, and see photograph of bullet, HSCA VII.390.)

209 de Mohrenschildt remark about Walker shooting: Report p. 724; (Marina version) XXII.777; HSCA II.234; (de Mohrenschildt version) Report p. 282.

Oswald after JFK shooting: III.252; III.225.

Note 66: For full analysis of the "gun in closet" incident, see also Meagher, *op. cit.,* p. 127.

210 Gun incident "in 1962": HSCA XII.52.

Marina on Oswald using rifles: XXII.763; XXII.785; XXIII.393; XXIII.402; XXII.778; I.14; XXII.197; XXII.785; V.397-9; HSCA II.229, 231.

de Mohrenschildts on Oswald use of rifle: IX.249; IX.316.

1967 photograph find: author's interviews with Jeanne de Mohrenschildt; George de Mohrenschildt letter of April 17, 1967, cited by McMillan, *op. cit.,* p. 489n9; back of photograph is shown HSCA VI.151; (Oswald's handwriting) HSCA II.396; (translation) HSCA II.388; (overwriting in pencil) HSCA II.386 and 388; (Marina does not remember signing) HSCA II.295-, 243, 306, 315; (Oswald showed to de Mohrenschildt) HSCA XII.336.

211 *Note 67:* The Assassinations Committee panel found that Oswald wrote the dedication on the back of the photograph. That may well be right. This, however, may be a suitable point to caution the reader against placing excessive emphasis on handwriting evidence (which features a great deal in the over-all story). Document examiners are the first to admit they are not infallible and that forgery can go undetected. The corollary, perhaps, is an example from the work of the HSCA's handwriting panel. It concluded that two Oswald signatures differed in many details from other Oswald signatures (HSCA VIII.235). The two signatures in question are on receipts for wages at Oswald's Dallas place of work—surely most likely to have indeed been signed by Oswald.

Another point on the same lines arises from a further inscription on the back of the photograph, presumably written since 1967. It reads "copyright G. de M." The HSCA experts did not think it had been written by de Mohrenschildt (HSCA II.385). De Mohrenschildt's lawyer, however, states that de Mohrenschildt told him—as indeed seems most probably—that he did write the notation (letter of Patrick Russell to author, June 18, 1979). Handwriting evidence should always be weighed in the light of other available evidence.

Note 68: During Assassinations Committee hearings, one Congressman wondered whether the unusual style of the inscription date was drawn from naval custom (HSCA II.292). The Marines do write dates in the order day, month, year but do not use Roman numerals. As stated, no similar trace of Roman-numeral usage can be found in Oswald's writings. The date on the back of the photograph, 5/IV/63, would normally mean May 4, 1963, according to the usual American ordering of dates. Oswald, though, was in New Orleans by that time. It is highly unlikely that he signed the picture there and mailed it along with a large pile of records to Texas (which is how Jeanne de Mohrenschildt suggests the photograph reached their effects). Nor, surely, would Marina (who stayed on in Texas for a while) have signed or made a joke of the photograph at this time. That would have been the height of foolhardiness *after* the attack on Walker—if Oswald was responsible for it and if Marina realized he was. Marina's latest remark—about Oswald showing the picture to de Mohrenschildt—may also indicate the occasion de Mohrenschildt actually obtained his signed copy (HSCA XII.336).

213 Oswald repayments: Report, Appendix XIV; XVII.646; XVIII.277 and 316; XIX.252; XXII.86 and 122; XXI.163; V.316; HSCA XII.338.

Oswald earnings in seven-week period: XXII.227 and 380.

Oswald purchase of money order for rifle: Report p. 119.

Time of purchase: VII.295—testimony of postal inspector Harry Holmes.

Oswald time sheet: XXIII.605.

Note 69: It has been suggested (McMillan, *op. cit.,* p. 485, note 8) that Oswald actually went to work only *after* picking up the rifle and filled in a false time on his time sheet to make it appear he had started work at 8:00 A.M. In fact, a check of Oswald's time sheets (XXIII.538) reveals an instruction to employees that "time shown hereon must agree with *clock register.*" If Oswald had to abide by some mechanical clocking-device, it would have been difficult to falsify his arrival time at work.

Coleman: HSCA Report p. 98n4; see also XXVI.437; XXVI.753.

214 *Note 70:* I have drawn on the Assassinations Committee summary of Walter Coleman's evidence, because it is the most up-to-date account. However, it should be noted that there are minor discrepancies between this and the documents on the matter in the Warren Commission volumes. In these reports, the Ford was "white or beige" and older. One of the Warren versions refers to the Ford leaving at speed; the other does not (XXVI.437-; XVI.753; HSCA Report p. 98n4).

Oswald's driving capability: Report p.321.

Surrey: V.446; HSCA Report p. 98n4.

Claunch: interview with Gary Shaw, independent researcher.

Car photograph: (mutilated) XVI.7; (police opinion) XXII.582, statements of Stovall and Rose; (Marina) XI.294; (in Curry book) Curry, *op. cit.,* p. 113, Exhibit 55.

215 HSCA and Walker: HSCA Report p. 61n15 and p. 98n.

216 Police call re Chevrolet: XXIII.888.

Walker's "holy hell": interview with author, 1979.

Seven Days in May and JFK: *The Celluloid Muse* by Higham and Greenberg, p. 92; *The Imperial Presidency* by Arthur Schlesinger, pp. 198 and 417; *Seven Days in May* by Fletcher Knebel and Charles W. Bailey; New York: Harper and Row, 1962.

Surrey and leaflets: Report p. 298; XVIII.646.

217 Walker arouses exiles: XXVI.738 (statement of Mrs. Connell).

October meetings: (Oswald) FBI file 205.646—statement of Edwin Steig; (Walker) *ibid* 647—statement of Sarah Costillo; (Oswald on October 23) II.408—testimony of Michael Paine.

Walker address in Oswald address book: XXV.862.

Dallas friend: II.418 (Michael Paine).

de Mohrenschildt activity re Haiti: HSCA XII.55—(including CIA document 431-154B); (Kail) HSCA XII.57 and HSCA X.42; (plot) Herbert Atkin, quoted in "Three Witnesses," article by Dick Russell in *New Times,* June 24, 1977.

219 *Note 71:* The HSCA source who knew de Mohrenschildt in Haiti, stockbroker Joseph Dryer, recognized the name William Avery Hyde as one mentioned by de Mohrenschildt. Hyde was the father of Ruth Paine, the woman with whom Marina Oswald lived before the assassination. The reference is interesting, because both Ruth Paine and de Mohrenschildt said after the assassination that they had met only once at a party (HSCA XII.61). It was an intercepted phone call between the phone numbers of Ruth Paine and her husband Michael—after the assassination—

which picked up the curious remark "We both know who is responsible" (*other than Oswald*). (CD 206 and this book's Chapter 7, "A Sphinx for Texas.")

Postcard: author's interview of Jeanne de Mohrenschildt, 1978.

13. The Company and the Crooks

223 Assassinations Committee staff report: HSCA X.3.

224 Hunt forms CRC: Hunt in *Give Us This Day, op. cit.,* pp. 40-50, 182-89.

Hunt plan: *ibid.,* p. 38.

Nixon account: "Cuba, Castro and John F. Kennedy" by R. Nixon in *Reader's Digest,* November 1964.

Nixon tape: White House taped conversation of Nixon talking with H. R. Haldeman, July 23, 1972.

Hunt: Unless otherwise indicated, all subsequent Hunt quotations are from Hunt's interview with the author, 1978.

225 Dulles misleading JFK: *Robert Kennedy and His Times* by Arthur Schlesinger, p. 452.

CIA intelligence reports on uprising: Hunt interview with author, 1978.

226 "treason": Robert Kennedy, interview with John Martin for JFK Oral History program, March 1, 1964.

Kennedy and CIA: *New Times,* April 25, 1966, p. 20, col. 3.

Harvey: Sen. Int. Cttee. *Assassination Plots,* p. 66; author's interview of Howard Hunt, 1978.

227 Pepe San Roman: interviewed in CBS TV documentary "The CIA's Secret Army," June 10, 1977; HSCA X.9; Haynes Johnson, *op. cit.,* p. 17.

Kohly: interview with author, 1978.

No long-term living with Castro: Cuba Study Group, Recommendation 6, June 13, 1961, *Schlesinger Papers.*

228 "Low key": General Maxwell Taylor, interviewed by L. Hackman. October 22, 1969, JFK Oral History Program.

RFK enthusiasm: Sen. Int. Cttee. *Assassination Plots,* p. 141.

JM/WAVE: HSCA X.11; (statistics: Thomas Powers, *op. cit.,* pp. 136 and 139n16).

229 Kennedy concern for prisoners: *Robert Kennedy and His Times* by Arthur Schlesinger, Chapter 21.

Miami speech: JFK *Public Papers* (1962), pp. 911-12; "not in script"—*Robert Kennedy and His Times* by Arthur Schlesinger, p. 538.

U.S. assurances: Schlesinger, *Robert Kennedy and His Times,* p. 257.

JFK on Republican reaction: journal of Arthur Schlesinger, October 30, 1962.

230 CIA and missile crisis: Robert Kennedy, April 30, 1964, in interview with J. B. Martin for JFK Oral History Program; Sen. Int. Cttee. *Assassination Plots* p. 148.

Clamp-down on exile raids: generally see Report of Sen. Int. Cttee., *Performance of Intelligence Agencies,* p. 11-; raid of March 17-18 and State Department reaction reported in *Dallas Times-Herald* March 19; March 21 JFK press conference reported in *Dallas Times-Herald,* March 22; March 26 raid—Albert Newman, *op. cit.,* p. 326; U.S.S.R.—"Cuba protests," *Dallas Times-Herald,* March 28, 29, 30; "U.S. Acts" *Dallas Times-Herald,* March 31; boat seizures—*Dallas Times-Herald,* April 1; JFK key statement on raids—JFK *Public Papers* (1963) for April 1; JFK on April 12—*ibid.,* for April 12 press conference.

232 Veteran: HSCA X.65.

Ayers: *op. cit.,* p. 53.

Krulak: Ayers, *op. cit.,* p. 14 (Ayers calls him "Kartak").

RFK and Cuban operations, 1963: *Robert Kennedy and His Times* by Arthur Schlesinger, pp. 544-6.

233 Soviet pullout from Cuba: *Dallas Times-Herald,* March 22, 1963; JFK press conference, JFK *Public Papers* (1963) for April 3.

Nixon speeches: to American Society of Newspaper Editors, April 20; and *Dallas Morning News,* April 21; HSCA X.13.

Cuban Revolutionary Council funds cut: *Robert Kennedy and His Times* by Arthur Schlesinger, p. 540; CRC leader resigns—Albert Newman, *op. cit.,* p. 333; HSCA X.13.

234 Sapp memo: to Assistant Chief of Police Anderson, April 4, 1963; author's interview with Sapp, 1978.

Handout: Manchester, *op. cit.,* p. 53.

CIA-Mafia collaboration: author's interview with participant (anonymous at his request), 1978; also Sen. Int. Cttee. *Assassination Plots* report, 1975. Also HSCA X.151-; HSCA IV.126; HSCA Report p. 114-. References hereafter to CIA-Mafia plots are from these sources unless otherwise indicated.

236 ONI and OSS contact with Mafia: *Luciano* by Thomas Sciacca (NY: Pinnacle Books, 1975); *The Secret History of America's First Central Intelligence Agency* NY: Delta Books, 1973); *the Secret War Report of the OSS,* edited by Anthony Cave Brown (NY: Berkley Publishing Corporation, 1976).

Lansky, Trafficante, and Cuba: "The Hughes-Nixon-Lansky Connection," article by Howard Kohn in *Rolling Stone*, May 20, 1976; also Ed Reid, *op. cit.*

Initial mob plotting: HSCA X.175-, 194n213.

238 Dulles: HSCA XI.66.

Maheu background: Sen. Int. Cttee. *Assassination Plots*, p. 74n4.

Giancana and Cuba: Hougan, *op. cit.*, pp. 335 and 337.

Note 72: The identity of the fourth man is well known to official investigators and has been published in reports. I have preserved his anonymity because that was the basis on which he granted me an interview.

239 Trafficante as "Pecora": HSCA V.257.

Trafficante background: Ed Reid, *op. cit.*; Sen. Int. Cttee. *Assassination Plots*; Hearings of McClellan Committee, 1959, p. 124-32; *Politics of Heroin in Southeast Asia* by Alfred W. McCoy (Harper Colophon Books, 1972), pp. 27 and 55; *Lansky* by Hank Messick (Berkley Medallion Books, 1971, pp. 195 and 215); HSCA V.419-.

240 De Varona: *The Hoffa Wars* by Dan Moldea (Paddington Press, Ltd., NY and London, 1978, p. 133) HSCA speculation: HSCA Report p. 114.

Szulc: "Cuba on Our Mind" by Tad Szulc, in *Esquire*, February 1974.

241 Smathers: "Were Trujillo, Diem, CIA Targets Too?" by Jack Anderson, UFS syndicated article in *Miami Herald*, January 19, 1971; conversation with the author, 1978; and interview by D. M. Wilson for JFK Oral History Program, March 31, 1964.

RFK, Giancana, and plots: Sen. Int. Cttee. *Assassination Plots*, p. 129-; HSCA X.187.

RFK "stops" plot: Seymour Hersh article, *New York Times*, March 10, 1975; also interview of Frank Mankiewicz, October 20, 1969, for RFK Oral History Program.

242 *Note 73:* Former Warren Commission Chief Counsel Lee Rankin told the Assassinations Committee he believed the CIA is probably still concealing information about the Castro murder plots—even today. He feels "there is a considerable amount being withheld and there may be a lot of false testimony in some of the information furnished . . . " (HSCA XI.71.)

14. The Mob Loses Patience

243 Trafficante quote: interview of author with Jose Aleman, 1978; originally quoted in *Washington Post*, May 16, 1976 (explained and documented later in this chapter).

RFK atrocity story: Robert F. Kennedy, *op. cit.*, p. 8.
244 Warren on Teamsters: *New York Times*, October 14, 1952.
Hoffa on juries: Robert F. Kennedy, *op. cit.*, p. 62.
Hoffa on RFK: "bastard"—*Hoffa: The Real Story*, by James R. Hoffa, as told to Oscar Fraley (New York, Stein and Day, 1975). pp. 107-115, "monster"—*Hoffa and the Teamsters* by Ralph James and Estelle James (Princeton, van Nostrand, 1965); "brat"—BBC interview with Hoffa, 1975.
245 Hoffa to Teamster on RFK: *International Teamster*, February 1959.
JFK order: "The Mafia, the CIA, and the Kennedy Assassination," Milton Viorst, *Washingtonian*, 1975.
246 RFK on pressure during campaign: Robert Kennedy, *op. cit.*, p. 170.
RFK on gangsters: Robert F. Kennedy, *op. cit.*, p. 240.
RFK on Hoffa associates and syndicate: Robert F. Kennedy, *op. cit.*, p. 75.
RFK on Baker: Robert F. Kennedy, *op. cit.*, p. 60.
Lansky: Robert F. Kennedy, *op. cit.*, pp. 89 and 247.
RFK on organized crime: Robert Kennedy to Senate Government Operations Committee, September 25, 1963.
247 Judicial assault on Hoffa: *The Fall and Rise of Jimmy Hoffa* by Walter Sheridan (New York, 1972), p. 193.
Hoffa's "seamy" information on Kennedys: cited Jim Hougan, *op. cit.*, p. 119.
Monroe and RFK: *ibid.*, p. 111-.
Exner, Giancana, and JFK: Sen. Int. Cttee. *Assassination Plots*, p. 129; *My Story* by Judith Exner as told to Ovid Demaris (New York, Grove, 1977); *"Jack, Judy, Sam and Johnny"* by Robert Sam Anson, in *New Times*, January 23, 1976.
248 Exner on being "used": *New York Post*, December 22, 1975.
Giancana boast: article by Robert Sam Anson, *New Times*, January 23, 1976.
249 Dalitz and Hoffa: Robert F. Kennedy, *op. cit.*, p. 97; *The Fall and Rise of Jimmy Hoffa* by Walter Sheridan (*op. cit.*), p. 528; *Los Angeles Times*, March 30, 1974; Ed Reid, *op. cit.*, p. 223; *New Times* article on Exner affair, January 23, 1976.
Giancana and RFK: McClellan Committee hearing June 9, 1959, 86 Cong., 1 Sess., 18672-.
Giancana crime career: *New Times* article on Exner affair, January 23, 1976, and Professor Robert Blakey, information to author 1979.
250 Kennedy prosecution record: Department of Justice figures, as pub-

lished in Assassinations Committee, V.435; Congressional Record, March 11, 1969, S2642; research of Katherine Kinsella for author, 1978; HSCA V.434-.

Salerno: quoted in *JILE,* Indiana Police Association journal, spring 1979.

Bruno wiretap: HSCA V.443; V.458.

251 Fithian: article in *JILE* Indiana Police Association journal, spring 1979.

HSCA finding: HSCA Report p. 161.

FBI surveillance of Giancana: HSCA V.447.

252 Partin episode: author's interviews with Judge Hawk Daniels, 1978; author's interview with Edward Partin, 1978; "An Insider's Chilling Story of Hoffa's Savage Kingdom" by Edward Partin, *Life,* May 15, 1964; HSCA Report p. 176-.

Bradlee and Hoffa plot: *Conversations with Kennedy* by Benjamin C. Bradlee (New York: W. W. Norton, Pocket Edition, 1976), p. 125-.

254 Trafficante and RFK: McClellan Committee Hearings, 1959 (p. 12432).

254 Aleman episode: author's interview with Jose Aleman, 1978; originally reported by George Crile in *Washington Post,* May 16, 1976; Aleman testimony to HSCA, HSCA V.301 (incorporating staff reports); HSCA Chief Counsel, HSCA V.345; HSCA Report p. 172-; Moldea, *op. cit.,* p. 427n46.

Note 74: the date of the alleged Aleman-Trafficante conversation is unclear. It was first reported (*Washington Post,* May 16, 1976) as September 1962. Aleman himself is unsure because he had at least three meetings with Trafficante during that general period. In his testimony to the Assassinations Committee he spoke of June-July 1963 (HSCA V.303).

Hoffa millionaire: Hoffa quoted in *Playboy,* December 1975.

256 Marcello: Ed Reid quoting Aaron Kohn), *op. cit.,* p. 156; (syndicate income) HSCA IX.65; (elusive;) *ibid.,* p. 154-; (Cuban involvement) Jim Hougan, *op. cit.,* p. 335 (quoting FBI); link to Hoffa—Judge Daniels interview with author, 1978; Marcello, Hoffa and Nixon contribution, Moldea, *op. cit.,* 108; bribe in Hoffa case—Ed Reid, *op. cit.,* pp. 159-60; birth and deportation—Ed Reid, *op. cit.,* p. 151-; (influence) HSCA IX.52 and 88n52; and Aaron Kohn, quoted by Fensterwald-Ewing, *op. cit.,* p. 307.

257 *Note 75:* One report says Marcello was picked up by two CIA agents posing as Justice Department officers (Hougan, *op. cit.,* p. 113). The Assassinations Committee staff report, however, specifies that they were Immigration Service officers (HSCA IX.71).

Marcello alleged threat: author's conversation with Edward Becker, 1978; originally revealed by Ed Reid, *op. cit.*, p. 161-; interviewed by Scott Malone, 1979; by Earl Golz, *Dallas Morning News*, December 1978; HSCA Report p. 171-; HSCA IX.75.

259 *Note 76:* Ed Reid, who first reported the alleged Marcello threat in his book *The Grim Reapers* (see bibliography), is the winner of many journalism awards, including a Pulitzer Prize in 1951. He became an acknowledged specialist on organized-crime operations for that period.

260 Marcello "sociopath": quoted in *The Courier*, New Orleans, September 30, 1976.

260 Blakey on mob guilt: *Newsweek*, July 30, 1979.

15. Three Options for History

262 Johnson predicts visit: *Dallas Times-Herald*, April 24, 1963 (reporting Johnson speech previous evening).
April 24 departure: II.459—testimony of Ruth Paine.
Murret and Oswald call: VIII.135—testimony of Lillian Murret; and VIII.164—Marilyn Murret.

263 Uncle's Mafia link: HSCA Report p. 170; HSCA IX.95.
HSCA on Soviets: HSCA Report p. 103.
Note 77: The thesis postulating Soviet involvement in the assassination has been expounded above all by the British writer Michael Eddowes in his book *The Oswald File* (see bibliography). Eddowes suggests that the real Oswald never returned from the Soviet Union but was replaced by a Soviet agent who returned to the United States posing as Oswald. Eddowes bases his theory mostly on discrepancies in the heights recorded for Oswald on official documents, which seem to show that the Oswald who returned from Russia was considerably shorter than the Oswald who served in the Marines. Eddowes believes that the fake Oswald killed President Kennedy on orders from the Soviet leader Khrushchev. The monstrous political implications aside, this theory founders on the fact that the fingerprints of Marine Oswald are identical with those of the Oswald who died in Dallas. To accept Eddowes' theory one would also have to believe that Oswald's mother was fooled by the fake Oswald on his arrival from Russia. Nevertheless, as this book went to press, Eddowes was pressing Texas courts to order the exhumation of Oswald's body and tests to determine whether the corpse is really his.
HSCA on Cuban role: HSCA Report p. 129.

265 Congressman Edwards: Fensterwald, *op. cit.,* p. 148.

Hart: *Denver Post,* May 2, 1976.

266 Chief Counsel: Professor Robert Blakey, in introduction to *The Final Assassinations Report* (see bibliography).

16. Viva Fidel?

268 Delgado: VIII.241.

Hemming: interview with author, 1978.

Oswald spring letter: XX.511—Oswald undated letter; date is best fixed between March 23 and April 2—see Newman, *op. cit.,* p. 328; also XXII.796—reports of policemen Harkness and Finigan, who observed "unidentified white male" with pro-Castro placard.

269 FBI reading FPCC mail: XVII.773—report by FBI agent Hosty, referring to information supplied by informant on April 21, 1963.

Old envelope: FBI exhibit 413 in National Archives—envelope from FPCC to Oswald, postmarked "1962," found among Oswald's effects after the assassination. The address on the envelope narrows the date down to the period August 4 and October 8, 1962.

May 26 letter to FPCC: XX.512.

FPCC reply: XX.514—letter is dated May 29.

Printing: (Jones) XXII.797; XXV.587 and 773; XX.771; (Mailer's) XXII.800; XXV.770-.

270 "Hidell": Report p. 578 and 615; (Marina signs) Report p. 578; (handwriting experts) HSCA VIII.238.

Worker letter: XX.257.

Port demonstration: XXII.806 (report of Patrolman Girod Ray).

271 Library visits: New Orleans FBI report dated November 27, 1963 (FBI file NO89-69).

Seminary visit: XXV.926-; (with Murret) HSCA IX.95.

Correspondence with Soviet Embassy: I.35; XVI.10-20; XVIII.506.

Bringuier visit: 35/76; XIX.240; XXV.773; (and next day) X.37; XXVI.768.

Oswald-Bringuier incident: XI.358; XXV.90/773/ XXVI.348/ 578/768; CD6.223; author's interview of Bringuier, 1978; Bringuier, *op. cit.,* p. 25-.

272 Police reaction: (Martello and Austin) James/Wardlaw, *op. cit.,* p. 12.

Oswald at newspaper: XXI.626.

Long John Nebel call: Lawrence (see bibliography) p. 66. August 16 incident: X.41, 61, 68; XVI.342; XXV.771; CD206.216-; CD114.629; CD75.69-.

272 Radio interview: X.49; XI.160-.
Debate: X.42; XI.171; XVII.763.
Warren Commission belief: Report p. 412.
273 Oswald-Bringuier episode: see source notes for p. 300, above.
274 Bringuier call to readers: XIX.175.
CIA and FBI subversion of FPCC: Sen. Int. Cttee., *Performance of Intelligence Agencies*, p. 66.
275 Army Intelligence file: HSCA Report p. 224; (history of spying) interview of John Marks, author of *CIA and the Cult of Intelligence* (see bibliography), quoted in Anson, *op. cit.*, p. 284.
276 Report on antisubversive operations; article in Dallas newspaper (uncited), filed by FBI, August 5, 1963, available from researcher Paul Hoch.
John Glenn: Hearings of Committee on Un-American Activities, November 18, 1963.
278 Bringuier and CIA: (DRE) HSCA X.81n; (CIA memo) addressed to Deputy Director for Support, May 1, 1967; (Domestic Contact service and D.O.D.) Marchetti-Marks, *op. cit.*, p. 220 and 227-; CIA document C5A, February 11, 1963.
278 Stuckey episode: McMillan, *op. cit.*, p. 352 (citing letters from Stuckey); and see source notes for p. 300 above.
Information Council of the Americas: XXII.826.
279 Report on Stuckey broadcast: Report p. 729.
Incorrect FBI report: XVII.763—report of Agent Kaack of October 22, 1963, says there was no FBI contact with Stuckey until August 30, 1963.
Quigley meeting: XXVI.95-; X.53; XVII.758.
Quigley review in 1961: IV.432 and 438—testimony of Quigley.
Oswald's request to see FBI: FBI item NO.100-16601-18—Quigley report of August 27, 1963.
FBI and Oswald security case: Sen. Int. Cttee., *Performance of Intelligence Agencies*, p. 89-.
280 Garner: interview with author, 1978.
Hoover and affidavits: XVII.816; affidavits entered into record at XVII.74; (not asked) HSCA Report p. 191n and 193n.
281 Walter: HSCA Report p. 191-.
Pena: XI.343, 356; XXV.671; XXVI.358; Weisberg, *Oswald in New Orleans*, *op. cit.*
Pena allegation about FBI: (on TV) *"the American Assassins"* (II) *CBS Reports*, November 26, 1975.
Note 78: Pena was eventually beaten up by somebody: it has been implied it was because of his allegations (*Oswald in New Orleans* by Harold Weisberg, *op. cit.*, p. 303).

Pena allegation denied: HSCA Report p. 193 and author's conversation with deBrueys, 1978.

Pena "posts bond': XI.358.

282 Alba: interview with author, 1978; reported in affidavit of private researcher Ian MacFarlane, December 23, 1975; *Dallas Morning News*, August 7, 1978; (HSCA comments) HSCA Report pp. 193- and 146.

283 Reily: *the Garrison Case: A Study in the Abuse of Power* by Milton Brener (Clarkson N. Potter, New York, 1969), p. 47.

FBI failure: (to use Cuban Section) HSCA Report p. 128.

17. Blind Man's Bluff in New Orleans

286 Oswald gives Quigley documents: XVII.758-62; IV.437; HSCA X.123.

544 Camp Street address on leaflet: XXVI.783.

287 CRC at Camp Street: Report p. 408 and substance of this chapter.

Second copy of leaflet: FBI document 97-74-67: CD 75.690-.

Note 79: This second copy of the leaflet bears the FBI notation 105-1095-129. This is the serial number also written on FBI documents concerning *anti*-Castro activities (e.g., CD 984b and FBI NO. 97-74-92).

FBI investigation of "544" leaflet: XVII.811; FBI serial 97-74-1A4 and 1A5; the most thorough study of FBI treatment of this area has been done by independent researcher Paul Hoch.

Report reference: Report p. 408.

HSCA criticism of FBI: HSCA X.126 and 124.

288 Newman inquiry: CD75, 680-; CD1.64.

Dallas copies: XXIV.332; XXIV.337; letter of February 7, 1968, from National Archives to Paul Hoch, states that of twenty copies seized in Dallas, nine bear no address, ten bear the Camp Street address, and one bears an illegible address.

Oswald to FPCC: XX.512 (May 26, 1963); XX.514 (FPCC reply); XX.518 (Oswald reply); XX.524 (Oswald on closure).

289 Newman: FBI serial No. 89-69; CD 75 p. 680-; CD1, p. 64; Secret Service reports December 3 and 9, 1963.

Rodriguez: XXIV.659; CD4.819; Secret Service, December 1, 1963 (of Rodriguez Sr.); interview of Rodriguez Jr., March 7, 1979, by Earl Golz of *Dallas Morning News*.

290 Banister: sources on Banister include HSCA X.123- and *Oswald in New Orleans* by Harold Weisberg (pp. 51, 327-, 337-, 364, 380, 391, 410); author's interviews with Banister's secretaries Dalphine Roberts (1978 and 1979) and Mary Brengel (1979);

Banister's brother Ross Banister (questioned by William Scott Malone, 1978); author's interview with Jack Martin, former Banister investigator, 1978; interview with Joe Newbrough, Banister investigator, by William Scott Malone, 1978; author's interview with attorney John Lanne, 1978; author's interview with Aaron Kohn, New Orleans Crime Commission, 1978; interview with Sam Newman by Malone, 1978.

291 Banister and "Friends of Democratic Cuba": from New Orleans Court records, FODC Articles of Incorporation, May 17, 1967.

292 Banister's address: CD75.683—report of FBI agent Wall, November 25, 1963; in 1967 independent researcher William Turner confirmed this was the same address as 544 Camp Street.

Note 80: For a full treatment of the Garrison investigation, see *American Grotesque* by James Kirkwood (Simon and Schuster, New York, 1970); *counterplot* by Edward Epstein (Viking Press, New York, 1968); *Plot or Politics?* by Rosemary James and Jack Wardlaw (Pelican, New Orleans, 1967); *The Kennedy Conspiracy: An Uncommissioned Report on the Jim Garrison Investigation* by Paris Flammonde (Meridith, New York, 1969); *The Garrison Enquiry* by Joachim Joesten (Peter Dawnay Ltd., London, 1967); see also articles in *Ramparts,* January 1968 by former FBI agent William Turner and *Playboy,* October 1967 (interview with District Attorney Garrison). Garrison also wrote a book, *A a Heritage of Stone* (Putnam, New York, 1970).

Banister's widow: interview of Mary Banister by Andrew Sciambra (New Orleans District Attorney's office), April 29-30, 1967.

Index cards and files: HSCA X.130-; and Garrison, *op. cit.,* p. 98-.

293 Banister spying on college students: HSCA X.127.

Campbell brothers: interviews with author, June 1979.

Note 81: Allen Campbell's 1969 statements are drawn from a May 14, 1969, interview by the New Orleans District Attorney's office, reported in Garrison, *op. cit.,* pp. 100 and 208n59. In his 1979 conversation with me, Allen Campbell claimed he had not actually been at 544 Camp Street in summer 1963. That time, however, is when his brother Daniel says Allen brought him into the Banister operation. Both brothers indicate they have more information to provide but are extremely nervous about doing so.

Banister angry: HSCA X.128 (Nitschke and Roberts).

Delphine Roberts: interviewed by author, 1978; (background) New Orleans *States-Item,* December 16, 1961, November 3, 1961, and January 18, 1962; and Roberts' election manifesto, January 27, 1962; HSCA X.128-; HSCA Report pp. 145, 146n.

296 Delphine Roberts' daughter: interviewed by the author, 1978.
Banister brother (Ross) and Nitschke: HSCA X.128.
Alba: HSCA Report p. 146.
297 FBI interview of Banister: HSCA X.126.
CIA and Banister: HSCA X.126.
Arcacha background: CIA document 1363-501, dated October 26,
1967; CD75.683—reports of FBI agent Wall, November 25, 1963;
interview of Mr. and Mrs. Richard Rolfe, New Orleans District
Attorney's office, January 13, 1968; Arcacha's own curriculum
vitae; CD 87; New Orleans Police Arrest Report, August 30,
1961 (item No. H-13903-61); HSCA X.110n and 61; (Banister
suggestion re Camp Street) December 3, 1963, report of Secret
Service agents Gerrets, Vial, and Counts; (Arcacha removed)
CIA document 1363-501, HSCA X.61.

Note 82: On March 9, 1962, the owner of 544 Camp Street, Sam
Newman, wrote to the CRC regarding rent arrears left behind by
Arcacha. The letter was addressed personally to Antonio de
Varona, the CRC leader who reportedly—at the initiative of
Santos Trafficante—played a part in the CIA-Mafia plots to
murder Castro (copy of letter is in files of William Scott Malone).

Note 83: The name of Arcacha Smith has come up in the strange
story of a woman who allegedly had foreknowledge of the President's murder. This was Rose Cheramie, a narcotics addict who
was hospitalized near Eunice, Louisiana, during the night of
November 20, 1963. A policeman who took custody of her,
former Lieutenant Francis Frugé, told me in 1978 that Cheramie
said she had been pushed from a car by two men, apparently of
Latin extraction. On the way to a hospital, Cheramie—Frugé told
me—mentioned that she had heard the two men discussing a plot
to kill the President in Dallas. Frugé thought little of this—given
that his charge was suffering from withdrawal symptoms—until
he heard the news of the President's death. He then arranged to
interview Cheramie in hospital as soon as possible. In essence,
her story was that, as a result of associations while working for
Ruby, she was involved in a drug run from Louisiana to Houston,
Texas. It was before her two companions dumped her, said
Cheramie, that she overheard them discussing an assassination
plot. She was also to claim that Ruby knew Lee Oswald. In 1979,
an Assassinations Committee report corroborated some aspects
of the story. In particular, a former doctor at the hospital, Victor
Weiss, recalled being told by a Dr. Bowers that Cheramie "had
stated before the assassination that President Kennedy was going

to be killed." It is Cheramie's supposed comments *before* the assassination which are of course the most significant aspects of the episode. Frugé says he contacted the Dallas police about Cheramie's information but found them wholly uninterested— given that Oswald was by then dead and universally regarded as having been the lone gunman. Frugé told the Committee that, during a later follow-up inquiry, he checked with the owner of the Silver Slipper Lounge—the brothel where Cheramie had been with her two companions. He examined a number of photographs shown to him by Frugé, and picked out one of Sergio Arcacha Smith and another of a Cuban exile Frugé named "Osanto." When I interviewed Frugé, he said he learned the identity of Cheramie's companions from her initial conversation with him. One of them was another known exile activist, other than Osanto. Arcacha Smith, the Committee's report on this matter notes, was a friend of David Ferrie, whose important role in the mystery was confirmed by the Committee's report. Both Arcacha Smith and Ferrie are reported to have had links with New Orleans Mafia boss Carlos Marcello. Arcacha Smith told the Committee he knew nothing about Cheramie or her allegations. Cheramie herself was killed in an automobile accident in 1965 by a driver who ran over her when she was lying in the road. Although the Committee found evidence that Cheramie had a history of mental illness and of providing false information to the authorities, the story cannot be entirely ignored. Whatever her reputation, the alleged fact that she apparently spoke of the President's murder in Dallas *in advance* is what matters evidentially. Some further research should be done, not least a check with Dr. Bowers to see whether he confirms that Cheramie talked of the murder plot to him before it occurred. (HSCA X.199; *Capital Times*, Madison, Wisconsin, February 1 and 2, 1967; files in office of New Orleans District Attorney; author's interviews with Lieutenant Frugé and other principals.)

298 Bartes: HSCA Report p. 144.

Quiroga: Secret Service report of Gerrets, Vial and Counts, December 3, 1963; XXVI.771- and X.42 (Quiroga information re Oswald).

Caire: XXII.828; (and Oswald) XXII.831.

Entries in Oswald address book: XVI.67; see *Oswald in New Orleans* by Harold Weisberg, p. 79.

Pena: interview with author 1978 (on Arcacha); (and FBI), same interview and interview of former FBI agent Warren deBrueys, *CBS Reports*, November 26, 1976; XI.354.

299 Ferrie background: HSCA X.105; HSCA IX.103; CIA document 1359-503, February 7, 1968; FBI reports from New Orleans November 26, 1963; CD75.287-; article in *New Republic*, "Is Garrison Faking?" by Fred Powledge, June 17, 1967; *Ramparts*, lead article, January 1968; July 18, 1961, letter of Arcacha to Eastern Airlines official Captain E. Rickenbacker; (bombing) article in *El Tiempo*, New York, March 1967.

Ferrie letter to Air Force: "Garrison's Case," *New York Review of Books*, September 14, 1967, p. 28.

300 Ferrie speech: James/Wardlaw, *op. cit.*, p. 46.

On President Kennedy: Secret Service report by agents Wall and Viater, November 27, 1963.

"On electorate": in notes found in Ferrie's effects after his death.

Banister: anecdote told by Aaron Kohn, New Orleans Crime Commission.

Ferrie demonstration: James/Wardlaw, *op. cit.*, p. 111.

301 Ferrie and Oswald: (CAP) HSCA IX.103; VIII.14; XXII.826; (Ferrie untruth re CRC) (HSCA X.132n; (Banister employee on Ferrie and Oswald) HSCA IX104—re Jack Martin; (Oswald, Marines and Socialism) Warren Report p. 383-; ("baloney") HSCA IX.107.

303 Andrews: XI.331 and 326-; XXVI.732 and 704.

Martin: HSCA IX.104.

304 HSCA on Oswald/Ferrie sighting: HSCA Report p. 142; HSCA IV.485.

Clinton incident: (background) *Robert Kennedy and His Times* by Arthur Schlesinger, p. 303; (incident) transcripts of evidence in trial, *State of Louisiana v. Clay Shaw*, February 6-7, 1969; author's interviews with Edwin McGehee (barber), John Manchester (town marshal), William Dunn (CORE worker), Henry Palmer (registrar of voters), Reeves Morgan (state representative), Maxine Kemp (hospital secretary), and former police intelligence officer Francis Frugé, 1978; HSCA Report p. 142.

308 COINTELPRO, etc.: *Robert Kennedy and His Times* by Arthur Schlesinger, p. 641-.

Note 84: Reeves Morgan, a member of the Louisiana State Legislature, says he informed the FBI of Oswald's presence in Clinton almost immediately after the assassination. It seems, however, that the FBI failed to investigate, and the Warren Commission never learned of the Clinton episode (HSCA Report p. 142 and author's interview of Morgan).

309 Ferrie and Marcello: (as pilot) HSCA Report p. 143n; (and Andrews) James/Wardlaw, *op. cit.,* p. 92; (Andrews and Marcello) testimony released by New Orleans grand jury, April 12, 1967; (Ferrie and Marcello case) CD 75 and HSCA X.105-; (Marcello opinion of Ferrie) interview of Joe Newbrough, former Banister investigator, by William Scott Malone, August 16, 1978.

310 Banister and Marcello: author's interview of Mary Brengel, 1978; HSCA X.127.
Oswald family's reported connections with organized-crime figures: HSCA IX93-103 and 115-.

311 Andrews: (asked to represent Oswald) XVI.331, 326; 339; (pseudonym) *Counterplot* by E. J. Epstein, p. 41n; (in fear of life) *Oswald in New Orleans* by Harold Weisberg, p. 139.

311 Clem Sehrt: HSCA IX.100.
Raoul Sere: HSCA IX.103.
Termine: HSCA IX.115.

312 Oswald obtaining bail: XXV.117; CD 75.159, FBI report of November 30, 1963; *Clandestine America,* III.2, p. 7, quoting New Orleans Crime Commission Director on Bruneau; CD6.104; VII.175; (Pecora) HSCA IX.192; HSCA Report p. 155.

313 *Note 85:* Banister's personal secretary, Delphine Roberts, offers one further clue to the way 544 Camp Street was caught up in the dirtier undercurrents of 1963 politics. She has come up with the names "Roselli' and "Maheu" as having had dealings with the Banister office. Robert Maheu was the man used by the CIA, as early as 1960, to enlist Mafia help in assassination plots against Fidel Castro. John Roselli was the first underworld figure Maheu recruited. Mrs. Roberts' claim that Banister was in touch with Maheu is not wholly implausible. Years previously the two men had been agents together in the Chicago office of the FBI, and Maheu admits he knew Banister. He denies, however, contacting Banister in 1963. Roselli has been identified as taking an active part in anti-Castro military operations in spring 1963. An exile training camp was being established in southern Louisiana at that time and with financing and support from organized crime. New Orleans would have been a natural enough place to find John Roselli. Delphine Roberts says she believes he was there and actually visited 544 Camp Street. If she is right, the covert activities of Guy Banister Associates assume even greater significance. (Author's interview with Roberts, 1978); (Maheu and Banister) Maheu conversation with William Scott Malone, 1979.
Marina and "Hidell": (on signing name) Warren Report p. 578

(denial) XXIII.402; (on hearing radio) V.401-; (transcript) Stuckey Exhibit 3.

HSCA on Marina: HSCA Report p. 55n.

314 Marina on Oswald affiliation: HSCA XII.394. (On other occasions Marina has stuck to the conventional line—that Oswald was firmly committed to the Castro side—e.g., HSCA XII.408.)

Schweiker: interviewed by author, 1978.

18. The Kennedy Legacy

316 American University speech: Public Papers of President Kennedy (1963), p. 45.

JFK address to nation: Public Papers of President Kennedy (1963), p. 606.

317 Revival of raids: Sen. Int. Cttee. *Assassination Plots*, p. 172, 337. *Robert Kennedy and His Times* by Arthur Schlesinger, p. 543-.

Exile leadership: Associated Press (Miami), May 10, 1963; CRC statement, June 21, 1963.

FBI seizures: Sen. Int. Cttee., *Performance of Intelligence Agencies*, p. 12-.

318 Lacombe: *ibid.* and New Orleans *States-Item* May 5, 1963; (Ferrie) James/Wardlaw, *op. cit.*, p. 131; (McLaney) *Washington Post*, August 1, 1963, HSCA X.185; HSCA X.72-.

Bringuier: memorandum from FBI New Orleans to HQ, May 11, 1964.

Interpen: *New York Times*, September 16, 1963.

319 Sturgis group financing: Fensterwald, *op. cit.*, p. 505.

Hall: (detained) *Oswald in New Orleans*, by Harold Weisberg, pp. 161, 273, 274, 276 and HSCA X.22; (Cuban jail) interview of Hall by Harold Weisberg, p. 92; ("Free Cuba") CD294, XVI.436; (Government crackdown in general) HSCA X.13.

Valle: (Trafficante) FBI 105-95677, quoting *Diario Las Americas*, February 25, 1967; (Ferrie) article in *El Tiempo* (New York), by Diego G. Tendedera, March 1967.

Senate Committee: Sen. Int. Cttee. *Assassination Plots*, p. 13.

"at peace": Associated Press (Mandeville, Louisiana) July 31, 1963.

CRC: June 21, 1963, statement by CRC.

320 Cuban protest: *Revolución*, Havana, August 19, 1963: (Castro) speech of July 26, 1963.

321 No U.S. expectation of toppling Castro: Sen. Int. Cttee. *Assassination Plots*, CIA/Cubela plotting: Sen. Int. Cttee. *Assassination*

Plots, p. 86- and 174-; author's interview with Rolando Cubela, Havana, 1978; HSCA X.157 and 162-; HSCA Report p. 111-.

Note 86: The Assassinations Committee Report (p. 113) said it could not confirm or deny that "AM/LASH" was Rolando Cubela. This may be so for the official record, but I have located no source which questions it.

324 Veciana: author's interviews with Veciana, Miami, 1978; HSCA X.37- and HSCA Report p. 135-; HSCA IV.476 and author's interviews of HSCA staff; "Dallas: the Cuban Connection," *Saturday Evening Post*, March 1976; *Washingtonian Magazine*, November 1980, article by former HSCA investigator Gaeton, Fonzi; research by David Leigh for *Washington Post*, June/July 1980.

Raids against Soviet ships: *Dallas Times-Herald*, March 19, 22, 27, 28, 29, 31, 1963.

331 Diosdado: author's interviews Veciana; interview of Diosdado by Susan Jetton, July 1980; *Washingtonian Magazine*, November 1980, pp. 182, 184.

335 Oswald at time of "Bishop" meeting: chronology of Oswald's activities prepared from Warren Commission documents by Mary Ferrell and Arch Kimbrough, Dallas researchers.

Oswald at Mexican consulate: XXIV.549;, 685; XXV.17, 811.

Passport: XXII.12; XXIV.509; (Knight) *New York Times*, March 23, 1966.

Tourist card numbers and FBI: FBI file SA 89-67, FBI report November 30, 1963 (Laredo, Texas); CD's 75/588/613/652.

336 Gaudet: interviews by author, 1977 and 1978; interviewed by Bernard Fensterwald 1975; and by Allen Stone (WRR, Dallas). May 7, 1975; CD's 75/588/613/652; HSCA Report p. 218-.

337 Gaudet and Banister: author's interview with Gaudet, 1978; HSCA Report p. 219n.

339 CIA/FBI and FPCC: Sen. Int. Cttee., *Performance of Intelligence Agencies*, p. 65.

Oswald summary of achievements: Report p. 731.

Oswald leaves New Orleans: XI.462-; XXIII.715, CD170.4/8; HSCA X.21.

Frontier stamp: XXV.16 and 819; XXIV.663.

19. Exits and Entrances in Mexico City

343 Parker: in interview with author Ed Reid.

Passengers on bus: XI.214 (McFarland); XI.215 (Mumford).

Bowen: XI.220 (seen); XXIV.576; XXV.42/45/75; (Report) Report p. 733.

Oswald as "Osborne": see source notes for page, "Printing."

344 Hotel Cuba: XI.223

Hotel Comercio: Report p. 733.

Mexico activity: (except where indicated) Report p. 299- and HSCA Report p. 121- and p. 248-.

Note 87: Marina Oswald has said that Oswald told her in advance he intended going to Mexico City and would visit the Cuban Embassy (HSCA II.257).

345 Oswald in Mexico: (seen with Cubans) XXVI.672; (exile haunt) Anson, *op. cit.,* p. 251.

Duran: interview with author in Mexico City, 1978, and subsequent contacts: XXV.586/634; XVI.33; XXIV.590; HSCA III.6-, Duran's suspicions—HSCA III.35, 58.

346 Azcue: XXIV.570; XXIV.563; author's research in Cuba; HSCA III.127; Report p. 301/734-.

Communist Party card: HSCA III.176, 155, 142.

347 CIA surveillance: David Phillips—speech to National Military Intelligence Association, 6.76; *The Night Watch* by David A. Phillips (Atheneum, New York, 1977); Agee, *op. cit.,* p. 543; author's interviews with Cuban Ministry of the Interior officials 1978 (including Nilvio Labrada, electronics specialist).

Intercepted conversations: *New York Times,* September 21, 1975, p. 1; *Washington Post,* November 26, 1976, p. 1; Secret Service document 104; State Department telegram 1201, November 28, 1963; Assassination Information Bureau briefing document "Oswald's Alleged Contacts with the Cuban and Soviet Embassies in Mexico City, 1978"; (with Soviets) Report p. 734; XXVI.149; XXVI.667-; CD1084d.5; CD1216; apparently CD347 (still withheld) reported in Coleman-Slawson draft.

348 Azcue: formal statement of Azcue for Havana public hearings on Kennedy case, July 29, 1978; Azcue testimony to Assassinations Committee, September 18, 1978.

Oswald height: XVII.285.

Description by Azcue: Havana statement July 29, 1978; and HSCA III.152; blond—HSCA III.136; belief—HSCA III.136; clothing—HSCA III.143.

Mirabal: HSCA III.174.

349 Azcue conviction: HSCA III.139.

Signature, etc.: HSCA III.172; HSCA Report p. 251.

Duran unsure: author's interview with Duran, 1978; HSCA III.29-39.

Azcue on possible lapse: HSCA III.153.

350 Duran name in Oswald's book: XVI.54.

Duran reaction to seeing film: interview with author, May 13, 1979; and letter, June 22, 1979.

351 Duran's height, etc.: HSCA III.103.

Duran on hair and eyes: HSCA III.69.

Contreras: interview with author, 1978; HSCA Report p. 124 and 125n17.

352 *Note 88:* Although the CIA failed to follow it up properly, Agency files show that in 1967 the Contreras story was considered "the first significant development in the investigation of the Kennedy assassination after 1965." Duran told the HSCA that she suggested "Oswald" should find a Mexican referee for his Cuban visa application. The HSCA also learned that the chairman of the university philosophy department sometimes held seminars at Duran's home. This, the Committee speculated, might explain why "Oswald" contacted Contreras—after he had attended a meeting in the philosophy department (HSCA Report p. 124-).

353 Mirabal: HSCA III.177.

CIA teletype, October 10: CD 631.

353 CIA on photograph: Report p. 364; XI.469; CD1287; CD631; CD1287; CD674; David Phillips in *The Night Watch* (see source notes for p. 384) has said there was no photograph of Oswald; see also document 948-927T, CIA/internal memorandum dated May 5, 1967.

Dallas FBI receive picture: Sen. Int. Cttee., *Performance of Intelligence Agencies,* p. 92.

CIA memo: CIA document 948-927T, dated May 12, 1967.

355 CIA possession of Oswald picture: CD692 CIA document 590-252, March 6, 1964 (memo to Warren Commission); (Minsk pictures) CIA document 614-261, March 20, 1964, XX.474, and see treatment in this book, Chapter 11, "The Man Who Was Perfectly All Right"; (picture sent from ONI) HSCA Report p. 224 and 225n.

356 CIA and "wait out": CIA document 579-250; HSCA IV.215; HSCA XI.63.

CIA to Commission in July: CD 1287.

Liebeler: *Inquest* by E. J. Epstein, p. 94.

357 1975 CIA explanations and Sprague: author's interview with Sprague, 1978.

Dozen pictures: CIA documents 929-;939, 927A-K (CIA Document Disposition Index); CIA has withheld another picture, 940-927L, supposedly of the same person; (October 1) CIA document 948-927T.

358 Phillips: in *The Night Watch* by David Phillips (Atheneum, New York, 1977), p. 142.

HSCA on CIA picture-taking: HSCA Report p. 125 and 125n18.

359 Colby: CBS Television, November 25, 1975.

Bugging: CD1084d.5; Coleman-Slawson memorandum, February 14, 1964; Odessa—CD1084d.4- and State Department telegram of November 28, 1963, from U.S. Ambassador Mann to Secretary of State; Duran—HSCA III.114; (Oswald's Russian) HSCA Report p. 251.

Phillips and Assassinations Committee: reported in *Washington Post,* May 6, 1977.

Transcribers: reported by Ronn Kessler for *Washington Post,* November 26, 1976.

360 Hoover report: HSCA Report p. 249-; Sen. Int. Cttee., *Performance of Intelligence Agencies,* p. 32; CD 87—Secret Service control No. 104 (cite uncertainly identified on document); (CIA plane) CIA document 14, letter from Mexico City to HQ, November 22, 1963 (released January 1976); (opinion on Shanklin and Hosty) HSCA Report p. 196; (HSCA conclusion on tape) HSCA Report p. 258.

361 HSCA Mexico conclusions: HSCA Report p. 250-252; ("source" in error) HSCA Report p. 122-123 on subject of Oswald statements at consulate; (CIA refusal) HSCA Report p. 124n15 re Garro (see Note 91).

362 CIA request to Navy: CD 631.

CIA message October 10: CIA document 7-2, HQ to Mexico City.

FBI 1963 reports to CIA: CIA document 590-252 (and CD 692) show that CIA was sent FBI reports (on Oswald's latest activities) on September 7, 10, and 24, 1963.

Note 89: There has apparently been little official concern about another man who certainly behaved as though he was on some sort of undercover mission in Mexico and whose movements ran parallel to Oswald's. This was Manuel Porras Rivera, a Costa Rican whose name appears on the list of travelers leaving Mexico on October 3, the same day as Oswald. Porras obtained entry permits for the United States and Mexico four days before Oswald got his Mexico permit in New Orleans. He traveled first to Miami, the main center of Cuban exile activity, and there—by his own admission—had meetings with anti-Castro activists. Porras then proceeded to Mexico City with the intention of obtaining a Cuban entry visa. In yet another of those coincidences which dog the Oswald affair, he visited the Cuban Embassy on Saturday, September 28, a day when Oswald was also there. Porras gave an improbable account of this, claiming that he found the consulate closed and then, having come all the way from Costa Rica specifically to obtain a Cuban visa, simply gave up. He said he did not return on Monday, when the offices were open, and left Mexico by bus on October 3. Once back in the United States, said Porras, he traveled to Dallas and then New Orleans—the other main American center for exile activities. Costa Rican intelligence revealed just a little more about this traveler. They were aware of his anti-Castro activity and that he planned to infiltrate Cuba.

Porras was somewhat older than Oswald and was, like the man remembered by witnesses in Mexico, only 5' 7" tall. It would be interesting to see his photographs and learn how well he spoke English in 1963. Certainly Porras' bizarre journey, his anti-Castro associates, and his aborted mission, deserved greater investigation (CD 963.17/19).

Phillips' and transcribers' account: *Washington Post,* November 26, 1976.

363 Rodriguez: *Dallas Morning News,* September 24, 1975 (reprinted from *Los Angeles Times* story by Charles Ashman).

Clark story: (in U.S.A.) *National Enquirer* article, "Fidel Castro Says He Knew of Oswald Threat to Kill JFK," October 15, 1967 (it seems the alleged interview took place in July); Assassinations Committee commentary on Clark, September 19, 1978, HSCA III.283; HSCA Report pp. 122 and 123.

364 *Note 90:* The Assassinations Committee also considered another allegation that Oswald had compromising links with staff of the Cuban Embassy. In 1964, *after* the publication of the Warren Report, a Mexican woman called Elena Garro came forward with an allegation that Oswald and two companions had attended a party at the home of relative of Sylvia Duran, the secretary from the Cuban consulate. U.S. intelligence agencies failed to investigate this allegation thoroughly when it was made. The Committee tried, and so did I, in 1978. Garro has said that she wanted to come forward with her story immediately after the assassination but was told not to and was sequestered in a hotel by one "Manuel Calvillo." The CIA; did find that she had stayed at the hotel. Duran does recall a party at a relative's home, attended by Garro, in September 1963. There, though, the facts wear thin. Research indicates it is extremely unlikely that Oswald was at the

party or discussed matters with Cuban officials present—as alleged by Garro. The question today is, rather, why did Garro
come up with the story? If she was primed to do so after the
assassination, why was she defused and by whom? Garro, whose
whereabouts in Europe are known, refuses to testify. A State
Department report in 1969 described her as "a professional anti-
Communist." (HSCA III.291). Former associates in Mexico City
told me they suspected her, on quite separate matters, of liaising
with and acting on behalf of U.S. intelligence—in the propaganda
field. The Committee found that its Garro inquiry was "inhibited
by the refusal of the CIA to make available its sources . . . on the
allegation." This, it seems to me, is outrageous. A State Department officer, who tried to investigate the Garro matter in 1964,
was later mistakenly dismissed and eventually committed suicide.
The Garro episode should now be thoroughly investigated anew,
with a keen interest in learning Garro's reason for spreading the
anti-Castro allegation and the identity of others who may have
put her up to it as early as 1963, then aborted the operation.
Taken together with other allegations which falsely linked Oswald to the Cubans (see Chapter 22, "The First Stone"), the
Garro case is disturbing. (Garro—HSCA Report p. 124 and
HSCA III.285.)

Phillips: (and "Bishop"): HSCA X.46- and HSCA Report p. 136
and 136n23.

Note 91: Whereas the HSCA Report referred only to "a retired
officer" being considered as "Bishop," he is repeatedly named as
Phillips in the Appendix to the Hearings, Vol. X.46.

365 Schweiker: interview by Michael Cockerell and author for BBC-TV
1978.

Veciana: references as when previously mentioned.

366 *Note 92:* The Assassinations Committee talked to Veciana's cousin,
Ruiz, in Cuba. He spoke badly of Veciana and suggested he had
had psychiatric problems. Ruiz suggested the Committee contact
another Veciana relative, a doctor, who would attest to Veciana's
psychiatric trouble. The Committee did so and found on the
contrary that the doctor attested to Veciana's "sound mental
condition." He knew, in addition, that Veciana had had to undergo vigorous tests for his work in the banking business. Another
family member confirmed Veciana's mental health. There is no
evidence whatsoever of any disorder of the sort Ruiz suggested.
Veciana has alleged that Ruiz was once approached for recruit-

ment by the CIA, and his slandering of Veciana may be an overkill reaction to that (HSCA X.45).

Veciana's reputation: HSCA X.42.

20. Double Image in Dallas

368 Oswald's return to USA: XXIV.549/569/571: (YMCA) X.281-; XI.478; XXII.159/207; (visits wife) XXIII.509; XXIV.702.

Book Depository job: CD5.325; CD3.34/121; III.121/212.

Rented rooms: XXIII.390; XXVI.538; (Beckley) X.294; VI.436.

Note 93: Most of Oswald's calls to his wife were made from the phone in his roominghouse. However, according to the manager of the garage across the street, Oswald made at least two long-distance phone calls from the pay phone at the garage. The manager, Jerry Duncan, remembered Oswald twice asking for change for the calls, about six weeks before the assassination. Although the recent calls on the phone were traced, none threw light on whom Oswald had been calling. This probably deserves reinvestigation (XXVI.250).

Birthday: I.53; III.40; XVII.189; McMillan, *op. cit.*, p. 379.

369 Supervisor: III.216.

Prospects: I.68; McMillan, *op. cit.*, p. 379.

IRS letter: FBI Exhibit 274, reported at length in *Dallas Morning News*, May 1, 1977; IRS records closed: refusal sent to Dallas researcher, June 22, 1968, on grounds that, being dead, Oswald could not give permission to make his returns public (sections 6103 and 7213 of Internal Revenue Code and 18 U.S.C. 1905, cited by Archivist of U.S.A.).

Hosty: Report 327/419/435/437/660/739; analysis of Hosty involvement in Sen. Int. Cttee., *Performance of Intelligence Agencies*, Appendix A; (November 1) IV.449; I.48; III.92/96-; (November 5) I.56; II.15; Hearings on FBI Oversight before House Subcommittee on Civil and Constitutional Rights, Serial 2, Pt. 3, pp. 143 and 145; HSCA Report p. 194-.

370 Women had phone number: III.43; XI.53.

Hosty and Oswald note: II.18 (Mrs. Paine); HSCA Report p. 195-; Sen. Int. Cttee., *Performance of Intelligence Agencies*, Appendix B; (testimony of Hosty, Fenner, Shanklin, Howe, etc.) Hearings on FBI Oversight before House Subcommittee on Civil and Constitutional Rights, Serial 2, pt. 3, October 21 and December 11-12, 1975.

372 *Note 94:* Congress' Assassinations Committee investigated another instance of strange FBI behavior regarding Oswald and Agent Hosty. Oswald's address book, seized after his arrest, contained Hosty's name, address, telephone number, and car license number. This was not necessarily compromising, for it had quickly become known that Hosty visited Marina in search of Oswald shortly before the assassination, and Marina was to explain that she passed on information about Hosty to her husband. Nevertheless, in the information about the address contents which first reached the Warren Commission, the reference to Hosty was missing. Only later, following independent reports and in the light of Commission interest in Oswald's relationship with the FBI, did the Bureau confirm the existence of the Hosty notation. In 1979 the Assassinations Committee investigated the omission in depth and concluded that "one or more FBI agents sought to protect Hosty from personal embarrassment by trying . . . to exclude his name from the reporting." The Committee found the incident regrettable but trivial in the wider context. This conclusion seems reasonable enough. (HSCA Report p. 186-); see also Report p. 327 and CD 205, CD 385, V.112, V.242; and Malley, HSCA III.507-.

Hosty and "bombs": interview with Earl Golz, *Dallas Morning News,* August 30, 1978; (Chief Counsel comment) HSCA III.512.

373 Letter to Soviet Embassy: Report p. 739; (on Mrs. Paine's desk) III.14-; (text) XVI.443; XVI.33 and 443.

374 PO box: XXII.717.
ACLU meeting and Paine: XI.403 and II.408.
Oswald writes to Communist Party: XXII.170.

375 Mail forwarding: VII.289-308/525-530.

376 Dannelly: Report p. 732; XXIV.729-.
Hutchinson: XXVI.178; X.327; (barber) X.309.

377 Car showroom: XXVI.430/577; Report 320 and 840; X.345, XXVI.450; X.347-; (Bogard) XXVI.682, 702, 703, 704, 664; (Pizzo) X.340.
Western Union: Report 332; XI.311; X.412; XXI.744, 745, 752-; Exhibits 3005, 3006, 3015; *Dallas Times-Herald,* November 30, 1963; *Dallas Morning News,* December 1, 1963.
Oswald and library card: Report 616.

378 Morrow: CD385.138-; CD950.
Morgan's Gunshop: XXIV.704.
Furniture store: XI.253; XI.262; Report p. 317; XXII.546-; XXVI.456.

379 Irving Sports Shop: XXIV.329-; Report 315; XXII.525/531; XI.224-; (screws) I.483.

Sports Drome: Report p. 318; X.370-; X.380; X.357/373; XXIV.304.

Dr. Wood: interview with author, 1978; XXVI.368; X.386; XX-III.403.

381 Mrs. Penn: Interview of Mrs. Penn by Texas researcher Penn Jones, June 1975; and Mannlicher bullet—CD205.182.

382 "Spanish" Oswalds: see source references for later mentions, this chapter.

"Oswald" at DRE meeting: CD205.646-.

Abilene incident: article by Earl Golz, *Dallas Morning News,* June 10, 1979.

382 *Note 95:* On November 15, 1963, one week before the assassination, de Varona attended a Cuban Revolutionary Council meeting in New Orleans. It is of note that he stayed at the home of Agustin Guitart, the uncle of Silvia Odio. Odio, as discussed in the latter part of this chapter, was visited in September 1963 by men claiming to be anti-Castro fighters. One of their number looked exactly like Oswald and was introduced as "Leon Oswald." One of the party later called Odio and made comments apparently designed to ensure that she remembered "Oswald." The caller said that Oswald thought the President should have been shot (see this chapter and HSCA X.62).

Inspector: Sen. Int. Cttee., *Performance of Intelligence Agencies,* p. 91.

Deslatte: CD75.677; interviewed by New Orleans District Attorney's office, 1967.

384 "Friends of Democratic Cuba": (Banister) Articles of incorporation of FODC., filed at Louisiana Secretary of State's office, May 17, 1967; (purchase form) FBI 89-69-1A6, released 1979.

385 Official impostor warning: (Hoover) CD 294B, Hoover memo to State Department Office of Security, June 3, 1960; (Department of State memo) Edward Hickey to John White, March 31, 1961; and XVIII.373, State Department document July 11, 1961.

385 Retail Merchants' Credit Association: XXII.99; XVII.728; XVII.685.

Frank/Slawson: *New York Times,* February 23, 1975.

386 Odio: interviews with author, 1978 and 1979; HSCA Report p. 137- and HSCA X.19-; also Warren XI.327/386; XXVI.362/472; see especially study in Meagher, *op. cit.,* p. 376-; XVI.834; CD 1553; "Dallas: The Cuban Connection," article in *Saturday Evening Post,* March 1976.

389 *Note 96:* Silvia Odio has explained that she suffered from blackouts at various periods of her life. The cause has been diagnosed medically since 1963, and she now appears better, if not wholly out of risk. Her apparent shock on the day of the assassination does not, against that background, seem farfetched. There were many, perhaps thousands, who wept openly when they heard the traumatic news of the Kennedy assassination. With Odio's recent visitation and disturbing phone call about "Oswald," her reaction seems understandable enough. There is no doubt she did pass out, and she was hospitalized. The way the Odio incident emerged is highly complex and the result of a series of conversations for which her sister Sarita was originally responsible. In the event, the FBI became interested because of information about Ruby, not Odio. (For full exposition, see HSCA X.24.) The person with whom Silvia Odio discussed the incident before the assassination was Dr. Burton Einspruch, her psychiatrist. He recalls that, in the normal course of a session with him, she told him the events of the preceding week—including the fact that she had been visited by two Latins and one "Anglo." There is no suggestion that, because Odio was visiting a psychiatrist, her reliability is diminished. Dr. Einspruch explains that Odio was a young woman of wealthy birth, transferred abruptly from affluence in Cuba to hard times as an exile. She had been deserted by her husband and left with young children to raise and other family members to help. She came to him, as would so many in America, to talk out her problems. Dr. Einspruch has said, from the start, that he has "great faith in Mrs. Odio's story of having met Lee Harvey Oswald." (Author's interviews with Odio and HSCA X.29.)

390 Correspondence with father: XX.690-. (Odio's own letter, sent to her father on October 27, did not survive. She clearly did write it because we have her father's reply—at Christmas—referring specifically to the strange visitors.)

391 Rankin: XXVI.834.

Hoover information on Hall: XXVI.834; (collapse of Hall story) CD.1553; HSCA XI.600.

HSCA on Oswald travel: HSCA Report p. 139 and HSCA X.21 and 32.

HSCA speculation: HSCA Report p. 140; (conclusion) HSCA Report p. 139.

393 Father's letter: XX.690; HSCA X.29.

JURE: (leaders nonplussed) XXVI.839; HSCA X.31.

Hall: (1967) interview for article in *National Enquirer,* September 1,

1968; (and HSCA) *Washington Post,* May 21, 1977; (immunized testimony) quoted at HSCA X.22-; ("fabrication") HSCA Report p. 138; (detained) HSCA X.22 and *Oswald in New Orleans,* by Harold Weisberg, pp. 161, 273, 274, 276; (Interpen and Hemming) memo of William Scott Malone to HSCA chief investigator C. Fenton, June 3, 1977; see also Hemming in this book, Chapter 9, "The Cracks in the Canvas"; (and Trafficante) see Hall interview with Harold Weisberg, p. 92, Malone memo *supra,* and memo of Mark Allen to HSCA staffer Donovan Gay, June 2, 1977.

393   Alpha 66 report: XIX.534 (report of Deputy Sheriff B. Walthers, November 23, 1963). See also CD3.315—there is confusion over two phonetically similar addresses. The correct address was probably 3126 Hollandale, Farmer's Branch.

21. Countdown to Conspiracy

394   Attwood episode: author's interviews with William Attwood, 1978 and 1979; *The Reds and the Blacks* by William Attwood (New York, 1967), pp. 142-144; *Robert Kennedy and His Times* by Arthur Schlesinger, p. 550-; author's interview with Arthur Schlesinger 1978; Sen. Int. Cttee. *Assassination Plots*, p. 173-; HSCA Report p. 127.

395   Bundy: Sen. Int. Cttee. *Assassination Plots*, p. 173.

Donovan: *Robert Kennedy and His Times* by Arthur Schlesinger, p. 541.

Vietnam: (1,000 to be withdrawn) *A Thousand Days* by Arthur Schlesinger, p. 908; Public Papers of President Kennedy (1963), p. 760. For detailed study of Kennedy policy on Vietnam withdrawal, see *Robert Kennedy and His Times* by Arthur Schlesinger, p. 712-; (CIA) Prouty, *op. cit.; The Pentagon Papers* by Peter Dale Scott (Senator Gravel, ed., Boston, 1971), Vol. 5, p. 215-.

396   President and CIA: *New Republic,* December 11, 1965, article on CIA by Harry Rowe Ransom.

Advisory group on Cuba: Sen. Int. Cttee. *Assassination Plots*, p. 173.

Howard and Castro: CIA debriefing of Lisa Howard, May 1, 1963.

397   Dallas visit announcements: (predicted) *Dallas Times-Herald,* September 13, 1963; (precise date) IV.348; XXII.619; *Dallas Morning News,* September 26, 1963.

398   Cubela: Sen. Int. Cttee. *Assassination Plots*, p. 86- and p. 174-.

Daniel: author's interview with William Attwood, 1978; *L'Express* (Paris), December 6, 1963; *New Republic,* December 7 and 14, 1963.

399 Miami speech: JFK Public Papers, 1963 (Washington, 1964), p. 875-; (Schlesinger) *Robert Kennedy and His Times* by Arthur Schlesinger, p. 554n; and interview with author, 1978; (American visitor) RFK Papers—CIA debriefing of Lisa Howard, May 1, 1963.

400 Cubela: Sen. Int. Cttee. *Assassination Plots*, p. 86- and p. 174; author's interview with Cubela, Havana, 1978.

401 *Note 97:* Former CIA officers, and other consultants, confirm that calls to Cuba were monitored, along with other systems of communication. A future inquiry, with access to classified material, could find it productive to examine records and working systems for the period. The National Security Agency is an obvious starting point. See also Sen. Int. Cttee. Supp., *Detailed Staff Reports on Intelligence Activities and the Rights of Americans,* Report 94-755, Book III.145 (1976).

402 Odio and father: XX.690.

Farmers Branch meeting: copy of original sound tape obtained in 1978 by the author from retired Dallas police lieutenant George Butler; also obtained by HSCA (see HSCA Report pp. 132 and 613n39); copy of tape held in files of Mary Ferrell, Dallas researcher; see also *Dallas Morning News,* August 14, 1978.

403 Chicago and Miami threats: HSCA Report p. 230- and notes; author's interviews with retired Miami Police Intelligence Captain Charles Sapp and former Lieutenant Everett Kay (who holds original surveillance tape of Milteer), 1978; article in *Miami News* by Bill Barry, February 2, 1967; "JFK, King: The Dade County Links," in *Miami Magazine,* September 1976; author's interview with member of Presidential party in Miami; CD's 1347/20p4 (which omits mention of tape recording); (earlier Sapp warning) Sapp memo to Assistant Chief of Police Anderson, April 4, 1963, as referred to elsewhere; (Chicago) "The Plot to kill JFK in Chicago," *Chicago Independent,* November, 1975; Warren XXVI.441; and HSCA sources as for Miami threat *supra*; (Bolden) Fensterwald/Ewing, *op. cit.,* p. 56.

Note 98: Bolden left the Secret Service under a cloud, and served time in prison for offenses allegedly committed during his government service. He, however, says the charges were trumped up. Washington lawyer Bernard Fensterwald believes Bolden's claim about a Kennedy threat in Chicago may well be credible.

405 *Note 99:* The President left Miami at 9:13 P.M., according to Dave

Powers, curator of John F. Kennedy Library (in 1979 letter to author).

406 Daniel: *New Republic,* December 7 and 14, 1963.

22. The First Stone

408 Shakespeare quote: *The Rape of Lucrece,* II.939-40.

Johnson summons Warren: Manchester, *op. cit.,* p. 730; Warren Commission internal memorandum by Melvin Eisenberg, February 17, 1964.

Warren Commission says no foreign involvement: Report p. 21.

Cuban official statement: statement by Carlos Lechuga, reprinted p. 115, *Four Days,* historical record of the death of President Kennedy (American Heritage Publishing Co., 1964).

Daniel: *New Republic,* December 7, 1963.

409 U.S. reaction: (Alexander) Manchester, *op. cit.,* p. 326; (editorials) *Dallas Morning News,* November 26, 1963; (poll) *Dallas Morning News,* December 6, 1963.

Warren and "Castro plot" in 1967: Sen. Int. Cttee., *Performance of International Agencies,* p. 80.

410 HSCA on Roselli allegations: HSCA Report p. 114.

Morgan: "The CIA's Secret Army," CBS-TV, Friday, June 10, 1977.

411 CIA and "Castro threat": CIA memo to David Belin, director of Rockefeller Commission on CIA Activities Within the United States, May 30, 1975.

Castro (interviewed by HSCA, April 3, 1978): HSCA III.216, 220; (HSCA conclusions) HSCA Report pp. 129, 123, and see HSCA X.170-.

413 Warren Commission and Castro influence on Oswald: Warren Report p. 414.

Oswald's feelings on Castro, etc.: (under questioning) Report p. 609; (radio debate) XXI.641; (Martello) X.60; (Commission) Warren Report p. 415; (HSCA) HSCA Report p. 1.

414 Castro interview: transcripts of interview by Frank Mankiewicz and Kirby Jones. (Their Castro interviews, conducted in 1974 and 1975, are published in *With Fidel* by Mankiewicz and Jones (Ballantine Books, New York, 1975); and HSCA III.238.

415 Alvarado episode: Sen. Int. Cttee., *Performance of Intelligence Agencies,* pp. 28- and 41-; Report p. 308-; XXV.647, author's interview with former U.S. Ambassador to Mexico Thomas Mann, 1978; *The Night Watch* by David Phillips (Atheneum,

New York, 1977), p. 141-; author's interviews with former staff at U.S. Embassy in Mexico; (Mann background) *Robert Kennedy and His Times* by Arthur Schlesinger, pp. 630-36; (Mann on Oswald's motivation, etc.) Mann cable to Secretary of State Rusk, November 28, 1963.

Note 100: The timing of Alvarado's visit to the Embassy is important. Whether he made up the story of his own volition or at the suggestion of others, he did so very quickly after the fact of an Oswald visit to Mexico became public knowledge. Although the story was slow in making news in the United States, it was in the Mexican newspaper *Excelsior* on the evening of November 24. Alvarado was telling his story about Oswald at the U.S. Embassy the next day at noon. Until the appearance of the *Excelsior* story, the Oswald visit to Mexico was theoretically known only to Oswald's wife, Cuban consulate staff, and U.S. intelligence. *Excelsior* cited a "high source" as the origin of its story. This was probably a Mexican government source, who in turn had learned the information from U.S. officials.

417 Nicaragua: Prouty, *op. cit.*, pp. 29, 41-, 388-; (Artime) "The Curious Intrigues of Cuban Miami" by Horace Sutton, *Saturday Review/World*, September 11, 1973; "Cuba on Our Mind" by Tad Szulc, *Esquire*, February 1974; article by Szulc, *New York Times*, June 9, 1973; (camps) HSCA X.67.

"Hunt in Mexico": *Compulsive Spy* by Tad Szulc (Viking Press, New York, 1974); Szulc letter to author, January 19, 1979.

419 Ford recollection: HSCA III.569.

Gutierrez: CD 564; Warren Commission staff memo by Coleman/ Slawson, April 1, 1964; CD 566.3-, CD 663.4; CD 896.3; CD 1029; CIA documents 965-927 AK, 972-927AR, 1179-995.

Cuban plane: Sen. Int. Cttee., *Performance of Intelligence Agencies*, p. 30; HSCA Report p. 117.

Lopez: HSCA Report p. 118.

420 Luce: author's interviews with Clare Boothe Luce, 1978; HSCA X.83; and interview by Earl Golz of *Dallas Morning News*, 1979; *Washington Star* (C-3), November 16, 1975; *ibid.* January 25, 1976.

422 Parrot Jungle: CD829; CD246.

November 26 news story: Pompano *Sun Sentinel;* also *Sun Sentinel* December 4; CD59; CD395; CD1020; CD810.

423 FBI memo re Sturgis: L. Patrick Gray to H.R. Haldeman, June 19, 1972 (Gray hearings, p. 47).

Note 101: There were other, more blatantly false attempts to attach

blame to the Castro regime. The Secret Service in Dallas intercepted a letter to Oswald mailed from Havana on November 28,
1963, and signed by one "Pedro Charles." "Charles" indicated in
the letter that Oswald had been hired by him to carry out a
mission involving "accurate shooting." (XXVI.148) Meanwhile,
another letter was sent to Robert Kennedy by a third party,
appearing to corroborate the supposed Oswald-Charles plot.
"Charles" was identified as a Castro agent (XXVI.148). Examination quickly established that the letters were mischievous,
when FBI tests showed they had been written on the same
typewriter. Like other letters sent as early as 1962 (HSCA
III.401-), the notes appear to have been a clumsy attempt at
fraud. They are certainly less sophisticated than some of the
other "Castro-did-it" leads.

Martino linked to Oswald Miami story: CD1020; Secret Service
report CO234030; FBI document 105-82555-2704; CD 691.2.

424 Martino background: FBI document 64-44828, dated July 31, 1959
(includes Martino-Trafficante connection); (hotel operated by
Trafficante) *Miami Herald*, July 9, 1959.

Bayo-Pawley Affair: article of that name by Miguel Acoca and
Robert K. Brown, *Soldier of Fortune*, spring 1976; article by
Gary Shaw and Larry Harris, *The Continuing Inquiry*, June 22,
1977; (Pawley and Dulles) HSCA X.83; see also UPI on Bayo-
Pawley, January 8, 1976.

426 Martino and Odio: XI.380; XXVI.738.

Luce: (Pawley) HSCA X.83; *Washingtonian Magazine*, Nov. 1980,
p. 224.

427 Martino FBI reports: CD 1020; CD 561; CD 961; CD 1169; (Castro
reference) CD 691; (electronics) Secret Service report
CD234030; FBI documents 105-8342, 105-82555-2704; (CIA electronics firm as cover) X.11.

Martino and Claasen: Claasen interview with Earl Golz of *Dallas
Morning News*, 1978.

428 Attwood efforts terminated: *The Red and the Blacks* by William
Attwood (Harper & Row, New York, 1967), p. 144; interview of
Attwood by author, 1978.

No acoustics analysis: HSCA Report p. 66 n1.

Rankin remark: *Inquest* by Edward Epstein, p. 103.

23. The Good Ole Boy

430 "Good Ole Boy" chapter title: This phrase is used in the South to
refer, somewhat affectionately, to a local "character." Detective

Combest of the Dallas police, whom I interviewed in 1978, described Ruby thus.

Chapter quote: HSCA Report p. 156.

Note 102: The most valuable investigative book on the Ruby case is *Who Was Jack Ruby?* (Everest House, New York, 1978) by the Washington correspondent Seth Kantor. Kantor was in Dallas on the day of the assassination and met Ruby, whom he knew from past journalism in Dallas, at Parkland Hospital. Goaded by the fact that the Warren Commission said he was wrong about seeing Ruby, Kantor researched the Ruby case for years. I am indebted to him for material in his book. Another industrious student of the Ruby area is Washington journalist William Scott Malone. Malone, who received grants for his work from the Fund for Investigative Journalism and the Center for National Security Studies, has worked on the case for the BBC, CBC, and CBS. I thank him, too, for his help.

Ruby interrogation: IV.196; V.181-.

431 Hubert/Griffin: memorandum to Willens and Rankin, May 14, 1964.

Griffin comment: Kantor, *op. cit.*, p. 159.

Hubert resignation: Kantor, *op. cit.*, p. 2.

Ruby request to go to Washington: V.194-.

432 Warren conclusion: Report p. 373.

HSCA: HSCA Report p. 147-.

Warren: (on organized crime) Report p. 801; (on Cuba) Report p. 369.

Youth: Report p. 786-; Kantor, *op. cit.*, p. 96.

433 Capone: XXIII.423.

Chicago union episode: Report p. 695; XXIII.433; Kantor, *op. cit.*, p. 99-.

RFK on Dorfman: Robert Kennedy, *op. cit.*, p. 84.

Ruby on leaving union: V.200; (stays on) Kantor, *op. cit.*, p. 100.

Ignored report: CD 1306 (FBI interview of Paul Roland Jones, June 26, 1964).

434 Miller: interview with author, 1978; also XXII.476 and CD 105.120 (FBI report, December 17, 1963).

Kutner: Moldea, *op. cit.*, p. 167.

Jones scheme: Third Interim Report, Kefauver Senate Committee, 82nd Congress, 1st Session; cited by Gus Taylor, *Organized Crime in America* (University of Michigan Press, 1973), p. 337-; Warren Report p. 793; (Guthrie) XXII.360; (Butler) Warren Report p. 793; (first Butler report) XXVI.342; (records missing) XXV.514-; HSCA Report p. 149; HSCA IX.513; (Butler) HSCA IX.153 and 158; (HSCA on Jones) HSCA IX.513; (Jones and

Ruby family) see *supra* and Warren Report p. 793; XXII.375. XXIII.203/374; (first Dallas club—Silver Spur) XXII.302.

Note 103: The HSCA Report dates the Jones bribery scheme as 1947 (HSCA Report p. 149). It actually took place at the end of 1946 (HSCA IX.516).

435 Labriola and Weinberg: XXII.300; (killed) *Captive City* by Ovid Demaris (Lyle Stuart, New York, 1969), pp. 5, 17, 169-.

Clubs: Report p. 794-.

Police: Report p. 800; Kantor p. 109; XXIII.78; XXV.290; HSCA IX.128; HSCA Report p. 156.

"pay-off man": "The Mafia, the CIA and the Kennedy Assassination" by Milton Viorst, in *The Washingtonian*, November 1975. "man with fix": XXIII.372.

436 Drug smuggling: XXIII.369.

Beard: interviewed by Earl Golz for *Dallas Morning News*, August 18, 1978; FBI document 602-982-243, June 10, 1976.

Note 104: After the assassination a woman reported meeting a man, who sounds like Ruby, in the Florida Keys in summer 1958. The man, whose name was "Jack," was then about to "run some guns to Cuba." He was described as a Dallas nightclub owner who came originally from Chicago. On the original evidence there was considerable doubt about this account because of inconsistencies in its telling. However, the FBI failed to find the witness' brother, James Woodard. In 1977, when he was traced, Woodard asserted that Ruby had been running guns. (XXVI.644; CD 360; interview with James Woodard by William Scott Malone, September 22-23 and October 10, 1977; author's interview with Woodard, 1978.)

FBI informant: XXVI.634—report of interview with Blaney Mack Johnson, December 1, 1963; article, "The Secret Life of Jack Ruby," by William Scott Malone, *New Times*, January 23, 1978; (Rothman's work) research of William Scott Malone.

437 McKeown: XXIII.158-; interview with author, 1978; HSCA Report p. 152; HSCA IX.587; *New Times*, June 24, 1977; Warren Commission memo by Hubert and Griffin, March 20, 1964; (date of McKeown-Ruby encounters) *ibid.*, and notes of interview of McKeown by Sen. Int. Cttee. investigator, 1975.

Note 105: The credibility of McKeown was rightly queried by the Assassinations Committee, due largely to his demeanor under interview. He has also claimed in recent years to have been visited by Lee Oswald—and that does not seem likely. McKeown first said this for television. His original remarks about Ruby, however, are to some extent corroborated by other evidence—in particular that of a police officer who helped a man—supposedly Ruby—to contact McKeown. I find him basically credible on the Ruby account.

Ruby on Cuba trip: V.200-; Report p. 801/812/370.

McWillie: "closest friend"—XXIII.166; V.201; "manager"—HSCA V.3; Rothman ownership—*Ramparts*, November 1973, p. 53; (syndicate connections) CD686D; (on Ruby visit) XXIII.37 and XXIII.170; HSCA V.2-.

Note 106: McWillie has said (HSCA V.10 and 26- and 167) that he arranged to bring over to Cuba Jack Ruby and a columnist called Tony Zoppi. His hope was that Zoppi would write useful publicity for the Tropicana, and Ruby's role was to persuade Zoppi to come. In the event Zoppi was unable to come, but Ruby, says McWillie, came anyway. As evidence to support this explanation of the Ruby trip, McWillie showed the Assassinations Committee a letter on the subject apparently written by Zoppi in 1976. (HSCA V.26) Zoppi himself gave an interview to Assassinations Committee staff (HSCA V.171) that throws doubt on McWillie's story. Zoppi confirms there was a plan to go to Cuba with Ruby, but it was planned for the winter, not the summer. His statement strongly suggests that Ruby's actual travel to Cuba was quite separate from the planned joint excursion (HSCA IX.164, 167).

438 Mynier: CD84.215, reporting interview with Mynier, November 26, 1963; also CD84.216.

McWillie response: HSCA V.154; (contradiction on phone) HSCA V.235.

Travel record: Havana arrival August 8—HSCA V.196 and 197; (September 11) HSCA Report p. 151 and see HSCA IX.159-; Agent—CD302.159; Labor Day—HSCA V.191 and Warren Report p. 802; postcard—HSCA V.195; exit card, September 11—HSCA V.197; return to Cuba—HSCA V.197; Mynier—CD 84.216; agent—CD 302.159; in Dallas (August 10)—XXIII.10 (August 21); HSCA V.204 (August 31); HSCA V.218; HSCA conclusion—HSCA Report p. 151; Panitz—CD 360.64; establishment frequented by Trafficante, etc.—research of William Scott Malone; by Baker—HSCA IX.323; HSCA and "Courier"—HSCA IX.177 and HSCA Report p. 152.

440 John Wilson: CIA document 206-83, November 26, 1963; FBI document 44-24016-255, November 26, 1963; CIA document 385-736, December 12, 1963; HSCA Report p. 153 and HSCA IX.175; Kantor, *op. cit.*, p. 132; (press accounts) *New York Times*, July 1, 1959; (detained with Wilson) Captain Paul Hughes, *ibid.* and FBI document 87-8756, October 23, 1959; (detention-camp superintendent) HSCA V.333; (Wilson on food) FBI document 44-24016-255; (two witnesses) Loran Hall in *Village Voice* article, October 3, 1977, and camp superintendent HSCA V.338; (Ruby at Capri) HSCA V.196; (Trafficante and Capri) *Time* magazine, March 2, 1959.

Note 107. In one of Ruby's notebooks, seized after he shot Oswald, police found the entry "October 29, 1963—John Wilson bond." (XIX.59, Armstrong Exhibit 5305Q). The note remains unexplained.

McWillie: on camp visits—HSCA V.166-; on Trafficante—HSCA IX.164 and HSCA V.165.

Trafficante: on Ruby—HSCA V.371; on McWillie—HSCA V.370.

441 HSCA on Ruby-Trafficante meeting: HSCA Report pp. 153 and 173.

Ruby-Trafficante associates: (Matthews) HSCA IX.524 and Report p. 173; *Dallas Morning News*, April 6, 1978; CD 86.198; (own lawyer) Frank Wright, interviewed by Dallas researcher Larry Harris, December 28, 1977; (Cuba plots) HSCA IX.532; interview by Harris of Alonzo Hudkins, January 3, 1978; HSCA IX.532; (Curry) *Dallas Morning News*, June 13, 1961; (Deauville) FBI document DL 44-1639, December 13, 1963; (operated by Trafficante) *Miami Herald*, July 9, 1959; (Dolan) HSCA Report pp. 156, and 173; HSCA IX.418-; (Todd) HSCA Report p. 173; HSCA IX.989.

442 Wilson never questioned, etc.: HSCA Report p. 153.

Ruby and Flynn: HSCA Report p. 151; HSCA V.218; CD 732; electronic purchases—"Rubygate" by William Scott Malone, *New Times*, January 23, 1978, citing Secret Service and FBI reports; conversation overheard—CD 302.159.

444 Edwards: Fensterwald-Ewing, *op. cit.*, p. 148.

Gaudet tip: CD 4.649, FBI document 44-2064; XXVI.337; author's interview with Gaudet, 1978; and see other Gaudet references in this book.

445 Former employee re guns: XXIV.345; HSCA IX.188.

Anti-Castro sentiments: FBI document DL44-1639, November 26, 1963, interview of B.J. Willis.

Ruby's fear: HSCA IX.162; and New York *Daily News*, July 18, 1976, p. 2, interview of Wally Weston.

Lawyer's note: Belli, *op. cit.*, p. 49.

445 Jail letter: *Ramparts*, February 1967, p. 26 (16-page letter to former jailmate).
Psychiatrist: "Examination of Jack Ruby," reported by Werner Tuteur, M.D.
Gangsters gather: Kantor, *op. cit.*, p. 20.
Phone records: HSCA Report p. 154: HSCA IX.188-; HSCA IV.496 and 562; (HSCA finding on calls) HSCA Report p. 156; (McWillie) CD84.212 and HSCA V.153; (Matthews' wife) HSCA IX.528 and 193; (Weiner) HSCA IX. 1042, 1054, 1062, 1057, and Moldea, *op. cit.*, p. 155; (Baker) HSCA Report p. 155 and see HSCA IX.274-; XXV.247; HSCA IV.566; (Kennedy and "lice") quoted in Kantor, *op. cit.*, p. 30; ("violence") Robert Kennedy, *op. cit.*, p. 60; (Baker call) XXV.244; (Ruby explanation of Baker call) V.200; (Baker version) HSCA IV.566; (Miller) HSCA Report p. 155 and HSCA IV.499 and HSCA IX.195; (Baker) HSCA Report p. 155 and see IX.274-; (Miller) HSCA Report p. 155 and HSCA IV.499 and HSCA IX.195.

446 *Note 108:* Ruby reportedly also spoke, in summer 1963 or later, with Lenny Patrick, firmly identified by the Assassinations Committee as one of two "executioners for the Chicago mob." The other was David Yaras, and both Patrick and Yaras had known Ruby since their youth in Chicago. Yaras was reportedly a hit man for Sam Giancana, the Chicago mob leader prominent in CIA-Mafia plots against Castro, and had himself been involved in Havana gambling operations before the Castro revolution. Yaras, who was also close to Jimmy Hoffa, was a target for investigation by Robert Kennedy's Justice Department team. On the eve of the assassination Yaras, like Ruby a week or so earlier, would talk by phone with the feared Barney Baker, Hoffa's aide. HSCA Report p. 150, HSCA IX.942, Warren XIV.443-, CD 1299, *Newsweek*, October 9, 1950, *Captive City*, by Ovid Demaris (Lyle Stuart, New York, 1969), p. 130; Moldea, *op. cit.*, p. 124; (and Hoffa) see reference in Moldea, *op. cit.*, and Kantor, *op. cit.*, p. 31; (call on eve of assassination) HSCA IV.567.

447 *Note 109:* It is conceivable that Ruby made a quick trip out of Dallas just before the assassination. According to witnesses interviewed by the FBI, he was seen in Las Vegas on November 17. McWillie, Ruby's friend and Cuban casino operator, lived there. The Warren Report dismissed such reports. However, while there is confusion about the precise date, it is not impossible that the visit took place. It may be significant that those who recalled the visit were employees of Las Vegas establishments, while those who denied it tend to have underworld connections. (XXIII.74-85 and Warren Report p. 802.)

Ruby habits: (keep fit) Warren Report p. 84; Kantor, *op. cit.*, p. 37; (pills) Kantor, *op. cit.*, pp. 31 and 24; HSCA IV.504.

Gruber/Jones episode: Kantor, *op. cit.*, p. 22 and HSCA IX.431; (Jones and Dallas) XXII.302; CD1262.10.

Purpose of calls: HSCA Report p. 155; (Weiner, Baker unsatisfactory replies) *ibid.;* (Hoffa Jr.) interviewed by Dan Moldea, December 27, 1977—in Moldea, *op. cit.*, p. 427n; (Hoffa threats) see Chapter 14, "The Mob Loses Patience."

448 *Note 110:* Whilst many of Ruby's calls may have concerned his troubles with the union AGVA, the Assassinations Committee noted that: "According to FBI records, AGVA has been used frequently by members of organized crime as a front for criminal activities;; (HSCA Report p. 156n).

Pecora: HSCA Report p. 155- and HSCA IX.192 and 194; and see *Clandestine America*, III.2, P. 7.

450 Ruby's finances: Warren Report p. 797-; Kantor p. 18; HSCA Report p. 156; (club for sale) XXIII.117; (call to IRS agent) XXIII.303, 383; (safe) Kantor, *op. cit.*, p. 24; (tax lawyer) Kantor, *op. cit.*, p. 24; (bank visit) *Dallas Morning News*, October 12, 1978.

Note 111: When arrested for the murder of Oswald, Ruby was carrying $3,000 (HSCA IX.2-7).

451 Paul dinner: Report p. 334; HSCA IX.978-; ("Connors") *Dallas Morning News*, March 9, 1978.

Campisi: HSCA Report p. 171n9 and HSCA IX.335-.

Civello: HSCA Report p. 171; *Clandestine America*, III.2, p. 7.

Meyers: Warren Report p. 334; XXV.191; XV.620; (seen in October) XXIII.85; HSCA IX.805; XXV.190; XXV.193.

Note 112: In 1978, Meyers told the Assassinations Committee he dined with Ruby on Saturday night, the eve of the Oswald murder. The Committee could not square this with Ruby's other known activities (HSCA IX.807).

Cabana Motel: Fensterwald, *op. cit.*, p. 288.

2.30 A.M. call: XXV.322.

452 Brading/Braden: (at Cabana) Brading statement to police, November 22, 1963; XXIV.202; XXV.626; (record) Miami Police Report (Eugene Brading), February 24, 1941; FBI report on Brading, August 11, 1951 (New York); Los Angeles police records, 1956 investigation of Arthur Clark, Brading; Federal Strike Force on Organized Crime, investigative records on Jim Braden, La Costa investigation 1971 and 1972; Noyes, *op. cit.*, Kantor, *op. cit.*, p. 32; (B. and Pereira case) Pereira *et al. v.* U.S.-347USI; (Dolan) HSCA, IX.424, HSCA Report pp. 156, 173; (detention of Brading) CD's 385/401/816; Dallas police report of Deputy C. L. Lewis, November 22, 1963; statement of Jim Braden, November 22, 1963; (departure of Brown) Kantor, *op. cit.*, p. 36, and Cabana Motel records researched by Earl Golz: (Braden on license) California Department of Motor Vehicles, License, Report of Jim Braden, 1963, H7511755; Request for license name change of Eugene Brading, September 19, 1963; (claimed visit to courthouse) Noyes, *op. cit.*, p. 73, and Moldea, *op. cit.*, p. 160; (Ferrie background) see *supra* Chapter 17, "Blind Man's Bluff in New Orleans"; (Père Marquette Building) Federal Parole Records, Eugene H. Brading; leasing and rental records, Père Marquette Building, 1963; CD 75; Noyes, *op. cit.*, p. 157-.

453 Ferrie and Chicago calls: Bell Telephone records in New Orleans, September 24, 1963, call from Ferrie (524-0147) to Chicago (312) WH4-4970; CE 2350; (West at Cabana) XXV.191.

Note 113: Research has suggested, as I have written, that the Chicago number Ferrie called was the apartment *block* Jean Aese West lived in, not necessarily the line to her apartment itself. However, in a public hearing, the Assassinations Committee Chief Counsel spoke as though the Committee had found it was the actual apartment number. This, HSCA sources state, was in error. Whether Ferrie's call actually went to West remains unknown. West is reportedly alive, outside the U.S.A., and clearly should be questioned. (HSCA IV.499 and 567; and HSCA IX.806.)

454 Ruby on November 22 (morning): Warren Report p. 334; Kantor, *op. cit.*, p. 38-; note for Ruby's movements see generally HSCA IX.1080 and 1101.

Ruby at hospital: Kantor, *op. cit.*, p. 41; and see HSCA V.179 and HSCA Report p. 158.

455 *Note 114:* Ruby himself denied visiting Parkland Hospital (HSCA V.179), and the Warren Commission chose to take his word for it rather than believe Kantor's statement that he saw Ruby there (Report p. 335-). However, following Kantor's researches, the

Assassinations Committee and former Warren Commission counsel Burt Griffin decided Kantor's version was more likely to be correct (HSCA Report p. 159 and Griffin letter to Kantor, May 2, 1977, cited by Kantor, *op. cit.*, p. 202). Kantor, a respected correspondent, knew Ruby quite well from his working days in Dallas and had no reason to make up the story. The significance of the incident today is that Ruby denied the hospital encounter with Kantor. Why did he lie about this apparently minor detail? And what does the lie imply about his veracity on other points concerning his activities in those vital days?

Ruby's emotional performance: Report p. 337-; (to rabbi) Report p. 340; (at radio station) Report p. 343: (Ainsworth) FBI document DL-441639, report of November 25, 1963.

Gruber call: Report p. 337.

Paul call: Report p. 337.

456 Police station sightings: Report p. 340-; analyzed by Kantor, *op. cit.*, p. 45, and by Meagher, *op. cit.*, Chapter 25.

Ruby on Fair Play for Cuba: Report p. 342.

Gun on person, November 22: CD1252.9; HSCA V.179.

At radio station: Report p. 343.

457 Olsen: Report p. 343.

Note 115: It may be that Ruby met with Olsen for much more than an hour. They talked in a garage, and the garage attendant's statement—coupled with the fact that Ruby omitted the episode in answers given to the FBI—suggests to some researchers that this was no casual encounter (XXV.521 and CD 1252.10 and CD 1253.4). Ruby was at radio station KLIF at 2.00 A.M. and at the Dallas *Times-Herald* around 4.00 A.M. (XV.254, 483, 532; XXIV.126, 162; XXV.228; XV.557, 566; XXVI.238; XXV.232; CD 360. 132; CD 105.325).

Olsen—renting room from Cheek: Shaw-Harris, *op. cit.*, p. 102; Jones, *op. cit.*, Vol. I.92-; (Cheek meeting Ruby) Report p. 363; (Olsen at time of Tippit shooting) XIV.264; (leaves Dallas) Jones, *op. cit.*, Vol. I.85-.

Note 116: Apart from Mrs. Cheek's acquaintance with Jack Ruby, it is of interest that she was known to take Cuban lodgers. One FBI report, albeit referring to a time well before the assassination, refers to wealthy Cubans who stayed at the house and may have been politically involved. One was arrested during his stay (CD 205.453).

Night movements: Report p. 344.

Officers discuss move: Kantor, *op. cit.*, p. 53.

Ruby inquiries: Report p. 346.

Ruby at police station at 4.00 P.M.: Meagher, *op. cit.*, Chapter 25; Kantor, *op. cit.*, p. 54-.

Meyers call: Report p. 349.

458 Call sequence starting 10:44 P.M.: CD1138.3; XIII.247; XIV.620; XXV.251; CD75.227.290; CD301.86; XXV.251; XXV.252; CD360.132; CD1252.12; XIV.605; XIV.620; CD223.82-; CD1253.6; XXV.251; Report p. 350; (and Paul) HSCA IX.780.

Note 117: Evidence gathered by Congress' Assassinations Committee raises new questions about Ralph Paul aside from his activities during the assassination weekend. This concerns Officer Tippit, the policeman killed in a shooting incident soon after the President's murder. Apart from his business connection with the Bull Pen at Arlington, Paul had long been associated with Austin's Bar-B-Cue. Tippit worked as a Peace Officer at the Bar-B-Cue for three years, and was still working there in November 1963. He had been having a protracted affair with a Bar-B-Cue female employee. Like Paul, Tippit lived near the Bar-B-Cue. In view of all this they must surely have known each other. It is an acquaintance which, in the light of Paul's contacts with Ruby at the time of the assassination, deserves further investigation. (Paul died in 1974.) (HSCA XII.36-42, Texas Attorney General's files, 9.)

Ferrie: (movements) *Counterplot* by Edward Epstein, p. 37; CD75; *Ramparts*, January 1968; "The Persecution of Clay Shaw," *Look*, August 29, 1969; FBI reports from New Orleans, November 26, 1963. (*Note*, Jack Ruby, in Dallas, also frequented skating rinks [XXIII.344].)

459 Ruby on November 24: Report p. 353; (cleaning lady) XIII.231-; (TV men) analyzed by Meagher, *op. cit.*, p. 449; (minister) XII.75 and 294; (stripper call) Report p. 353.

Senator reaction to news: Kantor, *op. cit.*, p. 217; XXIV.164-330; XXVI.569-.

460 Ruby and cash: Kantor, *op. cit.*, p. 64-.

Western Union transaction: Report p. 219; (possible slight time error) HSCA IV.587 (Revill).

Howard: XXIV.135.

Combest: Doubleday edition of Warren Report, New York, 1964 (caption to picture of Oswald shooting).

461 Ruby on intending three shots: Kantor, p. 113.

Howard: Kantor, p. 76.

Ruby note: *Newsweek*, March 27, 1967; HSCA Report p. 158;

interview with Joe Tonahill by William Scott Malone, 1978.
Ruby means of entry findings: (police report) HSCA IV.578; (Warren) Warren Report p. 216; (HSCA) HSCA Report p. 157.
Vaughn: XII.359; (four policemen) Pierce XII.340; (Putnam) CE 5073; (Maxey) XII.287; (Flusche) *Dallas Morning News*, March 25, 1979, HSCA IV.595-; (taxi driver) Tasker—XXIV.488; (journalist) McGarry—XXIV.465; incident analyzed HSCA Report p. 156 and HSCA and see latest analysis in depth by HSCA, HSCA IX.132; also Meagher, *op. cit.*, Chapter 24.

462 Sorrels: HSCA IX.137; and Kantor, *op. cit.*, p. 70.
Hall: XV.64-7 and HSCA IX.137.
Ruby refusals: HSCA IX.137-; HSCA Report p. 157n7; HSCA IV.589.
Dean report: XII.432, 439. (the report was filed on November 26, but in his Warren Commission testimony Dean said he had actually dictated that report on the preceding day.)
McMillon, Clardy, Archer: XX.564; XII.412; XII.403; Archer exhibits analyzed in Meagher, *op. cit.*, p. 407-.

463 *Note 118:* A former policeman, Napoleon Daniels, had gone to the police station to watch the transfer and was in the street near the ramp. He made a number of statements and at some points has appeared to suggest that he saw a man like Ruby slip down the ramp. The Warren Commission discounted his statements, which included numerous inconsistencies (HSCA IX.135-). See also HSCA IV.531 and 590.
Griffin: Kantor, *op. cit.*, p. 144; ("damned liar") XII.329; (Dean questioning) author's interviews with Griffin and Dean, 1978; Warren Commission memo for files, March 30 and 31, 1964; *Dallas Times-Herald*, April 5, 1964; (Dean on test) HSCA Report p. 158, and *Dallas Morning News*, March 25, 1979; (Vaughn test) Kantor, *op. cit.*, p. 74; (Commission lawyer on Dean) Kantor, *op. cit.*, p. 154.
Ruby and police: Meagher, *op. cit.*, p. 422-; HSCA IX.128; Kantor, *op. cit.*, pp. 148, 56; (Dean) Tyler *Courier-Times-Telegraph* (1000N069), 1977; *Dallas Morning News*, March 25, 1979; (on protecting officers) Kantor, *op. cit.*, p. 216, quoting Dallas police report of December 4, 1963.

465 9:00 A.M. orders: Kantor, *op. cit.*, p. 60-.
Harrison: (Ruby sheltering) Kantor, *op. cit.*, p. 71; (analysis) Kantor, *op. cit.*, pp. 60 and 145-; (Revill) XXII.81; (Miller) Kantor, *op. cit.*, p. 146-.

466 *Note 119:* Kantor (*op. cit.*, p. 61) says the result of Harrison's lie-detector test was "not conclusive." Captain Revill of the Dallas police says he passed the test (HSCA IV.589). Perhaps, given that this was in passing in testimony, Revill meant that Harrison passed the test on the specific point of whether Harrison noticed Ruby behind him just before the shooting. (He said he did not.)

467 Butler: Meagher, *op. cit.*, p. 423-.

Dean: (and Civello) *Dallas Morning News*, March 25, 1979; (Civello and) HSCA Report p. 171; (Civello and Ruby according to mutual employee) CD84.91-; (Jones) report of FBI agents Underhill and Morgan, June 26, 1964; (dinner) *Dallas Morning News*, March 25, 1979.

468 HSCA decision on ramp: HSCA Report p. 157 and HSCA IX.143-; (Dean on door) HSCA IX.144.

Dean and HSCA: HSCA IX139; (Ruby and assistance) HSCA Report p. 157 and HSCA IX.146.

Note 120: During the testimony of police Captain Revill to the Assassinations Committee, there was discussion suggesting that Dean removed guards from an interior door into the basement—about twenty minutes before Ruby shot Oswald (HSCA IV.590).

469 Ruby statements: ("used for purpose") Kantor, *op. cit.*, p. 209; (psychiatrist) "Examination of Jack Ruby," reported by Werner Tuteur M.D.; (during transfer) Meagher, *op. cit.*, p. 453.

Murtaugh: interview with Earl Golz of *Dallas Morning News*, 1979 (unpublished); interview with William Scott Malone, 1979; Zodiac News Service, August 24, 1974; interview by Sarah Holland, 1980.

Doyle interest: FBI documents 44-1559, April 24, 1964; 44-24016 471, November 29, 1963; 44-24016 624, December 10, 1963; unnumbered document November 30, 1963.

Note 121: Browder also crops up in the Assassinations Committee staff study of George de Mohrenschildt, Oswald's mentor in Dallas. In the months before the assassination, de Mohrenschildt was involved with Haitian banker Charles Clemard in discussions with U.S. Army Intelligence. Some time after the assassination, and while de Mohrenschildt was still in Haiti, Charles paid $24,000 to Browder. Browder, on being asked about his activity by the Assassinations Committee, confirmed that he did run munitions and aircraft in the anti-Castro Cuban cause. He asserted that these activities included assistance from the CIA (HSCA XII.59).

470 Commission request to CIA re Ruby: XXVI.467-; CIA document

442, memo from Karamessines to Rankin, September 15, 1964; and see HSCA XI.286, 456.

Davis: HSCA IX.183; Ruby mention of Davis—Warren Commission internal memo, March 19, 1964, by Hubert and Griffin; Kantor, *op. cit.*, pp. 14-129, 137-; author's interview with Seth Kantor, 1979; FBI document (NI) 105-82555, December 20, 1963.

470 QJ/WIN: Sen. Int. Cttee. *Assassination Plots*, pp. 37, 43-, 182.

Note 122: the agent QJ/WIN has yet to be publicly identified. In 1979 researcher Gary Shaw tentatively suggested he may be former French army captain, alleged narcotics smuggler, and OAS activist Jean Souêtre. CIA records suggest that Souêtre was in the Dallas area on the day of the Kennedy assassination and left precipitately afterward. The FBI, however, has said the man in Dallas was not Souêtre but Michel Roux, another Frenchman whose name happens to coincide with an alias Souêtre used. (*Continuing Inquiry*, III.10; CIA document 632-796; FBI documents 105-128529-4; interview with FBI by Earl Golz of *Dallas Morning News*, 1979.)

Note 123: Robert McKeown, who said Ruby once came to him for help connected with Cuba, has been quoted (long before the Thomas Davis matter was known publicly) as saying that Ruby thought McKeown's name was Davis when he visited in 1959 (HSCA IX.591).

Davis death: Kantor, *op. cit.*, p. 16.

CIA failure to tell Commission re Ruby/Trafficante allegation: HSCA Report p. 153.

Helms secrecy re plots: Sen. Int. Cttee. *Assassination Plots* p. 92 *et seq.*

Roselli on Ruby: quoted by Jack Anderson in *Washington Post*, September 7, 1976.

Note 124: In 1978 Roselli's name was linked to Ruby's in a press report quoting Army Intelligence and Justice Department sources. The report said that Ruby was identified meeting Roselli in Miami hotels during the two months before the Kennedy assassination. The report remains unsubstantiated. ("The Secret Life of Jack Ruby" by William Scott Malone, *New Times*, January 23, 1978.)

471 Ruby TV interview: KTVT, Fort Worth, Texas, September 9, 1965 (taped in Dallas County Courthouse).

24. Aftermath

473 Hoover quote: V.100 (Hoover testimony to Warren Commission).

Media reaction to HSCA Report: *Dallas Morning News*, July 22, 1979; *Newsweek*, July 30, 1979; *Time*, July 30, 1979; *New York Times Magazine*, July 15, 1979.

Blakey: int. for DIR radio, New York, August 1979—full transcript in *Clandestine America*, vol. III, no. 3, Jan/Feb 1980.

Acoustics/Barber: NAS Report, 1982; (Barber) *Nova* program on PBS, Nov 15 1988.

Barger: int, May 3 1989.

Blakey: int. May 3 1989.

Inside Edition, July 1989.

477 "Two coffins" & medical controversy: see Lifton, David, in Bibliography. The 1988 edition of his book contains autopsy photographs, and all interviews here, except where indicated; vital supportive reporting from *JFK: An Unsolved Murder*, reported by Sylvia Chase, and produced by Stanhope Gould, KRON TV (San Francisco), November 1988; see also Thompson, Josiah, in Bibliography, for thorough early study of medical area; McClelland—VI.33, (drawing) Thompson, 140; Clark—Lifton, 318; Parkland descriptions—see Lifton & Livingstone/Groden (cf. Bibliography); bone fragment—Lifton, 316; Hill—Livingstone/Groden, 388; Jacqueline Kennedy—Lifton, 312 & *Nova* (PBS TV), Nov. 15 1988; Bashour—Livingstone/Groden, 39; Sibert/O'Neill Report—Lifton, 172; & author's Sibert conversation, Sept 28 1985; Parkland doctors on PBS—*Nova* program, Nov 15 1988; McClelland int., May 4 1989; Gould & Chase—ints., May 4 1989; McClelland re. "Plot"—Livingstone/Groden 394 & int. May 4 1989.

Tippit: research summary prepared for author by Larry Harris, April 1989; & see Hurt, pp. 163-167.

488 *Note 125:* Congress' Assassinations Committee staff studied deaths of witnesses or potential witnesses in the Kennedy case and concluded that there was no evidence to link the deaths with the case itself. A much-quoted London *Sunday Times* report—suggesting the deaths were actuarially improbable—was shown to be erroneous (HSCA IV.454-).

489 Banister: author's interview with Delphine Roberts.

Ferrie: (Martin) HSCA Report p. 143; HSCA X.129-; (search, etc.) Secret Service report (Control No. 620; N.O. Police report K-126 34-63; N.O. FBI file 89-69; CD 75; HSCA X.105-; (former neighbor) HSCA X.114; (landlady) HSCA X.113; (Marcello hearing—alibi) HSCA X.114; HSCA X.105; HSCA IX.74 and HSCA Report p. 170, HSCA X.127; (ties to end of life) HSCA X.111; (1966) Garrison, *op. cit.*, p. 110, and *Counterplot* by Edward Epstein, p. 37-; (death) Garrison, *op. cit.*, p. 111, and James/

Wardlaw, *op. cit.*, p. 40; (Garrison and Roselli) HSCA
X.190n55.

Note 126: Oswald's library reading has thrown up several tantalizing
leads. Perhaps the most intriguing—and frustrating—concerns a
politically left-wing book called *The Shark and the Sardines* by
Dr. Juan Arevalo, former President of Guatemala. An FBI check
in February 1964 (XXV.901) established that Oswald took the
book out of the Dallas Public Library on November 6, 1963, and
should have returned it on the 13th. The book was still overdue
months later and was not among his effects found in Dallas. An
independent researcher discovered, however, that some unknown person did return the book after the FBI check. Had the
FBI ordered a watch for the book's return, one might have
identified some unknown acquaintance of the alleged assassin.
No such precaution was taken, and the return of the book remains mysterious (see Newman, *op. cit.*, pp. 107-, 124, 486-.).

del Valle: Miami Police Homicide Report, February 23, 1967; *National Enquirer*, April 27, 1967; *New York Daily News*, January
8, 1961 (background); (link to Trafficante) FBI document
105-95677; (sought) Fensterwald, *op. cit.*, p. 303.

491 Brading/Braden: see sources for Brading/Braden in sourcing of
Chapter 23; current situation—HSCA sources.

Hall: (1978) *Dallas Morning News*, September 17, 1978; (money
offer) *National Enquirer* interview with Hall, September 1, 1968;
("fabrication") HSCA Report p. 138.

Note 127: Joseph Milteer, the right-wing extremist who said two
weeks before the assassination that the President's murder was
"in the working," told a police informant afterward that "Everything ran true to form. I guess you thought I was kidding you
when I said he would be killed from a window with a high-
powered rifle." Asked whether he was guessing when he made
the original remark, Milteer replied, "I don't do any guessing."
According to the informant, Milteer said there was no need "to
'worry about Lee Harvey Oswald getting caught because he
doesn't know anything." The right wing, said Milteer, was "in the
clear," adding that "the patriots have outsmarted the Communist
group in order that the Communists would carry out the plan
without the right wing becoming involved." When the FBI questioned Milteer a few days after the assassination, he denied
making all these remarks. He died in 1974 and William Somer-
sett, the informant, is also dead. The Assassinations Committee
was unable to establish any connection between Milteer and

other elements of the case. HSCA Report p. 234n3 and 232-; CD.137.120; CD 1347.121; this page withheld till 1976; (denial) Cd 20.24; author's interview with former Miami police intelligence captain, Charles Sapp, 1978; HSCA III.447.

492 de Mohrenschildt: *Fort Worth Star-Telegram*, May 11, 1978; UPI, July 27, 1978; *Washington Star*, March 31, 1977; author's interviews with Assassinations Committee member and staff; author's interview with Jeanne de Mohrenschildt.

Note 128: The Assassinations Committee noted information that a large sum of money (allegedly at least $200,000) was paid into a de Mohrenschildt account in Haiti shortly after the assassination. The original source of this allegation is apparently Jacqueline Lancelot, a businesswoman reportedly associated with a number of intelligence personnel. The money was subsequently paid out, but not necessarily to de Mohrenschildt. Lancelot has not been interviewed in person, and the story is secondhand (HSCA XII.61).

Carlos Prio: HSCA staff source; *Rolling Stone*, June 2, 1977; *Yipster Times*, spring 1977; letter from FBI Director Hoover to Warren Commission chief counsel, April 17, 1964, *True*, August 1974.

493 Hoffa: (death) Moldea, *op. cit.*; "Provenzano Comeback Reported," *New York Times*, December 6, 1975; *Clandestine America*, Vol. III, NO. 1, p. 9, spring 1979; Sheridan, *op. cit.*, p. 300/356/408; (RFK suspicions) *Dallas Times-Herald*, March 17, 1979; (comment on JFK's death) Schlesinger, *op. cit.*, p. 616.

Crimaldi: Moldea, *op. cit.*, pp. 386-, 402; and see Crimaldi biography by J. Kidner (in bibliography).

494 Granello and Plumeri: Moldea, *op. cit.*, pp. 277, 386.

Yaras: (dead) Moldea, *op. cit.*, p. 387.

Nicoletti: *Rolling Stone*, June 2, 1977.

Weiner: HSCA Report pp. 155 and 159.

Giancana: *Chicago Daily News*, June 20, 1975; *Chicago Tribune*, June 20, 1975; *Washington Star*, December 29, 1975; Hougan, *op. cit.*, p. 346; author's interview with former 1975 witness before Sen. Int. Cttee. *Assassination Plots*. Witness, whose name is known to investigators, preferred to remain anonymous here.

Crimaldi: (on Giancana death) Moldea, *op. cit.*, p. 402.

495 Moceri: Moldea, *op. cit.*, p. 401-.

Roselli: *Washington Post*, August 5 and 22, and (Style section). September 12, 1976; Hougan, *op. cit.*, p. 348; research of William Scott Malone, Miami, 1978; (information to government) *Washington Post*, August 22, 1976, and *ibid.*; (Jack Anderson).

September 7 1976; (dining with Trafficante and lured to death) HSCA V.366; *New York Times*, February 25, 1977; *Robert Kennedy and His Times*, by Arthur Schlesinger, p. 549; (boat) Moldea, *op. cit.*, p. 433n; (Costa Rica) Hougan, *op. cit.*, p. 345-.

496 Regis Kennedy: (Ferrie alibi) HSCA pp. 105 and 114n5; (and Marcello) HSCA IX.70; (and threat) HSCA IX.81.

Sullivan: (death) *Washington Star*, July 16, 1978; (reply to question) HSCA III.488, Thomas Powers, *op. cit.*, p. 365n22.

Pawley: *Washington Post*, January 9, 1977.

Hunt: (Guatemala) Howard Hunt, *op. cit.*, (Banister) *Ramparts*, June 1967; (Mexico City) letter to author from Tad Szulc, January 19, 1979.

498 *Note 129:* In 1975 the name "Hunt"—for whatever reason—featured in a bizarre development. An anonymous sender in Mexico City sent U.S. researchers a copy of a letter purportedly written by Lee Oswald on November 8, 1963, two weeks before the Kennedy assassination. It reads:

"Dear Mr. Hunt,

I would like information concerding [*sic*] my position.

I am asking only for information

I am asking that we discuss the matter fully before any steps are taken by me or anyone else.

Thank you,

Lee Harvey Oswald"

Three handwriting experts in 1977 concluded that the letter was "the authentic writing of Lee Harvey Oswald and was written by him." In 1978, experts commissioned by Congress' Assassinations Committee expressed doubts but were unable to reach any firm conclusion about the authenticity of the letter. However, the misspelling of "concerning" mirrors an identical error in a letter Oswald wrote in 1961.

If the letter is genuine, Oswald wrote it two days after visiting the Dallas office of the FBI to leave the note the FBI destroyed before the assassination. There is nothing to indicate the identity of the "Hunt" to whom the letter—bogus or genuine—is supposedly addressed. Speculation has linked it as much to right-wing Dallas millionaire H. L. Hunt, whose offices Jack Ruby visited the day before the assassination, as to former CIA officer and Watergate burglar Howard Hunt. H. L. Hunt is dead. (Anonymous note) mailed August 18, 1975, to three researchers; (facsimile of note) HSCA IV.337; (1977 conclusion) *Dallas Morning News*, September 26, 1978, reporting conclusions of experts retained by that newspaper; (1978 conclusions of HSCA panel) HSCA IV357; ("uncertain") IV.361; (H. L. Hunt office visit by Ruby) XXV.194; (authentic 1961 letter) XVI.705— undated letter of May 1961.

Note 130: Extensive research into Frank A. Fiorini's assumption of the name "Sturgis" has been done by A. J. Weberman, co-author of *Coup d'Etat in America* (Third Press, New York, 1975). Weberman notes today that Fiorini's parents split up in the 1920s, and his mother took a second husband called Sturgis in 1937. From that time on, therefore, it would have been normal enough for Fiorini to have started using the name Sturgis. Weberman notes that Sturgis' legal adoption of the name Sturgis—in 1952— may well therefore have postdated his actual usage of the name by many years. Weberman believes this is compelling evidence— in addition to other material—that Frank Fiorini/Sturgis is the Hank Sturgis of Hunt's book *Bimini run*, published in 1949.

Sturgis/Fiorini: (Hunt on meeting) *New York Post*, February 6, 1975; (Sturgis version) interview by Andrew St. George. *True magazine, August 1974 (p. 76); (on November 22) Canfield and Weberman, op. cit.*, p. 103; (Cellula Fantasma operation) HSCA X.42.

499 Trafficante: (death) briefing for author by former HSCA investigator Gaeton Fonzi, April 1989; (HSCA hearing of March 16, 1977; (replies in 1978) HSCA V.375, 373, 371; (FBI surveillance) HSCA source who heard tape, in interview with author, May 1989.

Marcello: interview John Davis, May 2 1989, & Davis' book *Mafia Kingfish*, see Bibliography; (tomato salesman) *supra* and HSCA IX.65; (Defense Department) *Clandestine America*, III.2, p. 5; (Ferrie) HSCA Report p. 170; (denial) HSCA IX.84; (lawyer's visit to FBI) FBI (Tampa, Florida) report to Director, April 11, 1967, on interview with lawyer Frank Ragano.

500 Marcello (and HSCA): HSCA Report p. 169.

De Laparra, Tregle, Sumner, Hauser, surveillance etc.: see John Davis' *Mafia Kingfish, op. cit.;* also author's int. Davis, May 2 1989.

Blakey disappointment: int. May 3 1989.

Veciana shooting: *Miami Herald*, September 22 and 23, 1979.

"Bishop": HSCA Report pp. 135, 136n23, and n24, 197n2; HSCA X.37-; author's interviews with Antonio Veciana, 1978, and with HSCA staff, 1979 and 1989; Kail & de Mohrenschildt) HSCA XII.57; int. Sen. Schweiker, 1979: Who Killed JFK?, by Gaeton Fonzi, November 1980; research by David Leigh for *Washington*

Post, June/July 1980; (Sturgis name in Hunt book) *Bimini Run* by Howard Hunt, 1949; (Phillips on "Knight") Phillips, *op. cit.*, p. 88n; (Helms as Knight) Thomas Powers *op. cit.*, see Phillips refs.; interview Blakey, 1979.

512 *Note 131:* As noted, although the Assassinations Committee calls Phillips merely "the retired officer" in its Report (p. 136), the staff report to which it relates names Phillips clearly (HSCA X.46).

"Bishop"/Veciana intermediary: author's research and int. "Fabiola", Puerto Rico, May 28 1980; (Prewett) interview June 1980; int. "Cross", June 1980; (Terpil) interview & notes of Jim Hougan, 1983; (disinformation contacts of Phillips) interviews HSCA staff, 1980 & 1989; (Phillips on "conspiracy") information supplied by Kevin Walsh to author, May 1989; former wife interview, 1980.

Mexico City: interviews HSCA staff, 1980 & 1989; (Blakey) ints. 1980 & 1989; ("car" at border) cited as Control 16552, from Mexico City to Secretary of State, Nov. 23 1963, 11.32 p.m., in research for Assassinations Archives and Research Center by Ginger Lawson, Aug. 31 1988; (footnote re destruction of photos) HSCA Report p. 125.n18.

David/Nicoli scenario: author's conversations with Steve Rivele and James Lesar, 1987-1989.

Exner: *People* magazine, February 29 1988, and subsequent research by author and Mark Allen, 1988; & Phil Donahue TV show transcript 030188 (1988); (Why folly?) see *People* supra, & *Goddess, The Secret Lives of Marilyn Monroe*, by Anthony Summers, Macmillan N.Y., 1985, p. 237.

Harvey: *Washington Post*, October 10, 1976; & author's interviews with HSCA staff, 1980 & 1989; (Harvey in missile crisis) RFK, in recorded interview by J. B. Martin, April 30, 1964, Vol. III, p. 22-; JFK Oral History Program; Senate Intelligence Committee, *Assassination Plots*, p. 148n; *Robert Kennedy and His Times* by Arthur Schlesinger, p. 979; ("Executive Action") Sen. Intelligence Cttee. *Assassination Plots*, p. 181; (Castro plots) *ibid.*, p. 83-; Thomas Powers, *op. cit.*, p. 142.

"Bender": HSCA X.15; & Johnson, *op. cit.*, p. 75-.

Note 132: A footnote in later editions of *The Bay of Pigs* by Haynes Johnson (W. W. Norton & Co., Inc., first ed., 1964) states that on initial publication of the book, "the CIA let it be known that Frank Bender denied—in writing—making such statements." This reported denial need not be taken as a convincing refutation of the story—as the categorical nature of the quotation by the Assassinations Committee indicates (HSCA X.15 and 18n103).

Kennedy and McCone: as told by Walter Sheridan in recorded interview by Roberta Green, June 12, 1970. RFK Oral History Program.

McCone on two gunmen: journal of Arthur Schlesinger, December 9, 1963.

Griffin: BBC TV interview for *Panorama* Michael Cockerell and the author, January 1977.

Committee on CIA-Mafia-Cuban plots: HSCA Report p. 115.

Blakey on nuclear crisis: conversation with author, 1980.

Warren: Warren Commission internal memorandum by Melvin Eisenberg, February 17, 1964. "not in your lifetime": New York *Times*, February 5, 1964, p. 19, col. 7.

Assassinations Committee records dispute: House rule No. 36. first Blakey quote—affidavit for Civil Action No. 81-1206. Mark Allen v. F.B.I. et al., Feb. 15 1982; second Blakey quote—interview with Earl Golz, 1979; Blakey opposition—interview Kevin Walsh, & interview Blakey, June 1989; former staff—interviews of five members, July 1989; Blakey on "embarrassment"—Golz interview *supra*; "64 Congressmen"—supporters of H. Res. 160 (April 13 1983), & of H. Res. 173 (May 15 1985).

Cronkite: *Nova* program, PBS TV, November 15, 1980.

Lopez: in response to request for summary response, May 18 1989.

Fonzi: The *Washingtonian*, November 1980.

Blakey: DIR radio interview, *supra*.

Odio: filmed interview with author, 1978.

Bibliography

Works Related to the Assassination

Anson, Robert Sam, *They've Killed the President.* New York: Bantam, 1975.

Belin, David W., *November 22, 1963: You Are the Jury.* New York: Quadrangle Books, 1973.

——*Final Disclosure,* New York: Scribners, 1988.

Bishop, Jim, *The Day Kennedy Was Shot.* New York: Funk & Wagnalls, 1968; Bantam, 1969.

Blakey, Robert, and Richard Billings, *The Plot to Kill The President,* New York: Times Books, 1981.

Blumenthal, Sid, with Harvey Yazijian, *Government by Gunplay: Assassination Conspiracy Theories from Dallas to Today.* New York: Signet, 1976.

Bringuier, Carlos, *Red Friday: November 22, 1963.* Chicago: C. Hallberg, 1969.

Buchanan, Thomas C. *Who Killed Kennedy?* New York: Putnam, 1964; London: Secker & Warburg, 1964; New York: MacFadden, 1965.

Canfield, Michael, with Alan J. Weberman, *Coup d'Etat in America: The CIA and the Assassination of John F. Kennedy.* New York: Third Press, 1975.

Curry, Jesse, *JFK Assassination File: Retired Dallas Police Chief Jesse Curry Reveals His Personal File.* American Poster and Publishing Co., 1969.

Cutler, Robert B. *The Flight of CE-399: Evidence of Conspiracy.* Omni-Print, 1969; Beverly, Mass: Cutler Designs, 1970.

Davis, John H., *Mafia Kingfish: Carlos Marcello and the Assassination of John F. Kennedy,* New York: McGraw-Hill, 1988.

Eddowes, Michael, *Khrushchev Killed Kennedy.* Dallas: self-published, 1975.

November 22, How They Killed Kennedy. London: Neville Spearman Ltd., 1976.

———, *The Oswald File.* New York: Clarkson N. Potter, 1977; New York: Ace, 1978.

Epstein, Edward J., *Counterplot.* New York: Viking, 1969.

———, *Inquest: The Warren Commission and the Establishment of Truth.* New York: Bantam, 1966; Viking, 1969.

———, *Legend: The Secret World of Lee Harvey Oswald.* New York: McGraw-Hill, 1978; London: Hutchinson, 1978, and Arrow, 1978.

Feldman, Harold, *Fifty-one Witnesses: The Grassy Knoll.* San Francisco: Idlewild Publishers, 1965.

Fensterwald, Bernard Jr., with Michael Ewing, *Coincidence or Conspiracy?* (for the Committee to Investigate Assassinations). New York: Zebra Books, 1977.

Flammonde, Paris, *The Kennedy Conspiracy: an Uncommissioned Report on the Jim Garrison Investigation.* New York: Meridith, 1969.

Ford, Gerald R., with John R. Stiles, *Portrait of the Assassin.* New York: Simon & Schuster, 1965; Ballantine, 1966.

Fox, Sylvan, *The Unanswered Questions About President Kennedy's Assassination.* New York: Award Books, 1965 and 1975.

Garrison, Jim, *A Heritage of Stone.* New York: Putnam, 1970; Berkeley, 1972.

———*On the Trail of the Assassins,* Sheridan Square Press, 1988.

Groden, Robert J. & Livingstone, Harrison E., *High Treason, The Assassination of President John F. Kennedy—What Really Happened,* N.Y.: Conservatory Press, 1989.

Hannibal, Edward, with Robert Boris, *Blood Feud.* New York: Ballantine, 1979.

Hepburn, James (pseudonym), *Farewell America.* Liechtenstein: Frontiers Publishing Co., 1968.

Hockberg, Sandy, with James T. Vallière, *The Conspirators (The Garrison Case).* New York: special edition of *Win* magazine, February 1, 1969.

Hurt, Henry, *Reasonable Doubt,* New York: Holt, Rinehart and Winston, 1985.

James, Rosemary, with Jack Wardlaw, *Plot or Politics? The Garrison Case and Its Cast.* New Orleans: Pelican Publishing, 1967.

Joesten, Joachim, *The Garrison Enquiry: Truth & Consequences.* London: Peter Dawnay, 1967.

———, *Marina Oswald.* London: Peter Dawnay, 1967.

———, *Oswald, Assassin or Fall-guy?* New York: Marzani and Munsell, 1964.

———, *Oswald: The Truth*. London: Peter Dawnay, 1967.

Jones, Penn Jr., *Forgive My Grief* (Vols. I-IV). *Midlothian* (Texas) *Mirror*. Available from Penn Jones.

Kirkwood, James, *American Grotesque: An Account of the Clay Shaw-Jim Garrison Affair in New Orleans*. New York: Simon & Schuster, 1970.

Lane, Mark, *Rush to Judgment*. New York: Holt, Rinehart & Winston, 1966; London: Bodley Head, 1966.

———, *A Citizen's Dissent*. New York: Holt, Rinehart & Winston, 1966; Fawcett Crest, 1967; Dell, 1975.

Leek, Sybil, and Bert R. Sugar, *The Assassination Chain*. New York: Corwin Books, 1976.

Lifton, David S., *Best Evidence: Deception and Disguise in the Assassination of John F. Kennedy,* New York: Macmillan, 1981, and with update New York: Carroll & Graf, 1988.

McDonald, Hugh C., as told to Geoffrey Bocca, *Appointment in Dallas: The Final Solution to the Assassination of JFK*. New York: Zebra Books, 1975.

McDonald, Hugh, with Robin Moore, *L.B.J. and the J.F.K. Conspiracy*. Westport, Conn.: Condor, 1978.

McKinley, James, *Assassination in America*. New York: Harper & Row, 1977.

McMillan, Priscilla Johnson, *Marina and Lee*. New York: Harper & Row, 1978.

Manchester, William, *The Death of a President: November 20-25, 1963*. New York: Harper & Row, 1967; Popular Library, 1968.

Marcus, Raymond, *The Bastard Bullet: A Search for Legitimacy for Commission Exhibit 399*. Randall Publications, 1966.

Mayo, John B., *Bulletin from Dallas: The President Is Dead*. New York: Exposition Press, 1967.

Meagher, Sylvia, *Accessories after the Fact: the Warren Commission, the Authorities, and the Report*. New York: Bobbs-Merrill, 1967; Vintage, 1976.

———, *Subject Index to the Warren Report and Hearings and Exhibits*. New York: Scarecrow Press 1966; Ann Arbor, Michigan: University Microfilms, 1971.

Miller, Tom, *The Assassination Please Almanac*. Chicago: Henry Regnery Co., 1977.

Model, Peter, with Robert J. Groden, *JFK: The Case for Conspiracy*. New York: Manor Books, 1976.

Morrow, Robert D., *Betrayal: A Reconstruction of Certain Clandestine Events from the Bay of Pigs to the Assassination of John F. Kennedy.* Chicago: Henry Regnery Co., 1976.

Murr, Gary, *The Murder of Police Officer J. D. Tippit.* 1971 (unpublished manuscript), Canada, 1971.

Newman, Albert H., *The Assassination of John F. Kennedy: The Reasons Why.* New York: Potter, 1970.

Noyes, Peter, *Legacy of Doubt.* New York: Pinnacle Books, 1973.

Oglesby, Carl, *The Yankee and Cowboy War.* Mission, Kansas: Sheed, Andrews and McMeel, 1976.

Oltmans, Willem, *Reportage over de Moordenaars.* Utrecht, Holland: Bruna & Zoon, 1977.

Oswald, Robert L., with Myrick and Barbara Land, *Lee: A Portrait of Lee Harvey Oswald.* New York: Coward-McCann, 1967.

O'Toole, George, *The Assassination Tapes: An Electronic Probe into the Muder of John F. Kennedy and the Dallas Cover-up.* New York: Penthouse Press, 1975.

Popkin, Richard H., *The Second Oswald.* New York: Avon Books, 1966.

Rand, Michael, with Howard Loxton and Len Deighton, *The Assassination of President Kennedy.* London: Jonathan Cape, 1967.

Roffman, Howard, *Presumed Guilty.* Cranbury, New Jersey: Fairleigh Dickinson Press, 1975; London: Thomas Yoselaff, 1976; New York: A. S. Barnes & Co., 1976.

Sauvage, Leo, *The Oswald Affair: An Examination of the Contradictions and Omissions of the Warren Report.* Cleveland: World Publishing Co., 1966.

Scheim, David, *Contract on America: The Mafia Murders of John and Robert Kennedy,* New York: Shapolsky Books, 1988.

Scott, Peter Dale, with Paul Hoch and Russell Stetler, *The Assassinations: Dallas and Beyond—A Guide to Cover-ups and Investigations.* New York: Random House, Vintage Press, 1976.

Scott, Peter Dale, *Crime and Cover-up: the CIA, the Mafia, and the Dallas-Watergate Connection.* Berkeley, California: Westworks, 1977.

———, *The Dallas Conspiracy,* unpublished manuscript. (Much used as research tool by serious students of the Kennedy case.)

Shaw, J. Gary, and Larry R. Harris, *Cover-up: The Governmental Conspiracy to Conceal the Facts about the Public Execution of John Kennedy.* Cleburne, Texas, 1976 (available from its authors).

Stafford, Jean, *A Mother in History: Mrs. Marguerite Oswald.* New York: Farrar, Straus & Giroux, 1966; Bantam, 1966.

Thompson, Josiah, *Six Seconds in Dallas: A Microstudy of the Kennedy Assassination*. New York: Bernard Geis Associates, 1967; (revised) Berkeley, 1976.

Thornley, Kerry, *Oswald*. Chicago: New Classics House, 1965.

United Press International and *American Heritage* magazine, *Four Days*. New York: American Heritage Publishing Company, 1964.

Weisberg, Harold, *Oswald in New Orleans—Case for Conspiracy with the CIA*. New York: Canyon Books, 1967.

———, *Post-Mortem*. Frederick, Maryland, 1975 (self-published—available from author).

———, *Whitewash* (Vols. I-IV). Hyattstown, Maryland, 1965, 1967 (self-published); and (Vols I&II) New York: Dell, 1966-1967.

White, Stephen, *Should We Now Believe the Warren Report?* New York: Macmillan, 1968.

Wise, Dan, with Marietta Maxfield, *The Day Kennedy Died*. San Antonio: Naylor, 1964.

See also *The Assassination Story* (collected clippings from Dallas newspapers). American Eagle Publishing Co., 1964.

On Jack Ruby

Belli, Melvin, with Maurice Carroll, *Dallas Justice*. New York: David McKay, 1964.

Denson, R.B., *Destiny in Dallas*. Dallas: Denco Corporation, 1964.

Gertz, Elmer, *Moment of Madness: The People vs. Jack Ruby*. Chicago: Follett Publishing Co., 1968.

Hunter, Diana, with Alice Anderson, *Jack Ruby's Girls*. Atlanta: Hallux Inc., 1970.

Kantor, Seth, *Who Was Jack Ruby?* New York: Everest House, 1978.

Kaplan, John, with Jon R. Waltz; *The Trial of Jack Ruby: A Classic Study of Courtroom Strategies*. New York: Macmillan, 1965.

Wills, Gary, and Ovid Demaris, *Jack Ruby: The Man Who Killed the Man Who Killed Kennedy*. New York: New American Library, 1967; New American Library paperback, 1968.

On Forensic Science

Houts, Marshall, *Where Death Delights*. New York: Dell, 1967.

Medico-Legal Journal (Vol. 4, December 1964), *Trauma*. New York: Matthew Bender & Co., 1964.

On Intelligence

Abel, Elie, *The Missiles of October.* London: MacGibbon & Kee, 1969.
Agee, Philip, *Inside the Company: CIA Diary.* New York: Bantam, 1976.
Ashman, Charles, *The CIA-Mafia Link.* New York: Manor Books, 1975.
Barron, John, *KGB.* New York: Reader's Digest Press, 1974.
Bowart, Walter, *Operation Mind Control.* New York: Delacorte, 1977.
Dulles, Allen, *The Craft of Intelligence.* New York: Harper & Row, 1963.
Hougan, Jim, *Spooks.* New York: William Morrow, 1978.
Kirkpatrick, Lyman B., *The Real CIA.* New York: Macmillan, 1968.
Marchetti, Victor, and John Marks, *The CIA and the Cult of Intelligence.* New York: Alfred A. Knopf, 1974; Dell, 1975.
New York Times, The Pentagon Papers. June 13, 14, 15, & July 1, 1971.
Phillips, David, *The Night Watch.* New York: Atheneum, 1977.
Powers, Gary, with Curt Gentry, *Operation Overflight.* Holt, Rinehart & Winston, 1970; London, Hodder & Stoughton, 1970.
Powers, Thomas, *The Man Who Kept the Secrets: Richard Helms and the CIA.* New York: Alfred A. Knopf, 1979.
Prouty, L. Fletcher, *The Secret Team.* Englewood Cliffs, New Jersey: Prentice-Hall, 1973.
Rositzke, Harry, *The CIA's Secret Operations.* New York: Reader's Digest Press, 1977.
Wise, David, and Thomas B. Ross, *The Invisible Government.* New York: Random House, 1964.
————, *The Espionage Establishment.* New York: Random House, 1967.

Subjects related to Organized Crime (selected sources)

Exner, Judith, *My Story* (as told to Ovid Demaris). New York: Grove, 1977.
Kennedy, Robert F., *The Enemy Within.* New York: Harper & Row, 1960.
Kidner, John, *Crimaldi, Contract Killer.* Washington D.C.: Acropolis Books, 1976.
McClellan, John, *Crime Without Punishment.* New York: Duell, Sloan & Pearce, 1962.
Messick, Hank, and Burt Goldblatt, *The Mobs and the Mafia.* New York: Ballantine, 1973.
Moldea, Dan E., *The Hoffa Wars.* New York and London: Paddington Press, 1978.

Reid, Ed, *The Grim Reapers*. Chicago: Henry Regnery Co., 1969; New York: Bantam, 1969.

Reid, Ed, and Ovid Demaris, *The Green Felt Jungle*. New York: Trident Press, 1963.

Sheridan, Walter, *The Fall and Rise of Jimmy Hoffa*. New York: Saturday Review Press, 1973.

Talese, Gay, *Honor Thy Father*. Cleveland and New York: World Publishing Co., 1971.

Teresa, Vincent, with Thomas C. Renner, *My Life in the Mafia*. London: Hart-Davis, McGibbon, 1973; Panther, 1974.

Other

Attwood, William, *The Reds and the Blacks*. New York: Harper & Row, 1967.

Ayers, Bradley Earl, *The War That Never Was*. New York: Bobbs-Merrill, 1976.

Eisenhower, Dwight, *The White House Years: Waging Peace, 1956-1961*. New York: Doubleday, 1965.

Haldeman, H. R., with Joseph Di Mona, *The Ends of Power*. New York: Times Book Co., 1978.

Hunt, E. Howard, *Give Us This Day*. New York: Arlington House, 1973.

Johnson, Haynes, *Bay of Pigs*. New York: Norton, 1964.

Kennedy, John F., (speeches), *Public Papers of the Presidents of the United States*. Washington, D.C.: U.S. Government Printing Office, 1962-1964.

Lasky, Victor, *It Didn't Start with Watergate*. New York: Dell, 1978.

Lawrence, Lincoln (pseudonym). *Were We Controlled?* New Hyde Park, New York: University Books, 1967.

Schlesinger, Arthur, *A Thousand Days: John F. Kennedy in the White House*. Boston: Houghton Mifflin Co., 1965.

———, *Robert Kennedy and His Times*. Boston: Houghton Mifflin Co., 1978.

Schorr, Daniel, *Clearing the Air*. Boston: Houghton Mifflin Co., 1977; New York: Berkeley, 1978.

Sorensen, Theodore, *The Kennedy Legacy*. New York: New American Library, 1970.

White, Theodore, *The Making of the President*. New York: Atheneum, 1965.

Official Reports

Alleged Assassination Plots Involving Foreign Leaders, Interim Report of the Select Committee to Study Governmental Operations, with Respect to Intelligence Activities, U.S. Senate. Washington D.C.: U.S. Government Printing Office, 1975 (subsequent listings are also published by U.S. Government Printing Office unless otherwise described).

Hearings Before the Sub-Committee on Civil and Constitutional Rights of the Committee on the Judiciary, House of Representatives, on FBI Oversight (Serial No. 2, Part III), 1976.

Investigation of the Assassination of President John F. Kennedy, Book V, Final Report of the Select Committee to Study Governmental Operations, with Respect to Intelligence Activities, U.S. Senate, 1976.

Report of the President's Commission on the Assassination of President John F. Kennedy, and 26 accompanying volumes of Hearings and Exhibits, 1964; published by U.S. Government Printing Office and also Doubleday, McGraw-Hill, Bantam, Popular Library, and Associated Press, 1964.

Report of the Select Committee on Assassinations, U.S. House of Representatives, and 12 accompanying volumes of Hearings and Appendices (on Kennedy case as opposed to Martin Luther King assassination), 1979, published by U.S. Government Printing Office; and *Report* (only) by Bantam, New York, 1979, under title *The Final Assassinations Report.*

Report to the President by the Commission on CIA Activities Within the United States. Also published by Manor Books (New York), 1976.

Texas Supplemental Report on the Assassination of President John F. Kennedy and the Serious Wounding of Governor John B. Connally, November 22, 1963, by Texas Attorney General Waggoner Carr, Austin, Texas, 1964.

Illustration Credits

For permission to reproduce photographs, referred to here by caption number, the author and publishers are grateful to: Mrs. L. Boggs (*14*); Capital City Press—photo by John Boss (*24*—Partin); CIA (*17*); Cuban Government intelligence photos (*27*); Judge Daniels (*24*—Daniels); HSCA (*26*—"Bishop"); Jim Marrs (*20*); National Archives (*6, 7, 8, 9, 10, 25*—Oswald, *28, 29*); Ronan O'Rahilly (*25*—Roberts); Congressman Preyer (*16*); Senator Schweiker (*15*); Gary Shaw (*25*—Banister); Rick Solberg (*19*); UPI (*2, 18, 23*—Roselli, *24*—RFK and Hoffa); U.S. Government Printing Office (*5*); U.S. Senate (*13*); Jeff Wallace (*4*); *Washington Post*—photo by J.K. Atherton (*26*—Phillips); Jack Weaver (*1, 2*). Photograph of President Kennedy by George Tame, *New York Times*. Frontispiece and photograph 59a courtesy David Lifton and Mark Crouch; original source: Secret Service employee Jack Fox.

The author and publishers apologize to those photograph owners who have not, despite efforts, been traced, and who are therefore not credited here.

Index